Third New Jersey Regiment, Continental Line, 1777. (Private)

First Pennsylvania Battalion, 1775-1776 (Sergeant)

Haslet's Delaware Regiment, 1776 (Private)

Captain John Lamb's New York Artillery Company, 1775. (Gunner)

Second Massachusetts Regiment, Continental Line, 1777. (Private)

Second Rhode Island Regiment, Continental Line, 1779. (Private)

Virginia Light Dragoons, (Private of Captain Theodorick Bland's Troop)

Second Maryland Regiment, Continental Line, 1777. (Private)

The Spirit of 'Seventy-Six

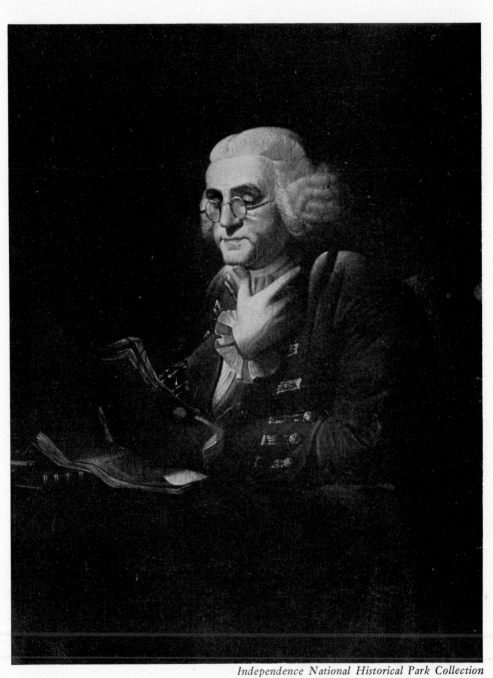

BENJAMIN FRANKLIN

David Rent Etter, after Martin

The Spirit
of
'Seventy-Six

THE STORY OF THE AMERICAN REVOLUTION

AS TOLD BY PARTICIPANTS

EDITED BY

Henry Steele Commager

AND

Richard B. Morris

VOLUME

II

THE BOBBS-MERRILL COMPANY, INC.

publishers

INDIANAPOLIS   NEW YORK

Table of Contents

(Names of authors are indicated by italics)

v

List of Illustrations

List of Maps

The Spirit of 'Seventy-Six

CHAPTER FIFTEEN

France Comes In

For ALMOST *a century the nations of Europe had been engaged in an inter-mittent conflict spread over a world stage. Generally called the Second Hun-dred Years' War, that conflict had turned on dynastic rivalries, colonial in-terests, and the maintenance of the balance of power. In the four great wars which had ended in 1763 England and France were always on opposing sides, and in each war the North American continent was a theater of operations. The last of these four wars, called in America the French and Indian, saw France stripped of her major possessions in North America and the neat bal-ance of power upon which statesmen had rested their hopes for peace tem-porarily destroyed.*

Would the American Revolution turn into a world war? Would France again take sides against her ancient enemy? Would the European absolute monarchies support a revolution against a king? Both Britain and her rebelli-ous colonies were keenly aware that aid from the uncommitted foreign powers could tip the scales. Although Great Britain tried desperately to keep the Revolution from turning into a world conflict, she acted precipitately in secur-ing military assistance from various German states. The American Congress in turn looked at once to France for aid short of war, then for a full-scale military alliance.

The diplomats with whom the American commissioners came in contact were experts in the techniques of secret diplomacy, procrastination, evasion and duplicity. But the inexperienced Americans did not behave precisely like innocents abroad. They themselves could be shrewd, subtle and suspicious— unfortunately of each other as well as of foreign chancelleries—and when American interest dictated, they could be forthright and moralistic. They soon learned that national interest governed the decisions of the major Euro-pean powers and the extent of their involvement in the American conflict.

The story of the war on the diplomatic front, involving transparent sub-terfuge, plots and counterplots, espionage and counterespionage, and most of all a grand public-relations effort, is told in several chapters in this volume. It introduces America's greatest diplomat, the scientist-philosopher Benjamin Franklin, with the "universal reputation"; the underestimated and traduced Silas Deane, whose early services were indispensable to the cause of inde-

*pendence; and brings to the fore two hard-headed and first-rate negotiators,
John Jay and John Adams.*

I. AMERICA SEEKS FOREIGN AID WITHOUT
ENTANGLING ALLIANCES

*To win the war against Great Britain the Patriot leaders quickly accepted
the need for foreign aid in some form, but at the start many of them were
wary of European alliances. On July 7, 1775, Franklin wrote Priestley: "We
have not yet applied to any foreign power for assistance, nor offered our
commerce for their friendship. Perhaps we never may; yet it is natural to
think of it, if we are pressed." In his* Common Sense *Tom Paine insisted that
independence would free the former colonies from being dragged at the heels
of England into European wars that were no concern of theirs.*

*No Patriot expressed this view more forthrightly and consistently than
did America's stalwart isolationist, John Adams. Arguing in the fall of 1775
that France was bound to come into the war anyhow, he warned that America
must avoid alliances which would entangle her in future European wars.
"When I first made these observations in Congress," wrote Adams with characteristic complacency, "I never saw a greater impression made upon that
assembly or any other."*

*By the end of November of '75 Congress was ready to make cautious
advances to the European powers. Their petition to the King had been disregarded, Americans were proclaimed rebels, and word had come that German troops were to be hired to crush the rebellion. On November 29 Congress set up a five-man secret Committee of Correspondence to get in touch
with "our friends" abroad. One of the members, Benjamin Franklin, began
almost at once to put out feelers as to the possibility of foreign aid or even an
alliance.*

*By June of 1776 Franklin's position was taken for granted by Richard
Henry Lee, who insisted that only by a declaration of independence could a
foreign alliance be obtained, and that an alliance with a despotic power would
not damage America's interests. As Robert Morris saw it, the issue was not
so much that of avoiding entanglements as in dragging all Europe into war
to help the cause of the Revolution. "Can this be morally right?" he asked
John Jay in September 1776, "or have morality and polity nothing to do with
each other?" America's diplomatic representatives abroad found varying answers to this question.*

1. AVOID ALLIANCES "WHICH WOULD ENTANGLE US," JOHN ADAMS WARNS

From the Autobiography.

[September 1775]

Some gentlemen doubted of the sentiments of France; thought she would
frown upon us as rebels, and be afraid to countenance the example. I replied
to those gentlemen that I apprehended they had not attended to the relative
situation of France and England; that it was the unquestionable interest of
France that the British Continental Colonies should be independent; that
Britain, by the conquest of Canada and her naval triumphs during the last

war, and by her vast possessions in America and the East Indies, was exalted to the height of power and pre-eminence that France must envy and could not endure.

But there was much more than pride and jealousy in the case. Her rank, her consideration in Europe and even her safety and independence were at stake. The Navy of Great Britain was now mistress of the seas, all over the globe. The Navy of France almost annihilated, its inferiority was so great and obvious that all the dominions of France, in the West Indies and in the East Indies, lay at the mercy of Great Britain, and must remain so as long as North America belonged to Great Britain, and afforded them so many harbors abounding with naval stores and resources of all kinds, and so many men and seamen ready to assist them and man their ships; that interest could not lie; that the interest of France was so obvious, and her motives so cogent, that nothing but a judicial infatuation of her councils could restrain her from embracing us; that our negotiations with France ought, however, to be conducted with great caution, and with all the foresight we could possibly obtain; that we ought not to enter into any alliance with her which should entangle us in any future wars in Europe; that we ought to lay it down as a first principle and a maxim never to be forgotten, to maintain an entire neutrality in all future European wars; that it never could be our interest to unite with France in the destruction of England, or in any measures to break her spirit or reduce her to a situation in which she could not support her independence.

On the other hand, it could never be our duty to unite with Britain in too great a humiliation of France; that our real, if not our nominal, independence would consist in our neutrality. If we united with either nation in any future war, we must become too subordinate and dependent on the nation, and should be involved in all European wars, as we had been hitherto; that foreign powers would find means to corrupt our people, to influence our councils, and, in fine, we should be little better than puppets, danced on the wires of the cabinets of Europe. We should be the sport of European intrigues and politics; that, therefore, in preparing treaties to be proposed to foreign powers, and in the instructions to be given to our ministers, we ought to confine ourselves strictly to a treaty of commerce; that such a treaty would be an ample compensation to France for all the aid we should want from her. The opening of American trade to her would be a vast resource for her commerce and naval power, and a great assistance to her in protecting her East and West India possessions, as well as her fisheries; but that the bare dismemberment of the British empire would be to her an incalculable security and benefit, worth more than all the exertions we should require of her, even if it should draw her into another eight or ten years' war.

—ADAMS, ed., *Works of John Adams*, II, 504-506.

2. FRANKLIN PUTS OUT FEELERS FOR ALLIANCES

Benjamin Franklin to his friend Charles William Dumas, at The Hague.

Philadelphia, December 9, 1775

. . . We are threatened from England with a very powerful force to come next year against us. We are making all the provision in our power here to prevent that force, and we hope we shall be able to defend ourselves. But as the events of war are always uncertain, possibly after another campaign we may find it necessary to ask aid of some foreign power. It gives us great pleasure to learn from you that "all Europe wishes us the best success in the maintenance of our liberty." But we wish to know whether any one of them, from principles of humanity, is disposed magnanimously to step in for the relief of an oppressed people, or whether if, as it seems likely to happen, we should be obliged to break off all connection with Britain and declare ourselves an independent people, there is any state or power in Europe who would be willing to enter into an alliance with us for the benefit of our commerce, which amounted, before the war, to near seven millions sterling per annum, and must continually increase, as our people increase most rapidly.

Confiding, my dear friend, in your good will to us and our cause, and in your sagacity and abilities for business, the committee of Congress, appointed for the purpose of establishing and conducting a correspondence with our friends in Europe, of which committee I have the honor to be a member, have directed me to request of you that, as you are situated at The Hague, where ambassadors from all courts reside, you would make use of the opportunity which that situation affords you of discovering, if possible, the disposition of the several courts with respect to such assistance or alliance, if we should apply for the one or propose for the other. As it may possibly be necessary, in particular instances, that you should, for this purpose, confer directly with some great ministers, and show them this letter as your credential, we only recommend it to your discretion that you proceed therein with such caution as to keep the same from the knowledge of the English ambassador, and prevent any public appearance, at present, of your being employed in any such business, as thereby, we imagine, many inconveniences may be avoided, and your means of rendering us service increased. . . .

We have hitherto applied to no foreign power. We are using the utmost industry in endeavoring to make saltpeter, and with daily increasing success. Our artificers are also everywhere busy in fabricating small arms, casting cannon, etc. Yet both arms and ammunition are much wanted. Any merchants who would venture to send ships laden with those articles might make great profit; such is the demand in every colony, and such generous prices are, and will be, given, of which, and of the manner of conducting such a voyage, the bearer, Mr. Story, can more fully inform you. And whoever brings in those articles is allowed to carry off the value in provisions to our West Indies, where they will fetch a very high price, the general exportation from North America being stopped. This you will see more particularly in a printed resolution of the Congress.

We are in great want of good engineers and wish you could engage and send us two able ones in time for the next campaign, one acquainted with field service, sieges, etc., and the other with fortifying sea ports. They will, if well recommended, be made very welcome and have honorable appointments, besides the expenses of their voyage hither, in which Mr. Story can also advise them. As what we now request of you, besides taking up your time, may put you to some expense, we send you, for the present, inclosed a bill for one hundred pounds sterling to defray such expenses, and desire you to be assured that your services will be considered and honorably rewarded by the Congress. . . .

—WHARTON, *Revolutionary Diplomatic Correspondence*, II, 64-67.

II. FRANCE GIVES AID SHORT OF WAR

The Seven Years' War, a crushing defeat for France, impelled her statesmen to reassess her diplomatic position and to consider anew ways of weakening Great Britain. In 1767 the Duc de Choiseul, France's foreign minister, dispatched Johann de Kalb, later to serve in the Patriot army, to report on the state of discontent in the American colonies. His report was negative and disappointing to his superiors. Thenceforth it became a cardinal point in French foreign policy that disaffection in America would weaken British power. A successful revolt might well restore the balance of power so rudely upset by the overwhelming British victory in 1763. By calling into existence the New World, France would "redress the balance of the Old."

Thus reasoned that prudent diplomat, the Comte de Vergennes, who became France's foreign minister when Louis XVI ascended the throne in 1774. His views were supported, probably in some measure shaped, by an extraordinary adventurer and master of backstairs intrigue, the talented playwright Pierre Augustin Caron, who wrote Figaro and other plays under the pseudonym of Beaumarchais. The playwright had a talent for publicity, both good and bad. At the time the Revolution began he was under a sentence of the Parlement of Paris, which deprived him of his civil rights for attempting to bribe a judge. The American cause aroused his enthusiasm and challenged his audacity. The result was a practical plan for aiding America.

The curtain for the first act rose in London in September 1775, when Beaumarchais dispatched to his King an exaggerated account of the Patriots' will to resist. ("I say, Sire, that such a nation must be invincible.") On his next visit to England he prepared a second paper for the King, which went through Vergennes's hands. In it he advocated assistance short of war. Beaumarchais discussed his plans with Arthur Lee, the Virginian then resident in England who had been authorized to collect information for the Congress as to the disposition of foreign powers, but who was without power to negotiate. On June 12 the Frenchman wrote Lee that he was setting up a private company to "send help to your friend in the shape of powder and ammunition in exchange for tobacco." This company was to conduct its operations under the name of Roderigue Hortalez et Compagnie.

In July 1776, Silas Deane arrived in Paris in the guise of a businessman. The Connecticut merchant Patriot had been commissioned by the secret Committee of Correspondence to buy military and other supplies and to probe the possibilities of securing more extensive assistance on the part of France. Deane was indefatigable in procuring needed supplies and recruiting officers abroad for the American army, perhaps overly generous in recognizing the rank and talents of some of the European applicants.

In September Congress appointed a diplomatic mission composed of Frank-

lin, Arthur Lee, and Deane himself to secure additional material aid from France, the recognition of independence, and treaties of commerce and alliance. Dr. Bancroft will appear repeatedly.

1. The Author of *Figaro* Comes to the Rescue of the Colonies

Pierre Augustin Caron de Beaumarchais to Louis XVI alone (given unclosed to M. de Vergennes).

February 29, 1776

Sire,—The famous quarrel between America and England, which will soon divide the world and change the system of Europe, imposes upon each power the necessity of examining well in what manner the event of this separation can influence it, and either serve it or injure it. . . .

At present, when a violent crisis is approaching with great rapidity, I am obliged to warn Your Majesty that the preservation of our possessions in America, and the peace which Your Majesty appears to desire so much, depend solely upon this one proposition: *the Americans must be assisted.* I will now demonstrate it.

The King of England, the ministers of the Parliament, the opposition, the nation, the English people, all the parties, in fine, who are tearing this state asunder, agree that they ought no longer to hope to regain the Americans, and that not even the great efforts which are being now made to subject them can ever reduce them with success. Thence, sire, these violent debates between the ministry and the opposition, this flux and reflux of opinions admitted or rejected, which, as they do not advance matters, only serve to put the question in a plainer and a clearer light. . . .

Let us submit all possible hypotheses, and let us reason.

What follows is very important.

Either England will have the most complete success in America during the campaign;

Or the Americans will repel the English with loss.

Either England will come to the determination already adopted by the king of abandoning the colonies to themselves, or parting from them in a friendly manner;

Or the opposition, in taking possession of the government, will answer for the submission of the colonies on condition of their being restored to the position they were in in 1763.

Here are all the possibilities collected together. Is there a single one of them which does not instantly give you the war you wish to avoid? Sire, in the name of God, deign to examine the matter with me.

First, if England triumphs over America, she can only do so by an enormous expenditure of men and money. Now the only compensation the English propose to themselves for so many losses is to take possession on their return of the French islands, and thus make themselves the exclusive vendors of the valuable supply of sugar, which can alone repair all the injuries done to their commerce, and this capture would also render them forever the absolute possessors of the advantages derived from the contraband commerce carried on by the Continent with these islands.

Then, Sire, there would remain to you nothing but the option of commencing at a later period an unprofitable war, or of sacrificing to the most shameful of inactive peaces all your American colonies, and of losing 280 millions of capital, and more than 30 millions of revenue.

2. If the Americans are victorious, they instantly become free, and the English, in despair at seeing their existence diminished by three quarters, will only be the more anxious, the more eager to seek a compensation, which will have become indispensable, in the easy capture of our American possessions; and we may be certain that they will not fail to do so.

3. If the English consider themselves forced to abandon the colonies to themselves without striking a blow, as it is the secret wish of the king they should do, the loss being the same for their existence, and their commerce being equally ruined, the result for us would be similar to the preceeding one, except that the English, less weakened by this amicable surrender than by a bloody and ruinous campaign, would only derive from it more means and facilities for gaining possession of our islands, which they would then be unable to do without if they wished to preserve their own and to keep any footing in America.

4. If the opposition takes possession of the government and concludes a treaty of reunion with the colonies, the Americans, indignant with France, whose refusal will alone have caused them to submit to the mother country, threaten us from the present moment to unite all their forces with England in order to take possession of our islands. They will, indeed, only reunite with the mother country on this condition, and Heaven knows with what joy the ministry, composed of Lords Chatham, Shelburne and Rockingham, whose dispositions toward us are publicly known, would adopt the resentment of the Americans, and carry on against you without cessation the most obstinate and cruel war.

What, then, is to be done in this extremity, so as to have peace and preserve our islands?

You will only preserve the peace you desire, Sire, by preventing it at all price from being made between England and America, and in preventing one from completely triumphing over the other; and the only means of attaining this end is by giving assistance to the Americans which will put their forces on an equality with those of England, but nothing beyond. And believe me, Sire, that the economy of a few millions at present may, before long, cost a great deal of blood and money to France.

—De Lomenie, *Beaumarchais*, III, 117-123.

2. Congress Instructs Deane in the Negotiation with France

The Committee of Secret Correspondence to Silas Deane.

Philadelphia, March 3, 1776

On your arrival in France, you will for some time be engaged in the business of providing goods for the Indian trade. This will give good countenance to your appearing in the character of a merchant, which we wish you continually to retain among the French, in general, it being probable that the court of France may not like it should be known publicly that any agent from the Colonies is in that country. When you come to Paris, by delivering Dr. Franklin's letter to Monsieur Le Roy at the Louvre, and M. Dubourg, you will be introduced to a set of acquaintances, all friends to the Americans. By conversing with them, you will have a good opportunity of acquiring Parisian French, and you will find in M. Dubourg a man prudent, faithful, secret, intelligent in affairs, and capable of giving you very sage advice.

It is scarce necessary to pretend any other business at Paris than the gratifying of that curiosity which draws numbers thither yearly, merely to see so famous a city. With the assistance of Monsieur Dubourg, who understands English, you will be able to make immediate application to Monsieur de Vergennes, *Ministre des Affaires Etrangères*, either personally or by letter, if M. Dubourg adopts that method, acquainting him that you are in France upon business of the American Congress, in the character of a merchant, having something to communicate to him that may be mutually beneficial to France and the North American Colonies; that you request an audience of him, and that he would be pleased to appoint the time and place.

At this audience if agreed to, it may be well to show him first your letter of credence, and then acquaint him that, the Congress finding that in the common course of commerce it was not practicable to furnish the continent of America with the quantity of arms and ammunition necessary for its defence (the Ministry of Great Britain having been extremely industrious to prevent it), you had been despatched by their authority to apply to some European power for a supply. That France had been pitched on for the first application, from an opinion that if we should, as there is a great appearance we shall, come to a total separation from Great Britain, France would be looked upon as the power whose friendship it would be fittest for us to obtain and cultivate. That the commercial advantages Britain has enjoyed with the Colonies had contributed greatly to her late wealth and importance. That it is likely great part of our commerce will naturally fall to the share of France; especially if she favors us in this application, as that will be a means of gaining and securing the friendship of the Colonies; and that as our trade was rapidly increasing with our increase of people, and in a greater proportion, her part of it will be extremely valuable. That the supply we at present want is clothing and arms for twenty-five thousand men with a suitable quantity of ammunition, and one hundred field pieces. That we mean to pay for the same by remittances to France or through Spain, Portugal or the French Islands, as soon as our navigation can be protected by ourselves or friends; and that we besides want great quantities of linens and woollens, with other articles for the Indian trade, which you are now actually purchasing, and for which you ask no credit, and that the whole, if France should grant the other supplies, would make a cargo which it might be well to secure by a convoy of two or three ships of war.

If you should find M. de Vergennes reserved and not inclined to enter into free conversation with you, it may be well to shorten your visit, request him to consider what you have proposed, acquaint him with your place of lodging, that you may yet stay some time at Paris, and that knowing how precious his time is, you do not presume to ask another audience, but that if he should have any commands for you, you will upon the least notice immediately wait upon him.

If at a future conference he should be more free, and you find a disposition to favor the Colonies, it may be proper to acquaint him that they must necessarily be anxious to know the disposition of France on certain points, which, with his permission, you would mention, such as whether if the Colonies should be forced to form themselves into an independent state, France would probably acknowledge them as such, receive their ambassadors, enter into any treaty or alliance with them, for commerce or defence, or both? If so, on what principal conditions? Intimating that you shall speedily have an opportunity of sending to America, if you do not immediately return, and that he may be assured of your fidelity and secrecy in transmitting carefully any thing he would wish conveyed to the Congress on that subject.

In subsequent conversations you may, as you find it convenient, enlarge on these topics that have been the subjects of our conferences with you, to which you may occasionally add the well-known substantial answers we usually give to the several calumnies thrown out against us. If these supplies on the credit of the Congress should be refused, you are then to endeavor the obtaining a permission of purchasing those articles, or as much of them as you can find credit for. . . .

You will endeavor to procure a meeting with Mr. Bancroft by writing a letter to him, under cover to Mr. Griffiths at Turnham Green, near London, and desiring him to come over to you, in France or Holland, on the score of old acquaintance. From him you may obtain a good deal of information of what is now going forward in England, and settle a mode of continuing a correspondence. It may be well to remit him a small bill to defray his expenses in coming to you, and avoid all political matters in your letter to him. You will also endeavor to correspond with Mr. Arthur Lee, agent of the Colonies in London. . . .

—DEANE, "Correspondence," *Conn. Hist. Soc. Coll.,* II, 365-368.

3. "I AM ABOUT TO ENTER ON THE GREAT STAGE OF EUROPE"

Silas Deane to Mrs. Deane.

March 3, 1776

You will not imagine I am unfeeling on this occasion—but to what purpose would it be to let my tender passions govern, except to distress you? I shall take every precaution, and if I fall into the enemie's hands, doubt not of good usage, as their sending Commissioners will be a security to me; but I am prepared even for the worst, not wishing to survive my country's fate, and confident, while that is safe, I shall be happy in almost any situation.

I have, in one of the most solemn acts of my life, committed my son and what I have to your care and the care of my brother, confident you will be to him a real mother, which you ever have been, and for my sake, as well as from the truly maternal affection you have ever borne for him, guard his youth from any thing dangerous or dishonorable. I can but feel for the pain I must give you by this adventure, but on all occasions you will have this satisfaction, that let what will happen, you have in every situation discharged your duty as one of the best of partners and wives, while on my part, by a peculiar fatality attending me from my first entrance into public life, I have ever been involved in one scheme and adventure after another, so as to keep my mind in constant agitation and my attention fixed on other objects than my own immediate interests.

The present object is great. I am about to enter on the great stage of Europe, and the consideration of the importance of quitting myself well weighs me down, without the addition of more tender scenes; but I am

"Safe in the hand of that protecting Power,
Who ruled my natal, and must fix my mortal hour."

It matters but little, my dear, what part we act, or where, if we act it well. I wish as much as any man for the enjoyments of domestic ease, peace and society, but am forbid expecting them soon; indeed, must be criminal in my own eyes, did I balance them one moment in opposition to the public good and the calls of my country.

I do not recollect any thing to add; it is a late hour, and to-morrow will be a busy day with me, as I hope to sail on Tuesday. May God Almighty protect you safe thro' the vicissitudes of times!

Yours, thro' life and all its scenes,

S. D.

P.S. Confident this letter will go safe, I venture to say that a concern, different from my contract, is to support me. I have agreed that all expenses of every kind shall be paid, and referred my salary to be determined hereafter, in consequence of which it is agreed that I have five hundred pounds sterling to carry with me for that purpose, and the same sum is to be remitted to me at the end of six months.

Should any accident happen to me, you will find this entered on the Committee of Secret Correspondence's books. The members are: Dr. Franklin, Mr. Dickinson, Mr. Jay, Mr. Morris, Col. Harrison, and Mr. Johnson. But you must not communicate this to any one except to my brother. This will explain my saying that I have a commission of two thousand pounds free of charge, as my charge will be amply provided for by the other way. And now, my dear, are not the ways of Providence dark and inscrutable to us, shortsighted mortals? Surely they are. My enemies thought to triumph over me and bring me down, yet all they did has been turned to the opening a door for the greatest and most extensive usefulness, if I succeed; but if I fail—why then the cause I am engaged in, and the important part I have undertaken, will justify my adventuring. . . .

—Deane, "Correspondence," *Conn. Hist. Soc. Coll.*, II, 362-363.

4. Beaumarchais Explains His Secret Supply System

To the Committee of Secret Correspondence of the Continental Congress.

Paris, August 18, 1776

The respectful esteem that I bear towards that brave people who so well defend their liberty under your conduct has induced me to form a plan concurring in this great work, by establishing an extensive commercial house, solely for the purpose of serving you in Europe, there to supply you with necessaries of every sort, to furnish you expeditiously and certainly with all articles—clothes, linens, powder, ammunition, muskets, cannon, or even gold for the payment of your troops, and in general every thing that can be useful for the honorable war in which you are engaged. Your deputies, gentlemen, will find in me a sure friend, an asylum in my house, money in my coffers, and every means of facilitating their operations, whether of a public or secret nature. I will, if possible, remove all obstacles that may oppose your wishes from the politics of Europe.

At this very time, and without waiting for any answer from you, I have procured for you about two hundred pieces of brass cannon, four-pounders, which will be sent to you by the nearest way, two hundred thousand pounds of cannon powder, twenty thousand excellent fusils, some brass mortars, bombs, cannon balls, bayonets, platines, clothes, linens, etc., for the clothing of your troops, and lead for musket balls. An officer* of the greatest merit for artillery and genius, accompanied by lieutenants, officers, artillerists, cannoniers, etc., whom we think necessary for the service, will go for Philadelphia even before you have received my first despatches. This gentlemen is one of the greatest presents that my attachment can offer you. Your deputy, Mr. Deane, agrees with me in the treatment which he thinks suitable to his office; and I have found the power of this deputy sufficient that I should prevail with this officer to depart under the sole engagement of the deputy respecting him, the terms of which I have not the least doubt but Congress will comply with.

The secrecy necessary in some part of the operation which I have undertaken for your service requires also, on your part, a formal resolution that all the vessels and their demands should be constantly directed to our house alone, in order that there may be no idle chattering or time lost—two things that are the ruin of affairs. You will advise me what the vessels contain which you shall send into our ports. I shall choose so much of their loading, in return for what I have sent, as shall be suitable to me when I have not been able beforehand to inform you of the cargoes which I wish. I shall facilitate to you the loading, sale and disposal of the rest.

For instance, five American vessels have just arrived in the port of Bordeaux, laden with salt fish. Though this merchandise, coming from strangers, is prohibited in our ports, yet as soon as your deputy had told me that these vessels were sent to him by you to raise money from the sale for aiding him in his purchases in Europe, I took so much care that I secretly obtained from the Farmers-General an order for landing it without any notice being taken of it. I could even, if the case had so happened, have taken on my own account these cargoes of salted fish, though it is no way useful to me, and charged myself with its sale and disposal, to simplify the operation and lessen the embarrassments of the merchants and of your deputy.

I shall have a correspondent in each of our seaport towns who, on the

---

* Charles Tronson du Coudray, who caused Washington embarrassment by insisting that he be given command of the artillery, superseding Knox. He was drowned in the Schuylkill, whether accidentally or by suicide has never been determined.

arrival of your vessels, shall wait on the captains and offer every service in my power. He will receive their letters, bills of lading, and transmit the whole to me. Even things which you may wish to arrive safely in any country in Europe, after having conferred about them with your deputy, I shall cause to be kept in some secure place. Even the answers shall go with great punctuality through me, and this way will save much anxiety and many delays. I request of you, gentlemen, to send me next spring, if it is possible for you, ten or twelve thousand hogsheads, or more if you can, of tobacco from Virginia of the best quality. . . .

Notwithstanding the open opposition which the King of France, his ministers and the agents of administration show, and ought to show, to everything that carries the least appearance of violating foreign treaties and the internal ordinances of the kingdom, I dare promise to you, gentlemen, that my indefatigable zeal shall never be wanting to clear up difficulties, soften prohibitions, and, in short, facilitate all operations of a commerce which my advantage, much less than yours, has made me undertake with you. What I have just informed you of is only a general sketch, subject to all the augmentations and restrictions which events may point out to us.

One thing can never vary or diminish: it is the avowed and ardent desire I have of serving you to the utmost of my power. You will recollect my signature, that one of your friends in London, some time ago, informed you of my favorable disposition towards you and my attachment to your interest. Look upon my house, then, gentlemen, from henceforward as the chief of all useful operations to you in Europe, and my person as one of the most zealous partisans of your cause. . . .

—WHARTON, *Revolutionary Diplomatic Correspondence*, II, 129-131.

5. BEAUMARCHAIS AND THE MYSTERY OF THE "LOST MILLION"

Shrouded in mystery are the operations of the colorful and devious Beaumarchais. In furnishing arms and supplies to the American cause through his dummy firm, Beaumarchais was not entirely forthright as to whether the supplies were a gift for which nominal payments in produce were made to disguise the transactions as commercial, or whether Congress was expected to pay for them. On the basis of early conversations with Beaumarchais in London, Arthur Lee was to insist that the supplies were a gift. On the other hand, Deane acted on the assumption that America was expected to pay, and was so instructed by Congress. Beaumarchais entered into a business agreement with Deane according to which Congress was required to pay for the arms and other supplies in produce or money at a date not fixed.

What complicates the whole transaction is the fact that Beaumarchais received a secret subsidy from the Kings of France and Spain in 1776 amounting to two million livres (the livre was replaced by the franc at the time of the French Revolution), and another million the following year. After the war Beaumarchais claimed that the United States government owed him 3,600,000 livres, but payment was put off when it was discovered that the American commissioners at Paris had given receipts to the French government for one million livres more than they had received. The million livres had been given to Beaumarchais by the French government and the United States insisted on the right to set it off against Beaumarchais's claim.

Beaumarchais's accounts were reviewed several times. His arch-foe, Arthur Lee, reported that he owed the United States 1,800,000 livres. Hamilton, when Secretary of the Treasury, restored a balance in his favor, but the French Revolutionary regime failed to support his claim. Beaumarchais's heirs in 1835 received 800,000 francs out of monies due to the United States for spoliations committed in the Napoleonic period in accordance with the treaty of 1831.

A. BEAUMARCHAIS SIGNS A RECEIPT FOR THE MILLION LIVRES

Vergennes refused the request of the United States to give up Beaumarchais's receipt, but after the French Revolution, on application of Gouverneur Morris, then minister to France, a copy of the receipt was turned over, and it is reproduced here in original and translation.

[1776]

J'ai reçu de Monsieur Du Vergier,—Conformément aux ordres de Monsieur le Comte de Vergennes en date du 5. courant que je lui ai remis. La somme d'un million, dont je rendrai compte à monditsieur Comte de Vergennes à Paris ce 10. juin 1776.

Signé: CARON DE BEAUMARCHAIS. Bon pour un million de livres tournois. Pour copie conforme.

Le commissaire de relations Extérieures.

BUCHOT

TRANSLATION: I have received from M. Du Vergier, in conformity with the instructions from the Count de Vergennes under date of the 5th current, which I have remitted to him. The sum of one million, for which I will give an accounting to the Count de Vergennes. At Paris the 10th June 1776.

Signed: Caron de Beaumarchais. For one million livres, Tours currency. [Worth about 10 d.]

A true copy.

The commissioner of foreign affairs.

—Gouverneur Morris Collection.

B. "AMERICANS, I DIE YOUR CREDITOR"

Beaumarchais to the American people.

Hamburg, April 10, 1795

Americans, I have served you with unwearied zeal; I have received during my life nothing but bitterness for my recompense, and I die your creditor. Suffer me, then, in dying, to bequeath to you my daughter to endow with a portion of what you owe me. Perhaps, after me, through the injustice of other persons, from which I shall no longer be able to defend myself, there will remain nothing in the world for her; and perhaps Providence has wished to procure for her, through your delay in paying me, a resource after my death against complete misfortune. Adopt her as a worthy child of the state!

Her mother—equally unhappy, and my widow—her mother will conduct her to you. Let her be looked upon among you as the daughter of a citizen.

But if, after this last effort, after all I have just said, contrary to all that seems possible, I could fear you would again reject my petition—if I could fear that to me or to my heirs you would refuse arbitrators, desperate, ruined as I am, as much through Europe as through you, and as your country is the only one where I can, without shame, extend my hand to the inhabitants, what remains for me to do except to supplicate Heaven to restore me for a short time to health, so as to permit me to travel to America? Arrived in the midst of you, with mind and body weakened, unable to maintain my rights, would it be necessary then that, with my proofs in my hand, I should be carried on a stool to the entrance of your national assemblies, and that, holding out to all the cap of liberty, with which no man has helped more than myself to decorate your heads, I should exclaim to you, "Americans, bestow alms on your friend, whose accumulated services have received but this reward? *Date obolum Belisario!*"

—De Lomenie, *Beaumarchais*, III, 217-218.

III. FRANCE ENTERS THE WAR

Three circumstances conspired to bring France into the war as an ally of America. First of all, there was Franklin's enormous prestige and popularity, a universal reputation to which even John Adams paid grudging tribute. This esteem is illustrated by two different accounts of a celebrated meeting between Franklin and Voltaire. The fur-capped Philadelphian epitomized all the virtues of an eighteenth-century Cincinnatus. His New World prestige was buttressed by Old World diplomatic skill and by his unique talents as a propagandist. Second came the victory at Saratoga, which made it clear that France could now get into the war on the winning side. Thirdly, the British efforts at conciliation with the colonies frightened France into taking hasty action without waiting upon her major ally, Spain.

After Saratoga, Vergennes was alarmed that he might miss the boat. "The power that will first recognize the independence of the Americans will be the one that will reap the fruits of this war," he wrote, paraphrasing Beaumarchais. Pressed by the American commissioners, who were receiving peace feelers from England, and in spite of Spain's refusal to join such an alliance, a French royal council on January 7, 1778, declared unanimously for a treaty of amity and commerce with the United States and then for a treaty of alliance on February 6.

The treaty of alliance had as its avowed end the "absolute and unlimited independence of the United States." It bound each of the allies to guarantee to the other the American possessions that it might hold at the end of the war. Hence, France was bound to defend American territory in North America, and the United States to come to the defense of the French West Indies. The treaty further provided that neither party should sign a treaty of peace with the common enemy without the consent of the other.

The treaty of amity and commerce defined the privileges to be enjoyed by the ships and commerce of both countries during a war in which one was neutral while the other was belligerent. The ships of the neutral should be free to carry noncontraband merchandise not only to the unblockaded ports of an enemy but from one enemy port to another. Free ships were to make free goods. Contraband was narrowly defined to consist almost entirely of arms and ammunition. All else was noncontraband. In addition, armed ships of the belligerent ally were to be allowed special privileges in the ports of the neutral, while they were to be denied to the ships of the opposing belligerent. This included the belligerent's right to bring prizes into the ports of the neutral and to depart with them without interference. These provisions were to plague the Federalist administration of Washington in the years ahead.

If to Vergennes France's entry into the war was sweet revenge, his counterpart in the negotiations, Benjamin Franklin, must have nursed emotions not unsimilar. Bancroft, the British secret agent and Franklin's secretary, later told the story that at the signing ceremony the Philadelphian wore the same suit of Manchester velvet that he had worn in London on that day in 1774 when he was subject to the savage examination of Attorney General Wedderburn for having made public certain letters of Governor Hutchinson—an event which was followed by Franklin's dismissal from his office of deputy postmaster general in America. Franklin never wore these clothes again. They had served their purpose.

1. THE REPUTATION AND INFLUENCE OF BENJAMIN FRANKLIN

A. SOLON AND SOPHOCLES EMBRACE

The diary of John Adams.

April 29, 1778. After dinner we went to the Academy of Sciences and heard M. d'Alembert, as perpetual secretary, pronounce eulogies on several of their members, lately deceased. Voltaire and Franklin were both present, and there presently arose a general cry that M. Voltaire and M. Franklin should be introduced to each other. This was done, and they bowed and spoke to each other. This was no satisfaction; there must be something more. Neither of our philosophers seemed to divine what was wished or expected; they, however, took each other by the hand. But this was not enough; the clamor continued, until the explanation came out. "*Il faut s'embrasser, à la Française.*" The two aged actors upon this great theatre of philosophy and frivolity then embraced each other, by hugging one another in their arms, kissing each other's cheeks, and then the tumult subsided. And the cry immediately spread through the whole kingdom, and, I suppose, over all Europe, "*Qu'il était charmant de voir embrasser Solon et Sophocle!*" . . .

—ADAMS, ed., *Works of John Adams*, III, 147.

B. CONDORCET RECOUNTS THE MEETING OF FRANKLIN AND VOLTAIRE

They then went to a public meeting of the Academy of Sciences. The scene was a moving one: Placed side by side, these two men, born in different worlds, venerated for their years, their reputations, the things they had done with their lives, and both delighting in the influence they had exerted in their age.

They embraced each other amid shouts of approval. Some one said that Solon was embracing Sophocles. But the French Sophocles had demolished error and advanced the reign of reason, while the Solon from Philadelphia, resting the constitution of his country on the unshakable foundation of the rights of man, had no occasion to fear that he would see during his lifetime doubtful laws fashioning chains for his country and opening the door to tyranny.

—CONDORCET, "Vie de Voltaire," *Oeuvres de Voltaire*, I, 290.

C. "MORE UNIVERSAL THAN NEWTON, FREDERICK OR VOLTAIRE, BUT——"

John Adams writes in May 1811 about Franklin's reputation.

Mr. Jefferson has said that Dr. Franklin was an honor to human nature. And so, indeed, he was. Had he been an ordinary man, I should never have taken the trouble to expose the turpitude of his intrigues, or to vindicate my reputation against his vilifications and calumnies. But the temple of human nature has two great apartments: the intellectual and the moral. If there is not a mutual friendship and strict alliance between these, degradation to the whole building must be the consequence. There may be blots on the disk of the most refulgent luminary, almost sufficient to eclipse it. And it is of great importance to the rising generation in this country that they be put upon their guard against being dazzled by the surrounding blaze into an idolatry to the spots. If the affable archangel understood the standard of merit, that

"Great or bright infers not excellence,"

Franklin's character can neither be applauded nor condemned, without discrimination and many limitations.

To all those talents and qualities for the foundation of a great and lasting character, which were held up to the view of the whole world by the University of Oxford, the Royal Society of London and the Royal Academy of Sciences in Paris, were added, it is believed, more artificial modes of diffusing, celebrating and exaggerating his reputation than were ever before or since practiced in favor of any individual.

His reputation was more universal than that of Leibnitz or Newton, Frederick or Voltaire, and his character more beloved and esteemed than any or all of them. Newton had astonished perhaps forty or fifty men in Europe; for not more than that number, probably, at any one time had read him and understood him by his discoveries and demonstrations. And these being held in admiration in their respective countries as at the head of the philosophers, had spread among scientific people a mysterious wonder at the genius of this perhaps the greatest man that ever lived. But this fame was confined to men of letters. The common people knew little and cared nothing about such a recluse philosopher. Leibnitz's name was more confined still. Frederick was hated by more than half of Europe as much as Louis XIV was, and as Napoleon is. Voltaire, whose name was more universal than any of those before mentioned, was considered as a vain, profligate wit, and not much esteemed or beloved by anybody, though admired by all who knew his works.

But Franklin's fame was universal. His name was familiar to government and people, to kings, courtiers, nobility, clergy and philosophers, as well as plebeians, to such a degree that there was scarcely a peasant or a citizen, a *valet de chambre*, coachman or footman, a lady's chambermaid or a scullion in a kitchen who was not familiar with it, and who did not consider him as a friend to human kind. When they spoke of him, they seemed to think he was to restore the golden age. They seemed enraptured enough to exclaim

Aspice, venturo laetentur ut omnia saeclo.

To develop that complication of causes which conspired to produce so singular a phenomenon is far beyond my means or forces. Perhaps it can never be done without a complete history of the philosophy and politics of the eighteenth century. Such a work would be one of the most important that ever was written; much more interesting to this and future ages than the *Decline and Fall of the Roman Empire*, splendid and useful as that is. . . . He [Franklin] was considered as a citizen of the world, a friend to all men and an enemy to none. His rigorous taciturnity was very favorable to this singular felicity. He conversed only with individuals, and freely only with confidential friends. In company he was totally silent. . . .

Franklin had a great genius, original, sagacious and inventive, capable of discoveries in science no less than of improvements in the fine arts and the mechanic arts. He had a vast imagination, equal to the comprehension of the greatest objects, and capable of a steady and cool comprehension of them. He had wit at will. He had humor that, when he pleased, was delicate and delightful. He had a satire that was good-natured or caustic, Horace or Juvenal, Swift or Rabelais, at his pleasure. He had talents for irony, allegory and fable that he could adapt with great skill to the promotion of moral and political truth. He was master of that infantine simplicity which the French call *naïveté*, which never fails to charm, in *Phaedrus* and La Fontaine, from the cradle to the grave. Had he been blessed with the same advantages of scholastic education in his early youth, and pursued a course of studies as unembarrassed with occupations of public and private life, as Sir Isaac Newton, he might have emulated the first philosopher. Although I am not ignorant that most of his positions and hypotheses have been controverted, I cannot but think he has added much to the mass of natural knowledge, and contributed largely to the progress of the human mind, both by his own writings and by the controversies and experiments he has excited in all parts of Europe. . . .

—ADAMS, ed., *Works of John Adams*, I, 659-661, 663-664.

2. SARATOGA WORKS A REVOLUTION IN THE FRENCH ATTITUDE

Journal of Arthur Lee.

27 *Nov.* [*1777*]. The commissioners met to consult on their despatches to Congress. Mr. D[eane] began the discourse; he remarked upon the proceedings of this court, with a good deal of ill-humour and discontent, said he thought it was our duty to state the whole to Congress, that things seem to be going very bad in America, they would be less provided for next campaign, and more pressed than ever. He therefore was of opinion we should lay before this court such a statement as would produce a categorical answer to the

proposition of an alliance, or satisfy them that without an immediate interposition, we must accommodate with Great Britain.

Dr. F[ranklin] was of a different opinion; he could not consent to state
that we must give up the contest without their interposition, because the effect
of such a declaration upon them was uncertain. It might be taken as a menace.
It might make them abandon us in despair or in anger. Besides he did not think
it true. He was clearly of opinion that we could maintain the contest, and
successfully too, without any European assistance; he was satisfied, as he had
said formerly, that the less commerce or dependence we had upon Europe,
the better, for that we should do better without any connexion with it.

Mr. Lee was against any such declaration, lest it might deprive them of
the assistance they now received instead of increasing it. He thought this
court had acted uniformly and consistently with their declarations; that the
violent things done were of necessity, and compelled by the bad conduct of
our people; that we ought to instruct those who were going to America to
avoid speaking with bitterness against this country, but rather to soften the
resentment of others, arising from considering the injuries and not the benefits
we had received from France; he was of opinion that if the credit of their
funds was maintained, all would go well. . . .

[*Dec.*] *6th*. Mons. Gérard, first secretary to Count Vergennes, met the
commissioners at Passy. He said he came from the counts Maurepas* and
Vergennes, to congratulate the commissioners upon the news [of the American victory at Saratoga], to assure them of the great pleasure it gave at Versailles, and to desire on the part of the king any farther particulars they might
have. He was informed that extracts were making from all the papers, which
should be sent the moment it was finished; and Mr. L. promised to send
extracts from his brother's letter, which contained some farther particulars.
Mr. Gérard said they might depend on three millions of livres also from
Spain, but he believed it would be through the Havannah and New-Orleans.
He said as there now appeared no doubt of the ability and resolution of the
states to maintain their independency, he could assure them it was wished
they would reassume their former proposition of an alliance, or any new one
they might have, and that it could not be done too soon; that the court of
Spain must be consulted, that they might act in harmony, and prepare for war
in a few months.

—R. H. LEE, *Life of Arthur Lee*, I, 354-355, 357-358.

3. NEGOTIATING AN ALLIANCE WITH VERGENNES

Journal of Arthur Lee.

Dec. 12th, [*1777*]. My colleagues did not reach Versailles till half after
eleven o'clock, when, upon sending notice by a servant to Mr. Girard, his
servant came with a hackney coach and carried us to a house about half a mile
from Versailles, where we found Count Vergennes and his secretary. . . .

The minister took our last memorial from his secretary and read it. He
then desired we would give him the information it promised, and any thing

---

* Count Jean Frédéric de Maurepas, Principal Minister in the Cabinet of Louis XVI.

we had new to offer. Dr. F[ranklin] said that the entering into the treaty proposed was the object, and that if there were any objections to it, we were ready to consider them. The count said that it was the resolution of his court to take no advantage of our situation, to desire no terms of which we might afterwards repent and endeavour to retract; but to found whatever they did so much upon the basis of mutual interest as to make it last as long as human institutions would endure. He said that entering into a treaty with us would be declaring our independency, and necessarily draw on a war. In this, therefore, Spain must be consulted, without whose concurrence nothing could be done. . . .

The next objection was that Spain would not be satisfied with the indeterminate boundary between their dominions and the United States, for that the state of Virginia, being supposed to run to the South Sea, might trench upon California. It was answered that the line drawn by the last treaty of peace with England, the Mississippi, would be adopted and would prevent all disputes. For that, though its source was not yet known, yet it might be agreed that a line drawn straight from its source, when found, should continue the boundary. This was admitted, as adjusting the matter properly. . . . It was, too, a first principle with us that fishing was free to all.

The conference ended with the count's observing that we must consider our independence as yet in the womb, and must not endeavour to hasten its birth immaturely. That he would despatch a courier to Spain, and it would be three weeks before his return. That the order for presenting clearances for the United States was recalled, and he would speak with Mons. de Sartine [Minister of Marine] about giving us a convoy for our supplies.

–R. H. Lee, *Life of Arthur Lee,* I, 360-362.

4. It Is Now or Never If France and Spain Are to Profit

Comte de Vergennes to Comte Armand de Montmorin, French Ambassador at Madrid.

Versailles, December 13, 1777

. . . You will understand, Monsieur le Comte, that what I send today . . . must be communicated to the Minister. . . . I shall not recall here either the outlines or the reflections which you will find scattered there; I am sure you will seize in a masterly way the whole state of affairs, and add to the force they so naturally present. There are, however, some considerations I did not wish to insert, which I have reserved for you, and which you will appropriate if you think them worth the trouble.

The first is that Spain's interest in this matter is at least ten times as much as ours; our islands are little likely to tempt the cupidity of the English, who have enough of them themselves. They want treasure, and it is only on the mainland that they can gather it. That being the case, it is easy to estimate, on the one hand, the infinite advantage to Spain of the absolute separation of new and old England, and the safety and peace which would be procured by the guarantee of the former; and, on the other hand, the incessantly arising uneasiness and dangers with which she would be threatened by too close a political coalition between the two nations.

A second reflection may bear on the fresh advantages which Spain may obtain. Perhaps she regrets the loss of Florida, which gives too easy access to the Gulf of Mexico, and would see that province with as much pain in the hands of the United States of America as in those of England. I do not know what the Americans may think on this subject; I have not taken measures to find out; but it is natural to suppose that they cannot care much about a thing which they do not yet possess, and which does not even seem of major importance to them. They are still too young to have ambitious views about opening up an interloping trade for themselves; being without any manufactures suitable for the use of the West Indies, they cannot aspire to carry their goods to lands which would be in a position to furnish them with the same.

A third reflection, which seems a natural consequence of the preceding ones, is that the interest for separating the English Colonies from their mother country and preventing them from ever being re-identified in any manner whatever is so important that even if it had to be purchased at the price of a somewhat disadvantageous war, if the two Crowns brought about that separation, it seems that they should not regret that war, whatever the issue may be.

The King our master is fully convinced, Sir, of these truths; they are so impressed on his mind that although exempt from that cruel ambition which causes the unhappiness of a country, having no views of conquest whatever, His Majesty would not hesitate to declare himself openly and be beforehand with the English, if his extreme delicacy and his warm attachment to the King his uncle did not cause his own interests to give way to the deference which he professes in his heart for that Prince whose enlightenment he admires and whose experience he reveres.

Take for your device, Monsieur le Comte, and cause it to be adopted where you are, *aut nunc aut nunquam* [now or never]. Events have surprised us; they have marched more rapidly than we could have expected. The time lost, if any, is not entirely our fault, but there is no more to be lost. I am pleased to think that no breach has yet been committed, and that if Spain will be good enough to tell us her decision, and the right one, we shall be beforehand with the English, or at least shall cross them: if, against all expectation, we disdain or neglect the most important conjuncture which Heaven could offer, the reproaches of the present generation and those of posterity will for ever accuse our culpable indifference.

—*Stevens' Facsimiles*, No. 1775.

5. VERGENNES AGREES TO A TREATY OF ALLIANCE

Narrative of Conrad Gérard, Secretary to Vergennes, of a conference with the American commissioners.

January 9, 1778

Count de Maurepas and Count de Vergennes having been good enough to commission me to announce to the American Deputies the resolutions taken by the King in adopting the memorandum intended for Spain, . . . we agreed to meet yesterday evening at six o'clock at Mr. Deane's house in Paris. . . .

I opened the conference by announcing that I was charged with a message which would begin to realise the hopes and the assurances which the King and his Ministry had caused to be given them, . . . but [as] in so important a matter most absolute secrecy should be observed, I must before all things beg them to be good enough to promise that, whatever might be the result of our conference and of the whole negotiation, they would not confide my message to anyone soever. . . .

I was allowed to continue to hold forth in this strain, Mr. Deane sometimes supporting my reasoning, and I then formally repeated my proposal. Dr. Franklin finally said, "I promise," and Mr. Lee and Mr. Deane repeated the same formula. Considering the distrust entertained of the Doctor's views, I think I gained a very important point.

Then I declared that, being now able to speak to them without reserve, I would announce to them that the King, being henceforth persuaded that the United States were resolved to maintain their independence, had decided to co-operate efficaciously to uphold it and to cause it to be firmly established; that the very deliberation which His Majesty had observed in coming to this decision, guaranteed the sincerity of his disposition and the firmness which he would bring to the carrying out of his resolutions; that they were exempt from all views of ambition and aggrandisement; that he only desired to bring about irrevocably and completely the independence of the United States; that he would find therein his essential interest in the weakening of his natural enemy, and that this important and permanent interest would render the American cause in future common to France; that His Majesty could not yet take nor announce a decisive course, which depended on combinations personal to himself, and on matters which he could not concert with the Deputies; but that I hoped that the specific and positive assurances I was authorised to give them would cause the most entire confidence in His Majesty's sentiments and in the disposition of His Ministry; that I consequently expected that the Deputies would in future unreservedly disclose their views; that we must at the present moment consider in this way two things which might be distinct: 1st, the decisive means for ending this great quarrel, the examination and employment of which would require time and would depend on events; and 2nd, the necessity of immediately preventing the effect of all the traps and manoeuvres which England employs to seduce the Deputies, and perhaps Congress, by the bait of a false peace and a mutilated or precarious independence; that they must not be mistaken; that England felt that the Americans were really in possession of their independence and would strive to allow only the shadow of it to exist, and that it would perhaps be limited to exclusive commercial advantages; but that it would suffice her to preserve some sort of thread of dependence and obligation, in order to put afterwards the liberty and tranquillity of the Colonies in danger; that they must not deceive themselves; and that the most clear-sighted people had felt, from the beginning of the troubles, that it was a commercial war, and that the least advantage saved for the mother country would decide the contest in her favour. . . .

Mr. Franklin briefly took up my speech, and spoke in a sense which inferred an immediate war.

As soon as I saw him bear on that idea, I stopped him, and stated that the immediate declaration of war did not enter into the present policy of the

King, and that amongst the means we sought, that one must be absolutely excluded. . . . I thought right to press him by telling him that the most urgent point depended on them—the Deputies—since it was a question of knowing what they, as zealous and enlightened citizens, would consider sufficient to reject all the proposals of England which did not include the recognition of full and absolute independence both in politics and trade, and that my second question was—what would they consider equally necessary to produce the same effect on Congress, and on the American people?

Mr. Franklin again spoke of war, and said afterwards that my two questions presented great difficulties, which would require time to settle, and he wished to defer giving me his reply to another day. I told him that I did not know when I could return, but that it seemed to me he might at least answer me as to their personal views. . . .

The Doctor . . . said that he would like to be able to settle the reply together. I . . . said that it was for me to leave them to deliberate without restraint, that I would go away and return. . . . It was agreed that I should return in an hour.

On my return, I found Mr. Franklin writing; he told me they were agreed as to the first point of my request, but that they had not yet come to a decision on the second. I was going to withdraw again, but Mr. Deane stopped me, saying that the manner in which I should explain the first point might facilitate their agreement on the second. I consequently proposed to the Doctor that he should read their first decision. He . . . read an article to the effect that *the immediate conclusion of a treaty of commerce and alliance would induce the Deputies to close their ears to any proposal which should not have as its basis entire liberty and independence, both political and commercial.*

I then declared that the King and his Ministry having presumed that such would be the desire of the Deputies, I had been authorised to tell them that whenever they should judge that treaty to be necessary His Majesty was resolved to conclude it at once, and that it would be begun as soon as they wished.

The Doctor, already softened by this resolution, which he did not appear to expect, observed that this was what they had proposed and solicited vainly for a year past. . . .

I . . . explained to him that two treaties might be concluded: the first, of peace, friendship and commerce, and the second, of eventual alliance; that the first would only contain clauses tending to regulate and confirm good feeling and commerce, that it would be permanent, would only contain harmless clauses, but that it would involve the recognition of independence. . . .

I added that the King, not wishing to make a war of ambition did not think he ought to require the United States to procure him any advantages or any increase of dominion; that the strengthening of the independence forming the principal object of his efforts, everything else would be accessory only; and that the compensation which France might justly claim would depend on events, without embarrassing the alliance with clauses the nonfulfillment of which (often impossible to carry out) only leads to dissatisfaction; that if nevertheless plans were formed on both sides they could agree as to the help to be furnished mutually as well as the advantages destined to form the compensation; that good policy would perhaps demand that they should agree not to cease war until the English were expelled from the continent of North America; that I did not know whether the King would make this a condition, or whether the States themselves would consider themselves in a position to carry out an enterprise on which their security and tranquillity appeared to depend.

The Deputies applauded this recital with a sort of transport. . . .

—Stevens' Facsimiles, No. 1831.

CHAPTER SIXTEEN

England Seeks Reconciliation

ALTHOUGH BY THE end of *1774* George III was determined that blows would decide the issue, conciliatory moves were nonetheless attempted before the actual outbreak of hostilities. They were initiated both in the colonies and in England. We have already seen how the Plan of Union, offered by the Loyalist Joseph Galloway and based substantially upon Franklin's plan of *1754,* was barely defeated in the First Continental Congress. Galloway's proposal would have set up a subordinate legislature in America, in effect creating a dominion status for the colonies. In February *1775,* Chatham offered a bill legalizing the forthcoming meeting of the Second Continental Congress and denying Parliament's right to tax the colonies for revenue purposes, but nothing came of it. Instead, Lord North's own plan of reconciliation was endorsed by the Commons; by its terms Parliament would "forbear" to lay any but regulatory taxes upon any American colony. Since this proposal was coupled with legislation restraining New Englanders in trading and fishing, it was hardly issued in a conciliatory spirit. Still, despite the bloodshed at Lexington and Bunker's Hill, Congress in July of '75 adopted the Olive Branch Petition professing the attachment of the American people to George III, but that monarch refused even to receive it and issued instead his Proclamation of Rebellion.

Having spurned Congress' original offer of conciliation, the North ministry suffered a change of heart and sent the olive branch to America on two separate occasions. The Howe mission, as we have already seen, was launched unpropitiously after the Declaration of Independence had been adopted. Its offer of conciliation was backed by what then seemed to be overwhelming force, and still it was rejected. The next occasion upon which the British formally presented conciliation terms was when the prospects of France's entry into the war on the side of the colonies seemed imminent. Since any proposal short of independence was not acceptable in the summer of '76, it should have seemed futile to even the most obtuse British cabinet officer to propose reconciliation when the Patriots had shown unexpected power on the battlefield and considerable success in securing foreign aid. True, the liberal terms which the Carlisle Commission was prepared to offer would have resolved all the major issues leading to the Revolution had they been *proposed back in '74, but now it was too late. This chapter deals with Britain's persistent efforts to end the conflict by negotiation, intrigue or bribery.*

I. THE ATTEMPT TO WOO FRANKLIN

The same desperate urgency that characterized French overtures to America after Saratoga marked British efforts both on the continent and in America to bring about reconciliation in order to prevent the alliance, and, when that was a fait accompli, *to split the allies. In January 1778, James Hutton, an English Moravian, approached Franklin with peace feelers, but was quickly rebuked. Another Englishman, William Pulteney, followed suit. Franklin in March of '78 reminded him: "I see by the propositions you have communicated to me that the ministers cannot yet divest themselves of the idea that the power of Parliament over us is constitutionally absolute and unlimited." Acknowledgment of independence, he reminded Pulteney, was a* sine qua non *for ending hostilities. Finally, on July 1, he contemptuously rejected the proposals contained in a letter from "Charles de Weissenstein," believed by Franklin to be from King George, and containing peace proposals. It contained the suggestion that the American leaders might be bought with promises of peerages and substantial pensions. Franklin's reply was never sent, but instead was deposited at the French Foreign Office. Apprised that "M. Weissenstein" might show up at Notre Dame Cathedral to receive Franklin's answer, the French secret service reported seeing a mysterious stranger who lurked about the church for two hours and then disappeared.*

1. FRANKLIN SPURNS PEACE FEELERS

A. JAMES HUTTON TO BENJAMIN FRANKLIN

London, January 27, 1778

I got to my own house in seventy-three hours from Paris. I shall never forget your kindness to me and your kind intention to serve my Brethren. The sensation I had of the certain miseries of war, that would attend all parties embarked in it, caused my heart almost to break. I always thought it a sad misfortune that there was such a thing as war upon earth.

When I left England I fancied that you and Mr. Deane could treat about peace. I wished it ardently; but having no commission, nor anything to offer, I was sorry to hear nothing of your side that I could mention as ground to treat upon, to such as I fancied could give it weight. I was a loving volunteer, loving both people with common ardour; a friend of peace; a hater of discord, with horror at all bloodshed, wishing you secure in your liberties, and guarded forever against all apprehensions. I did before I set out, and I do now still at this moment, and I think on better grounds, believe that anything short of absolute independency would almost be practicable, and could take place. There is such a spirit and temper now in the nation that I cannot think independency could be successfully proposed. If you and Mr. Deane could give me a hint of anything practicable, you considering not only your own case but ours, I would venture to try what could be done.

I know your hand writing as well as I do your heart. Direct your answer to me Queen's Row, Pimlico, Westminister, under the cover to M. Count de Gebelin, Rue Pompei, Paris, who will put a cover over it, and my friend Mr. Fullerton will without examination forward it to me in the packet of Mr. Stormont.

B. BENJAMIN FRANKLIN TO JAMES HUTTON

Passy, February 1, 1778

My Dear Old Friend,

You desired that if I had no proposition to make, I would at least give my advice. I think it is Ariosto who says that all things lost on earth are to be found in the moon; on which somebody remarked that there must be a great deal of good advice in the moon. If so, there is a good deal of mine, formerly given and lost in this business. I will, however, at your request, give a little more, but without the least expectation that it will be followed; for none but God can at the same time give good counsel and wisdom to make use of it.

You have lost by this mad war, and the barbarity with which it has been carried on, not only the Government and commerce of America, and the public revenues and private wealth arising from that commerce; but what is more, you have lost the esteem, respect, friendship and affection of all that great and growing people, who consider you at present, and whose posterity will consider you, as the worst and wickedest nation upon earth. A peace you may undoubtedly obtain by dropping all your pretensions to govern us; and to your superior skill in huckstering negociations, you may possibly make such an apparently advantageous bargain as shall be applauded in your Parliament; but if you cannot, with the peace, recover the affections of that people, it will not be a lasting nor a profitable one, nor will it afford you any part of that strength which you once had by your union with them, and might (if you had been wise enough to take advice) have still retained.

To recover their respect and affection, you must tread back the steps you have taken. Instead of honouring and rewarding the . . . advisers and promoters of this war, you should disgrace them, with all those who have influenced the nation against America by their malicious writings, and all the ministers and generals who have prosecuted the war with such inhumanity. This would show a national change of disposition and a disapprobation of what had passed.

In proposing terms, you should not only grant such as the necessity of your affairs may evidently oblige you to grant, but such additional ones as may shew your generosity, and thereby demonstrate your good will. For instance, perhaps you might by your treaty, retain all Canada, Nova Scotia and the Floridas. But if you would have a really friendly, as well as able ally in America, and avoid all occasion of future discord, which will otherwise be continually arising on your American frontiers, you should throw in those countries. And you may call it, if you please, an indemnification for the burning of their towns, which indemnification will, otherwise, be some time or other demanded.

I know your people will not see the utility of such measures and will never follow them, and even call it insolence and impudence in me to mention them. I have, however, complied with your desire.

—HUTTON, "Account of Hutton's Visit to Franklin," *Penn. Mag. of Hist. and Biog.*, XXXII, 228-230.

2. FRANKLIN SCORNS AN ATTEMPT TO WIN PEACE BY BRIBERY

Benjamin Franklin to "Charles de Weissenstein."

Passy, July 1, 1778

I received your letter, dated at Brussels the 16th past. My vanity might possibly be flattered by your expressions of compliment to my understanding, if your *proposals* did not more clearly manifest a mean opinion of it.

You conjure me, in the name of the omniscient and just God before whom I must appear, and by my hopes of future fame, to consider if some expedient cannot be found to put a stop to the desolation of America, and prevent the miseries of a general war. As I am conscious of having taken every step in my power to prevent the breach, and no one to widen it, I can appear cheerfully before that God, fearing nothing from his justice in this particular though I have much occasion for his mercy in many others. As to my future fame, I am content to rest it on my past and present conduct, without seeking an addition to it in the crooked, dark paths you propose to me, where I should most certainly lose it. This your solemn address would therefore have been more properly made to your sovereign and his venal Parliament. He and they, who wickedly began, and madly continue, a war for the desolation of America, are alone accountable for the consequences. . . .

You think we flatter ourselves and are deceived into an opinion that England *must* acknowledge our independency. We, on the other hand, think you flatter yourselves in imagining such an acknowledgement a vast boon, which we strongly desire, and which you may gain some great advantage by granting or withholding. We have never asked it of you; we only tell you that you can have no treaty with us but as an independent state; and you may please yourselves and your children with the rattle of your right to govern us, as long as you have done with that of your King's being King of France, without giving us the least concern if you do not attempt to exercise it. That this pretended right is indisputable, as you say, we utterly deny. Your Parliament never had a right to govern us, and your King has forfeited it by his bloody tyranny. But I thank you for letting me know a little of your mind, that, even if the Parliament should acknowledge our independency, the act would not be binding to posterity, and that your nation would resume and prosecute the claim as soon as they found it convenient from the influence of your passions, and your present malice against us. We suspected before that you would not be actually bound by your conciliatory acts longer than till they had served their purpose of inducing us to disband our forces; but we were not certain that you were knaves by principle, and that we ought not to have the least confidence in your offers, promises, or treaties, though confirmed by Parliament. . . .

One main drift of your letter seems to be to impress me with an idea of your own impartiality, by just censures of your ministers and measures, and to draw from me propositions of peace, or approbations of those you have inclosed to me, which you intimate may by your means be conveyed to the King directly, without the intervention of those ministers. You would have me give them to, or drop them for, a stranger, whom I may find next Monday in the church of Notre Dame, to be known by a rose in his hat. You yourself, Sir, are quite unknown to me; you have not trusted me with your true name. Our taking the least step towards a treaty with England through you, might, if you are an enemy, be made use of to ruin us with our new and good friends. I may be indiscreet enough in many things; but certainly, if I were disposed to make propositions (which I cannot do, having none committed to me to make), I should never think of delivering them to the Lord knows who, to be carried to the Lord knows where, to serve no one knows what purposes. Being at this time one of the most remarkable figures in Paris, even my appearance in the church of Notre Dame, where I cannot have any conceivable business, and especially being seen to leave or drop any letter to any person there, would be a matter of some speculation, and might, from the suspicions it must naturally give, have very mischievous consequences to our credit here. . . .

This proposition of delivering ourselves, bound and gagged, ready for hanging, without even a right to complain, and without a friend to be found afterwards among all mankind, you would have us embrace upon the faith of an act of Parliament! Good God! An act of your Parliament! This demonstrates that you do not yet know us, and that you fancy we do not know you; but it is not merely this flimsy faith that we are to act upon; you offer us *hope*, the hope of PLACES, PENSIONS and PEERAGES. These, judging from yourselves, you think are motives irresistible. This offer to corrupt us, Sir, is with me your credential, and convinces me that you are not a private volunteer in your application. It bears the stamp of British Court character. It is even the signature of your King. But think for a moment in what light it must be viewed in America. By PLACES, you mean places among us, for you take care by a special article to secure your own to yourselves. We must then pay the salaries in order to enrich ourselves with these places. But you will give us PENSIONS, probably to be paid too out of your expected American revenue, and which none of us can accept without deserving, and perhaps obtaining, a sus-*pension*. PEERAGES! alas! Sir, our long observation of the vast servile majority of your peers, voting constantly for every measure proposed by a minister, however weak or wicked, leaves us small respect for that title. We consider it as a sort of *tar-and-feather* honour, or a mixture of foulness and folly, which every man among us who should accept it from your King would be obliged to renounce, or exchange for that conferred by the mobs of their own country, or wear it with everlasting infamy.

—SMYTH, ed., *Writings of Franklin*, VII, 166-172.

II. THE CARLISLE COMMISSION

Failing to thwart the American commissioners in Paris, the British deemed more direct overtures immediately required. On February 17, 1778, before the existence of the Franco-American treaty had been announced to the British court, although its actuality had already leaked out, Lord North introduced in the House of Commons his proposals for conciliation. There followed a memorable scene which Horace Walpole caustically describes. An important bloc in the opposition ranks led by Rockingham would have given America her freedom and ended the contest. But not so Chatham, who in his last speech melodramatically opposed renouncing the sovereignty of America, collapsed, and was borne from the House a dying man. Notwithstanding strong opposition the well-trained cohorts of Lord North accepted this plan for reconciliation and he promptly dispatched a commission to go to America.

The Carlisle Commission took its name from one of its members, Frederick, Earl of Carlisle. To Horace Walpole, Carlisle cut a ridiculous figure. He described him as "a young man of pleasure and fashion, fond of dress and gaming, by which he had greatly hurt his fortune, as totally unacquainted with business, and though not void of ambition, [one who] had but moderate parts, and less application." The originator of the conciliation move was another member of the Commission, William Eden, who drafted North's legislation. The third member of the team was George Johnstone, onetime governor of Florida, a man innocent alike of abilities and of real integrity.

No intimation was given to the Commission of the military or naval plans afoot, although Germain did tell Carlisle to go to New York instead of Philadelphia. "Perhaps that city may not by your arrival be in our hands," he intimated. This was a slip, but the Commission reached Philadelphia in June 1778, just as Sir Henry Clinton was evacuating the city. Loyalist morale and British prestige were at their nadir in that area. Carlisle in a letter to his wife written from his ship, the Trident, *on the Delaware River conceded that the position of the Commission was already "desperate." "As long as we had the army to back us," he explained, "we had hopes of success; but this turning our backs upon Mr. Washington will certainly make them reject offers that perhaps the fear of what that army could have done would have made them listen to."*

Carlisle proved himself a better prophet than a negotiator. Congress refused to appoint commissioners to confer with the British, and the Commission itself made the fatal error of trying to bribe prominent Americans, and then of appealing over the head of the Congress to the people. The mission failed because it came too late, offered too little, and conducted itself in a pompous and even an offensive manner. What is perhaps most astonishing is that British officials deluded themselves that men like Washington, Franklin and Joseph Reed were susceptible to bribery, and that their peace overtures would be "gladly embraced" by the American people.

The British offer was—by British standards—farsighted and liberal; had it been proposed in 1775 or 1776 it would doubtless have satisfied all but the most extreme of the Patriots. Under its terms Britain agreed to keep no stand-

ing army in the colonies in time of peace, to make no change in colonial char-
ters save at the request of the assemblies concerned, to appoint judges during
good behavior, to consider American representation in Parliament or—if
Americans preferred—to recognize the American Congress as a permanent
institution. These concessions would have transformed the British Empire
into something very much like a commonwealth.

1. "An Unequalled Confession of Criminality in the Ministers"

The Journal of Horace Walpole.

Feb. 17, 1778. Disappointed, defeated, disgraced, alarmed, but still depending on a majority in both Houses, and on the blindness and indifference
of the nation, the Administration ventured on taking the very opposite part
to all they had been doing; and as if there was no shame but in losing their
places, presumed to tell the three Kingdoms that they must abandon all the
high views with which they had been lulled, and must stoop to beg peace of
America *at any rate.*

This was the substance of Lord North's opening his plan, which the very
night before had not been fixed, or not fully opened to a meeting of the principal Members at Lord North's—yet even then it had given disgust. The
Attorney-General Thurlow had protested he would take no part in it—and
did at last take but a very cold one. Lord North, who seldom shone when he
could not jest, made a sorry figure except in assurance. He declared he would
treat with the Congress, with anybody—*would even allow the independence*
of the Colonies—not verbally, yet virtually. He owned all his disappointments
—yet recurred to his usual defence, that every act had been the Act of the
Parliament. All the comfort he gave the country gentlemen was some hopes
that America might be persuaded to contribute some pecuniary assistance. He
allowed till the following June twelvemonth for the duration of the negotiation. . . .

The astonishment of a great part of the House at such extensive offers
precluded all expression. The Opposition felt honestly that they could not
decently disapprove a pacification they had so much recommended; and
during the course of the bill the Ministers had the satisfaction of finding this
integrity operate on some of the most upright but least clear-sighted, as Lord
George Cavendish and Frederick Montague pressed the Ministers not to lose
a moment in passing the bills—an instance of more virtue than judgement; for
the duplicity of the Court ought to have made them suspect fraud, and to
weigh every tittle of bills which were likely to be insidious, and the more concise the more capable of sinister interpretations.

The Tories, who could not like concessions so inadequate to their hopes,
and so repugnant to their high-flown attachment to the Prerogative, seeing
the intemperate zeal of the Opposition, were ashamed to mark themselves as
an obstinate and weak party, which they would be if they separated from the
Court when approved by the Opposition. Burke and Charles Fox yielded to
and seconded the torrent; but the latter threw a bomb that much disconcerted
though it did not disappoint the Minister. My cousin Thomas Walpole had

acquainted me that the treaty with France was signed. We agreed to inform Charles Fox; but as we both distrusted Burke, and feared the childish fluctuations of Lord Rockingham, we determined that Fox should know nothing of the secret till an hour or two before the House met. Accordingly, T. Walpole communicated the notice of the treaty to the Duke of Grafton on the 16th, and engaged him to acquaint Charles Fox, but just before the House should meet the next day. This was done most exactly, and Burke knew nothing of the matter till he came into the House.

As soon as Lord North had opened his two bills, Charles Fox rose, and after pluming himself on having sat there till he had brought the noble Lord to concur in sentiments with him and his friends, he astonished his Lordship with asking him whether a commercial treaty with France had not been signed by the American agents at Paris within the last ten days! If so, said he, the Administration is beaten by ten days—a situation so threatening that in such a time of danger the whole House must concur with the propositions, though probably now they would have no effect. Lord North was thunderstruck, and would not rise. . . .

George Grenville, with more sagacity than the rest, showed he felt the ignominious posture of his country in such humiliating concessions. He spoke with energy and weight, said he had been deceived by Administration, and the country had been so too. He would worship any man as the saviour of his country who could make peace; but he did not think these propositions would have that effect. He had seen an extract of a letter from Dr. Franklin, which asserted the treaty as a fact:—what then would be our situation with France? Were these our triumphs?—this the dignity of Parliament? *He felt the humiliating blush that must spread the cheek of his Sovereign when he should be called to give his assent to these bills.* He thought the Parliament had not been to bend, but to assert.

Gilbert, an agent of Lord Gower, proposed rather to tax placemen to carry on the war.

Burke maintained that Lord North had taken precisely the plan that he (Burke) had offered two years before; and he called on his Lordship to answer to the fact of the treaty.

Still the Minister was silent; till George Saville rose and told him it would be criminal to withhold a reply, and a matter of impeachment, and ended with crying, "An answer! an answer! an answer!"

Lord North, thus forced up, owned he had heard the report of a treaty, but desired to give no answer to the House at that moment. He had no official intelligence on that subject. The report might be vague. Some time ago the Ministers of France had denied it.

Such evasive answers rather convinced everybody of the truth. (Three days after this, Lord Mansfield, at Lady Gower's, said openly that the Ministers did not speak truth if they denied the treaty, for it was certainly signed!) Leave was then given, *nemine contradicente*, for the two bills to be brought in.

Such an avowal, in effect, of criminality, ignorance, and incapacity in the Ministers had never been equalled—nor, since King John surrendered his

Crown at the Nuncio's feet, could a more ignominious instance of the debasement of a great monarch be quoted. The Ministers had stigmatized the whole body of colonists as cowards, and boasted they could traverse the whole continent of America with 5000 men; and in four years stooped to offer terms infinitely beyond what would have glutted the most sanguine or presumptuous wishes of the insurgents but two years ago! No matter whether sincere their offers or not: *if insincere, it was but another infamy.* But how could England but fall into disgrace and contempt, when Ministers, by turns so audacious, so criminal, and so mean, remained yet undisturbed in their posts? Their cruelty, injustice, defeats had revolted few. Few showed either joy or indignation at their recantation. The Scots at first inveighed against the pacific spirit, but soon grew so silent that no doubt they were let into the secret of the insincerity of the Court—and both the King and the Scots enjoyed any ignominy that fell on the Parliament.

—WALPOLE, *Journal*, II, 200 *et seq.*

2. SIR JOHN DALRYMPLE SUGGESTS A DUKEDOM FOR WASHINGTON

[*c*. March 1778]

"Thoughts on instructions to the American Commissioners."

... 4thly, America will desire that the laws be repealed which cramp her internal manufactures for the advantages of the British manufactures. It is also full time for England to recover her dream on this head. These laws are of no use to England, because they are not executable in America. They are unpopular, in their eyes they are unjust, and therefore the juries on whom the execution of them depends never did and never will give effect to them.

5thly, America will ask that the laws be repealed which have interfered in their internal police; for example, which have declared that a tender of paper payment shall not be a legal tender. It is the busy, meddling, officious, practmatical [*sic*]—I had almost said Parliamentary—turn of England which has brought the present mischief upon us; is it worth our while to maintain a war to prevent the Americans from cheating each other, or even a few of ourselves, in their modes of payments? If our merchants are cheated, they will stop giving credits to the cheaters and then the cheaters will grow honest to recover their credits with our merchants. . . .

I presume to suggest another thing. From all accounts of General Washington's character there is a resemblance between his character and General Monk's, for he is silent, keeps his mind to himself, has plain understanding, and is a man of principle. Besides this, he has no son, daughter, brother or sister, so that his ambition must be limited to himself. Charles the II owed his kingdom to his personal application to Monk, delivered by one of Monk's own friends. Might not the Ministers treating by the King's command or the King himself write a private letter to Washington to remind him of the similarity between his situation and Monk's, desiring him to ask terms for America fair and just, and they should be granted, and that the terms for himself should be the dukedom that was given to Monk, and a revenue to support it in order to give dignity to the man who generously gave up his own power to save his country?

If the Minister has not a man he can trust with such a commission, I can find one. I mean Mr. Lloyd Delany, the bosom friend of General Washington, a man of fortune in Maryland, now in London; two of whose family are now with General Howe, and who has given proofs of his secrecy, as he was one of those who knew of a scheme of mine relating to the paper money of America.

> —GR. BRIT. HIST. MSS. COMM., *Stopford-Sackville Manuscripts,*
> II, 103-104.

3. "THE GENEROUS TERMS NOW HELD OUT WILL BE GLADLY EMBRACED"

Lord George Germain to Sir Henry Clinton—"Most Secret."

Whitehall, March 8, 1778

In my last letter I informed you that the command resigned by Sir William Howe had, by the King's wish, been delivered over to yourself, which shows in the highest degree the great confidence felt by his Majesty in your abilities. My circular letter of this day's date will inform you of what has been done by the King and Parliament towards opening the way for the return of peace, and if that be true which has been so repeatedly declared by the Colony Assemblies, and is still asserted by many persons who pretend to be well informed of the dispositions of the inhabitants, that the generality of the people desire nothing more than a full security for the enjoyment of all their rights and liberties under the British Constitution, there can be no room to doubt that the generous terms now held out to them will be gladly embraced, and that a negociation will immediately take place upon the arrival of the New Commission, and be so far advanced before the season will admit of military operations as to supersede the necessity of another campaign. So speedy and happy a termination of the war could not fail to give the greatest pleasure to the King, as the peace, prosperity, and happiness of all his subjects has ever been the most ardent wish of his royal breast. . . .

> —GR. BRIT. HIST. MSS. COMM., *Stopford-SackvilleManuscripts,*
> II, 94-95.

4. CHATHAM: "IF WE MUST FALL, LET US FALL LIKE MEN!"

Chatham's last appeal, in the House of Lords, April 7, 1778.

Earl of Chatham. His Lordship began by lamenting that his bodily infirmities had so long, and especially at so important a crisis, prevented his attendance on the duties of Parliament. He declared that he had made an effort almost beyond the powers of his constitution to come down to the House on this day (perhaps the last time he should ever be able to enter its walls) to express the indignation he felt at an idea which he understood was gone forth, of yielding up the sovereignty of America!

My Lords, continued he, I rejoice that the grave has not closed upon me; that I am still alive to lift up my voice against the dismemberment of this ancient and most noble monarchy! Pressed down as I am by the hand of infirmity, I am little able to assist my country in this most perilous conjuncture; but, my Lords, while I have sense and memory, I will never consent to deprive the royal offspring of the House of Brunswick, the heirs of the Princess

Sophia, of their fairest inheritance. Where is the man that will dare to advise such a measure? My Lords, his Majesty succeeded to an empire as great in extent as its reputation was unsullied. Shall we tarnish the lustre of this nation by an ignominious surrender of its rights and fairest possessions? Shall this great kingdom, that has survived whole and entire the Danish depredations, the Scottish inroads, and the Norman conquest, that has stood the threatened invasion of the Spanish Armada, now fall prostrate before the House of Bourbon? Surely, my Lords, this nation is no longer what it was! Shall a people that seventeen years ago was the terror of the world, now stoop so low as to tell its ancient inveterate enemy, Take all we have only give us peace? It is impossible!

I wage war with no man, or set of men. I wish for none of their employments; nor would I co-operate with men who still persist in unretracted error; or who, instead of acting on a firm decisive line of conduct, halt between two opinions, where there is no middle path. In God's name, if it is absolutely necessary to declare either for peace or war, and the former cannot be preserved with honour, why is not the latter commenced without hesitation? I am not, I confess, well informed of the resources of this kingdom; but I trust it has still sufficient to maintain its just rights, tho' I know them not. But, my Lords, any state is better than despair. Let us at least make one effort; and if we must fall, let us fall like men!

—ALMON, *Parliamentary Register*, X, 369-370.

5. The Peace Commissioners Submit Their Proposals

The Earl of Carlisle, W. Eden, G. Johnstone, to his excellency Henry Laurens, the President, and other Members of Congress.

June 13, 1778

Gentlemen, With an earnest desire to stop the further effusion of blood and the calamities of war, we communicate to you, with the least possible delay after our arrival in this city, a copy of the communication with which his Majesty is pleased to honour us, as also the acts of parliament on which it is founded; and at the same time that we assure you of our most earnest desire to re-establish, on the basis of equal freedom and mutual safety, the tranquillity of this once happy empire, you will observe that we are vested with powers equal to the purpose, and such as are even unprecedented in the annals of our history. . . .

More effectually to demonstrate our good intentions, we think proper to declare, even in this our first communication, that we are disposed to concur in every satisfactory and just arrangement towards the following among other purposes:

To consent to a cessation of hostilities, both by sea and land. To restore free intercourse, to revive mutual affection, and restore the common benefits of naturalisation through the several parts of this empire. To extend every freedom to trade that our respective interests can require. To agree that no military force shall be kept up in the different states of North America, without the consent of the general congress, or particular assemblies. To concur in measures calculated to discharge the debts of America, and raise the value and credit of the paper circulation.

To perpetuate our union by a reciprocal deputation of an agent or agents from the different states, who shall have the privilege of a seat and voice in the parliament of Great Britain; or, if sent from Britain, to have in that case a seat and voice in the assemblies of the different states to which they may be deputed respectively, in order to attend to the several interests of those by whom they are deputed.

In short, to establish the power of the respective legislatures in each particular state, to settle its revenue, its civil and military establishment, and to exercise a perfect freedom of legislation and internal government, so that the British states throughout North America, acting with us in peace and war, under our common sovereign, may have the irrevocable enjoyment of every privilege that is short of a total separation of interest, or consistent with that union of force on which the safety of our common religion and liberty depends.

In our anxiety for preserving those sacred and essential interests, we cannot help taking notice of the insidious interposition of a power which has from the first settlement of these colonies been actuated with enmity to us both. And notwithstanding the pretended date, or present form, of the French offers to America, yet it is notorious that these were made in consequence of the plans of accommodation previously concerted in Great Britain, and with a view to prevent our reconcilion, and to prolong this destructive war.

But we trust that the inhabitants of North-America, connected with us by the nearest ties of consanguinity, speaking the same language, interested in the preservation of similar institutions, remembering the former happy intercourse of good offices, and forgetting recent animosities, will shrink from the thought of becoming an accession of force to our late mutual enemy, and will prefer a firm, free and perpetual coalition with the parent state to an insincere and unnatural foreign alliance. . . .

If after the time that may be necessary to consider of this communication and transmit your answer, the horrors and devastations of war should continue, we call God and the world to witness that the evils which must follow are not to be imputed to Great Britain; and we cannot without the most real sorrow anticipate the prospect of calamities which we feel the most ardent desire to prevent. We are, with perfect respect, Gentlemen, your most obedient and most humble servants.

—Annual Register for 1778, pp. 327-329.

6. THE BRITISH PEACE PROPOSALS: TOO LITTLE AND TOO LATE

Henry Laurens of the Continental Congress to General Horatio Gates.

York, Pennsylvania, June 17, 1778

. . . If all the fine things now offered had been tendered some time ago, admitting their solidity, there can be no doubt but that the people of America would joyfully have embraced the proposition, but now what answer can be given but that which was returned to the foolish Virgins?—"the door is shut"—More especially when we reflect that there is no solidity, because all is to be transmitted to Parliament for ratification, "and until such ratification no such regulation, matter or thing shall have any other force or effect or be carried further into execution than is hereafter mentioned." Here a boy's card house [is] tumbled down by a breath.

"If," say Lord Carlisle, William Eden and Geo. Johnstone, Esquires, "after the time that may be necessary to consider this communication and transmit your answer, the horrors and devastations of war should continue, we call God and the world to witness that the evils which must follow are not to be imputed to Great Britain." To whom are the past to be imputed? But are they not now, in the very moment of pretended attempts to establish peace, burning, ravaging and murdering?

They seem to mistake our understanding as once they did our resolution.

—BURNETT, *Letters of Members of the Continental Congress,* III, 298-299.

7. CONGRESS REJECTS THE CARLISLE PROPOSALS

Henry Laurens to the Earl of Carlisle and the other British commissioners.

June 17, 1778

I have received the letter from your excellencies of the 9th instant, with the enclosures, and laid them before Congress. Nothing but an earnest desire to spare the further effusion of human blood could have induced them to read a paper containing expressions so disrespectful to his most Christian majesty, the good and great ally of these states, or to consider propositions so derogatory to the honor of an independent nation.

The acts of the British parliament, the commission from your sovereign, and your letter suppose the people of these states to be subjects of the crown of Great Britain, and are founded on the idea of dependence, which is utterly inadmissible.

I am further directed to inform your excellencies that Congress are inclined to peace, notwithstanding the unjust claims from which this war originated and the savage manner in which it hath been conducted. They will, therefore, be ready to enter upon the consideration of a treaty of peace and commerce not inconsistent with treaties already subsisting, when the king of Great Britain shall demonstrate a sincere disposition for that purpose. The only solid proof of this disposition will be an explicit acknowledgment of the independence of these states, or the withdrawing his fleets and armies.

—*Journals of the Continental Congress,* XI, 615.

8. "WE CAN FIND NO SAFETY BUT IN BRITAIN'S RUIN"

Patrick Henry to Richard Henry Lee.

Williamsburg, June 18, 1778

I look at the past condition of America as at a dreadful precipice from which we have escaped by means of the generous French, to whom I will be everlastingly bound by the most heartfelt gratitude. But I must mistake matters, if some of those men who traduce you do not prefer the offers of Britain. You will have a different game to play now with the commissioners. How comes Governor Johnstone there? I do not see how it comports with his past life. Surely Congress will never recede from our French friends. Salvation to America depends upon our holding fast our attachment to them. I shall date our ruin from the moment that it is exchanged for anything Great Britain can say or do. She can never be cordial with us. Baffled, defeated, disgraced by her colonies, she will ever meditate revenge. We can find no safety but in her ruin, or at least in her extreme humiliation, which has not happened, and cannot happen until she is deluged with blood, or thoroughly purged by a revolution, which shall wipe from existence the present king with his connexions, and the present system, with those who aid and abet it. For God's sake, my dear sir, quit not the councils of your country until you see us forever disjointed from Great Britain. *The old leaven still works. The flesh pots of Egypt are still savoury to degenerate palates.* Again, we are undone if the French alliance is not religiously observed.

Excuse my freedom. I know your love to our country, and this is my motive. May heaven give you health and prosperity.

—WIRT, *Life of Henry,* I, 564-565.

9. JOSEPH REED SPURNS A BRIBE FROM THE KING

On the 18th of June [1778], the city of Philadelphia was evacuated by the British troops, and I came to town the same day, having sent Governor Johnstone's letter to me to the Congress, then sitting at York-Town. On Sunday the 21st of June, at General Arnold's quarters, I received the following letter from Mrs. [Elizabeth] Ferguson, a lady of family and reputation, and who had, before the war, married a gentleman attached to the British interests, and then a commissary of prisoners in their army:

"Having occasion, on particular business, to go to Lancaster, I purpose setting off on Monday morning from this place. It would afford me considerable satisfaction, could I be favoured with an hour's conversation with you, Sir, previous to my being at Lancaster. In order to effect this, I propose going near the camp, where, if you will be good enough to meet me at any place you will name, within a mile or two of Valley-Forge, it would vastly oblige me. I should have been at Lancaster last week, but being in the city to take leave of my husband, I was refused a pass on the day I purposed leaving the town. I enclose a letter Col. Boudinot had from General Roberdeau, pointing out the necessity of being soon at Lancaster. I also enclose a letter Mr. Stockton has wrote, relative to Mr. Ferguson's proscription, which I must beg the favour of you to consider and give your advice on when we meet.

"At all events, I would wish much to see you before I go. If one day would suit you better than another, I would postpone or forward a day, in order to see you, though Monday is the time proposed. The Valley-Forge is about twenty-four miles from this, so that if I set off from this in the morning, I shall be able to see you in the afternoon. Be so obliging as to appoint the place; but I would wish to avoid passing through the camp; but any little cottage or farm-house would be agreeable to me to see you in. However it may affect my own private concerns, I cannot avoid sincerely congratulating you, Sir, on the prospect of your entering once more your own house in the city. . . .

"P. S. Since writing the above, I hear the camp is moved; therefore, if this should reach you, I beg you will be so good as to point out where I shall see you, as writing will not do."

I enquired of the servant who delivered me the letter where Mrs. Ferguson was, and was informed she had come to town that morning; upon which I wrote a short billet, mentioning that being engaged to dinner, I could not come so early as she seemed to wish, but would certainly wait on her in the evening, when I left the company with whom I dined. I accordingly did so, and found her in all appearance waiting for me. She opened the conversation by relating the difficulties and perplexities in which she found herself, what advice had been given her respecting Mr. Ferguson, and what her intentions had been. The particulars I did not recollect when I first committed this transaction to writing, nor have I since, as it seemed to be only introductory; or, perhaps, the subsequent conversation being more interesting, the other did not make the usual impression.

From this subject, we imperceptibly slid into that of the British Commissioners, their business and characters, when Mrs. Ferguson mentioned Governor Johnstone's lodging in that very house with her, and that she had frequently conversed with him on public affairs. She described him as a gentleman of great abilities and address, and possessed of many amiable qualities; that he had sketched out a plan of settlement of our disputes, on his passage, which he had permitted her to see, and that she had made some extracts from it, which she gave me expectations she would communicate to me on another occasion. She then added that he had expressed the most favourable sentiments of me, and the part I had acted in this great contest. Upon which I mentioned my having received a letter from him at the Valley-Forge, and acknowledged his civility in sending my packets with unbroken seals.

Mrs. Ferguson then went on to say that Governor Johnstone expressed great anxiety to see me, and particularly wished to engage my interest to promote the object of their commission, *viz.* a reunion between the two countries, if it was consistent with my principles and judgment; and in such case, it could not be deemed improper or unbecoming in Government to take a favourable notice of such conduct; and in this instance I might have £10,000 sterling and any office in the colonies in his Majesty's gift.

I found an answer was expected, and gave one: "That I was not worth purchasing, but such as I was, the King of Great-Britain was not rich enough to do it." By this time the evening was pretty far advanced, and no reply being made, I rose to take my leave, which I did, after expressing my concern for her private misfortunes, and left the house, with a mind much agitated with this new and unexpected scene.

At this time I had not seen Governor Johnstone's letters to Mr. Morris and Mr. Dana, which would probably have determined me sooner as to the part I ought to act: besides which, the Congress was yet at York-Town, the Executive Council at Lancaster, I was about to join the army again; the battle of

Monmouth and other important events succeeded, which engrossed the public attention and my own, and prevented my return to Congress till the month of July. In the mean time I was deliberating what steps I ought to pursue: On the one hand, the duty I owed to my country seemed to demand a full disclosure; on the other, a reluctance to expose the lady to a criminal prosecution, or popular resentment, and myself to the imputation of vanity and ostentatious integrity, kept me silent, except to General Washington and two or three other gentlemen. But the more I reflected upon the nature of the proposition, and the danger of negotiation in such hands, private considerations gave way to public duty, and on the 18th of July I made a full disclosure of the whole transaction to Congress, only concealing the name of the lady.

—REED, *Remarks on Johnstone's Speech*, pp. 16-22.

10. LORD CARLISLE CONCLUDES HIS MISSION IS RIDICULOUS

To Lady Carlisle.

New York, July 21, 1778

The arrival of this [French] fleet makes every hope of success in our business ridiculous; the address by proclamation to the people ought and has been tried; a certain time will show its effects, but in truth the compliance with our instructions in this particular is the mere obedience to a form. The leaders on the enemy's side are too powerful; the common people hate us in their hearts, notwithstanding all that is said of their secret attachment to the mother country. I cannot give you a better proof of their unanimity against us than in our last march; in the whole country there was not found one single man capable of bearing arms at home; they left their dwellings unprotected, and after having cut all the ropes of the wells had fled to Gen. Washinton. Formerly, when things went better for us, there was an appearance of friendship by their coming in for pardons, that might have deceived even those who have been the most acquainted with them. But no sooner our situation was the least altered for the worse, but these friends were the first to fire upon us, and many were taken with the pardons in our [their] pockets. Beat Gen. Washinton, drive away Monsr. d'Estaing, and we should have friends enough in this country; but in our present condition the only friends we have, or are likely to have, are those who are absolutely ruined for us, and in such distress I leave you to judge what possible use they can be to us.

But don't you say now—if all this is as hopeless as you represent, what is the use of remaining? To tell you fairly, I think none; but as everybody in the world will not be ruled perhaps by my opinions, we must stay till there is not a possibility of doubt upon that subject. God knows what may happen in the course of the next month; we must regulate our conduct by circumstances; the necessity of the times may impel us to steps we at present have not in idea. . . .

—GR. BRIT. HIST. MSS. COMM., *Fifteenth Report*, Appendix, VI, 356-357.

III. FORLORN HOPES OF PEACE

Despite the ridiculous bungling of the Carlisle Commission some Englishmen still felt that peace could be made with America. The Dean of Glou-

cester had the absurd notion that America could be divided into fragments,
and Admiral Rodney was so remote from American public opinion as to ven-
ture the suggestion that Benedict Arnold, whom he assumed had retained his
immense popularity with the American troops despite his treasonable be-
havior, should be given an important command, and that Washington could
still be bought.

1. The Dean of Gloucester Proposes to Fragmentize America

John Adams to the President of the Congress.

Paris, May 9th, 1780

I have the honor to enclose to Congress proposals for a general pacification, by the Dean of Gloucester.

"Proposals to the English, Americans, French, and Spaniards, now at war.

"First. That Great Britain shall retain Newfoundland, with the desert
coasts of Labradore; also Canada, Nova Scotia, and the country bordering on
the Bay of Fundy, as far as the bay and river of Penobscot.

"Secondly. That all the country from the Penobscot River to the River
Connecticut, containing almost all the four populous Provinces of New England, shall be ceded to the Americans.

"Thirdly. That all the country from the Connecticut to the River Delaware, containing the whole of New York, Long Island and the Jerseys, with
some parts of two other Provinces indenting with them, shall return to Great
Britain.

"Fourthly. That all the country from the Delaware to the northern boundary of South Carolina, containing the greatest part of Pennsylvania, all Maryland, Virginia and North Carolina, shall be ceded to the Americans.

"Fifthly. That all the country from the northern boundary of South
Carolina to the extreme point of the eastern Florida, containing three whole
Provinces, shall be retained by Great Britain.

"Sixthly. That West Florida, chiefly barren sand, and the Fortress of Gibraltar (totally useless) shall be ceded to Spain, in order to satisfy the punctilio
of that nation, and that the Spaniards shall give Porto Rico in exchange, an
island on which they seem to set no value, and which indeed is of no use to
them, though large in itself, stored with good ports, well situated, and capable
(in the hands of the English) of great improvements.

"Seventhly. Lastly, that the English shall give up the conquests they have
made on the French in the East Indies, who shall do the like to the English
in the West Indies."

I shall make no remarks upon this plan, but there is no Englishman who
thinks of a wiser, or at least who dares propose one. All who talk of propositions throw out something as absurd and idle as this, which will convince Congress that we shall have no peace for some time.

The French armament, which sailed from Brest the 2d of May, under the
command of M. de Rochambeau, of the troops, and M. de Ternay, of the
fleet, and the armament from Cadiz, of twelve ships of the line, besides frigates
and other armed vessels, with eleven thousand five hundred land forces, with

a fine train of artillery, which were to sail about the same time, or earlier, both destined for America, as it is supposed, will I hope bring the English to think of some plan a little more rational.

—SPARKS, *Diplomatic History of the Revolution*, V, 84-86.

2. ADMIRAL RODNEY STILL THINKS WASHINGTON CAN BE BOUGHT!

Sir George Rodney to Lord George Germain—"Private."

Sandwich, St. Lucia, December 22, 1780

Believe me, my dear Lord, you must not expect an end of the American war till you can find a general of active spirit, and who hates the Americans from principle. Such a man with the sword of war and justice on his side will do wonders, for in this war I am convinced the sword should cut deep. Nothing but making the Americans feel every calamity their perfidy deserves can bring them to their senses. . . .

The war in America is now turned to a war of posts, and, unhappily for England, when they have taken posts of infinite advantage, they have been unaccountably evacuated without one good reason assigned. Such was the Highlands up Hudson's River, and which cut off all communication between the southern and northern provinces, and which with little difficulty might have opened a passage from Canada. This is the post Arnold was to have betrayed, and which he assured me, as he did the General, he would answer with his head should be taken in ten days. But, to my infinite surprize, cold water was immediately thrown upon it, notwithstanding it had but a few days before the arrival of Arnold been told me that it was of infinite consequence, and if taken would ruin the rebels.

Believe me, my Lord, this man Arnold, with whom I had many conferences, will do more towards the suppressing the rebellion than all our generals put together. He perfectly knows every inch of the country, is greatly beloved by the American troops, and if entrusted with a body of what is called Royalists will induce great part of [the] rebels to desert. I am perfectly of his opinion that upon a certainty of their being paid their arrears and a portion of land given after the war, Washington would soon have no army. Jealousy, my Lord, unless commands from home signifies his Majesty's pleasure, will prevent Arnold being employed to advantage. He certainly may be trusted, as the Americans never forgive, and the Congress to a man are his personal enemies. Give him but a command and thousands will join him who are sick of the war and have a great opinion of his generalship. . . .

Thus, my Lord, have I endeavoured to make you truly acquainted with affairs at present in America, but believe me the acting in North Carolina will only prolong the war. The Northern Colonies should feel the fatal results of their treason. There and there only the war must be finished. I cannot conclude without being of opinion that a new Commission with the same powers of Lord Carlisle's, taking care the majority of Commissioners are not *military men*, may have such effect as to bring about a peace. Washington is certainly to be bought—honours will do it.

—GR. BRIT. HIST. MSS. COMM., *Stopford-Sackville Manuscripts*, II, 192-194.

CHAPTER SEVENTEEN

The Patriots Seize the Initiative in the Middle States

WITH THE WITHDRAWAL *in June of '78 of British troops from Philadelphia, a story related toward the close of our first volume, the initiative in the Middle States passed from the British to the Patriots. Not that the Patriots had been entirely inert before that time, but their activities had been largely defensive actions or sporadic raids to throw the enemy off balance, destroy stores, or pick off key personnel. One such raid, holding a larger significance for a later full-scale engagement, was staged near Newport in midsummer of '77, when Major General Richard Prescott, commander of the British troops in Rhode Island, was caught in bed in embarrassing circumstances. His seizure made it possible to effect an exchange of an American prisoner of equal rank, Major General Charles Lee.*

Even before the British evacuation of Philadelphia, Congress, without consultation with Washington, embarked on "one of the maddest of all mad projects," another ill-planned invasion of Canada. This expedition was to be placed under the command of Lafayette, with the trouble-maker Conway as his immediate subordinate. After a midwinter journey to Albany, the young Frenchman found that the troops which were promised him were not at hand. In bitter disillusionment he called off the enterprise. "I am sure I will be very ridiculous and laughed at," he confessed.

When Clinton withdrew his forces across Jersey, Washington pursued him in what proved a futile effort to trap him and cut the British army to pieces. Subsequently, in midsummer of '78, an ill-starred Franco-American amphibious operation was launched against Newport, Rhode Island. The British hold on the lower Hudson was shaken by the Patriots' temporary recapture of Stony Point and the Paulus Hook raid. In January of 1780 Stirling staged what he hoped would be a surprise attack on a British camp on Staten Island, but the enemy was not surprised, and the Patriots withdrew with little or no net profit.

The British in turn threw counterpunches at the Americans. Banastre Tarleton struck at Poundridge, near Bedford, against militia operating in Westchester County and put a church and other buildings to the torch. In New Jersey a British-Hessian force moved from Staten Island and struck in strength at the American army, but was hurled back at Springfield. Raids were staged on New Haven and Norwalk, and the turncoat, Benedict Ar-

704

GEORGE WASHINGTON

Portrait by James Peale

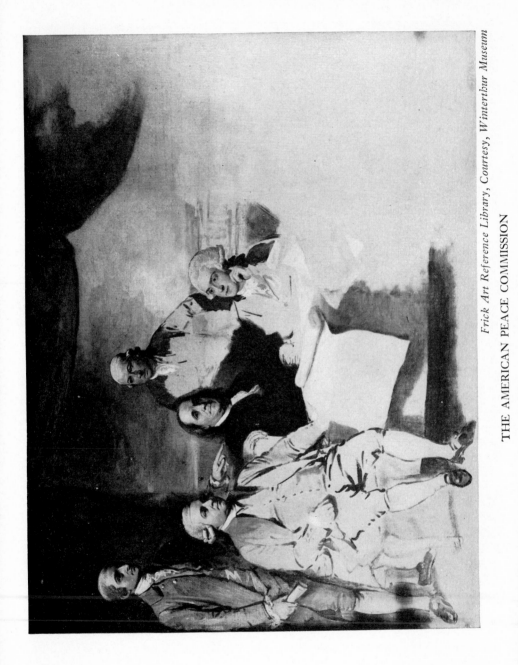

THE AMERICAN PEACE COMMISSION

nold, made an especially savage raid on New London that outraged the Patriots.

The effect of these offensive and counteroffensive moves was to tie a huge
British army down to New York City, while the decisive operations of the
war were being determined in the Southern theater.

I. GENERAL PRESCOTT IS CAPTURED

Prescott's capture amused two continents. The London Chronicle *for
September 27-30, 1777, spoke of the general as having been carried off "naked,
unanointed, unanealed," and put in rhyme some of the gossip that was not
reported in the American newspaper account:*

> What various lures there are to ruin man;
> Woman, the first and foremost, all bewitches!
> A nymph once spoiled a General's mighty plan,
> And gave him to the foe—without his breeches.

*Elias Boudinot, in charge of prisoner exchanges, negotiated the swap of
Prescott for Lee. His Journal records a significant conversation with Lee,
who, following his capture, was outspoken about the folly of Congress' hoping to withstand the British troops, criticized Washington as "ignorant," and
had the ridiculous plan of assembling civilians—the wealthy, the elderly and
children—inside a fortress to be built at Pittsburgh. Boudinot had strong reser-
vations about Lee. "Whenever anything on a very large scale struck him,"
he remarked in his Journal, "a partial lunacy took place." Unfortunately
Washington was not aware of the strange indecision and doubtful loyalty of
which Lee's mind was a curious compound, nor did he learn that on June 4,
1778, two weeks after rejoining the Patriot army, Lee wrote a letter to Sir
Henry Clinton congratulating him on his promotion to succeed Howe!*

1. THE BRITISH SOUND THE ALARM AFTER "THE BIRD HAS FLED"

Providence, July 12, 1777: Thursday evening last a party of 38 men, of the
troops belonging to this State, under the command of Lieut. Col. William
Barton, of this town, accompanied by Major Adams of the Train, Capt.
Philips, Lieutenants Potter and Badcock, and Ensigns Stanton and Wilcocks,
went in five boats from Warwick-Neck, with a view to take Major-General
Prescot, Commander in Chief of the British and foreign troops on Rhode
Island, whose headquarters were then at a house about four miles from Newport. The colonel and his party, after passing the enemy's ships and guard
boats, landed about twelve at night, and with *"infinite address and gallantry"*
got to Prescot's quarters undiscovered. A centinel at the door hailed, but was
immediately secured, and the party, instantly breaking the doors and entering
the house, took the general in bed. His aid-de-camp leaped from a window in
his shirt and attempted to escape, but was taken a few rods from the house.

The party soon after returned to their boats with the prisoners, and some
time after they had put off the enemy fired rockets from their several posts as
signals for an alarm, but *too late—the bird had fled.* The prisoners were safely

landed about day-break at Warwick-Neck. On receiving intelligence here, a coach was immediately sent, and the general with his aid-de-camp, attended by Col. Barton and some other officers, arrived in town at twelve o'clock.

This bold and important enterprize must reflect the highest honor on Col. Barton and his little party. A lieut. col. of Horse, with at least 70 Light Dragoons, took Major General Lee (betrayed by a Tory) five miles from his troops. A lieutenant colonel of Foot, with only 38 privates and 6 officers, has taken a Chief Commander, when almost incircled by an army and navy.

—Continental Journal and Weekly Advertiser, July 17, 1777.

2. Lee's Triumphal Return with "a Miserable Dirty Hussy"

Journal of Elias Boudinot.

Dec. 1778: I endeavoured to negotiate his [General Lee's] exchange, and it was agreed (hypothetically) that it should take place for Major Genl Prescott, subject to Genl Howe's approbation. Genl Howe objected, and ordered Genl Lee round by sea to Philadelphia, that he might be exchanged under his own eye. Genl Lee (abhoring the sea) applied to me by letter and most earnestly requested that he might be permitted to go thro' New Jersey, under the care of a British officer, to which Genl Washington consented, and he accordingly went to Philadelphia, but no consent was obtained to the exchange.

In the spring of 1778 a proposition was made by both parties for a partial exchange of prisoners, and I was ordered to Germantown to meet the British commissory to attempt the business. When I was setting off from camp, Genl Washington called me into his room and in the most earnest manner intreated of me, if I wished to gratify him, that I would obtain the exchange of Genl Lee, for he never was more wanted by him than at the present moment, and desired that I would not suffer trifles to prevent it. I accordingly went, and made a pretty considerable exchange of prisoners, but quite new propositions were made for the exchange of Genl Lee, which neither the General or myself had ever thought of; after reducing the terms to as favourable a scale as I thought right, I agreed to it on condition that if General Washington was not pleased with the new plan and notice was given of his refusal within 24 hours, the exchange was to be void, without any charge of failure on my part.

I arrived at head quarters about 6 o'clock P. M. and going in to the General began to tell him of my success. When he interrupted me with much eagerness and asked me if I had exchanged Genl Lee, I informed him of what had been done; he replied, "Sit down at this table and write a letter informing of my confirmation of the exchange and send one of my horse guards immediately to the enemies lines with it." I assured him that next day would be time enough, but he insisted on its being immediately done, and I sent him accordingly, fixing the next day but one for Genl Lee's coming out to us.

When the day arrived the greatest preparations were made for his reception. All the principal officers of the army were drawn up in two lines, advanced of the camp about 2 miles towards the enemy. Then the troops with the inferior officers formed a line quite to head quarters. All the music of the army attended. The General, with a great number of principal officers and their suites, rode about four miles on the road towards Philadelphia and waited till Genl Lee appeared. Gen Washington dismounted and received Gen Lee as if he had been his brother. He passed thro' the lines of officers and the army, who all paid him the highest military honors, to head quarters, where Mrs Washington was, and there he was entertained with an elegant dinner, and the music playing the whole time. A room was assigned him back of Mrs Washington's sitting room, and all his baggage was stowed in it.

The next morning he lay very late, and breakfast was detained for him. When he came out, he looked as dirty as if he had been in the street all night. Soon after I discovered that he had brought a miserable dirty hussy with him from Philadelphia (a British sergeant's wife) and had actually taken her into his room by a back door and she had slept with him that night.

—BOUDINOT, *Journal or Historical Recollections*, pp. 76-78.

II. LAFAYETTE'S ABORTIVE EXPEDITION TO CANADA

Memoirs of the Marquis de Lafayette.

The 22nd of January [1778], Congress resolved that Canada should be entered, and the choice fell upon M. de Lafayette. The Generals Conway and Stark were placed under him. Hoping to intoxicate and govern so young a commander, the war-office, without consulting the commander-in-chief, wrote to him to go and await his further instructions at Albany. But after having won over by his arguments the committee which Congress had sent to the camp, M. de Lafayette hastened to Yorktown, and declared there "that he required circumstantial orders, a statement of the means to be employed, the certainty of not deceiving the Canadians, an augmentation of generals, and rank for several Frenchmen, fully impressed," he added, "with the various duties and advantages they derived from their name; but the first condition he demanded was, not to be made, like Gates, independent of General Washington." At Gates's own house he braved the whole party, and threw them into confusion by making them drink the health of their general. In Congress he was supported by President Laurens, and he obtained all that he demanded.

His instructions from the war-office promised that 2500 men should be assembled at Albany, and a large corps of militia at Co[h]o[e]s; that he should have two millions in paper money, some hard specie, and all means supplied for crossing Lake Champlain upon the ice, whence, after having burnt the English flotilla, he was to proceed to Montreal and act there as circumstances might require.

Repassing then, not without some danger, the Susquehannah, which was filled with floating masses of ice, M. de Lafayette set out for Albany, and, in spite of the obstacles offered by ice and snow, rapidly traversed an extent of four hundred miles. . . .

M. de Lafayette, on arriving at Albany, experienced some disappointments. Instead of 2500 men, there were not 1200. Stark's militia had not even received a summons. Clothes, provisions, magazines, sledges, all were insufficient for that glacial expedition. By making better preparations and appointing the general earlier, success would probably have been secured. Several Canadians began to make a movement, and from that moment they testified

great interest in M. de Lafayette; but two months were requisite to collect all
that was necessary, and towards the middle of March the lakes began to thaw.
M. de Lafayette, general, at twenty years of age, of a small army, charged with
an important and very difficult operation, authorized by the orders of Congress, animated by the expectations now felt in America and which, he knew,
would ere long be felt likewise in Europe, had many motives for becoming
adventurous; but, on the other hand, his resources were slender, the time
allowed him was short, the enemy was in a good position, and Lieutenant-
General Carleton was preparing for him another Saratoga. Forced to take a
decisive step immediately, he wrote a calm letter to Congress, and with a
heavy sigh abandoned the enterprise. . . .

—LAFAYETTE, *Memoirs, Correspondence and Manuscripts*, pp. 38-41.

III. MONMOUTH

*On June 17, 1778, Washington called a council of war at Valley Forge in
which he informed the officers of Clinton's evident intention of evacuating
Philadelphia and asked advice as to the course he should pursue. In the march
across Jersey Clinton seemed to be heading for Sandy Hook, whence he could
embark his troops to New York. This meant taking a northeasterly route to
New Brunswick, and then cutting across to Monmouth Courthouse, a short
distance from the coast. Major General Lee opposed bringing on a full-scale
action as "criminal," and won a majority of the leading officers over to his
views. It was voted to strengthen Maxwell's and Dickinson's forces hanging
on Clinton's left flank, but to avoid a general engagement with the main army.
Hamilton, who kept the minutes of the council, observed that the results of
their deliberations "would have done honor to the most honorable society of
midwives, and to them only." Nathanael Greene also dissented from the decision. "People expect something from us and our strength demands it," he
wrote Washington.*

*The American commander decided to dispatch an advance guard to estab-
lish contact with the enemy and to place it under the command of someone
who favored the offensive. He named Lafayette. Lee agreed to the choice,
then reasserted his command, then wavered again, and at the moment of contact with the enemy took over the reins once more. When, early in the morning of June 28, word came to Washington that the British were preparing to
leave Monmouth Courthouse, Washington determined to strike. Lee was
ordered to fall upon the rear of the enemy, but reports coming in indicated
that, oddly enough, Lee was falling back. The British, who had received intelligence from an American deserter of Washington's intent to hit their rear,
wheeled about and attacked first. Washington put spurs to his horse, and soon
came upon the retreating troops. He confronted Lee, demanded to know the
reason for the situation, and received a lame explanation. Whether or not he
called Lee "a damned poltroon" as tradition would have it, he was in a tower-
ing rage and reputedly swore "till the leaves shook on the trees." Taking command of the situation himself, he ordered the soldiers to take cover behind a
hedgerow, and Wayne's brigade was placed where it could hold off the*

From The American Revolution   *Courtesy of Harper & Brothers*
by John Richard Alden

enemy. American fire swept back a British cavalry charge, the British were driven back, but a counterstroke was halted because, as Major Henry Dearborn explained, the men were "beat out with heat and fatigue." The next morning the enemy was gone.

At the end of the day most American officers were agreed with John Laurens, who wrote his father Henry, then President of Congress: "General Lee, I think, must be tried for misconduct." In that letter Lee was depicted as paralyzed by indecision, his orders constantly countermanded, and "all this disgraceful retreating passed without the firing of a musket, over ground which might have been disputed inch by inch." Washington moved fast against Lee. In his letter to Congress of July 1, reporting the battle, he singled out Wayne for commendation, but as regards Lee he commented: "The peculiar situation of General Lee at this time requires that I should say nothing of his conduct. He is now in arrest. The charges against him, with such sentence as the court-martial may decree in his case, shall be transmitted, for the approbation or disapprobation of Congress, as soon as it shall be passed." Although Hamilton believed that Lee's friends would see to it that he was cleared, this was not to be the case. Lee was found guilty and suspended from his command for one year, and then dropped from the army. A repercussion of the affair was a duel between Hamilton's bosom friend, John Laurens, Washington's aide, and Lee, who had made disparaging remarks about the general. Lee received a slight wound, and the affair of honor was terminated.

One colorful incident during that torrid day was the appearance on the battlefield of Molly Hays, a Pennsylvania Dutch girl, who accompanied her husband John, an artilleryman, and brought pitcher after pitcher of water to the parched troops. When John fell wounded, Molly grasped the rammer staff from his hands, swabbed and loaded it, and stood at her post under fire. Her feat is commemorated on the Monmouth battle monument, and artillerymen still offer a toast

> *. . . Drunk in a beverage richer*
> *And stronger than was poured that day*
> *From Molly Pitcher's pitcher.*

1. Lee Urges "a Bridge of Gold" to Let the Enemy Escape

Memoirs of the Marquis de Lafayette.

On the 17th of June [1778], Philadelphia was evacuated. The invalids, magazines and heavy ammunition of the British were embarked with the general; the commissioners of conciliation alone remained behind. Passing over to Gloucester, the army marched, in two columns, each consisting of seven thousand men, commanded by Clinton and Knyphausen, towards New York. The army of the United States, which was of nearly equal force, directed itself from Valley Forge to Coryell's Ferry, and from thence to King's Town, within a march of the enemy; it was thus left at the option of the Americans, either to follow on their track or to repair to White Plains.

In a council held on this subject, Lee very eloquently endeavoured to prove that it was necessary to erect a bridge of gold for the enemy; that while on the very point of forming an alliance with them, every thing ought not to be placed at hazard; that the English army had never been so excellent and so well disciplined; he declared himself to be for White Plains: his speech influenced the opinion of Lord Stirling and of the brigadiers-general.

M. de Lafayette, placed on the other side, spoke late, and asserted that it would be disgraceful for the chiefs, and humiliating for the troops, to allow the enemy to traverse the Jerseys tranquilly; that, without running any improper risk, the rear guard might be attacked; that it was necessary to follow the English, manoeuvre with prudence, take advantage of a temporary separation, and, in short, seize the most favourable opportunities and situations. This advice was approved by many of the council, and above all by M. du Portail, chief of the engineers, and a very distinguished officer. The majority were, however, in favour of Lee; but M. de Lafayette spoke again to the general on this subject in the evening, and was seconded by Hamilton, and by Greene, who had been lately named quarter-master in place of Mifflin.

Several of the general officers changed their opinion; and the troops having already begun their march, they were halted in order to form a detachment. When united, there were 3,000 continentalists and 1,200 militia; the command fell to the share of Lee, but, by the express desire of the general, M. de Lafayette succeeded in obtaining it. Everything was going on extremely well, when Lee changed his mind and chose to command the troops himself; having again yielded this point, he rechanged once more; and as the general wished him to adhere to his first decision—"It is my fortune and honour," said Lee to M. de Lafayette, "that I place in your hands; you are too generous to cause the loss of both!" This tone succeeded better, and M. de Lafayette promised to ask for him the next day.

The enemy, unfortunately, continued their march; M. de Lafayette was delayed by want of provisions; and it was not until the 26th, at a quarter to twelve at night, that he could ask for Lee, who was sent with a detachment of one thousand men to Englishtown on the left side of the enemy. The first corps had advanced upon their right; and M. de Lafayette, by Lee's especial order, joined him at midday, within reach of the enemy, from whom he fortunately succeeded in concealing this movement. The two columns of the English army had united together at Monmouth Courthouse, from whence they departed on the morning of the 28th.

—LAFAYETTE, *Memoirs, Correspondence, and Manuscripts*, pp. 50-52.

2. "BY GOD! THEY ARE FLYING FROM A SHADOW!"

Testimony of Lieutenant Colonel Richard Harrison of the Continental Army at the court-martial of General Lee.

On the 28th of June, as one of His Excellency's [General Washington's] suite, I marched with him till we passed the Meetinghouse near Monmouth. . . . When we came to where the roads forked, His Excellency made a halt for a few minutes, in order to direct a disposition of the army. The wing under General Greene was then ordered to go to the right to prevent the enemy's turning our right flank.

After order was given in this matter, and His Excellency was proceeding down the road, we met a fifer, who appeared to be a good deal frighted. The General asked him whether he was a soldier belonging to the army, and the cause of his returning that way; he answered that he was a soldier, and that the Continental troops that had been advanced were retreating. On this answer the General seemed to be exceedingly surprized, and rather more exasperated, appearing to discredit the account, and threatened the man, if he mentioned a thing of the sort, he would have him whipped.

We then moved on a few paces forward (perhaps about fifty yards) where we met two or three persons more on that road; one was, I think, in the habit of a soldier. The General asked them from whence they came, and whether they belonged to the army; one of them replied that he did, and that all the troops that had been advanced, the whole of them, were retreating. His Excellency still appeared to discredit the account, having not heard any firing except a few cannon a considerable time before. However, the General, or some gentleman in company, observed that, as the report came by different persons, it might be well not wholly to disregard it.

Upon this I offered my services to the General to go forward and to bring him a true account of the situation of matters, and requested that Colonel Fitzgerald might go with me. After riding a very short distance, at the bridge in front of the line that was afterwards formed on the heights, I met part of Colonel Grayson's regiment, as I took it, from some of the officers that I knew. As I was in pursuit of information, I addressed myself to Captain Jones of that regiment and asked him the cause of the retreat, whether it was general, or whether it was only a particular part of the troops that were coming off. I do not precisely recollect the answer that he gave me; but I think, to the best of my knowledge, he said, "Yonder are a great many more troops in the same situation."

I proceeded and fell in with Lieutenant-Colonel Parke. These troops were rather disordered. The next officer that I was acquainted with was Lieutenant-Colonel William Smith. I addressed myself to Colonel Smith and asked him what was the cause of the troops retreating, as I had come to gain information? who replied that he could not tell, that they had lost but one man. I then proceeded down the line, determined to go to the rear of the retreating troops, and met with Colonel Ogden. I asked him the same question, whether he could assign the cause or give me any information why the troops retreated. He appeared to be exceedingly exasperated and said, "By God! they are flying from a shadow."

I fell in immediately after with Captain Mercer, who is aid-de-camp to Major-General Lee, and, expecting to derive some information from him, I put the same question to him. Captain Mercer seemed, by the manner of his answer (as I addressed myself to him, saying, "For God's sake, what is the cause of this retreat?"), to be displeased; his answer was, "If you will proceed, you will see the cause; you will see several columns of foot and horse." I replied to Captain Mercer that I presumed that the enemy was not in greater force than when they left Philadelphia, and we came to that field to meet columns of foot and horse.

The next field-officer I met was Lieutenant-Colonel Rhea, of New Jersey, who appeared to be conducting a regiment. I asked him uniformly the same question for information, and he appeared to be very much agitated, expressed his disapprobation of the retreat, and seemed to be equally concerned (or perhaps more) that he had no place assigned to go where the troops were to halt.

About this time I met with General Maxwell; and, agreeable to the General's direction to get intelligence, I asked him the cause. He appeared to be as much at a loss as Lieutenant-Colonel Rhea or any other officer I had met with; and intimated that he had received no orders upon the occasion and was totally in the dark what line of conduct to pursue.

I think nearly opposite to the point of wood where the first stand was made, I saw General Lee. I do not recollect that anything passed between us, but General Lee's asking me where General Washington was, and my telling him that he was in the rear advancing.

I then went to the extreme of the retreating troops, which were formed of Colonel Stewart's regiment, and found them in the field where the enemy retreated to, just beyond the defile. I addressed myself to General Wayne, General Scott and, I believe, to Colonel Stewart, and to several other officers who were there; and asked General Wayne the cause of the retreat, who seemed no otherwise concerned than at the retreat itself, told me he believed it was impossible to tell the cause; and while we were standing together, which I supposed might be three or four minutes, the enemy's light infantry and grenadiers came issuing out of the wood, pressing very hard upon us at about two or three or four hundred yards distance. The troops that had been halted were put in motion.

I had some conversation with General Wayne relative to a disposition of the troops, if nothing could be done to check the advance of the enemy, who seemed to consider the matter exceedingly practicable, provided any effort or exertion was made for the purpose, alledging that a very select body of men had been that day drawn off from a body far inferior in number. General Wayne then told me that as General Washington might not be perfectly well acquainted with the country, it might be well to advise him of a road, if I met him, that led by Taylor's Tavern, on which it would be necessary to throw a body of troops, in case the enemy should attempt to turn our right flank.

I, upon this, left General Wayne and galloped down the line to meet General Washington, to report to him the state of our troops and the progress of the enemy. I met General Washington at the point of wood, or near it, where the first stand was made, and reported to him what I had seen, adding that the enemy was pressing hard and would be upon him in a march of fifteen minutes; which (I have since understood) was the first information he received of the enemy being so close upon our retreating troops. We remained there a few minutes until the extreme rear of our retreating troops got up.

—HARRISON, Testimony, *N. Y. Hist. Soc. Coll.,* VI, 71-75.

3. LEE'S RETREAT ROUSES WASHINGTON TO FURY

Narrative attributed to James Sullivan Martin.

After all things were put in order, we marched, but halted a few minutes in the village, where we were joined by a few other troops and then proceeded on. We now heard a few reports of cannon ahead; we went in a road running through a deep narrow valley, which was for a considerable way covered with thick wood; we were some time in passing this defile. While in the wood we heard a volley or two of musketry, and upon inquiry we found it to be a party of our troops who had fired upon a party of British horse; but there was no fear of horse in the place in which we then were.

It was ten or eleven o'clock before we got through these woods and came into the open fields. The first cleared land we came to was an Indian corn-field, surrounded on the east, west and north sides by thick tall trees; the sun shining full upon the field, the soil of which was sandy, the mouth of a heated oven seemed to me to be but a trifle hotter than this ploughed field; it was almost impossible to breathe. We had to fall back again as soon as we could, into the woods; by the time we had got under the shade of the trees, and had taken breath, of which we had been almost deprived, we received orders to re-treat, as all the left wing of the army (that part being under the command of Gen. Lee) were retreating. Grating as this order was to our feelings, we were obliged to comply.

We had not retreated far before we came to a defile, a muddy sloughy brook; while the artillery were passing this place, we sat down by the road side;—in a few minutes the Commander-in-chief and suit crossed the road just where we were sitting. I heard him ask our officers, "by whose order the troops were retreating," and being answered, "by Gen. Lee's," he said some-thing, but as he was moving forward all the time this was passing, he was too far off for me to hear it distinctly; those that were nearer to him said that his words were—"D—n him"; whether he did thus express himself or not I do not know; it was certainly very unlike him, but he seemed at the instant to be in a great passion; his looks if not his words seemed to indicate as much.

After passing us, he rode on to the plain field and took an observation of the advancing enemy; he remained there some time upon his old English charger, while the shot from the British artillery were rending up the earth all around him. After he had taken a view of the enemy, he returned and ordered the two Connecticut brigades to make a stand at a fence, in order to keep the enemy in check while the artillery and other troops crossed the before-men-tioned defile.

—MARTIN (?), *Narrative of a Revolutionary Soldier*, pp. 91-95.

4. "MOLLY PITCHER" MANS A GUN AT MONMOUTH

Narrative attributed to Joseph P. Martin.

One little incident happened during the heat of the cannonade, which I was eye-witness to, and which I think would be unpardonable not to men-tion. A woman whose husband belonged to the Artillery, and who was then attached to a piece in the engagement, attended with her husband at the piece the whole time. While in the act of reaching a cartridge and having one of her feet as far before the other as she could step, a cannon shot from the enemy passed directly between her legs without doing any other damage than carry-ing away all the lower part of her petticoat. Looking at it with apparent unconcern, she observed that it was lucky it did not pass a little higher, for in that case it might have carried away something else, and continued her occupation.

—MARTIN(?), *Narrative of a Revolutionary Soldier,* pp. 96-97.

IV. THE RHODE ISLAND CAMPAIGN OF 1778

A French fleet under Count d'Estaing arrived before New York too late to prevent Lord Howe from ferrying Clinton's forces across to Manhattan. A naval attack against New York seemed hazardous because D'Estaing's huge ships of war drew too much water to take them into the bay as the channel across Sandy Hook bar was not dredged until modern times. Not knowing where the French fleet or Washington's army might strike, the British seemed temporarily paralyzed. As Captain Mackenzie of the Royal Welsh Fusiliers commented somewhat inaccurately in his diary:

> *So extraordinary an event as the present certainly never before occurred in the history of Britain! An army of 50,000 men, and a fleet of nearly 100 ships and armed vessels, are prevented from acting offensively by the appearance on the American coast of a French squadron of 12 sail of the line and 4 frigates, without troops. Some unpardonable faults have been committed somewhere; and those whose duty it is to watch the motions of the enemy in every quarter should answer with their heads for risquing the fate of so large a portion of the national force by their supineness and total want of intelligence.*

The most feasible place to use this amphibious force (4,000 French soldiers were transported with the fleet), it was soon decided, was to be against the British in Rhode Island, in a joint operation with American troops under General Sullivan. Sullivan's army, divided between Greene and Lafayette, with the New Hampshireman in supreme command, marched to a rendezvous with the French some miles north of Newport. But New England militia reinforcements failed to arrive until some ten days after D'Estaing appeared off Newport. By that time Clinton had sent an expeditionary force in Lord Howe's fleet to the relief of General Pigot, commanding the Newport defenses.

The Franco-American campaign was marked at the start by maladroit moves, bad luck and lack of co-operation. When the British fleet appeared off Newport, D'Estaing, in order to keep his front together and drive off the enemy, re-embarked the French troops over Sullivan's protest. But the naval engagement never took place, for a violent storm on the night of August 11 scattered both squadrons and forced Sullivan to abandon his ground attack. Howe put back to New York for repairs. D'Estaing sailed to Boston to refit.

Sullivan's temper, which he always had such difficulty in controlling, now got out of hand. The American general published an order condemning the French move. The lowered Patriot morale, to which both commanders had contributed in different ways, caused some five thousand militiamen to go back home. Now that Sullivan's forces were weakened, Pigot attacked, but the Patriot troops refused to give ground. Under cover of night Sullivan ferried his men over to Tiverton and Bristol.

SIEGE OF NEWPORT

In the Newport venture both sides suffered equally, about two hundred and fifty casualties apiece, but for the grand alliance it was an inauspicious start. An anti-French riot broke out in Boston, and it took the combined arts of John Hancock, Nathanael Greene and Alexander Hamilton to heal the wounds to Gallic pride. Lafayette was temporarily embittered. Writing a friend at this time, he declared: "I begin to see that, seduced by a false enthusiasm, I made a mistake to leave everything and run to America. But it would be a greater one to return. My cup is filled; I must drink it to the dregs, but the dregs can already be tasted."

The Newport fiasco set off fierce polemics. Writing to a critic, the Rhode Island merchant John Brown, on September 6, Greene controverted Brown's assertion that the expedition had been "the worst concerted and executed of the war." The plan of attack had been to land on the northern part of the island to lull the enemy into a belief that the Americans intended to storm the garrison by regular approaches. But Greene pointed out that they really intended to re-embark the troops and land on the southern part of the island, and he maintained this would have been successful "had our strength been sufficient and the disembarkation covered by the fleet." Defending Sullivan's conduct, Greene held that "an attack with militia, in an open country where they could retire after defeat, might be very prudent, which would be very rash and unwarrantable upon an island." This was probably a judicious analysis. The risks had become too great, and Sullivan did the best he could in extricating his forces from disaster.

1. THE FRENCH ADMIRAL SENDS EFFUSIVE GREETINGS

Count d'Estaing to General Washington.

At sea, July 8, 1778

I have the honor of imparting to Your Excellency the arrival of the King's fleet, charged by His Majesty with the glorious task of giving his allies, the United States of America, the most striking proofs of his affection. Nothing will be wanting to my happiness, if I can succeed in it. It is augmented by the consideration of concerting my operations with a general such as Your Excellency. The talents and great actions of General Washington have insured him, in the eyes of all Europe, the title, truly sublime, of Deliverer of America. Accept, Sir, the homage that every man, that every military man, owes you; and be not displeased that I solicit, even in the first moment of intercourse, with military and maritime frankness, a friendship so flattering as yours. I will try to render myself worthy of it by my respectful devotion for your country. It is prescribed to me by orders, and my heart inspires it. . . .

—SPARKS, *Correspondence of the American Revolution*, II, 155-156.

2. "ALL OUR HOPES OF ASSISTANCE ARE AT AN END"

General John Sullivan to George Washington.

Head Quarters on Rhode Island, August 13, 1778

In my last I had the honor to inform your Excellency of my being in possession of the enemies works on the north part of Rhode Island, and of the arrival of the British fleet the moment we had landed, as also of the sailing of Count Destaing in quest of them. As this unfortunate circumstance deprived us of the assistance we promised ourselves from the French troops, I found it necessary to wait on the ground till the tenth at night; when, finding my own troops numbers had increased sufficiently to warrant my advancing to the town without waiting the return of the fleet, I issued orders for the army to march the 11th at six in the morning, but Fortune, still determined to sport longer with us, brought on a storm so violent that it last night blew down, tore and almost ruined all the tents I had. The arms of course were rendered useless, and almost the whole of our ammunition ruined. The much greater part of the army have no kind of covering, nor would tents if they had them prove a sufficient security against the severity of the storm. My men are mostly lying under the fences, half covered with water, without ammunition, and arms rendered useless; the communication between us and the main cut off by the violence of the wind which will scarcely permit a whale boat to pass. Should the enemy come out to attack us our dependance must be upon the superiority of our numbers and the point of the bayonet. How our militia may behave on such an occasion I am unable to determine. To retreat is impossible; therefore we must conquer or perish.

Perhaps under these circumstances an attack upon us might be of great advantage. Several men have perished with the severity of the weather and I expect more will as I see no probability of the storm ceasing. All our hopes of assistance from the French fleet are at an end as this storm must have driven them far off from this port and, I am very apprehensive, quite far off the coast.

To combat all these misfortunes and to surmount all those difficulties requires a degree of temper and persevering fortitude which I could never boast of, and which few possess in so ample a manner. Your Excellency, I will however endeavour by emulating the example to rise superior to the malevolence of Fortune and my present lamentable situation as quick as possible and, if Heaven will cease to frown, endeavor to gratify your Excellencys desires. . . .

—HAMMOND, ed., *Letters and Papers of Sullivan*, II, 205-207.

3. "EVERY VOICE IS RAISED AGAINST THE FRENCH NATION"

General Sullivan to Henry Laurens.

Camp before Newport, August 16th, 1778

My dear Sir: I have been honoured with your Excellency's favour of the 8th inst., with the gazette inclosed. I most sincerely thank you for the licence you have given me to communicate intelligence to your Excellency by private letter, and also for your promise to retaliate in kind. My letters to General Washington, copies of which he is to convey to Congress from time to time, must have informed you of the return of the French fleet, the loss it sustained in the storm, and their sudden departure for Boston. This movement has raised every voice against the French nation, revived all those ancient prejudices against the faith and sincerity of that people, and inclines them most heartily to curse the new alliance. These are only the first sallies of passion, which will in a few days subside.

I confess that I do most cordially resent the conduct of the Count, or rather the conduct of his officers, who have, it seems, compelled him to go to Boston and leave us on an island without any certain means of retreat; and what surprises me exceedingly is that the Count could be persuaded that it was necessary for ten sail of the line to lay in the harbour to attend one which is refitting.

I begged the Count to remain only twenty-four hours, and I would agree to dismiss him, but in vain. He well knew that the original plan was for him to land his own troops with a large detachment of mine within their lines, under fire of some of his ships, while with the rest I made an attack in front, but his departure has reduced me to the necessity of attacking their works in front or of doing nothing. They have double lines across the island in two places, at near quarter of a mile distance. The outer line is covered in front by redoubts within musket-shot of each other; the second in the same manner by redoubts thrown up between the lines. Besides this there is an inaccessible pond which covers more than half of the first line. A strong fortress on Tominy Hill overlooks and commands the whole adjacent country.

The enemy have about six thousand men within these works. I have eight thousand one hundred and seventy-four. With this force I am to carry their lines or retire with disgrace. Near seven thousand of my men are militia, unaccustomed to the noise of arms. Should I throw my men by strategem within these lines it must be my best troops. Should they be defeated the want of ships will render their retreat impracticable, and most of the army must be sacrificed. You will, therefore, judge of my feelings, and of the situation which my inconstant ally and coadjutor has thrown me into. My feelings as a man press me to make the desperate attempt. My feelings as an officer cause me to hesitate.

I have submitted the considerations to my officers; how they will declare I know not. I feel disgrace will attend this fatal expedition, though it gave at first the most pleasing presages of success.

—HAMMOND, ed., *Letters and Papers of Sullivan*, II, 218-220.

4. "WE SOON PUT THE ENEMY TO ROUT"

Nathanael Greene to George Washington.

Camp Tiverton, August 31, 1778

On the evening of the 29th the army fell back to the north end of the island [Rhode Island]. The next morning the enemy advanced upon us in two columns upon the east and west road. Our light troops, commanded by Colonel Livingston and Colonel Laurens, attacked the heads of the columns about seven o'clock in the morning but were beat back; they were reinforced with a regiment upon each road. The enemy still proved too strong. General Sullivan formed the army in order of battle, and resolved to wait their approach upon the ground we were encamped on, and sent orders to the light troops to fall back. The enemy came up and formed upon Quaker Hill, a very strong piece of ground within about one mile and a quarter of our line. We were well posted with strong works in our rear, and a strong redoubt in front, partly upon the right of the line.

In this position a warm cannonade commenced and lasted for several hours, with continual skirmishes in front of both lines. About two o'clock the enemy began to advance in force upon our right, as if they intended to dislodge us from the advanced redoubt. I had the command of the right wing. After advancing four regiments and finding the enemy still gaining ground, I advanced with two more regiments of regular troops and a brigade of militia, and at the same time General Sullivan ordered Colonel Livingston, with the light troops under his command, to advance. We soon put the enemy to the rout, and I had the pleasure to see them run in worse disorder than they did at the battle of Monmouth. Our troops behaved with great spirit; and the brigade of militia under the command of General Lovell advanced with great resolution and in good order, and stood the fire of the enemy with great firmness. Lieutenant-colonel Livingston, Colonel Jackson and Colonel Henry B. Livingston did themselves great honor in the transactions of the day, but it's not in my power to do justice to Colonel Laurens who acted both the general and partisan. His command of regular troops was small, but he did everything possible to be done by their numbers; he had two most excellent officers with him—Lieutenant-colonel Henry and Major Talbot.

The enemy fell back to their strong ground, and the day terminated with a cannonade and skirmishes. Both armies continued in their position all day yesterday, cannonading each other every now and then. Last night we effected a very good retreat without the loss of men or stores.

We have not collected an account of the killed and wounded, but we judge our loss amounts to between two and three hundred, and that of the enemy to much more.

We are going to be posted all round the shores as guard upon them, and in that state to wait for the return of the fleet, which, by the way, I think will not be in a hurry.

It is reported that Lord Howe arrived last night with his fleet and the reinforcement mentioned in your Excellency's letter to General Sullivan. If the report is true we got off the island in very good season.

—GREENE, *Life of Nathanael Greene*, II, 130-132.

5. BOSTON RIOTS AGAINST THE FRENCH FLEET

Petersfield, February, 1784

A most violent affray, in which numbers on both sides were engaged and the French seem to have been very roughly treated, happened on the 17th of September, 1778, at night, in Boston. Some of the French were said to have been killed, and several were certainly wounded; among whom were some officers, and one particularly of considerable distinction. As both D'Estaing and the government of Boston were eager to accommodate matters in such a manner as that no sting should remain behind on either side, a great reserve was observed with respect to the particulars of the riot, as well as of the circumstances which led to it; and the cursory imperfect sketches that were published showed evidently that they were not to be relied upon.

A proclamation was issued by the council of state on the following day, strictly urging the magistrates to use their utmost endeavours for bringing the offenders to justice, and offering a reward of 300 dollars for the discovery of any of the parties concerned in the riot. And to remove the impression of its arising from any popular animosity to the French, the Boston prints laboured to fix it upon some unknown captured British seamen and deserters from Burgoyne's army, who had enlisted in their privateers. D'Estaing had the address to give into this idea, and to appear thoroughly satisfied with the satisfaction he received. The high reward produced no manner of discovery.

The same spirit operated just about the same time and in the same manner, but much more violent in degree, and fatal in consequence between the American and French seamen, in the city and port of Charlestown, South Carolina. The quarrel there began, as at Boston, ashore and at night, and ended in the last extreme of hostility, an open fight with cannon and small arms; the French firing from their ships, whither they had been hastily driven from the town, and Americans from the adjoining wharfs and shore. Several lives were acknowledged to be lost, and a much greater number were, of course, wounded. . . .

—*Universal Magazine*, LXXIV, 87.

6. Yankee Doodle's Expedition to Rhode Island

A Tory Satire

From Lewis, Monsieur Gérard came,
    To Congress in this town, sir,
They bowed to him, and he to them,
    And then they all sat down, sir.

Begar, said Monsieur, one grand coup
    You shall bientot behold, sir;
This was believed as gospel true,
    And Jonathan felt bold, sir.

So Yankee Doodle did forget
    The sound of British drum, sir,
How oft it made him quake and sweat,
    In spite of Yankee rum, sir.

He took his wallet on his back,
    His rifle on his shoulder,
And veowed Rhode Island to attack
    Before he was much older.

In dread array their tattered crew
    Advanced with colors spread, sir.
Their fifes played Yankee doodle, doo,
    King Hancock at their head, sir. . . .

They swore they'd make bold Pigot squeak,
    So did their good ally, sir,
And take him prisoner in a week,
    But that was all my eye, sir.

As Jonathan so much desired
    To shine in martial story,
D'Estaing with politesse retired,
    To leave him all the glory.

He left him what was better yet,
    At least it was more use, sir,
He left him for a quick retreat,
    A very good excuse, sir. . . .

Another cause with these combined,
    To throw him in the dumps, sir,
For Clinton's name alarmed his mind
    And made him stir his stumps, sir.
                —Rivington's *Royal Gazette*, October 3, 1778.

V. STONY POINT

Stony Point, on the west side of the Hudson, and Verplanck's Point across the river were likened by Washington to the Pillars of Hercules. He considered them "the key to the Continent." But before the Patriots had completed fortifying these approaches to West Point, they were seized by Clinton in the spring of 1779. The British immediately set about erecting formidable fortifications. Washington asked Anthony Wayne to get a trustworthy officer into the British works to find out whatever he could about them. The man selected was Allen McLane, and the way in which he got inside the fort at Stony Point is told in his manuscript journal. After further reconnaissance of the area, Washington designated Anthony Wayne to attack with a force of 1,350 men. They were to use bayonets, and, except in one battalion, not a musket was loaded. It was to be Paoli in reverse. The plan was skillfully executed, and the fort was taken. The British losses: 63 killed, 70 or more wounded, 543 captured, along with artillery and military equipment. The Americans lost 15 killed, 80 wounded.

Believing that "it would require more men to maintain it than we can afford," Washington had the fort dismantled, and Clinton moved in again. The effects, then, of Stony Point were largely psychological. With the bayonet alone, the Americans had successfully attacked British regulars in a fortified position, and by that achievement won new respect from their enemy.

1. A SPY GETS INSIDE BRITISH-HELD STONY POINT

Journal of Captain Allen McLane of Pennsylvania.

Friday the 2 July [1779].—By Genl. Washington's orders went in with a flag to conduct Mrs. Smith to see her sons. [Elsewhere in the Journal appears the following memorandum: "McLane discovered the unfinished situation of the works on Stony Point while accompanying Mrs. Smith with a flag and communicated his observations to head quarter, which discovery determined Genl. Washington to carry it by storm on the night of the 17th July, 1779."]

Saturday, 3d of July.—Took post at the short clove, nothing occurring this day. At 8 o'clock moved down towards Stony Point—lay close to the works. All quiet this night.

Tuesday, July 6th.—Lay on the line all this day. His Exclly. Genl. Washington reconnoitred the enemy's works.

Wednesday, July 14.—Moved down to the hills in front of Stony Point—took the widow Calhoon and another widow going to the enemy with chickens and greens—drove off 20 head of horned cattle from the enemy's pasture, the property of John Deinke, Saml. Calhoon and Jacob Rose—gave them their cattle.

Lay in the woods this night near Captain Hutchinsons.

Thursday, July 15th.—This morning mustered my company at Hutchins' house—at ten o'clock rode with Majors Posey and Lee to reconnoitre the enemy's lines. Genl. Waine moved down from the forest to the ground near the lines. At 8 o'clock at night moved my company close to the enemy's sentrys in order to intersept intelligence. At 30 minutes past 12 o'clock the light infantry began the attack on the lines, Genl. Waine at their head. They rushed on with fixed bayonets and carried the lines in 25 minutes—killed one capt., 21 privates, wounded 4 subalterns, 66 privates, took one colonel, 4 captains, 15 subalterns, 468 men. At the same time a feint was made against Verplank's Point.

—McLane Papers, Lib. II, N.Y. Hist. Soc.

2. Wayne's Troops Take the Fort at Bayonet Point

Nathanael Greene to Colonel Cox.

Stoney-Point, King's Ferry, July 17, 1779

I wrote you a hasty account yesterday morning of a surprize Gen. Wayne had effected upon the garrison at this place. He marched about two o'clock in the afternoon from Fort Montgomery with part of the light infantry of the army, amounting to about 1,400 men. The garrison consisted of between 5 and 600 men, including officers. The attack was made about midnight and conducted with great spirit and enterprise, the troops marching up in the face of an exceeding heavy fire with cannon and musketry, without discharging a gun. This is thought to be the perfection of discipline and will for ever immortalize Gen. Wayne, as it would do honor to the first general in Europe. The place is as difficult of access as any you ever saw, strongly fortified with lines and secured with a double row of abatis. The post actually looks more formidable on the ground than it can be made by description, and, contrary to almost all other events of this nature, increases our surprize by viewing the place and the circumstances.

The darkness of the night favoured the attack and made our loss much less than might have been expected. The whole business was done with fixed bayonets. Our loss in killed and wounded amounted to 90 men, including officers—eight only of which were killed. Gen. Wayne got a slight wound (upon the side of his head) and three or four other officers—among the number is Lieut. Col. Hay, of Pennsylvania—but they are all in a fair way of recovery.

The enemy's loss is not certainly known, neither have we any certain account of the number of prisoners, as they were sent away in the dark and in a hurry, but it is said they amount to 440; about 30 or 40 were left behind unable to march, and upwards of 30 were buried.

The enemy made little resistance after our people got into the works; their cry was, "Mercy, mercy, dear, dear Americans!"

—JOHNSTON, *Storming of Stony Point*, pp. 174-175.

3. "The Enterprise Was Really a Gallant One"

Journal of Commodore George Collier.

A very disagreeable event, however, put a stop to the favourite expedition against New London; and this was the surprisal (in the night) of the strong post of Stony Point, in the North River, which was carried by the rebels with very little loss and the garrison all made prisoners or killed. The enterprise was really a gallant one, and as bravely executed. The rebel troops, under a General Wayne, formed two attacks with fixed bayonets and unloaded arms during the darkness and silence of the night; it was said that they had taken the precaution to kill every dog two days before that was within some miles round the post, to prevent their approach being discovered by their barking. They began to march from their camp, eleven miles off, soon after dusk, proceeding with celerity and silence; and soon after midnight fell in with the British piquets, whom they surprised and bayonetted a number of them; the rest hastily retreated, keeping up a straggling fire, though to very little purpose, for the rebels followed close at their heels. Their forlorn hope consisted of forty men, and were followed by a party with hooks on long poles, to pull aside the abattis and thereby give an entrance to the column behind. The works of Stony Point were not half completed; and as one part of its strength at that time consisted in the abattis, the rebels found no great difficulty in getting into the body of a work which was quite open, though on an eminence.

A young man of the name of Johnson, who was Lieut.-Colonel of the 17th Regiment, was left with the charge of this important post; he was reckoned a brave and good officer for his years, but the force was certainly inadequate to its defence. On the first alarm from the piquets he ran down with the main guard to defend the abattis and support them. The rebel column was stopped for a few minutes, and a brisk firing took place on both sides; but to Colonel Johnson's grief and surprise, he heard a cry of "Victory" on the heights above him and the "Fort's our own" (which was the rebel watchword). He very soon learned by some of his officers that the enemy were in full possession of the body of the place. It was certainly so. The column which was destined for making the other attack took a short detour around, and climbed up the perpendicular height, which being over the river, nobody expected an enemy on that side; and the surprise of the King's troops at seeing them in possession of the works was extreme.

The laws of war give a right to the assailants of putting all to death who are found in arms; justice is certainly due to all men, and commendation should be given where it is deserved. The rebels had made the attack with a bravery they never before exhibited, and they showed at this moment a generosity and clemency which during the course of the rebellion had no parallel. There was light sufficient after getting up the heights to show them many of the British troops with arms in their hands; instead of putting them to death, they called to them "to throw their arms down if they expected any quarter." It was too late then to resist; they submitted, and the strong post of Stony Point fell again into possession of the rebels.

The loss of the King's troops, considering the place was taken by storm, was very small, Captain Tew being the only officer killed and thirty-two men; forty-three were wounded, and the rest were made prisoners. The enemy found here many brass mortars, many pieces of large cannon, together with the ammunition necessary for them—an unlucky piece of business and fatal to the reputation of a gallant young man, who was certainly left with a force very inadequate to the purpose for which he was placed at Stony Point. . . .

On the receipt of this disagreeable news, the Commodore sent orders to discontinue the blockade of the harbour at New London, and immediately proceeded back to New York with all the men-of-war and transports, getting through that most dangerous pass called Hell Gates, luckily without losing any of the ships. . . .

The fleet was no sooner descried from Stony Point than the rebels set fire to everything there that would burn, and went off with their usual alertness; they had conveyed away some of the cannon and mortars, but the greatest part of them were loaded on a galley, with which they proposed going up the river to their strong post at West Point; but as the galley was beginning to move she was luckily sunk. . . .

—JOHNSTON, *Storming of Stony Point,* pp. 134-136.

VI. PAULUS HOOK

In his letter of July 27, 1779, to Washington reporting on the capture of Stony Point, Wayne omitted mentioning the role of Allen McLane. Nor did he single out for special commendation Major Henry Lee ("Light-Horse Harry"), whose corps had played a minor role in that engagement. So high-spirited an officer as Lee was certain to make his own bid for glory. As Washington Irving later put it, "Stony Point had piqued his emulation."

Lee's objective was Paulus Hook, a fort directly opposite New York City at what is now Jersey City. McLane scouted the territory, reported that the garrison numbered little over 200, and guided Lee's men through the complex approaches to the fort. Time was of the essence, as the fort was protected by a deep ditch which could be crossed only at low tide. Lee's offensive moves began on the morning of August 18, but a defection of Virginians reduced his forces, and it was four o'clock of the following morning before he approached the marshlands leading to the ditch. A rising tide would soon make it impassable. The Americans staged a gallant bayonet attack and took the fort in a few minutes, with only two killed and three wounded. But alarm guns on the New York side were arousing the British, and Lee had to pull out with some 158 prisoners.

After Paulus Hook, Lee was charged with having taken precedence over
officers senior in rank, but a court-martial exonerated him. Hamilton's com-
ment on the charges is worth noting. In a letter to John Laurens, dated
September 11, 1779, he wrote:

> *The Philadelphia papers will tell you of a handsome stroke by Lee at*
> *Powle's Hook. Some folks in the Virginia line, jealous of his glory, had*
> *the folly to get him arrested. He has been tried and acquitted with the*
> *highest honor. Lee unfolds himself more and more to be an officer of*
> *great capacity, and if he had not a little spice of the Julius Caesar or*
> *Cromwell in him, he would be a very clever fellow.*

1. ALLEN MCLANE RECONNOITERS PAULUS HOOK

Monday, August 16. Moved toward Powles Hook to reconeter. Took
two prisoners on Hobuck. . . . Returned with the party to Hackinsack. This
night lay at Storms house.

Tusday, 17 Aug. Drew four days' provisions. Detached two sergeants
[?] with 12 men eatch to lay in Bergain Woods. This night lay near the
liberty pole.

Wensday, 18 August. This morning received orders from Maj. Lee to
take post in the wood near Bargan in order to intercept the communication
between Powles Hook and the [?] and to join him at a sertain place in the
woods near the Three Pidgeons in order to conduct him to attack Powles
Hook. Met him and after some deficalty arrived at the works half past three
in morning. Stormed them without more loss than two men killed and five
wounded who killed about fifty, took 150 prisoner, 9 officers

Thursday 19, 1779 August. and then retired to the new bridge the distance
of 22 miles. . . .

—McLane Papers, Lib. II, N.Y. Historical Soc.

2. A PATRIOT VIEW: "THE GREATEST ENTERPRISE EVER UNDERTAKEN"

Captain Levin Handy to George Handy.

Paramus, 22 August, 1779

Before this reaches you, I doubt not but you have heard of our success
at Powles Hook, where the enemy had a very strong fort, within one and
a quarter miles from New York. We started from this place on Wednesday
last half after ten o'clock, taking our route by a place called New Bridge on
Hackensac River, where my two companies were joined by three hundred
Virginians and a company of dismounted Dragoons, commanded by Captain
McLane. We took up our line of march about 5 o'clock in the evening from
the bridge, the nearest route with safety, to Powles, distant then about twenty
miles, with my detachment in front, the whole under command of the gallant Major Lee. The works were to be carried by storm—the whole to advance
in three columns, one of which I had the honour to command.

The attack was to commence at one half after 12 o'clock, but having been
greatly embarrassed on our march, and having a number of difficulties to
surmount, did not arrive at the point of attack till after four o'clock in the
morning, when, after a small fire from them, we gained their works and put

about fifty of them to the bayonet, took one hundred and fifty-seven prisoners, exclusive of seven commanding officers; this was completed in less than thirty minutes, and a retreat ordered, as we had every reason to suppose unless timely it would be cut off. Our situation was so difficult that we could not bring off any stores. We had a morass to pass of upwards two miles, the greatest part of which we were obliged to pass by files, and several canals to ford up to our breast in water. We advanced with bayonets, pans open, cocks fallen, to prevent any fire from our side; and believe me when I assure you we did not fire a musket.

You will see a more particular account of it in the papers than it is in my power to give you at present. It is thought to be the greatest enterprise ever undertaken in America. Our loss is so inconsiderable that I do not mention it.

—REED, *Life and Correspondence of Reed*, II, 125-126.

3. A TORY VIEW: THE PATRIOTS FAILED TO EXPLOIT THEIR VICTORY

Nearly half an hour after two, the Rebels in three divisions (exceeding 400 men) passed the ditch in front of the abatis, about 20 yards from the abatis, where they were fired upon by a few centries, but having seized immediately on the block house guards (who, in place of defending their post, ran out to see what was the matter) they proceeded to the work, which they soon became masters of, with the cannon, etc. But they were so confused and alarmed, they neither spiked the cannon nor damaged the barracks, or made any other use of their victory than carrying off about 100 prisoners, among whom there are about ten Hessians (whose loss is much regretted) and four officers of Colonel Buskirk's battalion, and plundering a few women.

This panic (amongst them) was occasioned by an incessant fire kept on them from a small redoubt into which Major Sutherland threw himself with a captain subaltern and 25 gallant Hessians on the first alarm. The Rebels repeatedly challenged the redoubt to surrender, or they would bayonet them, to which they received a fire and "No," for answer. About half after 8 o'clock Major Sutherland was joined by one Light Infantry company of the Guards, under the command of Captain Dundass, with which he immediately marched, and Captain Maynard was shortly after ordered to follow Major Sutherland by Colonel Gordon, on which Major Sutherland marched both companies in order to succour Colonel Buskirk, and after going about 15 miles, he found that Colonel Buskirk had a smart engagement with the Rebels some time before and had returned. There were a few prisoners made, amongst whom is a Captain Meale, who was found asleep from the great fatigue he underwent; and surely unless he had been a Livingston, Laurens or Adams, he could not in that situation forfeit his claim to British valor and humanity. The Light Infantry rested here for an hour, during which Dr. Gordon gallantly charged two Rebels, who had fired at him, and took one of them.

Major Sutherland, finding one object of his march answered by Colonel Buskirk's being safe, and 100 men not sufficient to answer his other intentions, returned, this charming body of men having made a march of about 30 miles in less than 10 hours.

—*New York Gazette and Mercury*, August 23, 1779.

VII. SPRINGFIELD

In the spring of 1780 the British had evidence that there was much discontent in the Patriot ranks. Civilian morale was depreciating along with the Continental currency. Washington found that his half-starved army stationed at Morristown was increasingly reluctant to re-enlist. Among the Headquarters Papers in the Clements Library is an undated memorandum from Knyphausen to Clinton:

Having received intelligence that Washington's army was very discontented, that many of them wished to have an opportunity given them of coming in to join the royal army, and that he had detached the York Brigade towards Albany to oppose the incursions of the Indians—these reasons induced General Knyphausen to make a move into Jersey with 6,000 men.

Knyphausen's force crossed over from Staten Island to Elizabethtown and marched to the village of Connecticut Farms, burned the church and other buildings and accidentally killed the wife of the Reverend James Caldwell. To Knyphausen's surprise the militia turned out and disputed his crossing of the Rahway River. That story is told by Sylvanus Seeley, a colonel in the New Jersey state militia, who proved especially useful to Washington in transmitting intelligence regarding British troop and ship movements around New York harbor. With the militia reinforced by Continental troops, Knyphausen faced about and retired to Elizabethtown.

To save face he decided to try once again. On June 23 his forces marched to the Jersey town of Springfield, but were obstinately resisted by Patriot troops under Nathanael Greene. After seizing the town, Knyphausen pushed a column to the American left, threatening Greene's rear. The American general withdrew his troops to higher ground and stopped the British column cold. Outnumbered five or six to one, the Americans had fought the British and Hessian troops to a standstill. The burning and looting of Springfield, following hard on the atrocities at Connecticut Farms, roused the countryside against the British, who attempted no further operations in New Jersey.

1. THE PRELIMINARY BATTLE OF CONNECTICUT FARMS

Diary of Colonel Sylvanus Seeley, of the New Jersey militia.

7th June 1780: Had an alarm and the enemy came out as far as Springfield Bridge. The Militia colected fast and joining Maxwells brigade stopt the enemy and after sum fire at long shot the enemy retired to a breast work they had threw up on an advantagious pice of ground on this side the farm meeting hous. About 3 this aftarnoon they set fire to about 30 buildings, one of which is the meeting hous. We have had about 15 killed and 40 wounded, among the latter my brother Saml, slightly. I had orders and marched my regiment to Thompsons Mills whare we lay all night.

8th: This morning about ½ after 12 the rear of the enemy left the ground. About 8 o'clock received orders to follow them and on ower march receive[d] inteligence that the enemy are going, but when we got to town find a guard in the woods back of Decon Ogdens hous and at the forks of the road. Aftar sum time here and being joined by Lord Stirlings troopes he orders us to advance in three colloms, one on the main road, the Continental troops of Col. Cortland on the left, myself in the centor. We advanced, and the troop under my command behaved exceeding well, altho at a certain time one platoon fell back a little, but after being ordered to com up came up and stood thare ground well. We took about 20 prisoners and advance through the woods whare the enemy open upon us with a number of field pieces, and finding they ware true [too?] heavy for us General Hand ordered a retreat, which was performed in good order. I had one man killed and three wounded. After retiring about half a mile we lay on ower armes untill evening and then returned to the north end of town and staid all night.

22d. [23d]: This day the enemy came out and burnt Springfield and returned about 3 o'clock P.M., pursewed by ower people. The enemies loss this day is thought to be considerable. Owers is about 15 killed and 40 wounded. I got home about 10 at night.

—SEELEY, *Diary*, Morristown National Historical Park.

2. "THE ENEMY WERE OBSTINATELY OPPOSED"

Lieutenant Colonel Lewis Morris, Jr., to his father, Brigadier General Lewis Morris.

Springfield, June 24th, 1780

My Dear Sir,

I have only time to inform you that I got neither wound or bruise in the conflict of yesterday. The enemy advanced with their whole force about sunrise in two columns, one upon the Vauxhall road, the other upon the Springfield road. Genl. Greene, who was left here for the security of the post and protection of the country with two brigades and the militia, formed his little army judiciously and to the best advantage at the bridge leading into town. The enemy were obstinately opposed and several times repulsed, but after a fire of forty minutes, both artillery and musquetry, our brave fellows were obliged to yield to superior numbers.

To cover this retreat the General had posted Col. Smith with a regiment in an orchard about the center of the town and thrown a small party into a stone house upon his left flank. Here the enemy met with a second check and lost a considerable number of men About a quarter of a mile from this the troops rallied and the artillery being posted upon commanding ground, a warm cannonade commenced, but the enemy would not advance near enough for our musquetry. The troops being greatly exposed in this position to the fire of their artillery, the general thought it most prudent to retire to an eminence about three hundred yards in the rear, where we continued spectators to the melancholy, general conflagration of Springfield, till they retreated, and then followed them into Elizabeth Town. About twelve at night they crossed their bridge, cut it away and are now secure upon Staten Island.

I will not recapitulate the scene of destruction and distress which I have been witness to. I dont wish to wound your humanity—happy I am that your family has never fallen in the track of such barbarians. It is a sweet consolation to me that they paid so dearly for their conquest. You may depend upon it that they lost a considerable number of both officers and men—I will not pretend to say how many, but from the numbers engaged you may rate them great. Let my friends in Philadelphia know this as I am in haste and cannot write. My love to you and God bless you also.

—LEWIS MORRIS, JR., Ms. Letter, Morristown National Historical Park.

VIII. BENEDICT ARNOLD FIRES NEW LONDON

When it was known that Washington's army was heading southward to trap Cornwallis, Benedict Arnold, rewarded for his treason with a commission as brigadier general, proposed an expedition against Connecticut in order to force Washington to leave some of his forces in the North. The raid was as ferocious as any conducted by British and Tories in the entire war. Arnold's forces landed on the morning of September 6, 1781, one division on each side of the harbor, and drove the defenders from Fort Trumbull on the west side of the Thames River. Fort Griswold on the opposite bank was valiantly defended by Lieutenant Colonel William Ledyard, who finally surrendered to overwhelming numbers, only to be bayoneted by Lieutenant Colonel Van Buskirk of the New Jersey Volunteers. Tories, Hessians and British joined in indiscriminate slaughter of the garrison after it had surrendered. Before embarking his troops for New York, Arnold put the town to the torch, in all some 143 buildings, with an estimated loss of a half-million dollars. It is said that Arnold stood in the church belfry and watched the conflagration with as much satisfaction as Nero. This was Arnold's last act of spite against his own people and his native land. He had been born in Norwich, a dozen miles away.

1. COLONEL LEDYARD IS BAYONETED WHILE SURRENDERING

Memoirs of Major General William Heath.

September 10, 1781

Intelligence was received from Governor Trumbull that the enemy had made a descent on New London, on the [morning] of the 6th with about two thousand infantry and three hundred light horse. Their fleet consisted of about forty sail of ships-of-war and transports; they plundered the inhabitants of property to a large amount, and burnt a great part of the town. The militia behaved very gallantly, and a number of very valuable citizens were killed; among others Col. Ledyard, Captains Saltonstall and Richards. The enemy in three assaults on the fort on Groton side of the river were repulsed, but on the fourth attempt carried it. . . .

In Governor Trumbull's letter, the enemy were charged with behaving in a wanton and barbarous manner; and that of between seventy and eighty men who were killed, three only were killed before the enemy entered the fort and the garrison had submitted; that on Col. Ledyard's delivering his sword reversed to the commanding officer who entered the fort, the officer immediately plunged it into the colonel's body, on which several soldiers bayoneted him. It is also asserted that upon the foregoing taking place, an

American officer, who stood near to Col. Ledyard, instantly stabbed the British officer who stabbed the colonel; on which the British indiscriminately bayoneted a great number of Americans. . . .

Arnold himself continued on the New London side and, while his troops were plundering and burning, was said to have been at a house where he was treated very politely; that while he was sitting with the gentleman [Christopher Christophers] regaling himself, the latter observed that he hoped his house and property would be safe; he was answered that while he [Arnold] was there it would not be touched; but the house, except the room in which they were, was soon plundered and found to be on fire.

During the plunder of the town, the British . . . were in great confusion, setting their arms against trees and fences while they were collecting and carrying off their plunder; in this situation they might easily have been defeated. . . .

—HEATH, *Memoirs*, pp. 282-284.

2. ARNOLD CLAIMS THAT THE BURNING OF THE TOWN WAS ACCIDENTAL

Benedict Arnold to Sir Henry Clinton.

Sound, off Plumb Island, September 8, 1781

. . . At one o'clock the next morning, we arrived off the harbour [New London], when the wind suddenly shifted to the northward, and it was nine o'clock before the transports could beat in. At ten o'clock, the troops in two divisions, and in four debarkations, were landed: one on each side the harbour, about three miles from New London.

. . . Lieutenant Col. Eyre had sent Captain Beckwith with a flag to demand a surrender of the fort, which was peremptorily refused, and the attack had commenced. After a most obstinate defense of near forty minutes, the fort was carried by the superior bravery and perseverance of the assailants. The attack was judicious and spirited and reflects the highest honor on the officers and troops engaged, who seemed to vie with each other in being first in danger. The troops approached on three sides of the work, which was a square with flanks, made a lodgment in the ditch and under a heavy fire, which they kept up on the works, effected a second lodgment on the friezing, which was attended with great difficulty, as only a few pickets could be forced out or broken in a place, and was so high that the soldiers could not ascend without assisting each other. Here the coolness and bravery of the troops were very conspicuous, as the first who ascended the frieze were obliged to silence a nine-pounder, which infiladed the place on which they stood, until a sufficient body had collected to enter the works, which was done with fixed bayonets through the embrazures, where they were opposed with great obstinacy by the garrison with long spears. . . .

Our loss, though very considerable, is very short of the enemy's who lost most of their officers, among whom was their commander, Col. Ledyard. Eighty-five men were found dead in Fort Griswold, and 60 wounded, most of them mortally; their loss on the opposite side must have been considerable, but cannot be ascertained. I believe we have about 70 prisoners, besides the wounded, who were left paroled.

Ten or twelve of the enemy's ships were burned, ... one loaded with naval stores. An immense quantity of European and West India goods were found in the stores, ... the whole of which was burnt with the stores, which proved to contain a large quantity of powder, unknown to us; the explosion of the powder and change of wind soon after the stores were fired, communicated the flames to a part of the town, which was, notwithstanding every effort to prevent it, unfortunately destroyed.

—ARNOLD, *Life of Benedict Arnold*, pp. 349-351.

CHAPTER EIGHTEEN

Spies, Treason and Mutiny

As WE HAVE *already observed in connection with the British background to the American war, and the position of the Loyalists, the American Revolution was a rather special kind of war, one in which we cannot glibly apply the familiar standards of wars between nations. In the first place it was very difficult to know at just what point the conflict between colonies and mother country became a war between America and Britain, and at what point, therefore, lack of enthusiasm for separation, or for war, became treason. Galloway, for example, remained Loyalist too long; Dickinson, who was almost as lukewarm in the beginning, changed in the nick of time. Second, the Revolution was still an eighteenth-century war, one which attracted mercenaries, adventurers and soldiers of fortune, men like Charles Lee and General von Steuben and even the beloved Montgomery and—on the other side—Dr. Church and Dr. Bancroft. Were these men guilty of treason, or were they merely following accepted practices of the day? Were the Hessians who left the British Army deserters, or were they free of any obligations to the foreign masters who had hired their services from their princes? Third, and most pervasive, the circumstances of the war were such as to make it difficult to know just what constituted comfort to the enemy, and what constituted aid, even more difficult to hold comfort or aid treasonable, and almost impossible to punish it as treason. It was, indeed, a very mixed-up war: one in which participants flowed in and out, as it were; one in which absence without leave and desertion were hopelessly blended; one in which it was almost impossible for civilians to escape involvement with whatever army happened to be in the vicinity and to levy on provisions, shelter and information.*

Espionage, treason and mutiny—these things had meanings and connotations different from those which we attach to them today. By modern standards men like Charles Lee and Silas Deane were subversives if not traitors, but then so, too, were Fox, Camden, Barré, Wilkes and others who championed the American cause in Parliament. By modern standards armies that melted away after battles (or sometimes before them) were guilty of desertion. By modern standards refusal to obey officers, refusal to abide by rules, refusal to fight except after approval by military town meetings as it were—these things were all mutinous. But it is best to put aside modern standards, and take the Revolution on its own terms.

Recent wars have depended much on intelligence and counterintelligence, espionage and counterespionage, security, underground movements and so

*forth, but there was little of this in the American Revolution, which was, in a
sense, a much less sophisticated war. Where thousands of Loyalists were prepared to tell what they knew, why hire spies? Where tens of thousands of
Americans were prepared to inform on the invaders, why build up an espionage system? There were spies, there was an espionage system, but these
never mattered very much. Almost the only place where espionage was important was Europe, and London and Paris swarmed with spies and informers
in the best cloak-and-dagger tradition.*

*What of treason? Here Benedict Arnold looms up in lonely and awful
infamy. There were, in fact, other traitors—Benjamin Thompson, for example, or Dr. Church—but Arnold alone is remembered and execrated. Washington was right when he said that "this is the first instance of treason of this
kind" and that "nothing is so high an ornament to the characters of the American soldiers as their withstanding all the arts and seductions of an insidious
enemy." Arnold almost cost Americans their Revolution—it was a close
thing—yet we cannot but be wryly grateful for our only genuine villain;
what, after all, would we do without him?*

*Not only was treason rare, but mutiny, too. The American soldiers were
not professionals and they clung, many of them, to their amateur standing.
They were oftentimes required to serve far longer than they had bargained
for, and often, too, without pay, or with pay in worthless currency; they
were exposed to danger and to harsh discipline, to summer heat and winter
blizzards, to starvation and nakedness, to misery and disease. Yet there were
few mutinies, and those that did occur—chiefly in 1781—were merely desperate protests against conditions that had become intolerable, not shifts of allegiance to the British cause.*

*We give, in this chapter, a few indications of espionage and of plots and
counterplots; a more circumstantial account of the most notorious treason in
our history, and with it the touching story of John André; and finally some
accounts of the famous mutiny in January 1781 and its peaceful outcome.*

I. DR. CHURCH GOES OVER TO THE ENEMY

*Colonel Benjamin Church was the hero of King Philip's War, and one of
the notable figures in the history of the Plymouth Colony; something of his
fame was transmitted to his grandson, Benjamin Church of Rhode Island,
who managed to tarnish it. A graduate of Harvard College, Church studied
medicine in London, and returned to Massachusetts to an established position
and a handsome practice. One of the inner circle of Patriot leaders, he had
been appointed to the First Continental Congress and then made director and
chief physician to the American army outside Boston. Yet from the beginning his conduct had been a bit ambiguous, and Paul Revere, for one, suspected
that his patriotism was by no means pure. For reasons never wholly explained
Dr. Church entered into questionable—if not treasonable—correspondence
with General Gage. A cipher letter giving information on American military
arrangements was intercepted by Henry Ward of Rhode Island. Unable to
explain it away, Dr. Church was condemned by a court-martial to imprison-*

ment, then released on parole. The next year he sailed for the West Indies in search of health, and was lost at sea; his family was pensioned by George III.

1. "AN EVENT WHICH GIVES ME MUCH UNEASINESS"

James Warren to John Adams.

Watertown, October 1, 1775

An event has lately taken place here which makes much noise, and gives me much uneasiness, not only as it affects the character, and may prove the ruin of a man who I used to have a tolerable opinion of, but as it may be the cause of many suspicions and jealousies, and what is still worse, have a tendency to discredit the recommendations of my friends at the Congress. Dr. Church has been detected in a correspondence with the enemy, at least so far that a letter wrote by him in curious cypher and directed to Major Cane (who is an officer in the Royal army and one of Gage's family) has been intercepted.

The history of the whole matter is this. The Doctor, having formed an infamous connection with an infamous hussey to the disgrace of his own reputation, and probable ruin of his family, wrote this letter last July, and sent it by her to Newport with orders to give it to Wallace, or Dudley to deliver to Wallace, for conveyance to Boston. She, not finding an opportunity very readily, trusted it with a friend of hers to perform the orders, and came away and left it in his hands. He kept it some time and, having some suspicions of wickedness, had some qualms of conscience about executing his commissions, after some time consulted his friend. One result was to open the letter, which was done. The appearance of the letter increasing their suspicions, the next question after determining not to send it to Boston was, what should be done with it. After various conferences at divers times, they concluded to deliver it to General Washington.

Accordingly the man came with it last Thursday. After collecting many circumstances, the man was employed to draw from the girl, by using the confidence she had in him, the whole secret, but without success. She is a subtle, shrewd jade. She was then taken into custody and brought to the General's quarters that night. It was not till the next day that anything could be got from her. She then confessed that the Doctor wrote and sent her with the letter as above.

Upon this, the General sent a note desiring Major Hawley and me to come immediately to Cambridge. We all thought the suspicion quite sufficient to justify an arrest of him and his papers, which was done, and he is now under a guard. He owns the writing and sending the letter, says it was for Flemming in answer to one he wrote to him, and is calculated by magnifying the numbers of the army, their regularity, their provisions and ammunition, etc., to do great service to us. He declares his conduct tho' indiscreet was not wicked. There are, however, many circumstances, new and old, which time won't permit me to mention, that are much against him. The letter, I suppose, is now decyphering, and when done will either condemn, or in some measure excuse him. Thus much for this long story.

—*Warren-Adams Letters*, I, 121-122.

2. "What Punishment Can Equal Such Horrid Crimes!"

Governor Samuel Ward of Rhode Island to Henry Ward.

Philadelphia 11th October 1775

Dear Brother

I received yours of 3rd inst. and very readily allow it to ballance our literary accounts to that time.

Dr. Church, who could have thought or even suspected it, a man who seemed to be all animation in the cause of his country, highly connected, employed in several very honorable and lucrative departments, and in full possession of the confidence of his country—what a complication of madness and wickedness must a soul be filled with to be capable of such perfidy, what punishment can equal such horrid crimes! I communicated the affair to the Massachusetts delegates; they could hardly conceive it possible. They soon after received some account of the matter themselves. A letter from Mr. Secretary Read says upon searching his papers nothing amiss was found in them; his friends from thence would infer his innocence; he pretends that the letters sent through [Captain James] Wallace were wrote to his brother in law Fleming (late partner with Mein) and contained accounts favourable to our cause; such letters as these might have been sent in every week without interruption; of course there could be no occasion for that expensive roundabout and suspicious way of conveyance which he took.

I am obliged to you for the circumstantial account of the matter as it throws light on the subject. How happy it is that he is discovered before he had done us any considerable mischief! The greatest that I am apprehensive of is that it may induce suspicions and lessen that confidence which is necessary to a cordial union and our mutual support; this ought carefully to be guarded against as fatal, and at the same time the utmost vigilance is necessary least we should be betrayed. . . .

—Ward, *Correspondence*, pp. 99-100.

II. ARSON IN AMERICA AND ENGLAND

The Revolution had its quota of plots and counterplots, some of them sensible enough, some melodramatic, some the products of a fevered imagination. The first of these was known as the Hickey Plot after the ringleader, Thomas Hickey, one of Washington's guards, who was hanged in June 1776. Its purported objective was the assassination of the general. Another is the orgy of arson attributed to "John the Painter" in England. The accused claimed that Silas Deane encouraged him during the early months of his Paris residence to set on fire the Portsmouth dockyard. Deane's complicity has never been proved.

1. "A Most Barbarous and Infernal Plot among the Tories"

Extract of a letter.

New York, June 24, 1776

My last to you was by Friday's post, since which a most barbarous and infernal plot has been discovered among our Tories, the particulars of which

Courtesy, Pennsylvania Academy of the Fine Arts

ROBERT MORRIS

Portrait by Charles Willson Peale

Courtesy, National Gallery of Art, Washington, D. C.
Gift of Miss Marian B. Maurice

THOMAS PAINE

Portrait by John Wesley Jarvis

BATTLE OF GERMANTOWN: ATTACK ON THE CHEW HOUSE

I cannot give you, as the Committee of Examination consists of but three, who are sworn to secrecy. Two of Washington's guards are concerned; the third they tempted to join them made the first discovery. The general report of their design is as follows: Upon the arrival of the troops they were to murder all the staff officers, blow up the magazines, and secure the passes of the town. Gilbert Forbes, gunsmith in the Broadway, was taken between two and three o'clock on Saturday morning, and carried before our Provincial Congress, who were then sitting, but refusing to make any discovery, he was sent to jail and put in irons. Young Mr. Livingstone went to see him early in the morning, and told him he was sorry to find he had been concerned, and, as his time was very short, not having above three days to live, advised him to prepare himself. This had the desired effect; he asked to be carried before Congress again, and he would discover all he knew. Several have been since taken (between twenty and thirty), among them our Mayor, who are all now under confinement. It is said their party consisted of about five hundred.

I have just heard the Mayor has confessed bringing money from Tryon to pay for rifle-guns that Forbes had made. Burgoyne is arrived at Quebeck with his fleet.

—FORCE, *American Archives*, 4th Series, VI, 1054.

2. JOHN THE PAINTER TRIES TO BURN PORTSMOUTH AND BRISTOL

Towards the close of the year [1776], and in the beginning of the ensuing, much confusion, apprehension, and suspicion was excited by the machinery of a wretched enthusiast and incendiary, since well known by the appellation of John the Painter, but whose real name was James Aitken. This man, who was born in Edinburgh, and bred a painter, possessing an extraordinary spirit of rambling, with a strong propensity to vice, had passed in the course of a few years thro' an uncommon variety of those scenes which attend the most profligate and abandoned state of a vagabond life—a kind of life for which a manual trade, however followed, affords the most perfect opportunity and cover.

Among his other exploits, he had passed through several marching regiments of foot, from each of which he deserted as soon as opportunity served, after receiving the bounty money. In his various peregrinations through the different parts of England, he alternately committed highway robberies, burglaries, petty thefts, rapes, and worked at his trade, as occasion invited, villainy prompted, or fear or necessity operated. Whether it proceeded from the apprehension of punishment, or that the original bent of his genius led him to new scenes of action, whatever was the operative motive, he shipped himself off for America, where he continued for two or three years. His being of a melancholy solitary nature, which neither sought for associates in crimes, nor admitted of partners in pleasure, as it contributed much to his preservation for so long a time from the justice of those laws which he was constantly breaking, served equally to throw in utter darkness all those parts of his life which he did not himself think fitting or necessary to communicate. His transactions in America are accordingly unknown, any further than that he traversed, and worked at his trade in, several of the colonies.

As his pilgrimage on that continent was in the beginning, and during the progress, of the present troubles, it may well be imagined that the violence of the language and sentiments held in political matters by that order of the people with whom he lived and conversed gave birth to that madness of enthusiasm in him which afterwards became so dangerous. He accordingly returned to England with the most deadly antipathy to the government and nation, and soon after, if not originally, adopted the design of subverting, in his own single person, that power which he so much abhorred.

The scheme was as detestable as could even be expected from the villainous character of the framer. It was to destroy the maritime force of this country, as well as its internal strength and riches, by setting fire to the royal dock-yards, and burning the principal trading cities and towns, with their shipping, of whatever sort, so far as it could possibly be done. In the prosecution of this atrocious design, he traversed the kingdom to discover the state of the several docks, and the nature of the watch by which they were guarded, which he in general found to be as lax and insufficient as he could have wished. He also took wonderful pains in the construction of fireworks, machines and combustibles for the purpose, but was strangely unsuccessful in all his attempts of this nature.

It was owing to this unaccountable failure in his machines that the nation was saved from receiving some dreadful, if not irretrievable shock. One of them, which extinguished of its own accord, without any human interference, was found, several weeks after it had been laid, in the center of a prodigious quantity of one of the most combustible substances, in the great hemp house at Portsmouth. He, however, succeeded in setting fire to the rope house in that yard, and had an opportunity, for several miles in his flight to London, to feast the malignity of his nature in the contemplation of that dreadful conflagration which he had excited, and which from its prodigious appearance he imagined had spread to all the magazines, buildings and docks. The fire was happily subdued, with no other loss than that of the rope house and its contents.

The incendiary still pursued his design, but failed in his attempts upon the royal docks, and narrowly escaped being taken at Plymouth. The city of Bristol was at that time greatly divided between the two numerous parties of Tories and Whigs, as they were called, the former of which eagerly supported, and the latter as highly detested, the present court measures against America. The former carried up an address of congratulation upon the late successes of his Majesty's arms, which the latter condemned in the strongest terms, representing it as an act highly indecent, unchristian and impious to exhibit any marks of triumph and rejoicing in the slaughter and destruction of their fellow-subjects.

In this state of party and political disunion among the inhabitants, John the Painter, in the month of January 1777, attempted first to burn the shipping, and afterwards the city itself. A deep and narrow chasm, which is nearly dry when the tide is out, fronts a great part of the quay in Bristol, which is generally crowded with a prodigious number of vessels, all lying so close together, and so free from water in that season, that the first thing which strikes the attention of a stranger is a surprize how they could be so lodged, and the second, a conviction of the fatal and irremediable consequences both to the shipping and the city, which a fire must inevitably produce. The incendiary, failing in his attempt to set two or three of those vessels on fire, found so strict a watch kept afterwards that he was obliged to change his mode of operation, and to secure the destruction of the ships by beginning with the houses. After some failures in his attempts this way, in which, as in all others, the findings of his ineffective apparatus afforded full evidence of the atrociousness of the design, he at length succeeded so far as to set fire to some warehouses in the vicinity of the quay, six or seven of which were consumed.

These facts and circumstances afforded a full scope to all the rage and virulence of party to blaze out in their utmost violence. The most bigotted and furious, and consequently the most ignorant, on the one side, attributed them to the disaffection, the republican and American principles, of the other; whilst those on an equal scale of understanding and prejudice on that, were fully convinced that they were malicious acts or inventions of the Tories, merely for the purpose of calumniating and blackening their adversaries.

The reign of the incendiary was not much longer. He was taken up soon after his departure from Bristol, upon some suspicious circumstances, and behaved with great boldness, art and an uncommon government in point of speech upon his several examinations, refusing peremptorily to answer any questions which admitted even of a doubt in the remotest tendency that the answer could by any construction be wrested to his own crimination; nor was he at all disconcerted or embarrassed by the appearance, or the questions proposed to him, by some of the Lords and other principal officers of the admiralty. . . .

The news of his commitment was soon spread; and it having been reported that he had been in America, and had worked there as a painter, Earl Temple desired one Baldwin, a painter who had likewise been in America and had done business there, to attend his examination before Sir John Fielding, to see if he could recollect him. But Baldwin, upon looking at the man and being asked the question, frankly declared that he had never before seen him in his life.

This open declaration, after others, as he said, had borne false witness against him, prejudiced the prisoner in favour of Baldwin, and he expressed a strong desire to cultivate an acquaintance with him, which Baldwin did not decline, being encouraged to visit him as often as opportunity offered, in order, if possible, to bring him to confession. This had the desired effect, and brought the whole scene of iniquity to light.

After a regular attendance on him for 15 days, sometimes once a day and sometimes twice, the prisoner at length began to trust him and to speak openly. He told him he had been in France; that he had there seen Silas Deane; that Silas Deane had given him some money; had encouraged him to set fire to the dock-yards at Portsmouth, Plymouth, Woolwich, etc. as the best means of distressing Great-Britain; that he had promised to reward him according to the service he should do to the American cause; and that, as an earnest of what should follow, he had given him a recommendation to, and bills upon, a merchant in London to the amount of 300 *l.*, which, however, he had found it necessary to burn, to prevent a discovery; that, in consequence of this encouragement, he procured a passport from the French king; which passport he lamented that he had left at Portsmouth, with other things, in a bundle. That from France he came to Canterbury, where he devised the machine which had been found in the hemp house, and had it there constructed; that before he left Canterbury he had a quarrel with a dragoon; and that when he removed from thence he directed his course to Portsmouth, where he prepared the combustibles with which he afterwards set the place on fire; that he disclosed to him (Baldwin) the secret of making the composition, and the manner of his applying it; told him the circumstance of his being locked in the rope-house; of his quarreling with his landlady on account of the interruption she gave him in his operations; of her forcibly turning him out of her house; of his taking another lodging; of the difficulty he had in lighting his matches; of his purchasing other matches; of his flight from Portsmouth in a woman's cart; with many other particulars, all of which were confirmed on his trial by the testimony of the persons, respectively, who were any ways employed by him, or with whom he had any thing to do in the business. The boy who made the cannister, the dragoon with whom he quarrelled at Canterbury, the woman at whose house he lodged at Portsmouth, the man who let him out of the rope-house, the persons who saw him in the dock-yard, the woman who sold him the matches, the woman who took him up in her cart in his flight from Portsmouth, and last of all the bundle in which was his passport from France, with the identical articles in it which he had specifically mentioned to Baldwin; all these were produced against him, and, as the judge observed, in summing up the evidence, that from a chain of circumstances attentively put together, such a body of evidence may be drawn as would be abundantly stronger than where two or three witnesses swear to a positive fact.

It is no wonder, therefore, that the jury, without going out of court, pronounced the prisoner GUILTY; and he being asked in the usual form what he had to say, why sentence of death should not be passed upon him, replied *he had nothing to say.*

—*Annual Register for 1777,* pp. 28-31, 246-247.

III. A REGIUS PROFESSOR REMAINS LOYAL TO HIS KING

John Vardill, rector of Trinity Church and professor at King's College, was—so it would seem—loyal to his King because he was so deeply loyal to the Anglican Church. He had gone to England in 1774 and remained there throughout the war, spying on American sympathizers and, on one occasion, arranging for the theft of the whole of Silas Deane's correspondence with the French Court. He was well paid for these activities, but thought that he ought to have his various American salaries as well.

The Memorial of John Vardill.

November 16, 1783

Sheweth:

That he is a native of New York, and was late Professor of Natural Law and Moral Philosophy in King's College, and Assistant Preacher and Lecturer in the Episcopal Churches and Chapels in that city. He has been long obnoxious to the Rebels from his uniform opposition to their measures. . . .

In consequence of these and such like services and to give the Loyalists at New York a proof of the attention and rewards which would follow their zeal and loyalty, Administration were pleased to appoint him Regius Professor of Divinity at King's College, and he was ordered to acquaint the President of the College with this instance of royal patronage, and that the establishment of the professorship and his appointment should make a clause in the Charter then to be granted. The intelligence was accordingly inserted in the New York *Gazette* of 1775, but the national disappointments which ensued have prevented the grant of that Charter.

In 1775 the Rebels having gained the ascendancy at New York, and being much incensed by letters against him from London, and by their knowledge of his character and conduct in general, he could not return to New York with any safety, and Government was therefore pleased to give him his present allowance of £200 per annum with the most direct and explicit promise that he should be no loser by his loyalty and services, and that the allowance should be other ways provided for, or [he be] able to return to New York with honour and advantage to them and himself. Relying on this, instead of returning into the country or employing himself in the line of his profession, he devoted his time, from 1775 to 1781, to the service of government: and not to mention various periodical pieces and pamphlets which he wrote, or furnished materials for, as well as intelligence supplied from an extensive American correspondence; waiving these and hoping that the necessity will apologize for this free communication:

In 1777 your Memorialist detected a gentleman in London employed by Dr. Franklin, among other purposes, to purchase cutters for packet boats, in which he and a Capt. Nicholson were to sail from France to America. Your Memorialist perswaded him to unbosom himself, and at the desire of the late Lord Suffolk went down with Col. Smith after him to Dover; where, after obtaining a full discovery, the Captain was engaged to proceed to France, to furnish all the intelligence he could collect and to deliver the letters from time to time committed to him. This he faithfully did for two years, whereby many vessels bound to America were taken and much useful information obtained. A gentleman of distinction was also sent over to him to direct and receive information and he proceeded (thro the Captain) very far in a negotiation for peace with Dr. Franklin; but the capture of Burgoyne blasted it.

Your Memorialist having also discovered that a mistress of Dr. Bancroft, Secy. to Dr. Franklin, was about to leave London for Paris, he formed an acquaintance with her, and found, as he suspected, that she had letters to convey from the factions in this country, on which he proposed a plan, and procured a person to accompany her to Brighthelmston who there obtained a coppy of the most material contents of the letters, for the use of Government.

Hearing about the same time that an American vessel was taken and brought into Portsmouth by a mutiny of the sailors, and finding that the Captain was an acquaintance, your Memorialist invited him to his house, and led him to confess that he was bound to Amsterdam, that he had a number of letters (come from the Board of War at Boston) to people in Holland, France and England. These he delivered to your Memorialist who gave them to Mr. Eden, by which means, among other particulars, Government was informed of the articles most wanted by Congress, of the houses and persons with whom they corresponded and of the ships employed for the purpose.

In 1777 your Memorialist also met accidentally in London with an American fellow student, a gentleman of birth, fortune and considerable confidence with Dr. Franklin, who, after much perswasion and promise, confessed that he was here on Congress business, had brought letters from Dr. Franklin and others at Paris, and was about to return with some from hence; he was prevailed on by your Memorialist to disclose them and for a certain reward to continue his residence at Paris and to give all the information he could to Lord Stormont, occasionally visiting this country to convey letters to and from Paris. This gentleman often dined with Dr. Franklin and was intimate with all the American leaders. He among other things informed Government of the fict[it]ious titles and directions under which the Rebel correspondents have received their letters.

These services were not without expence to your Memorialist and in one instance endangered his life and drew on him the hatred of many of his countrymen, especially the trimmers and false Loyalists. As a reward for these and other services, Government was pleased to give him an immediate appointment, by warrant in 1777 (the Charter being unavoidably postponed), to the Regius Professorship of Divinity with a full promise and purpose of granting him at the same time a direct, certain and permanent provision for life, by annexing to it a salary of £200 per annum. But thro' the changes and misfortunes of the times, this engagement has not yet been fulfilled.

In 1778 at the request of one of the commissioners then embarking for America, he drew up an account of the characters of the leading Rebels and Loyalists and supplied him with letters of introduction to Messrs. Jay, Livingston, Duane and Morris, of the Congress; and to Messrs. Benson, Harper, Jones and Custis, who had great influence in the Rebel states.

In 1779 he went down to Yorkshire and opposed the Association in a series of papers called "The Alarm" and signed *Cassandra*, which he caused to be printed and circulated thro' the counties. For these he had the thanks of the nobility and gentlemen of the county, and a letter of high approbation from a distinguished person in Administration.

In 1780 he also published a pamphlet against the Associations, and assisted in writing another entitled "The Declaration and Address, from the Loyalists to the People of America," which was extensively circulated thro' the Colonies; not to mention that for three years he supplied (without reward) a morning paper with paragraphs and essays in support of Government.

Your Memorialist has lost, by his loyalty, by the services above recited and others of the same nature, and by the unfortunate issue of the war, his income as Professor of Natural Law and Moral Philosophy at King's College, £100 stg., exclusively of fees for private pupils, which from his station and established character would have been numerous, and the use of chambers, a cellar, yard and garden; the salary as assistant minister and lecturer in the church at New York £200 stg., not to mention that he was next in order to the Rector, and would have succeeded (as was the established rule) on his death or removal; the salary which Government engaged to annex to his Regius Professorship £200 stg. . . .

Having thus briefly stated his services and losses, your Memorialist therefore prays that his case may be taken into your consideration in order that your Memorialist may be enabled, under your report, to receive such aid and relief as his services and loses may be found to deserve.

—American Loyalist Audit Office Transcripts, Vol. 42, pp. 37-46, N. Y. Public Lib.

IV. DR. BANCROFT GIVES THE HISTORY OF HIS CAREER AS A SPY

Dr. Edward Bancroft was not only a spy but a double spy, and a highly accomplished one at that. A Massachusetts Yankee, he had, like Dr. Church, studied medicine in England; unlike Church he decided to settle down in England and there pursue his scientific and literary interests. There he made the acquaintance of Franklin, and it was on this acquaintance that he later capitalized. When Franklin went to France, Bancroft arranged to act as his spy; later he made the same arrangements with Silas Deane, to whom he had been commended by the Committee of Secret Correspondence and with whom he became on terms of intimacy. Meantime Bancroft had been appointed agent for the British government—at the handsome salary of £1,000 per year—and a most successful agent he was. Just to add to his interests—and rewards—he speculated heavily on the secret information which he obtained through espionage. To top it, Bancroft had himself appointed secretary of the American Peace Commission which negotiated the final settlement with England! After the war Bancroft devoted himself for many years—he lived until 1821—to scientific and literary pursuits. His espionage was not suspected until a century after his death.

Letter from Edward Bancroft, "British-American spy," to the Marquis of Carmarthen, British Foreign Secretary.

Duke Street, London, September 17, 1784

In the month of June 1776, Mr. Silas Deane arrived in France, and pursuant to an instruction given him by the Secret Committee of Congress, wrote to me in London, requesting an interview in Paris, where I accordingly went early in July and was made acquainted with the purposes of his mission and with everything which passed between him and the French Ministry. After staying two or three weeks there, I returned to England, convinced that the Government of France would endeavour to promote an absolute separation of the then United Colonies from Great Britain, unless a speedy termination of the revolt, by reconciliation or conquest, should frustrate this project.

I had then resided near ten years, and expected to reside the rest of my life, in England; and all my views, interests and inclinations were adverse to the independancy of the Colonies, though I had advocated some of their claims from a persuasion of their being founded in justice. I therefore wished that the Government of this country might be informed of the danger of French interference, though I could not resolve to become the informant. But Mr. Paul Wentworth having gained some general knowledge of my journey to France and of my intercourse with Mr. Deane, and having induced me to believe that the British Ministry were likewise informed on this subject, I at length consented to meet the then Secretaries of State, Lords Weymouth and Suffolk, and give them all the information in my power; which I did with the most disinterested views, for I not only did not ask, but expressly rejected, every idea of any reward.

The Declaration of Independancy was not then known in Europe, and I hoped that Government, thus informed of the danger, would prevent it by some accomodation with the Colonies, or by other means. It had been my original intention to stop after this first communication; but having given the first notice of a beginning intercourse between France and the United Colonies, I was urged on to watch and disclose the progress of it; for which purpose I made several journeys to Paris and maintained a regular correspondence with Mr. Deane through the couriers of the French Government. And in this way I became *entangled* and obliged to proceed in a kind of business as repugnant to my feelings as it had been to my original intentions.

Being thus devoted to the service of Government, I consented, like others, to accept such emoluments as my situation indeed required. And in Feb'y 1777, Lord Suffolk, to whom by Lord Weymouth's consent my communications were then made, formally promised me, in the King's name, a pension for life of £200 per annum, to commence from the Christmas preceeding. This was for services *then rendered;* and as an inducement for me to go over and reside in France and continue my services there until the revolt should terminate or an open rupture with that nation ensue, his Lordship farther promised that when either of these events should happen, my permanent pension of £200 per annum should be increased to £500 *at least.*

Confiding in this promise, I went to Paris, and during the first year resided in the same house with Dr. Franklin, Mr. Deane, etc., and regularly informed this Government of every transaction of the American Commissioners; of every step and vessel taken to supply the revolted Colonies with artillery, arms, etc.; of every part of their intercourse with the French and other European courts; of the powers and instructions given by Congress to the Commissioners, and their correspondence with the Secret Committees, etc.; and when the Government of France at length determined openly to support the revolted Colonies, I gave notice of this determination, and of the progress made in forming the two Treaties of Alliance and Commerce, and when these were signed, on the evening of the 6th of Feb'y, I at my own expence, by a special messenger and with unexampled dispatch conveyed this intelligence to this city, and to the King's Ministers, within 42 hours from the instant of their signature, a piece of information for which many individuals here would, for purposes of speculation, have given me more than all that I have received from Government. Afterwards, when that decisive measure of sending Count d'Estaing with the fleet from Toulon to commence hostilities at the Delaware and New York was adopted, I sent intelligence of the direct object and plan of the expedition. . . .

—BANCROFT, "Letter," *American Historical Review*, XXIX, 493-494.

V. THE TREASON OF BENEDICT ARNOLD

Benedict Arnold has the distinction of being the one villain of American history whose villainy is universally recognized and conceded. He is not, to be sure, our only traitor, nor the only American soldier or official who took money from foreign governments; his villainy did not seriously injure the American cause; he had, before his day of infamy, contributed greatly to the American cause. What, then, is the explanation of his singular notoriety? It is in part because the stakes were so high and it was so near a thing—had he succeeded the American cause might well have been lost. It is in part because his betrayal was so cold-blooded and calculated; in part because it involved such cherished institutions as West Point (not yet an Academy) and Washington; in part because he was not punished for his perfidy, but richly rewarded. But beyond all this there is a happier reason that, as Washington himself observed, villainy and treason were rare in the Revolution and have remained rare in our history. Arnold, in short, has no very serious competitors, none, certainly, who played so melodramatically for such high stakes.

The story of Arnold's treason is too familiar for elaboration; its essentials are told in our letters and documents. Arnold is, in any event, already a familiar figure: we have seen him sharing in the capture of Ticonderoga, fighting his way through the Maine wilderness, leading a desperate attack on Quebec, engaged in furious combat on Lake Champlain, emerging out of arrest to win victory at Saratoga. No wonder Washington thought highly of him; he might have said, as Lincoln said of Grant, "he fights." He was given command of Philadelphia; he asked for and obtained command at West Point; there was nothing, it seemed, that he could not have.

Why, then, did he go over to the enemy? His own explanation—that he was outraged by the French alliance and in despair over the American cause—cannot be accepted; it came too late. Aside from this rationalization there were two motives or pressures to which Arnold responded: resentment against real and imagined slights by the Congress and by the authorities of Pennsylvania; reckless extravagance and a desperate need for money. A court-martial had only just reprimanded him for improper conduct bordering on corruption. Yet all American generals who felt slighted and who needed money did not turn traitor; in fact none did but Arnold. Clearly the ultimate explanation is to be found in the mysterious realm of personality. Arnold was a man without principles or convictions, a gambler, hot-blooded, reckless, arrogant and ambitious.

We know that treason is heinous and should be punished, and that such treason as Arnold's should bring odium and remorse. There is no evidence that it did. Arnold was extremely well paid for his betrayal—much too well paid considering how little the British got out of it; he saw to it, too, that his

wife and his sons were amply taken care of by the British government. Leg-
end has him suffering the agonies of the damned and, on his deathbed, calling
for his old uniform, but the legend is baseless. The virtue of many of Arnold's
companions in arms was its own reward, but Arnold's treason was handsomely
rewarded.

The documents which we present here tell their own story, and need
neither explanation nor elaboration, nor do their authors need further intro-
duction: André, Clinton, Wayne, Lafayette—these are old familiars. Joseph
Stansbury, Loyalist poet and halfhearted spy, was sufficiently involved in the
treason to be arrested by the Americans but not sufficiently involved to be
rewarded by the British. When, after the war, he claimed compensation for
his services, his claims were disallowed with the nasty observation that "how-
ever you may like the treason it is impossible to approve the traitor." Andrew
Elliot, another British agent, was uncle to William Eden of the Carlisle Com-
mission. The "Mr. Moore" referred to in a letter is Arnold himself, and "John
Anderson" is of course André, as Elliot explains.

1. Arnold and André Complete Their Business Arrangements

A. draft of a letter from major john andré to joseph stansbury,
british agent in philadelphia

May 10, 1779

Altho I think we understood each other clearly this morning and nothing
was omitted which I could have to say on the subject, it is, or may be, of too
much importance not to take further pains that all may be perfectly well comprehended.

On our part we meet ["ArnGen" deleted] Monk's ouvertures with full
reliance on his honourable intentions and disclose to him with the strongest assurances of our sincerity that no thought is entertained of abandoning the
point we have in view. That on the contrary powerfull means are expected
for accomplishing our end. We likewise assure him that in the very first instance of receiving the tidings or good offices we expect from him, our liberality will be evinced; that in case any partial but important blow should by his
means be struck or aimed, upon the strength of just and pointed information
and cooperation, rewards equal at least to what such service can be estimated
at will be given, but should the abilities and zeal of that able and enterprizing
gentleman amount to the seizing an obnoxious band of men, to the delivering
into our power or enabling us to attack to advantage and by judicious assistance compleately to defeat ["our Enemy" deleted] a numerous body, then
would the generosity of the nation exceed even his own most sanguine hopes,
and in the expectation of this he may rely on that *honour* he now trusts in his
present advances. Should his manifest efforts be foiled and after every zealous
attempt flight be at length necessary, the cause in which he suffers will hold
itself bound to indemnify him for his losses and receive him with the honour
his conduct deserves. His own judgment will point out the services required,
but for his satisfaction we give the following hints. . . .

THE TREASON COUNTRY

West Point

Newburgh
(approx. 8
air miles)

Fishkill
(approx. 7
air miles)

N

Robinson House
(Arnold's headquarters)

North Salem
(approx. 9
air miles)

Fort Montgomery

Arnold flees to Vulture, Sept. 25

Fort Clinton

Peekskill

South Salem
(approx. 11
air miles)

VERPLANCK'S POINT

Pine's Bridge
(where Smith
left André)

KINGS FERRY

Fort Lafayette

HUDSON

Croton River

Stony Point

Smith's House

Haverstraw Bay

Haverstraw

Vulture

Arnold and André confer,
night of Sept. 21-22

Tellers Point

RIVER

Arnold sails for New York on Vulture, Sept. 26

André's route

Scale of Miles

0 1 2 3 4 5

Tappan Sea

André captured, Sept. 23

Tarrytown

NEW YORK

NEW JERSEY

White Plains

Tappan

André hanged,
Oct. 2

Dobbs Ferry

From Traitorous Hero
by Willard M. Wallace

Courtesy of Willard M. Wallace

B. DECODED COPY OF A LETTER FROM GENERAL ARNOLD TO MAJOR ANDRÉ

May 23, 1779

Our friend S[tansbury] acquaints me that the proposals made by him in my name are agreeable to S[ir] H[enry] C[linton], and that S[ir] H[enry] engages to answer my warmest expectations for any services rendered. As I esteem the interest of America and Great Britain inseparable S[ir] H[enry] may depend on my exertions and intelligence. It will be impossible to cooperate unless there is a mutual confidence. S[ir] H[enry] shall be convinced on every occasion that his is not misplaced.

Gen. W[ashington] and the army move to the North River as soon as forage can be obtained. C[ongress] have given up Ch[arle]s Town if attempted. They are in want of arms, ammunition and men to defend it. 3 or 4 thousand Militia is the most that can be mustered to fight on any emergency. Seizing papers is impossible. Their contents can be known from a Member of Congress. 4 months since, the French Minister required Congress to vest their agents with powers to negotiate peace with Britain. The time is elapsed in disputing if they shall demand independency with their original terms or insist on the addition of Newfoundland. No decision, no measure taken to prevent the depreciation of money; no foreign loan obtained. France refused to become surety; no encouragement from Spain. The French fleet has co[nditional] orders to return to this continent. They depend on great part of their provision from hence. A transport originally a 64 and a foreign 28 guns and daily expected here for provision.

I will cooperate when an opportunity offers, and as life and every thing is at stake I will expect some certainty, my property here secure and a revenue equivalent to the risk and service done. I cannot promise success; I will deserve it. Inform me what I may expect. Could I know S[ir] H[enry's] intentions he should never be at a loss for intelligence. I shall expect a particular answer thro our friend S[tansbur]y.

Madam Ar[nold] presents you her particular compliments.

C. DECODED COPY OF A LETTER FROM GENERAL ARNOLD TO MAJOR ANDRÉ,
ADDRESSED TO JOHN ANDERSON

July 12, 1780

... General W[ashington] expects on the arrival of the F[rench] troops to collect 30,000 troops to act in conjunction; if not disappointed, N. York is fixed on as the first object; if his numbers are not sufficient for that object, Can-a- is the second; of which I can inform you in time, as well as of every other design. I have accepted the command at W[est] P[oint] as a post in which I can render the most essential services, and which will be in my disposal. The mass of the people are heartily tired of the war and wish to be on their former footing. They are promised great events from this year's exertion. If disappointed, you have only to persevere and the contest will soon be at an end. The present struggles are like the pangs of a dying man, violent but of a short duration.

As life and fortune are risked by serving His Majesty, it is necessary that the latter shall be secured as well as the emoluments I give up, and a compensation for services agreed on, and a sum advanced for that purpose—which I have mentioned in a letter which accompanies this, which Sir Henry will not, I believe, think unreasonable.

P. S. I have great confidence in the bearer, but beg Sir Henry will threaten him with his resentment in case he abuses the confidence placed in him, which will bring certain ruin on me. The bearer will bring me 20 guineas, and pay the remainder to Captain A—— who is requested to receive the deposit for Mr. Moore.

D. DECODED COPY OF A LETTER FROM GENERAL ARNOLD TO MAJOR ANDRÉ

July 15, 1780

Two days since I received a letter without date or signature, informing me that S[ir] Henry —— was obliged to me for the intelligence communicated, and that he placed a full confidence in the sincerity of my intentions, etc., etc. On the 13th instant I addressed a letter to you expressing my sentiments and expectations, viz, that the following preliminaries be settled previous to cooperating. First, that S[ir] Henry secure to me my property, valued at ten thousand pounds sterling, to be paid to me or my heirs in case of loss; and, as soon as that shall happen, —— hundred pounds per annum to be secured to me for life, in lieu of the pay and emoluments I give up, for my services as they shall deserve. If I point out a plan of cooperation by which S[ir] H[enry] shall possess himself of West Point, the garrison, etc., etc., etc., twenty thousand pounds sterling I think will be a cheap purchase for an object of so much importance. At the same time I request a thousand pounds to be paid my agent. I expect a full and explicit answer. The 20th I set off for West Point. A personal interview with an officer that you can confide in is absolutely necessary to plan matters. In the mean time I shall communicate to our mutual friend S[tansbur]y all the intelligence in my power, until I have the pleasure of your answer.

—VAN DOREN, *Secret History of the Revolution,*
439-440, 441-442, 463-464, 464-465.

2. CLINTON EMBRACES "A PLAN OF SUCH INFINITE EFFECT"

Sir Henry Clinton to Lord George Germain.

New York, October 11, 1780

About eighteen months since, I had some reason to conceive that the American Major General Arnold was desirous of quitting the rebel service and joining the cause of Great Britain. A secret correspondence which I conceived to be from this officer, which expressed a displeasure at the alliance between America and France, engaged me to pursue every means of ascertaining the identity of the person who was thus opening himself to me, and from whom I had on every occasion received, during the whole of our correspondence, most material intelligence....

The correspondence was continued up to July, 1780, when Major General Arnold obtained the command of all the rebel forts in the Highlands, garrisoned with near 4000 men. And it seemed to me, by the correspondence in question, that it was certainly that officer who made the offers under the description I have given. The getting possession of these posts with their garrisons, cannon, stores, vessels, gunboats, etc., etc., appeared to me an object of the highest importance, which must be attended with the best consequences to His Majesty's service—among others that of opening the navigation of the North River and the communication, in a certain degree, with Albany, as appears by the enclosed copy of a letter from G[eneral] Haldimand to me.

The very particular situation of the campaign at this period will mark of what great import such an event would prove. A French fleet and a considerable land force had arrived at Rhode Island. Mr. Washington had very much augmented his army, and was drawing additional strength to it daily by every strained exertion upon the country and the militia of it. There was great reason, from information, to suppose that an attempt was intended upon New York, that Mr. Washington with his army was to have moved upon Kings Bridge and Morrisania while a corps threatened—perhaps attacked—Staten Island, at the same time that the French would have invaded Long Island and have moved upon New York by that inroad. To have pursued these plans large magazines of every nature must have been formed by the rebels, and it is beyond doubt that the principal rebel depot must have been made at West Point and its dependent forts.

From this description, which I have reason to believe just, will be seen of what great consequence would be the encouraging and closing in with a plan of such infinite effect, if carried into execution, toward the success of the campaign, and that it was to be pursued at every risk and at every expense....

Many projects for a meeting were formed, and in consequence several appointments made, in all which General Arnold seemed extremely desirous that some person who had my particular confidence might be sent to him—some man, as he described in writing, of *his own mensuration.* I had thought of a person under this immediate description, who would have cheerfully undertaken it but that his peculiar situation at the time (from which I could not then release him) precluded him from engaging in it [ed. note—"Maj. Gen. William Phillips, who had been captured at Saratoga and was on parole in New York"]. General Arnold finally insisted that the person sent to confer with him should be the Adjutant General, Major André, who indeed had been the person on my part who managed and carried on the secret correspondence.

—Clinton, *The American Rebellion,* pp. 462-465.

3. Arnold's Plans Go Awry

Extract from an intelligence report of Andrew Elliot of New York, October 4-5, 1780.

... General Arnold with whom a secret correspondence has been carrying on for a considerable time without the least suspicion, about three months ago got the command of the forts and troops up the North River. His head quarters was at Colonel Robinsons house on this side the North River, which is near West Point, and about twelve miles above Stoney Point.

A meeting with the French generals was appointed by General Washington at Hartford, which took place near three weeks ago. When Washington set off, General Arnold had the sole command. He in consequence of his correspondence and intentions appointed a meeting with Colonel Robinson and Major André, now Adjutant General; it was to take place first on this side the river a little above Tarry Town, or on the water near the *Vulture* sloop of war that generally lays at Spitendevil, but as there was no trusting the secret with any body, unfortunately the *Vulture* had sent her boats up the river the very night of the intended meeting. Colonel Robinson and André got to the place appointed and waited many hours; they got safe back.

Arnold . . . immediately proposed by letter a meeting at Haverstraw near Mr. William Smiths home. Colonel Robinson and Major André went on board the *Vulture;* she proceeded by way of a cruise up the river; on the night appointed Mr. Joseph Smith, brother to William Smith, came to the *Vulture* with a flag of truce from General Arnold, and a pass for Mr. John Anderson to go up the river to meet him (John Anderson was the name André had corresponded under for some time past). Colonel Robinson unfortunately was not mentioned in the pass, so staid on board the *Vulture*.

John Anderson left the *Vulture* about one o'clock on Thursday morning, met General Arnold on the shore within three miles of Smiths house, the conversation passed, but it was thought necessary that John Anderson should bring down plans of the forts, the grounds that commanded them, the approaches, etc. These done in General Arnolds own hand were lodged at Smiths house; there they went. General Arnold *says* he thought it would be dangerous for John Anderson to return by water, as they had spyboats always plying on the river when our armed vessels were advanced from their usual station (but if Anderson had been taken by them he would have been brought directly to Arnold, and as papers were *necessary* to be sent, they could have easily been sunk). Whether it was a desire of doing too much or *fate*, it was therefore determined that André, still as John Anderson, should pass the river and go by land to Kingsbridge, with a pass from General Arnold, Mr. Smith (who all this time Arnold declares knew nothing of his plan) to conduct him and pass him over the new bridge on Croton River and there leave him, all which was happily effected, and Smith returned.

André, before he set out by land, had at the express desire of General Arnold changed his cloaths, left his uniform at Smiths, was there furnished with other cloaths, and a horse and saddle from Arnold. The day after André parted with Smith, he was met by a party of militia near Tarry Town, stopt, suspected, taken, searched, the papers found under his stockings; he [was] sent up the country, and the papers dispatched to Washington who was expected back from Hartford at Robinsons home Sunday the 24th September.

Fryday André was taken, Washington was delayed. We know not how or when he got Andrés papers, but on Monday the 25th two of Washingtons aid de camps came to Arnold at Robinsons house at breakfast time, and told the general that Washington would dine there. Arnold had then heard nothing of André, but just as the aid de camps set down to breakfast Arnold went out of the room to give some orders. He was met by an officer with a letter from the commander of the militia who had taken André, telling him the event and of his having sent the papers to Washington as they were of so dangerous a nature (this officer must have been Arnolds friend as he must know his hand).

Arnold desired the messenger to stay for an answer, ran out and ordered an horse saddled, and sent a servant down the hill to order his barge's crew to man the boat (they were just returned from buying a suit of new sails). He then went to Mrs. Arnold (formerly Miss Peggy Shippen of Philadelphia). The two aid de camps had just left her to get peaches. He told her he must fly to save his life without having time to explain (she was ignorant of all). He jumped on his horse and, as he turned the stable, met four Light Horse men who told him His Excellency was just coming up the road. Arnold told them to put up their horses, and then galloped down almost a precipice (the short road), threw his saddle with his pistols into the boat, and desired the men to pull away as he was obliged to go to Stoney Point and was anxious to return to meet his Excellency.

Just as he set off an armed boat from West Point came to the landing (supposed to be ordered by Washington to carry off Arnold). General Arnold called to them to go up to the house to get refreshment and tell his Excellency when he arrived that he would be back before dinner. He was not three hundred yards from the wharf when he saw the armed vessel put off after him, but having new sails got soon from them. When he was as far as Stoney Point he told his men particular business from His Excellency to the Captain of the *Vulture* obliged him to go on board. He promised them two gallons of rum and they rowed on, but never were men so surprised when they found their general was to stay, and that they were prisoners.

Col. Robinson was on board the *Vulture* waiting for André, ignorant of his fate. Arnolds arrival unfolded all. Arnold sent back his boatswain with a letter to Washington assuring him his wife and aid de camps and all his family were ignorant of his proceedings and intentions, that he would soon make his reasons public (which will be done this week; the printers here have been *prevented* saying any thing till Arnold wrote his own sentiments). He also declared that André at his desire came in a flag from the *Vulture* with his pass, under the name he had desired him to assume, that at his desire he had at Smiths house changed his uniform for other cloaths, and set off with his pass, his guide and horse and saddle for Kingsbridge, that as he was then Commanding Officer he had a right to do all this, and André every reason in the world to depend on such protection and to act as he did as it was by his orders.

Robinson and Arnold arrived to the amazement of all here on Tuesday the twenty sixth. The General was thrown into the greatest distress from the failure of so well concerted a plan, so near ending the rebellion, as it would have given us all the forts, half the army, and cut off all communication with the Southern and Eastern Provinces as also the French. Andrés situation gives the General great distress. He immediately wrote Washington, enclosed another letter from Arnold to the same purpose as above, and demanded his Adjutant General.

—*Stevens' Facsimiles*, No. 739.

4. BENEDICT ARNOLD IS CONSCIOUS OF HIS OWN RECTITUDE

Arnold to Washington.

Vulture, September 25, 1780

Sir: The heart which is conscious of its own rectitude cannot attempt to palliate a step which the world may censure as wrong; I have ever acted from a principle of love to my country since the commencement of the present unhappy contest between Great-Britain and the Colonies; the same principle of love to my country actuates my present conduct, however it may appear inconsistent to the world, who very seldom judge right of any man's actions.

I have no favour to ask for myself. I have too often experienced the ingratitude of my country to attempt it; but from the known humanity of your Excellency, I am induced to ask your protection for Mrs. Arnold from every insult and injury that the mistaken vengeance of my country may expose her to. It ought to fall only on me; she is as good and as innocent as an angel, and is incapable of doing wrong. I beg she may be permitted to return to her friends in Philadelphia, or to come to me as she may choose; from your Excellency I have no fears on her account, but she may suffer from the mistaken fury of the country.

I have to request that the inclosed letter may be delivered to Mrs. Arnold, and she be permitted to write to me.

I have also to ask that my cloaths and baggage, which are of little consequence, may be sent to me; if required their value shall be paid in money.

—ANDRÉ, *Papers*, pp. 26-27.

5. WAYNE'S VETERANS HURRY TO THE DEFENSE OF WEST POINT

General Anthony Wayne to H. A. Sheel.

Haverstraw near Stoney Point, October 2, 1780

I am confident that the perfidy of Gen. Arnold will astonish the multitude. . . . The dirty, dirty acts which he has been capable of committing beggar all description, and are of such a nature as would cause the *Infernals to blush* were they accused with the invention or execution of them.

The detached and debilitated state of the garrison of West Point insured success to the assailants. The enemy were all in perfect readiness for the enterprize, and the discovery of the treason only prevented an immediate attempt by open force to carry those works which perfidy would have effected the fall of by a slower and less sanguine mode. Our army was out of protecting distance, the troops in the possession of the works of a spiritless miserable *Vulgus* in whose hands the fate of America seemed suspended. In this situation his Excellency (in imitation of Caesar and his Tenth Legion) called for his *veterans;* the summons arrived at one o'clock in the morning, and we took up our line of march at 2 and by sunrise arrived at this place distant from our former camp 16 miles, the whole performed in four hours in a dark night, without a single halt or a man left behind.

When our approach was announced to the General he thought it fabulous, but when convinced of the reality he received us like a god, and retiring to take a short repose exclaimed, "All is safe, and I again am happy." May he long, very long, continue so!

—STILLÉ, *Wayne and the Pennsylvania Line*, pp. 236-237.

6. LaFayette Asks: What Will the French Officers Say?

LaFayette to the Chevalier de la Luzerne.

West Point, 25 September 1780

When I left you yesterday morning, M. le Chevalier, to come here to take breakfast with General Arnold, we were very far from thinking of the event which I am now about to announce to you. You will shudder at the danger we have run. You will be astonished at the miraculous chain of accidents and circumstances by which we have been saved. But you will be still more greatly surprised when you learn by what instrument this conspiracy was being carried on. West Point was sold, and it was sold by Arnold! That same man who had covered himself with glory by rendering valuable services to his country, had lately formed a horrid compact with the enemy. And, but for the chance which brought us here at a certain time, but for the chance which, by a combination of accidents, caused the Adjutant General of the English army to fall into the hands of some countrymen, beyond the line of our own posts, West Point and the North River would probably be in the possession of our enemies.

When we left Fishkill we were preceded by one of my aides-de-camp and General Knox's aide, who found General and Mrs. Arnold at table and who sat down to breakfast with them. During that time two letters were brought to General Arnold giving him information of the capture of the spy. He ordered a horse saddled, went to his wife's room and told her that he was lost, and directed one of his aides-de-camp to say to General Washington that he had gone to West Point and should return in an hour.

Upon our arrival here, we crossed the river and went to look at the works. Judge of our astonishment when, upon our return, we were informed that the captured spy was Major André, the Adjutant General of the English army, and that among the papers found upon him was a copy of a very important council of war, a statement of the strength of the garrison and of the works, and certain observations upon the methods of attack and defence, all in General Arnold's handwriting. The English Adjutant-General wrote also to the General, admitting his rank and his name. A search was made for Arnold, but he had escaped in a boat on board the sloop of war *Vulture*, and, as nobody suspected his flight, no sentry could have thought of arresting him. Colonel Hamilton, . . . who had gone in quest of Arnold, received soon afterward a flag of truce with a letter from Arnold for the General, in which he made no effort to justify his treason, and a letter from the English Commandant, Robertson [Robinson], who in a most insolent manner demanded the surrender of the Adjutant-General, upon the ground that he had been acting under the permission of General Arnold.

The first care of General Washington was to return to West Point the troops whom Arnold had dispersed under various pretexts. We remained here to insure the safety of a fort which the English would value less if they knew it better. The Continental troops are being brought here, and, as the advice of Arnold may induce Clinton to make a sudden movement, orders have been given to the army to hold itself in readiness to march at a moment's notice.

I cannot describe to you, M. le Chevalier, to what degree I am astounded by this piece of news. In the course of a revolution such as ours it is natural that a few traitors should be found, and every conflict which resembles a civil war of the first order ... must necessarily bring to light some great virtues and some great crimes. Our struggles have brought forward some heroes (General Washington for instance) who would otherwise have been merely private citizens. They have also developed some great scoundrels who would otherwise have remained merely obscure rogues. But that an Arnold, a man who, although not so highly esteemed as has been supposed in Europe, had nevertheless given proof of talent, of patriotism, and especially of the most brilliant courage, should at once destroy his very existence and should sell his country to the tyrants whom he had fought against with glory, is an event, M. le Chevalier, which confounds and distresses me, and, if I must confess it, humiliates me to a degree that I cannot express. I would give anything in the world if Arnold had not shared our labors with us, and if this man, whom it still pains me to call a scoundrel, had not shed his blood in the American cause. My knowledge of his personal courage led me to expect that he would decide to blow his brains out (this was my first hope); at all events, it is probable that he will do so when he reaches New York, whither the English sloop proceeded immediately upon receiving Arnold on board. That vessel had come up the river in connection with this despicable conspiracy, and the house of the Chevalier Smith, which is in our possession, was the place of rendezvous. . . .

Unaccustomed as they are to the convulsions of a revolution, what will the officers of the French army say when they see a general abandon and basely sell his country after having defended it so well! You can bear witness, M. le Chevalier, that this is the first atrocity that has been heard of in our army. . . .

—Tower, *La Fayette in the American Revolution*, II, 164-167.

7. "Treason of the Blackest Dye"

Nathanael Greene's Order of the Day, September 26, 1780.

Treason of the blackest dye was yesterday discovered. General Arnold, who commanded at West Point, lost to every sentiment of honor, of public and private obligation, was about to deliver up that important fort into the hands of the enemy. Such an event must have given the American cause a deadly wound if not a fatal stab. Happily the scheme was timely discovered to prevent the final misfortune. The providential train of circumstances which led to it affords the most convincing proofs that the liberties of America are the object of divine protection. At the same time the treason is so regretted the General cannot help congratulating the army on the happy discovery.

Our enemies, despairing of carrying their point by force, are practising every base art to effect, by bribery and corruption, what they cannot accomplish in a manly way. Great honor is due to the American army that this is the first instance of treason of this kind, where many were to be expected from the nature of the dispute, and nothing is so high an ornament to the characters of the American soldiers as their withstanding all the arts and seductions of an insidious enemy.

Arnold the traitor has made his escape to the enemy, but Mr. André, Adjutant-General to the British army, who came out as a spy to negotiate the business, is our prisoner.

His Excellency the Commander-in-Chief has arrived at West Point from Hartford, and is now doubtless taking proper steps to unravel fully so hellish a plot.

—MOORE, *Diary of the American Revolution*, II, 323.

8. WASHINGTON RECALLS THE HISTORY OF ARNOLD'S TREASON

Diary of Tobias Lear, private secretary to Washington.

Oct. 23, 1786. Mr. Drayton and Mr. Izard here all day. After dinner General Washington was, in the course of conversation, led to speak of Arnold's treachery, when he gave the following account of it, which I shall put in his own words, thus:

"I confess I had a good opinion of Arnold before his treachery was brought to light; had that not been the case, I should have had some reason to suspect him sooner, for when he commanded in Philadelphia, the Marquis la Fayette brought accounts from France of the armament which was to be sent to co-operate with us in the ensuing campaign. Soon after this was known, Arnold pretended to have some private business to transact in Connecticut, and on his way there he called at my quarters, and in the course of conversation expressed a desire of quitting Philadelphia and joining the army the ensuing campaign. I told him that it was probable we should have a very active one, and that if his wound and state of health would permit, I should be extremely glad of his services with the army. He replied that he did not think his wound would permit him to take a very active part; but still he persisted in his desire of being with the army.

"He went on to Connecticut, and on his return called again upon me. He renewed his request of being with me next campaign, and I made him the same answer I had done before. He again repeated that he did not think his wound would permit him to do active duty, and intimated a desire to have the command at West Point. I told him I did not think that would suit him, as I should leave none in the garrison but invalids, because it would be entirely covered by the main army. The subject was dropt at that time, and he returned to Philadelphia. It then appeared somewhat strange to me that a man of Arnold's known activity and enterprise should be desirous of taking so inactive a part. I however thought no more of the matter.

"When the French troops arrived at Rhode Island, I had intelligence from New York that General Clinton intended to make an attack upon them before they could get themselves settled and fortified. In consequence of that, I was determined to attack New York, which would be left much exposed by his drawing off the British troops; and accordingly formed my line of battle, and moved down with the whole army to King's Ferry, which we passed. Arnold came to camp at that time, and having no command, and consequently no quarters (all the houses thereabouts being occupied by the army), he was obliged to seek lodgings at some distance from the camp. While the army was crossing at King's Ferry, I was going to see the last detachment over and met Arnold, who asked me if I had thought of anything for him. I told him that he was to have the command of the light troops, which was a post of honor, and which his rank indeed entitled him to. Upon this information his countenance changed, and he appeared to be quite fallen; and instead of thanking me, or expressing any pleasure at the appointment, never opened his mouth. I desired him to go on to my quarters and get something to refresh himself, and I would meet him there soon. He did so.

"Upon his arrival there, he found Col. Tilghman, whom he took a-one side, and mentioning what I had told him, seemed to express great uneasiness at it—as his leg, he said, would not permit him to be long on horse-back; and intimated a great desire to have the command at West Point. When I returned to my quarters, Col. Tilghman informed me of what had passed. I made no reply to it—but his behavior struck me as strange and unaccountable. In the course of that night, however, I received information from New York that General Clinton had altered his plan and was debarking his troops. This information obliged me likewise to alter my disposition and return to my former station, where I could better cover the country. I then determined to comply with Arnold's desire, and accordingly gave him the command of the garrison at West Point.

"Things remained in this situation about a fortnight, when I wrote to the Count Rochambeau desiring to meet him at some intermediate place (as we could neither of us be long enough from our respective commands to visit the other), in order to lay the plan for the siege of Yorktown, and proposed Hartford, where I accordingly went and met the Count. On my return I met the Chevalier Luzerne towards evening, within about 15 miles of West Point (on his way to join the Count at Rhode Island), which I intended to reach that night, but he insisted upon turning back with me to the next public house; where, in politeness to him, I could not but stay all night, determining, however, to get to West Point to breakfast very early. I sent off my baggage, and desired Colonel Hamilton to go forward and inform General Arnold that I would breakfast with him.

"Soon after he arrived at Arnold's quarters, a letter was delivered to Arnold which threw him into the greatest confusion. He told Colonel Hamilton that something required his immediate attendance at the garrison, which was on the opposite side of the river to his quarters; and immediately ordered a horse to take him to the river, and the barge, which he kept to cross, to be ready; and desired Major Franks, his aid, to inform me when I should arrive that he was gone over the river and would return immediately.

"When I got to his quarters and did not find him there, I desired Major Franks to order me some breakfast; and as I intended to visit the fortifications I would see General Arnold there. After I had breakfasted, I went over the river, and inquiring for Arnold, the commanding officer told me that he had not been there. I likewise inquired at the several redoubts, but no one could give me any information where he was. The impropriety of his conduct when he knew I was to be there, struck me very forcibly, and my mind misgave me; but I had not the least idea of the real cause.

"When I returned to Arnold's quarters about two hours after and told Colonel Hamilton that I had not seen him, he gave me a packet which had just arrived for me from Col. Jemmison, which immediately brought the matter to light. I ordered Colonel Hamilton to mount his horse and proceed with the greatest despatch to a post on the river about eight miles below, in order to stop the barge if she had not passed; but it was too late.

"It seems that the letter Arnold received which threw him in such confusion was from Col. Jemmison, informing him that André was taken and that the papers found upon him were in his possession. Col. Jemmison, when André was taken with these papers, could not believe that Arnold was a traitor, but rather thought it was an imposition of the British in order to destroy our confidence in Arnold. He, however, immediately on their being taken, despatched an express after me, ordering him to ride night and day till he came up with me. The express went the lower road, which was the road by which I had gone to Connecticut, expecting that I would return by the same route, and that he would meet me; but before he had proceeded far, he was informed that I was returning by the upper road. He then cut across the country and followed in my track till I arrived at West Point. He arrived about two hours after and brought the above packet.

"When Arnold got down to the barge, he ordered his men, who were very clever fellows and some of the better sort of soldiery, to proceed immediately on board the *Vulture* sloop of war, as a flag, which was lying down the river; saying that they must be very expeditious, as he must return in a short time to meet me, and promised them two gallons of rum if they would exert themselves. They did accordingly; but when they got on board the *Vulture*, instead of their two gallons of rum, he ordered the coxswain to be called down into the cabin and informed him that he and the men must consider themselves as prisoners. The coxswain was very much astonished and told him that they came on board under the sanction of a flag. He answered that that was nothing to the purpose; they were prisoners. But the Captain of the *Vulture* had more generosity than this pitiful scoundrel and told the coxswain that he would take his parole for going on shore to get clothes and whatever else was wanted for himself and his companions. He accordingly came, got his clothes and returned on board. When they got to New York, General Clinton, ashamed of so low and mean an action, set them all at liberty."

—RICHARD RUSH, *Occasional Productions*, pp. 79-85.

VI. THE CAPTURE AND EXECUTION OF ANDRÉ

Dramatically André is, of course, the foil to Arnold. All that Arnold was not, André was—or seemed to be. Young, handsome, brilliant, charming, loyal, high-minded, he was to be the sacrifice to evil, or to fate, that mythology demands. He is, indeed, so nearly legendary a character that had he not existed, legend must inevitably have created him. Born in London, the son of a Genevese merchant, educated in Geneva, he was something of a soldier of fortune.

He was, in addition, a minor poet, a dramatist and actor, and an amateur artist. General Clinton loved him; his fellow officers regarded him with admiration and affection. He won the respect of all the Americans who came to know him, not least young Alexander Hamilton, who wrote a secret letter to Clinton urging the exchange of André for Arnold.

Should Washington have pardoned him, or allowed him a soldier's death? Certainly these would have been the easier decisions, and may have been the right ones. But it is worth quoting the conclusion of R. E. Graves, author of the article on André in the (English) Dictionary of National Biography, *on this vexatious question: "Washington has been unreasonably censured for not having granted him a more honourable death. To have done so would have implied a doubt as to the justice of his conviction. . . . Washington and André deserve equal honour: André for having accepted a terrible risk for his country and borne the consequences of failure with unshrinking courage; and Washington for having performed his duty to his own country at a great sacrifice of his feelings."*

1. Colonel Hamilton Describes the Capture of André

Alexander Hamilton to John Laurens.

October 1780

Arnold employed one Smith to go on board the *Vulture* on the night of the twenty-second, to bring André on shore with a pass for Mr. John Anderson. André came ashore accordingly, and was conducted within a picket of ours to the house of Smith, where Arnold and he remained together in close conference all that night and the day following.

At daylight in the morning, the commanding officer at King's Ferry, without the privity of Arnold, moved a couple of pieces of cannon to a point opposite to where the *Vulture* lay, and obliged her to take a more remote station. This event, or some lurking distrust, made the boatmen refuse to convey the two passengers back, and disconcerted Arnold so much that, by one of those strokes of infatuation which often confound the schemes of men conscious of guilt, he insisted on André's exchanging his uniform for a disguise, and returning in a mode different from that in which he came. André, who had been undesignedly brought within our posts in the first instance, remonstrated warmly against this new and dangerous expedient. But Arnold persisting in declaring it impossible for him to return as he came, he at length reluctantly yielded to his direction and consented to change his dress and take the route he recommended. Smith furnished the disguise, and in the evening passed King's Ferry with him and proceeded to Crompond, where they stopped the remainder of the night, at the instance of a militia officer, to avoid being suspected by him.

The next morning they resumed their journey, Smith accompanying André a little beyond Pine's Bridge, where he left him. He had reached Tarrytown when he was taken up by three militiamen, who rushed out of the woods and seized his horse.

At this critical moment his presence of mind forsook him. Instead of producing his pass, which would have extricated him from our parties and could have done him no harm with his own, he asked the militiamen if they were of the *upper* or *lower* party—descriptive appellations known among the enemy's refugee corps. The militiamen replied they were of the lower party, upon which he told them he was a British officer and pressed them not to detain him, as he was upon urgent business. This confession removed all doubts, and it was in vain he afterwards produced his pass.

He was instantly forced off to a place of greater security, where, after a careful search, there were found concealed in the feet of his stockings several papers of importance, delivered to him by Arnold! Among these were a plan of the fortifications of West Point; a memorial from the engineer on the attack and defence of the place; returns of the garrison, cannon and stores; copy of the minutes of a council of war held by General Washington a few weeks before.

The prisoner at first was inadvertently ordered to Arnold, but on recollection, while still on the way, he was countermanded and sent to Old Salem. The papers were enclosed in a letter to General Washington, which, having taken a route different from that by which he returned, made a circuit that afforded leisure for another letter, through an ill-judged delicacy, written to Arnold with information of Anderson's capture, to get to him an hour before General Washington arrived at his quarters; time enough to elude the fate that awaited him. He went down the river on his barge to the *Vulture* with such precipitate confusion that he did not take with him a single paper useful to the enemy. On the first notice of the affair he was pursued but much too late to be overtaken.

—LODGE, ed., *Works of Hamilton*, IX, 210 ff.

2. "BETRAYED INTO THE VILE CONDITION OF AN ENEMY IN DISGUISE"

John André to George Washington.

Salem, September 24, 1780

I beg your Excellency will be persuaded that no alteration in the temper of my mind, or apprehension for my safety, induces me to take the step of addressing you, but that it is to secure myself from an imputation of having assumed a mean character for treacherous purposes or self interest, a conduct incompatible with the principles that actuated me, as well as with my condition in life.

It is to vindicate my fame that I speak and not to solicit security.

The person in your possession is Major John André, Adjutant General to the British army.

The influence of one commander in the army of his adversary is an advantage taken in war. A correspondence for this purpose I held, as confidential (in the present instance) with his Excellency Sir Henry Clinton.

To favor it, I agreed to meet, upon ground not within posts of either army, a person who was to give me intelligence; I came up in the *Vulture* man of war for this effect, and was fetched by a boat from the shore to the beach. Being there I was told that the approach of day would prevent my return, and that I must be concealed until the next night. I was in my regimentals and had fairly risked my person.

Against my stipulation, my intention and without my knowledge before hand, I was conducted within one of your posts. Your Excellency may conceive my sensation on this occasion and will imagine how much more I must have been affected by a refusal to reconduct me back the next night as I had been brought. Thus become a prisoner I had to concert my escape. *I quitted my uniform* and was passed another way in the night without the American posts to neutral ground, and informed I was beyond all armed parties and left to press for New-York. I was taken at Tarry Town by some volunteers.

Thus as I have had the honor to relate was I betrayed (being Adjutant General of the British army) into the vile condition of an enemy in disguise within your posts.

Having avowed myself a British officer I have nothing to reveal but what relates to myself, which is true on the honor of an officer and a gentleman.

The request I have to make your Excellency, and I am conscious I address myself well, is, that in any rigor policy may dictate, a decency of conduct towards me may mark that though unfortunate I am branded with nothing dishonourable, as no motive could be mine but the service of my king and as I was involuntarily an imposter. . . .

—ANDRÉ, *Papers*, pp. 20-22.

3. "YOUR EXCELLENCY WILL DIRECT THIS OFFICER TO RETURN!"

Sir Henry Clinton to George Washington.

New York, September 26, 1780

Being informed that the King's Adjutant General in America has been stopt, under Major General Arnold's passports, and is detained a prisoner in your Excellency's army, I have the honour to inform you, Sir, that I permitted Major André to go to Major General Arnold at the particular request of that general officer. You will perceive, Sir, by the inclosed paper, that a flag of truce was sent to receive Major André, and passports granted for his return. I therefore can have no doubt but your Excellency will immediately direct that this officer has permission to return to my orders at New-York.

—ANDRÉ, *Papers*, pp. 27-28.

4. "MAJOR ANDRÉ . . . OUGHT TO BE CONSIDERED AS A SPY"

George Washington to Sir Henry Clinton.

Head Quarters, September 30, 1780

In answer to Your Excellency's Letter of the 26th Instant, which I had the honor to receive, I am to inform You, that Major André was taken under such circumstances as would have justified the most summary proceedings against him. I determined however to refer his case to the examination and decision of a Board of General Officers, who have reported, on his free and voluntary confession and Letters; "That he came on Shore from the *Vulture* Sloop of war in the night of the Twenty first of September Instant on an interview with General Arnold in a private and secret manner. Secondly that he changed his dress within our lines, and under a feigned name and in a disguised habit passed our Works at Stoney and Verplanks points the Evening of the Twenty second of September Instant, at Tarry Town, in a disguised habit, being then on his way to New York, and when taken he had in his possession Several papers which contained intelligence for the Enemy. The Board having maturely considered these Facts do also report to His Excellency General Washington, that Major André Adjutant General to the British Army ought to be considered as a Spy from the Enemy, and that agreable to the Law and usage of Nations it is their opinion he ought to suffer death."

From these proceedings it is evident Major André was employed in the execution of measures very foreign to the Objects of Flags of truce and such as they were never meant to authorise or countenance in the most distant degree; and this Gentleman confessed with the greatest candor in the course of his examination, "that it was impossible for him to suppose he came on shore under the sanction of a Flag."

—FITZPATRICK, ed., *Writings of Washington*, XX, 103-104.

5. "I Shall Think Myself Bound to Retaliate"

Arnold to George Washington.

New York, October 1, 1780

If after this just and candid representation of Major André's case the board of general officers adhere to their former opinion, I shall suppose it dictated by passion and resentment. And if that gentleman should suffer the severity of their sentence, I shall think myself bound by every tie of duty and honour to retaliate on such unhappy persons of your army as may fall within my power—that the respect due to flags and to the law of nations may be better understood and observed.

I have further to observe that forty of the principal inhabitants of South Carolina have justly forfeited their lives, which have hitherto been spared by the clemency of His Excellency Sir Henry Clinton. Sir Henry could not in justice extend his mercy to them any longer, if Major André suffers; which in all probability will open a scene of blood at which humanity will revolt.

Suffer me to entreat your Excellency, for your own and the honour of humanity, and the love you have of justice, that you suffer not an unjust sentence to touch the life of Major André. But if this warning should be disregarded, and he should suffer, I call heaven and earth to witness that your Excellency will be justly answerable for the torrent of blood that may be spilt in consequence.

—VAN DOREN, *Secret History of the Revolution*, pp. 369-370.

6. "Adopt My Death to the Feelings of a Man of Honour"

John André to George Washington.

Tappan, October 1, 1780

Buoyed above the terror of death by the consciousness of a life devoted to honourable pursuits, and stained with no action that can give me remorse, I trust that the request I make to your Excellency at this serious period, and which is to soften my last moments, will not be rejected.

Sympathy towards a soldier will surely induce your Excellency and a military tribunal to adopt the mode of my death to the feelings of a man of honour.

Let me hope, Sir, that if aught in my character impresses you with esteem towards me, if aught in my misfortunes marks me as the victim of policy and not of resentment, I shall experience the operation of these feelings in your breast, by being informed that I am not to die on a gibbet.

—ANDRÉ, *Papers*, p. 40.

7. REMORSELESS WASHINGTON!

A Monody on the Death of André
by Ann Seward
Oh Washington! I thought thee great and good,
Nor knew thy Nero thirst for guiltless blood:
Severe to use the power that fortune gave,
Thou cool determined murderer of the brave.
Remorseless Washington! the day shall come
Of deep repentance for this barbarous doom;
When injured André's mem'ry shall inspire
A kindling army with resistless fire,
Each falchion sharpen that the Britons wield,
And lead their fiercest lion to the field;
Then, when each hope of thine shall end in night,
When dubious dread and unavailing flight
Impel your haste, thy guilt-upbraided soul
Shall wish, untouched, the precious life you stole;
And when thy heart, appalled and vanquished pride,
Shall vainly ask the mercy you denied,
With horror shalt thou meet the fate thou gave,
Nor pity gild the darkness of thy grave.

—NILES, ed., *Principles and Acts*, p. 497.

8. NEVER WAS DEATH SUFFERED WITH MORE JUSTICE OR LESS DESERT

Alexander Hamilton to John Laurens.

October 1780

André was, without loss of time, conducted to the headquarters of the army, where he was immediately brought before a board of general officers to prevent all possibility of misrepresentation, or cavil on the part of the enemy. The board reported that he ought to be considered as a spy, and, according to the laws of nations, to suffer death, which was executed two days after.

Never, perhaps, did a man suffer death with more justice, or deserve it less. The first step he took after his capture was to write a letter to General Washington, conceived in terms of dignity without insolence, and apology without meanness. The scope of it was to vindicate himself from the imputation of having assumed a mean character for treacherous or interested purposes; asserting that he had been involuntarily an imposter; that contrary to his intention, which was to meet a person for intelligence on neutral ground, he had been betrayed within our posts, and forced into the vile condition of an enemy in disguise; soliciting only that, to whatever rigor policy might devote him, a decency of treatment might be observed, due to a person who, though unfortunate, had been guilty of nothing dishonorable. His request was granted in its full extent; for, in the whole progress of the affair, he was treated with the most scrupulous delicacy. When brought before the board of officers he met with every mark of indulgence, and was required to answer no interrogatory which could even embarrass his feelings. On his part, while he carefully concealed every thing that might involve others, he frankly confessed all the facts relating to himself; and, upon his confession, without the trouble of examining a witness, the board made their report. The members of it were not more impressed with the candor and firmness, mixed with a becoming sensibility, which he displayed, than he was penetrated with their liberality and politeness. He acknowledged the generosity of the behavior towards him in every respect, but particularly in this, in the strongest terms of manly gratitude. In a conversation with a gentleman who visited him after his trial, he said he flattered himself he had never been illiberal; but if there were any remains of prejudice in his mind, his present experience must obliterate them.

In one of the visits I made to him (and I saw him several times during his confinement), he begged me to be the bearer of a request to the General, for permission to send an open letter to Sir Henry Clinton. "I foresee my fate," said he, "and though I pretend not to play the hero, or to be indifferent about life, yet I am reconciled to whatever may happen, conscious that misfortune, not guilt, has brought it upon me. There is only one thing that disturbs my tranquillity. Sir Henry Clinton has been too good to me; he has been lavish of his kindness. I am bound to him by too many obligations, and love him too well, to bear the thought that he should reproach himself, or that others should reproach him, on the supposition of my having conceived myself obliged by his instructions to run the risk I did. I would not for the world leave a sting in his mind that should imbitter his future days." He could scarce finish the sentence, bursting into tears in spite of his efforts to suppress them, and with difficulty collected himself enough afterwards to add, "I wish to be permitted to assure him I did not act under this impression, but submitted to a necessity imposed upon me, as contrary to my own inclination as by his orders." His request was readily complied with, and he wrote the letter annexed, with which I dare say you will be as much pleased as I am, both for the diction and sentiment.

When his sentence was announced to him he remarked that since it was his lot to die, there was still a choice in the mode, which would make a material difference in his feelings, and he would be happy, if possible, to be indulged with a professional death. He made a second application, by letter, in concise but persuasive terms. It was thought this indulgence, being incompatible with the customs of war, could not be granted, and it was therefore determined, in both cases, to evade an answer, to spare him the sensations which a certain knowledge of the intended mode would inflict.

In going to the place of execution, he bowed familiarly as he went along to all those with whom he had been acquainted in his confinement. A smile of complacency expressed the serene fortitude of his mind. Arrived at the fatal spot, he asked, with some emotion, "Must I then die in this manner?" He was told that it had been unavoidable. "I am reconciled to my fate," said he, "but not to the mode." Soon, however, recollecting himself, he added: "It will be but a momentary pang," and, springing upon the cart, performed the last offices to himself with a composure that excited the admiration and melted the hearts of the beholders. Upon being told that the final moment was at hand, and asked if he had anything to say, he answered: "Nothing but to request you will witness to the world that I die like a brave man." Among the extraordinary circumstances that attended him, in the midst of his enemies, he died universally esteemed and universally regretted.

There was something singularly interesting in the character and fortunes of André. To an excellent understanding, well improved by education and travel, he united a peculiar elegance of mind and manners, and the advantage of a pleasing person. 'Tis said he possessed a pretty taste for the fine arts, and had himself attained some proficiency in poetry, music and painting. His knowledge appeared without ostentation, and embellished by a diffidence that rarely accompanies so many talents and accomplishments: which left you to suppose more than appeared. His sentiments were elevated, and inspired esteem: they had a softness that conciliated affection. His elocution was handsome; his address easy, polite and insinuating. By his merit he had acquired the unlimited confidence of his general, and was making a rapid progress in military rank and reputation. But in the height of his career, flushed with new hopes from the execution of a project the most beneficial to his party that could be devised, he was at once precipitated from the summit of prosperity and saw all the expectations of his ambition blasted, and himself ruined.

—Lodge, ed., *Works of Hamilton*, IX, 216 ff.

9. "Melancholy and Gloom Affected All Ranks"

Journal of Dr. James Thacher.

October 2d, 1780.—Major André is no more among the living. I have just witnessed his exit. It was a tragical scene of the deepest interest. During his confinement and trial, he exhibited those proud and elevated sensibilities which designate greatness and dignity of mind. Not a murmur or a sigh ever escaped him, and the civilities and attentions bestowed on him were politely acknowledged. Having left a mother and two sisters in England, he was heard to mention them in terms of the tenderest affection, and in his letter to Sir Henry Clinton he recommended them to his particular attention.

The principal guard officer, who was constantly in the room with the prisoner, relates that when the hour of his execution was announced to him in the morning, he received it without emotion, and while all present were affected with silent gloom, he retained a firm countenance, with calmness and composure of mind. Observing his servant enter the room in tears, he exclaimed, "Leave me till you can show yourself more manly!" His breakfast being sent to him from the table of General Washington, which had been done every day of his confinement, he partook of it as usual, and having shaved and dressed himself, he placed his hat on the table and cheerfully said to the guard officers, "I am ready at any moment, gentlemen, to wait on you."

The fatal hour having arrived, a large detachment of troops was paraded, and an immense concourse of people assembled; almost all our general and field officers, excepting His Excellency and his staff, were present on horseback; melancholy and gloom pervaded all ranks, and the scene was affectingly awful. I was so near during the solemn march to the fateful spot as to observe every movement and participate in every emotion which the melancholy scene was calculated to produce. Major André walked from the stone house, in which he had been confined, between two of our subaltern officers, arm in arm. The eyes of the immense multitude were fixed on him, who, rising superior to the fears of death, appeared as if conscious of the dignified deportment which he displayed. He betrayed no want of fortitude, but retained a complacent smile on his countenance, and politely bowed to several gentlemen whom he knew, which was respectfully returned.

It was his earnest desire to be shot, as being the mode of death most conformable to the feelings of a military man, and he had indulged the hope that his request would be granted. At the moment, therefore, when suddenly he came in view of the gallows, he involuntarily started backward and made a pause.

"Why this emotion, sir?" said an officer by his side.

Instantly recovering his composure, he said, "I am reconciled to my death, but I detest the mode."

While waiting and standing near the gallows, I observed some degree of trepidation: placing his foot on a stone and rolling it over, and choking in his throat as if attempting to swallow. So soon, however, as he perceived that things were in readiness, he stepped quickly into the wagon, and at this moment he appeared to shrink, but instantly elevating his head with firmness, he said, "It will be but a momentary pang," and taking from his pocket two white handkerchiefs, the provost-marshal, with one, loosely pinioned his arms, and with the other, the victim, after taking off his hat and stock, bandaged his own eyes with perfect firmness, which melted the hearts and moistened the cheeks, not only of his servant, but of the throng of spectators.

The rope being appended to the gallows, he slipped the noose over his head and adjusted it to his neck, without the assistance of the awkward executioner. Colonel Scammel now informed him that he had an opportunity to speak, if he desired it. He raised the handkerchief from his eyes, and said, "I pray you to bear me witness that I meet my fate like a brave man." The wagon being now removed from under him, he was suspended, and instantly expired; it proved indeed "but a momentary pang." He was dressed in his royal regiments and boots, and his remains, in the same dress, were placed in an ordinary coffin and interred at the foot of the gallows; and the spot was consecrated by the tears of thousands.

Thus died, in the bloom of life, the accomplished Major André, the pride of the Royal Army, and the valued friend of Sir Henry Clinton. He was about twenty-nine years of age, in his person well proportioned, tall, genteel and graceful. His mien respectable and dignified. His countenance mild, expressive and prepossessing, indicative of an intelligent and amiable mind. His talents are said to have been of a superior cast, and, being cultivated in early life, he had made very considerable proficiency in literary attainments. . . . Military glory was the mainspring of his actions and the sole object of his pursuits, and he was advancing rapidly in the gratification of his ambitious views till by a misguided zeal he became a devoted victim.

—THACHER, *Military Journal*, pp. 226-231.

VII. MUTINY

The year of Arnold's treason was also one of mutinies and dissension. There had been a minor mutiny in Washington's army at Morristown in May 1780, when two Connecticut regiments had defied their officers and demanded their back pay; they were disarmed by Pennsylvania troops. Next January it was the turn of the Pennsylvania Line. These soldiers had genuine grievances. They had gone for months without pay; they were in rags; they were reduced to dry bread and cold water. Worst of all many of them who had enlisted for "three years or the duration of the war" found, to their indignation, that this meant the longer rather than the shorter of the two periods. The particular occasion of their mutiny, the night of January 1, 1781, was the appearance in camp of recruiting agents offering $25 in specie for new recruits! Some 2,400 men were involved in this mutiny—a formidable force. On January 3 they made camp at Princeton and chose spokesmen to present their case to Congress. Pennsylvania's President Reed ended the mutiny by acceding to most of their terms. Meantime word of the outbreak had reached Clinton, who promptly sent two spies to seduce the Americans from their allegiance; these were seized by the men themselves and promptly hanged.

A few weeks later three New Jersey regiments mutinied; this time Washington acted promptly and harshly. The mutiny was put down by arms, and the ringleaders executed. Again in June—after the war was over—some three hundred troops demonstrated in front of Independence Hall in Philadelphia; Congress promptly escaped to Princeton.

The most astonishing aspect of this whole matter is that there were, over the years, so few mutinies, and that so many soldiers—nonprofessionals—endured so much for so long.

1. THE SUFFERINGS AND GRIEVANCES OF THE PENNSYLVANIA LINE

Anthony Wayne to President Joseph Reed.

Mount Kemble, N. J., December 16, 1780

. . . I don't mean to cast any reflection upon the conduct of your Excellency or the Honourable Council; on the contrary, I am but too well convinced that nothing on your part was omitted to render the situation of the officers and soldiers as comfortable as the exhausted state of the treasury and other circumstances would admit of; and although they were not equal to your wishes or their merits and expectations, yet they have been such as afforded great relief to both officers and soldiers. But those comforts being for some time totally consumed, we are reduced to dry bread and beef for our food, and to cold water for our drink. Neither officers or soldiers have received a single drop of spirituous liquors from the public magazines since the 10th of October last, except one gill per man some time in November; this, together with the old worn out coats and tattered linen overalls, and what was once a poor substitute for a blanket (now divided among three soldiers), is but very wretched living and shelter against the winter's piercing cold, drifting snows and chilling sleets.

Our soldiery are not devoid of reasoning faculties, nor are they callous to the first feelings of nature; they have now served their country with fidelity for near five years, poorly clothed, badly fed and worse paid; of the last article, trifling as it is, they have not seen a paper dollar in the way of pay for near *twelve months*.

In this situation the enemy began to work upon their passions and have found means to circulate some proclamations among them. Capt. Zeigler will be able to inform your Excellency of matters which I don't choose to commit to paper. However, I don't despair of being able to restore harmony and content, and to defeat every machination of the public foe and the more dangerous lurking incendiary, if aided by your Excellency in a timely supply of stores and clothing. But what will insure success is the immediate passing of the act for making good the depreciation. Give your soldiery a landed property, make their interest and the interest of America reciprocal, and I will answer for their bleeding to *death*, drop by drop, to establish the independency of this country. On the contrary, should we neglect rewarding their past services, and not do justice to their more than Roman virtue, have we nothing to apprehend from their defection? Believe me, my dear sir, that if something is not immediately done to give them a local attachment to this country and to quiet their minds, we have not yet seen the worst side of the picture.

The officers in general, as well as myself, find it necessary to stand for hours every day, exposed to wind and weather, among the poor naked fellows, while they are working at their huts and redoubts, often assisting with our own hands, in order to produce a conviction to their minds that we share and more than share every vicissitude in common with them, sometimes asking to participate of their bread or water. The good effect this conduct has is very conspicuous and prevents them murmuring in public; but the delicate mind and eye of humanity are hurt, very much hurt, at their visible distress and private complainings. Be assured, sir, that we depend much upon your interest (and we flatter ourselves that that dependence is well founded) to remove those difficulties and alleviate the distresses they now experience.

An immediate supply of hard cash to pay the bounty to the recruits we have enlisted for the war out of the seven months' men is absolutely necessary; I think the number is already about one hundred. We could have retained every man we wished, had we been furnished with specie in time. I fear it is now too late; the mode of recruiting will probably be by classing the inhabitants, and obliging those classes to furnish a given number of men for the war by a certain day, which I wish the earliest possible, to the end that we may have it in our power to reduce them to some degree of discipline before the opening of the campaign, as we shall probably take the field in conjunction with the first corps of France.

—REED, *Life and Correspondence of Reed*, II, 315-317.

2. MUTINY IN JANUARY

Lieutenant Enos Reeves of the Pennsylvania Line.

Mount Kemble, N. J., January 2, 1781

Yesterday being the last time we (the officers of the regiment) expected to be together, as the arrangement was to take place this day, we had an elegant regimental dinner and entertainment, at which all the field and other officers were present, with a few from the German regiment, who had arrived with the men of their regiment that belong to the Penna. Line. We spent the day very pleasantly and the evening till about ten o'clock as cheerfully as we could wish, when we were disturbed by the huzzas of the soldiers upon the Right Division, answered by those on the Left.

I went on the Parade and found numbers in small groups whispering and busily running up and down the line. In a short time a gun was fired upon the right and answered by one on the right of the Second Brigade, and a skyrocket thrown from the center of the first, which was accompanied by a general huzza throughout the line, and the soldiers running out with their arms, accoutrements and knapsacks.

I immediately found it was a mutiny, and that the guns and skyrocket were the signals. The officers in general exerted themselves to keep the men quiet, and keep them from turning out. We each applied himself to his own company, endeavored to keep them in their huts and lay by their arms, which they would do while we were present, but the moment we left one hut to go to another, they would be out again. Their excuse was they thought it was an alarm and the enemy coming on.

Next they began to move in crowds to the Parade, going up to the right, which was the place appointed for their rendezvous. Lieut. White of our regiment, in endeavoring to stop one of those crowds, was shot through the thigh, and Capt. Samuel Tolbert in opposing another party was shot through the body, of which he is very ill. They continued huzzaing and firing in a riotous manner, so that it soon became dangerous for an officer to oppose them by force. We then left them to go their own way.

Hearing a confused noise to the right, between the line of huts and Mrs. Wicks, curiosity led me that way, and it being dark in the orchard I mixed among the crowd and found they had broken open the magazine and were preparing to take off the cannon.

In taking possession of the cannon they forced the sentinel from his post and placed one of their own men. One of the mutineers coming officiously up to force him away (thinking him to be one of our sentinels) received a ball through the head and died instantly.

A dispute arose among the mutineers about firing the alarms with the cannon, and continued for a considerable time—one party aledging that it would arouse the timid soldiery, the other objected because it would alarm the inhabitants. For a while I expected the dispute would be decided by the bayonet, but the gunner in the meantime slipped up to the piece and put a match to it, which ended the affair. Every discharge of the cannon was accompanied by a confused huzza and a general discharge of musketry.

About this time Gen. Wayne and several field officers (mounted) arrived. Gen. Wayne and Col. Richard Butler spoke to them for a considerable time, but it had no effect. Their answer was, they had been wronged and were determined to see themselves righted. He replied that he would right them as far as in his power. They rejoined, it was out of his power; their business was not with the officers, but with Congress and the Governor and Council of the State; 'twas they had wronged and they must right. With that, several platoons fired over the General's head. The General called out, "If you mean to kill me, shoot me at once—here's my breast!" opening his coat. They replied that it was not their intention to hurt or disturb an officer of the Line (two or three individuals excepted); that they had nothing against their officers, and they would oppose any person that would attempt anything of the kind.

A part of the Fourth Regiment was paraded and led on by Capt. Campbell, to recapture the cannon; they were ordered to charge and rush on. They charged but would not advance, then dispersed and left the officer alone. Soon after a soldier from the mob made a charge upon Lieut. Col. William Butler, who was obliged to retreat between the huts to save his life. He went around one hut and the soldier around another to head him, met Capt. Bettin who was coming down the alley, who seeing a man coming towards him on a charge, charged his espontoon to oppose him, when the fellow fired his piece and shot the captain through the body and he died two hours later.

About twelve o'clock they sent parties to relieve or seize the old camp guard, and posted sentinels all round the camp. At one o'clock they moved off towards the left of the line with the cannon and when they reached the centre they fired a shot. As they came down the line, they turned the soldiers out of every hut, and those who would not go with them were obliged to hide till they were gone. They continued huzzaing and a disorderly firing till they went off, about two o'clock, with drums and fifes playing, under command of the sergeants, in regular platoons, with a front and rear guard.

Gen. Wayne met them as they were marching off and endeavored to persuade them back, but to no purpose; he then inquired which way they were going, and they replied either to Trenton or Philadelphia. He begged them not to attempt to go to the enemy. They declared it was not their intention, and that they would hang any man who would attempt it, and for that, if the enemy should come out in consequence of this revolt, they would turn back and fight them. "If that is your sentiments," said the General, "I'll not leave you, and if you wont allow me to march in your front, I'll follow in your rear."

This day Col. Stewart and Richard Butler joined Gen. Wayne in hopes they could turn them when they grew cooler, being much agitated with liquor when they went off; it being New Years Day, they had drawn half a pint per man. The men have continued going off in small parties all day. About one o'clock one hundred head of cattle came in from the eastward, which they drove off to their main body, which lay in a wood near Vealtown, leaving a few behind for the use of the officers.

When we came to draw provisions and State stores this day, we found that near half of the men of our regiment had remained.

The men went off very civily last night to what might have been expected from such a mob. They did not attempt to plunder our officers' huts or insult them in the least, except those who were obstinate in opposing them. They did not attempt to take with them any part of the State stores, which appears to me a little extraordinary, for men when they get but little want more.

The militia are called out—they are to assemble at Chatham—in order to oppose the enemy if they come out, or the mutineers if they attempt going to them.

—REEVES, "Extracts," *Penn. Mag. of Hist. and Biog.*, XXI, 72-75.

3. THE BRITISH PLAN TO PROFIT BY THE MUTINY

Diary of Captain Frederick Mackenzie of the Royal Welsh Fusiliers.

January 4, 1781. Thick weather, and heavy rain from 5 this evening.

Undoubted intelligence received that the whole Pennsylvania Line have mutinied. They began on Monday the 1st instant by seizing all the artillery, military stores and provisions, and marched that evening from their huts at Morristown to an advantageous piece of ground about 7 miles from thence, where they took post. In moving off, they passed General Waynes quarters, where they huzzaed for officers and soldiers without pay, clothing or provisions; then for Thirteen Kings without breeches. Wayne desired to know what they would have, and what they intended; they said they were determined to go to the Congress at Philadelphia, to demand their arrears of pay, clothing and provisions, and their dismission.

On Tuesday they marched on to Middlebrook, and yesterday to Brunswick. They amount to about 1200 men. Two companies of riflemen from Bottle Hill marched off to join them, without the militia daring to molest them. All the boats on the Delaware have been secured so as to prevent the mutineers from making use of them to pass the river to Philadelphia. The country is in great confusion, and the persons in authority under Congress dread the effects of this revolt, as the people in general are tired of the oppression and difficulties they suffer and earnestly wish for a return of peace and the old Government.

In consequence of this information the Commander in Chief has ordered the British Grenadiers and Light Infantry, three battalions of Hessian Grenadiers, and the Jagers, to march at day break tomorrow towards Denyces Ferry, from whence if there is occasion he intends to go with them to South Amboy, in Jersey, to favor the revolt and keep the militia back.

A person has been sent to them to assure the mutineers that in this struggle for their just rights and liberties, they will be assisted by a body of British troops; that if they will lay down their arms they shall be pardoned all past offences, be paid all the pay due them by Congress, and not be required to serve unless they chuse it. They are desired to send Commissioners to Amboy to treat for them, to whom safe conduct shall be given, and to whom the sincerity of these proposals shall be explained. They are advised to move and take post behind South River, in which situation nothing can approach them, and where they can be immediately supported from hence. They are desired to consider the total inability of Congress to satisfy their just demands, even if they were inclined to grant them, and they are warned of the severity with which numbers of them will be punished, if they suffer themselves to be satisfied with the promises of Congress, and return to their service.

This letter is addressed, "To the persons chosen by the Pennsylvania Line to head them in their struggle for their rights."

'Tis said they have chosen a British serjeant (a deserter) for their leader, and have given him the rank of Major General.

—MACKENZIE, *Diary*, II, 442-444.

4."THIS SURPRIZING AFFAIR HAS BEEN BROUGHT TO A HAPPY ISSUE"

General John Sullivan to the French minister.

Trenton, N. J., January 13, 1781

The soldiers in general shew no disposition to injure their officers though some who were intoxicated with liquors discharged their muskets, killed one officer and wounded three or four. Part of the division moved a few miles that evening [January 1], and the remainder followed them the next morning, when the whole assumed a military order under the command of their sergeants, and marched without offering the least insult to the inhabitants, except in one instance for which the culprit was immediately apprehended and delivered over to the civil power. The inhabitants say that on their march they never suffered the soldiers to enter their houses even for water, nor was any article taken from them during their march.

Upon their taking post at Princeton it began to be suspected that their intentions were to join the enemy, but they persevered in declaring their detestation of the British and their attachment to the cause of their country. They said they were only seeking a redress of grievances, which when obtained they would cheerfully return to their duty. And if the enemy appeared in the interim they would fight them with desperation.

This however was not fully credited untill they seized and brought to Gen. Waine, who with Col. Butler and Stewart remained among them without command, two British emissaries from Sir Henry Clinton with a written invitation promising them great rewards if they would march to South River about 20 miles distant from Princeton where he would cover them with a body of British troops. The spies were delivered over to Gen. Waine and, after Governor Reeds arrival, to him, but afterwards by their request returned to them. The board of sergeants, who had assumed the command, issued orders next morning, stating the facts and declaring that the Pennsylvania Line dispised a treachery and meanness like that of Benedict Arnold, that their views were honorable and their attachment to the cause of their country unalterable, and they were only seeking redress of grievances from men of honor. When Governor Reed came to Princeton they received him with every mark of respect and esteem. They mentioned to him the grounds of their complaints which were principally the two first mentioned.

He made them some proposals and communications from the Committee of Congress which were readily accepted. They were then requested to march to Trenton, which they agreed to, and delivered to the Committee of Congress the two spies sent from Sir Henry Clinton, who were tried by a board of officers, condemned and executed on the 11th instant. The Committee of Congress have appointed Commissioners to determine respecting their inlistments, to discharge such as are entitled thereto, and to give them the necessary certificates. This seems to be perfectly satisfactory to them; many of those discharged are now offering to reinlist upon having a furlough for a short time.

Thus, Sir, has this surprizing affair been brought to a happy issue. Perhaps history does not furnish an instance of so large a body of troops revolting from the command of their officers, marching in such exact order, without doing the least injury to individuals, and remaining in this situation for such a length of time, without division or confusion among themselves, and then returning to their duty as soon as their reasonable demands were complied with. This conduct ought to convince the British how much they mistake the disposition of the Americans at large when they assert that they would willingly join them if not overawed by their tyrannic rulers. Here was a large body composed as well of foreigners as natives, having no officer to command them and no force to prevent their joining the enemy for which they had repeated invitations, yet, though they well knew they were liable to the severest punishment for their revolt, they disdained the British offers with a firmness that would have done honor to the antient Romans, and through the whole have shown the greatest respect to the Committee of Congress, to the Governor and members of the Council for the State of Pensylvania, and expressed the highest confidence in the justice of their civil rulers and have not through the whole deviated from that order and regularity which upon other occasions must have done honor to military discipline.

P. S. One circumstance ought not to be omitted which in my opinion does the insurgents much honor. When they delivered up the British emissaries Governor Reed offered them a hundred gold guineas, which they refused, saying that what they did was only a duty they owed that country, and that they neither received nor would receive any reward but the approbation of that country for which they had so often fought and bled.

—HAMMOND, ed., *Letters and Papers of Sullivan*, XV, 263-265.

5. WASHINGTON DEALS FIRMLY WITH THE JERSEY MUTINEERS

George Washington to the Commission for Redressing the Grievances of the New Jersey Line.

Ringwood, January 27, 1781

Gentlemen: The fatal tendency of that spirit which has shown itself in the Pensylvania and Jersey lines, and which derived so much encouragement from impunity in the case of the former determined me at all events to pursue a different conduct with respect to the latter. For this purpose I detached a body of troops under Major Genl. Howe with orders to compel the mutineers to unconditional submission and execute on the spot a few of the principal incendiaries. This has been effected this morning; and we have reason to believe the mutinous disposition of the troops is now completely subdued and suceeded by a genuine penitence.

But having punished guilt and supported authority, it now becomes proper to do justice. I therefore wish the Commissioners, as soon as convenient to enter upon the objects for which they have been appointed. But I think it my duty to observe to them the necessity of the greatest caution in discussing one article, the terms of the inlistments of the troops. In transacting this with the Pensylvanians for want of proper care, the greatest part of the line has been dismissed, though only a small proportion was intitled to a dismission. Authentic and unequivocal proofs have been since found, that a majority of the discharged men were fairly and explicitly inlisted for the war. This evil arose from admitting the oaths of the individuals themselves, before the vouchers could be assembled. From the temper of the soldiery who will scruple no means of getting rid of the service it becomes necessary to admit none but the most unsuspicious evidence in their favour. Generally on investigation the complaints on this head have appeared ill founded, and as the presumption is strong against the soldier, the proofs of an unfair detention ought to be equally strong. Men are extremely wanted, it is at an infinite expence they are procured and they ought not lightly to be released from their engagements.

Whenever a complaint has been made to me, I have invariably directed an inquiry, for I have ever considered it as not less impolitic than unjust in our service to use fraud in engaging or retaining men; but as I mentioned above, the complaint has much oftner. been found to originate in the levity of the soldier than in truth. I have the honor etc.

—FITZPATRICK, ed., *Writings of Washington*, XXI, 147-148.

CHAPTER NINETEEN

The Home Front in the War

IT DID NOT *take long for the Patriot leaders to realize that there was much more to winning the war than ambushing Redcoats. The war had to be fought on the home front as well as on the battlefield. Committees of safety, state governments, and the Continental Congress had not only to raise men for the army, but to supply them with arms, powder, equipment, medicines, food, clothing and a hundred other necessities. To keep the armies properly supplied without a central fiscal system, or an effective machinery of taxation, required heroic exertions. Desperate efforts were made on various levels, local, state and interstate, to hold the price and wage line in the face of printing-press inflation, for military and civilian leaders alike recognized that unless prices and wages were brought under control, the cost of fighting the war would be prohibitive. At the same time speculation, profiteering, cornering the market and hoarding posed heavy problems for the military who, from time to time, had to impress the goods and services of civilians.*

Central to the problem was the lack of a taxing power by Congress, which had merely the power to levy requisitions; when the states proved delinquent in meeting these—as they all did—paper currency seemed the only way out. Inevitably it depreciated, and eventually the phrase "not worth a Continental" became a part of the American vocabulary. Foreign loans helped stave off total bankruptcy, but inflation and repudiation left ugly scars. Yet in the perspective of history paper money seems not only the inevitable solution, but probably that one which spread the costs of the war most equitably over the population at large.

I. MUNITIONS, SUPPLIES AND IMPRESSMENT

From the first, the Patriot leaders were concerned with the desperate need for gunpowder, of which saltpeter (potassium nitrate) was a major component, and for arms. Pennsylvania, a center for arms manufacturing, rushed production as soon as hostilities began. But as prices for materials and parts mounted, arms makers found it necessary to seek an upward revision of their contracts. As a result of higher domestic costs muskets made under contract in Pennsylvania averaged $12 apiece as against 24 livres or about five dollars for those imported from France. Fortunately for the Patriot army the cheaper French arms were quickly made available; well over 100,000 French arms were imported during the Revolution for the use of the Continental forces.

From time to time it was necessary to impress supplies, provisions, wagons and horses for carrying on the war. But the Patriot authorities, reluctant to antagonize civilians or jeopardize property rights, trod softly. Washington told the Continental Congress in December 1777, "I confess I have felt myself greatly embarrassed with respect to a vigorous exercise of military power. An ill-placed humanity perhaps and a reluctance to give distress may have restrained me too far." In 1780 he justified impressment on the ground that "Our affairs are in so deplorable a condition (on the score of provisions) as to fill the mind with the most anxious fears. . . . Men half-starved, imperfectly cloathed, riotous, and robbing the country people of their subsistence from shear necessity."

During his campaign in the South, Nathanael Greene found it necessary to seize wagons when wagoners proved unco-operative. But the most desperate need was for horses. After Guilford Courthouse, Cornwallis began his retreat to the North Carolina coast on March 18, 1781. A month later he headed north for Virginia, having seized swift-blooded horses to mount the dragoons of Tarleton. Greene was handicapped in his pursuit as he found that Marion and his partisans were impressing horses for themselves rather than turning them over to the regular army. In desperation Greene's officers began to seize horses wherever they could locate them. On March 24, 1781, Governor Jefferson wrote Greene complaining that his officers had made illegal impressments, and on April 1 enclosed a set of resolutions of the Virginia legislature demanding restitution. Greene sent back a stinging rebuke.

1. "I Am Determined Never to Have Salt Petre out of My Mind"

John Adams to James Warren.

October 21, 1775

We must bend our attention to salt petre. We must make it. While Britain is Mistress of the Sea and has so much influence with foreign courts we cannot depend upon a supply from abroad.

It is certain that it can be made here, because it is certain that it has been formerly and more latterly. Dr. Graham, of White Plains in the Colony of New York, told me that he has made some thousands of pounds weight many years ago, by means of a German servant whom he bought and found to be good for nothing else.

Messrs. De Witts—one of Windham, the other of Norwich—have made a considerable quantity, a sample of which has been shewn me by Col. Dyer, and they have made a large collection of materials for making more.

Mr. Wisner of New York informs me that his son has made a quantity of very good, also by the method published by the Continental Congress.

Two persons belonging to York Town in this Colony have made one hundred and twenty weight, have received the premium and are making more.

A gentleman in Maryland made some last June from tobacco house earth.

Mr. Randolph, our venerable President, affirms to me that every planter almost in that Colony has made it from tobacco house earth. That the process is so simple that a child can make it. It consists in nothing but making a lixivium from the earth which is impregnated with it, and then evaporating the lixivium. That there is certainly discovered in Virginia a vast quantity of the rocks of salt petre. That there are salt petre rocks, he says, all chemists and naturalists who have written agree, and that he was informed by many gentlemen in Virginia, cautious, incredulous men, of strict honour and veracity, that they have been to see the rocks and tryed them and found them by experiment to be the very rock of salt petre.

The old gentleman, in short, who is not credulous nor inthusiastical but very steady, solid and grave, is as sanguine and confident as you can conceive, that it is the easiest thing in the world to make it, and that the tobacco colonies alone are sufficient to supply the Continent forever.

Every Colony, my friend, must set up works at the public expense.

I am determined never to have salt petre out of mind, but to insert some stoke or other about it in every letter for the future. It must be had.

—Warren-Adams Letters, I, 158-159.

2. PRICES AND WAGES ADD TO GUNSMITHS' DIFFICULTIES

[December 1776]

The Gunlock Makers to the Honorable the Committee of Safety.

The humble address and petition of James Walsh and Samuel Kinder, gunlock makers of the City of Philadelphia, sheweth:

That your Petitioners, from many unforeseen difficulties attending their business, and the extravagant advance on the necessities of life, have been obliged to solicit your honorable board for redress.

At the commencement they had materials to procure which were new and uncommon; hands to instruct who were strangers and unlearned, and even those to purchase at double their value; steel to provide, in which article their loss is manifest to their acquaintance. Still hoping that their perseverance would surmount every difficulty, they continued with labour and assiduity. Notwithstanding which, they now find it impossible to subsist, as their most painful endeavors bear no proportion to the present rate of things. Files are now double what they have been, and some treble; vices, double; steel, scarce any to be found good; thirty to forty shillings advance on one hundred bushels of coal; journeymen's wages still rising; your Petitioners limited; and the enormous price of every other necessity too well known to trouble your Honors with a repetition.

Your Petitioners humbly beg your Honors to take their case into consideration and act therein as to your Honors shall seem meet, and your Petitioners, as in duty bound, etc.

JAMES WALSH
SAMUEL KINDER
—Archives, Pennsylvania Historical Commission.

3. "ARE HORSES DEARER THAN THE LIBERTIES OF THE PEOPLE?"

Nathanael Greene to Governor Thomas Jefferson.

April 28, 1781

... I was very particular in giving my orders to guard against the evils complained of ... and I have no wish to screen a single officer who has wantonly invaded the property of the people or offered any insult to the inhabitants; but I wish the improper conduct of a few officers may not be made to operate as a punishment upon the whole army. Particular situations and particular circumstances often make measures necessary that have the specious show of oppression, because they carry with them consequences pointed and distressing to individuals. It is to be lamented that this is the case; but pressing circumstances make it political and sometimes unavoidable.

When we retired over the Dan, our force was too small to stop the progress of the enemy, or mark the limits of their approach. We appealed to the only means left us to save your country and prevent the destruction of a virtuous little army. Men were called for; they turned out with a spirit that did honor to themselves and their country. Horses were wanted to mount our dragoons; they could not be procured but by virtue of impress warrants. You was convinced of the fact, and therefore furnished me with the warrants for the purpose. I took the most advisable and, as I thought, most effectual means to have the business conducted with propriety; and I cannot but think the gentlemen generally who were intrusted with the execution of my orders were governed entirely by a principle of public good. Some mistakes and several abuses appear to have happened in impressing stud-horses instead of geldings; but those mistakes arose from the necessity of mounting our dragoons in such a manner as to give us an immediate superiority over the enemy, as well as in the quality of the horses as their number. The people complained; I was ready to redress their grievances; some of the most valuable horses were returned; and I shall direct some others to be restored, notwithstanding the great inconvenience which must inevitably attend this army by it. The Assembly of your State appear to have taken up the matter from a principle acknowledged to be virtuous, but from its tendency must be allowed to be impolitic.

The rights of individuals are as dear to me as to any man; but the safety of a community I have ever considered as an object more valuable. In politics, as well as in everything else, a received and established maxim is, that greater evils should, in every instance, give way to lesser misfortunes. In war it is often impossible to conform to all the ceremonies of law and equal justice; and to attempt it would be productive of greater misfortunes to the public from the delay than all the inconveniences which individuals may suffer.

Your Excellency must be sensible of the innumerable inconveniences I had to labor under at the time, and the variety of difficulties that still surround us. Nothing but light-horse can enable us, with the little army we have, to appear in the field; and nothing but a superiority in cavalry can prevent the enemy from cutting to pieces every detachment coming to join the army or employed in collecting supplies. From the open state of this country their services are particularly necessary, and unless we can keep up the corps of cavalry, and constantly support a superiority, it will be out of our power to act or to prevent the enemy from overrunning the country and commanding all its resources.

The Assembly, I fear, by their resolves have destroyed my hopes and expectations on this head. Under the law as it at present stands, it is certain nothing can be done. By limiting dragoon horses to the narrow price of five thousand pounds, it amounts only to a prohibition, and cuts off the prospect of any future supplies. At this moment the enemy are greatly superior to us; and unless Virginia will spring immediately to the most generous exertions, they will indubitably continue so. It is in vain to expect protection from an army which is not supported, or make feeble efforts upon narrow principles of prudence or economy; they only serve to procrastinate the war, and tire out the patience of the people. Already have we experienced, in many instances, the ill consequences of neglecting the army when surrounded with difficulties and threatened with ruin. Great expense of blood and treasure have attended this policy; and to redress the grievances of a few individuals when it will entail a calamity on the community, will be neither political or just. If horses are dearer to the inhabitants than the lives of subjects, or the liberties of the people, there will be no doubt of the Assembly persevering in their late resolution; otherwise I hope they will reconsider the matter, and not oblige me to take a measure which cannot fail to bring ruin upon the army, and fresh misfortunes upon the country.

—GREENE, *Life of Nathanael Greene*, III, 288-290.

II. HOLDING THE PRICE AND WAGES LINE

On the verge of hostilities Congress not only imposed nonimportation regulations but fixed schedules to restrain the increase in the prices of articles already imported. Alexander Hamilton, the fiery young Patriot, applauded Congress' action in his treatise A Full Vindication *(December 1774). Nonetheless the war years were marked by a rapid rise in the cost of living, an astonishing decline in the value of Continental paper money, and an orgy of profiteering and black-marketeering. To meet this threat the New England states sent delegates to a convention at Providence toward the close of 1776, where a formula was adopted for curbing wages and prices. This action was defended on the ground that something had to be done to sustain the morale of the armed forces, increasingly resentful of profiteering back home by farmer, merchant and laborer. The resentment of the soldier to high prices and profiteering was expressed by Nathanael Greene early in the war.*

1. "THE FARMERS ARE EXTORTIONATE"

Nathanael Greene to Governor Samuel Ward of Rhode Island.

Camp on Prospect Hill, December 31, 1775

... You misunderstood me, Dear Sir, or I wrote what I did not mean. It was not the lower class of people that I meant to complain of, but the merchants and wealthy planters, who I think does not exert themselves as they ought. This is no time for giting riches but to secure what we have got. Every shadow of oppresseon and extortion ought to disappear, but instead of that we find many articles of merchandise multiplied four fold their original value, and most cent per cent [100%]. The farmers are extortionate where ever their situation furnishes them with an opportunity. These are the people that I complain mostly of; they are wounding the cause.

When people are in distress its natural for them to try every thing and every where to get relief, and to find oppresseon instead of relief from these two orders of men will go near to driving the poorer sort to desperation. It will be good policey in the United Colonies to render the poorer sort of people as easy and happy under their present circumstances as possible, for they are creatures of a day, and present gain and gratification, tho small, has more weight with them than such greater advantagies at a distance. A good politician must and will consider the temper of the times and the prejudices of the people he has to deal with, when he takes his measures to execute any great design. The current sentiment in the New England Colonies greatly favors the opposition, but if the distresses of the people are multiplied their oppinions may change. They naturally look back upon their former happy situation and contrast that with their present wretched condition, and conclude that the source of all their misery originates in the despute with Great Britain. . . .

We have suffered prodigeously for want of wood; many regiments has been obliged to eat their provision raw for want of fireing to cook, and notwithstanding we have burnt up all the fences and cut down all the trees for a mile round the camp, our suffering has been inconceivable. The barracks has been greatly delayed for want of stuff; many of the troops are yet in their tents and will be for some time, especially the officers. The fatigues of the campaign, the suffering for want of wood and cloathing, has made abundance of the soldiers heartily sick of service.

The Connecticut troops went off in spite of all that could be done to prevent it; but they met with such an unfavorable reception at home that many are returning to camp again already. The people upon the roads exprest so much abhorrence at their conduct for quiting the army that it was with difficulty they got provisions. I wish all the troops now going home may meet with the same contempt.

—Greene Papers.

2. WAGE AND PRICE REGULATION BY THE PROVIDENCE CONVENTION

December 31, 1776

This Committee taking into consideration the unbounded avarice of many persons, by daily adding to the now most intollerable exhorbitant price of every necessary and convenient article of life, and also the most extravagant price of labour in general, which at this time of distress, unless a speedy and effectual stop be put thereto, will be attended with the most fatal and pernicious consequences, as it not only disheartens and disaffects the soldiers who have nobly entered into service, for the best of causes, by obliging them to give such unreasonable prices for those things that are absolutely needful for their very existence that their pay is not sufficient to subsist them, but it is also very detrimental to the country in general.

Wherefore it is recommended by this Committee, that the rates and prices hereafter enumerated be affixed and settled within the respective states in New England, to wit:

Farming Labour in the summer season shall not exceed three shillings and four pence per diem, and so in the usual proportion at other seasons of the year, and the labour of mechanics and tradesmen and other labour to be computed according to the usages and customs that have heretofore been adopted and practised in different parts of the several states compared with farming labour. . . .

—CONVENTION OF THE NEW ENGLAND STATES, Journals.

The states represented at the meeting acted with commendable speed. New Hampshire, Massachusetts, Connecticut and Rhode Island almost immediately enacted legislation incorporating the wage and price schedule recommended by the Providence Convention. In addition to fixing the scale of wages for farm labor Rhode Island set maximum wages as follows:

[1777]
per diem

Teaming work, the teamster finding himself and cattle, for one hand
    with cart or waggon, one yoke of oxen, and a good draught-horse,
    or two yoke of oxen . . . . 13s.
Teaming to and from sea port markets and for the army per ton per
    mile, if not more than one mile 4s. For every mile after the first
    mile out 1s. 6d.
Horse-keeping, at sea port towns per night or 24 hours, 2s. 6d.
Horse-shoeing all round, with steel corks, heel and toe, 6s.
Ox-shoeing and other blacksmith's work in the same proportion.
Ships iron-work—weight-work at 3d. per lb. and all light work in the
    same proportion, excepting cast iron.
House-carpenters, finding themselves . . . . 5s.
Ship carpenters, finding themselves . . . . 6s.
Caulkers, finding themselves . . . . 7s.
Masons, finding themselves . . . . 6s. 6d.
Taylors making a plain suit of best broadcloth cloths, 24s. and their
    daily wage, the employer finding them at . . . . 3s.
Trucking, 1s. 6d. per hogshead, and other things in proportion
Best beaver hats at 42s. best felt hats at 8s.
Coopers, finding themselves . . . . 5s.
    setting and finding hogshead hoops, 3d. each
    setting and finding barrel hoops, 2d. each
Barbers for shaving, 3d.

—Rhode Island Records, 1772-1777, pp. 641 *et seq.,*
State Archives, Providence.

3. A LEARNED DOCTOR OPPOSES PRICE CONTROLS

The proceedings of the Providence Convention were laid before Congress on January 28, 1777, and evoked a spirited debate. On February 4, a resolution of the Committee of the Whole was debated setting forth the opinion of the committee

that the peculiar situation of the New England states, whose communication with Congress was in a great measure cut off, and who were invaded

or threatened with an immediate invasion by the enemy, rendered the ap-
pointment and meetings of the Committee proper and necessary, and con-
sequently worthy of the approbation of Congress.

The motion was carried that day, but, on reconsideration, was defeated by
one vote, only to be reopened on February 14. The debates of that day were
carefully preserved in the diary of one of the chief participants, Dr. Benjamin
Rush, whom we have already met on several occasions. They were strikingly
parallel to the arguments following the close of World War II between those
who favored continuing price controls and rationing and those who main-
tained that artificial price controls were ineffective so long as bank credit was
permitted to expand at a disturbing rate.

From the Diary of Dr. Benjamin Rush.

February 14, 1777

Upon the question whether the Congress should recommend to the States
to adopt the plan for reducing and regulating the price of labor, manufactures,
imports, and provisions which had been adopted in the four New England
states:

It was said in the negative by *Mr. James Smith*, that such a recommendation would interfere with the domestic policies of each State, which were of
too delicate a nature to be touched by the Congress.

Dr. Rush: I am against the whole of the resolution. It is founded in the
contrary of justice, policy and necessity as has been declared in the resolution. The wisdom and power of government have been employed in all ages
to regulate the price of necessaries to no purpose. It was attempted in England
in the reign of Edward II by the English parliament, but without effect. The
laws for limiting the price of everything were repealed, and Mr. Hume who
mentions this fact records even the very attempt as a monument of human
folly.

The Congress with all its authority has failed in a former instance of regulating the price of goods. You have limited Bohea tea to ¾ of a dollar, and
yet it is daily sold before your eyes for 30s. The Committee of Philadelphia
limited the price of West India goods about a year ago. But what was the
consequence? The merchants, it is true, sold their rum, sugar and molasses at
the price limited by the committee, but they charged a heavy profit upon the
barrel, or the paper which contained the rum or the sugar.

Consider, Sir, the danger of failing in this experiment. The salvation of
this continent depends upon the authority of this Congress being held as sacred as the cause of liberty itself. Suppose we should fail of producing the
effects we wish for by the resolution before you. Have we any character to
spare? Have we committed no mistakes in the management of the public
affairs of America? We have, Sir. It becomes us therefore to be careful of
the remains of our authority and character.

It is a common thing to cry aloud of the rapacity and extortion in every
branch of business, etc., among every class of men. This has led some people
to decry the *public virtue* of this country. We estimate our virtue by a false
barometer when we measure it by the price of goods. The extortion we com-

plain of arises only from the excessive quantity of our money. Now, Sir, a failure in this attempt to regulate the price of goods will encrease the clamors against the rapacity of dealers, and thus depreciate our public virtue.

Consider, Sir, the consequence of measuring our virtue by this false standard. You will add weight to the arguments used at St. James's to explode patriotism altogether, and by denying its existence in this country destroy it forever. Persuade a woman that there is no such thing as chastity, and, if there is, that she does not possess it, and she may be easily seduced if she was as chaste as Diana. Sir, the price of goods may be compared to a number of light substances in a bason of water. The hand may keep them down for a while, but nothing can detain them on the bottom of the bason but an abstraction of the water. The continent labours under a universal malady. From the crown of her head to the sole of her feet she is full of disorders. She requires the most powerful tonic medicines. The resolution before you is nothing but an opiate. It may compose the continent for a night, but she will soon awaken again to a fresh sense of her pain and misery.

Colonel Richard Lee, in the affirmative. Mr. President, the learned Doctor has mistook the disorder of the continent. She labours under a spasm, and spasms, he knows, require *palliative* medicine. I look upon the resolution before you only as a temporary remedy. But it is absolutely necessary. It is true the regulations formerly recommended by Congress were not faithfully carried into execution, but this was owing to the want of regular government. New and regular governments have been instituted in every part of America, and these will enable all classes of people to carry the resolution into execution.

Mr. Samuel Chase, in the affirmative. Mr. President, this is a necessary resolution. It is true it failed formerly in Philadelphia because it abounded with Tories. But it succeeded in Maryland. It must be done. The mines of Peru would not support a war at the present high price of the necessaries of life. Your soldiers cannot live on their pay. It must be raised unless we limit the price of the clothing and other articles necessary for them.

Mr. Seargant, Negative. The price of goods cannot be regulated while the quantity of our money and the articles of life are allowed to fluctuate.

Colonel James Wilson, Negative. There are certain things, Sir, which absolute power cannot do. The whole power of the Roman emperors could not add a single letter to the alphabet. Augustus could not compel old bachelors to marry. He found out his error, and wisely repealed his edict lest he should bring his authority into contempt. Let us recommend the resolution to the *consideration* of the States only without giving our opinion on it, that they may discuss it with unbiassed minds.

Dr. Witherspoon, Negative. Sir, it is a wise maxim to avoid those things which our enemies wish us to practise. Now I find that our enemies have published the act of the assembly of Connecticut for regulating the price of necessaries in the New York paper in order to show our distress from that quarter. Remember, laws are not almighty. It is beyond the power of despotic princes to regulate the price of goods. I fear if we fail in this measure we shall weaken the authority of Congress. We shall do mischief by teaching the continent to *rest* upon it. If we limit *one* article, we must limit *every* thing, and this is impossible.

Mr. John Adams, Negative. Perhaps I may here speak against the sense of my constituents, but I cannot help it. I much doubt the justice, policy and necessity of the resolution. The high price of many articles arises from their scarcity. If we regulate the price of imports we shall immediately put a stop to them forever.

Dr. Rush. Sir, it has been said that the high price of goods in Philadelphia arose from the monopolies and extortion of the Tories. Here I must say the Tories are blamed without cause. A similar spirit of speculation prevails among the Whigs in Philadelphia. They are disposed to realise their money in lands or goods. But this is not owing to any timidity or disaffection among them. They fear the further depreciation of your money by future emissions. Stop your emissions of money and you will stop speculation. I am not apt to reply to *words*, much less to *play* upon them. The gentleman from Virginia has miscalled the malady of the continent. It is not a spasm, but a dropsy. I beg leave to prescribe two remedies for it. (1) Raising the interest of the money we borrow to six per cent. This, like a cold bath, will give an immediate *spring* to our affairs; and (2) *taxation*. This, like *tapping*, will diminish the quantity of our money, and give a proper value to what remains.

The resolution was amended. The plan of the four New England States was *referred* only to the other States, to act as they thought proper.

—RUSH, Diary. Library Company of Philadelphia, Ridgeway Branch.

III. FURTHER EFFORTS TO HOLD THE PRICE LINE

In November 1777, after the New England states had found it expedient to scuttle their price and wage codes, Congress recommended a broad scheme of price and wage regulations. A call for three regional conventions was issued. Of these, only one was held and set schedules for labor and commodities—a Northern and Middle States convention at New Haven. "Why do we complain of a partial infringement of liberty manifestly tending to the preservation of the whole?" the convention asked. "Must the lunatick run uncontrouled to the destruction of himself and neighbours merely because he is under the operation of medicines which may in time work his cure?"

The problem was exigent and demanded the attention of Congress, of interstate conventions, of state legislatures and of town conventions, as well as of theoreticians. The delicate balance between prices and wages was carefully analyzed by one writer in the New Jersey Gazette. *Conceding that in general "trade can best regulate its own prices," this writer contended that on extraordinary occasions legislative intervention was justifiable. Such schedules, he urged, should bear equitably on all groups in the community and should favor the production of necessaries.*

In addition to state laws and town regulations, local courts, Revolutionary committees and self-appointed vigilante groups sought to enforce price and wage controls, and to punish profiteers and monopolizers. At Fishkill, New York, a group of housewives took the law into their own hands, weighed out their own purchases, and remitted the money to the Dutchess County Com-

mittee. A Schenectady weaver was denounced for charging too much for weaving linen, and a Boston hatter who exceeded the regulated price was named "an enemy of his country." In Boston five "Tory villains" were punished for profiteering by a vigilante group under the leadership of a masked man called "Joyce Junior," a veteran agitator, and a new order of "female mobility" disciplined the Boston merchant, Thomas Boylston.

1. JOYCE JUNIOR RIDES AGAIN

Letter of Abigail Adams.

April 20, 1777

About eleven o'clock yesterday William Jackson, Dick Green, Harry Perkins and Sargent, of Cape Ann, and A. Carry, of Charlestown, were carted out of Boston under the direction of Joice junior, who was mounted on horseback with a red coat, a white wig and a drawn sword, with drum and fife following. A concourse of people to the amount of five hundred followed. They proceeded as far as Roxbury, when he ordered the cart to be tipped up, then told them if they were ever caught in town again it should be at the expense of their lives. He then ordered his gang to return, which they did immediately without any disturbance.

Monday, 21st

Have now learned the crime of the carted Tories. It seems they have refused to take paper money, and offered their goods lower for silver than for paper; bought up articles at a dear rate and then would not part with them for paper.

—ADAMS, *Familiar Letters*, pp. 262-263.

2. "TRADE CAN BEST REGULATE ITS OWN PRICES"

From the *New Jersey Gazette*, March 11, 1778.

. . . in order to find out how to proportion the limitations duly, it may be necessary to have recourse to calculation.

By the law lately passed for regulating prices, the legislature seem to have aimed at fixing most of the articles of internal produce at double the former prices. This may perhaps be a proper standard for some articles; but when the matter is fairly considered, it will be found that the same reasons which require the prices of some things to be doubled, will call for a similar advance on some others, and on others again a much greater. Of the latter kind are such articles as derive their value chiefly from labour, and require the use of some commodity, either imported from abroad or which, from its scarcity, cannot be obtained but at a very high price. To explain my meaning I shall subjoin a few calculations.

I. As to farmers. Let us suppose a farm, the annual produce of
which is for sale, exclusive of what was necessary for the consumption of such parts of the family as do not labour, would sell
in former time for £300.0.0
It is said to be a large allowance to admit that one half of this value is
paid for labour, supposing the whole to be done on hire . . 150.0.0
Annual profit remaining 150.0.0

Supposing the price of labour to be doubled, the labour on the same
farm will be worth 300.0.0
The consumption of the family will be the same, and allow the same
annual profit as formerly 150.0.0
The extraordinary price of salt may be 15.0.0
Allow, moreover, the use of as much rum, tea, sugar and other lux-
uries that will cost extra 35.0.0
_____
£500.0.0

The farmer ought therefore to have for his produce on an average
now 5s. for what he would formerly have sold for 3s., or 1s. 8 now
for 1s. formerly.

II. As to labourers. Let us suppose a labourer, finding his own provisions and cloathing, formerly earned per annum 45.0.0

That his provisions cost him 20.0.0
And his cloathing 10.0.0
Profit toward maintenance of his family 15.0.0
_____
45.0.0

Provisions at double price will be 40.0.0
Cloathing will cost at least three times the old price 30.0.0
His profit for the use of his family ought to be at least double as they
must purchase all they consume 30.0.0
_____
£100.0.0

His wages therefore ought to be increased to 10s. for every 4s.6 he
would formerly have received; or 1s.8 now for 9d. formerly.

The same proportion will be requisite for mechanicks, handicraftsmen,
lawyers, clerks, etc., so far as their several productions derive their value from
labour; making the proper additions or deductions for what the prices of their
respective materials may exceed or fall short of that proportion.

It will be observed that I have stated the price of labour at double the
former price to the farmer, though I have shewn it must cost more to others;
and that I have stated provisions at double to labourers, etc., though I have said
the farmer ought to sell them at a lower rate. A little reflection will justify
these diversities. As to the first, the farmer, having the advantage of feeding
and, in a great measure, clothing and paying his labourers from his own produce without purchase (to say nothing of the advantage he may derive from
the labour of his children and servants), can always procure at a much cheaper
rate than a person of any other class. And as to the second—suppose the price
of the common articles of provisions should be fixed at the rate of 5s. now, for
3s. formerly, as above stated, if we move but a small allowance for the extraordinary prices of salt, sugar, tea, rum, etc. . . . . we shall find the average price of
provisions to labourers, mechanicks, etc., will not be less than doubled. I have
heard it remarked that a great majority of the members of the legislature being
farmers, their limitations are calculated greatly in favour of that class of men.
If there is any truth in the remark, I am persuaded it must arise from their want

of proper information, as I cannot suppose they would designedly oppress others for their own emolument. As faithful representatives of the people, I should suppose they would be particularly watchful that no just ground should be given for a suspicion of this kind. . . .

—*New Jersey Gazette*, March 11, 1778.

3. THE LADIES OF BOSTON STAGE A BOSTON COFFEE PARTY

Abigail to John Adams.

Boston, July 31 [1777]

I have nothing new to entertain you with, unless it is an account of a new set of mobility, which has lately taken the lead in Boston. You must know that there is a great scarcity of sugar and coffee, articles which the female part of the state is very loath to give up, especially whilst they consider the scarcity occasioned by the merchants having secreted a large quantity. There had been much rout and noise in the town for several weeks. Some stores had been opened by a number of people, and the coffee and sugar carried into the market and dealt out by pounds. It was rumored that an eminent, wealthy, stingy merchant (who is a bachelor) had a hogshead of coffee in his store, which he refused to sell to the committee under six shillings per pound.

A number of females, some say a hundred, some say more, assembled with a cart and trucks, marched down to the warehouse and demanded the keys, which he refused to deliver. Upon which, one of them seized him by his neck and tossed him into the cart. Upon his finding no quarter, he delivered the keys, when they tipped up the cart and discharged him; then opened the warehouse, hoisted out the coffee themselves, put it into the truck and drove off.

It was reported that he had personal chastisement among them; but this, I believe, was not true. A large concourse of men stood amazed, silent spectators of the whole transaction. . . .

—ADAMS, ed., *Letters of Mrs. Adams*, I, 109-110.

IV. THE ISSUANCE AND CONTROL OF THE CURRENCY

Lacking the power to tax, dependent on the states for requisitions which they grudgingly met in only small part, and rescued from total bankruptcy by timely foreign loans, Congress found it necessary to turn to the printing presses to finance the war. As the contest proved long and increasingly costly, the government issued twice as much Continental money in the year 1778 as in the three preceding years, and the year 1779 saw that figure increased another two-and-a-half-fold. In addition the states issued around $210 million in paper notes, the overwhelming portion by the Southern states. The indebtedness of the United States government was estimated by a committee of Congress in 1783, and the cost of operating the war by Hamilton in a report to Congress in 1790.

Since currency depreciation set in almost at once, the Patriot authorities, federal, state and local, sought to make paper money legal tender in business transactions. Wherever they could, farmers and merchants tried to get specie, like the brazen tavern keeper for whose story we are indebted to Joseph White, an orderly sergeant in an artillery regiment, who participated in the battles of Trenton and Princeton and received an enlisted man's eight-dollar-a-month pension in 1819. It goes without saying that price and wage controls could not hold up, were people to demand more in paper than in specie, and those who did were held to be enemies of their country, at times punished criminally, and at other times denounced publicly. The unequal struggle to maintain the paper standard in the early period of depreciation is reported by Robert Morton, son of a Philadelphia merchant, who kept a diary during the British occupation of Philadelphia. At the time of these entries he was just seventeen years of age. Newspaper accounts ranged from satirical Tory and British stories ridiculing the effort to maintain the worthless paper, to serious proposals by Patriots for stabilizing the economy.

1. DEBTS AND INFLATION

A. ESTIMATE OF THE DEBT OF THE UNITED STATES, 1783

As reported by the Grand Committee of Congress, April 8, 1783.

Foreign Debt

To the Farmers General of France	. .	Livres	1,000,000
To Beaumarchais	. .		3,000,000
To the King of France, to the end of 1782 .	. .		28,000,000
To ditto for 1783	. .		6,000,000
		Livres 38,000,000 =	$7,037,037
Received on loan in Holland, 1,678,000 florins	. . . . .		671,200
Borrowed in Spain by Mr. Jay	. . .		150,000
Interest on Dutch one year, at 4 per cent	. . . .		26,848
Total foreign debt	. . . . .		$7,885,085

Domestic Debt

Loan Office	$11,463,802	
Interest unpaid for 1781	190,000	
Ditto 1782	687,828	
Credit to sundry persons on		
Treasurey books	638,042	
Army debt to 31 December 1782 . . .	5,635,618	
Unliquidated ditto	8,000,000	
Deficiencies in 1783	2,000,000	
Total domestic debt		$28,615,290
Aggregate debt		$36,500,375

Interest

On foreign debt, 7,885,085, at 4 per cent		315,403
On domestic debt, 28,615,290, at 6 per cent		1,716,917
On commutation of half-pay, estimated at 5,000,000 at 6 per cent		300,000
Bounty to be paid, estimated at 5,000,000 at 6 per cent . . .		30,000
Aggregate of interest		$2,362,320

—HUNT, ed., *Writings of Madison*, I, 443.

B. ALEXANDER HAMILTON'S ESTIMATE OF THE COST OF THE WAR (1790)

Transactions of the Treasury

	Bills of credit	New emissions	Total specie value
1775 and 1776	$ 20,964,666	. . . .	$20,064,666
1777	26,426,333	. . . .	24,986,646
1778	66,965,269	. . . .	24,289,438
1779	149,703,856	. . . .	10,794,620
1780	82,908,320	$ 891,236	3,000,000
1781*	11,408,095	1,179,249	1,942,465
1782	. . . .	. . . .	3,632,745
1783	. . . .	. . . .	3,226,583
Total	$357,476,541	$2,070,485	$91,937,168

Total Expenditures

Expenditures at the treasury . . . . $ 91,937,168
Outstanding certificates of indebtedness 16,708,009
Expended in Europe 5,000,000
State debts 21,000,000
  Total cost of war $134,645,177

—BULLOCK, *Finances of the U. S.*, pp. 174-175.

C. PRICES RISE FANTASTICALLY AS PAPER MONEY SHRINKS IN VALUE

Quantity of Certain Staples That Could Be Purchased in Pennsylvania for £100 in paper currency.

April	Flour cwt.	Sugar cwt.	Iron cwt.	Beef bbl.
1774	105.9	36.4	76.9	36.4
1775	133.3	39.5	77.9	33.3
1776	143.3	30.8	74.8	26.7
1777	83.8	8.89	40.0	10.5
1778	63.2	2.75	11.8	9.78
1779	6.67	0.84	2.65	1.82
1780	1.15	0.30	0.88	0.22
1781	0.71	0.21	0.52	0.11

cwt. = 112 lbs.; bbl. = 225 lbs.

—BEZANSON, *Prices and Inflation during the Revolution*, p. 321.

2. THE DEPRECIATION OF THE CURRENCY THREATENS TOTAL RUIN

Robert Morris to the Commissioners in France.
                                   Philadelphia, December 21, 1776
  Gentlemen: . . . I must add to this gloomy picture one circumstance, more distressing than all the rest, because it threatens instant and total ruin to the

---

* In the year 1781 the finances were restored to a specie basis.

American cause, unless some radical cure is applied, and that speedily; I mean the depreciation of the Continental currency. The enormous pay of our Army, the immense expenses at which they are supplied with provisions, clothing and other necessaries, and, in short, the extravagance that has prevailed in most departments of the publick service, have called forth prodigious emissions of paper money, both Continental and Colonial. Our internal enemies, who, alas! are numerous and rich, have always been undermining its value by various artifices, and now that our distresses are wrought to a pitch by the success and near approach of the enemy, they speak plainer and many peremptorily refuse to take it at any rate. Those that do receive it, do it with fear and trembling; and you may judge of its value, even amongst those, when I tell you that £250 Continental money, or 666 2-3 dollars, is given for a bill of exchange of £100 sterling, sixteen dollars for a half-johannes, two paper dollars for one of silver, three dollars for a pair of shoes, twelve dollars for a hat, and so on; a common labourer asks two dollars a day for his work and idles half his time.

All this amounts to real depreciation of the money. The war must be carried on at an expense proportioned to this value, which must inevitably call for immense emissions, and, of course, still further depreciations must ensue. This can only be prevented by borrowing in the money now in circulation. The attempt is made, and I hope will succeed by loan or lottery. The present troubles interrupt those measures here, and as yet I am not informed how they go on in other States, but something more is necessary; force must be inevitably employed, and I fear to see that day. We have already calamities sufficient for any country, and the measure will be full when one part of the American people is obliged to dragoon another, at the same time that they are opposing a most powerful external foe. . . .

—FORCE, *American Archives*, 5th Series, III, 1334.

3. "I DO NOT LIKE YOUR REBEL MONEY"

Narrative of Joseph White, sergeant of artillery in the Continental Army.

[December, 1776]

After crossing the [Delaware] river, we were put into the back part of a tavern; the tavernkeeper refused to take rebel money, as he called it. I went to General Putnam and told him that he had everything he wanted, "but he will not take paper money. He calls it rebel money."

"You go and tell him, from me, that if he refuses to take our money, take what you want without any pay."

I went and told the man what the General said.

"Your Yankee general dare not give such orders," said he.

I placed two men at the cellar door, as centries. "Let nobody whatever go down," I said. I called for a light, and two men to go down cellar with me. We found it full of good things, a large pile of cheeses, hams of bacon, a large tub of honey, barrels of cider, and 1 barrel marked cider-royal, which was very strong; also, all kinds of spirit. The owner went to the General to complain.

"The sergeant told me," said the General, "that you refused to take paper money."

"So I did," said he. "I do not like your rebel money."

The General flew round like a top. He called for a file of men. A corporal and four men came. "Take this Tory rascal to the main guard house."

I sent a ham of bacon, one large cheese and a bucket full of cider-royal to General Putnam. He asked who sent them. He told him the sergeant that he gave leave to take them.

"Tell him I thank him," said he.

—WHITE, *Narrative*.

4. "MORE TO FEAR FROM PAPER MONEY THAN FROM BRITISH GENERALS"

Joseph Eggleston, Jr., to Joseph Eggleston, Amelia County, Virginia.

State of Delaware, September 2, 1777

I sit down to answer your letter by Mr. Ellison which he delivered to me this day. He tells me he came from Philadelphia for that purpose, and seems to be pleased with the thoughts of having it in his power to return your favor of lending him the horse to ride to Richmond. I have written twice in answer to those letters which Peter Berry brought out; in those letters I informed Messrs. Cocke and Hardaway that Old Figure was on Staten Island and in possession of the enemy, and therefore not to be purchased by any person among us. I should have been much pleased if it had been in my power to have assisted Berry in purchasing any firm horse for them, but it would have been impracticable if I had seen him.

The horse you mentioned called Bay Richmond could not be had for less than £1500. The prices of every kind of article here would astonish you. You desire I would procure you a good beaver hatt and some other articles. In answer to which part of your letter I would inform you that goods are 200 per cent dearer than they were in Virginia when I left it. I was obliged to buy a hat a few days past, and paid 18 dollars for one of an inferior kind. Boots sell for the *moderate* price of 21 dollars; broad cloth £12 a yard. Rum is 20/ the quart; whiskey 10/. Every other article bears a proportionate price.

But I turn from this prospect to one that can be contemplated with much greater pleasure. I mean our military affairs; for it is my fixed opinion that America has much more to fear from the effects of the large quantities of paper money than from the operations of Howe and all the British generals. Burgoyne has been defeated by General Arnold, has lost his tents, baggage, etc., and is retreating with his broken forces towards Ticonderoga. We are this moment alarmed with some movements of the enemy which the Light Horse must attend to and therefore my letter will be much shorter than it would have been. I will just inform you that the whole army, from General Washington downwards, are in high spirits and make no doubt of keeping the enemy from Philadelphia. . . .

—EGGLESTON, Letter, Morgan Library.

5. THE BANEFUL INFLUENCE OF PAPER MONEY

From the diary of Robert Morton of Philadelphia.

Nov. 27th, 28th, 29th, 30th [1777].—These 4 days the fleet [has been] coming up in great numbers. Some part of the army have marched over

Schuylkill, and reports are prevalent that the main part of the army will soon move off. The Americans are moving off their heavy cannon. Gen'l Washington, it is said, is going to Virginia in a few weeks, and the command [is] to devolve upon Gen'l Gates. Great exertions are making, both by the men and women of this city, to support the credit of the paper money legally issued. The women are determined to purchase no goods with hard money. Some of those who agreed to receive paper money have refused it for their goods, and among the rest some of our Society [of Friends].

Dec. 1st, 2nd, 3rd.—Numbers of the fleet [are] daily arriving. None of the large ships have yet come up. A contest has subsisted in this city since the arrival of the fleet, concerning the legal paper currency. The English merchants that came in the fleet will not dispose of their goods without hard money, alleging that no bills are to be bought, no produce to be obtained, and no method can be adopted by which they can send remittances. Numbers of the most respectable inhabitants are using all their influence to support it, and numbers of others who have no regard for the public good are giving out the hard money for what they want for immediate use, thus purchasing momentary gratifications at the expense of the public, for if the circulation of this money should be stopt, many who have no legal money but paper and have no means of obtaining gold and silver, will be reduced to beggary and want, and those who are so lost to every sense of honor, to the happiness of their fellow citizens, and eventually their own good, as to give out their hard money, either for the goods of those who are newcomers, or in the public market where it is now exacted for provisions, will, by their evil example, oblige those who possess hard money, to advance it and ruin the credit of the other money for the present. The consequence of which must be that we shall be shortly drained of our hard cash, the other money rendered useless, no trade by which we can get a fresh supply; our ruin must therefore be certain and inevitable.

This depreciation of the paper currency will not only extend its baneful influence over this city, but over all the continent, as the friends of government and others have been collecting this legal tender for several months past, expecting that in those places in the possession of the British Army it will be of equal value with gold and silver. But from the enemies of the British constitution among ourselves, who give out their hard money for goods, from the almost universal preference of private interest to the public good, and from a deficiency of public virtue, it is highly probable the paper money will fall, and those newcomers, having extracted all our hard money, will leave us in a situation not long to survive our ruin. . . .

—Morton, "Diary," *Penn. Mag. of Hist. and Biog.*, I, 31-33.

V. AN END TO DEPRECIATION:
THE FORTY-TO-ONE FORMULA

By 1779 the depreciation of the Continental currency had become alarming, rising from 8 to 1 in January to 38½ to 1 by November. But besides the "Continentals" additional millions were outstanding in quartermaster certificates, which were receipts given in payment by the Army for supplies it requisitioned, in loan-office certificates, and in certificates given soldiers for back pay. Repudiation of the paper had long been urged. Congress finally decided to face reality, which in fact meant repudiation or bankruptcy. On March 18, 1780, it retired the bills in circulation by accepting them in payments due it from the states at one-fortieth of their face value. This wiped the federal-currency slate clean. A timely subsidy from France in May 1781, and French backing for a large loan from the Netherlands forthcoming in November, enabled Robert Morris to make some progress toward returning the country to a specie basis before the war came to an end.

1. Repudiation "to Save Our Estates and Liberties"

March 12, 1778

To the Inhabitants of the United States, from "A Naturalized American."

The hopes of our enemies are now built upon the expences they are putting us to. The question is no more who are poltroons? but whose resources will fail soonest? We must put the trial upon this issue. . . .

The debt of America, though much larger than it need to have been had honesty, economy and good sense prevailed in every department, is not in itself alarming. The Continent, from its different climates and being so well cultivated, hath those internal advantages that most of the necessaries wanted may be furnished out of its own produce; and were patriotic societies to be formed in every State for encouraging the most *useful* arts and manufactures, within a few years it might support itself without going to any foreign market whatsoever.

But, it will be inquired, how are the high prices of things to be reduced in the mean while, without which the war cannot be carried on much longer? This brings me to the main source of our present difficulties—the depreciation of the currency—which must be remedied or we are undone. I doubt not to assert that the *grand* occasion of such depreciation hath been a *redundancy* through the amazing quantities that have been emitted. New emissions must decrease its value yet more. Borrowing what hath been emitted upon loan-office tickets, bearing interest, and then circulating it afresh, continues the evil while it increases our debt.

The only sovereign remedy that can produce a radical cure is the lessening of the currency till there is barely sufficient for circulation—all others are mere temporary palliatives. It is to be feared that the currency exceeds the quantity wanted for circulation by two-thirds, if not four-fifths. Let the Continent agree then to sink the redundancy—or that will sink the Continent. We shall be no losers; the remainder will be worth the whole nominal sum. Can an individual with a single dollar purchase after the proposed diminution what he must otherwise give five for; and with equal ease can he procure the one as the five; he is no real sufferer by the diminution, while the public is a great gainer, for the *fluctuating* value of the currency is cured.

But how is this diminution to be fairly brought about? I humbly apprehend, gentlemen, it may be done as follows, viz. Let one or more, or all the emissions of the *United Colonies*, after certain days, be no longer legal tenders

through the Continent—let the bills be paid by every holder to his town col-
lector, as a part of his tax for the current year, or, if more, for future ones, till
the whole is exhausted (whatever may be advanced not to be taxed as a part
of his estate, and in case of his death to be accounted for in like mode to his
successors)—let the bills thus collected be paid to the respective Treasurer of
each State, to be by him defaced, and then to be put into the hands of the
Continental Treasurer, who shall credit the State for the same as its quota for
past, present or future taxes. There would be still in circulation all the emissions of the *United States*, which, if not sufficient, would leave room for all
that might be further necessary. . . .

The scheme, gentlemen, is practicable, have we but spirit but to adopt it,
for we have *all* the paper among us, the circulation being confined to ourselves. The matter is near a crisis: we have our choice either to part with
our paper and so to save our estates and liberties, or to retain it and so doing lose all. We must either submit to the necessity of the day and tax
ourselves voluntarily, or we must submit to the parliament of Great-Britain
and be taxed for the little property they may leave us, just as their *omni-
potence* shall direct. . . .

—*Independent Chronicle*, March 12, 1778.

2. THE STAMPEDE TO PAY OFF DEBTS IN PAPER—AN ENGLISH VIEW

November 6, 1780.—A writer in London says:—The incredible fall of
continental currency in America may be understood from the following
notorious fact, viz.: Ten thousand pounds Maryland currency *was* worth six
thousand sterling; ten thousand pounds continental money *is* worth one hundred pounds. The difference makes a loss of five thousand nine hundred
pounds sterling, being as sixty to one.

This was the exchange at Philadelphia in June last, and as they had not then
heard of Gates's defeat*, it must be now lower. Actions commenced for considerable sums by creditors have been obliged to be withdrawn, or a non-suit
suffered; a lawyer of eminence not opening his mouth in a trial of consequence, under a fee of *one thousand pounds*, though the legal fee is about
forty, and the debt, if recovered, being paid in continental money, dollar for
dollar, worth now but a penny, the difference between a penny and 4s. 6d.
sterling, is lost to the receiver. The Congress having called in the former emissions, forty dollars for one, and giving that *one* in paper, cut off every hope
it will hereafter *appreciate*. The freight of a hogshead of tobacco is three
hundred pounds, or one hogshead for the carriage of another; instead of the
creditor pursuing the debtor with an arrest, the debtor pursues the creditor
with a *tender* of continental money and forces the bond out of his hand.

Hence it appears what the best fortunes in that country are reduced to; an
unpleasing reflection it must be! for time, which lightens all other losses, ag-
gravates the loss of fortune. Every day we feel it more, because we stand
more in want of the conveniences we have been used to. On the other hand,
new fortunes are made on the ruin of old ones.

* At Camden, August 16, 1780.

War, which keeps the spirits in motion, has diffused a taste for gayety and dissipation. The French Resident at Philadelphia gives a rout twice a week to the ladies of that city, amongst whom French hair-dressers, milliners and dances are all the *ton*. The Virginia jig has given place to the cotillon, and minuet-de-la-cour.

The Congress are fallen into general contempt, for their want of credit and power; the army is absolute and has declared it will not submit to a peace made by Congress; the people grumble, but are obliged to surrender one piece of furniture after another, even to their beds, to pay their taxes.

After all, a power drawn from such distant and dissonant parts cannot form a permanent union. The force of this kingdom, moving uniformly from one centre, must in all human probability ultimately prevail; or an accident may produce, in an instant, what the most powerful efforts require time and perseverance to accomplish.

–MOORE, *Diary of the American Revolution*, II, 343-344.

3. A TORY EXULTS: "THE CONGRESS IS FINALLY BANKRUPT!"

From Rivington's *Royal Gazette* for May 12, 1781.

May 7, [1781]–The Congress is finally bankrupt! Last Saturday a large body of the inhabitants with paper dollars in their hats by way of cockades paraded the streets of Philadelphia, carrying colors flying, with a DOG TARRED, and instead of the usual appendage and ornament of feathers, his back was covered with the Congress' paper dollars. This example of disaffection, immediately under the eyes of the rulers of the revolted provinces, in solemn session at the State House assembled, was directly followed by the jailer, who refused accepting the bills in purchase of a glass of rum, and afterwards by the traders of the city, who shut up their shops, declining to sell any more goods but for gold or silver. It was declared also by the popular voice that if the opposition to Great Britain was not in future carried on by solid money instead of paper bills, all further assistance to the mother country were vain and must be given up.

–MOORE, *Diary of the American Revolution*, II, 425-426.

4. "WE HAVE PURSUED OUR PAPER PROJECTS AS FAR AS IS PRUDENT"

James Madison, the writer of this letter, was already gaining a reputation as a leading Nationalist in Congress. His addressee was to be the author of an early history of the United States.

James Madison to Philip Mazzei, a European intellectual.

Philadelphia, July 7, 1781

The vicissitudes which our finances have undergone are as great as those of the war, the depreciation of the old continental bills having arrived at forty, fifty and sixty for one. Congress, on the 18th of March, 1780, resolved to displace them entirely from circulation, and substitute another currency, to be issued on better funds, and redeemable at a shorter period. For this purpose they fixed the relative value of paper and specie at forty for one; directed the States to sink by taxes the whole two hundred millions in one year, and to provide proper funds for sinking in six years a new currency which was not to exceed ten millions of dollars, which was redeemable within that period and to bear an interest of five per cent., payable in bills of exchange on Europe or hard money. The loan-office certificates granted by Congress are to be discharged at the value of the money at the time of the loan, a scale of depreciation being fixed by Congress for that purpose.

This scheme has not yet been carried into full execution. The old bills are still unredeemed, in part, in some of the States, where they have depreciated to two, three and four hundred for one. The new bills, which were to be issued only as the old ones were taken in, are consequently in a great degree still unissued; and the depreciation which they have already suffered has determined Congress and the States to issue as few more of them as possible.

We seem to have pursued our paper projects as far as prudence will warrant. Our medium in future will be principally specie. The States are already levying taxes in it. As the paper disappears, the hard money comes forward into circulation. This revolution will also be greatly facilitated by the influx of Spanish dollars from the Havannah, where the Spanish forces employed against the Floridas consume immense quantities of our flour and remit their dollars in payment. We also receive considerable assistance from the direct aids of our ally and from the money expended among us by his auxiliary troops.

These advantages, as they have been and are likely to be improved by the skill of Mr. Robert Morris, whom we have constituted minister of our finances, afford a more flattering prospect in this department of our affairs than has existed at any period of the war.

—HUNT, ed., *Writings of Madison*, I, 144-145.

VI. THE BANK AND THE FINANCIER

In the closing years of the Revolution the government was heading for a financial crisis. Various proposals were made to expedite raising money for the war. One of the earliest, and certainly the most thoroughgoing, was the series of proposals drawn up by Washington's aide, Alexander Hamilton. We give here a portion of an undated letter, probably written by Hamilton some time in 1780, and addressed "To a Member of Congress." Although some historians have named Robert Morris as the addressee, he was not in Congress at this time. Hamilton's letter takes on deeper significance in view of his later plan for a national bank, which he proposed when he became Secretary of the Treasury, and his later efforts to attach the financial and commercial interests to the new nation on the basis of self-interest. His two bank plans had a common end, but the later was less grandiose and at the same time more clearly under private control than that envisioned in the earlier proposal.

In the following letter Hamilton suggests that a foreign loan be procured that would be convertible into merchandise and imported on public account. To obtain the full support of the moneyed men behind the government he recommended that a national bank be set up, the ownership of which was to be evenly divided between the government and private capital. When on

February 20, 1781, Robert Morris was named by Congress to the post of Superintendent of Finance, Hamilton pressed the matter once more. But Morris was less venturesome and instead pushed through Congress a charter for the Bank of North America, which was to perform the functions of discount and deposit. In addition, Hamilton's bank would have coined money, issued paper currency, and have charge of contracts for supplying the armed forces.

When, in June 1781 Robert Morris entered upon his duties as Superintendent of Finance, his only available resources were bills of exchange that Congress from time to time drew on foreign envoys, optimistically assuming that funds existed in Europe for meeting the bills. Almost immediately Morris was called upon by Washington to finance the Yorktown campaign. The financier managed to provide the army with transportation from the head of the Chesapeake, to advance a month's pay to the soldiers, and to forward needed supplies. The arrival in August of almost a half million dollars in specie from France eased his burdens. Nonetheless, Morris seems to have personally advanced $12,000 toward the expenses of the Yorktown campaign.

Following the suggestions of Hamilton, Gouverneur Morris and others, Robert Morris secured the consent of Congress to establishing a bank. Incorporated in 1782 both by Congress and the State of Pennsylvania, the Bank of North America rendered valuable assistance to the government, lending the United States $1,249,000 during Morris' regime.

Morris employed his personal credit to secure the notes issued to the army at the time of its disbanding. As his letter to Washington reveals, the army's demands constituted merely a small part of his fiscal problems. Needless to say he—and his policies—encountered heavy criticism. Finding it impossible to carry through his program, he resigned in despair. We include some letters of his supporters and one written by a puzzled critic.

1. HAMILTON ENLISTS "THE INTEREST OF THE MONEYED MEN"

Alexander Hamilton to "a Member of Congress."

[1780]

The present conjuncture is by all allowed to be peculiarly critical. . . . The object of principal concern is the state of our currency. In my opinion, all our speculations on this head have been founded in error. Most people think that the depreciation might have been avoided by provident arrangements in the beginning without [any aid] from abroad; and a great many of our [sanguine] politicians, till very lately, imagined the [money] might still be restored by expedients with [in our] selves. Hence the delay in attempting [to procure] a foreign loan.

This idea proceeded from [an igno]rance of the real extent of our resources. The war, particularly in the first periods, [required] exertions beyond our strength, to which [neither] our population nor riches were equal. . . .

The public expenditures, from the dearness of everything, necessarily became immense; great[er] in proportion than in other countries; and much beyond any revenues which the best concerted scheme of finance could have extracted from the natural funds of the State. No taxes, which the people were capable of bearing, on that quantity of money which is deemed a proper medium for this country (had it been gold instead of paper), would have been sufficient for the current exigencies of government.

The most opulent states of Europe, in a war of any duration, are commonly obliged to have recourse to foreign loans or subsidies. [Here Hamilton cited the huge debts of foreign nations.] How, then, could we expect to do without them, and not augment the quantity of our artificial wealth beyond those bounds which were proper to preserve its credit? The idea was chimerical. . . .

Could a loan have been obtained, and judiciously applied, assisted by a vigorous system of taxation, we might have avoided that excess of emissions which has ruined the paper. The credit of such a fund would have procured loans from the moneyed and trading men within ourselves; because it might have been so directed as to have been beneficial to them in their commercial transactions abroad. (This will appear from the plan which will be proposed.)

The necessity for a foreign loan is now greater than ever. Nothing else will retrieve our affairs. . . .

How this loan is to be employed is now the question; and its difficulty equal to its importance. Two plans have been proposed: one, to purchase up at once, in specie or sterling bills, all superfluous paper; and to endeavor, by taxes, loans and economy, to hinder its returning into circulation. The remainder, it is supposed, would then recover its value. This, it is said, will reduce our public debt to the sterling cost of the paper. . . .

The other plan proposed is to convert the loan into merchandise and import it on public account. This plan is incomparably better than the former. Instead of losing on the sale of its specie or bills, the public would gain a considerable profit on the commodities imported. The loan would go much further this way towards supplying the expenses of the war; and a large stock of valuable commodities, useful to the army and to the country, would be introduced. This would affect the prices of things in general and assist the currency. But the arts of monopolizers would prevent its having so extensive and durable an influence as it ought to have.

A great impediment to the success of this, as well as the former scheme, will be the vast sums requisite for the current expenses. . . .

The only plan that can preserve the currency is one that will make it the *immediate* interest of the moneyed men to cooperate with government in its support. . . .

The plan I would propose is that of an American bank, instituted by authority of Congress for ten years, under the denomination of The Bank of the United States. . . .

I give one half of the whole property of the bank to the United States, because it is not only just but desirable to both parties. The United States contribute a great part of the stock; their authority is essential to the existence of the bank; their credit is pledged for its support. The plan would ultimately fail if the terms were too favorable to the company and too hard upon government. It might be encumbered with a debt which it could never pay and be obliged to take refuge in a bankruptcy. The share which the State has in the profits will induce it to grant more ample privileges, without which the trade of the company might often be under restrictions injurious to its success. . . .

It may be objected that this plan will be prejudicial to trade by making the government a party with a trading company; which may be a temptation to arrogate exclusive privileges and thereby fetter that spirit of enterprise and competition on which the prosperity of commerce depends. But Congress may satisfy the jealousies on this head by a solemn resolution not to grant exclusive privileges, which alone can make the objection valid. . . .

—Hamilton Papers, 1st Series, Lib. of Congress.

2. Morris and the "Art Magick"—Some Washington Comments

George Washington to Robert Morris.

New Windsor, June 4, 1781

The present conveyance is sudden and unexpected; I have only time therefore to acknowledge the receipt of your favors of the 29th. Ulto. and to assure you, that I felt a most sensible pleasure, when I heard of your acceptance of the late appointment of Congress to regulate the Finances of this Country. My hand and heart shall be with you, and as far as my assistance will, or can go, command it.

Washington to John Mathews.

New Windsor, June 7, 1781

. . . I have great expectations from the appointment of Mr. Morris, but they are not unreasonable ones; for I do not suppose that by Art magick, he can do more than recover us, by degrees, from the labyrinth into which our finance is plunged.

Washington to the Chevalier de la Luzerne.

New Windsor, June 8, 1781

I presage the happiest Consequences from the Appointment of a Gentleman of Mr. Morris's Character and Abilities to the Superintendance of our Finance. I wait impatiently for his making me the Visit which he proposes, as many very essential Matters in the Operations of the Campaign will depend upon the Assistance which he will be able to afford us.

—Fitzpatrick, *Writings of Washington*, XXII, 159, 177, 181.

3. Joseph Reed Calls Morris "a Pecuniary Dictator"

Joseph Reed to Nathanael Greene.

November 1, 1781

. . . It would add too much to this already tedious letter to enter into a detail of the events which have put us into our present state, but in brief it may be ascribed to the failure of public credit, the non-production of taxes, and consequent poverty of Congress, which was, indeed, truly abject and distressing; in this wretched extremity, it became necessary to appoint what I may properly call a pecuniary dictator. The qualities required were ability of mind, some money in hand, and a private credit for more. I believe I ought to have put the latter qualities first, for if Sully had been here without them, he would not have been thought of.

Mr. Morris, who had been long pursuing a gainful traffic from which others were excluded by embargo and restrictions, . . . naturally presented himself as combining the necessary qualities; but his terms were high, and at first blush inadmissible. He claimed a right of continuing in private trade, of dismissing all Continental officers, handling public money at pleasure, with many lesser privileges amounting to little less than an engrossment of all those powers of Congress which had been deemed incommunicable, and which we have sometimes thought they exercised with rather too much hauteur. However, Mr. Morris was inexorable, Congress at mercy, and, finally, the appointment made with little relaxation in the original conditions, since which the business of that august body has been extremely simplified, Mr. Morris having relieved them from all business of deliberation or executive difficulty with which money is in any respect connected.

—REED, *Life and Correspondence of Reed*, II, 374-375.

4. MORRIS IS "CONCILIATING FAST THE SUPPORT OF MONEYED MEN"

Alexander Hamilton to Marquis de Noailles.

[1782]

There has been no material change in our internal situation since you left us. The capital successes we have had have served rather to increase the hopes than the exertions of the particular States. But in one respect we are in a mending way. Our financier has hitherto conducted himself with great ability, has acquired an entire personal confidence, revived in some measure the public credit, and is conciliating fast the support of the moneyed men. His operations have hitherto hinged chiefly on the seasonable aids from your country; but he is urging the establishment of permanent funds among ourselves; and though, from the nature and temper of our governments, his applications will meet with a dilatory compliance, it is to be hoped they will by degrees succeed. . . .

Upon the whole, however, if the war continues another year, it will be necessary that Congress should again recur to the generosity of France for pecuniary assistance. The plans of the financier cannot be so matured as to enable us by any possibility to dispense with this; and if he should fail for want of support, we must replunge into that confusion and distress which had liked to have proved fatal to us, and out of which we are slowly emerging. The cure, on a relapse, would be infinitely more difficult than ever.

—J. C. HAMILTON, ed., *Writings of Hamilton*, I, 314-317.

5. "NO OTHER MAN COULD HAVE KEPT THE MONEY MACHINE A-GOING"

Alexander Hamilton to George Washington.

April [9,] 1783

As to Mr. Morris, I will give your Excellency a true explanation of his conduct. He had been for some time pressing Congress to endeavor to obtain funds, and had found a great backwardness in the business. He found the taxes unproductive in the different States; he found the loans in Europe making a very slow progress; he found himself pressed on all hands for supplies; he found himself, in short, reduced to this alternative: either of making en-

FIRST RECOGNITION OF THE AMERICAN FLAG BY A FOREIGN GOVERNMENT

Salute to the U.S.S. *Ranger* in command of John Paul Jones in the harbor of Quiberon, France, February 13, 1778

THE MEMORABLE ENGAGEMENT OF THE *SERAPIS* AND THE *BON HOMME RICHARD*

gagements which he could not fulfill, or declaring his resignation in case funds were not established by a given time. Had he followed the first course, the bubble must soon have burst; he must have sacrificed his credit and his character, and public credit, already in a ruinous condition, would have lost its last support.

He wisely judged it better to resign. This might increase the embarrassments of the moment; but the necessity of the case, it was to be hoped, would produce the proper measures; and he might then resume the direction of the machine with advantage and success.

He also had some hope that his resignation would prove a stimulus to Congress.

He was, however, ill advised in the publication of his letters of resignation. This was an imprudent step and has given a handle to his personal enemies, who, by playing upon the passions of others, have drawn some well-meaning men into the cry against him. But Mr. Morris certainly deserves a great deal from his country. I believe no man in this country but himself could have kept the money machine a-going during the period he has been in office. From every thing that appears, his administration has been upright as well as able.

The truth is, the old leaven of Deane and Lee is, at this day, working against Mr. Morris. He happened, in that dispute, to have been on the side of Deane; and certain men can never forgive him. A man whom I once esteemed, and whom I will rather suppose *duped* than wicked, is the second actor in this business.

—Hamilton Papers, 1st Series, Lib. of Congress.

Robert Morris to George Washington.

The Office of Finance, November 26, 1783

I have been honored with the receipt of your Excellency's letter of the eighteenth instant and in consequence shall send this to the City of New York which I hope and expect is now in our possession. It is unnecessary to assure you, Sir, how pleasing it would be to comply with the wishes of the officers now in service, as expressed in their memorial of the seventeenth instant: because I am sure both you and they must be convinced of my disposition to render justice to every part of the Army. But alas, Sir, the good will is all which I have in my power. The means of making payment is not, on the contrary. I am constantly involved in scenes of distress to keep pace with those engagements which I have already taken for the subsistence and pay which the Army have heretofore received.

Those engagements, which I dreaded at the time, were taken under various considerations. The relief of the Army then to be discharged—your Excellency's earnest desire—the orders of Congress and in particular the urgency of the committee appointed to treat with me on that subject and my own desire to render service to the Army—these were amongst the motives which induced me to hazard an anticipation of above a million of dollars on the public account. My solicitude to fulfill those engagements is extreme, but my calls for help are disregarded, and under such circumstances it cannot be expected that I shall make new engagements—and there is not any money in the Treasury. I lament the situation of the officers and am truly sorry that the States are so inattentive to the finances of the Union.

—Robert Morris Papers.

VII. PROFITEERS AND PROFITEERING

1. The Operations of "the Tribe of Profiteers"

The American Revolution brought to the fore a handful of dedicated leaders of unimpeachable integrity, and it disclosed, too, devotion and integrity in the people at large. But as in all wars there were "patrioteers" who profited while their fellow men fought and sacrificed. If the Revolution as a whole were to be judged in moral terms, it would appear a triumph of character over venality. But the venality was there, it was pervasive, it was continuous. We give here some of the innumerable protests against that "spirit of avarice" which threatened the liberties of the young nation.

A. "monopolizers are our worst oppressors"

"P.W." on monopolies.

Needham, Massachusetts, October 29, 1776

If the traders in this town and land had managed their commerical business with any tolerable regard to the good of the publick, as they might have done in consistency with seeking their own profit so far as it was fit and proper they should, being members of one and the same political body, we should have been at this day in happy circumstances, compared with what we now are. Our traders, considered in general, are, in the view of all considerate persons, as grand oppressors, and as truly and extensively so, in proportion to the sphere in which they move, as our ministerial oppressors in England; and unless they are soon restrained, either from a virtuous principle within or from some extensive power, they will be the destroyers of the poor, the widow, the fatherless, and all others whose situation in life is such as renders it impossible for them to do justice to themselves. To what can it be attributed but the excessive love traders have to their own precious selves, that they put such an extravagant price upon the commodities they have to sell?

And what an unspeakable damage has this been to the publick! It has occasioned the undue rise of everything we depend upon for the support and comfort of life. Farmers, manufacturers in their several occupations, and labourers in all their kinds, excuse their high demands for what is wanted in their way from the still higher demands of traders for what they have to sell. In very truth, our traders, both in town and country, are the real cause of the monstrously high price of every thing; and the love of their own interest, in opposition to the interest of all others and to the subversion of it, if they may get by it, is that shameful principle by which they are governed in this whole affair.

Monopolizers in this day of common calamity are our worst oppressors. Those among them, in special, are so, who, not content with the thousands they are righteously entitled to, in consequence of the prizes the commissioned vessels they own have brought in, have been unduly influenced, from an avaricious disposition, to make a monopoly of as much of the effects of those prizes as their cunning would enable them to do, that, by an excessively enhanced price they might by and by get that from others, however poor and destitute, which both reason and revelation unite in calling the gain of oppression. These extortioners are not only sordidly unjust, but basely wanting in gratitude to that Providence which has distinguished them from most others in this day of general distress; and they ought to be restrained by Government within the limits of what is right and fit; and unless some measures are soon authoritatively come into to effect so righteous and valuable an end, it may be feared whether undesirable consequences will not take place, as a general clamour begins to be loudly heard.

–Force, *American Archives*, 5th Series, II, 1288-1289.

B. that "pernicious practice" of engrossing

John Penn to Governor Richard Caswell of North Carolina.

Philadelphia, June 25th, 1777

In my way to this place I was informed that salt sold in Maryland for 20 dollars a bushill. There are a considerable number of merchants in this and that State that make it their business to buy up all the necessaries of life in order to fix what price they please afterwards.

I suspect some of that tribe will be soon in N. Carolina to ingross all our salt and other things. Would it not be proper to keep a look out and prevent if possible such a pernicious practice? . . .

–Emmett Collection, Facsimile 3933, N. Y. Public Lib.

C. the spirit of avarice threatens the liberties of america

John Harvie to Thomas Jefferson.

York Town, December the 29th, 1777

. . . If the late generous spirit of Virginia in their Act of cloathing and measures for preventing of forestalling does not inspire the other States with a virtuous emulation, the avarice of individuals will be more fatal to the liberties of America than the sword of the enemy. I have a great while past shuddered at the rapid strides of this monster in society, but lately he has broke through every feeble fort opposed to him, and threatens us with inevitable destruction unless his carrier [career] is immediatly checked by the joint efforts of the United States. In short the avarice and disaffection of the people here is so great that they refuse any price that we can give for the necessary provisions for the army, and the General's last letter, couched in terms strong and pathetic, holds out a probability of the army desolveing unless they are more fully and constantly supplied.

You would execrate this State if you were in it. The supporters of this government are a set of weak men without any weight of character. No kind of respect is paid by the people either to their laws or advice, and instead of checking they in many instances countenance the exactions of their constituents, being otherwise fearful of looseing their present shadow of power. Two thirds of the State of Delaware are notoriously known in their hearts to be with our enemys. They have not at present the shadow of government amongst them, and their representation to Congress has been withdrawn a considerable time before I had a seat in it. From this you must foresee that these execrable States clogg the operations of the Continent in an alarming degree.

Then what is to be done? Are we with this conviction upon our minds to suffer them, for the want of virtue and vigour in their governments, to involve the whole in the worst of calamitys or will not Congress be justifyable (from the necessity of the case as guardians to the sacred rights of the people at large) in pursueing such measures as will eventually save this Continent from perdition? The feelings of my own heart tells me they will. Yet I revere the sovereignty of the States and civil rights of the people as much as any man liveing who is not capable of more refined and deeper reflections than myself. Such I acknowledge see things of this delicate nature in a more enlarged comprehensive point of view and by such I ardently wish to be instructed.

Indeed, my honored friend, for such I esteem you, the present state and condition of this Continent, oweing to the alarming disaffection in this quarter, an almost universal discontent in the army, a reformation therein meditated by Congress to commence and be carryed into effect this winter, with numberless other matters that I am not at liberty to disclose even to you, requires the wisdom of the first characters amongst us to give them weight and efficacy.

—Boyd, ed., *Writings of Thomas Jefferson*, II, 125-126.

D. WASHINGTON: "HUNT THEM DOWN AS PESTS OF SOCIETY"

George Washington to Joseph Reed.

December 12, 1778

It gives me very sincere pleasure to find that there is likely to be a coalition of the Whigs in your State (a few only excepted) and that the assembly of it, are so well disposed to second your endeavours in bringing those murderers of our cause (the monopolizers, forestallers, and engrossers) to condign punishment. It is much to be lamented that each State long ere this has not hunted them down as the pests of society, and the greatest Enemys we have to the happiness of America. I would to God that one of the most attrocious of each State was hung in Gibbets upon a gallows five times as high as the one prepared by Haman. No punishment in my opinion is too great for the Man who can build his greatness upon his Country's ruin.

—Fitzpatrick, ed., *Writings of Washington*, XIII, 383.

E. "AMERICANS SEEM TO HAVE LOST THEIR OLD NOBLE PRINCIPLES"

Samuel Shaw to Francis and Mary Shaw.

28th of June, 1779

I wish, seriously, that the ensuing campaign may terminate the war. The people of America seem to have lost sight entirely of the noble principle which animated them at the commencement of it. That patriotic ardor which then inspired each breast; that glorious, I had almost said godlike, enthusiasm—has given place to avarice, and every rascally practice which tends to the gratification of that sordid and most disgraceful passion. I don't know as it would be too bold an assertion to say that its depreciation is equal to that of the currency—*thirty for one*. You may perhaps charitably think that I strain the matter, but I do not. I speak *feelingly*. By the arts of monopolizers and extortioners, and the little, the very little, attention by authority to counteract them, our currency is reduced to a mere name.

Pernicious soever as this is to the community at large, its baneful effect is more immediately experienced by the *poor* soldier. I am myself an instance of it. For my services I receive a nominal sum, —— dollars at *eight* shillings, in a country where they pass at the utmost for *fourpence* only. If it did not look too much like self-applause, I might say that I engaged in the cause of my country from the purest motives. However, be this as it may, my continuance in it has brought me to poverty and rags; and, had I fortune of my own, I should glory in persevering, though it should occasion a sacrifice of the last penny. But, when I consider my situation—my pay inadequate to my support, though within the line of the strictest economy; no private purse of my own—and reflect that the best of parents, who, I am persuaded, have the tenderest affection for their son and wish to support him in character, have not the means of doing it, and may, perhaps, be pressed themselves—when these considerations occur to my mind, as they frequently do, they make me serious; more so than my natural disposition would lead me to be. The loss of my horse, by any accident whatever (unless he was actually killed in battle, and then I should be entitled only to about one third of his value), would plunge me in inextricable misfortune; two years' pay and subsistence would not replace him. Yet the nature of my office renders it indispensable that I should keep a horse. These are some of the emoluments annexed to a military station. I hardly thought there were so many before I began the detail; but I find several more might be added, though I think I have mentioned full enough.

Believe me, my dear and honored parents, that I have not enumerated these matters with a view to render you uneasy. Nothing would give me more pain, should they have that effect; but I think communicating one's difficulties always lessens, and, of course, makes them more tolerable; and I fancy it has already had some influence on me. I feel much easier than when I began to write, and more reconciled to my lot. It is true I shall see many persons grown rich at the end of the war, who at the commencement of it had no more than myself; but I shall not envy them.

I must, notwithstanding, repeat my wish that this campaign may put an end to the war, for I much doubt the virtue of the people at large for carrying it on another year. Had the same spirit which glowed in the breast of every true American at the beginning of the controversy been properly cherished, the country, long ere now, had been in full enjoyment of the object of our warfare—"peace, liberty, and safety." But, as matters are at present circumstanced, it is to be feared these blessings are yet at a distance. Much remains to be done for the attainment of them. The recommendations of Congress, in their late address to the inhabitants of the States, should be in good earnest attended to. We are not to stand still and wait for salvation, but we must exert ourselves—be industrious in the use and application of those means with which Heaven has furnished us, and then we may reasonably hope for success.

—SHAW, *Journals*, pp. 58-60.

2. SPECULATION IN HIGH PLACES

That distinction which now, in principle at least, obtains between public and private interest was at best dimly perceived in the era of the Revolution. Robert Morris, who conducted the major business operations for the Congress, engaged, too, in extensive business operations on his own, especially with Silas Deane, American agent in Paris. Congressman Samuel Chase of Maryland, who had earlier favored price and wage controls, took advantage of inside information to make a secret purchase of grain for the French fleet— conduct which aroused young Hamilton to a public denunciation of the transaction. Officers of the Army trafficked with the enemy, and General Greene himself engaged in wartime speculations—with the brother of Silas Deane. It is some satisfaction to recall that few of the speculators came out ahead in their dubious ventures.

A. ROBERT MORRIS ADVISES DEANE NOT TO MISS A CHANCE FOR A KILLING

Philadelphia, February 27, 1777

You will receive herewith copy of a letter I wrote you the 11th January on commercial matters, also copy of one dated 31st January respecting my brother; the contents of both are hereby confirmed, and I am sorry it is not in my power to own receipt of any fresh letters from you or him. The state of suspense I am left in makes me very uneasy, especially on his account; however, I must wait with patience to have my doubts cleared up, and hope it will be done more to my satisfaction than my present fears suggest.

I have not received any goods from you or him. Neither have I heard of any being sent by you either for this place or the West Indies. If you have, from any cause that I am unacquainted with, neglected doing it, you may have leisure to repent hereafter that you missed so fine an opportunity of making a fortune. The prices of all imported articles have been enormously high. I could have sold any quantity of European manufactures for 500 to 700 per cent and bought tobacco for 25s. to 30s. per ct. It is not too late, but goods are becoming rather more plenty and tobacco is rising, but there is plenty of room to make as much money as you please, and if insurance could be obtained in Europe it might be reduced to a certainty even if you gave a premium of 50 per cent, which, however, is vastly too high. I think some good hand might be found to go over to London and manage such insurances there. They love high premiums and will insure anything for money, but this really would be to their advantage, as I don't think we have lost above one fourth or at most one third of our inward-bound vessells.

I am sorry to inform you that there are now two or three British men of war in Chesapeak Bay. They have taken the ship *Farmer*, Captain Dashiel, which had on board 500 hhds. of tobacco on the public account and 50 hhds.

on my account; was bound for Nantes, consigned to Messrs. Pliarne Penet & Co. They have for the present blocked up several others there, but we shall get them away by and by. . . .

—DEANE, *Papers*, XX, 14-15.

B. YOUNG HAMILTON DENOUNCES THE WAR PROFITEERS

Alexander Hamilton to John Holt, Printer.

Poughkeepsie, October 19, 1778

SIR:—While every method is taken to bring to justice those men whose principles and practices have been hostile to the present revolution, it is to be lamented that the conduct of another class, equally criminal, and, if possible, more mischievous, has hitherto passed with impunity, and almost without notice. I mean that tribe who, taking advantage of the times, have carried the spirit of monopoly and extortion to an excess which scarcely admits of a parallel. Emboldened by the success of progressive impositions, it has extended to all the necessaries of life. The exorbitant price of every article, and the depreciation upon our currency, are evils derived essentially from this source. When avarice takes the lead in a state, it is commonly the forerunner of its fall. How shocking is it to discover among ourselves, even at this early period, the strongest symptoms of this fatal disease! . . .

When a man appointed to be the guardian of the state and the depositary of the happiness and morals of the people, forgetful of the solemn relation in which he stands, descends to the dishonest artifices of a mercantile projector and sacrifices his conscience and his trust to pecuniary motives, there is no strain of abhorrence of which the human mind is capable, no punishment the vengeance of the people can inflict, which may not be applied to him with justice. If it should have happened that a member of C——ss had been this degenerate character, and has been known to turn the knowledge of secrets to which his office gave him access to the purposes of private profit, by employing emissaries to engross an article of immediate necessity to the public service, he ought to feel the utmost rigor of public resentment and be detested as a traitor of the worst and most dangerous kind.

October 26, 1778

SIR:— . . . When you resolved to avail yourself of the extraordinary demand for the article of flour which the wants of the French fleet must produce, and which your official situation early impressed on your attention, to form connections for monopolizing that article, and raising the price upon the public more than an hundred per cent; when by your intrigues and studied delays you protracted the determination of the C—tt—e of C——ss on the proposals made by Mr W—sw—th, C—s—y G—n—l [Jeremiah Wadsworth, Commissary General], for procuring the necessary supplies for the public use, to give your agents time to complete their purchases;—I say when you were doing all this, and engaging in a traffic infamous in itself, repugnant to your station, and ruinous to your country, did you pause and allow yourself a moment's reflection on the consequences? Were you infatuated enough to imagine you would be able to conceal the part you were acting? Or had you conceived a thorough contempt of reputation, and a total indifference to the opinion of the world? Enveloped in the promised gratifications of your avarice, you probably forgot to consult your understanding and lost sight of every consideration that ought to have regulated the man, the citizen or the statesman. . . .

—*New York Journal and General Advertiser*, Oct. 19 and Oct. 26, 1778.

C. GREENE INSISTS HIS BUSINESS PARTNERSHIP BE KEPT SECRET

Nathanael Greene to Colonel Jeremiah Wadsworth.

Camp, April 30th, 1779

You may remember I wrote you sometime since that I was desirous that this copartnership between Mr. Dean, you and myself should be kept a secret. I must beg leave to impress this matter upon you again; and to request you to enjoin it upon Mr Dean. The nearest friend I have in the world shall not know it from me; and it is my wish that no mortal should be acquainted with the persons forming the Company except us three. I would not wish Mr Dean even to let his brother know it. Not that I apprehend any injury from him, but he may inadvertently let it out into the broad world, and then I am persuaded it would work us a public injury.

While we continue in the offices which we hold, I think it is prudent to appear as little in trade as possible. For however just and upright our conduct may be, the world will have suspicions to our disadvantage.

By keeping the affair a secret I am confident we shall have it more in our power to serve the commercial connection than by publishing it.

I have wrote to my brother Jacob Greene to pay you £5000 without informing him for what purpose or on what account. If you could advance the other 5000 until you come to Camp, it would be very agreeable to me. If not I must take some other way of sending it. . . .

Camp, April 30th, 1779

I have received your two last letters with the inclosed alphabet of figures to correspond with. The plan is very agreeable which is proposed. But in addition to it will it not be best to take upon us a fictitious name? This will draw another shade of obscurity over the business and render it impossible to find out the connection. The busy world will be prying into the connection and nature of the business; and more especially as a letter of Mr Deane's has lately been intercepted in which it is pretended great things are discovered and dangerous combinations formed. Whether there has been any letter intercepted and if there has whether it contains anything of the kind that is represented, I am by no means certain. It is said he is forming one of the greatest commercial houses in the world; and has a plan for land jobing of equal extent. I know not what it all means; but believe it is the effects of malice and detraction; which I can assure you was never more prevalent. . . .

Morristown, 11th of April, 1780
...How stands our 298.37 [company affair] with B. D. [Barnabas Deane]? Let me know as particularly as you can. Send the information in one letter and what you say upon it in another.

Yours
You Know Who

—GREENE, "Letters," *Penn. Mag. of Hist. and Biog.*, XXII, 211-216.

D. AMERICAN OFFICERS TRAFFIC WITH THE ENEMY

Governor William Livingston of New Jersey to General John Sullivan.

Morris Town, August 19, 1779

I have sufficient evidence to believe that constant communication and commercial intercourse has for a considerable time past been held by many of the County of Essex; that those communications have been principally supported by means of flaggs and passports obtained from divers officers of the Army belonging to the United States, who for some time past have been stationed at Elizabeth Town, Newark and other places in that neighbourhood.

Under colour of their flaggs, which from their frequency must be supposed (to use the softest term) to have been imprudently granted, great mischiefs have arisen to those parts of the country—mischiefs, I imagine, greatly superior to the advantages that may be pretended to be derived from any intelligence that can be gained thereby. Persons of dubious political characters, as I am informed, have been sent over; provisions for the aid and comfort of the British troops furnished; a pernicious and unlawful traffic carried on; the little specie left among us collected with the greatest avidity to maintain this execrable trade; and the Continental currency by that means further depreciated; opportunities afforded the enemy for circulating their counterfeit bills, and the disaffected of conveying to them intelligence of every movement and designed operation of our troops; the confidence of the people in the integrity of our officers diminished, and a universal murmuring excited among the friends of the common cause.

It is made capital by an Act of our legislature for any subject of this state to go into the enemy's lines with a passport from any officer under the rank of a Brigadier General of the Continental Army or of our militia, or of the Governor of this state.

To prevent the further abuse of those flags by the officers of our militia, I have given the strictest orders and issued a proclamation for the purpose. I have also represented the matter to his Excellency General Washington, that he may take such measure to discountenance the practice in the officers under his command as he shall think best calculated to answer the end.

I am credibly informed that no person is guilty of a greater prostitution of passports than Doctor Barnet, a captain of horse, who is not a little suspected of disaffection. He is at all events a very improper person to be trusted with blank flaggs (as I am told he is), being much addicted to strong drink, and having very little discretion when sober.

If he has any of those blanks from you, I hope you will caution him against using them for the future but upon the most important occasion, and indeed I believe it was not the intent of our law that the person thereby authorized to grant passports should delegate that power to any other, it being a personal trust reposed in them who from their stations the law presumed would always use it with prudence.

I do not pretend that our legislature supposed that the officers of the Army of the United States wanted any authority from them to grant flaggs, but they have made it felony for the subjects of this state to go with any other than the Act has appointed, which they had a right to do, and consequently any inferior officer granting them thereby deludes the person into a capital crime.

You will excuse my earnestness on this subject as I am a daily witness of the inexpressible mischiefs resulting from the abuse I complain of.

—HAMMOND, ed., *Letters and Papers of Sullivan*, XIII, 433-435.

3. WAR ON THE PROFITEERS: THE ATTACK ON "FORT WILSON"

The radical party in Pennsylvania sought in vain to have Congress halt the depreciation of Continental money by reducing emissions, imposing additional taxes, and obtaining new loans. Congress took no effective action, and soaring prices and scarcities caused widespread discontent. A mass meeting in the Statehouse yard authorized a new committee to fix a schedule of prices, and to discipline merchants and financiers who failed to co-operate.

During the summer and fall of '79 popular feeling against the speculators ran high. On October 4 a mob attacked the residence of James Wilson, the lawyer who had incurred the special animosity of the radicals by serving as counsel for the Penn family in their suit against the state, and by defending merchants before price-control committees. Wilson's own speculative propensities were notorious; even later, when he had become justice of the Supreme Court, he was deeply involved in land speculation and on the run from creditors. A number of merchants, war speculators and conservatives sought refuge from the mob in Wilson's house, which was then dubbed "Fort Wilson"; they were joined there by Wilson's friend General Mifflin.

We give two eyewitness accounts of the attack on "Fort Wilson"—one by the distinguished artist, Charles Willson Peale; the other by the dashing hero of Stony Point, Allen McLane.

A. "THE MILITIA WOULD HAVE KILLED EVERY ONE ASSEMBLED"

Statement of Charles Willson Peale.

The rapidity of the depreciation of the Continental money was at this period such that those who retained it a few days could not purchase near the value which they had given for it.

This being a grievance greatly felt by those who had been most active in favour of the Revolution, and among them those who had on every occasion rendered their personal service in the militia, many of whom thought that this continual depreciation of their favourite paper was brought about by the machinations of their internal enemies. Very few indeed could trace the real or principal cause to its true source, viz. that of too great a quantity being issued and put into circulation. Taxation being too slow to obtain the necessary supply for the support of an army, Congress were continually obliged to be issuing more, although there was already so much in use as to have totally banished gold and silver in common dealings.

At the meeting of the militia of Philadelphia on the commons in 1779, a number of those active Whigs whose zeal would carry them any length in their favourite cause, and whose tempers had now become soured by the many insults they had met with from the Tories, assembled at Burns' tavern, and after they had come to some resolutions, more passionate than judicious, that of sending away the wives and children of those men who had gone with the British, or were within the British lines, was adopted.

After these zealots had formed this design, they then began to devise the mode of carrying it into execution, and proposed to put themselves under some commander, and accordingly sent a messenger to request Captain Peale to attend them. But so soon as he was made acquainted with the business, he told them that he could not approve of the measure, as it would in the practice be found a difficult and dangerous undertaking; that the taking of women and children from their homes would cause much affliction and grief; that, when seen, the humanity of their fellow-citizens would be roused into an opposition to such a measure; that such attempts must of course fail. But all his arguments were in vain; they could not see these difficulties with a *determined* band. He then told them that the danger in case of a failure in such an attempt would be imminent to the commander of such a party. The reply was that General Washington could not take his command without running some risks, and that they in this undertaking would sacrifice their lives or effect it.

Captain Peale was at last obliged to refuse, and made the excuse that he was applied to by some of his friends to stand as a candidate at the then approaching election for members of the General Assembly; after which all further entreaty ceased, and he left them, and did not hear anything further of their proceedings until the Thursday following, when he received a notice that desired him, with Col. Bull, Major Boyd and Dr. Hutchinson, to meet the militia on the Monday following at Mrs. Burns' tavern on the common. Those persons so noticed having consulted together, all of them disapproved of the violent proceedings of the militia. Dr. Hutchinson said he would not attend the meeting; Peale and the other gentlemen conceived that they as good citizens were in duty bound to go and use their best endeavours to restrain, as far as they might be able, any violent and improper proceedings, and, in duty to themselves, at least to remonstrate in a public manner against having any part in the business.

After further consideration, Dr. Hutchinson agreed to meet them; Col. Bull, being dangerously ill, could not attend.

Accordingly, on that memorable Monday Dr. Hutchinson, Major Boyd and Captain Peale went to Mrs. Burns' tavern (where great numbers of the militia had already asembled), and they did use every argument in their power to prevent any further proceedings in that vain and dangerous undertaking. They represented the difficulty of selecting such characters as all could agree to be obnoxious amongst such a body of the people; that in such an attempt they must infallibly differ as to the object—of course no good purpose could be answered.

Among the militia were many Germans, whose attachment to the American cause was such that they disregarded every danger, and whose resentment at this time was most violently inveterate against all Tories. They only looked straight forward, regardless of consequences. In short, to reason with a multitude of devoted patriots assembled on such an occasion was in vain; and after Peale found all that could be said availed nought, he left them and went to his home, and afterwards to the President's, General Reed, whom he found was preparing to go out in order to prevent mischief, which he said was to be feared from the tidings then brought him. Captain Peale immediately returned to his home, where he had not long been before he heard the firing of small arms. He then began to think that he ought to prepare himself by getting his fire-arms in order, in case he should be under the necessity of making use of them; for no man could now know where the affair would end; and finding his wife and family very uneasy, he determined to stay within his own doors for the present time.

Shortly that tragical scene was ended, and very fortunately no more lives were lost.

The militia having taken two men who they conceived were inimical to the American cause, they were parading them up Walnut Street, and when they had got opposite James Wilson, Esq.'s house at the corner of Third Street, where a considerable number of gentlemen to the number of about thirty had collected and had armed themselves, amongst them Captain Campbell, commander of an invalid corps, this unfortunate person hoisted a window with a pistol in his hand, and some conversation having passed between him and the passing militia, a firing began, and poor Campbell was killed; a Negro boy at some distance from the house was also killed, and four or five persons badly wounded. The militia had now become highly exasperated, and had just broke into the house, and most probably would have killed every one assembled within those walls; but, very fortunately for them, General Reed with a number of the light horse appeared at this fortunate juncture and dispersed the militia. Numbers of them were taken and committed to the common jail, and a guard placed to prevent a rescue.

The next morning the officers of the militia and numbers of the people assembled at the Court House in Market Street, and the minds of the citizens generally seemed to be much distressed.

The militia of Germantown were beginning to assemble, and General Reed had sent Mr. Matlack, the Secretary of Council, to the officers of the militia, then assembled in Market Street, as above mentioned, to endeavour to keep them waiting until he could address the militia of Germantown, after which he would be with them.

Peale, hearing of this meeting at the Court House, went there, and found that the officers were exceedingly warm and full of resentment that any of the militia should be kept in durance in the jail; they appeared to be ripe for undertaking the release of the prisoners, and all Mr. Matlack's arguments, perhaps, would have been insufficient to keep them much longer from being active.

Several of the magistrates were present, and Peale whispered Mr. Matlack to know if he did not think it would be prudent to propose the taking bail for the persons and let them be released by the magistrates then present. This opinion was approved of as the most certain means to prevent disorder and perhaps a further shedding of blood. This measure being offered to the officers of the militia, they readily entered security for the personal appearance of the militia then confined at any future time for trial, and, in consequence, the prisoners were released by the magistrates' orders.

General Reed, having succeeded in preventing the Germantown militia from entering the city, came expecting to find things in the situation he had left them, and was not a little mortified to find that Mr. Matlack could not do as he had ordered. The people were assembled at the State House, and he publicly harangued them, after which, amongst a number of the officers and his particular acquaintance, he was blaming Mr. Matlack for not doing as he had requested him. Peale then told the General that Mr. Matlack ought not to suffer blame, for if the measure was wrong, that he was the unlucky person who had proposed that measure, which he then conceived was the best expedient, as it had the appearance of being a judicial act.

C.W.P.

—REED, *Life and Correspondence of Reed*, II, 423-426.

B. "THE LABORING PART OF THE CITY HAD BECOME DESPERATE"

Journal of Allen McLane.

I was standing on the front steps of my house in Walnut Street and observed Colonel Grayson beckoning to me from the door of the War Office. I went to him, and he told me he was glad I had not left the city, for that he had great apprehensions that several of our most respectable citizens, then assembled at Mr. Wilson's house, would be massacred, as they were determined to defend themselves against the armed mob that had assembled on the Commons this morning and were moving down Second Street, expecting to find Mr. Wilson and his friends at the City Tavern, but they were within pistol shot of the War Office. I listened to the sound of the drum and fife, could distinctly hear the sound in Second Street, and in a few minutes observed the front of those in arms appeared in Walnut Street, moving up the street; by this time the front of the mob was near Dock Street, in Walnut Street.

The colonel asked me if I knew those in front of the armed men; I answered I thought the leader was Captain Faulkner, a militia officer. The colonel proposed that we should meet and persuade them to turn up Dock to Third Street, which we did attempt. I introduced Colonel Grayson to Captain Faulkner, as a member of the Board of War. Grayson addressed him and expressed his fears as to the consequence of attacking Mr. Wilson in his house. Faulkner observed, they had no intention to meddle with Mr. Wilson or his house; their object was to support the constitution, the laws and the Committee of Trade. The labouring part of the City had become desperate from the high price of the necessaries of life.

The halt in front brought a great press from the rear; two men, Pickering and Bonham, ran up to the front, armed with muskets and bayonets fixed, and inquired the cause of the halt, at the same time ordered Faulkner to move up Walnut Street. Grayson addressed Bonham, and I addressed Pickering, who answered me with the threat of a bayonet, sometimes bringing himself in the attitude of a charge from trailed arms. Captain Faulkner and Mr. John Haverstadt interfered, to pacify Pickering and Bonham. Then word was given to pass up Walnut Street. By this time the press of the mob was so great that it was difficult to keep our feet, and we were crowded among the citizen prisoners, which they had taken into custody in their march through the city. Colonel Grayson and myself linked arms and determined to clear ourselves from the press when we reached the War Office.

As we passed my house, I saw my wife and Mrs. Forrest at the window of the second story. The moment she saw me in the crowd she screamed out and fainted. It was impossible then to escape. We were then within pistol-shot of Wilson's house. I saw Captain Campbell, of Colonel Hazen's regiment of the Continental Army, at one of the upper windows at Wilson's house; heard him distinctly call out to those in arms to pass on. Musketry was immediately discharged from the street and from the house, the mob gave way and fled in all directions, and left Grayson and myself under the eaves of the house in Third Street, exposed to the fire of those in the street at a distance. We concluded we would run into Wilson's garden, but there we found ourselves exposed to the fire of both the mob in the neighbours' yards, as well as those of Wilson's friends in the house.

In a few minutes we were discovered by General Mifflin, who recognised us as officers of the Continental Army, and ordered one of the doors of the back building to be opened; at this moment several persons in the house became much alarmed, and jumped out of the second-story windows. The back door of the house was immediately opened, and we entered. General Mifflin and Thompson met us on the lower floor, and requested us to follow them up stairs, observing that Mr. Wilson and his friends were about retiring to the upper rooms, which we did. When I reached the third story, I looked out of one of the windows in Third Street, looked up Third Street, could see no person in the street nearer than Dock Street, where the mob had dragged a field-piece. I looked down Third Street and saw a number of desperate-looking men in their shirt sleeves coming out of Pear Street, moving towards Wilson's house, armed with bars of iron and large hammers, and in a minute reached the house and began to force the doors and windows; they presently made a breach in Third Street, but on entering the house, they received a fire from the staircases and cellar windows, which dropped several of them; the others broke and dispersed, leaving their wounded in the house. Some of Wilson's friends ran down stairs, shut the doors and barricaded them. . . .

In a few minutes, Governor Reed, with a detachment of the first troop of City Horse, appeared. Wilson and his friends in the house sallied out. I moved with them, and the first person I recognised in the street was Governor Reed, who called upon me, by name, to aid in seizing the rioters.

—McLane Journal, N. Y. Historical Soc.

CHAPTER TWENTY

Health, Hospitals and Medicine

JOHN ADAMS *and Benjamin Rush did not always see eye to eye, but on one subject they were in agreement. "Disease," wrote Adams, "has destroyed ten men for us where the sword of the enemy has killed one." And Rush said that "hospitals are the sinks of human life in an army. They robbed the United States of more citizens than the sword." Unfortunately we do not have reliable statistics by which to test the accuracy of these generalizations, but it is reasonably clear that even Adams was not exaggerating. That the battlefield was safer than the hospital was an accepted fact in eighteenth-century warfare, and even in nineteenth-century. In the course of the Seven Years' War, for example, the British lost 1512 killed in battle and 134,000 from disease; even in our own Civil War deaths in action in the Union armies came to 67,000 while 224,000 died from disease.*

The explanation of the heavy mortality in the Revolutionary armies is to be found partly in the condition of medicine in the eighteenth century generally, partly in the situation that obtained in the American states during the war. Medicine was still more medieval than modern; there was no understanding of infection or knowledge of asepsis; only a primitive form of inoculation against smallpox; no proper safeguards against typhus, diphtheria, malaria or even scurvy; surgery was primitive, and anesthetics were unknown. As for the American situation, most of the soldiers were young and strong, and conditions of army life were, on the whole, healthy; soldiers lived mostly outdoors, managed generally to get enough vegetables; and were not so exposed to venereal diseases as were soldiers in the armies of the Old World. On the other hand the American states boasted very few well-trained doctors, almost no hospital facilities, and a desperate want of medicines, surgical instruments, bandages, bedding and other necessities.

Congress undertook early to provide some kind of medical establishment, but lacked understanding of the nature or dimensions of the problem. The original plan was shockingly inadequate; here, as elsewhere, Congress was trying to wage a cheap war. Charles Lee denounced the "little, narrow dirty economy in all things relating to the hospitals," and even Washington, who served without compensation, exclaimed that the pay of physicians was so low that "no man, sustaining the Character of a Gentleman . . . can think of accepting it." Not only were the rates of pay for physicians, nurses, orderlies and other medical personnel scandalously low, but arrangements for hospitals, food, clothing, bedding and medicines were likewise niggardly.

Congress was unfortunate, too, in its choice of director-generals. The first choice was Dr. Benjamin Church, who shortly went over to the enemy. As his successor Congress appointed Dr. John Morgan. He had studied at that seat of medical learning, Edinburgh, and on the continent; held membership in many professional and scientific societies; helped found the Philadelphia College of Medicine; and was generally regarded as the first doctor in the country. But within a year Dr. Morgan had fallen victim to a combination of professional jealousy and impossible conditions of work, and was cavalierly dismissed. His successor was the almost equally famous Dr. William Shippen, also of Philadelphia, also a graduate of Edinburgh, and also a professor at the new medical school. Though he lasted longer, he too, in the end, fell victim to the unavoidable difficulties of his position, and to the vindictiveness of his professional rivals, notably the third member of the Philadelphia fraternity, Dr. Benjamin Rush. Shippen was succeeded by Dr. Cochran of New Jersey, who was happily divorced from the internecine bickering of the Philadelphia medicos and survived the war.

Of the many other doctors who served as "physician-in-chief" for the various departments, the most famous was undoubtedly Benjamin Rush, doctor, teacher, reformer, educator, politician, signer of the Declaration, friend and patron of Tom Paine, critic of Washington, proponent of a new system of medicine, and the most articulate of all the doctors of the Revolution.

It is to Rush that we owe the most comprehensive and the most perspicacious commentary on medicine during the Revolution. Some of the other doctors were ready enough with the pen, but used it either to defend themselves against what they thought scurrilous attacks upon their integrity, or to display the breadth of their interests. Thus Dr. Morgan devoted a good deal of energy to presenting his defense against Shippen; thus Dr. James Thacher left a substantial "Military Journal" which says next to nothing about health, hospitals or medical practices. Surprisingly enough we do not have a single good comprehensive printed journal, diary, memoir or autobiography from the pen of a doctor active in the war. By all odds our best source is the correspondence of Benjamin Rush, and some of his official and semiofficial papers, and on these we have relied heavily.

In the beginning Congress provided only for medical departments of New England and the North; only very late in the war did it get around to organizing a Southern department. All of the director-generals came from the North—Church from New England, Morgan and Shippen from Pennsylvania, and Cochran from New Jersey—and so did most of the physicians-in-chief. The story of health and hospitals is therefore very largely that of the Northern campaigns—particularly the ill-omened Canadian campaign.

We present our fragmentary material here largely in chronological sequence—which is also the sequence of the military campaigns.

I. SETTING UP A MEDICAL ESTABLISHMENT

Congress wrestled with the medical problem throughout the war, but never very energetically and never successfully. From time to time it pro-

vided elaborate medical establishments, but almost always on paper. Appropriations for medical services were parsimonious; the wages provided for in the resolution of July 27 could scarcely be expected to attract talent, and though these wages—it would be improper to call them salaries—were from time to time increased, they never remotely approached what might be called a living wage. Thus as late as July 1782—when Continental money had depreciated heavily—the director of the hospital was given a salary of $122 a month, hospital surgeons $96 a month, and stewards $30 a month.

Nor were efforts to insure skillful and experienced medical help more successful. There was provision for examinations for appointment to the position of physician, but there simply were not enough trained doctors to go around, and as for assistants, stewards and nurses, it was pretty much a matter of making out with what came along. The British medical services, it should be noted, were not much better; there was no examination for appointment to army physician, and many officers, and even sergeants (like the famous Sergeant Lamb), wholly without any medical training, nevertheless performed medical duties.

1. CONGRESS MAKES PROVISION

July 27, 1775

The Congress took into consideration the report of the committee on establishing an hospital, and the same being debated, was agreed to as follows:

That for the establishment of an hospital for an army consisting of 20,000 men, the following officers and other attendants be appointed, with the following allowance or pay, viz.:

One director general and chief physician, his pay per day, 4 dollars.

Four surgeons, per diem each, one and one third of a dollar.

One apothecary, one and one third of a dollar.

Twenty [surgeons'] mates, each, two thirds of a dollar.

Two storekeepers, each four dollars per month.

One nurse to every 10 sick, one fifteenth of a dollar per day, or 2 dollars per month.

Labourers occasionally.

The duty of the above officers: viz.:

Director to furnish medicines, bedding and all other necessaries, to pay for the same, superintend the whole, and make his report to, and receive orders from the commander in chief.

Surgeons, apothecary and mates: to visit and attend the sick, and the mates to obey apothecary and the orders of the physicians, surgeons and apothecary.

Matron: to superintend the nurses, bedding, etc.

Nurses: to attend the sick and obey the matron's orders.

Clerk: to keep accounts for the director and storekeepers.

Storekeeper: to receive and deliver the bedding and other necessaries by order of the director. . . .

—*Journals of the Continental Congress*, II, 207-208.

2. Appointing Surgeons for the Revolutionary Army

Diary of Dr. James Thacher.

July 1775. On the day appointed, the medical candidates, sixteen in number, were summoned before the board for examination. This business occupied about four hours; the subjects were anatomy, physiology, surgery and medicine. It was not long after that I was happily relieved from suspense by receiving the sanction and acceptance of the board, with some acceptable instructions relative to the faithful discharge of duty, and the humane treatment of those soldiers who may have the misfortune to require my assistance. Six of our number were privately rejected as being found unqualified. The examination was in a considerable degree close and severe, which occasioned not a little agitation in our ranks. But it was on another occason, as I am told, that a candidate under examination was agitated into a state of perspiration, and being required to describe the mode of treatment in rheumatism, among other remedies he would promote a sweat, and being asked how he would effect this with his patient, after some hesitation he replied, "I would have him examined by a medical committee."

I was so fortunate as to obtain the office of surgeon's mate in the provincial hospital at Cambridge, Dr. John Warren being the senior surgeon. He was the brother and pupil of the gallant General Joseph Warren, who was slain in the memorable battle on Breed's Hill. This gentleman has acquired great reputation in his profession, and is distinguished for his humanity and attention to the sick and wounded soldiers, and for his amiable disposition. Having received my appointment by the Provincial Congress, I commenced my duty in the hospital July 15th. Several private but commodious houses in Cambridge are occupied for hospitals, and a considerable number of soldiers who were wounded at Breed's Hill, and a greater number of sick of various diseases, require all our attention. Dr. Isaac Foster, late of Charlestown, is also appointed a senior hospital surgeon; and his student, Mr. Josiah Bartlet, officiates as his mate; Dr. Benjamin Church is director-general of the hospital. . . .

—Thacher, *Military Journal,* pp. 28-29.

II. THE RAVAGES OF SMALLPOX ON THE EXPEDITION AGAINST CANADA

Smallpox, wrote John Adams, was "ten times more terrible than Britons, Canadians and Indians together." It was, in all probability, the worst killer during the Revolution. It was still almost a quarter of a century to Edward Jenner's discovery of inoculation with cowpox, but the practice of inoculation with smallpox itself was widespread—and sometimes successful. The worst ravages of the smallpox were on the Canadian campaign, and after. Dr. Lewis Beebe, from whose journal we take this account of that campaign, was a Massachusetts Jack-of-all-trades; for a time a doctor, he shifted later to the ministry, and ended up keeping a liquor shop in New York City.

"Nothing to Be Heard but 'Doctor! Doctor! Doctor!' "

Sunday 19th of May [1776]: In the afternoon was entertained with a sermon by one of the chaplains; midling morallity.

On Thursday, general orders were given by Gen. Arnold for innoculation; accordingly Col. Porters regiment was innoculated. On Fryday Gen. Thomas arrived at head quarters from Quebeck and gave counter orders: that it should be death for any person to innoculate, and that every person innoculated should be sent immediately to Montreal. . . . General Thomas this day is under great indisposition of body.

Monday 20th: General Thomas remained poorly, with many symptoms of the small pox. Early this morning 2 privates received the lash for desertion. Express orders were sent early this morning to the Three Rivers for all there to repair immediately to Sorrell. This day an express arrived to Gen. Thomas from Gen. Schuyler informing of 4000 Hanoverians laying of[f] Boston, 1000 more being gone to New York. Also another express from Maj. Sherburn who went with 140 men of Colo. Pattersons regiment from Montreal to reinforce Colo. Beadle, informing that Capt. Bliss was taken prisoner by a party of 100 regulars, 1000 savages, but received the most humane treatment, contrary to the expectation of all. . . .

Saturday 25: This day Colo. Poor arrived from Sorrell, and marched the same immediately for St. Johns. He gave me an invitation to join his regiment as surgeons mate, of which I accepted, etc.

Sunday 26: Parts of different regiments arrived from Sorrell, all being ignorant of their destination, but very few general orders, and they usually countermanded within few hours after given. Yesterday and today I have been much unwell, troubled with the quick step, attended with severe gripings. If ever I had a compassionate feeling for my fellow creatures who were objects in distress, I think it was this day; to see large barns filled with men in the very heighth of the small pox and not the least thing to make them comfortable, was almost sufficient to excite the pity of brutes. . . .

Sunday 2d. June: This morning a little after the first dawnings of the day Gen. Thomas expired; this was the 13th day after the eruption first appeared.

> Thomas is dead, that pious man,
> Where all our hopes were laid.
> Had it been one, now in command,
> My heart should not be grieved. . . .

Tuesday 4th: One of our regiment died this morning very suddenly, and was intered in the afternoon without so much as a coffin and with little or no ceremony. Among hundreds of men it was difficult to procure 8 or 10 to bear the corps about 15 rods. Death is a subject not to be attended to by soldiers; Hell and Damnation is in allmost every ones mouth from the time they awake till they fall asleep again; the stupidity of mankind in this situation is beyond all description. This day Majr. Brewer, Majr. Thomas and Majr. Sedgwick left this place for New England.

Wednesday 5th: For 10 days past I have been greatly troubled with the dysentery, and for three days it has been very severe. Took physic in the morning. Hope for some relief. In the afternoon went across the river to visit Col. Reed who I found to have the disorder very light. The number of sick with the pekot on this side is about 300, the greater part of which have it by innoculation and like to do well. I accidentally met, near night, a little, great, proud, self-conceited, foppish quack; the coxcomb appeared very haughty and insolent, but after some time in a stiff, starched and a most exalted manner says, "How do you do, Mr. Beebe." After a few complements had passed between us, I asked if he could let me have a little physic; says he, "I have plenty of physic but God damn my soul if I let you have an atom!" Here our conversation ended. . . .

Friday 7: Last evening one died of the small pox, and early this morning one of the colic; at 10 A.M. one of the nervous fever. Here in the hospital is to be seen at the same time some dead, some dying, others at the point of death, some whistling, some singing and many cursing and swearing. This is a strange composition and its chief intention has not as yet been discovered; however it appears very plain that it is wonderfully calculated for a campaign, and, if applied properly and in time, is very efficatious to prevent anything that is serious or concerning futurity. Visited many of the sick in the hospital —was moved with a compassionate feeling for poor distressed soldiers, [who,] when they are taken sick, are thrown into this dirty, stinking place and left to take care of themselves. No attendance, no provision made, but what must be loathed and abhorred by all both well and sick. . . .

Monday 10th: This day died two in Colo. Pattersons regiment with the small pox. No intelligence of importance comes to hand this day, except orders, from the great Mr. Brigadier Gen. Arnold, for Colo. Poor with his regiment to proceed to Sorrell immediately. Is not this a politick plan, especially since there is not ten men in the regiment but what has either now got the small pox or taken the infection? Some men love to command, however ridiculous their orders may appear. But I am apt to think we shall remain in this garrison for the present. It is enough to confuse and distract a rational man to be surgeon to a regiment. Nothing to be heard from morning to night but "Doctor! Doctor! Doctor!" from every side till one is deaf, dumb and blind, and almost dead; add to all this, we have nothing to eat; thus poor soldiers live sometimes better, but never worse. . . .

Thursday 13th: Arose this morning at the revilee beat, put on my morning dress, walked abroad and found the camp in a most profound silence, the whole being buried in sleep, but it was not long before the whole camp echoed with execrations upon the musketoes; was not a little pleased to hear the characters of particular persons handled in the most familiar manner, and thought many observations which were made upon particular persons were very pertinent and just. Extracted one tooth a little after sunrise, which caused one hearty "O! Dear." About 10 A.M. extracted another tooth. Bought a fowl and some fresh butter, with which we had a very good dinner. The great Gen. Arnold arrived here yesterday and began to give his inconsistent orders today for his great pity and concern for the sick; in the first place gave particular orders that every sick man, together with everyone returned not fit for duty, should draw but half allowance. In this order is discovered that superior wisdom which is necessary for a man in his exalted station in life to be possessed of. . . .

Monday 17: This morning had Colo. Poors orders to repair to Isle aux Naux to take care of the sick there; accordingly sailed in a batteau, and arrived there about 3 P.M. Was struck with amazement upon my arrival to see the vast crowds of poor distressed creatures. Language cannot describe nor imagination paint the scenes of misery and distress the soldiery endure. Scarcely a tent upon this isle but what contains one or more in distress and continually groaning and calling for relief, but in vain! Requests of this nature are as little regarded as the singing of crickets in a summers evening. The most shocking of all spectacles was to see a large barn crowded full of men with this disorder, many of which could not see, speak or walk. One—nay two —had large maggots, an inch long, crawl out of their ears, were on almost every part of the body. No mortal will ever believe what these suffered unless they were eye witnesses. Fuller appeared to be near his end. Gen. Sullivan set fire to all the armed vessels, 3 gundalows and fort at Chambly, and at evening came all his army, with all the stores and baggage, to St. Johns. . . .

Wednesday 26: The regiment is in a most deplorable situation, between 4 and 500 now in the height of the small pox. Death is now become a daily visitant in the camps, but as little regarded as the singing of birds. It appears, and really is so, that one great lesson to be learnt from Death is wholly forgot: (viz) that therein we discover our own picture; we have here pointed out our own mortality in the most lively colours. Strange that the frequent instances of so solemn a scene as this should have such an effect that it should harden, and render us stupid, and make us wholly insensible of the great importance of so serious a matter, but herein is discovered the amazing blindness and stupidity which naturally possess our minds. 40 to 50 batteaus sailed this morning for Isle aux Naux, to bring the remainder of the army; having a fair wind they cut a pretty figure. This day had intelligence that the Congress had agreed to raise an army of 72 thousand men for the year 1777. Visited many of the sick, see many curious cases, find in general that I can effect greater cures by words than by medicine.

Thursday 27: Buried two of our regiment this day. The hot weather proves very unfriendly to those who have the small pox. A large schooner arrived from Isle aux Naux, deeply loaded with stores. One thing, by the way, is somewhat remarkable, that a regiment so distressed with sickness as ours is should be so engaged in fatigue and doing duty that they can by no means find time to attend prayers night and morning or even preaching upon the Sabbath; the regiments are generally supplied with chaplains, who are as destitute of employ in their way as a parson who is dismissed from his people for the most scandalous of crimes. . . .

Saturday 29th: Buried 4 this day, 3 belonging to our regiment on the other side; they generally lose more than double to what we do here. Alas! What will become of our distressed army? Death reigns triumphant. God seems to be greatly angry with us; He appears to be incensed against us for our abominable wickedness—and in all probability will sweep away a great part of our army to destruction.

'Tis enough to make humane nature shudder only to hear the army in general blaspheme the holy name of God. This sin alone is sufficient to draw down the vengeance of an angry God upon a guilty and wicked army. But what is still melancholy, and to be greatly lamented is, amidst all the tokens of Gods holy displeasure, we remain insensible of our danger, and grow harder and harder in wickedness, and are ripening fast for utter destruction.

Sunday 30: I hardly know what to say. I have visited many of the sick. We have a great variety of sore arms and abscesses forming in all parts of the body, proceeding from the small pox, occasioned by the want of physic to cleanse the patients from the disorder. However we had none so bad as yet but what we have been able to cure, except the disorder otherwise was too obstinate. Buried two today. No preaching or praying as usual. The small pox rather abates in the regiments. A number are employed the other side almost the whole of the day to dig graves and bury the dead. . . .

Wednesday 3d. [*July, 1776*]: Had prayer last evening and this morning; hope the regiment will take a new turn of mind and for the future give steady attendance. Buried 3 this day. How strange it is that we have death sent into our camp so repeatedly, every day! And we take so little notice of it! Nay, it will not prevent cursing and swearing in the same tent with the corps. Several were confined the other side for quarreling; some of their party came to relieve them, which they effected by pulling down the guard house; upon which Gen. Sullivan paraded the whole army. Confined a number of offenders under a guard of every 4th man in the regiment. A special court is ordered to sit to-morrow. Since I have been writing, one more of our men has made his exit. Death visits us every hour. . . .

Friday 12: Felt some better as to my health. Walked to visit some of the sick in the neighborhood. Dined at Colo. Strongs with Colo. Gilman and others. Returned soon to camp. Notwithstanding the regiment as a body are on the gaining hand, yet found 6 or 8 in the most deplorable situation that ever mortals were in; it is in vain to pretend to give any just description of their unhappy circumstances, as language cannot describe, nor imagination paint, their distresses. It is impossible for [a] person that has any feeling for humane nature to enter their tents without droping a tear of pity over them.

Saturday 13: Buried 3 yesterday and 2 today—a number more lay at the point of death. Last evening heard of the death of Colo. Williams. He left this place about 10 days past for Ruport, to regain his health, being much troubled with the dysentery. He arrived at Skenesboro and grew so ill that he was unable to proceed any further, and there died July 10th, 1776, half after one in mane [morning?]. General orders for all the sick to be removed to-morrow morning to Ticonderoga. . . .

Friday 19: Last evening we had one of the most severe showers of rain ever known; it continued almost the whole night, with unremitted violence; many of their tents were ancle deep in water. Many of the sick lay their whole lengths in the water, with one blankett only to cover them. One man having the small pox bad, and unable to help himself, and being in a tent alone, which was on ground descending, the current of water came thro his tent in such plenty that it covered his head, by which means he drowned. This is the care that officers take of their sick. Such attention is paid to the distrest, who are destitute of friends. Buried two yesterday, and two more today. Cursing and damning to be heard, and idleness to be seen throughout the army as usual. . . .

Tuesday October 1st: After breakfast and waiting upon the hospital as usual, crossed to head quarters, took a view of the gundolas and rowgallies, two of which were just going to sail, in order to join the fleet; in which goes Gen. Waterbury. In the afternoon it made my heart ache to visit the hospital, to see the dysentery rage with unabated fury among many of them when I had not one article calculated for their assistance; one with this disorder, and two with the scurvey, were on the brink of the grave. Doctor Mingo is much as was a few days past, his disorder rather abates. Mr. Coxcomb is a little poorly. I almost wish sometimes that he was a good deal so, but this I know does not discover a good disposition. . . .

—BEEBE, "Journal," *Penn. Mag. of Hist. and Biog.*, LIX, 328-350.

III. THE BREAKDOWN OF HOSPITAL SERVICES

In time Congress was to establish a series of hospitals—some on paper, and some real—but at first the regional directors had to improvise hospitals as best they could. For the first few years of the war these hospitals were notoriously lacking in the most elementary necessities. Sometimes they were without heat; sometimes without food; sometimes without bedding for the sick. There were never enough doctors or nurses or orderlies, and rarely enough medicines and bandages. Eventually the French made good American deficiencies, but to the end of the war the hospitals were a cause for discontentment. The conditions described here cannot, therefore, be blamed on the doctors in charge of the medical services of the Northern Department. Actually both Dr. Stringer and Dr. Potts were professionally competent, and both were honest and well intentioned. But they had placed on them an intolerable burden of tending to the victims of the unfortunate Canadian campaign, and, a little later, of the Long Island and New York campaign. Dr. Stringer was dismissed along with Dr. Morgan; Potts succeeded him and managed the Department until after Saratoga.

1. DR. STRINGER FAILS THE NORTHERN ARMY

A. "IN THE NAME OF GOD WHAT SHALL WE DO WITH THE SICK?"

Samuel Stringer to Horatio Gates.

Fort George, July 24, 1776

Sir: . . . On my return yesterday evening I found Major Stewart's letter on the 18th, also one from Colonel Trumbull of the same date, requesting a return of the sick, etc., who I find are greatly increased, insomuch that we are in the utmost distress for both assistants and medicines. . . .

At the same time that I wrote to General Washington, I requested an augmentation of the hospital surgeons and mates, and sent a list for such a supply of medicines as I thought necessary for the campaign; and, from a letter I received from Mr. Giles, Apothecary-General, before I departed, I expected the medicines to be forwarded immediately; but, to my great mortification, except a few that Dr. Potts brought with him, none are arrived, not even a quantity that the doctor informed me were to come from Philadelphia, under the care of Mr. McHenry. What we are to do, under these shocking circumstances, I know not; I say shocking, because nothing can appear more so than our present situation—men dying for want of assistance that we are not empowered to give. Besides a want of surgeons, I am not furnished with clerks or stewards; one clerk, that I took upon myself to appoint, with General Schuyler's concurrence, is not now capable of going through the business he is obliged to take charge of. As our men's lives are thus wasted, would it be improper (as writing answers no end) that I should leave the care of the sick to Dr. Potts, and go to York myself, and see the medicines forthwith forwarded by land, until they can be safely conveyed by water, and from thence wait on Congress in person, lay our situation before them, and endeavour to have my powers enlarged, or at least get their consent to provide the number of assistants that are requisite? If, sir, you should approve of such a step, I should be much obliged to you for a letter enforcing the necessity of the application. I should not, at this time of distress, hesitate to engage surgeons, had not General Schuyler received an answer in the winter to the purport of my letter above mentioned, which was contained in a fresh resolve, "that the resolve (now enclosed) was sufficient." . . .

Dr. Potts informed me that there were twenty half-chests of medicines, already put up at York, to be sent off by the first sloop, for ten battalions in this department. I made at Albany the strictest inquiry about them, and find they are not come. Whence such a dilatoriness arises, I cannot account; but there certainly is a remissness somewhere that ought to be removed, if possible.

Just now Lieutenant Diffendorff arrived, and acquaints us that a large number of sick are coming, in addition to what we already have (about fifteen hundred). In the name of *God*, what shall we do with them all, my dear General?

             —FORCE, *American Archives*, 5th Series, I, 651-652.

     B. "NONE OF THE TEN CHESTS OF MEDICINE HAS EVER BEEN RECEIVED"

Horatio Gates to Egbert Benson.

                      Tyconderoga, August 22, 1776

Dear Sir: The 29th ultimo I granted Doctor Stringer, at his earnest request, a permission to go to New York with all expedition, to procure medicines for the General Hospital and Army in this department. He made me a solemn promise he would not delay an instant in returning to his duty with the medicinal stores so much wanted, and which the troops here are almost ready to mutiny to obtain. I am this day informed that Doctor Stringer, instead of fulfilling his promises and returning with all imaginable despatch to his duty, is gone a preferment hunting to the Congress at Philadelphia, while the troops here are suffering inexpressible distress for want of medicines.

I entreat, sir, you will instantly lay this letter before General Washington, and receive his commands for sending a supply of medicines to Doctor Potts at Lake George. Not one of the ten chests of medicines, which you told me at New York were sent to the ten regiments that marched in the spring from thence, have ever been received by either of those regiments; therefore be sure you send the supply now demanded by some person whose particular duty it will be to see it delivered to Doctor Potts. Many of the regimental surgeons here have not any medicines, nor do I believe there is a pound of bark in the whole camp.

I cannot be long answerable for the consequences of the shameful neglect of the Army in this department. The United States expect the same good service from their troops here as everywhere else. This they cannot have unless they command the same attention to be paid the health of their soldiers here as elsewhere.

—FORCE, *American Archives*, 5th Series, I, 1114.

2. "THE SITUATION OF THE SICK IS NOT TO BE DESCRIBED"

Dr. Jonathan Potts to Dr. John Morgan.

Fort George, August 10, 1776

... The distressed situation of the sick here is not to be described: without clothing, without bedding or a shelter sufficient to screen them from the weather.

I am sure your known humanity will be affected when I tell you we have at present upwards of one thousand sick crowded into sheds and laboring under the various and cruel disorders of dysenteries, bilious putrid fevers and the effects of a confluent smallpox; to attend this large number we have four seniors and four mates, exclusive of myself, and our little shop does not afford a grain of jalap, ipecac, bark, salt, opium and sundry other capital articles and nothing of the kind to be had in this quarter; in this dilemma our inventions are exhausted for substitutes, but we shall go on doing the best we can in hopes of speedy supply. . . .

—GIBSON, *Dr. Otto and the Medical Background of the Revolution*, p. 107.

3. "IT WOULD MELT A HEART OF STONE TO HEAR THE MOANS"

Samuel Wigglesworth to the New Hampshire Committee of Safety.

Mount Independence, opposite Ticonderoga, September 27, 1776

Gentlemen: When I waited upon you to receive a commission for Doctor Mooers, if I am not mistaken Colonel Thornton informed me that there would be a supply of medicines proper for the campaign without fail. In hopes that it would be so I appeased the troops at Number-Four, but alas! how have we found ourselves mistaken. Gentlemen, I wish you could transport yourselves to this place for a moment, to see the distressed situation of these troops, and no medicines. Near half of this regiment is entirely incapable of any service, some dying almost every day. Colonel Wymans regiment in the same unhappy situation. There are no medicines of any avail in the Continental chest; such as are there are in their native state, unprepared; no emetic nor cathartic; no mercurial or antimonial remedy; no opiate or elixir tincture, nor even any capital medicine. It would make a heart of stone melt to hear the moans and see the distresses of the sick and dying. I scarce pass a tent but I hear men solemnly declaring that they will never engage another campaign without being assured of a better supply of medicines.

The above, gentlemen, is this real state of this army. Now, sirs, think how much more unhappy and distressed the condition of these troops must be, should the enemy attack our lines. Numbers of wounded, which is the never failing consequences of obstinate battles, and nothing suitable wherewith to dress their wounds.

Gentlemen, you will excuse the freedom I have used in transmitting to you the state of this army in the above respect, and thought it my duty to acquaint you therewith.

I am, gentlemen, with great respect, your humble servant,

SAMUEL WIGGLESWORTH

—FORCE, *American Archives*, 5th Series, II, 574.

4. THE HOSPITALS AT TICONDEROGA

Report of the Committee sent to the Northern Department.

November 27, 1776

... Your Committee ... beg leave further to report that they have visited the General Hospital for the Northern Army, situated at Fort George; that there is a range of buildings erected convenient for the purpose, which ... contained about four hundred sick, including those wounded and sent from General Arnold's fleet; that they were sufficiently supplied with fresh mutton and Indian meal, but wanted vegetables; that the Director-General in that department obtained a large supply of medicines, but that the sick suffered much for want of good female nurses and comfortable bedding; many of those poor creatures being obliged to lay upon the bare boards. Your Committee endeavored to secure straw as the best temporary expedient; but they earnestly recommended it to the attention of Congress that a quantity of bedding be speedily furnished. ...

A hospital, in the opinion of your committee, should be continued at Fort George for the reception of persons infected with contagious disorders; but your Committee are clearly of the opinion that the General Hospital for the army stationed at Tyconderoga ought to be erected on the opposite grounds, called Mount Independence, Fort George being at much too great a distance. Your Committee recommended that a quantity of vegetables be sent to Tyconderoga without delay. ... Your Committee cannot omit mentioning, under this head, the complaints which they have received from persons of all ranks, in and out of the army, respecting the neglect and ill-treatment of the sick. It is shocking to the feelings of humanity, as well as ruinous to the publick service, that so deadly an evil hath been so long without a remedy....

—FORCE, *American Archives*, 5th Series, III, 1584.

5. SMALLWOOD COMPLAINS OF THE INHUMAN NEGLECT OF THE SICK

Colonel William Smallwood to the Maryland Council of Safety.

Philips's Heights, [New York,] October, 1776

... We want medicine much; none can be had here. Our sick have and are now suffering extremely. The number you'll observe from the list is very considerable, owing in a great measure to the bad provision made for and care taken of them, the men being often moved, and have been exposed to lie on the cold ground ever since they came here; often lying without their tents for several nights, as is now the case, having been five nights and days without them, being ever since the enemy landed up here. . . .

Our next greatest suffering proceeds from the great neglect of the sick; and his [Washington's] orders . . . are most salutary, were they to be duly attended to; but here, too, there is not only a shameful but even an inhuman neglect daily exhibited. The Directors of the General Hospitals supply and provide for the sick, who are extremely remiss and inattentive to the well-being and comfort of these unhappy men; out of this train they cannot be taken. I have withdrawn all mine long ago, and had them placed in a comfortable house in the country, and supplied with only the common rations; even this is preferable to the fare of a General Hospital. Two of these Regimental Hospitals, after I have had them put in order, one has been taken away by the Directors for a General Hospital, and my people turned out of doors, and the other would have been taken in the same manner, had I not have applied to General Washington, who told me to keep it. The misfortune is that every supply to the Regimental Hospital of necessaries suitable for the sick must come from an order from these Directors, and is very seldom obtained. I have more than once applied that my Quartermaster might furnish and make a charge for what was supplied, by which means I could have rendered the situation of the sick much more comfortable, at a less expense, but could not be allowed. I wish this could be obtained.

I foresee the evils arising from the shameful neglect in this department. One good-seasoned and well-trained soldier, recovered to health, is worth a dozen new recruits, and is often easier recovered than to get a recruit, exclusive of which this neglect is very discouraging to the soldiery and must injure the service upon the new inlistments after the troops go into winter quarters.
—FORCE, *American Archives*, 5th Series, II, 1099-1100.

6. DR. MORGAN REFUSES MEDICINES TO THE MARYLAND TROOPS

John Pine to James Tighlman, Esq.

Camp at White-Plains, November 7th, 1776

Dear Sir: I arrived here on Monday, the 28th of last month, about four in the afternoon, while our people were engaged in a very hot battle, the particulars of which I suppose you'll hear before this comes to hand. Colonel Smallwood's battalion suffered a good deal; the Colonel himself wounded in two places; the number of killed and wounded, as the report is in the camp, amounts only to about ninety, but from the wounded I saw myself in the hospital and adjacent houses, there must at least be an hundred and twenty or thirty wounded; the number of killed I don't know.

The day after I came here I waited on Doctor Morgan, Director-General of the hospitals here, for medicines, etc. He told me he had nothing to say to the Maryland troops, and that it was not his business to supply the regimental surgeons with medicines, and that it must have been a mistake of the Convention or Council of Safety of Maryland to send their surgeons here without them and think they were to be supplied here. Upon this, I went to Colonel Smallwood, who is about fifteen miles from this, near the hospital, and told him the case, and what condition I found the sick in, both the Regular and Flying-Camp, Maryland troops, without the least morsel of physick of any sort, although a great many of them in a very pitiable condition, upon which the Colonel gave me a letter to Doctor Morgan. The doctor then told me I might have some few things if I could go to New York for them, which is about eighty miles from this. I told him by the time I went there and got back, that the time of most of the Maryland troops would be expired. He told me he could not help it, and that medicines were very hard to be got.

I should be glad this matter was communicated to the Council of Safety. Since I came here I have been of what service I could to the Maryland troops; all their surgeons are over in the Jerseys with their sick, and a great number are still sick here.

—FORCE, *American Archives*, 5th Series, III, 836-837.

7. "OUR HOSPITAL BEGGARS DESCRIPTION AND SHOCKS HUMANITY"

Anthony Wayne to Horatio Gates.

Ticonderoga, 1 December, 1776

I must take the liberty to remind you that the term for which the Pennsylvanians are engaged expires the 5th of next month; no time is therefore to be lost in relieving them. We shall be hard set to get the sick away; our hospital, or rather house of carnage, beggars all description, and shocks humanity to visit. The cause is obvious: no medicine or regimen on the ground suitable for the sick; no beds or straw to lay on; no covering to keep them warm, other than their own thin wretched clothing. We can't send them to Fort George as usual, the hospital being removed from thence to Albany, and the weather is so intensely cold that before they would reach there they would perish. It lays much in your power, by a proper representation to Congress, to have these defects supplied, and many other abuses redressed that tend to render the service almost intolerable to men and officers. But as you are a much better judge of those matters than me, I shall say no more on the subject.

—FORCE, *American Archives*, 5th Series, III, 1031.

8. "THEY WENT, AND FOUND NO HOSPITAL"

Court-Martial of Caleb Green.

Tavern near Peekskill, 25 December, 1776

Caleb Green, a soldier in Colonel Thomas's regiment and my company, confined for desertion: Samuel Townsend, Captain, to the officer of the main guard. Peekskill, 9th December, 1776.

The prisoner to the crime pleads not guilty.

Abraham Egburt, on oath, testifies that himself and the prisoner had liberty to go to the hospital, to recover their health. They went, and found no doctor, nor any body to assist them; from the hospital the prisoner went to his own home, about two miles, and that he has not seen him since, till he returned to his own company, the 8th of December.

William Brown, on oath, testifies that he was sent to order the prisoner to camp, but on being informed by his neighbours that he was unable to go to camp, never went to him. I was sent to him a second time, about the beginning of this month. I forwarded the order by the prisoner's brother, and the prisoner made no delay in coming.

Nathan Merrit testifies that he agrees with William Brown, and further saith that about the 25th of last November he was at the prisoner's house, and that he appeared very unwell.

Daniel Lewis, on oath, agrees with Nathan Merrit respecting the prisoner's health.

The Court, having heard the evidence offered, do unanimously adjudge the prisoner not guilty of the crime laid to his charge.

SAM'L WYLLYS, *President*

W. HEATH. I do hereby approve the sentence.

—FORCE, *American Archives*, 5th Series, III, 1421.

IV. DR. SHIPPEN AND DR. RUSH TRY TO BRING ORDER OUT OF CHAOS

In October 1776 Dr. Shippen was promoted to the post of Director-General of the hospitals west of the Hudson. Shocked by the conditions that he discovered, he promptly wrote his friend, R. H. Lee, a proposal for the reorganization of the medical services; this proposal contained, implicitly, criticism of his superior, Dr. Morgan. The following spring Shippen submitted to the Congress a formal plan for a general reorganization of the medical services of the Army; Congress adopted the plan and appointed its author to be Director-General of all the hospitals.

Meantime a new star was rising on the medical horizon. Benjamin Rush was younger than Dr. Morgan or Dr. Shippen, but did not suffer his youthfulness to embarrass him. Professor of Chemistry at the College of Philadelphia, he counted medicine merely one of his many interests. He was a leader in the Patriot cause; as we have seen, he sponsored Thomas Paine and limned the Founding Fathers; he signed the Declaration of Independence; he wrote antislavery pamphlets; he championed popular education, and even education for girls; he tried a variety of religious faiths; he was, in short, a universal genius. He was, in addition, ambitious and vindictive. In April 1777 he was appointed Surgeon General of the armies of the Middle Department, and signalized his appointment by producing an eminently sensible manual for preserving the health of soldiers. No less disturbed by incompetence than Shippen had been, he now blamed Shippen for the distressing condition of army medical services, and lodged a formal complaint against his superior. Congress investigated, sustained Dr. Shippen, and Rush resigned, returning to teaching, private practice and politics.

We give here extracts from some of the many letters of accusation and complaint—letters which, for all their querulousness and partisanship, provide us with authentic information.

1. Dr. Shippen Proposes a Plan of Reorganization

Dr. William Shippen, Jr., to Richard Henry Lee.

Bethlehem, Tuesday, December 17, 1776

From a tedious experience I have learned what is necessary in a military hospital, and I think it my duty to give my opinion thereon to my friends in Congress. I have attended to this matter more carefully, because I saw on my first entering the Army that many more brave Americans fell a sacrifice to neglect and iniquity in the medical department than fell by the sword of the enemy. I saw Directors, but no direction; physicians and surgeons, but too much about their business, and the care of the sick committed to young boys in the character of mates, quite ignorant, and, as I am informed, hired at half price, etc., etc., etc. Some I found honestly doing the duty of their stations.

How far my own department has been better filled does not become me to say, and I am not ashamed to own that I am conscious of many imperfections, but flatter myself that none of them have arisen from want of care and integrity in the Director, or skill and industry in his physicians, surgeons and mates; all the latter, he can with pleasure declare, have done more than their duty cheerfully. Some have arisen from my inexperience, some from the scarcity of many articles necessary for the sick, and some from the distracted, flying state of the army. All these causes, I persuade myself, will in a great measure be removed in the next campaign, if our cruel enemies risk another.

I would humbly propose the following arrangements as necessary and, I hope, adequate to making the sick soldiery comfortable and happy: Suppose three armies, a Northern, Middle and Southern; to each of these the following officers:

   1 Director and Surgeon General
   3 Sub or Assistant Directors
  10 Surgeons or Physicians
  20 Mates
   1 Apothecary General
   4 Mates
   1 to act as Quartermaster General
      and Commissary General
   3 Deputies, or one to every hundred sick
   1 Steward to every hundred sick
   1 Matron to . . . ditto . . .
   1 Ward-Master to ditto . . .
   1 Nurse to every fifteen sick,
   1 to act as Secretary and Storekeeper
      to every hospital

The Directors-General and Sub-Directors to be chosen by the Congress; the Physicians and Surgeons, after a strict examination; all other officers by the Directors.

Not less than this, in my opinion, will induce men properly qualified to engage; and any others will be dear at any price.

—Force, *American Archives*, 5th Series, III, 1259.

2. Dr. Rush Contrasts British and American Establishments

A. benjamin rush to john adams

Trenton, October 1st, 1777

Dear Sir:

They [the British] pay a supreme regard to the cleanliness and health of their men. After the battle on the 11th of last month, the soldiers were strictly forbidden to touch any of the blankets belonging to the dead or wounded of our army lest they should contract the "rebel distempers." One of their officers, a subaltern, observed to me that his soldiers were infants that required constant attendance, and said as a proof of it that although they had blankets tied to their backs, yet such was their laziness that they would sleep in the dew and cold without them rather than have the trouble of untying and opening them. He said his business every night before he slept was to see that no soldier in his company laid down without a blanket.

Great pains were taken to procure vegetables for the army, and I observed everywhere a great quantity of them about the soldiers' tents. The deputy quartermasters and deputy commissaries in Howe's army are composed chiefly of old and reputable officers, and not of the vagrants and bankrupts of the country.

There is the utmost order and contentment in their hospitals. The wounded whom we brought off from the field were not half so well treated as those whom we left in General Howe's hands. Our officers and soldiers spoke with gratitude and affection of their surgeons. An orderly man was allotted to every ten of our wounded, and British officers called every morning upon our officers to know whether their surgeons did their duty. You must not attribute this to their humanity. They hate us in every shape we appear to them. Their care of our wounded was entirely the effect of the perfection of their medical establishment, which mechanically forced happiness and satisfaction upon our countrymen perhaps without a single wish in the officers of the hospital to make their situation comfortable.

It would take a volume to tell you of the many things I saw and heard which tend to show the extreme regard that our enemies pay to discipline, order, economy and cleanliness among their soldiers.

In my way to this place I passed through General Washington's army. To my great mortification I arrived at the headquarters of a general on an outpost without being challenged by a single sentry. . . . Our hospital opened a continuation of the confused scenes I had beheld in the army. The waste, the peculation, the unnecessary officers, etc. (all the effects of *our* medical establishment), are enough to sink our country without the weights which oppress it from other quarters. It is now universally said that the system was formed for the Director General and not for the benefit of the sick and wounded. Such unlimited powers and no checks would have suited an angel. The sick suffer, but no redress can be had for them. Upwards of 100 of them were drunk last night. We have no guards to prevent this evil. In Howe's army a captain's guard mounts over every 200 sick. Besides keeping their men from contracting and prolonging distempers by rambling, drinking, and whoring, guards keep up at all times in the minds of the sick a sense of military sub-ordination. A soldier should never forget for a single hour that he has a master. One month in our hospitals would undo all the discipline of a year, provided our soldiers brought it with them from the army.

I know it is common to blame our subalterns for all these vices. But we must investigate their source in the higher departments of the army. . . .

The present management of our army would depopulate America if men grew among us as speedily and spontaneously as blades of grass. The "wealth of worlds" could not support the expense of the medical department alone above two or three years. . . .

B. BENJAMIN RUSH TO JOHN ADAMS

Reading, October 21, 1777

My dear Friend:

. . . Our hospital affairs grow worse and worse. There are several hundred wounded soldiers in this place who would have perished had they not been supported by the voluntary and benevolent contributions of some pious whigs. The fault is both in the establishment and in the Director General. He is both *ignorant* and *negligent* of his duty. There is but *one* right system for a military hospital, and that is the one made use of by the British army. It was once introduced by Dr. Church at Cambridge, and Dr. McKnight informs me that he never has seen order, economy or happiness in a hospital since it was banished by Dr. Morgan and his successor. My heart is almost broken at seeing the distresses of my countrymen without a power to remedy them. Dr. S. never sets his foot in a hospital. Tell me, are there any hopes of our plan being mended? Dr. Brown and every medical officer in the hospital execrate it. If it cannot be altered, and that soon, I shall trouble you with my resignation, and my reasons shall afterwards be given to the public for it. The British system would save half a million a year to the continent, and what is more, would produce perfect satisfaction and happiness.

A surgeon general is wanted in the northern department. Give me leave to recommend Dr. McKnight, a senior surgeon in the flying hospital, for that office. He has skill, industry and humanity, and has served with unequaled reputation since the beginning of the war. . . .

C. BENJAMIN RUSH TO WILLIAM DUER, DELEGATE TO CONGRESS FROM NEW YORK

Princeton, December 8th, 1777

Dear Sir,

I beg leave to trouble you for a few minutes with some remarks upon the medical establishment, which in spite of the munificence and good intentions of the Congress has not produced that happiness which was expected. The reason of it appears from experience to be owing to your having deviated from the plans used in all European armies, and in particular from that most excellent one which is now in use in the British army. It is as follows:

1. There is an inspector general and chief physician, whose only business it is to visit all the hospitals, to examine into the quantity and quality of the medicines, stores, instruments, etc., and to receive and deliver reports of the number of sick and wounded to the commander in chief.

THE REDOUBTABLE JOHN PAUL JONES

Captain Jones shoots a sailor who attempted to strike his colors in an engagement

English mezzotint, 1780

THE ATTACK ON FORT MOULTRIE, JUNE 28, 1776

2. There is a purveyor general, whose business it is to provide hospitals, medicines, stores, beds, blankets, straw, and necessaries of all kinds for the sick and wounded. He is allowed as many deputies as there are hospitals. He has nothing to do with the care of the sick.

3. There are physicians and surgeons general, whose business it is to administer the stores provided by the purveyor general and to direct everything necessary for the recovery, the convenience and happiness of the sick. The purveyor is subject to all their orders, which are always made in writing to serve as vouchers for the expenditures of the purveyor. As an additional check upon the purveyor, none of his accounts are passed until they are certified by the physicians and surgeons general. This renders it impossible to defraud the sick of anything prescribed or purchased for them. The physicians and surgeons general have their deputies under them who are called *seniors* and *mates*.

This is a short account of the outlines of the British system, which is said to be the most perfect in the world. I shall now compare it with the establishment now in use in the American hospitals.

The director general possesses all the powers of the above officers. He is chief physician, inspector general, purveyor or commissary general, physician and surgeon general. All reports come through his hands, by which means the number of sick, wounded and dead may always be proportioned to his expenditures and to his fears of alarming Congress with accounts of the mortality of diseases. He can be present only in one place at a time but is supposed to be acquainted with all the wants of his hospitals. This is impossible. The sick therefore must suffer, for the surgeons of hospitals have no right to *demand* supplies for them, the director general being the only judge of their wants. Lastly, his accounts are *not* certified by the physicians and surgeons general, so that the sick have no security for the stores and medicines intended for them. A director general may sell them to the amount of a million a year without a possibility of being detected by your present establishment. All that the Congress requires of him are receipts for the purchase of the articles intended for the sick.

These ample and *incompatible* powers thus lodged in the hands of *one* man appear to be absurd as if General Washington had been made quartermaster, commissary and adjutant general of your whole army. And your having invested him with a power to direct the physicians and surgeons in anything while he acts as purveyor is as absurd as it would be to give the commissary general a power to command your commander in chief. To do the duty of purveyor general *only*, requires a share of industry and a capacity for business which falls to the lot of few men in the world. What can be expected then from one who, added to that office, is responsible for every life in the army?

D. BENJAMIN RUSH TO WILLIAM DUER

Princeton, December 13, 1777

Dear Sir,

In my letter to you a few days ago I informed you that we had 3000 patients in our hospitals. Since the dating of that letter I have discovered that they now amount to 5000. They consist chiefly of southern army, and amount to near one half of the number of troops which composed that army during the last campaign.

I have heard with great pleasure that you are about to new-model the army. For God's sake, do not forget to take the medical system under your consideration. It is a mass of corruption and tyranny and has wholly disappointed the benevolence and munificence of the Congress. It would take up a volume to unfold all the disorders and miseries of the hospitals. What do you think of 5000 being supported with stores, hospital furniture, etc., sufficient for only 1500 men? What do you think of 600 men in a village without a single officer to mount a guard over them or punish irregularities? This is the case at this time in Princetown, and the consequences are: Old disorders are prolonged, new ones are contracted, the discipline of the soldiers (contracted at camp) is destroyed, the inhabitants are plundered, and the blankets, clothes, shoes, etc., of the soldiers are stolen or exchanged in every tavern and hut for spiritous liquors.

I have witnessed these things for these six months and have complained of them to the Director General, to the Congress, and to the generals of the army to no effect. What do you think of 400 sick being crowded into a house large enough (according to the calculations of Pringle, Monroe and Dr. Jones, who have all written upon military hospitals) for only 150? This has been done in one place, and the consequences of it was a putrid fever was generated which carried off 12 soldiers in three days (who all came into the hospital with other diseases) and many more in the space of two weeks. Upon my complaining to the Director General that he had crowded too many sick into one house, he told me "he was the *only* judge of that, and that my *only* business was to take care of all he sent there." Your system justified his making me this answer, although it does not oblige him ever to go *inside* of a hospital or to expose himself to the least danger of being infected by a fever. Six surgeons have died since last spring of fevers contracted in our hospitals, and there is scarcely one who has not been ill in a greater or lesser degree with it.

Nothing like this has happened in the northern department. The reasons of which are these. Dr. Potts has confined himself *solely* to the purveying business, and Dr. Treat, who served as a surgeon in the British hospitals last war, has introduced the British system in its *most minute parts* into the hospitals under his direction.

I wish some members of Congress (not related to Dr. S——n) would visit our hospitals and converse with the principal surgeons in them. Although Dr. S——n has taken great pains to extort the power of appointing them out of the physician and surgeon generals' hands, and has made some of them dependent upon his will, yet I believe you will not find more than *one* man among them who does not reprobate our system and who will not ring peals of distress and villainy in your ears much louder than anything you have heard from me.

I bequeath you these broken hints as a legacy, being determined, as soon as I can with honor and a clear conscience leave my present charge, to send you my commission. I beg leave to repeat my solicitation in favor of Dr.

Jones (of New York) being appointed *inspector general* of your hospitals. He will save you millions of dollars, and what are more estimable, thousands of lives in a year. I would rather serve as a mate in a hospital under him with the British system than share with the present Director General in all his power and glory. . . .

—BUTTERFIELD, ed., *Letters of Benjamin Rush*, I, 154-176 *passim*.

V. THE IMPACT OF THE WAR ON MEDICINE

War tends to specialize and restrict science, but does provide doctors with clinical facilities in a highly concentrated form, and some opportunity for medical experimentation. The American Revolution stimulated both thinking and writing in the field of medicine. At its outset Dr. John Jones of New York published a useful volume on the treatment of wounds and fractures; the Baron Van Swieten's The Diseases Incident to Armies *was published in Philadelphia; a Dr. William Brown of Virginia published a pharmacopoeia; and the chief physician for Rochambeau's army, Jean Coste, brought out a pharmacopoeia for the use of the French hospitals; Dr. Morgan wrote on inoculation against the smallpox and so did Benjamin Rush; and a Dr. Barnabas Binney studied a "Remarkable Case of a Gun-Shot Wound"—the remarkable thing being that the patient recovered.*

We give here four examples of the impact of war on medical thought and practice. The first is by Dr. Ebenezer Beardsley, who thought he found the cause, if not the cure, for dysentery, and submitted his findings (after the war) to the newly organized American Academy of Arts and Sciences. The second is from the indefatigable pen of Dr. Rush: Directions for Preserving the Health of Soldiers; *it has some claim to being considered the most important of his medical writings. Third are two brief extracts from Dr. James Thacher's often disappointing* Journal of the American Revolution: *an account of Saratoga as a clinical laboratory, and a description of wholesale inoculation against the dread smallpox. And last a letter to the Earl of Sandwich, First Lord of the Admiralty, tells us some of the measures taken in the British Navy to overcome scurvy.*

1. AN AMERICAN DOCTOR TRIES TO FIND THE CAUSE OF DYSENTERY

[1783]

By Dr. Ebenezer Beardsley.

About the beginning of April 1776, the American army, under the command of his Excellency General Washington, marched from Boston for New York, at which place they arrived near the middle of the month. The sick and invalids having been left behind, the whole army were in perfect health. They took up their quarters in the barracks and houses of the citizens till about the first of May, when they all went into tents, except the 22nd Regiment, under the command of Colonel William Wyllys, who for want of tents continued in their quarters in Smith Street. This regiment was very healthy until about the middle of the month, when upwards of one hundred of the men were taken down with the dysentery in the space of one week.

Such a sudden invasion of this formidable disease alarmed me greatly. As I found upon inquiry that there was not a single dysenteric patient besides in the whole army, I concluded that the disease arose from some cause peculiar to the city; but after a careful inquiry, I could not find that there was a single inhabitant in the whole city that was sick with the distemper. Those who lived in the same street, and many of them in the same houses with us, were entirely free from this, or indeed any other disease.

For several days I was much perplexed and greatly at a loss as to the cause. At length I observed that not only the citizens with whom we lived were free from the disease, but that some whole companies of the same regiment had nothing of it. This led me to consider more minutely the situation and circumstances of those who were sick; all of whom, I found, lived either in low underground rooms, or else in garrets, so situated as not to admit of a free circulation of air. The rooms were also considerably less in proportion to the number of men than usual. Struck with these discoveries, I concluded at once that the difference arose from a confined stagnant air, deprived by this means of its natural elacticity, and loaded with putrid effluvia from the bodies of the unhappy people who lived in it.

Having communicated my discoveries to the Colonel, I requested that the men (both sick and well) might be removed out of those rooms into such as were more airy and capacious. This measure was attended with the most salutary consequences. Those who were sick recovered in a short time, except one or two that died; and no more being seized with the disease, in a few weeks the regiment became entirely healthy. . . .

The discovery of this singular instance of the pernicious effects of confined stagnant air was of great use to me in the course of the campaign. In the months of July and August, the dysentery, bilious and other fevers of the putrid kind became very rife both in the army and the country. Great pains were taken to procure for our men who were sick with any of those disorders, large rooms, and to have them well ventilated. Yet, under these circumstances, I frequently observed that the sick who lay in and near the corners of the rooms were handled much more severely than those which lay in the middle of them.

—BEARDSLEY, "Effects of Stagnant Air," *Memoirs of
Academy of Arts and Sciences*, I, 542.

2. DR. RUSH INSTRUCTS OFFICERS IN SOLDIERS' HEALTH

To the Officers in the Army of the United American States: Directions for Preserving the Health of Soldiers.

April 22d, 1777

. . . The art of preserving the health of a soldier consists in attending to the following particulars: I. Dress. II. Diet. III. Cleanliness. And IV. Encampments.

I. *The Dress* of a soldier has a great influence upon his health. It is to be lamented that the peculiar situation of our country, from the infancy of our foreign trade and domestic manufactures, has obliged us to clothe our soldiers chiefly in linen. It is a well-known fact that the perspiration of the body, by attaching itself to linen and afterwards by mixing with rain, is disposed to form miasmata which produce fevers. Upon this account I could wish the rifle shirt was banished from our army. Besides accumulating putrid miasmata, it conceals filth and prevents a due regard being paid to cleanliness. The Roman soldiers wore flannel shirts next to their skins. This was one among other causes of the healthiness of the Roman armies. During the last war in America, Gen. (then Col.) Gage obliged the soldiers of his regiment to wear flannel shirts from an accidental want of linen, and it was remarkable during a sickly campaign on the Lakes not a single soldier belonging to the said regiment was ever seen in any of the military hospitals. I have known several instances where the yearly visits of the intermitting fever have stayed in the State of Pennsylvania, in places most subject to the disorder, by nothing else but the use of flannel shirts.

The hair by being long uncombed is apt to accumulate the perspiration of the head, which by becoming putrid sometimes produces diseases. There are two methods of guarding against this evil: the first is by combing and dressing the hair every day; the second is by wearing it thin and short in the neck. The former is attended with delays often incompatible with the duty of a soldier, and therefore the latter is to be preferred to it. This easy mode of wearing the hair is strongly recommended by Count Saxe and by all modern writers on the military art.

II. *The Diet* of soldiers should consist *chiefly* of vegetables. The nature of their duty, as well as their former habits of life, require it. If every tree on the continent of America produced Jesuits bark, it would not be sufficient to preserve or restore the health of soldiers who eat two or three pounds of flesh in a day. Their vegetables should be well cooked. It is of the last consequence that damaged flour should not be used in the camp. It is the seed of many disorders. It is of equal consequence that good flour should not be rendered unwholesome by an error in making it into bread. Perhaps it was the danger to which flour was always exposed of being damaged in a camp, or being rendered unwholesome from the manner of baking it, that led the Roman generals to use wheat instead of flour for the daily food of their soldiers. Caesar fed his troops with wheat only, in his expedition into Gaul. It was prepared by being well boiled, and was eaten with spoons in the room of bread. If a little sugar or molasses is added to wheat prepared in this manner, it forms not only a most wholesome food but a most agreeable repast.

What shall I say to the custom of drinking spirituous liquors which prevails so generally in our army? I am aware of the prejudices in favor of it. It requires an arm more powerful than mine—the arm of a Hercules—to encounter them. The common apology for the use of rum in our army is that it is necessary to guard against the effects of heat and cold. But I maintain that in no case whatever does rum abate the effects of either of them upon the constitution. On the contrary, I believe it always increases them. The temporary elevation of spirits in summer and the temporary generation of warmth in winter produced by rum always leaves the body languid and more liable to be affected with heat and cold afterwards. Happy would it be for our soldiers if the evil ended here! The use of rum, by gradually wearing away the powers of the system, lays the foundation of fevers, fluxes, jaundices, and all the train of diseases which occur in military hospitals. It is a vulgar error to suppose that the fatigue arising from violent exercise or hard labor is relieved by the use of spirituous liquors. The principles of animal life are the same in a horse as in a man, and horses, we find, undergo the severest labor with no other liquor than cool water. There are many instances where even reapers have been forced to acknowledge that plentiful draughts of milk and water have enabled them to go through the fatigues of harvest with more pleasure and fewer inconveniences to their health than ever they experienced from the use of a mixture of rum and water.

Spirituous liquors were unknown to the armies of ancient Rome. The canteen of every soldier was filled with nothing but vinegar, and it was by frequently drinking a small quantity of this wholesome liquor mixed with water that the Roman soldiers were enabled to sustain tedious marches through scorching sands without being subject to sickness of any kind. The vinegar effectually resists that tendency to putrefaction to which heat and labor dispose the fluids. It moreover calms the inordinate action of the solids which is created by hard duty. It would be foreign to my purpose, or I might show that the abstraction of rum from our soldiers would contribute greatly to promote discipline and a faithful discharge of duty among them. Gen. Wolfe, who was a philosopher as well as a general, never suffered a drop of spirits to be drank by his soldiers except when they served as sentries or upon fatigue duty in rainy weather. Perhaps these are the only cases in which a small quantity of rum may be useful. It will be of the most essential service if it be mixed with three or four times its quantity of water.

III. Too much cannot be said in favor of *Cleanliness*. If it were possible to convert every blade of grass on the continent into an American soldier, the want of cleanliness would reduce them in two or three campaigns to a handful of men. It should extend 1. To the *body* of a soldier. He should be obliged to wash his hands and face at least once every day, and his whole body twice or three times a week, especially in summer. The cold bath was part of the military discipline of the Roman soldiers and contributed much to preserve their health. 2. It should extend to the *clothes* of a soldier. Frequent changes of linen are indispensably necessary, and unless a strict regard is paid to this article, all our pains to preserve the health of our soldiers will be to no purpose. 3. It should extend to the *food* of a soldier. Great care should be taken that the vessels in which he cooks his victuals should be carefully washed after each time of their being used.

Too many soldiers should not be allowed on any pretense whatever to crowd into the same tent or quarter. The jail fever is the offspring of the perspiration and respiration of human bodies brought into a compass too narrow to be diluted and rendered inert by a mixture with the atmosphere.

The straw or hay which composes the bed of a soldier should be often changed, and his blanket should be exposed every day to the sun. This will prevent the perspiration from becoming morbid and dangerous by accumulating upon it.

The commanding officer should take the utmost care never to suffer a soldier to sleep or even to sit down in his tent with wet clothes, nor to lie down in a wet blanket or upon damp straw. The utmost vigilance will be necessary to guard against this fruitful source of disorders among soldiers.

The environs of each tent and of the camp in general should be kept perfectly clean of the offals of animals and of filth of all kinds. They should be buried or carefully removed every day beyond the neighborhood of the camp.

IV. The formation of an *Encampment* is of the utmost importance to the health of an army. It is to no purpose to seek for security from an enemy in the wisest disposition of troops in a country where marshes and millponds let loose intermitting fevers upon them. Sometimes it may be necessary to encamp an army upon the side of a river. Previous to this step, it is the duty of the quartermaster to inquire from what quarter the winds come at the season of his encampment. If they pass across the river before they reach his army, they will probably bring with them the seeds of bilious and intermitting fevers, and this will more especially be the case in the fall of the year. The British troops at Pensacola, by shifting their quarters every year so as to avoid the winds that come over a river in the neighborhood of the town at a certain season, have preserved their health in a manner scarcely to be paralleled in so warm a climate.

It is the duty of the commanding officer of a division or detachment of the army to avoid as much as possible exposing his troops to *unnecessary* fatigue or watchfulness. The daily exercises of the manual and maneuvers (which contribute to the health of soldiers), as also all marches, should be performed in the cool of the morning and evening in summer. Sentries should always be provided with watch coats, and they should be *often* relieved in very hot, cold, and rainy weather.

The fire and smoke of wood, as also the burning of sulphur and the explosion of gunpowder, have a singular efficacy in preserving and restoring the purity of the air. There was an instance in the last war between Britain and France of a ship in Sir Edward Hawke's fleet that had above one hundred men on board ill with a putrid fever. This ship was obliged to bear her part in the well-known battle between Sir Edward and Monsieur Conflans. A few days after the engagement, every man on board this ship recovered, and an entire stop was put to the progress of the disorder. This extraordinary event was thought to be occasioned by the explosion and effluvia of the gunpowder.

I shall conclude these directions by suggesting two hints which appear to be worthy of the attention of the gentlemen of the army. Consider in the first place that the principal study of an officer in the time of war should be to save the blood of his men. An heroic exploit is admired most when it has been performed with the loss of a few lives. But if it be meritorious to save the lives of soldiers by skill and attention in the field, why should it be thought less so to preserve them by skill and attention of another kind, in a march or an encampment? And on the contrary, if it be criminal in an officer to sacrifice the lives of thousands by his temerity in a battle, why should it be thought less so to sacrifice twice their number in a hospital by his negligence? Consider in the second place that an attention to the health of your soldiers is absolutely necessary to form a *great* military character.

Had it not been for this eminent quality, Xenophon would never have led ten thousand Greeks for sixteen months through a cold and most inhospitable country, nor would Fabius have kept that army together without it which conquered Hannibal and delivered Rome. . . .

—BUTTERFIELD, ed., *Letters of Benjamin Rush*, I, 141-145.

3. DR. THACHER FINDS SARATOGA A GOOD CLINICAL LABORATORY

October 24th, 1777.—This hospital is now crowded with officers and soldiers from the field of battle; those belonging to the British and Hessian troops are accommodated in the same hospital with our own men, and receive equal care and attention. The foreigners are under the care and management of their own surgeons. I have been present at some of their capital operations, and remarked that the English surgeons perform with skill and dexterity, but the Germans, with a few exceptions, do no credit to their profession; some of them are the most uncouth and clumsy operators I ever witnessed, and appear to be destitute of all sympathy and tenderness towards the suffering patient. Not less than one thousand wounded and sick are now in this city; the Dutch church and several private houses are occupied as hospitals. We have about thirty surgeons and mates; and all are constantly employed. I am obliged to devote the whole of my time, from eight o'clock in the morning to a late hour in the evening, to the care of our patients.

Here is a fine field for professional improvement. Amputating limbs, trepanning fractured skulls, and dressing the most formidable wounds, have familiarized my mind to scenes of woe. A military hospital is peculiarly calculated to afford example for profitable contemplation, and to interest our sympathy and commiseration. If I turn from beholding mutilated bodies, mangled limbs, and bleeding, incurable wounds, a spectacle no less revolting is presented, of miserable objects languishing under afflicting diseases of every description—here, are those in a mournful state of despair, exhibiting the awful harbingers of approaching dissolution—there, are those with emaciated bodies and ghastly visage, who begin to triumph over grim disease and just lift their feeble heads from the pillow of sorrow. . . .

It is my lot to have twenty wounded men committed to my care by Dr. Potts, our surgeon-general; one of whom, a young man, received a musket-ball through his cheeks, cutting its way through the teeth on each side and the substance of the tongue; his sufferings have been great, but he now begins to articulate tolerably well. Another had the whole side of his face torn off by a cannon-ball, laying his mouth and throat open to view. A brave soldier received a musket-ball in his forehead; observing that it did not penetrate deep, it was imagined that the ball rebounded and fell out; but after several days, on examination, I detected the ball laying flat on the bone, and spread under the skin, which I removed. No one can doubt but he received his wound while facing the enemy, and it is fortunate for the brave fellow that his skull proved too thick for the ball to penetrate. But in another instance, a soldier's wound was not so honorable; he received a ball in the bottom of his foot, which could not have happened unless when in the act of running from the enemy. This poor fellow is held in derision by his comrades, and is made a subject of their wit for having the mark of a coward. . . .

—THACHER, *Military Journal*, pp. 112-114.

4. HOW THE ARMY INOCULATED AGAINST SMALLPOX

April 20th (1781). All the soldiers, with the women and children, who have not had the small-pox, are now under inoculation. Of our regiment, one hundred and eighty seven were subjects of the disease. The old practice of previous preparation by a course of mercury and low diet has not been adopted on this occasion; a single dose of jalap and calomel, or the extract of butternut, *juglans cinerea,* is in general administered previous to the appearance of the symptoms. As to diet, we are so unfortunate as to be destitute of the necessary comfortable articles of food, and they subsist principally on their common rations of beef, bread, and salt pork. A small quantity of rice, sugar or molasses, and tea, are procured for those who are dangerously sick. Some instances have occurred of putrid fever supervening, either at the first onset or at the approach of the secondary stage, and a few cases have terminated fatally.

Many of our patients were improper subjects for the disease, but we were under the necessity of inoculating all, without exception, whatever might be their condition as to health. Of five hundred who have been inoculated, four only have died, but in other instances the proportion of deaths is much more considerable.

The extract of butternut is made by boiling down the inner bark of the tree; the discovery of this article is highly important, and it may be considered as a valuable acquisition to our materia medica. The country people have for some time been in the practice of using it, and Dr. Rush . . . has recommended the employment of it among our patients, as a mild yet sufficiently active cathartic, and a valuable and economical substitute for jalap. It operates without creating heat or irritation, and is found to be efficacious in cases of dysentery and bilious complaints. As the butternut tree abounds in our country, we may obtain at a very little expense a valuable domestic article of medicine. . . .

—THACHER, *Military Journal*, pp. 257-258.

5. A NAVAL SURGEON PRESCRIBES CITRUS FRUITS FOR SCURVY

Mr. Northcote, Surgeon, to the Earl of Sandwich.

Prudent, Sandy Hook, New York, August 19, 1781

I should not presume to address your Lordship was I not persuaded that whatever contributes to promote the health and happiness of so valuable a life as that of a British sailor cannot fail of meeting your Lordship's most gracious acceptance, which I flatter myself will in some measure apologize for the liberty I have taken, and that the justness of my intentions will excuse the freedom.

As the scurvy, my Lord, is the most prevalent and most destructive disease incident to seamen, and lemon and orange juice the grand specific in that most terrible malady, I humbly beg leave to recommend it to your Lordship's consideration whether it would not be of infinite more service to the Navy if the surgeons of his Majesty's ships were to be largely supplied with those most salutary vegetable acids instead of the present mineral acid (elixir of vitriol), which is of little or no use.

Two thirds of our seamen die of the scurvy and other diseases which take their rise from putrefaction, and for which the Peruvian bark, lemon and orange juice are the great and peculiar antiseptics. Therefore, if our seamen could be preserved free from those diseases, they would seldom be endangered by any other.

I beg to recall to your Lordship's memory that, by the returns made to the House of Commons in December 1760, out of 185,000 men raised for the sea service during the last war, above 130,000 died by diseases, and two thirds of those of the putrid kind.

If the seizures of tobacco (instead of being burnt) were always sent to the dockyards to supply the ships destined for foreign service, it would be of infinite service to fumigate the ships frequently therewith, whenever there was a contagious disorder on board, and this without any additional expense to the Government.

The vinegar supplied the Navy at present is good for little or nothing; it should always be the strongest that can be procured.

Good, sound, rough cyder would also be of infinite use to scorbutics; and every ship should be supplied with some for their use only. Essence of malt and sour khrout are also of great use. These and many other articles (which would be a means of saving the lives and preserving the health of our seamen, if put in execution), I recommended some years ago in an appendix to the *Marine Practice of Physic and Surgery*, to which I beg leave to refer your Lordship; and as the subject of this letter is a great national concern, I have the vanity to hope that it will not be disregarded.

—Barnes & Owens, eds., *Private Papers of Earl of Sandwich*, IV, 178-179.

6. The Hessian Doctor

In May 1780, Philip Freneau quit the New Jersey militia, where he had served briefly, and shipped on the cargo ship Aurora, *bound for St. Eustatius. On May 25 she was captured by an enemy sloop; Freneau was sentenced to imprisonment on the notorious prison ship* Scorpion *in the Hudson River. Falling ill, he was transferred to the hospital ship* Hunter, *more a charnal house than a prison. We give here some embittered lines on the Hessian doctor whose duty it was to care for the sick.*

> From Brooklyn heights a Hessian doctor came,
> Nor great his skill, nor greater much his fame:
> Fair Science never called the wretch her son,
> And Art disdained the stupid man to own. ....
> He on his charge the healing work begun
> With antinomial mixtures by the tun:
> Ten minutes was the time he deigned to stay,
> The time of grace allotted once a day:

He drenched us well with bitter draughts, 'tis true,
Nostrums from hell, and cortex from Peru:
Some with his pills he sent to Pluto's reign,
And some he blistered with his flies of Spain.
His Tartar doses walked their deadly round,
Till the lean patient at the potion frowned,
And swore that hemlock, death, or what you will,
Were nonsense to the drugs that stuffed his bill.
On those refusing he bestowed a kick,
Or menaced vengeance with his walking stick:
Here uncontrolled he exercised his trade,
And grew experienced by the deaths he made. . . .
Knave though he was, yet candor must confess
Not chief physician was this man of Hesse:
One master o'er the murdering tribe was placed,
By him the rest were honored or disgraced.
Once, and but once, by some strange fortune led,
He came to see the dying and the dead.
He came, but anger so inflamed his eye,
And such a faulchion glittered on his thigh,
And such a gloom his visage darkened o'er,
And two such pistols in his hands he bore,
That, by the gods, with such a load of steel,
We thought he came to murder, not to heal.
Rage in his heart, and mischief in his head,
He gloomed destruction, and had smote us dead
Had he so dared, but fear withheld his hand,
He came, blasphemed, and turned again to land.

—FRENEAU, *Poems,* pp. 48-49.

CHAPTER TWENTY-ONE

Prisons and Escapes

WE HAVE *a great many hardship and atrocity stories from prisoners, both American and British, but few facts and almost no reliable statistics. Just as neither the Americans nor the British were prepared to care for the sick and the wounded, so they were unprepared to care for prisoners; these elementary and familiar accompaniments of war seemed to take both sides by surprise. It cannot be said that either side ever got over its surprise; at the very close of the war both the British Cabinet and the Congress were playing fast and loose with their prisoners. Nor did either army, at any time during the war, make really adequate preparation for the care of prisoners, or for their orderly exchange or release.*

A miasmic air of incompetence, spite and brutality hangs over the whole story of Revolutionary War prisoners. From the beginning to the end of the war there was confusion on both sides about the status of prisoners. Because the British did not at first—or for a long time—concede the de jure *existence of the United States, they adopted the logical but untenable position that American prisoners were not in fact prisoners of war, but traitors in rebellion against their lawful sovereign. The circumstances of war, and the threat of retaliation, persuaded them not to insist on this position, or on its consequences; yet to the very end they refused to concede diplomatic immunity to Henry Laurens, who languished in the Tower until 1782. Americans were almost equally shortsighted toward the Loyalists who had the bad luck to be captured; they insisted that these were not ordinary prisoners, subject to exchange, but criminals who should be turned over to their states for punishment. To make the situation worse, neither side trusted the other. Thus some of the British officers held that they were not, in any event, bound by agreements with rebels, and that they could violate their parole with impunity. The Americans, in turn, dishonored General Gates's agreement with Burgoyne on the disposition of the so-called "Convention" troops.*

We simply do not know how many prisoners were taken by the rival armies, but there is some reason to believe that these numbers may have run about even. The Americans made three major hauls during the war: Trenton, Saratoga and Yorktown. Trenton accounted for 900 or 1,000 prisoners, Saratoga for about 6,000, and Yorktown for perhaps 8,000. The British captured not far from 4,000 in the fighting around New York City, and over 5,000 at Charleston, and British captures of American fishermen and seamen were substantial—over 1,000 of these were still held in English prisons at the close of the war. British and American captures in the hard-fought campaigns in the Carolinas, and along the far-flung frontiers, probably canceled out; in any event the inclination here was not to be bothered with prisoners, but to dispose of them in the speediest and most convenient way.

Neither side had made adequate provision for their prisoners. The Americans were constantly on the move and did not want to carry prisoners with them, and the few cities which they did hold with any degree of assurance were not prepared to take over responsibility for large numbers. The British had a firm base only in New York—or Quebec and Halifax—and did not have facilities there to take care of their large prisoner hauls. The obvious solution was an exchange, but insuperable difficulties obstructed this—not least that the British had more to gain by exchange than the Americans. Another solution was release on parole, but this was complicated by deep-seated mutual distrust. Indeed in a country as large as America, and with armies so unorganized and records so haphazardly kept, there were no satisfactory means of enforcing paroles.

Both sides therefore fell back on hastily improvised prisons: local jails, barracks, warehouses, churches, underground mines, ships—whatever was at hand. Conditions in these were almost always wretched and sometimes, as in the prison ships or the abandoned copper mines, barbarous. But it is sobering to remember that conditions in prisons were just as barbarous eighty years later, at Andersonville, Libby and Elmira. On the whole the lot of the prisoner in the Revolution was almost as desperate as the lot of the wounded; it is estimated that 7,000 Americans perished on the notorious prison ships in the Hudson.

Prison and escape narratives are often exciting individually but they tend to be monotonous collectively, for on horror stories the law of diminishing returns sets in very speedily. One imprisonment, after all, tends to be very much like another, and the bitterness and invective of the imprisoned, too, forms a pattern. We have tried here to present a variety of prison experiences rather than a large number of prison or escape narratives. We give a lively story of imprisonment in Boston during the siege. There are a handful of narratives from New York; a few descriptions of conditions on the terrible prison ships; some glimpses into the experience of the "Convention" troops from Saratoga to Charlottesville; some samples of British and Loyalist prison narratives; Henry Laurens' own story of his sufferings in the Tower; and, at the end, the dramatic story of Captain Asgill which moved two continents to tears.

I. STORMONT REJECTS FRANKLIN'S PLEA FOR MERCY TO PRISONERS

We begin with a document that illuminates the peculiar difficulties of prisoner exchange—the stiff-necked refusal of some British officials and officers to recognize the rebels even for purposes of negotiation: Franklin's proposal to the British Ambassador to France, Lord Stormont, for an exchange of prisoners, and Stormont's fatuous rejection of the overture. Franklin never forgave the British their ungenerous attitude toward American prisoners, and at one time he undertook to prepare a little illustrated book with 35 engravings, "each expressing one or more of the horrid facts to be inserted in the book, in order to impress the minds of children and posterity with a deep sense of your bloody and insatiable malice and wickedness." Perhaps happily for the future of Anglo-American relations no such book was ever published.

Paris, April 2, 1777

MY LORD:—We did ourselves the honor of writing some time ago to your lordship on the subject of exchanging prisoners. You did not condescend to give us any answer, and therefore we expect none to this. We, however, take the liberty of sending you copies of certain depositions, which we shall transmit to Congress, whereby it will be known to your court that the United States are not unacquainted with the barbarous treatment their people receive, when they have the misfortune of being your prisoners here in Europe; and that, if your conduct towards us is not altered, it is not unlikely that severe reprisals may be thought justifiable, from the necessity of putting some check to such abominable practices.

For the sake of humanity, it is to be wished that men would endeavor to alleviate, as much as possible, the unavoidable miseries attending a state of war. It has been said that, among the civilized nations of Europe, the ancient horrors of that state are much diminished; but the compelling men by chains, stripes and famine to fight against their friends and relations is a new mode of barbarity which your nation alone had the honor of inventing; and the sending American prisoners of war to Africa and Asia, remote from all probability of exchange, and where they can scarce hope ever to hear from their families, even if the unwholesomeness of the climate does not put a speedy end to their lives, is a manner of treating captives that you can justify by no other precedent of custom, except that of the black savages of Guinea. We are your lordship's most obedient, humble servants,

B. FRANKLIN, S. DEANE

Paris, 3 April, 1777

MY LORD:—In answer to a letter, which concerns some of the most material interests of humanity, and of the two nations, Great Britain and the United States of America, now at war, we received the enclosed *indecent* paper, as coming from your lordship, which we return for your lordship's most mature consideration.

B. FRANKLIN, S. DEANE

Lord Stormont's letter said:

"The King's Ambassador receives no applications from rebels, unless they come to implore his Majesty's mercy."

—BIGELOW, *Works of Franklin*, VII, 394n-395n.

II. JOHN LEACH AND HIS COMPANIONS SUFFER IN A BOSTON PRISON

The British did not bother to imprison many American civilians during their brief occupation of Boston. One of their victims was the remarkable

John Leach, accused, vaguely, of "being a spy and taking plans." Born in England, Leach had early gone to sea, and had circumnavigated the globe no less than three times. This experience suggested to him the propriety of con- ducting a school of navigation—probably the only one of its kind in Boston. His prison diary is as interesting for what it tells of the moral standards of stout Bostonians as for what it tells of the prisons.

A Journal kept in Boston Gaol, in 1775.

From Sunday, July 2d, to Monday, 17th. From the 2d July to the 17th a complicated scene of oaths, curses, debauchery and the most horrid blas- phemy, committed by the Provost Marshal, his deputy and soldiers, who were our guard, soldier prisoners, and sundry soldier women, confined for thefts, etc. We had some of the vilest women for our neighbors; some placed over our heads, and some in rooms each side of us; they acted such scenes as was shocking to nature, and used language horrible to hear, as if it came from the very suburbs of Hell. When our wives, children and friends came to see us (which was seldom they were permitted), we seemed to want them gone, notwithstanding we were so desirous of their company, as they were exposed to hear the most abandoned language, as was grating to the ears of all sober persons.

Friday, July 7th, my wife came to see me. She has attempted it since, but was denied sundry times, and I did not see her again till the 28th July. We are very close confined, having the doors open for air sometimes one hour in 24, and sometimes not at all.

Monday 17th, my son Tileston died, whom I left well in my house; I was not permitted to attend the funeral, notwithstanding my letter to the general this morning requesting the same, or dismission, or trial. This evening the Provost informed us there was to be held a garrison court of enquiry at Con- cert Hall to-morrow, in consequence of my letter. We were desirous to pre- pare for trial.

Wednesday, 19th. Escorted from gaol again, with the additional company of 3 sailors, thieves and house-breakers; surrounded by soldiers, we made a curious medley; the fly blowers examined, and the 3 sailors. Mr. Hunt, Mr. Edes and Mr. Starr were asked who prosecuted them, and one Capt. Symmes, of the Regulars, was summoned by Major Moncreif as an evidence against Mr. Lovell and myself. Till this time we did not know our crimes, on what account we were committed, but now we found Mr. Lovell was charged with "being a spy, and giving intelligence to the rebels," and my charge, "be- ing a spy, and suspected of taking plans." When Capt. Symmes appeared, he knew so little of us that he called me "Mr. Lovell"; he knew so little of us that instead of being a just evidence, he appeared ashamed and confounded, and went off. At 2 o'clock we were sent back to our stone edifice under a strong guard.

Thursday, 20th. Our 5 room companions were escorted as before with one Carpenter, a barber, who swam to Cambridge and back again. The said Carpenter and Mr. Hunt were examined. We were all sent back to gaol again under a strong guard. This makes 3 days we were carried out to trial,

4 hours each time (and nothing asked us) under all the disgrace and contempt they could contrive.

August 4. Mr. Gill, printer, was brought to prison and put in our room. He is charged with printing sedition, treason and rebellion.

August 9. Some small liberty of the yard. A poor painter, an inhabitant, was put in the dungeon and very ill used by the Provost and his deputy, Samuel Dyer; the then Provost turned him out and made him get down on his knees in the yard and say, "God bless the King!"

August 11. Close confined; the Provost would not suffer the doors to be opened to put our victuals in, but made us take it through the bars; and we ... are daily treated with fresh insults and abuses. To day Amos Fisk died; he was a Charlestown prisoner, and the Provost uttered the most horrid speeches of what would become of his soul and body. This afternoon my wife came and tarried some time in the gaol house before she was admitted, in which time the Provost insulted her by saying I was a damned rebel, and my family the damnest rebel family in the country. She was admitted into our room a few minutes, and a sergeant sent in with her to hear the conversation. The Provost told her she must not come again.

Sunday, 13th [August]. Close shut up; much swearing and blasphemy close under our window the whole day by the Provost, his deputy and our guard of soldiers. It seems to be done on purpose, as they knew it was grating to us to hear such language. This morning my wife sent me a note in the foot of a stocking rolled up. We are obliged to act with secrecy, as our victuals, cloaths and every thing are constantly searched for letters and papers. This note informed me that my friend and relation, Mrs. B——, was got well of the small pox in the country.

Tuesday, 15th. Close confined, the weather hot. Died, Capt. Walker, a country prisoner from Charlestown. Swearing began at 3 this morning, and held all day: the place seems to be an emblem of Hell. At 9 at night most horrid swearing and blasphemy; the worst man of war that ever I knew was nothing to compare with this diabolical place. Poor Mr. Lovell began to droop; he is very weakly. It gives us all great concern, as we were all more afraid of sickness in this dreadful place than anything else, but God wonderfully preserved our healths and spirits. I did not think we could possibly survive such treatment but our help was from above. They sometimes gave us water in the pail in the morning, and by the heat of the weather and our cell it grew very warm, and they would not change it, and damned us, saying we must have that or none. This night I watched with Mr. Lovell.

Thursday, 17th [August]. Kept close all day. One Mr. French, an inhabitant, confined in the dungeon all day, and at night let out, and was obliged to fall down on his knees to the Provost in the yard, and say, "God bless the King!" Today, Phineas Nevers, a Charlestown prisoner, died. James Dickey discharged, and to pay a dollar fees; he paid a pistareen and left his silver broach in pawn for 4 more; the Provost kept the broach and give Dyer the pistareen. Also 3 dollars was demanded of Dorrington, and the Provost kept his bed and bedding 6 days and then delivered them up. The old Dutchman who was discharged the 25th July, was confined for complaining of the soldiers robbing his garden, which was his whole living, and because he had not a dollar to pay his fees, the soldiers on guard were ordered, each, to give him a kick as he went away.

Saturday, 19th. Close confined; dreadful language from morning to night; Mr. Lovell continues poorlye. This afternoon my wife came to ask my advice about signing for buying meat, as none were to have it but friends of Government. I told her to sign nothing and trust to Providence, and ask no favours from such wretches. The poor sick and wounded prisoners fare very hard, are many days without the comforts of life. Doctor Brown complained to Mr. Lovell and me that they had no bread all that day and the day before. He spoke to the Provost, as he had the charge of serving the bread; he replied, they might eat the nail heads and gnaw the plank and be damned. The comforts that are sent us by our friends we are obliged to impart to these poor suffering friends, and see the soldiers and others with rum to carry it them by stealth, when we are close confined and cannot get to them. . . . Some of the limbs which have been taken off, it was said, were in a state of putrification; not one survived amputation.

Wednesday, 23d. This morning, when my son brought my breakfast, the Provost said to the soldiers on guard, "God damn that dog (meaning my child)! Don't let him come up the yard. That dog deserves to be shot." In the afternoon Serjeant Neal and Corporal Royal were confined prisoners by the Provost for giving us air and fresh water in his absence. They told him we were almost suffocated with heat; he replied, "God damn them, if they are dead and rotten, my orders to you is to keep them close."

Friday, 25th. Last night Thomas Forakers, boatbuilder, and his servant John Bouve were brought to gaol on suspicion of concealing a man that swam over from Chelsea, upon false information of a very wicked woman; and this morning the boy John Bouve (about 16 years of age) was put in irons, in the dungeon, as he had nothing to confess; he was examined by Major Sheriff and Major Rooke, and then hand cuffed and put in the dungeon again. We fed the boy from our room, and encouraged him to keep up his spirits by telling him they were a pack of cowardly scoundrels and dare not hurt the hair of his head. While his irons were putting on, close by our cell door, the Provost said to him, he was a man under sentence of death, and might choose his minister to come and see him, for he was to be hanged in the afternoon. At 5 in the afternoon, finding they could make nothing of him, they took his irons off and put him in a room next to ours, among some soldiers, thieves, etc. The weather very hot and we close confined all day.

—LEACH, "Journal," *New England Genealogical Register*, XIX, 255 ff.

III. THE SUFFERINGS OF AMERICAN PRISONERS IN NEW YORK

We give here three narratives of imprisonment in New York, headquarters of British prisons.

The accounts of Jonathan Gillett and Thomas Stone need little introduction. Both were from Connecticut; both were captured on Long Island, Gillett by the Hessians, Stone in the course of a raid on one of the British posts.

*Both suffered imprisonment on the Jersey prison ship before being trans-
ferred to the equally notorious Sugar House in New York. Their narratives
serve as an introduction to the story of the prison ships. Shocking conditions
among Patriot prisoners in New York and the benevolence of a courageous
Quaker lady are the subjects of the touching story told by Robert Keith,
chaplain aboard the ship that carried John Jay to Spain on his frustrating
mission for Congress. Jay had Chaplain Keith's statement entered in his
letter book.*

1. Captured by the Hessians!

Jonathan Gillett to Eliza Gillett at West Hartford.

New York, December 2nd, 1776

My Friends,

No doubt my misfortunes have reached your ears. Sad as it is, it is true
as sad. I was made prisoner the 27th day of August past by a people called
Heshens, and by a party called Yagers, the most inhuman of all mortals. I cant
give room to picture them here but thus much——I at first resolved not to be
taken, but by the impertunity of the seven taken with me, and being surrounded on all sides, I unhappily surendered; would to God I never had! Then
I should never [have] known there unmerciful cruelties; they first disarmed
me, then plundered me of all I had, watch, buckles, money and sum clothing,
after which they abused me by bruising my flesh with the butts of there
[guns]. They knocked me down; I got up and they [kept on] beating me
almost all the way to there [camp] where I got shot of them. The next thing
was I was allmost starved to death by them. I was kept here 8 days and then
sent on board a ship, where I continued 39 days, and by [them was treated]
much worse than when on shore.

After I was set on [shore] at New York, [I was] confined [under] a strong
guard till the 20th day of November, after which I have had my liberty to
walk part over the city between sun and sun. Notwithstanding there generous
allowance of food I must inevitably have perished with hunger had not sum
friends in this [city] relieved my extreme necessity, but I cant expect they can
always do it. What I shall do next I know not, being naked for clothes and
void of money, and winter present, and provisions very skerce; fresh meat one
shilling per pound, butter three shillings per pound, cheese two shillings, turnips and potatoes at a shilling a half peck, milk 15 coppers per quart, bread
equally as dear; and the General says he cant find us fuel thro' the winter, tho'
at present we receive sum cole.

I was after put on board siezed violently with the disentarry. It followed
me hard upwards of six weeks—after that a slow fever, but now am vastly
better. . . . my sincere love to you and my children. May God keep and preserve you at all times from sin, sickness, and death! . . .

I will endeavor to faintly lead you into the poor cituation the soldiers are
in, espechally those taken at Long Island where I was. In fact these cases are
deplorable and they are real objects of pitty. They are still confined and in
houses where there is no fire—poor mortals, with little or no clothes—perish-

ing with hunger, offering eight dollars in paper for one in silver to relieve there distressing hunger, occasioned for want of food. There natures are broke and gone, some almost loose there voices and some there hearing. They are crouded into churches and there guarded night and day. I cant paint the horable appearance they make. It is shocking to human nature to behold them. Could I draw the curtain from before you, there expose to your view a lean jawed mortal, hunger laid his skinny hand [upon him] and whet to keenest edge his stomach cravings, sorounded with tattred garments, rotten rags, close beset with unwelcome vermin—could I do this, I say, possable I might in some [small] manner fix your idea with what appearance sum hundreds of these poor creatures make in houses where once people attempted to implore God's blessings, etc. But I must say no more of there calamities. God be merciful to them—I cant afford them no relief. If I had money I soon would do it, but I have none for myself.

I wrote to you by Mr. Wells to see if some one would help me to hard money under my present necessity. I write no more; if I had the General would not allow it to go out, and if ever you write to me write very short or else I will never see it. What the Heshens robbed me of that day amounted to the value of seventy two dollars at least. . . .

—DANDRIDGE, *American Prisoners of the Revolution*, pp. 28-31.

2. THOMAS STONE CHARGES THAT PRISONERS WERE POISONED

Recollections of Thomas Stone.

About the 25th of Jan., 1778, we were taken from the ships to the Sugar House, which during the inclement season was more intolerable than the ships.

We left the floating Hell with joy, but alas, our joy was of short duration. Cold and famine were now our destiny. Not a pane of glass, nor even a board to a single window in the house, and no fire but once in three days to cook our small allowance of provision. There was a scene that truly tried body and soul. Old shoes were bought and eaten with as much relish as a pig or a turkey; a beef bone of four or five ounces, after it was picked clean, was sold by the British guard for as many coppers.

In the spring our misery increased; frozen feet began to mortify; by the first of April, death took from our numbers, and, I hope, from their misery, from seven to ten a day; and by the first of May out of sixty-nine taken with me only fifteen were alive, and eight out of that number unable to work.

Death stared the living in the face: we were now attacked by a fever which threatened to clear our walls of its miserable inhabitants.

About the 20th of July I made my escape from the prison-yard. Just before the lamps were lighted I got safely out of the city, passed all the guards, was often fired at, but still safe as to any injury done me; arrived at Harlem River eastward of King's Bridge.

Hope and fear were now in full exercise. The alarm was struck by the sentinels keeping firing at me. I arrived at the banks of Harlem—five men met me with their bayonets at my heart; to resist was instant death, and to give up, little better.

I was conducted to the main guard, kept there until morning, then started for New York with waiters with bayonets at my back, arrived at my old habitation about 1 o'clock P.M.; was introduced to the prison keeper who threatened me with instant death, gave me two heavy blows with his cane; I caught his arm and the guard interfered. Was driven to the provost, thrust into a dungeon—a stone floor, not a blanket, not a board, not a straw to rest on. Next day was visited by a refugee lieutenant, offered to enlist me, offered a bounty—I declined. Next day renewed the visit, made further offers, told me the general was determined I should starve to death where I was unless I would enter their service. I told him his general dare not do it. (I shall here omit the imprecations I gave him in charge.)

The third day I was visited by two British officers, offered me a sergeant's post, threatened me with death as before in case I refused.

I replied, "Death if they dare!"

In about ten minutes the door was opened, a guard took me to my old habitation the Sugar House, it being about the same time of day I left my cell that I entered it, being three days and nights without a morsel of food or a drop of water—all this for the crime of getting out of prison. When in the dungeon reflecting upon my situation, I thought if ever mortal could be justified in praying for the destruction of his enemies, I am the man.

After my escape the guard was augmented, and about this time a new prison keeper was appointed. Our situation became more tolerable.

The 16th of July was exchanged. Language would fail me to describe the joy of that hour; but it was transitory. On the morning of the 16th, some friends, or what is still more odious, some refugees, cast into the prison yard a quantity of warm bread, and it was devoured with greediness. The prison gate was opened, we marched out about the number of 250. Those belonging to the North and Eastern States were conducted to the North River and driven on board the flag ship, and landed at Elizabethtown, New Jersey. Those who ate of the bread soon sickened; there was death in the bread they had eaten. Some began to complain in about half an hour after eating the bread; one was taken sick after another in quick succession and the cry was, "Poison, poison!" I was taken sick about an hour after eating. When we landed, some could walk, and some could not. I walked to town about two miles, being led most of the way by two men. About one half of our number did not eat of the bread, as a report had been brought into the prison *that the prisoners taken at Fort Washington had been poisoned in the same way.*

The sick were conveyed in wagons to White Plains, where I expected to meet my regiment, but they had been on the march to Rhode Island, I believe, about a week. I was now in a real dilemma; I had not the vestige of a shirt to my body, was moneyless and friendless. What to do I knew not. Unable to walk, a gentleman—I think his name was Allen—offered to carry me to New Haven, which he did. The next day I was conveyed to Guilford, the place of my birth, but no near relative to help me. Here I learned that my father had died in the service the spring before. I was taken in by a hospitable uncle, but in moderate circumstances. Dr. Readfield attended me for about four months. I was salivated twice, but it had no good effect. They sent me 30 miles to Dr.

Little of East Haddam, who under kind Providence restored me to such a state of health that I joined my regiment in the spring following.

    —DANDRIDGE, *American Prisoners of the Revolution*, pp. 133-136.

3. A NEW YORK WIDOW BRAVES PERSECUTION TO SUCCOR PRISONERS

Statement of Robert Keith, chaplain to the *Confederacy*.

    On board the *Confederacy* at Martinico, 19th December, 1779

Mrs. Sarah Smith, widow of Mr. John Smith, cabinet maker, late of New York, being an elderly lady of a benevolent Christian disposition, was remarkably charitable and very serviceable to the American prisoners in the years 1776 and '77, to my certain knowledge. I, being one of that unfortunate number captivated at Fort Washington, was brought with the rest of my fellow sufferers to New York. In our approach to the city this good lady met us with her bounty and followed us to the several places of confinement with refreshments, which were very acceptable to us who had been three days destitute of the necessary supports of life.

When the officers had their parole of the city, she invited those whom she met with to come to her house and partake of such as she could afford them; and desired them to invite their acquaintance also to come and partake with them. Her house was kept open, and her table spread, almost constantly for several weeks. She bestowed both food and raiment with so hearty good will that relieving the distressed appeared to be her greatest satisfaction.

She greatly alleviated my misfortune by receiving me into her family as a boarder, where I had the best opportunity of being acquainted with her conduct. Her extraordinary liberality induced me sometimes to express my concern lest she would bring herself to poverty and distress:—to which she replied, she espoused the same cause in which they were suffering; therefore, while she had any thing to give, they should be welcome to share with her; and when it was out of her power to relieve them, she was willing to suffer with them. She not only entertained those who could come to her house, but also daily visited those who were kept in close confinement.

As she was comforting the disconsolate one day in the Provost, she bid them be of good cheer, the scale might turn, and the day might come when they would guard, in the same Provost, those who were now guarding them there. The guard, overhearing this address, shut her immediately in another room, saying that was the fittest place for such a d——d rebel.

After she got out of the gaol, she was likely to suffer for want of bread, and sent to see if I could procure her some flour on Long Island, where I was then upon parole. As I could procure but little, I wrote to Mr. Pintard, our agent there, to supply her out of the flour sent by Congress for the use of the American prisoners, which request he was kind enough to comply with. Her personal distresses did not yet make her forget the poor prisoners; but for their relief she went thro' the city, craving alms from the well disposed people of her acquaintance. This coming to the ears of the mayor and aldermen, they sent for her and examined her concerning it. She honestly confessed the fact, and they asked by what authority she acted.

She replied, "By the authority of the word of God."

Not being able to manage her, they turned her over to the general who also examined her, and received for answer as above. To prevent her future usefulness in this way, he ordered her not only to leave the city, but withdraw out of their lines, permitting her to take with her only one bed and her wearing apparel. When she had disposed of her property which she had not given away, she could not think of going out of the lines without visiting the prisoners on the island and inquiring into their necessities. Nor did she come empty handed, but dealt liberally both clothes and money to those who might never have opportunity to make her restitution. She left New York the latter part of '77, went up the North River to Clark's-town near Tappan Bay, where she was spending the remains of her small living when I had the last account from her.

—JAY, Letter Book, II (appendix), Columbia University Lib.

IV. THE HORRORS OF THE BRITISH PRISON SHIPS

We come now to the most harrowing chapter in the history of Revolutionary prisons, and perhaps in the history of the Revolution itself. What Andersonville was to the Civil War, the British prison ships were to the Revolution. Lacking adequate prisons in their one permanent headquarters, New York City, the British hit on the idea of using ships moored in the Hudson as prisons. This would, presumably, have a double advantage: the ships would be hard to escape from, and they would be clean and healthy. Both of these assumptions proved wrong. As for their presumed safety, prisoners who could swim could escape from them more easily than from a prison on land—if they had enough strength left to swim to shore. And as for their healthful character—they proved to be the most fatally unhealthful prisons ever devised. The fault here was not, to be sure, in the ships, but in the administration. Wretched food, or no food at all; frightful overcrowding in the fetid holds; a complete lack of medical care—these things condemned literally thousands of American prisoners to death. In the end the British prison ships probably killed more American soldiers than British rifles: the total estimate runs to 7,000 or 8,000.

We give here narratives by William Slade and Thomas Dring: Slade's is a contemporary narrative; the other was written up later and strains for literary effect. A Connecticut boy, William Slade had been captured at Fort Washington in November 1776, and imprisoned on the first of the prison ships, the Grosvenor; he introduces us to what is to be the familiar picture of smallpox, starvation and mistreatment. Thomas Dring was a sailor who passed from one prison ship to another; forty years later he set down his recollections of his dreadful experiences—with the help of one Albert Greene, who was doubtless responsible for the "literary" touches.

The suffering of American prisoners in New York was notorious, and late in 1777 Washington arranged to send his old friend and associate, Elias Boudinot, then commissary general of prisoners, to New York to investigate conditions. General Clinton gave Boudinot permission to see whatever was to be seen, and early in February he arrived "to inquire and find out the real state of our unfortunate brethren." On his return to Valley Forge he pre-

pared a report for General Washington. We have taken an excerpt from that report, and added to it a somewhat more systematic statement from Boudinot's later journal. Boudinot himself had a long and distinguished career in American public life: member and President of the Continental Congress; member of the first three United States Congresses; Director of the Mint; lawyer before the United States Supreme Court; and author of many theological tracts.

1. WILLIAM SLADE RECORDS LIFE AND DEATH ON THE PRISON SHIP

Fort Washington, the 16th day November, A. D. 1776. This day I, William Slade, was taken with 2,800 more. We was allowed honours of war. We then marched to Harlem under guard, where we were turned into a barn. We got little rest that night, being verry much crowded, as some trouble [illegible]. . . .

Sunday 17th. Such a Sabbath I never saw. We spent it in sorrow and hunger, having no mercy showed.

Munday 18th. We were called out while it was still dark, but was soon marched to New York, four deep, verry much frowned upon by all we saw. We was called Yankey Rebbels a-going to the gallows. We got to York at 9 o'clock, were paraded, counted off and marched to the North Church, where we were confined under guard.

Tuesday 19th. Still confined without provisions till almost night, when we got a little mouldy bisd [biscuit], about four per man. These four days we spent in hunger and sorrow being derided by everry one and calld Rebs.

Wednesday, 20th. We was reinforsd by 300 more. We had 500 before. This caused a continual noise and verry big huddle. Jest at night drawed 6 oz of pork per man. This we eat alone and raw.

Thursday, 21st. We passed the day in sorrow haveing nothing to eat or drink but pump water.

Friday, 22nd. We drawed ¾ lb of pork, ¾ lb of bisd, one gil of peas, a little rice and some kittels to cook in. Wet and cold.

Saturday, 23rd. We had camps stews plenty, it being all we had. We had now spent one week under confinement. Sad condition. . . .

Wednesday, 27th. Was spent in hunger. We are now dirty as hogs, lying any and every whare. Joys gone, sorrows increase. . . .

Sunday, 1st of Decembere, 1776. About 300 men was took out and carried on board the shipping. Sunday spent in vain.

Munday, 2nd. Early in the morning we was called out and stood in the cold, about one hour and then marched to the North River and went on board the *Grovnor* transport ship. Their was now 500 men on board; this made much confusion. We had to go to bed without supper. This night was verry long, hunger prevailed much. Sorrow more.

Saturday, 7th. We drawed 4 lb of bisd at noon, a piece of meat and rice. This day drawed 2 bisd per man for back allowance, (viz) for last Saturday at the church. This day the ships crew weighed anchor and fell down the river below Govnors Island and sailed up the East River to Turcle Bay [Turtle Bay is at the foot of 23rd Street], and cast anchor for winter months.

Sunday, 8th. This day we were almost discouraged, but considered that would not do. Cast off such thoughts. We drawed our bread and eat with sadness. At noon drawed meat and peas. We spent the day reading and in meditation, hopeing for good news. . . .

Thursday, 12th. We drawed bisd. This morning is the first time we see snow. At noon drawed a little meat and pea broth. Verry thin. We almost despair of being exchanged.

Friday, 13th. of Decr. 1776. We drawed bisd and butter. A little water broth. We now see nothing but the mercy of God to intercede for us. Sorrowful times, all faces look pale, discouraged, discouraged.

Saturday, 14th. We drawed bisd. Times look dark. Deaths prevail among us, also hunger and naked. We almost conclude [that we will have] to stay all winter. At noon drawed meat and rice. Cold increases. At night suffer with cold and hunger. Nights verry long and tiresome, weakness prevails.

Sunday, 15th. Drawed bisd. Paleness attends all faces. The melancholyst day I ever saw. At noon drawed meat and peas. Sunday gone and comfort. As sorrowfull times as I ever saw.

Munday, 16th of Decr. 1776. Drawed bisd and butter at noon. Burgo poor. Sorrow increases. The tender mercys of men are cruelty.

Tuesday, 17th. Drawed bisd. At noon meat and rice. No fire. Suffer with cold and hunger. We are treated worse than cattle and hogs. . . .

Saturday, 21st. Drawed bisd. Last night one of our regiment got on shore, but got catched. Troubles come on, comfort gone. At noon drawed meat and rice. Verry cold. Soldiers and sailors verry cross. Such melancholy times I never saw.

Sunday, 22nd. Last night nothing but grones all night of sick and dying. Men amazeing to behold. Such hardness, sickness prevails fast. Deaths multiply. Drawed bisd. At noon meat and peas. Weather cold. Sunday gone and no comfort. Had nothing but sorrow and sadness. All faces sad.

Munday, 23rd. Drawed bisd and butter. This morning Sergt Kieth, Job March and several others broke out with the small pox. About 20 gone from here today that listed in the King's service. Times look verry dark. But we are in hopes of an exchange. One dies almost every day. Cold but pleasant. Burgo for dinner. People gone bad with the pox.

Tuesday, 24th. Last night verry long and tiresome. Bisd. At noon rice and cornmeal. About 30 sick. [They] were carried to town. Cold but pleasant. No news. All faces gro pale and sad.

Wednesday, 25th. Last night was a sorrowful night. Nothing but grones and cries all night. Drawed bisd and butter. At noon peas. Capt. Benedict, Leiut Clark and Ensn Smith come on board and brought money for the prisoners. Sad times.

Thursday, 26th. Last night was spent in dying grones and cries. I now gro poorly. Terrible storm as ever I saw. High wind. Drawed bisd. At noon meat and peas. Verry cold and stormey.

Friday, 27th. Three men of our battalion died last night. The most melancholyest night I ever saw. Small pox increases fast. This day I was blooded. Drawed bisd and butter. Stomach all gone. At noon, burgo. Basset is verry sick. Not like to live I think.

Saturday, 28th. Drawed bisd. This morning about 10 o'clock Josiah Basset died. Ensn Smith come here about noon with orders to take me a shore. We got to shore about sunset. I now feel glad. Coffee and bread and cheese. . . .

Thursday, 2nd. Ensn Smith looked about and got something to ly on and in. A good deal poorly, but I endeavourd to keep up a good heart, considering that I should have it [the small pox] light, for it was verry thin and almost full. . . .

—DANDRIDGE, *American Prisoners of the Revolution*, pp. 494-499.

2. HEAT, STARVATION, VERMIN AND SMALLPOX ON THE *Jersey*

[1819]

Thomas Dring's narrative.

The First Night on Board

We had now reached the accommodation-ladder, which led to the gangway on the larboard side of the *Jersey*, and my station in the boat, as she hauled alongside, was exactly opposite to one of the air-ports in the side of the ship. From this aperture proceeded a strong current of foul vapor, of a kind to which I had been before accustomed while confined on board the *Good Hope;* the peculiarly disgusting smell of which I then recollected, after a lapse of three years. This was, however, far more foul and loathsome than anything which I had ever met with on board that ship; and it produced a sensation of nausea far beyond my powers of description.

Here, while waiting for orders to ascend on board, we were addressed by some of the prisoners, from the air-ports. We could not, however, discern their features, as it had now become so dark that we could not distinctly see any object in the interior of the ship. After some questions whence we came and respecting the manner of our capture, one of the prisoners said to me that it was "a lamentable thing to see so many young men in full strength, with the flush of health upon their countenances, about to enter that infernal place of abode." He then added in a tone and manner but little fitted to afford us much consolation: "Death has no relish for such skeleton carcasses as we are, but he will now have a feast upon you fresh-comers."

After lanterns had been lighted on board, for our examination, we ascended the accommodation-ladder to the upper deck, and passed through the barricade door, where we were examined and our bags of clothes inspected. These we were permitted to retain, provided they contained no money or weapons of any kind.

After each man had given his name and the capacity in which he had served on board the vessel in which he was captured, and the same had been duly registered, we were directed to pass through the other barricade door, on the starboard side, down the ladder leading to the main hatchway. I was detained but a short time with the examination, and was permitted to take my bag of clothes with me below; and passing down the hatchway, which was still open, through a guard of soldiers, I found myself among the wretched and disgusting multitude, a prisoner on board the *Jersey*.

The gratings were soon after placed over the hatchways and fastened down for the night; and I seated myself on the deck, holding my bag with a firm grasp, fearful of losing it among the crowd. I had now ample time to reflect on the horrors of the scene, and to consider the prospect before me. It was impossible to find one of my former shipmates in the darkness; and I had, of course, no one with whom to speak during the long hours of that dreadful night—surrounded by I knew not whom, except that they were beings as wretched as myself; with dismal sounds meeting my ears from every direction; a nauseous and putrid atmosphere filling my lungs at every breath; and a stifling and suffocating heat, which almost deprived me of sense, and even of life. . . .

The thought of sleep did not enter my mind. At length, discovering a glimmering of light through the iron gratings of one of the air-ports, I felt that it would be indeed a luxury if I could but obtain a situation near that place, in order to gain one breath of the exterior air. Clenching my hand firmly around my bag, which I dared not leave, I began to advance towards the side of the ship, but was soon greeted with the curses and imprecations of those who were lying on the deck, and whom I had disturbed in attempting to pass over them. I, however, persevered and at length arrived near the desired spot, but found it already occupied, and no persuasion would induce a single individual to relinquish his place for a moment.

Thus I passed the first dreadful night, waiting with sorrowful forebodings for the coming day. The dawn at length appeared, but came only to present new scenes of wretchedness, disease and woe. I found myself surrounded by a crowd of strange and unknown forms, with the lines of death and famine upon their faces. My former shipmates were all lost and mingled among the multitude, and it was not until we were permitted to ascend the deck, at eight o'clock, that I could discern a single individual whom I had ever seen before. Pale and meager, the throng came upon deck to view, for a few moments, the morning sun, and then to descend again, to pass another day of misery and wretchedness.

The First Day

After passing the weary and tedious night, to whose accumulated horrors I have but slightly alluded, I was permitted to ascend to the upper deck, where other objects, even more disgusting and loathsome, met my view. I found myself surrounded by a motley crew of wretches, with tattered garments and pallid visages, who had hurried from below for the luxury of a little fresh air. Among them I saw one ruddy and healthful countenance, and recognized the features of one of my late fellow-prisoners on board the *Belisarius*. But how different did he appear from the group around him, who had here been doomed to combat with disease and death! Men who, shrunken and decayed as they stood around him, had been but a short time before as strong, as healthful, and as vigorous as himself—men who had breathed the pure breezes of the ocean, or danced lightly in the flower-scented air of the meadow and the hill, and had from thence been hurried into the pent-up air of a crowded prison ship, pregnant with putrid fever, foul with deadly contagion; here to linger out the tedious and weary day, the disturbed and anxious night; to count over the days and weeks and months of a wearying and degrading captivity, unvaried but by new scenes of painful suffering, and new inflictions of remorseless cruelty—their brightest hope and their daily prayer, that death would not long delay to release them from their torments.

In the wretched groups around me, I saw but too faithful a picture of our own almost certain fate; and found that all which we had been taught to fear of this terrible place of abode was more than realized.

During the night, in addition to my other sufferings, I had been tormented with what I supposed to be vermin; and on coming upon deck, I found that a black silk handkerchief, which I wore around my neck, was completely spotted with them. Although this had often been mentioned as one of the miseries of the place, yet, as I had never before been in a situation to witness anything of the kind, the sight made me shudder; as I knew, at once, that so long as I should remain on board, these loathsome creatures would be my constant companions and unceasing tormentors.

The next disgusting object which met my sight was a man suffering with the smallpox; and in a few minutes I found myself surrounded by many others laboring under the same disease, in every stage of its progress.

As I had never had the smallpox, it became necessary that I should be inoculated; and there being no proper person on board to perform the operation, I concluded to act as my own physician. On looking about me, I soon found a man in the proper stage of the disease, and desired him to favor me with some of the matter for the purpose. He readily complied, observing that it was a necessary precaution on my part, and that my situation was an excellent one in regard to *diet*, as I might depend upon finding that *extremely moderate*. The only instrument which I could procure, for the purpose of inoculation, was a common pin. With this, having scarified the skin of my hand, between the thumb and forefinger, I applied the matter and bound up my hand. The next morning I found that the wound had begun to fester; a sure symptom that the application had taken effect.

Many of my former shipmates took the same precaution and were inoculated during the day. In my case the disorder came on but lightly, and its progress was favorable; and without the least medical advice or attention, by the blessing of Divine Providence, I soon recovered. . . .

In the course of the day, after the regulations of the ship had been made known to us, we divided ourselves into messes of six men each; and on the next morning we drew our scanty pittance of food with the rest of our companions.

The Fourth of July

A few days before the fourth of July, we had made such preparations as our circumstances would admit, for an observance of the anniversary of American Independence. We had procured some supplies wherewith to make ourselves merry on the occasion, and intended to spend the day in such innocent pastime and amusement as our situation would afford, not dreaming that our proceedings would give umbrage to our keepers, as it was far from our intention to trouble or insult them. We thought that, although prisoners, we had a right, on that day at least, to sing and be merry. As soon as we were permitted to go on deck in the morning, thirteen little national flags were displayed in a row upon the booms. We were soon ordered by the guard to take them away; and as we neglected to obey the command, they triumph-antly demolished, and trampled them underfoot.

Unfortunately for us, our guards at that time were Scotchmen, who, next to the refugees, were the objects of our greatest hatred; but their destruction of our flags was merely viewed in silence, with the contempt which it merited.

During the time we remained on deck, several patriotic songs were sung, and choruses were repeated; but not a word was intentionally spoken to give offense to our guards. They were, nevertheless, evidently dissatisfied with our proceedings, as will soon appear. Their moroseness was a prelude to what was to follow. We were, in a short time, forbidden to pass along the common gangways, and every attempt to do so was repelled by the bayonet. Although thus incommoded, our mirth still continued. Songs were still sung, accom-panied with occasional cheers. Things thus proceeded until about four o'clock, when the guards were turned out, and we received orders to descend between decks, where we were immediately driven at the point of the bayonet.

After being thus sent below in the greatest confusion, at that early and un-usual hour, and having heard the gratings closed and fastened above us, we suposed that the barbarous resentment of our guards was fully satisfied; but we were mistaken, for they had further vengeance in store, and merely waited for an opportunity to make us feel its weight.

The prisoners continued their singing between decks, and were, of course, more noisy than usual, but forbore, even under their existing temptations, to utter any insulting or aggravating expressions. At least, I heard nothing of the kind, unless our patriotic songs could be so construed.

In the course of the evening, we were ordered to desist from making any further noise. This order not being fully complied with, at about nine o'clock the gratings were removed, and the guards descended among us, with lanterns and drawn cutlasses in their hands. The poor, helpless prisoners retreated from the hatchways, as far as their crowded situation would permit; while their cowardly assailants followed as far as they dared, cutting and wounding ev-eryone within their reach, and then ascended to the upper deck, exulting in the gratification of their revenge.

Many of the prisoners were wounded; but, from the total darkness, neither their number nor their situation could be ascertained; and if this had been possible, it was not in the power of their companions to afford them the least relief. During the whole of that tragical night, their groans and lamentations were dreadful in the extreme. Being in the gun-room, I was at some distance from the immediate scene of this bloody outrage; but the distance was by no means far enough to prevent my hearing their continual cries from the ex-tremity of pain, their applications for assistance, and their curses upon the heads of their brutal assailants.

It had been the usual custom for each prisoner to carry below, when he descended at sunset, a pint of water, to quench his thirst during the night. But, on this occasion, we had thus been driven to our dungeons three hours before the setting of the sun, and without our usual supply of water.

Of this night I cannot describe the horrors. The day had been very sultry, and the heat was extreme throughout the ship. The unusual number of hours during which we had been crowded together between decks; the foul atmosphere and sickening heat; the additional excitement and restlessness caused by the wanton attack which had been made; above all the want of water, not a drop of which could we obtain during the whole night, to cool our parched tongues; the imprecations of those who were half distracted with their burning thirst; the shrieks and wailings of the wounded; the struggles and groans of the dying—together formed a combination of horrors which no pen can describe.

In the agonies of their suffering the prisoners invited, and even challenged, their inhuman guards to descend once more among them; but this they were prudent enough not to attempt.

Their cries and supplications for water were terrible, and were, of themselves, sufficient to render sleep impossible. Oppressed with the heat, I found my way to the grating of the main hatchway, where on former nights I had frequently passed some time, for the benefit of the little current of air which circulated through the bars. I obtained a place on the larboard side of the hatchway, where I stood facing the East, and endeavored, as much as possible, to draw my attention from the terrific sounds below me, by watching through the grating the progress of the stars. I there spent hour after hour in following with my eye the motion of a particular star as it rose and ascended, until it passed over beyond my sight.

How I longed for the day to dawn! At length the morning light began to appear, but still our torments were increasing every moment. As the usual hour for us to ascend to the upper deck approached, the working-party were mustered near the hatchway, and we were all anxiously waiting for the opportunity to cool our weary frames, to breathe for a while the pure air, and, above all, to procure water to quench our intolerable thirst. The time arrived, but still the gratings were not removed. Hour after hour passed on, and still we were not released. Our minds were at length seized with the horrible suspicion that our tyrants had determined to make a finishing stroke of their cruelty, and rid themselves of us altogether.

It was not until ten o'clock in the forenoon that the gratings were at length removed. We hurried on deck, and thronged to the water-cask, which was completely exhausted before our thirst was allayed. So great was the struggle around the cask that the guards were again turned out to disperse the crowd.

In a few hours, however, we received a new supply of water, but it seemed impossible to allay our thirst, and the applications at the cask were incessant until sunset.

Our rations were delivered to us, but, of course, not until long after the usual hour. During the whole day, however, no fire was kindled for cooking in the galley. All the food which we consumed that day we were obliged to swallow raw. Every thing, indeed, had been entirely deranged by the events of the past night, and several days elapsed before order was restored. This was at length obtained by a change of the guard, who, to our great joy, were relieved by a party of Hessians.

The average number who died on board during the period of twenty-four hours was about five; but on the morning of the fifth of July, eight or ten corpses were found below. Many had been badly wounded, to whom, in the total darkness of the night, it was impossible for their companions to render any assistance; and even during the next day they received no attention, except that which was afforded by their fellow prisoners, who had nothing to administer to their comfort, not even bandages for their wounds.

—DRING, *Recollections of the Jersey Prison Ship*, pp. 28-36, 89-94.

3. ELIAS BOUDINOT REPORTS TO WASHINGTON ON CONDITIONS IN NEW YORK

Draft of his report to George Washington.

Camp, March 2, 1778

Having been detained in New York on the business committed to me by your Excellency much longer than could have been expected, [I] think it my duty to take the earliest opportunity of communicating a report of my proceedings and the reasons of my conduct.

On my arrival in Jersey I wrote to Sir Henry Clinton for permission to pass to New York, for the purpose of visiting our prisoners . . . and received an answer through Mr. Loring [Commissary General of Prisoners, whose wife had been General Howe's mistress]. When arrived at the city, [I] was received with great politeness and civility and put under no other restraint than being informed that they trusted to my prudence for a proper behaviour.

My business here being to inquire and find out the real state of our unfortunate bretheren, and not to negotiate any general principles, I thought it prudent, in the first place, to make it a point to know the tempers and characters of the particular persons I had to do with, and then endeavour to improve it to the advantage of our miserable prisoners.

Having for several days visited the different places of their confinement, and made every inquiry in my power, I beg leave to report to your Excellency the results of the whole: That I found the hospitals in tollerable good order, neat and clean and the sick much better taken care of than I expected. That the Sugar House appeared comfortable and warm, having a stove in each story and shutters to the windows. The prisoners also, being well cloathed and each of them having a good blanket, may stand through the winter very well, especially as they are not crowded, being now reduced in the whole to about 400, two hundred of whom are in the Sugar House; the rest being in the different hospitals. Some of the privates appear to be a sett of sad villains, who rob each other of their cloaths and blanketts, and many of them sell their own shoes, blanketts and even shirts for rum. . . .

That in the Provoost I was greatly distressed with the wretched situation of so many of the human species. That on meeting all the prisoners of war together in a room, in company with Mr. Loring, I heard their complaints and took notes of the accusations on which they were severally confined in order to found a representation to Major General Robertson [James Robertson was commandant of New York City] in their favour. They repeated to me instances of the most shocking barbarity in presence of the keeper of the Provoost, whom they charged as the author: as the beating and knocking down officers of rank and distinction on the most triffling occasion, locking them up in dark, damp dungeons, for asking more water than usual in warm weather; or for not going to bed immediately on being order[ed] by the serjeant [Sergeant Keefe]. Officers have been locked up in the dungeon for examination, and left there without farther inquiry or any charge brought against them for many months. That besides prisoners of war, there are many inhabitants here, as Committee Men, Commissioners, Oppressors of the Friends of Government, etc., etc., who are wretched beyond description. That inhabitants and persons in civil departments when taken are sent to the Provoost without distinction, and at present there seems to be no redemption for them.

That on stating the case of each of these unhappy men . . . and delivering it to General Robertson, he very humanely agreed to the discharge of all the officers (except seven) on their parole; and gave me the strongest assurances that he would not allow of such a power on the serjeant of the Provoost, but would put a stop to it immediately. That the officers on Long Island are boarded out amongst the inhabitants in the most convenient manner, and appear to be very comfortable and healthy. They amount to about 250. . . .

That to answer the pressing necessities of our prisoners I have been obliged to stretch my credit to the utmost. That not being able to obtain the least aid from the State of Jersey, [I] have been put to the greatest difficulty to make remittances, not being able to procure above 300 barrells of flour for want of means of transportation; and although I have employed the best men I could meet with for the purpose, can get nothing done effectually without my personal attendance. . . .

That although the above appears now to be the state of the prisoners in New York, from my personal observation while visiting the several departments, yet I think it my duty nevertheless to add to this report [that] which I received from the unanimous representation of both officers and privates, viz. that this alteration has taken place within a short time past, in a great measure by the industry and attention of Mr. Pintard [Louis Pintard, a brother-in-law of Elias Boudinot], our agent in New York, who has employed special nurses in the hospitals, added to the supplies for the sick, and done every thing in his power for the relief of the unhappy sufferers. . . . But Mr. Pintard being forbid going to the Provoost, his care cannot extend to those confined there, except as to sending them provisions and fire wood. . . .

That after finishing the business of the military prisoners, I waited on Commodore [William] Hotham, and informed him that Mr. Pintard, having obtained provisions and cloathing for the sea prisoners, had been refused the liberty of sending them on board of the prison ships notwithstanding the pressing necessities of those suffering people. He informed me that he could not know Mr. Pintard, or any other person but his own Commissary, and that he would not suffer any cloaths purchased in New York to go on board without Lord Howe's express orders, but that any provisions sent to the Commissary appointed by him should be distributed. I applied then for the enlargement of the sea officers on parole, but he answered that this could not be done, as no sea prisoners were ever admitted to that indulgence. . . .

There are 58 officers and 62 sea men on board the prison ships, who suffer greatly and die daily. . . .

P. S. I had almost forgot to mention that, having receiving the fullest assurances from our officers that a poor woman* had saved the lives of a number of our prisoners by exerting herself in serving them at far beyond her abilities, and that she was now in a suffering condition for want of provision, I thought it prudent to send her a present of 5 barrels of flour.

—BOUDINOT, "Report," *William & Mary Quarterly*, 3rd ser., XIII, 379-387.

4. ELIAS BOUDINOT FINDS BRITISH PRISONS WORSE THAN REPORTED

February 4, 1778

. . . I waited on the General [Robertson] at breakfast. He behaved as before with the greatest civility and good humor. After breakfast he asked a great many questions about the news in our lines, and conversed on common topicks, but said nothing about my conduct while in the city, on which I at last introduced the business on which I had come: that I was a stranger to military rule; I knew that I was in a garrisoned town, and therefor wished to know what line of conduct it was expected that I should pursue.

The General answered me that he knew we had heard strange stories within our lines of their conduct to our prisoners; that he rejoiced that General Washington had taken the measure of sending me in to examine for ourselves, for that he was sure that we should find them a parcel of damned lies; that he had ordered every place I should choose to visit to be freely opened to me, and that as I was a gentleman, all that he expected was that I should behave as such, and that I might use my own pleasure and go where I pleased.

I confess I was surprised at this generous conduct, and immediately replied that I could not accept the gentlemanly offer. That I had come on a fair and open business. That I had no secrets to communicate and would not receive any from any person whatever. That I could not put myself so far in their power as after my departure to render it possible for them to charge me with improper behavior unworthy my character, by communicating or receiving secret intelligence to or from our officers. That my intentions were not only to be convinced myself of the truth of the treatment the prisoners had received, but if it had been cruel, that the General should be convinced of the fact also, as necessary towards their relief. That therefor I should not see a prisoner or have any communication with one but in the presence of a British officer, who I hoped he would oblige me by appointing to attend me.

The General expressed himself well pleased with the proposal, and appointed one accordingly, observing again that he was sure I should find the reports we had heard totally false.

Accordingly I went to the Provost with the officer, where we found near 30 officers, from colonels downwards, in close confinement in the gaol in New York. After some conversation with late Ethan Allen, I told him my errand, on which he was very free in his abuse of the British on account of

* Very possibly a Mrs. Deborah Franklin, banished from New York in November 1780 for her aid to American prisoners.

the cruel treatment he had received during —— months close confinement. We then proceeded up stairs to the room of their confinement. I had the officers drawn up in a ring and informed them of my mission: that I was determined to hear nothing in secret. That I therefore hoped they would each of them in their turn report to me faithfully and candidly the treatment they severally had received. That my design was to obtain them the proper redress, but if they kept back anything from an improper fear of their keepers, they would have themselves only to blame for their want of immediate redress. That for the purpose of their deliverance the British officer attended that the British General should be also well informed of facts.

On this after some little hesitation from a dread of their keeper, the Provost Martial, one of them began and informed us that they had been confined on the most frivolous pretenses: some for having been oppressors of the friends of Government—for taking refugees' property, while officers under command and in obedience to orders—for being out of their bounds of parole, the week after their return—some confined in the dungeon for a night to wait the censure of General to examine them, and forgot for months—for being Committee Men, etc., etc. That they had received the most cruel treatment from the Provost Martial, being locked up in the dungeon on the most trifling pretenses, such as asking for more water for drinking on a hotter day than usual—for sitting up a little longer in the evening than orders allowed—for writing a letter to the General making their complaints of ill usage and throwing out of the windows. That some of them were kept 10, 12 and 14 weeks in the dungeon on these trifling pretenses.

A Captain Vandyke had been confined 18 months for being concerned in setting fire to the city when, on my calling for the Provost books, it appeared that he had been made prisoner and closely confined in the Provost 4 days before the fire happened.

A Major Paine had been confined 11 months for killing a Capt. Campbell in the engagement when he was taken prisoner, when, on examination, it appeared that the captain had been killed in another part of the action. The charge was that Major Paine when taken had no commission tho' acknowledged by us as a major.

Captain —— was confined for breaking a soldier's thigh with the but of his gun after he was shot down, when the British surgeon on examination acknowledged that the thigh was broken by a ball, etc., etc., etc.

Most of the cases examined into turned out wholly false or too trifling to be regarded. It also appeared by the declaration of some of the gentlemen that their water would be sometimes, as the caprice of the Provost Martial led him, brought up to them in the tubs they used in their rooms, and when the weather was so hot that they must drink or perish.

On hearing a number of these instances of cruelty, I asked who was the author of them. They answered "the provost keeper." I desired the officer to call him up that we might have him face to face. He accordingly came in, and on being informed of what had passed, he was asked if the complaints were true. He with great insolence answered that every word was true—on which the British officer, abusing him very much, asked him how he dared to treat gentlemen in that cruel manner. He, insolently putting his hands to his side, swore that he was as absolute there as Gen'l Howe was at the head of his army. I observed to the officer that now there could be no dispute about facts as the fellow had acknowledged every word to be true.

I stated all the facts in substance and waited again on Gen'l Robertson, who hoped I was quite satisfied of the falsity of the reports I had heard. I then stated to him the facts and assured him that they turned out worse than anything we had heard. On his hesitating as to the truth of this assertion, I observed to him the propriety of having an officer with me, to whom I now appealed for the truth of the facts. He being present confirmed them—on which the General expressed great dissatisfaction, and promised that the author of them should be punished.

—BOUDINOT, *Journal or Historical Recollections*, pp. 13-17.

V. CONGRESS KEEPS THE "CONVENTION" TROOPS IN AMERICA

Article IV of the Convention (not Capitulation) between Generals Gates and Burgoyne provided that British troops (many of them Hessians) might march to the nearest port and there embark for Britain on the promise that they would not fight again in North America. Under this agreement there was nothing to prevent them from fighting elsewhere, in exchange for troops who could fight in America. No wonder Burgoyne boasted that he had dictated the terms, and that they did not constitute a surrender! The Congress was so delighted at the victory of Saratoga that at first it hastened to congratulate Gates on a "surrender upon terms honorable and advantageous to these states." Upon reflection, however, Congress changed its mind, and sought ways to qualify or evade the arrangements that Gates had made. A Committee of Congress promptly discovered several technicalities which appeared to justify delay. First, Burgoyne had failed to surrender all his arms. Second, he had complained that Congress had violated the terms of the Convention; the Committee argued that this complaint constituted a denunciation of the Convention. Third, there was no evidence that the King had ratified the Convention; when evidence was produced the Committee said that it might all be a forgery! Thus the Committee took refuge in subterfuges not creditable to their honor.

The "Convention" troops were marched to Boston, and encamped in near-by towns, and General Heath was informed that embarkation had been indefinitely postponed. General Burgoyne, however, was permitted to return to England, where he denounced what he rightly considered the violation of the terms of the Convention. In January and February the prisoners were marched south to barracks prepared for them near Charlottesville, Virginia; most of the Hessians melted away during their progress through Pennsylvania, which was just what the Americans wanted.

We give here three accounts of the experiences of the Convention troops. The first, from the lively pen of Hannah Winthrop—wife of the famous Harvard astronomer—to the equally lively Mercy Warren, tells of the arrival of the troops in Cambridge. The second, a long complaint about mistreatment, is written by Lieutenant Colonel Thomas Anburey who later published a volume of Travels Through the Interior Parts of America. *From the Baroness Riedesel, wife of the commander of the Hessian troops at Saratoga and best of all the women chroniclers of the Revolution, comes the story of the long march to Virginia.*

1. THE "CONVENTION" TROOPS MARCH THROUGH CAMBRIDGE

Hannah Winthrop to Mercy Warren.

Cambridge, November 11, 1777

Last Thursday, which was a very stormy day, a large number of British troops came softly thro the town via Watertown to Prospect Hill. On Friday we heard the Hessians were to make a procession in the same rout; we thought we should have nothing to do with them but view them as they passt. To be sure, the sight was truly astonishing. I never had the least idea that the Creation produced such a sordid set of creatures in human figure—poor, dirty, emaciated men, great numbers of women, who seemed to be the beasts of burthen, having a bushel basket on their back, by which they were bent double—the contents seemed to be pots and kettles, various sorts of furniture—children peeping thro' gridirons and other utensils, some very young infants who were born on the road; the women [with] bare feet, cloathed in dirty rags—such effluvia filled the air while they were passing, had they not been smoking all the time, I should have been apprehensive of being contaminated.

After a noble looking advanced guard Gen. J. Burgoyne headed this terrible group on horseback. The other general also, cloathed in blue cloaks. Hessians, Anspachers, Brunswickers, etc., etc., followed on. The Hessian general gave us a polite bow as they passed. Not so the British. Their baggage waggons [were] drawn by poor half starved horses. But to bring up the rear, another fine noble looking guard of American brawny victorious yeomanry, who assisted in bringing these sons of slavery to terms. Some of our waggons drawn by fat oxen, driven by joyous looking Yankees, closed the cavalcade.

The generals and other officers went to Bradishs, where they quarter at present. The privates trudged thro thick and thin to the hills, where we thought they were to be confined, but what was our surprise when in the morning we beheld an inundation of those disagreeable objects filling our streets! How mortifying is it—they in a manner demanding our houses and colleges for their genteel accommodations. Did the brave General Gates ever mean this? Did our legislature ever intend the military should prevail above the civil? Is there not a degree of unkindness in loading poor Cambridge, almost ruined before this great army seemed to be let loose upon us? And what will be the consequence time will discover.

Some polite ones say, we ought not to look on them as prisoners; they are persons of distinguished rank. Perhaps too we must not view them in the light of enemys. I fear this distinction will be soon lost. Surpriseing that our general or any of our colonels should insist on the first University in America being disbanded for their more genteel accomodation, and we poor oppressed people seek an asylum in the woods against a piercing winter! ... It is said we shall have not less than seven thousand persons to feed in Cambridge and its environs, more than its inhabitants. Two hundred and fifty cord of wood will not serve them a week. Think then how we must be distresst. Wood is risen to £5.10 pr. cord and but little to be purchased. I never thought I could lie down to sleep surrounded by these enemies, but we strangely become enured to those things which appear difficult when distant.

—*Warren-Adams Letters*, II, 451–452.

2. "Stupid Fools, They Might Perceive That We Were Officers!"

Letters from Lieutenant Colonel Thomas Anburey.

December 7, 1777

We are anxiously expecting the vessels, as our situation is not only very unpleasant but dangerous, both to officers and soldiers; the latter of whom are in continual broils with the American guards, which are composed of militia, who, not being under very great discipline, not only infringe their orders, which perhaps they do not comprehend, or else use their authority as they think proper. They have received orders not to let any officer pass without his side arms, and as many of them left their baggage in Canada, others lost them with their baggage during the campaign, this ignorant people will not let any one pass without a sword, drawling out, "I swear now you shan't pass, because you have not got a sword." At the same time, stupid fools, they might perceive by our cloaths and bayonets that we were officers. Much altercation has ensued, to remedy which the officers had passports signed by General Heath, but this did not avail, as very few of the centinels could read. At last it was ordered that any officer who wanted to pass the centinels was to go to the American guard, where the officer should send a soldier to pass him; this did not altogether remedy the evil, as many of the officers could not make out the passport.

When I describe to you the troops, you will not so much wonder at these embarrassments. In marching the party to relief, you will see an old man of sixty and a boy of sixteen; a black and an old decrepid man limping by his side; most of them wear great bushy wigs; in short, they would be a subject for the pencil of Hogarth; but, egad, they are ready enough in presenting their pieces, and if a soldier comes the least near them they level at him and say, "I swear now, if you attempt to pass, I'll blaze at you." . . .

January 19, 1778

It is impossible to describe with what a dejected mind I sit down to write, as not only the flattering hopes of shortly seeing my friend is done away, and every prospect vanished, but some years, perhaps, may elapse before the termination of this unhappy contest.

What was intended as an accommodation to the troops relative to their embarking at Rhode Island, has proved a most unfortunate circumstance indeed; for the Congress have not only denied that request, but have put a stop to any embarkation till the convention is ratified at home by the King and Parliament, an event that can never happen, as it would be allowing the authority of the Congress and the independence of the Americans. What renders our situation more distressing is that had the transports came round to Boston, the Council would have consented to our embarkation. . . .

Judge, my dear friend, what must be the feelings of every one, and how exasperated we must be at this treatment! We have no other hopes left but an exchange of prisoners, which, considering our numbers, will be some time before the whole can be effected. Our situation now becomes every day more and more mortifying, for, exclusive of the insults we continually meet with from the American soldiery, the officers, no doubt stimulated by this resolve of Congress, behave very tauntingly; and Colonel Henley, who commands the troops, has been guilty of great cruelty to the soldiers. That you may form an idea as to the natural ferocity of disposition in this man, and how deliberate he is in his barbarities, I shall state a few of them.

On the 19th of last month, he went up to the American barracks to release some of our soldiers; after calling over their names, he addressed himself to a Corporal Reeves, of the 9th Regiment, and told him "he had been confined for insulting a provincial officer."

Reeves made answer, "He was sorry for it; that he was in liquor, and would not have acted so had he known him to have been an officer, and was ready to ask his pardon."

Colonel Henley said, "By God, Sir, had you served me so, I would have run you through the body, and I believe you to be a great rascal."

Reeves made answer, "I am no rascal, but a good soldier, and my officers know it." Colonel Henley then demanded silence. Reeves repeated nearly the same words, adding, "That he hoped soon to carry arms under General Howe and fight for his King and country."

The colonel then replied, "Damn your King and country! When you had arms, you were willing enough to lay them down." Colonel Henley then ordered silence. Reeves repeating nearly the same words, the colonel ordered one of the guard to run him through for a scoundrel. The men of the guard not obeying his orders, he dismounted from his horse and, seizing a firelock with a fixed bayonet from one of the guard, stabbed Corporal Reeves in the left breast, and whilst he had the bayonet at his bosom, the colonel told him, "If he said another word, he would have it through his body."

Reeves then told him, "He did not care, he would stand by King and his country till he died."

Colonel Henley then made a second dart at him with the firelock and fixed bayonet, which two of the other prisoners threw up, and it passed over Reeves' shoulder. At the same time one of the men said to Colonel Henley, "That the man was his prisoner, that he had better not take his life, as he could do with him as with the other men who were in his custody."

Colonel Henley then returned the firelock and ordered him back into the guard-room, dismissing the rest of the prisoners. . . .

Do not be surprised after this if you should hear of a general massacre of all the British troops! But what more fully stamps the character of this most sanguinary man, and his ferocious disposition, is a most unaccountable expression he made to some soldiers without any provocation.

Our passes are renewable every month, for which purpose the quartermaster-serjeants of the different regiments attend at the American Deputy Adjutant-General's office; on the 16th of last month, as the serjeants attended at the office to apply for passes, Serjeant Fleming, of the 47th Regiment, not being acquainted with Colonel Henley, took him for Colonel Keith, the Deputy Adjutant-General, saluted him cap in hand, and was going to address him when Colonel Henley extended his arm towards him with his fist clenched, and said, "You rascals, I'll make damnation fly out of ye; for I will myself, one of these nights, go the rounds, and if I hear the least word or noise in your barracks, I'll put shot amongst you and make flames of Hell jump out of ye, and turn your barracks inside out"; declaring, if he was a centinel and any British soldiers looked sulky at him, he would blow their brains out!

Such glaring conduct could not escape the notice of General Burgoyne, who applied to General Heath for redress, and he instituted a Court of Enquiry to investigate the grounds of complaint, and reported it would be for the *honor* of Colonel Henley, as well as for the satisfaction of all interested, that the judgement of a court-martial should be taken on his conduct during his command at Cambridge, which court-martial is to sit to-morrow.

—ANBUREY, *Travels Through the Interior Parts of America,* II, 72-86.

3. Baroness Riedesel Takes the Long Road to Virginia

Before we passed the so-called Blue Mountains, we were forced to make a still further halt of eight days, that our troops might have time to collect together again. In the mean time such a great quantity of snow fell that four of our servants were obliged to go before my wagon on horseback, in order to make a path for it. We passed through a picturesque portion of the country, which, however, by reason of its wildness, inspired us with terror. Often we were in danger of our lives while going along these break-neck roads; and more than all this we suffered from cold and, what was still worse, from a lack of provisions.

When we arrived in Virginia and were only a day's journey from the place of our destination, we had actually nothing more remaining but our tea, and none of us could obtain any thing but bread and butter. A countryman whom we met on the way gave me only a hand full of acrid fruits. At noon we came to a dwelling where I begged for something to eat. They refused me with hard words, saying that there was nothing for dogs of Royalists. Seeing some Turkish [Indian] meal lying around, I begged for a couple of hands full, that I might mix it with water and make bread.

The woman answered me, "No, that is for our Negroes, who work for us, but you have wished to kill us." Captain Edmonston offered her from me two guineas for it, as my children were so hungry. But she said, "Not for a hundred would I give you any; and should you all die of hunger, it will be so much the better."

At this reply, the captain became so provoked that he wished to take it by force. I, however, entreated him, in order to prevent disturbance, to keep quiet, as we, perhaps, would soon come across better disposed people. But alas that did not happen! We did not once meet with even a hut. The roads were horrible, the horses completely tired out, my three children exhausted by hunger, very wan, and I for the first time was thoroughly disheartened. Captain Edmonston, exceedingly touched at this sight, went from man to man to see if he could not obtain something to eat. At last he received from one of the drivers of our baggage-wagons a piece of old bread, a quarter of a pound's weight, which had been considerably gnawed at, since, on account of its hardness, no one could bite off the smallest piece.

The instant he brought it to us, joy sparkled in the eyes of the children. I was about to give the first piece to Caroline as the youngest. "No," said the kind child, "my sisters are more hungry than I." Gustava and Frederica also refused to take it, wishing to leave it for their little sister. I therefore divided it and gave it to all three to eat. Tears ran down both my cheeks; and the good Edmonston was so affected that he was unable longer to endure the sight.

If I had at any time refused a piece of bread to the poor, I should have thought that God wished now to punish me for it. The kind driver, who had so willingly given us his last piece of bread, received a guinea from Captain Edmonston, and, on our arrival at the place of our destination, a large stock of bread for his return journey.

The place of our destination was Colle in Virginia, where my husband, who had gone ahead with our troops, awaited us with impatient longing. We arrived here about the middle of February, 1779, having, on our journey, passed through the provinces of Connecticut, New York, New Jersey, Pennsylvania and Maryland, and having traveled in twelve weeks six hundred and seventy-eight English miles. The house in which we lived and the entire estate belonged to an Italian, who, as he was to be absent for some time, gave it up to us. We looked forward longingly to the departure of himself, wife and daughter, for not only was the house small, but, more than all, the scarcity of provisions seemed to trouble them—a circumstance which caused the husband to exercise a kind of guardianship over us. Thus, when he had a ram killed, he gave us on the first day nothing more than the head, the neck and the giblets, although I represented to him that more than twenty persons were to make a meal off them. He assured me that a right good soup might be made of these articles, and gave us, besides, two heads of cabbage, with which, and half of a putrid ham, we were obliged to be satisfied.

The troops had been expected earlier, and accordingly many oxen and swine had been killed for food; and, as salt was very scarce, they cut the meat into quarters, placed it in a vault in the earth, and scattered between the pieces ashes instead of salt which answered equally as well. But as in this part of the country the sun, even in January, often shines out very warm, all the top layers were spoiled. The meat was brought to us on a wheel-barrow; but we were often obliged to throw the whole of it away, although sometimes we could wash it, in which case we salted and hung it up in smoke.

The day of our arrival, when I had scarcely enough for dinner to satisfy us alone, I saw, with tears, eight of our officers ride up just before dinner. What could we do but share with them the little we had?

The troops were stationed at Charlottesville, two hours ride from us. To reach them we were obliged to go through a very beautiful piece of woods. At first they endured many privations. They occupied block-houses, which, however, were without plaster and destitute of doors and windows, so that they were very cold inside. They worked, however, with great industry to build themselves better dwellings; and, in a short time, I saw a pretty little town spring up. Behind each barrack they laid out gardens and constructed pretty little inclosures for poultry. Afterwards, when the old provisions were consumed, they received fresh meat and meal enough to make bread. As this latter was Indian meal, it served them for omelets and dumplings; so that now they were in want of nothing but money. Very little of this latter commodity was sent to them by the English, and it was difficult sometimes to obtain credit—a circumstance which oftentimes gave great inconvenience to the common soldiers.

In the middle of the month of February the fruit trees, which were already in blossom, were all killed by the night-frost. As soon as the temperature of the air would allow, we had the garden and the field tilled and planted; and, as our landlord went off three weeks after, we took possession of everything— swine, wild turkeys, etc. Some of the latter weighed over fifty pounds and were perfectly tame; but when spring came, they all flew off to hatch their eggs, which they had laid in the forests. We gave them up for lost, but they all came back and brought with them a great number of young ones.

We had built for us a large house, with a great drawing-room in the centre, and upon each side two rooms, which cost my husband one hundred guineas. It was exceedingly pretty.

Many of the Negroes brought us everything that we needed in the shape of poultry and vegetables. Every week General Phillips and ourselves killed, by turns, an ox and two pigs. Very soon we wanted nothing. But the heat bothered us very much in summer; and we lived in constant terror of rattle-snakes. The fruits were also eaten into by three kinds of ticks. We had, more-over, very heavy thunderstorms, lasting for five or six days at a time, and accompanied by tempests which tore up by the roots more than one hundred trees in our vicinity. The trees stood very loosely, and their roots were lightly covered, as the strong winds blew away from them the earth, which was mostly sand. Besides all this, the Negroes and herdsmen often made fires un-der the trees, for which they cared nothing. By reason of this the trees were more easily blown down. Often whole forests were set on fire and burned down in order to obtain new land.

At night we were obliged to leave our windows open, that we might be able to draw in fresh air and sleep. Thereupon, three or four nasty bats, three times as large as with us, would wake us up, and we were obliged to spend half the night in chasing them around the room. On one occasion a person came in the night to my husband to tell him that the stable, which was a new one, was in danger of being blown down by the wind. Everyone ran out to prop it up, except myself, who was left alone with my children and women serv-ants. The wind continually grew stronger. A great piece of the chimney fell into the room; the whole house rocked; and I remained half the night in the greatest fear of being killed by a fragment. We were often frightened in this manner.

We had no chairs to sit on, only round blocks, which we also used for a table, laying boards upon them. In this manner we lived for three or four months, pretty contentedly.

—RIEDESEL, *Letters and Journals*, pp. 152-156.

VI. THE SUFFERINGS OF LOYALIST AND BRITISH PRISONERS

If British prisoners suffered less than American, it was not because Americans were more humane, but because they had so few facilities for imprisonment, and so little experience in the practice. They could not afford to maintain large bodies of prisoners, nor did they have enough food and fuel for proper maintenance. They made in fact little effort to detain the Hessians, confident that if they escaped it would not be back to their British masters, but to American farmers. Loyalists, on the other hand, fared hard. Some more extreme Patriots took the same attitude toward Loyalists that extreme English patriots took toward the rebels—they were traitors and should suffer the extreme penalty. This was, happily, impractical, and though—especially in the Carolinas—many of them doubtless were killed and not captured, they could console themselves that this procedure was irregular.

We give here the prison experience of one British soldier, and of two Loyalists. Ensign Hughes was an Old Etonian and a gentleman; he had bought an ensigncy in the 53d Regiment, and fought in Canada and New York. Captured at Ticonderoga, he was taken to Pepperell, Massachusetts—as much out of the world as the deserts of Arabia, he found, and inhabited by people "as ignorant as Hottentots." He was, however, allowed the freedom of the town; about the hardest thing he had to endure was that Americans had not "the least idea of a gentleman" and expected servants to sit down at table with their betters. Eventually Ensign Hughes was exchanged and returned to his native land. He died in Canada a few years later.

What the Jersey prison ship was to Americans, the Simsbury copper mines were to Loyalists, with the important difference that only a few Loyalists were imprisoned in the hideous mines. One of them was Joel Stone of Connecticut who escaped from his dungeon to Upper Canada. Escape was not, apparently, too difficult, for Rivington's Royal Gazette gives us many stories of successful prison breaks.

1. ENSIGN HUGHES ENJOYS "RURAL HAPPINESS" AT PEPPERELL

Oct. 12th [*1777*]. To pass off a tedious minute, I shall describe the passing of one day—which will serve for the whole, there being no variety. At 9 o'clock (arouse is the word) we jump up from the floor, and without the trouble of putting on our clothes, being always dressed, we fall to our breakfast, consisting of boiled rice sprinkled with salt and garnished with a few lumps of stinking butter, to prevent its sticking in the throat. This meal finished, we mount the quarter deck, which is almost five paces long; here we amuse ourselves with walking, sitting, and talking about the weather, wind, tide, etc., etc., till one o'clock, when a servant announces the dinner being ready. Our dinners always (like those of the foundation boys at Eaton) consist of one dish, with this trifling difference—theirs consists of mutton, ours salt pork, with ship biscuit. Our apparatus is first the top of a chest of drawers for table (rather the worse for wear); instead of table cloth, about an inch of grease and dirt. Our plates are formed of pieces of wood, our dish a wooden bowl; 3 one-pronged forks and two knives are laid in order (those that have knives to cut for the rest). Our drink is very small beer (generally sour) and water. After dinner one of the drawers receives the meat, which is laid by for supper. Our afternoon is the most tedious part of the day, so that by 8 o'clock we are heartily tired, when we take a slight repast and lay down on the floor of the cabin, thicker than three in a bed.

Oct. 15th. Two of our men made their escape by slipping unobserved into the boat, untying and letting her drive on shore, they laying at the bottom; this exploit was performed during a hard shower.

Oct. 17th. Most of the gentlemen being unwell, Capt. Davies having the fever and ague and myself a violent dysentery, occasioned by our confined situation and bad diet, we wrote to the Council of Boston and desired leave to go into the country on parole.

Oct. 18th. Our request being granted, a commissary brought us a parole for the town of Pepperell—but we are limited to a mile. . . .

Oct. 21st. Arrived at Pepperell, and were delivered over to the Committee of the town, who distributed us about the neighbourhood for this night. I lay at one Gibson's, who was formerly a cornet in the provincial service, the greatest blackguard and the greatest rebel I ever met with.

Oct. 22nd. Procured quarters in a house, in which I have agreed to pay two silver dollars pr week for board, etc., etc. The family are very civil—it consists of Father (who is almost deaf), Mother (a talkative old woman), and two daughters, who are of the order of old maids, confounded ugly, with beards an inch long.

Oct. 25th. This town is quite a new settlement and so little cleared that in some places the houses are a mile distant. We are almost as much out of the world here as if we were in the deserts of Arabia, and the inhabitants as ignorant as the Hottentots. I have been asked how often I have visited Jerusalem and if I did not live close by it, though I told them I lived in England; and then they asked if England was not a fine town. What a life am I to lead? I am sick of their absurdities.

Oct. 26th. I find that the people here have not the least idea of a gentleman. Our servants are treated just like ourselves, and they are surprised to find our men won't eat at the same table with us, to which they are always invited. Two of our gentlemen agreeing with some inhabitant about boarding, the only thing the people objected to was the article of washing. "Oh! if that is the only obstacle," says a Committee man, who went with them, "it is easily removed; send them a tub, and give them a little soap, and they can wash their own clothes."

November 1st. This life being such a one as perhaps I may never see again, I cannot refrain describing it. We have but one room to eat and sit in, which is in common with all the family, master, mistress and servant, and what to call it I know not, as it serves for parlour, kitchen and workroom. About 9 o'clock, Lt. Brown (who lives with me) and myself breakfast, but they all wonder how we can sleep so long. Our breakfast is bread and milk, or boiled Indian corn with butter and treacle spread over it. This is pretty substantial, and after it we generally walk into the woods, to gather chestnuts or throw stones at squirrels.

About 12 o'clock the whole family collects for dinner, which soon after smokes upon the board; and whilst it is cooling, Father shuts his eyes, mutters an unintelligible monstrous long grace, and down we all sit with no other distinction but Brown and me getting pewter plates—whereas the others have wooden platters. Our food is fat salt pork and sauce (the name they give to roots and greens). We never get fresh meat but when a fox or hawk seizes an unfortunate fowl, but, being discovered by the noise we make, is frightened and lets fall the prey, generally with the loss of a leg or wing. The fowl on this disaster is immediately pickt and put into the pot. The dinners are upon that free and easy mode that neither gentleman or lady use any ceremony—all hands in the dish at once—which gives many pretty opportunities for laughter, as two or three of us often catch hold of the same piece.

This meal over, another grace is said, and we all disperse to our different employments, theirs working and ours the best we can find. At night fall a large fire is made on the hearth, and the kitchen (or whatever it is) receives the whole family, which would present an high scene to an unconcerned spectator—Mother, Brown and me round the fire, she knitting and asking us silly questions; our servant at the opposite corner of the chimney from us; at our back two or three women spinning with large noisy wheels, and in the middle of the room sits Father, and one or two apprentice boys shelling Indian corn. We have no candles, but the room is lighted by splinters of pine wood flung into the fire. About 8 o'clock we get bread and milk for supper; a little after Father begins to yawn—upon which we stand up. He says prayers, and we depart to our beds.

Our apartment, or rather the place we lay in, extends over the whole house and is what is commonly called the garret. We have three beds in it—one of which contains Brown and me, in the second sleep our two young ladies, and close at their feet, in the third, rest the servant and apprentice. Our room is not the worse for being a repository of fruit and nuts, as we generally make an attack on the apples before we get up of a morn.

If this is the kind of life the poets say so much of and call Rural Happiness, I wish to my soul that they were here, and I in London.

—HUGHES, *Journal*, pp. 22-26.

2. A CONNECTICUT LOYALIST ESCAPES FROM HIS DISMAL DUNGEON

Narrative of Joel Stone.

November 8th, 1784

In the year 1776 I discovered that it was perfectly impracticable any longer to conceal my sentiments from the violent public. The agents of Congress acted with all the cunning and cruelty of inquisitors and peremptorily urged me to declare without further hesitation whether I would immediately take up arms against the British Government or procure a substitute to serve in the general insurrection.

I could no longer withhold any positive reply and unalterable resolution of declining to fulfil their request by joining in an act which I actually detested and which had been repeatedly deemed a rebellion by the public proclamation of General Howe. The leader of the faction then informed me that my conduct in consequence of such refusal would undergo the strictest scrutiny and that I might expect to meet the utmost severity to my person from those in authority and an incensed public.

Thus perpetually perplexed and harassed, I determined in my own mind to withdraw as soon as possible to the City of New York and there by joining his Majesty's forces cast what weight I was able into the opposite scale. But before I could carry my design into execution a warrant by order of the agents of Congress was issued out in order to seize my person. Being apprized of this and hearing that a party of men were actually on their way to my house, I packed up my books and bills, which I delivered to a careful friend to secrete, and left the care of my effects in the house to one of my sisters who had lived with me some time. Before the tumultuous mob which attended the party surrounded the premises, I had the good fortune to get away on horseback and, being in a dark night, happily eluded their search. But my sister, as I was afterwards given to understand, met the resentment of the mob, who from language the most opprobrious proceeded to actual violence, breaking open every lock in the house and seizing all the property they could discover. My goods and chattels thus confiscated they exposed to sale as soon as possible in opposition to the repeated remonstrances of my partner, declaring that the whole estate, real and personal, was become the property of the States.

But I soon found that my person was one principal object of their aim. Being informed to what place I had fled, a party of about twelve armed men with a constable came up and, seizing my horse, were proceeding into the house when I found an opportunity to slip from their hands. [It] was full fourteen days before I was perfectly secure, during which time several parties were detached after me, whom they were taught to consider as a traitor to the United States and unworthy to live. An invincible frenzy appeared to pervade the minds of the country people, and those very men who so recently had held one in the highest esteem became the most implacable enemies. I could not help considering my fate as peculiarly hard in thus being hunted as a common criminal and proscribed without cause in the very country that gave me birth, merely for performing my duty and asserting the rights of the British Constitution.

However, I had the unspeakable happiness to escape the utmost vigilance of my pursuers and at length reached Long Island. There I soon joined the King's army as a volunteer, in company with several gentlemen in the same persecuted situation, who also like myself had missed no opportunity of serving the royal cause but whose exertion had been greatly curbed by the popular party. I remained thus until the 15th April, 1778, when, finding my money just expended amidst so many enormous calls and dreading that the patience of my best friends would not hold out much longer however willing they had been to assist me, I accepted a warrant to raise a company (as stated in my memorial presented to the Right Honorable the Lords Commissioners of His Majesty's Treasury), with a view to be in pay, especially as but little prospect was presented of a speedy termination being put to the unhappy war.

On the night of the 12th of May, 1778, as I was lying at Huntingdon on Long Island in order to carry my purpose of recruiting further into execution, I was surprised whilst asleep by a company of whale boat men who took me prisoner and carried [me] over to Norwalk in Connecticut.

The magistrate before whom I was taken refused to consider me as a prisoner of war, which I claimed as a right, but charging me with the enormous crime of high treason against the States I was committed a close prisoner to Fairfield jail. I was there indicted, threatened with the vengeance of the law and warned solemnly for that death which most certainly would be inflicted upon me.

In a situation so perfectly horrible, perpetually exposed to the most barbarous insults of the populace and even some of the magistrates of the place, it may easily be supposed I would mediate [meditate] a recovery from a captivity so much to be dreaded. For a purpose so truly desirable I resolved to exert every effort of ingenuity that my mind could suggest. By the aid of my brother and other friends in that country I sent a flag to the commander of the king's army at or nigh King's Bridge in New York, soliciting immediate relief. This not producing the desired effect, I petitioned the Governor . . . that I might, agreeable to justice, be deemed a prisoner of war, treated as such and be permitted to appear before himself and Council in person to remove every objection to the late request. I freely offered to defray all the incidental expenses occasioned by my removal across the country. However, he hesitated some time but at last agreed to my proposal. I paid for the strong guard which attended me by the way and entertained some hope of my meeting a favorable reception from the Governor.

The result turned out quite contrary to my wish. My petition was rejected with the utmost disdain and I was reminded to prepare for that approaching fate which was irrevocably fixed, as I was afterwards informed by a decree which could not be thwarted.

On my return the captain and guard buoyed me up by the way with a distant view of clemency, which in a great measure prevented me from an attempt which by the aid of pecuniary means must have freed me from so dreadful a situation, as I discovered that these mercenaries were far from being invulnerable in the respect alluded to. But as that must have cost me a considerable sum, the notion that I should one day be exchanged soothed for the present my perturbed mind and prevented my immediate attempt to escape. But on my return to prison all my sanguine hopes vanished and left my mind in the utmost agitation. I began to renew my contrivances and intrigues in conjunction with my friends and resolved to spare no expense in my power to regain my liberty. Many of my schemes, though they cost large sums, proved unsuccessful, yet I did not despair of gaining my point. The dungeon was truly dismal, the walls strong and the place perpetually guarded, yet being in the prime of life my spirits were warm and my passions violent. I therefore firmly determined to effect an escape if I even should be obliged to sink the last shilling and go out naked into the world.

Communicating my final resolution to Mr. H——, a fellow prisoner, he readily approved of my plan and embraced the offered opportunity of being again free. By the generous aid of my friends and a judicious application of almost all the money I could raise we happily emerged from that place of horror July 23, 1778, and with quick despatch pursued our way into the wilderness of that country to wait the further assistance of our friends.

The whole country being immediately alarmed, a general hue and cry surrounded us, so that all our expected subsistence was cut off for two days and two nights, during which time we lived upon a fruit which grows spontaneously in those parts called Nurtle berries. When the alarm was somewhat subsided we met the help which we expected from our friends. They also instructed us how to proceed in the further completion of our plan. I found my strength much impaired by the close confinement, and so sudden a transition from a warm prison to be exposed to the dews and damps of the wood had like to have been attended with the most fatal consequences to my health. Amidst this sudden sickness we travelled every night, rested sometimes in caves of the rocks and sometimes on the cold ground in wild marshes. At the same time the heart of my companion failed him, and the dread of falling into the hands of the enemy struck him with an unmanly panic. His unparalleled pusilanimity reminded me of the travelling tribes of old who pressed their leader to return them to their late house of bondage. In vain I attempted to arouse his magnanimity, for it was all absorbed in a littleness of soul which rather would have trusted to the clemency of tyrants than improve the auspicious opportunity which fortune had put into our hands. . . .

—STONE, "Narrative," *Loyalist Narratives*, pp. 323-330.

VII. AMERICAN PRISONERS IN ENGLISH GAOLS

In the course of the war the British captured perhaps two thousand American seamen—crews of privateers and fishermen. Those taken in the coastal waters off Long Island were commonly confined in the prison ships; some were carried to Halifax and jailed there; those taken on the high seas were carried to England and imprisoned in Plymouth and elsewhere.

The British authorities—like the Union authorities in 1861—had trouble making up their minds about the status of these captured seamen. Were they pirates? or did they enjoy belligerent rights? Fear of retaliation rather than magnanimity persuaded the British to accord belligerent status to their American prisoners. These endured the usual privations and humiliations in their British gaols, but their lot was ameliorated by the generosity of many friends of the American cause who supplied them with small sums of money and with food. Throughout the war Franklin tried in vain to arrange an exchange between American prisoners in England, and British seamen held in France or in the States.

We do not have a great many prison or escape narratives from England,

*but those we have are of unusual interest. One of the best is that of the gifted
and distinguished Henry Laurens, President of the American Congress, Minister Plenipotentiary to Holland, and member of the American peace coi.mis-
sion. That the British were unprepared to accord him diplomatic immunity,
and wavered between treating him as a prisoner of war, subject to exchange,
and a traitor, guilty of high treason, reveals a great deal about their confused
attitude towards the Revolution as late as 1781.*

1. A PLEA FOR AMERICAN PRISONERS IN ENGLAND

Benjamin Franklin to David Hartley, M.P.

Passy, 14 October 1777

You in England, if you wish for peace, have at present the opportunity of
trying this means with regard to the prisoners now in your gaols. They complain of very severe treatment. They are far from their friends and families,
and winter is coming on, in which they must suffer extremely if continued in
their present situation: fed scantily on bad provisions, without warm lodging,
clothes, or fire, and not suffered to invite or receive visits from their friends,
or even from the humane and charitable of their enemies.

I can assure you from my own certain knowledge that your people, prisoners in America, have been treated with great kindness; they have been served
with the same rations of wholesome provisions with our own troops, comfortable lodgings have been provided for them, and they have been allov/ed
large bounds of villages in the healthy air, to walk and amuse themselves with
on their parole. Where you have thought fit to employ contractors to supply
your people, these contractors have been protected and aided in their operations. Some considerable act of kindness towards our people would take off
the reproach of inhumanity in that respect from the nation, and leave it where
it ought with more certainty to lie, on the conductors of your war in America.
This I hint to you, out of some remaining good-will to a nation I once loved
sincerely.

—BIGELOW, ed., *Works of Franklin*, VII, 227-228.

2. HENRY LAURENS IS IMPRISONED IN THE TOWER

*Henry Laurens was undoubtedly the most distinguished American cap-
tured by the British during the war. Charleston's leading merchant, and one
of South Carolina's most distinguished statesmen, he had been one of the
leaders in the Revolutionary movement in his state, helped write its conserva-
tive Constitution, served as member and then as President of the Continental
Congress. In 1779 he was appointed to negotiate a commercial agreement
with Holland. In August 1780 he sailed on the brig* Mercury, *only to be captured by the frigate* Vestal; *the diplomatic pouch which he threw overboard
failed to sink, was recovered by an English seaman, and its secret papers used
as a pretext for the British declaration of war against the Dutch.*

*Laurens was taken first to Dartmouth prison, then on to London where he
was examined by a group of High Commissioners, and held "on suspicion of
high treason." In October 1780 he was committed to the Tower, and there,
notwithstanding his proper claims for diplomatic immunity, and the protests*

of Franklin and others, kept in confinement for over a year. During his im-
prisonment he was subjected not only to hardships but to continuous efforts
to seduce him from his allegiance. After Yorktown he was released on parole,
and early in 1782 exchanged for Lord Cornwallis. He proceeded to Paris
where he participated in the final stages of negotiating the treaty of peace with
Britain.

Laurens' narrative, written 1780-1782.

About 11 o'clock at night I was sent under a strong guard, up three pair of stairs in Scotland Yard, into a very small chamber. Two king's messengers were placed for the whole night at one door, and a subaltern's guard of soldiers at the other. As I was, and had been for some days, so ill as to be incapable of getting into or out of a carriage, or up or down stairs, without help, I looked upon all this parade to be calculated for intimidation. My spirits were good, and I smiled inwardly. The next morning, 6th October [1780], from Scotland Yard I was conducted again under guard to the secretary's office, White Hall, where were present Lord Hillsborough, Lord Stormont, Lord George Germain, Mr. Chamberlain, Solicitor of the Treasury, Mr. Knox, Under-Secretary, Mr. Justice Addington, and others. I was first asked, by Lord Stormont, "If my name was Henry Laurens?"

"Certainly, my Lord, that is my name."

Capt. Keppel was asked, "If that was Mr. Laurens?" He answered in the affirmative.

His Lordship then said: "Mr. Laurens, we have a paper here—" holding the paper up—"purporting to be a commission from Congress to you, to borrow money in Europe for the use of Congress. It is signed Samuel Huntingdon, President, and attested by Charles Thomson, Secretary. We have already proved the handwriting of Charles Thomson."

I replied: "My Lords, your Lordships are in possession of the paper and will make such use of it as your Lordships shall judge proper." I had not destroyed this paper, as it would serve to establish the rank and character in which I was employed by the United States. Another question was asked me, which I did not rightly understand. I replied: "My Lords, I am determined to answer no questions but with the strictest truth; wherefore, I trust, your Lord-ships will ask me no questions which might ensnare me, and which I cannot with safety and propriety answer." No further questions were demanded. I was told by Lord Stormont, I was to be committed to the Tower of London on "suspicion of high treason." I asked, "If I had not a right to a copy of the commitment?"

Lord Stormont, after a pause said: "He hesitated on the word right," and the copy was not granted.

Mr. Chamberlain then very kindly said to me: "Mr. Laurens, you are to be sent to the Tower of London, not to a prison; you must have no idea of a prison."

I bowed thanks to the gentlemen, and thought of the new hotel, which had been recommended by my friends in Newfoundland. A commitment was made out by Mr. Justice Addington, and a warrant by their Lordships to the Lieutenant of the Tower to receive and confine me.

From White Hall, I was conducted in a close hackney coach, under the charge of Col. Williamson, a polite, genteel officer, and two of the illest-looking fellows I had ever seen. The coach was ordered to proceed by the most private ways to the Tower. It had been rumored that a rescue would be attempted. At the Tower the colonel delivered me to Major Gore, the residing Governor, who, as I was afterward well informed, had previously concerted a plan for mortifying me. He ordered rooms for me in the most conspicuous part of the Tower (the parade). The people of the house, particularly the mistress, entreated the Governor not to burthen them with a prisoner. He replied, "It is necessary. I am determined to expose him." This was, however, a lucky determination for me. The people were respectful and kindly attentive to me from the beginning of my confinement to the end; and I contrived, after being told of the Governor's humane declaration, so to garnish my windows by honeysuckles, and a grape-vine running under them, as to conceal myself entirely from the sight of starers, and at the same time to have myself a full view of them. Governor Gore conducted me to my apartments at a warder's house.

As I was entering the house I heard some of the people say: "Poor old gentleman, bowed down with infirmities. He is come to lay his bones here." My reflection was, "I shall not leave a bone with you."

I was very sick, but my spirits were good, and my mind foreboding good from the event of being a prisoner in London. Their Lordships' orders were: "To confine me a close prisoner; to be locked up every night; to be in the custody of two wardens, who were not to suffer me to be out of their sight *one moment*, day or night; to allow me no liberty of speaking to any person, nor to permit any person to speak to me; to deprive me of the use of pen and ink; to suffer no letter to be brought to me, nor any to go from me," etc. As an apology, I presume for their first rigor, the wardens gave me their orders to peruse. . . .

And now I found myself a close prisoner, indeed; shut up in two small rooms, which together made about twenty feet square; a warder my constant companion; and a fixed bayonet under my window; not a friend to converse with, and no prospect of a correspondence.

Next morning, 7th October, Gov. Gore came into my room with a workman and fixed iron bars to my windows; altogether unnecessary. The various guards were enough to secure my person. It was done, as I was informed, either to shake my mind or to mortify me. It had neither effect. I only thought of Mr. Chamberlain's consolation. I asked Mr. Gore, "What provision was to be made for my support?"

He replied, "He had no directions."

I said, "I can very well provide for myself, but I must be allowed means for obtaining money." He gave no answer.

In a word, I discovered I was to pay rent for my little rooms, find my own meat and drink, bedding, coals, candles, etc. This drew from me an observation to the gentleman jailer (the officer who locks up a prisoner every night), who would immediately report it to the Governor: "Whenever I caught a bird in America I found a cage and victuals for it."

What surprised me most was, although the Secretaries of State had seen the ill state of my health and must also have heard of my continuing ill by reports daily made to them, they never ordered, or caused to be provided for me, any medical assistance. The people around me thought, for a considerable time, my life in imminent danger. I was of a different opinion. When the Governor had retired from his iron bars, neither my servant nor baggage being yet arrived, I asked the warder, "If he could lend me a book for amusement?"

He gravely asked: "Will your honor be pleased to have *Drelincourt upon Death?*"

I quickly turned to his wife, who was passing from making up my bed. "Pray, Madam, can you recommend an honest goldsmith who will put a new head to my cane; you see this old head is much worn?"

"Yes, sir, I can."

The people understood me, and nothing more was said of *Drelincourt. . . .*

The 8th, Governor Gore, hypocritically kind, came and told me I had leave to walk about the Tower (he had received the order from General Vernon); but advised, I would only walk the parade before the door; "if you go farther," said he, "there will be such a rabble after you."

I treated his kindness with contempt, and refused to walk. The parade is the very place where he had predetermined to expose me. The order of General Vernon, received by him from the Secretaries of State, was "that I should be permitted to walk the Tower grounds." Mr. Gore attempted to supersede both. The Governor grew uneasy, and asked the wardens why I had not walked. They answered that I was lame with the gout.

Sunday, 12th November, hobbled out; a warder with a sword in his hand at my back; the warder informed me Governor Gore had ordered that I should walk only on the parade; I returned immediately to my little prison.

The 16th, the Governor, more uneasy, jealous and fearful of General Vernon, sent me notice I might walk the broad pavement (115 yards) before the great armory, and within the armory, all arbitrary on his part; but the walk within the building was very agreeable; it would afford sufficient exercise, and viewing the quantity and variety of military stores, etc., etc., was amusing. I visited the place almost every day, till the third December, when, going there, Lord George Gordon, [who] was also a prisoner in the Tower, unluckily met and asked me to walk with him. I declined it and returned instantly to my apartment. The Governor, being informed of this by one of his spies, although the warder explained and proved to him I was in no respect a transgressor, caught hold of the occasion and locked me up. I remained thus closely confined by his arbitrary will forty-seven days; if any, the fault was in Lord George, but the brutal Governor dared not lock him up. . . .

Sunday, 18th, General Vernon, having been fully informed by a friend in the Tower of the Governor's arbitrary locking me up from the third December, called and very kindly enquired if I took my walks abroad as usual.

I replied in the negative and candidly explained what had passed between the Governor and myself. He was exceedingly displeased and said aloud—the people below stairs heard him—"I'll take care to give orders that you may walk when you please and where you please!" He gave orders, not to the Governor, but to Mr. Kinghorn, an inferior officer.

The 22d February, walked abroad, first time since third December. The Governor very angry and much mortified; I must expect the effect of his ill nature in some other way; but I despise him.

Monday, 26th February, Mr. Oswald having solicited the Secretaries of State for my enlargement upon parole and offered to pledge "his whole fortune as surety for my good conduct," sent me the following message, in addition to the above by Mr. Kinghorn, the gentleman jailer: "Their Lordships say, if you will point out anything for the benefit of Great Britain in the present dispute with the Colonies, you shall be enlarged." The first part of the message overwhelmed me with feelings of gratitude, the latter filled me with indignation. I snatched up my pencil, and upon a sudden impulse wrote a note to Mr. Oswald as follows, and sent it by the same Mr. Kinghorn:

"I perceive, my dear friend, from the message you have sent me by Mr. Kinghorn, that if I were a rascal, I might presently get out of the Tower. I am not. You have pledged your word and fortune for my integrity. I will never dishonor you, nor myself. Yes, I could point out, but is this the place? If I had nothing in view but my own interest or convenience, promises and pointings out would be very prompt; but this is not a proper place. I could point out a doctrine, known to every old woman in the kingdom, 'A spoonful of honey will catch more flies than a ton of vinegar.' What I formerly predicted to you, came to pass. I can foresee, now, what will come to pass, *happen to me what may*. I fear no 'possible consequences.' I must have patience and submit to the will of God. I do not change with the times. My conduct has been consistent, and shall be so." . . .

The 7th March, Mr. Oswald visited and was left alone with me. It immediately occurred he had some extraordinary subject from White Hall for conversation, and so it appeared. Mr. Oswald began by saying, "I converse with you this morning not particularly as your friend, but as a friend to Great Britain." I thanked him for his candor. He proceeded: "I have certain propositions to make for obtaining your liberty, which I advise you should take time to consider. I showed the note you lately sent me to Lord Germain, who was at first very angry. He exclaimed, 'Rascals! rascals!—we want no rascals! Honey! honey!! vinegar! They have had too much honey, and too little vinegar! They shall have less honey and more vinegar for the future!'" I said to Mr. Oswald, I should be glad to taste a little of his lordship's vinegar; his lordship's honey had been very unpleasant; but Mr. Oswald said, "That note was written without a moment's deliberation, intended only for myself, and not for the eye of a minister." Mr. Oswald smiled, and said, "It has done you no harm."

I then replied, "I am as ready to give an answer to any proposition which you have to make to me at this moment as I shall be in any given time. An honest man requires no time to give an answer where his honor is concerned.

If the Secretaries of State will enlarge me upon parole, as it seems they can enlarge me if they please, I will strictly conform to my engagement to do nothing, directly or indirectly, to the hurt of this kingdom. I will return to America, or remain in any part of England which may be assigned, and render myself when demanded."

Mr. Oswald answered, "No, you must stay in London, among your friends. The ministers will often have occasion to send for and consult you; but observe, I say all this as from myself, not by particular direction or authority; but I know it will be so. You can write two or three lines to the ministers and barely say, you are sorry for what is past. A pardon will be granted. Every man has been wrong at some time or other of his life, and should not be ashamed to acknowledge it."

I now understood Mr. Oswald and could easily perceive my worthy friend was more than half ashamed of his mission. Without hesitation, I replied, "Sir, I will never subscribe to my own infamy, and to the dishonor of my children." Mr. Oswald then talked of long and painful confinement, which I should suffer, and repeated "possible consequences." "Permit me to repeat, Sir," said I, "I am afraid of no consequences but such as would flow from dishonorable acts."

Mr. Oswald desired "I would take time, weigh the matter properly in my mind, and let him hear from me."

I concluded by assuring him, "he never would hear from me in terms of compliance; if I could be so base, I was sure I should incur his contempt."

Mr. Oswald took leave with such expressions of regard and such a squeeze of the hand as induced me to believe he was not displeased with my determination.

In the course of this conversation, I asked, "Why ministers were so desirous of having me about their persons?"

Mr. Oswald said, "They thought I had great influence in America."

I answered, "I once had some influence in my own country; but it would be in me the highest degree of arrogance to pretend to have a general influence in America. I know but one man of whom this can be said; I mean General Washington. I will suppose, for a moment, the General should come over to your ministers. What would be the effect? He would instantly lose all his influence, and be called a rascal."

"Mr. Duché dreamed that he had an influence even over the General. What was the consequence of his apostasy? Was the course of American proceedings interrupted? By no means. He was execrated, and the Americans went forward." . . .

—LAURENS, "Narrative," *S.C. Hist. Soc. Coll.*, I, 24–34.

VIII. CAPTAIN ASGILL IS REPRIEVED AS A COMPLIMENT TO LOUIS XVI

For excitement, pathos and romance, the affaire Asgill ranks with the affaire André; here romance triumphs over pathos because it had a happy ending.

In March 1782 a group of Loyalist irregulars captured an American Patriot, one Joshua Huddy. Turned over to General Clinton in New York, Huddy was—at the request of the Associated Loyalists—returned by Clinton to his captors who, for reasons that appeared to them persuasive, promptly strung him up. Pinned on Huddy's breast was a placard reading:

We, the Refugees, having long with grief beheld the cruel murders of our brethren, and finding nothing but such measures daily carried into execution, therefore determined not to suffer without taking vengeance for the numerous cruelties; and thus begin, having made use of Captain Huddy as the first object to present to your view; and we further determine to hang man for man while there is a Refugee existing.

Washington, supported by a council of war, promptly decided on retaliation, and demanded that General Clinton turn over to him for punishment the officer who commanded at Huddy's execution. Clinton disowned the act of the Loyalists and refused to surrender one of his own officers as a victim. Washington then determined to retaliate on a British prisoner selected by lot, and the choice fell on Captain Charles Asgill, one of the thousands of prisoners surrendered at Yorktown.

The choice could not have been more unfortunate. By the terms of surrender, these prisoners were exempted from any punishment of this nature. And as for Captain Asgill, he was designed by Nature to excite sympathy: a lad not yet twenty, only son of Sir Charles Asgill—who was once Lord Mayor of London and was a long-time friend to the American cause—and his French Huguenot wife, Thérèse Prativiel. Young Captain Asgill himself had many American friends—he had been at Westminster School with three South Carolinians—and he was to win many more.

Soon the Asgill case became an international cause célèbre. That a charming young aristocrat should suffer death for a crime of which he was innocent, at a time when the war was clearly over, seemed to many, both in America and in Europe, an intolerable outrage. Pressure on General Washington to stay the execution was strong, and though he was adamant on the matter of release, he did yield on a stay. Meantime there were representations from at home and abroad—from General Rochambeau, from Richard Oswald in Paris, from young Alexander Hamilton. Secretary of Foreign Affairs Robert Livingston acknowledged that "the affair of Huddy . . . will need explanation in Europe." It did indeed; it promised to be a serious impediment to the new nation's campaign for diplomatic recognition and support.

Salvation—and rescue from a dangerously embarrassing situation—came in the nick of time. Distracted with grief, Lady Asgill had appealed to the French Court for help; Vergennes enlisted the sympathy of the King and Queen, and they in turn instructed him to appeal for mercy directly to General Washington. Such an appeal was, of course, irresistible. With deep relief Washington turned the correspondence over to the Congress which voted "that the life of Captain Asgill should be given as a compliment to the King of

France." Secretary Livingston, who was by now alarmed at the potentialities of the affair, wrote to John Adams:

> *The release of Captain Asgill was so exquisite a relief to my feelings that I have not much cared what interposition it was owing to. It would have been a horrid damp to the joys of peace, if we had received a disagreeable account of him.*

Finally, it should be pointed out that the deliberation and humanity manifest in the Asgill case contrasted sharply with the impulsive and vindictive behavior of the British at Charleston. Isaac Hayne, a prominent South Carolinian and a colonel in the militia, was hanged in the summer of 1781 without formal trial by Rawdon and Balfour on the technical charge of breaking his parole after the surrender of Charleston. Greene and Marion both felt that this action called for retaliation, but Greene waited until the Patriot leader Christopher Gadsden and other fellow prisoners were safe within American lines, then formally declared that the first regular British colonel captured should suffer the fate of Colonel Hayne. In fact, the threat was never carried out.

We give here half a dozen letters which tell the story of the Asgill affair, and an excerpt from the reminiscences of Elias Boudinot—he was a member of Congress at the time, and shortly elected to its Presidency.

1. "THE ENEMY HAVE INHUMANLY EXECUTED CAPTAIN JOSHUA HUDDY"

George Washington to Brigadier General Moses Hazen.

Head Quarters, May 3, 1782

Sir: The Enemy, persisting in that barbarous line of Conduct they have pursued during the course of this War, have lately most inhumanly executed Captain Joshua Huddy of the Jersey State Troops, taken Prisoner by them at a Post on Tom's River, and in consequence, I have written to the British Commander in Chief, that unless the Perpetrators of that horrid deed were delivered up I should be under the disagreeable necessity of Retaliating, as the only means left to put a stop to such inhuman proceedings.

You will therefore immediately on receipt of this designate, by Lot for the above purpose, a British Captain who is an unconditional Prisoner, if such a one is in your possession; if not, a Lieutenant under the same circumstances from among the Prisoners at any of the Posts either in Pennsylvania or Maryland. So soon as you have fixed on the Person, you will send him under a safe Guard to Philadelphia, where the Minister of War will order a proper Guard to receive and conduct him to the place of his Destination.

For your information respecting the Officers who are Prisoners in our possession I have ordered the Commisry of Prisoners to furnish you with a List of them; it will be forwarded with this. I need not mention to you that every possible tenderness, that is consistent with the Security of him, should be shewn to the person whose unfortunate Lot it may be to suffer.

—FITZPATRICK, ed., *Writings of Washington*, XXIV, 217-218.

2. "It Is Really a Melancholy Case"

Robert R. Livingston, Secretary for Foreign Affairs, to Benjamin Franklin.

Philadelphia, May 30, 1782

... I enclose a number of letters that have passed between Generals Washington, Clinton, Robinson, and Sir Guy Carleton, chiefly on the subject of Captain Huddy, who, having been taken prisoner and confined some time at New York, was carried by a Captain Lippincott and a party of soldiers to the Jersey shore, and there hanged without the least pretence. You will see an account of the whole transaction in some of the papers I sent. The General, in pursuance of his determination, has ordered the lot to be cast among the British captains. It has fallen upon the honorable Captain Asgill of the Guards, who is now on his way to camp. A friend of his, Captain Ludlow, is gone to New York to see if anything can be done to save him.

It is really a melancholy case, but the repeated cruelties of this kind that have been practiced, have rendered it absolutely necessary to execute the resolution to retaliate, which we have so often taken, and so frequently been prevented by our feelings from carrying into execution.

—WHARTON, ed., *Revolutionary Diplomatic Correspondence*, V, 462-463.

3. "Such a Sacrifice Is Repugnant to the Genius of the Age"

Alexander Hamilton to Henry Knox.

Albany, June 7, 1782

We are told that there is a British officer coming on from Cornwallis' army, to be executed by way of retaliation for the murder of Capt. Hudy. As this appears to me clearly to be an ill-timed proceeding, and if persisted in will be derogatory to the national character, I cannot forbear communicating to you my ideas upon the subject.

A sacrifice of this sort is entirely repugnant to the genius of the age we live in, and is without example in modern history, nor can it fail to be considered in Europe as wanton and unnecessary. It appears that the enemy (from necessity, I grant, but the operation is the same) have changed their system and adopted a more humane one; and, therefore, the only justifying motive of retaliation—the preventing a repetition of cruelty—ceases. But if this were not the case, so solemn and deliberate a sacrifice of the innocent for the guilty must be condemned on the present received notions of humanity, and encourage an opinion that we are, in a certain degree, in a state of barbarism.

Our affairs are now in a prosperous train, and so vigorous—I would rather say so violent—a measure would want the plea of necessity. It would argue that at this late stage of the war, in the midst of success, we should suddenly depart from that temper with which we have all along borne with a great and more frequent provocation. The death of André could not have been dispensed with, but it must still be viewed at a distance as an act of *rigid justice*. If we wreak our resentment on an innocent person, it will be suspected that we are too fond of executions. I am persuaded it will have an influence peculiarly unfavorable to the General's character. . . .

—LODGE, ed., *Works of Hamilton*, IX, 256-258.

4. "Nothing I Could Say Would Have the Least Effect"

Benjamin Franklin to Richard Oswald.

Passy, July 28, 1782

... The situation of Captain Asgill and his family afflicts me, but I do not see what can be done by any one here to relieve them. It can not be supposed that General Washington has the least desire of taking the life of that gentleman. His aim is to obtain the punishment of a deliberate murder, committed on a prisoner in cold blood by Captain Lippincott. If the English refuse to deliver up or punish this murderer, it is saying that they choose to preserve him rather than Captain Asgill. It seems to me, therefore, that the application should be made to the English ministers for positive orders directing General Carleton to deliver up Lippincott, which orders being obtained should be despatched immediately by a swift-sailing vessel. I do not think any other means can produce the effect desired.

The cruel murders of this kind, committed by the English on our people since the commencement of the war, are innumerable. The Congress and their generals, to satisfy the people, have often threatened retaliation, but have always hitherto forborne to execute it, and they have been often insultingly told by their enemies that this forbearance did not proceed from humanity but fear. General Greene, though he solemnly and publicly promised it in a proclamation, never made any retaliation for the murder of Colonel Haynes and many others in Carolina, and the people, who now think if he had fulfilled his promise this crime would not have been committed, clamor so loudly that I doubt General Washington can not well refuse what appears to them so just and necessary for their common security.

I am persuaded that nothing I could say to him on the occasion would have the least effect in changing his determination.

—Wharton, ed., *Revolutionary Diplomatic Correspondence*, V, 617-618.

5. "Let Your Feelings Plead for My Inexpressible Misery"

Lady Asgill to Count de Vergennes.

London, July 18, 1782

Sir: If the politeness of the French court will permit an application of a stranger, there can be no doubt but one in which all the tender feelings of an individual can be interested will meet with a favorable reception from a nobleman whose character does honor, not only to his own country, but to human nature. The subject, sir, on which I presume to implore your assistance is too heart-piercing for me to dwell on, and common fame has most probably informed you of it; it therefore renders the painful task unnecessary.

My son (an only son), as dear as he is brave, amiable as he is deserving to be so, only nineteen, a prisoner under the articles of capitulation of Yorktown, is now confined in America, an object of retaliation. Shall an innocent suffer for the guilty? Represent to yourself, sir, the situation of a family under these circumstances; surrounded as I am by objects of distress, distracted with fear and grief, no words can express my feeling or paint the scene: my husband given over by his physicians a few hours before the news arrived, and not in a state to be informed of the misfortune; my daughter seized with a fever and delirium, raving about her brother, and without one interval of reason, save to hear heart-alleviating circumstances.

Let your feelings, sir, suggest and plead for my inexpressible misery. A word from you, like a voice from heaven, will save us from distraction and wretchedness. I am well informed General Washington reveres your character. Say but to him you wish my son to be released, and he will restore him to his distracted family and render him to happiness. My son's virtue and bravery will justify the deed. His honor, sir, carried him to America. He was born to affluence, independence and the happiest prospects. Let me again supplicate your goodness; let me respectfully implore your high influence in behalf of innocence, in the cause of justice, of humanity, that you would, sir, despatch a letter to General Washington from France, and favor me with a copy of it to be sent from hence.

I am sensible of the liberty I have taken in making this request; but I am sensible, whether you comply with it or not, you will pity the distress that suggests it; your humanity will drop a tear on the fault and efface it. I will pray that heaven may grant you may never want the comfort it is in your power to bestow on

Asgill

—Wharton, ed., *Revolutionary Diplomatic Correspondence*, V, 635-636.

6. "Their Majesties Desire to Calm the Anxiety of a Mother"

Count de Vergennes to George Washington.

Versailles, July 29, 1782

Sir: it is not in quality of a King, the friend and ally of the United States (though with the knowledge and consent of His Majesty), that I now have the honor to write to Your Excellency. It is as a man of sensibility, and a tender father who feels all the force of paternal love, that I take the liberty to address to Your Excellency my earnest solicitations in favor of a mother and family in tears. Her situation seems the more worthy of notice on our part, as it is to the humanity of a nation at war with her own, that she has recourse for what she ought to receive from the impartial justice of her own generals.

I have the honor to enclose Your Excellency a copy of a letter which Lady Asgill has just wrote me. I am not known to her, nor was I acquainted that her son was the unhappy victim, destined by lot to expiate the odious crime that a formal denial of justice obliges you to revenge.

Your Excellency will not read this letter without being extremely affected; it had that effect upon the King and Queen, to whom I communicated it. The goodness of Their Majesties' hearts induces them to desire that the inquietudes of an unfortunate mother may be calmed, and her tenderness reassured. I felt, sir, that there are cases where humanity itself exacts the most extreme rigor; perhaps the one now in question may be of the number; but allowing reprisals to be just, it is not less horrid to those who are the victims; and the character of Your Excellency is too well known for me not to be persuaded that you desire nothing more than to be able to avoid the disagreeable necessity.

There is one consideration, sir, which, though it is not decisive, may have an influence on your resolution. Captain Asgill is doubtless your prisoner, but he is among those whom the arms of the King contributed to put into your hands at Yorktown. Although this circumstance does not operate as a safe-guard, it however justifies the interest I permit myself to take in this affair. If it is in your power, sir, to consider and have regard to it, you will do what is agreeable to Their Majesties; the danger of young Asgill, the tears, the despair of his mother, affect them sensibly; and they will see with pleasure the hope of consolation shine out for those unfortunate people.

In seeking to deliver Mr. Asgill from the fate which threatens him I am far from engaging you to seek another victim; the pardon, to be perfectly satisfactory, must be entire. I do not imagine it can be productive of any bad consequences. If the English general has not been able to punish the horrible crime you complain of in so exemplary a manner as he should, there is reason to think he will take the most efficacious measures to prevent the like in future.

I sincerely wish, sir, that my intercession may meet success; the sentiment which dictates it, and which you have not ceased to manifest on every occasion, assures me that you will not be indifferent to the prayers and to the tears of a family which has recourse to your clemency through me. It is rendering homage to your virtue to implore it.

I have the honor to be, with the most significant consideration, Sir, yours, etc.

VERGENNES

—WHARTON, ed., *Revolutionary Diplomatic Correspondence*, V, 634-635.

7. "THIS LETTER OPERATED LIKE AN ELECTRIC SHOCK"

Reminiscence of Elias Boudinot.

A very large majority of Congress were determined on his execution, and a motion was made for a resolution positively ordering the immediate execution. Mr. Duane and myself, considering the reasons assigned by the Commander in Chief conclusive, made all the opposition in our power. We urged every argument that the peculiarity of the case suggested, and spent three days in warm debate, during which more ill blood appeared in the House than I had seen. Near the close of the third day, when every argument was exhausted, without any appearance of success, the matter was brought to a close by the question being ordered to be taken. . . .

The next morning as soon as the minutes were read, the President announced a letter from the Commander in Chief. On its being read, he stated the receipt of a letter from the King and Queen of France, inclosing one from Mrs. Asgill, the mother of Capt. Asgill, to the Queen, that on the whole was enough to move the heart of a savage. The substance was asking the life of young Asgill.

This operated like an electrical shock—each member looking on his neighbor in surprise, as if saying "here is unfair play." It was suspected to be some scheme of the minority. The President was interrogated. The cover of the letters was called for. The General's signature was examined. In short, it looked so much like something supernatural that even the minority, who were so much pleased with it, could scarcely think it real.

After being fully convinced of the integrity of the transaction a motion was made that the life of Capt. Asgill should be given as a compliment to the King of France. This was unanimously carried, on which it was moved that the Commander in Chief should remand Capt. Asgill to his quarters at Lancaster. To this I objected that as we considered Capt. Asgill's life as forfeited, and we had given him to the King of France, he was now a free man, and therefore I moved that he should be immediately returned into New York, without exchange. This also was unanimously adopted, and thus we got clear of shedding innocent blood by a wonderful interposition of Providence.

—BOUDINOT, *Life and Letters*, I, 249-251.

CHAPTER TWENTY-TWO

Songs and Ballads of the Revolution

THE GENERAL LEVEL *of Revolutionary songs and ballads is low, but that is merely a reflection of the melancholy fact that the general level of poetry, both in America and in Britain, was low. In America this pervading mediocrity, to call it nothing worse, did not represent a descent from a lofty Parnassus but, if anything, an ascent; as a matter of fact Freneau, Trumbull, Dwight, Hopkinson and Barlow are an improvement on almost every poet who had gone before except Edward Taylor. In England, on the other hand, the decline from the previous generation was calamitous, and the contrast between the poetry of the period of the American Revolution and that of the next generation was so startling as to suggest something more than fortuity. During the years of the American Revolution England boasted not a single poet of even second rank, unless Cowper be admitted to this dubious category. And although the American poets, such as they were, confessed the inspiration of the war and tried their hands at some vision of Columbus, some tribute to Washington, some invocation of providential blessing, the English poets were apparently not sufficiently interested in the war to write about it at all.*

It is not, however, with formal poetry but with ballads and songs that we are concerned in this chapter; to be sure it is not always easy to distinguish the two categories. For all the volume of doggerel that cluttered up the press and filled the broadsides, the war itself produced nothing to compare with the songs of the American Civil War—not one, for example, that we sing today (as we still sing "Dixie" or "The Battle Hymn of the Republic" or "Marching through Georgia") unless it is "Yankee Doodle"—which probably came before the war. Yet here and there we come across a good ballad: "Yankee Doodle" itself, in almost any of its many forms; "The Volunteer Boys"; best of all, perhaps, the strangely moving "Nathan Hale" which has qualities of a genuine folk-ballad, and which we have given earlier.

One explanation of this is that Americans were not, as yet, a singing people, or a musical. Except among the Germans there was little church music, and no music in the schools, and few musical societies; Billings was trying to remedy that but with little success. The famous painting of "The Spirit of 'Seventy-Six" reminds us that there were drummers and fifers, but no army bands and no band music. For that matter the Revolutionary armies were not marching armies in any serious way, and it is the requirements of the march that produce the best military music. Except for a convivial song, here and there, set to traditional music, one cannot imagine the American soldiers actually singing the songs we have here: most of them are hothouse products.

For the most part we have inserted ballads and poems where they appear to belong in these volumes; thus Warren's stirring "Free America" is part of the chapter on the beginning of the Revolution; the beautiful ballad of Nathan Hale is inserted in the melancholy story of his execution; Hopkinson's "Battle of the Kegs" adorns the story of the battle for Philadelphia; and Freneau's "Prison Ship" adds its poetic testimony to the sufferings of hospitalized American prisoners, while Loyalist poetry has been levied upon to illustrate the attitude of the Tories. We include here, in a sense, what is left, and what does not seem to fit in elsewhere: ballads and songs and poems that are general rather than particular, that celebrate some larger cause or sing the praises of some universal hero rather than those that dramatize a particular battle or incident of war.

The songs themselves need little introduction. We have separated the Patriot and the Loyalist (and British) songs, and it is clear—as it is natural— that the Americans were more vocal than their enemies. We have thought it best, on the whole, to present the songs in chronological order, for there is no topical arrangement in poems and songs so few and so general. Where possible we have provided the date and the author, though these are sometimes in dispute, and often unknown.

Some of the poets' names here and elsewhere in the book are familiar and, by our standards, distinguished: Hopkinson, Dickinson, Paine, Trumbull, Freneau—but most of the songs collected by Frank Moore and other students of Revolutionary War poetry are by little-known or unknown men. Many of them have come down to us in altered form; there is no way of knowing what the soldiers actually sang, and we must be content with what is recorded, sometimes at a much later date.

I. PATRIOT

1. YANKEE DOODLE

The history of this, undoubtedly the most famous song of the Revolution, is, like the history of "Dixie," shrouded in obscurity and in controversy. One version was mentioned in the first American opera libretto, Andrew Barton's The Disappointment *(1767); another is attributed to one Dr. Shuckberg, a surgeon in the British Army, who wrote it—so it is alleged—to ridicule the American troops besieging Boston in 1775. If so, it soon got out of his control. No two versions agree, and the number of verses that got themselves added to the original is incalculable. In* The Contrast *Royall Tyler has his Yankee character Jonathan boast that while he knows only 190 of the verses of "Yankee Doodle," his sister Tabitha can sing them all.*

> Father and I went down to camp
>   Along with Captain Gooding,
> And there we see the men and boys
>   As thick as hasty pudding.

And there we see a thousand men,
    As rich as 'Squire David,
And what they wasted every day,
    I wish it could be savéd.

The 'lasses they eat every day
    Would keep a house a winter.
They have as much that I'll be bound,
    They eat it when they're a mind to.

And there we see a swamping gun,
    Big as a log of maple,
Upon a deuced little cart,
    A load for Father's cattle.

And every time they shoot it off
    It takes a horn of powder,
And makes a noise like Father's gun,
    Only a nation louder.

I went as nigh to one myself
    As Siah's underpinning,
And Father went as nigh again—
    I thought the deuce was in him.

Cousin Simon grew so bold
    I thought he would have cock't it;
It scared me so, I shrinked it off
    And hung by Father's pocket.

And Captain Davis had a gun,
    He kind of clapt his hand on't,
And stuck a crooked stabbing iron
    Upon the little end on't.

And there I see a pumkin shell
    As big as Mothers bason,
And every time they touched it off
    They scampered like the nation.

I see a little barrel too,
    The heads were made of leather,
They knocked upon't with little clubs,
    And called the folks together.

And there was Captain Washington,
    And gentlefolks about him.
They say he's grown so tarnal proud
    He will not go without 'em.

He got him on his meeting clothes,
    Upon a slapping stallion.
He set the world along in rows,
    In hundreds and in millions.

The flaming ribbons in his hat,
    They look'd so tearing fine ah,
I wanted pockily to get
    To give to my Jemimah.

I see another snarl of men
    A-digging graves, they told me,
So tarnal long, so tarnal deep,
    They 'tended they should hold me—

It scared me so I hooked it off,
    Nor stopt as I remember,
Nor turned about till I got home
    Locked up in Mother's chamber.

—STEDMAN AND HUTCHINSON, *Library of American Literature*, III, 338.

2. LIBERTY TREE

Thomas Paine, 1775
(Tune: "The Gods of Greece")

In a chariot of light, from the regions of day,
    The Goddess of Liberty came,
Ten thousand celestials directed her way,
    And hither conducted the dame.
A fair budding branch from the gardens above,
    Where millions with millions agree,
She brought in her hand as a pledge of her love,
    And the plant she named Liberty Tree. . . .

Beneath this fair tree, like the patriarchs of old,
    Their bread in contentment they ate,
Unvexed with the troubles of silver or gold,
    The cares of the grand and the great.
With timber and tar they Old England supplied,
    And supported her power on the sea:
Her battles they fought, without getting a groat,
    For the honor of Liberty Tree.

But hear, O ye swains ('tis a tale most profane),
    How all the tyrannical powers,
Kings, Commons and Lords, are uniting amain
    To cut down this guardian of ours.

From the East to the West blow the trumpet to arms,
　　Thro' the land let the sound of it flee:
Let the far and the near all unite with a cheer,
　　In defense of our Liberty Tree.
　　　　　　　　—FONER, ed., *Writings of Paine*, II, 1091.

3. BUNKER HILL, OR THE AMERICAN HERO

1775

*Nathaniel Niles, who wrote this "Sapphick Ode," called it "The American
Hero," but as "Bunker Hill" it was known then, and since. Niles himself was
a versatile Connecticut Yankee who had been educated at Harvard and the
College of New Jersey, tried preaching, law, medicine and politics, and in the
end combined invention and farming, first in Connecticut and then in Vermont where he had a long and notable career. Andrew Law, of Norwich,
Connecticut, put "The American Hero" to music; later he had a distinguished
career as a composer and musical critic. His* Essays on Music *was probably
the first book of musical criticism in our literature; it announced, at the
outset, that the musician must be "a linguist, an orator, a poet, a painter,
a mathematician, a philosopher, an architect, a Christian, a friend to God and
man." This song and Billings' "Chester" were among the most widely sung
of Revolutionary songs.*

Why should vain mortals tremble at the sight of
Death and destruction in the field of battle,
Where blood and carnage clothe the ground in crimson,
　　　　Sounding with death-groans?

Death will invade us by the means appointed,
And we must all bow to the King of Terrors;
Nor am I anxious, if I am preparéd,
　　　　What shape he comes in.

Infinite goodness teaches us submission;
Bids us be quiet under all His dealings:
Never repining, but forever praising
　　　　God our Creator.

Well may we praise Him, all His ways are perfect;
Though a resplendence infinitely glowing
Dazzles in glory on the sight of mortals,
　　　　Struck blind by lustre!

Good is Jehovah in bestowing sunshine,
Nor less His goodness in the storm and thunder:
Mercies and judgments both proceed from kindness—
　　　　Infinite kindness.

THE WYOMING MASSACRE
From the painting by Chappel

BENEDICT ARNOLD

O then exult that God forever reigneth.
Clouds, which around Him hinder our perception,
Bind us the stronger to exalt His name, and
　　　Shout louder praises!

Then to the wisdom of my Lord and Master
I will commit all that I have or wish for:
Sweetly as babes sleep will I give my life up
　　　When called to yield it.

Now, Mars, I dare thee, clad in smoky pillars,
Bursting from bomb-shells, roaring from the cannon,
Rattling in grape shot, like a storm of hailstones,
　　　Torturing Aether!

Up the black heavens, let the spreading flames rise,
Breaking like Aetna through the smoky columns,
Low'ring like Egypt o'er the falling city,
　　　Wantonly burnt down.

While all their hearts quick palpitate for havock,
Let slip your blood hounds, named the British lyons:
Dauntless as Death stares; nimble as the whirlwind;
　　　Dreadful as demons!

Let Oceans waft on all your floating castles,
Fraught with destruction, horrible to nature:
Then, with your sails filled by a storm of vengeance,
　　　Bear down to battle!

From the dire caverns made by ghostly miners,
Let the explosion, dreadful as vulcanoes,
Heave the broad town, with all its wealth and people,
　　　Quick to destruction!

Still shall the banner of the King of Heaven
Never advance where I'm afraid to follow:
While that precedes me with an open bosom,
　　　War, I defy thee.

Fame and dear freedom lure me on to battle,
While a fell despot, grimmer than a death's-head,
Stings me with serpents, fiercer than Medusa's,
　　　To the encounter.

Life, for my country and the cause of freedom,
Is but a trifle for a worm to part with;—
And if preservéd in so great a contest,
　　　Life is redoubled.

—STEDMAN AND HUTCHINSON, *Library of American Literature*, III, 263-264.

4. THE PENNSYLVANIA MARCH

1775

We are the troops that n'er did stoop
  To wretched slavery,
Nor shall our seed, by our base deed,
  Despiséd vassels be.
Freedom we will bequeath them
  Or we will bravely die;
Our greatest foe ere long shall know
  How much did Sandwich lie.

CHORUS: And all the world shall know
  Americans are free;
Nor slaves nor cowards will we prove,
  Great Britain soon shall see.

We'll not give up our birthright;
  Our foes shall find us men:
As good as they in any shape,
  The British troops shall ken;
Huzza, brave boys, we'll beat them
  On any hostile plain;
For freedom, wives, and children dear,
  The battle we'll maintain.

What? Can those British tyrants think
  Our fathers crossed the main,
And savage foes and danger met,
  To be enslaved by them?
If so, they are mistaken,
  For we will rather die;
And since they have become our foes,
  Their forces we defy.

—MOORE, *Songs and Ballads*, p. 90.

5. THE AMERICAN PATRIOT'S PRAYER

1776

This patriotic hymn is sometimes ascribed to Thomas Paine; it is unlikely that Paine should have written it, however. A substantial proportion of the songs of the Revolution were written as hymns—the "Soldier's Hymn" which follows, for example, and the famous "Chester."

Parent of all, omnipotent
  In heav'n and earth below,
Thro' all creation's bounds unspent,
  Whose streams of goodness flow,

Teach me to know from whence I rose,
    And unto what designed;
No private aims let me propose,
    Since linked with human kind.

But chief to hear my country's voice,
    May all my thoughts incline,
'Tis reason's law, 'tis virtue's choice,
    'Tis nature's call and thine.

Me from fair freedom's sacred cause,
    Let nothing e'er divide;
Grandeur, nor gold, nor vain applause,
    Nor friendship false misguide.

Let me not faction's partial hate
    Pursue to this land's woe;
Nor grasp the thunder of the state,
    To wound a private foe.

If, for the right, to wish the wrong
    My country shall combine,
Single to serve th' erron'ous throng,
    Spight of themselves, be mine.
        —PAINE, *Large Additions to Common Sense*,
        appended to *Common Sense*, p. 80.

6. THE AMERICAN SOLDIER'S HYMN

'Tis God that girds our armor on,
    And all our just designs fulfills;
Through Him our feet can swiftly run,
    And nimbly climb the steepest hills.

Lessons of war from Him we take,
    And manly weapons learn to wield.
Strong bows of steel with ease we break,
    Forced by our stronger arms to yield.

'Tis God that still supports our right,
    His just revenge our foes pursues;
'Tis He that with resistless might
    Fierce nations to His power subdues.

Our universal safeguard He!
    From Whom our lasting honours flow;
He made us great, and set us free
    From our remorseless bloody foe.

Therefore to celebrate His fame,
    Our grateful voice to Heaven we'll raise;
And nations, strangers to His name,
    Shall thus be taught to sing His praise.
            —MOORE, *Songs and Ballads*, pp. 221-222.

7. WASHINGTON

The apotheosis of Washington began in the Continental Congress and flourished all through the war—and after. It is a tribute to the judgment of the American people that they at once recognized Washington's superiority and did it homage. There are any number of poems about Washington during the war, and most of them are characterized by good judgment rather than by poetic talent. We give here two anonymous poems, and one—"The Toast"— by Francis Hopkinson. Lawyer, statesman, man of letters and poet, Francis Hopkinson was one of the most gifted men of his generation; it is perhaps fitting that his son, Joseph, should have written "Hail, Columbia!" which has some claim to being our first generally accepted national song. "A New Song" was probably composed in 1776, and "Thanksgiving Hymn" at the end of the war.

A. THE TOAST

Francis Hopkinson

'Tis Washington's health—fill a bumper around,
For he is our glory and pride;
Our arms shall in battle with conquest be crowned,
Whilst virtue and he's on our side.

'Tis Washington's health—and cannons should roar,
And trumpets the truth should proclaim;
There cannot be found, search the world all o'er,
His equal in virtue and fame.

'Tis Washington's health—our hero to bless,
May Heav'n look graciously down!
Oh! long may he live our hearts to possess,
And freedom still call him her own.
            —HOPKINSON, *Miscellaneous Essays*, III, 176.

B. A NEW SONG

(Tune: "The British Grenadiers")

Vain Britons, boast no longer with proud indignity
By land your conquering legions, your matchless strength at sea!
Since we your braver sons, incensed, our swords have girded on,
Huzza, huzza, huzza, huzza, for War and Washington!

Urged on by North and Vengeance, these valiant champions came,
And bellowing "Tea and Treason!" and George was all on flame!
As sacrilegious as it seems, we Rebels still live on
And laugh at all your empty puffs, and so does Washington!

Still deaf to mild intreaties, still blind to England's good,
You have for thirty pieces betrayed your country's blood;
Like Aesop's greedy cur, you'll gain a shadow for your bone,
Yet find us fearful shades indeed, inspired by Washington.

Mysterious! unexampled! incomprehensible!
The blundering schemes of Britain, their folly, pride and zeal!
Like lions how ye growl and threat! mere asses have ye shown,
And ye shall share an ass's fate and drudge for Washington!

Your dark, unfathomed councils our weakest heads defeat,
Our children rout your armies, our boats destroy your fleet!
And to compleat the dire disgrace, cooped up within a town,
You live the scorn of all our host, the slaves of Washington!

Great Heaven! is this the nation whose thundering arms were hurled
Thro' Europe, Afric, India? Whose Navy ruled the world?
The lustre of your former deeds—whole ages of renown—
Lost in a moment—or transferred to us and Washington!

Yet think not thirst of glory unsheaths our vengeful swords
To rend your bands asunder and cast away your cords.
'Tis Heaven-born Freedom fires us all and strengthens each brave son,
From him who humbly guides the plough to god-like Washington!

For this, O could our wishes your ancient rage inspire,
Your armies should be doubled in numbers, force and fire!
Then might the glorious conflict prove which best deserved the boon—
America or Albion—a George or Washington!

Fired with the great idea our fathers' shades would rise!
To view the stern contention, the gods desert their skies,
And Wolfe, mid hosts of heroes, superior, bending down,
Cry out with eager transport, "Well done, brave Washington!"

Should George, too choice of Britons, to foreign realms apply
And madly arm half Europe, yet still we would defy
Turk, Russian, Jew and Infidel, or all those powers in one,
While Hancock crowns our Senate—our camp great Washington.

Tho' warlike weapons failed us, disdaining slavish fears,
To swords we'd beat our plough-shares, our pruning hooks to spears,
And rush all desperate on our foe, nor breathe, till battle won;
Then shout and shout, "America and conquering Washington!"

Proud France should view with terror, and haughty Spain should fear,
While every warlike nation would court alliance here—
And George, his minions trembling round, dismounted from his Throne,
Pay homage to America and glorious Washington!
—*Columbia Magazine*, August 1789.

C. THANKSGIVING HYMN

1783

The Lord above, in tender love,
Hath saved us from our foes;
Through Washington the thing is done,
The war is at a close.

America has won the day,
Through Washington, our chief;
Come, let's rejoice with heart and voice,
And bid adieu to grief.

Now we have peace, and may increase
In number, wealth, and arts;
If every one, like Washington,
Will strive to do their parts.

Then let's agree, since we are free,
All needless things to shun;
And lay aside all pomp and pride,
Like our great Washington.

From present wars and future foes,
And all that we may fear;
While Washington, the great brave one,
Shall as our chief appear.

—MOORE, *Songs and Ballads,* p. 376.

8. COLUMBIA, COLUMBIA, TO GLORY ARISE

1777

*This well-known poem was written by Timothy Dwight while he was
serving as chaplain of General Parsons' Connecticut Continental Brigade.
Young Dwight had already embarked upon that literary career which was to
make him the leading figure of the Hartford Wits, and upon his theological
and public careers as well. His later work, "Greenfield Hill," reveals the same
patriotic enthusiasm for Columbia as is found here.*

Columbia, Columbia, to glory arise.
The queen of the world, and the child of the skies!
Thy genius commands thee; with rapture behold,
While ages on ages thy splendors unfold.
Thy reign is the last, and the noblest of time,
Most fruitful thy soil, most inviting thy clime;
Let the crimes of the east ne'er encrimson thy name,
Be freedom, and science, and virtue thy fame.

To conquest and slaughter let Europe aspire;
Whelm nations in blood, and wrap cities in fire;
Thy heroes the rights of mankind shall defend,
And triumph pursue them, and glory attend.

A world is thy realm: for a world be thy laws,
Enlarged as thine empire, and just as thy cause;
On Freedom's broad basis, that empire shall rise,
Extend with the main, and dissolve with the skies.

Fair Science her gates to thy sons shall unbar,
And the east see thy morn hide the beams of her star.
New bards, and new sages, unrivalled shall soar
To fame unextinguished, when time is no more;
To thee, the last refuge of virtue designed,
Shall fly from all nations the best of mankind;
Here, grateful to heaven, with transport shall bring
Their incense, more fragrant than odors of spring.

Nor less shall thy fair ones to glory ascend,
And genius and beauty in harmony blend;
The graces of form shall awake pure desire,
And the charms of the soul ever cherish the fire;
Their sweetness unmingled, their manners refined,
And virtue's bright image, instamped on the mind,
With peace and soft rapture shall teach life to glow,
And light up a smile in the aspect of woe.

Thy fleets to all regions thy power shall display,
The nations admire, and the ocean obey;
Each shore to thy glory its tribute unfold,
And the east and the south yield their spices and gold.
As the day-spring unbounded, thy splendor shall flow,
And earth's little kingdoms before thee shall bow:
While the ensigns of union, in triumph unfurled,
Hush the tumult of war, and give peace to the world.

Thus, as down a lone valley, with cedars o'erspread,
From war's dread confusion I pensively strayed—
The gloom from the face of fair heaven retired;
The winds ceased to murmur; the thunders expired;
Perfumes, as of Eden, flowed sweetly along,
And a voice, as of angels, enchantingly sung:
"Columbia, Columbia, to glory arise,
The queen of the world, and the child of the skies."

—STEDMAN AND HUTCHINSON, *Library of American Literature*, III, 480-481.

9. CHESTER

1778

This solemn hymn, by William Billings, was one of the most widely sung of all Revolutionary songs. Billings himself has some claim to be called the father of American music. Trained as a tanner, he was self-educated in music, and as early as 1770—he was twenty-four at the time—brought out the first of many books of music: The New England Psalm-Singer. *As music master,* composer and teacher he did much to reform and modernize the singing habits of the American people.

> Let tyrants shake their iron rod,
> And slavery clank her galling chains;
> We fear them not, we trust in God—
> New England's God for ever reigns.
>
> Howe and Burgoyne, and Clinton, too,
> With Prescott and Cornwallis joined;
> Together plot our overthrow,
> In one infernal league combined.
>
> When God inspired us for the fight,
> Their ranks were broke, their lines were forced;
> Their ships were shattered in our sight,
> Or swiftly driven from our coast.
>
> The foe comes on with haughty stride;
> Our troops advance with martial noise;
> Their veterans flee before our youth,
> And generals yield to beardless boys.
>
> What grateful offering shall we bring?
> What shall we render to the Lord?
> Loud hallelujahs let us sing,
> And praise his name on every chord.
>   —MOORE, ed., *Songs and Ballads*, pp. 241-242.

10. THE VOLUNTEER BOYS

1780

This is one of the best convivial songs produced during the American Revolution. Its authorship is attributed to Henry Archer, a young Scotsman of fortune who came to America in 1778 and enlisted as a volunteer in the Continental Army.

> Hence with the lover who sighs o'er his wine,
> Chloes and Phillises toasting;
> Hence with the slave who will whimper and whine,
> Of ardor and constancy boasting.
> Hence with love's joys,
> Follies and noise,
> The toast that I give is the Volunteer Boys.
>
> Nobles and beauties and such common toasts,
> Those who admire may drink, sir;
> Fill up the glass to the volunteer hosts,
> Who never from danger will shrink, sir.
> Let mirth appear,
> Every heart cheer,
> The toast I give is the brave volunteer.

Here's to the squire who goes to parade,
Here's to the citizen soldier;
Here's to the merchant who fights for his trade,
Whom danger increasing makes bolder.
Let mirth appear,
Union is here,
The toast that I give is the brave volunteer.

Here's to the lawyer, who leaving the bar,
Hastens where honor doth lead, sir,
Changing the gown for the ensigns of war,
The cause of his country to plead, sir.
Freedom appears,
Every heart cheers,
And calls for the health of the law volunteers.

Here's to the soldier, though battered in wars,
And safe to his farm-house retired;
When called by his country, ne'er thinks of his scars,
With ardor to join us inspired.
Bright fame appears,
Trophies uprear,
To veteran chiefs who became volunteers.
—MOORE, ed., *Songs and Ballads*, p. 285.

11. TWO SATIRICAL BALLADS

We conclude the American section with two poems, or ballads, which might fit just as well in the English. Both purport to be written by Englishmen; the first, "The Halcyon Days of Old England," was inspired by Burgoyne's defeat, and picked up somehow by Horace Walpole, who transcribed it in his Journal. The second, "Our Commanders," first appeared in a London paper; it might have been written by an American sympathizer, a follower of Wilkes or Grafton, or by a soured Loyalist.

A. THE HALCYON DAYS OF OLD ENGLAND

or

Wisdom of Administration Demonstrated
A Ballad
To the tune of "Ye Medley of Mortals"

1777

Give ear to my song, I'll now tell you a story,
This is the bright era of Old England's glory;
And though some may think us in pitiful plight,
I'll swear they're mistaken, for matters go right!
　　　　　　　　Sing tantarara, wise all, wise all,
　　　　　　　　Sing tantarara, wise all.

Let us laugh at the cavils of weak silly elves!
Our statesmen are wise men—they say so themselves!
And though little mortals may hear it with wonder,
'Tis consummate wisdom that causes each blunder!
　　　　　　　　　Sing tantarara, wise all, etc.

They now are conducting a glorious war!
(It began about tea, about feathers, and tar!)
With spirit they pushed when they plannéd with sense!
Forty millions they've spent for a tax of threepence!
　　　　　　　　　Sing tantarara, wise all, etc. . . .

What honours we're gaining by taking their forts,
Destroying batteaux and blocking up ports;
Burgoyne would have worked them—but for a mishap,
By Gates and one Arnold he's caught in a trap!
　　　　　　　　　Sing tantarara, wise all, etc. . . .

Oh, think us not cruel because our allies
Are savagely scalping men, women and boys!
Maternal affection to this step doth move us—
The more they are scalpéd, the more they will love us!
　　　　　　　　　Sing tantarara, wise all, etc.

Some folks are uneasy and make a great pother
For the loss of one army and half of another:
But, sirs, next campaign by ten thousands we'll slay them,
If we can but find soldiers and money to pay them!
　　　　　　　　　Sing tantarara, wise all, etc.

I've sung you my song, now I'll give you a pray'r:
May peace soon succeed to this horrible war!
Again may we live with our brethren in concord!
And the authors of mischief all hang in a strong cord!
　　　　　　　　　Sing tantarara, wise all, etc.
　　　　—Stone, ed., *Ballads and Poems Relating to the*
　　　　　Burgoyne Campaign, p. 69.

B. our commanders

Gage nothing did, and went to pot;
Howe lost one town, another got;
Guy nothing lost, and nothing won;
Dunmore was homewards forced to run;
Clinton was beat and got a garter,
And bouncing Burgoyne catch'd a tartar;
Thus all we gain for millions spent
Is to be laughed at, and repent.
　　　　　　—Stone, ed., *Ballads and Poems Relating to the*
　　　　　　　Burgoyne Campaign, p. 68.

II. LOYALIST AND BRITISH

The Tory and British songs and poems make a sorry show. Perhaps the best of them is the anonymous "How Happy the Soldier" which was almost as popular with the Americans as with the British, and which reappeared, with new words by Charles Jones, as "The Stars and Stripes," in the second war with Britain. The best of those which can be identified is doubtless Jonathan Odell's drinking song, "The Old Year and the New." It is interesting to note that so many of the British or Tory songs were drinking songs, and so few—none here—were religious.

1. How Happy the Soldier

How happy the soldier who lives on his pay
And spends half a crown out of six-pence a day;
Yet fears neither justices, warrants, nor bums,
But pays all his debts with the roll of his drums.
With row de dow, row de dow, row de dow, dow;
And he pays all his debts with the roll of his drums.

He cares not a marnedy how the world goes;
His King finds his quarters, and money, and clothes;
He laughs at all sorrow whenever it comes,
And rattles away with the roll of his drums,
With row de dow, row de dow, row de dow, dow;
And he pays all his debts with the roll of his drums.

The drum is his glory, his joy and delight,
It leads him to pleasure as well as to fight;
No girl, when she hears it, tho' ever so glum,
But packs up her tatters and follows the drum.
With row de dow, row de dow, row de dow, dow;
And he pays all his debts with the roll of his drums.

—Dolph, *Sound Off.*

2. The Rebels

1778

Captain Smyth, the author of this song, was an officer in Simcoe's Queen's Rangers, who wrote many songs which were published during the war. "The Rebels" first appeared in the Pennsylvania Ledger *as "a new song, to the tune of Black Joke," and later under its present title.*

Ye brave, honest subjects, who dare to be loyal
And have stood the brunt of every trial
  Of hunting-shirts and rifle-guns:
Come listen awhile, and I'll sing you a song;
I'll show you those Yankees are all in the wrong,
Who, with blustering look and most awkward gait,
'Gainst their lawful sovereign dare for to prate,
  With their hunting-shirts and rifle-guns.

The arch-rebels, barefooted tatterdemalions,
In baseness exceed all other rebellions,
   With their hunting-shirts and rifle-guns.
To rend the empire, the most infamous lies
Their mock-patriot Congress do always devise;
Independence, like the first of rebels, they claim,
But their plots will be damned in the annals of fame,
   With their hunting-shirts and rifle-guns.

Forgetting the mercies of Great Britain's king,
Who saved their forefathers' necks from the string;
   With their hunting-shirts and rifle-guns.
They renounce allegiance and take up their arms,
Assemble together like hornets in swarms.
So dirty their backs and so wretched their show
That carrion-crow follows wherever they go,
   With their hunting-shirts and rifle-guns.

With loud peals of laughter, your sides, sirs, would crack
To see General Convict and Colonel Shoe-black,
   With their hunting-shirts and rifle-guns.
See cobblers and quacks, rebel priests and the like,
Pettifoggers and barbers, with sword and with pike,
All strutting, the standard of Satan beside,
And honest names using, their black deeds to hide.
   With their hunting-shirts and rifle-guns.

This perjured banditti now ruin this land,
And o'er its poor people claim lawless command,
   With their hunting-shirts and rifle-guns.
Their pasteboard dollars prove a common curse;
They don't chink like silver and gold in our purse.
With nothing their leaders have paid their debts off;
Their honor's dishonor, and justice they scoff,
   With their hunting-shirts and rifle-guns.

For one lawful ruler, many tyrants we've got,
Who force young and old to their wars, to be shot,
   With their hunting-shirts and rifle-guns.
Our good king, God speed him! never uséd men so;
We then could speak, act, and like freemen could go;
But committees enslave us, our Liberty's gone,
Our trade and church murdered, our country's undone,
   By hunting-shirts and rifle-guns.

Come take up your glasses, each true loyal heart,
And may every rebel meet his due desert,
   With his hunting-shirt and rifle-gun.

May Congress, Conventions, those damn'd inquisitions,
Be fed with hot sulphur, from Lucifer's kitchens,
May commerce and peace again be restored,
And Americans own their true sovereign lord!
   Then oblivion to shirts and rifle-guns.
     God save the King!
       —MOORE, ed., *Songs and Ballads*, pp. 196-199.

3. A CONVIVIAL SONG

1779

"A song written by a refugee on reading the King's Speech, and sung at the Refugee Club in the City of New York."

Here's a bumper, brave boys, to the health of our king,
Long may he live, and long may we sing
In praise of a monarch who boldly defends
The laws of the realm and the cause of his friends.
   CHORUS
   Then cheer up, my lads, we have nothing to fear
     While we remain steady
     And always keep ready
   To add to the trophies of this happy year.

The Congress did boast of their mighty ally,
But George doth both France and the Congress defy,
And when Britons unite, there's no force can withstand
Their fleets and their armies, by sea and on land.
   CHORUS

Thus supported, our cause we will ever maintain,
And all treaties with rebels will ever disdain;
Till, reduced by our arms, they are forced to confess
While ruled by Great Britain they ne'er knew distress.
   CHORUS

Then let us, my boys, Britain's right e'er defend.
Who regards not her rights, we esteem not our friend;
Then, brave boys, we both France and the Congress defy,
And we'll fight for Great Britain and George till we die.
   CHORUS
       —MOORE, ed., *Songs and Ballads*, p. 253.

4. THE OLD YEAR AND THE NEW: A PROPHECY

Jonathan Odell, 1779-1780
What though last year be past and gone,
   Why should we grieve or mourn about it?
As good a year is now begun,
   And better, too—let no one doubt it.

'Tis New Year's morn; why should we part?
　　Why not enjoy what heaven has sent us?
Let wine expand the social heart,
　　Let friends, and mirth, and wine content us.

War's rude alarms disturbed last year;
　　Our country bled and wept around us;
But this each honest heart shall cheer,
　　And peace and plenty shall surround us. . . .

Last year saw many honest men
　　Torn from each dear and sweet connection;
But this shall see them home again
　　And happy in their king's protection. . . .

Last year rebellion proudly stood,
　　Elate, in her meridian glory;
But this shall quench her pride in blood;
　　George will avenge each martyred Tory. . . .

Then bring us wine, full bumpers bring;
　　Hail this New Year in joyful chorus;
God bless great George our Gracious King
　　And crush rebellion down before us!

'Tis New Year's morn; why should we part?
　　Why not enjoy what heaven has sent us?
Let wine expand the social heart,
　　Let friends, and mirth, and wine content us.

—SARGENT, ed., *Loyalist Poetry of the Revolution*, pp. 99-101.

5. THE VOLUNTEERS OF IRELAND

This song was written for the Loyalist regiment, the Volunteers of Ire-land, and sung on St. Patrick's Day of 1780 at a celebration provided by the colonel of the regiment, Lord Rawdon.

Success to the Shamrock, and all those who wear it;
　　Be honor their portion wherever they go:
May riches attend them, and stores of good claret,
　　For how to employ them sure none better know.
Every foe surveys them with terror,
But every silk petticoat wishes them nearer;
So Yankee keep off, or you'll soon learn your error,
　　For Paddy shall prostrate lay every foe.

This day, but the year I can't rightly determine,
　　St. Patrick the vipers did chase from the land;
Let's see if like him, we can't sweep off the vermin
　　Who dare 'gainst the sons of the shamrock to stand.

Hand in hand! Let's carol the chorus—
As long as the blessings of Ireland hang o'er us,
The crest of Rebellion shall tremble before us,
    Like brothers, while thus we march hand in hand.

St. George and St. Patrick, St. Andrew, St. David,
    Together may laugh at all Europe in arms.
Fair conquest her standard has o'er their heads wavéd,
    And glory has on them conferred all the charms.
War's alarms to us are a pleasure,
Since honour our danger repays in full measure,
And all those who join us shall find we have leisure
    To think of our sport even in war's alarms.
    —MOORE, *Diary of the American Revolution*, II, 261-262.

CHAPTER TWENTY-THREE

Sea Battles and Naval Raids

THE STORY *of the sea battles and naval campaigns of the American Revolution is a nautical version of David and Goliath. The British Navy enjoyed overwhelming superiority over the tiny Continental naval force, except perhaps for that comparatively brief period when the French Navy was effectively committed and boldly directed to advancing the military and amphibious operations of the allied forces in America. No American naval force could cope with the larger vessels and squadrons of the British Navy. The operations of the Continental cruisers were severely restricted to isolated skirmishes, often heroic in character, to providing a small degree of protection to American coastal shipping, and to making war on hostile privateers and smaller men-of-war. To a limited extent the Continental Navy co-operated with Patriot land forces around certain towns. It attacked the enemy's communications and overseas commerce and even raided the coasts of the British Isles and the outlying parts of the British Empire.*

The Continental and state navies put to sea some hundred ships. The British, in turn, increased their naval forces from 270 ships in 1775 to 468 in 1783, of which 174 carried sixty cannon or more, heavily outgunning the American frigates. Nevertheless, despite this vast superiority over the Americans the British suffered the loss of 200 ships sunk or captured by the Continental or state navies. Although by the end of the war the Continental Navy was virtually eliminated, the naval war was still fought fiercely on the high seas. The explanation is that the most punishing blows to British commerce were inflicted by American privateers, outfitted in huge numbers, readily manned with trained seamen, and easily replaced when sunk or captured. The privateers accounted for another 600 British ships sunk or captured. Paradoxically, then, there never was a period in the war when American naval operations, public and private, did not constitute a nuisance threat to the British merchant marine as they pinned down British squadrons, raised the price of imports to England, and even on occasion brought the war home to the British people.

Before France came into the war the British used their Navy largely in amphibious operations in America—to launch the Northern campaign down

Lake Champlain, to land and evacuate troops at Boston, to attack New York, Charleston, Narragansett Bay and Philadelphia, and to make sporadic raids against seaport towns like Bristol and Falmouth. Once France openly joined America, and then Spain joined France in alliance against England, large naval engagements were inevitable.

Down until the year 1781 French naval operations off North America were largely inconclusive. As a result of the procrastination of the French admiral, Count d'Estaing, the British fleet stationed at the mouth of the Delaware Bay managed to elude him and to get back to the safety of New York, which d'Estaing's larger vessels did not venture to enter. Instead, the French admiral participated in an inglorious amphibious operation against Newport, with General John Sullivan as commander of the land forces, an operation which is treated at length elsewhere in this volume.

In European waters Admiral Keppel's squadron clashed in an indecisive engagement with the French fleet of Admiral the Comte d'Orvilliers off Ushant. Similarly, in the West Indies, early operations were damaging to British naval power but not decisive. The French captured Dominica and Grenada and repulsed Vice-Admiral Byron's attempt to recapture the latter island with severe losses to the British, who in turn seized Martinique.

The French fleet was unable to prevent the British capture of Savannah or to effect its recapture or to prevent the great capitulation of Charleston to the British. The story was different in the year 1781, when the Count de Grasse, as we shall see in a later chapter, succeeded in bottling up the sea approaches to Yorktown. In other areas of naval operations the British were, however, far more successful. Rodney scored a smashing victory over De Grasse in the West Indies on April 12, 1782; Lord Howe successfully relieved Gibraltar; a British expedition captured the Dutch colony on the Cape of Good Hope; and inconclusive naval sparring off the Coromandel Coast of India took place between French and British squadrons. In fact, the ability of the British Navy to rebound in adversity made it possible for the British to stiffen the terms of peace with America and persuaded France and Spain to agree to a termination of the conflict.

As a preliminary to the story of the naval campaigns we give a collection of narratives and documents designed to illuminate the many political and administrative problems that emerged to perplex the Patriots—problems of Admiralty, prize courts, blockade, appointments, and so forth. It is interesting to note that the ubiquitous John Adams is almost as prominent here as in the political arena. The difficulties that confronted the Americans were natural, almost inevitable, in a country without a prior naval establishment, or a naval tradition. That so great a naval power as Great Britain experienced difficulties equally formidable is to be explained in part by the logistics of the war, but in large part by sheer incompetence and corruption.

I. FOUNDING THE AMERICAN NAVY

As might have been expected, the initiative for building a Navy came from seafaring New England, an area acutely conscious of the need for ob-

*taining security on the seas. The first proposal was advanced by Rhode Island.
The General Assembly, convened at Providence, adopted a resolution of in-
structions to the Rhode Island delegates to the Continental Congress on
August 26, 1775, which included a proposal for establishing an American
Navy. On October 3 the Rhode Island delegates to Congress introduced a
motion for setting up a Continental naval force. Two days later letters from
London were brought to the attention of Congress revealing that two brigs
containing arms, powder and other stores had sailed without convoy from
England on August 11 bound for Quebec. A motion was thereupon made that
a committee of three be appointed to prepare a plan for intercepting the brigs,
and a heated debate was set off. John Adams, who served on the enlarged
Committee for Fitting Out Armed Vessels formed shortly thereafter, recounts
the proceedings in Congress which led to the founding of the Navy.*

1. Rhode Island Calls on Congress to Build a Fleet

Resolutions of the General Assembly of Rhode Island.

August 26, 1775

Whereas, notwithstanding the humble and dutiful petition of the last Congress to the King, and otherwise pacific measures taken for obtaining a happy
reconciliation between Great Britain and the colonies; the ministry, lost to
every sentiment of justice, liberty and humanity, continue to send troops and
ships of war into America, which destroy our trade, plunder and burn our
towns, and murder the good people of these colonies——

It is therefore voted and resolved, that this colony most ardently wish to
see the former friendship, harmony and intercourse between Britain and these
colonies restored, and a happy and lasting connection established between
both countries, upon terms of just and equal liberty; and will concur with the
other colonies in all proper measures for obtaining those desirable blessings.

And as every principle, divine and human, require us to obey that great
and fundamental law of nature, self-preservation, until peace shall be restored
upon constitutional principles, this colony will most heartily exert the whole
power of government, in conjunction with the other colonies, for carrying
on this just and necessary war, and bringing the same to a happy issue.

And amongst other measures for obtaining this most desirable purpose,
this Assembly is persuaded that the building and equipping an American fleet,
as soon as possible, would greatly and essentially conduce to the preservation
of the lives, liberty and property of the good people of these colonies; and
therefore instruct their delegates to use their whole influence, at the ensuing
Congress, for building, at the Continental expense, a fleet of sufficient force
for the protection of these colonies, and for employing them in such a manner
and places as will most effectually annoy our enemies and contribute to the
common defence of these colonies.

—Rhode Island Records, VII, 368-369.

2. "The True Origin and Foundation of the American Navy"

From the Autobiography of John Adams.

[1775]

On Thursday, October 5th, 1775, sundry letters from London were laid before Congress and read, and a motion was made that it be

Resolved, That a committee of three be appointed to prepare a plan for intercepting two vessels which are on their way to Canada, laden with arms and powder, and that the committee proceed on this business immediately.

The secretary has omitted to insert the names of this committee on the journals, but as my memory has recorded them, they were Mr. Deane, Mr. Langdon, and myself, three members who had expressed much zeal in favor of the motion.

[*October 13, 1775*]. As a considerable part of my time, in the course of my profession, had been spent upon the sea-coast of Massachusetts, in attending the courts and lawsuits at Plymouth, Barnstable, Martha's Vineyard, to the southward, and in the counties of Essex, York and Cumberland to the eastward, I had conversed much with the gentlemen who conducted our cod and whale fisheries as well as the other navigation of the country, and had heard much of the activity, enterprise, patience, perseverance, and daring intrepidity of our seamen. I had formed a confident opinion that, if they were once let loose upon the ocean, they would contribute greatly to the relief of our wants, as well as to the distress of the enemy. I became therefore at once an ardent advocate for this motion, which we carried, not without great difficulty.

The opposition to it was very loud and vehement. Some of my own colleagues appeared greatly alarmed at it, and Mr. Edward Rutledge never displayed so much eloquence as against it. He never appeared to me to discover so much information and sagacity, which convinced me that he had been instructed out-of-doors by some of the most knowing merchants and statesmen in Philadelphia. It would require too much time and space to give this debate at large, if any memory could attempt it. Mine cannot. It was, however, represented as the most wild, visionary, mad project that ever had been imagined. It was an infant, taking a mad bull by his horns; and what was more profound and remote, it was said it would ruin the character, and corrupt the morals of all our seamen. It would make them selfish, piratical, mercenary, bent wholly upon plunder, etc., etc. These formidable arguments and this terrible rhetoric were answered by us by the best reasons we could allege, and the great advantage of distressing the enemy, supplying ourselves, and beginning a system of maritime and naval operations, were represented in colors as glowing and animating. The vote was carried, the committee went out, returned very soon and brought in the report. . . .

". . . Friday, October 13. The Congress, taking into consideration the report of the committee appointed to propose a plan, etc., after some debate,

"*Resolved*, That a swift sailing vessel, to carry ten carriage guns and a proportionable number of swivels, with eighty men, be fittted with all possible despatch for a cruise of three months, and that the commander be instructed to cruise eastward, for intercepting such transports as may be laden with war-like stores and other supplies for our enemies, and for such other purposes as the Congress shall direct. That a committee of three be appointed to prepare an estimate of the expense, and lay the same before the Congress, and to contract with proper persons to fit out the vessel.

"*Resolved*, That another vessel be fitted out for the same purposes, and that the said committee report their opinion of a proper vessel, and also an estimate of the expense.

"The following members were chosen to compose the committee: Mr. Deane, Mr. Langdon and Mr. Gadsden.

"*Resolved*, That the further consideration of the report be referred to Monday next.

"Monday, October 30. The committee appointed to prepare an estimate and to fit out the vessels, brought in their report, which, being taken into consideration,

"*Resolved*, That the second vessel, ordered to be fitted out on the 13th instant, be of such a size as to carry fourteen guns and a proportionate number of swivels and men.

"*Resolved*, That two more vessels be fitted out with all expedition, the one to carry not exceeding twenty guns, and the other not exceeding thirty-six guns, with a proportionable number of swivels and men, to be employed in such manner, for the protection and defence of the United Colonies, as the Congress shall direct.

"*Resolved*, That four members be chosen and added to the former committee of three, and that these seven be a committee to carry into execution, with all possible expedition, as well the resolutions of Congress, passed the 13th instant, as those passed this day, for fitting out armed vessels.

"The members chosen: Mr. Hopkins, Mr. Hewes, Mr. Richard Henry Lee and Mr. John Adams."

This committee immediately procured a room in a public house in the city and agreed to meet every evening at six o'clock in order to despatch this business with all possible celerity. . . .

On the 17th of November,

"A letter from General Washington, enclosing a letter and journal of Colonel Arnold and sundry papers, being received, the same were read, whereupon,—

"*Resolved*, That a committee of seven be appointed to take into consideration so much of the General's letter as relates to the disposal of such vessels and cargoes belonging to the enemy as shall fall into the hands of, or be taken by, the inhabitants of the United Colonies.

"The members chosen, Mr. Wythe, Mr. E. Rutledge, Mr. J. Adams, Mr. W. Livingston, Dr. Franklin, Mr. Wilson and Mr. Johnson.

"Thursday, November 23. The committee, for fitting out armed vessels, laid before Congress a draught of rules for the government of the American navy, and articles to be signed by the officers and men employed in that service, which were read, and ordered to lie on the table for the perusal of the members.

"Saturday, November 25. Congress resumed the consideration of the report of the committee on General Washington's letter, and the same being debated by paragraphs, was agreed to as follows.

"Whereas, it appears from undoubted information that many vessels which had cleared at the respective custom-houses in these Colonies, agreeable to the regulations established by Acts of the British Parliament, have in a lawless manner, without even the semblance of just authority, been seized by His Majesty's ships of war and carried into the harbor of Boston and other ports, where they have been rifled of their cargoes, by orders of His Majesty's naval and military officers there commanding, without the said vessels having been proceeded against by any form of trial, and without the charge of having offended against any law.

"And whereas orders have been issued in His Majesty's name, to the commanders of his ships of war, 'to proceed as in the case of actual rebellion against such of the seaport towns and places, being accessible to the King's ships, in which any troops shall be raised, or military works erected,' under color of which said orders, the commanders of His Majesty's said ships of war have already burned and destroyed the flourishing and populous town of Falmouth, and have fired upon and much injured several other towns within the United Colonies, and dispersed at a late season of the year hundreds of helpless women and children, with a savage hope that those may perish under the approaching rigors of the season, who may chance to escape destruction from fire and sword; a mode of warfare long exploded among civilized nations.

"And whereas the good people of these Colonies, sensibly affected by the destruction of their property, and other unprovoked injuries, have at last determined to prevent as much as possible a repetition thereof, and to procure some reparation for the same, by fitting out armed vessels and ships of force; in the execution of which commendable designs it is possible that those who have not been instrumental in the unwarrantable violences above mentioned may suffer, unless some laws be made to regulate, and tribunals erected competent to determine the propriety of captures.

"Therefore, *Resolved*,——

"1. That all such ships of war, frigates, sloops, cutters and armed vessels as are or shall be employed in the present cruel and unjust war against the United Colonies, and shall fall into the hands of, or be taken by, the inhabitants thereof, be seized and forfeited to and for the purposes hereinafter mentioned.

"2. That all transport vessels in the same service, having on board any troops, arms, ammunition, clothing, provisions, or military or naval stores, of what kind soever, and all vessels to whomsoever belonging that shall be employed in carrying provisions or other necessaries to the British army or armies or navy, that now are, or shall hereafter be, within any of the United

Colonies, or any goods, wares, or merchandises, for the use of such fleet or army, shall be liable to seizure, and with their cargoes shall be confiscated."

I have been particular in transcribing the proceedings of this day, November 25th, 1775, because they contain the true origin and foundation of the American Navy, and, as I had at least as great a share in producing them as any man living or dead. . . .

On Tuesday, November 28th, the Congress resumed the consideration of the rules and orders for the Navy of the United Colonies, and the same being debated by paragraphs were agreed to. . . . They were drawn up in the marine committee, and by my hand, but examined, discussed and corrected by the committee. In this place I will take the opportunity to observe that the pleasantest part of my labors for the four years I spent in Congress from 1774 to 1778 were in this naval committee. Mr. Lee, Mr. Gadsden were sensible men, and very cheerful, but Governor Hopkins of Rhode Island, about seventy years of age, kept us all alive. Upon business, his experience and judgment were very useful. But when the business of the evening was over, he kept us in conversation till eleven, and sometimes twelve o'clock. His custom was to drink nothing all day, nor till eight o'clock in the evening, and then his beverage was Jamaica spirit and water. It gave him wit, humor, anecdotes, science and learning. He had read Greek, Roman and British history, and was familiar with English poetry, particularly Pope, Thomson and Milton, and the flow of his soul made all his reading our own and seemed to bring to recollection in all of us all we had ever read. I could neither eat nor drink in these days. The other gentlemen were very temperate. Hopkins never drank to excess, but all he drank was immediately not only converted into wit, sense, knowledge and good humor, but inspired us with similar qualities.

This committee soon purchased and fitted five vessels. The first we named *Alfred*, in honor of the founder of the greatest navy that ever existed. The second, *Columbus*, after the discoverer of this quarter of the globe. The third, *Cabot*, for the discoverer of this northern part of the continent. The fourth, *Andrew Doria*, in memory of the great Genoese Admiral, and the fifth, *Providence*, for the town where she was purchased, the residence of Captain Hopkins and his brother Ezek, whom we appointed first captain. We appointed all the officers of all the ships. At the solicitation of Mr. Deane, we appointed his brother-in-law, Captain Saltonstall.

Sometime in December, worn down with long and uninterrupted labor, I asked and obtained leave to visit my State and family. Mr. Langdon did the same. Mr. Deane was left out of the delegation by his State, and some others of the naval committee were dispersed, when Congress appointed a committee of twelve, one from each State, for naval affairs, so that I had no longer any particular charge relative to them; but as long as I continued a member of Congress, I never failed to support all reasonable measures reported by the new committee.

—ADAMS, ed., *Works of John Adams*, III, 7-12.

II. CONGRESS RUNS THE NAVY

The Marine Committee set up by Congress applied itself at once to the conduct of naval affairs. While the rest of the committee were in Baltimore, Robert Morris proposed to Paul Jones a bold plan of attacking the British West Indies, Pensacola and St. Augustine, to draw the British Navy off the American coast. But most of Morris' colleagues were less sure of how to run the Navy and not agreed on the strategy to be employed.

Writing on November 7, 1776, to William Vernon, a member of the Navy Board, William Ellery of the Marine Committee confessed: "The conduct of the affairs of a navy as well as those of an army we are yet to learn." He asked that all knowledge of maritime and naval affairs be thrown "into the common stock," and particularly solicited advice about how the British Navy operated.

One of the first matters attended to by Congress was the setting up of Boards of Admiralty, which were regional naval boards. It was found necessary not to tie the regional boards down by too rigid instructions, but to give them some latitude in directing fleet operations. Washington, whose experience in the front lines had not augmented his stock of admiration for the way Congress handled military matters, felt much the same way about the Navy. This is made explicit in the exchange between the general and John Jay, at that time serving in Congress. The "certain commercial agent in Europe," to whom Jay refers in unflattering terms, was the paranoid Arthur Lee, and the "family compact" doubtless refers to the political alignments of the Virginia Lees, who generally opposed Deane, Franklin and Washington, and lined up on many questions with John Adams and a few of the New England malcontents in Congress.

The remaining letters in this section illustrate other problems confronting Congress or the regional Navy boards in handling naval affairs—running the blockade, protecting merchant ships, fixing on the size of naval vessels, and settling clashes over rank and seniority. John Paul Jones himself was the victim of the seniority system. In the spring of 1781 Congress recommended his promotion to the rank of Rear Admiral, but the action was blocked by rival officers. Captain Nicholson's letter to Captain Barry reveals the fierce jealousy that at times inspired ungenerous acts by America's first naval heroes.

1. JOHN PAUL JONES IS URGED TO CARRY THE WAR TO THE ENEMY

Robert Morris to John Paul Jones.

Philadelphia, February 1, 1777

... Destroying their settlements [the British West Indies and Pensacola], spreading alarms, showing and keeping up a spirit of enterprize that will oblige them to defend their extensive possessions at all points, is of infinitely more consequence to the United States of America than all the plunder that can be taken. If they divide their force we shall have elbow room and, that gained, we shall turn about and play our parts to the best advantage, which we cannot do now being constantly cramped in one part or an other.

It has long been clear to me that our infant fleet cannot protect our own coasts; and the only effectual relief it can afford us is to attack the enemies defenceless places and thereby oblige them to station more of their ships in their own countries, or to keep them employed in following ours, and either way we are relieved so far as they do it.

I do not pretend to give you any account of the coasts and harbours, strength of fortifications or mode of attack, for I cannot doubt your being well acquainted with these things, knowing as I do that you have been a commander in the West India trade, and at any rate your appearance will be unexpected and the enemy unprepared. They have no troops, and the very sound of a great gun will frighten them into submission. Governor Chester [Governor of West Florida] will no doubt know where the brass artillery are deposited and be glad to surrender them as a ransom for himself and his capital. When your business is done at Pensacola you may give them an alarm at St. Augustine, but they have some troops and you must be careful of your men. I think you should carry with you as many marines as possible, for they will be useful and necessary in all your land excursions.

The southern Colonies wish to see part of their Navy, and if you find it convenient and safe you might recruit and refit at Georgia, South or North Carolina, there make sale of such part of your prize goods, etc., as would be useful to them, learn where was the safest port to the northward, and then push along to such place of safety as might be necessary for refitting and re-manning the fleet. Should you prefer going to the coast of Africa you have the consent of the Marine Committee, but in that case I apprehend you only want the two ships and sloop *Providence*. Remember it is a long voyage—that you cannot destroy any English settlements there, and that if you meet any of their men of war in those seas they will be much superior to you in strength, etc. You may, it is true, do them much mischief, but the same may be done by cruizing to windward of Barbadoes as all their Guineamen fall in there. However, you are left to your choice and I am sure will choose for the best. Should there be a difficulty in getting all the vessels fully manned with so many seamen as you may think necessary, take the more Marines and you will get seamen from prizes in the course of your voyage. . . .

—Paullin, *Out-Letters of the Marine Committee*, I, 65-70.

2. Why Does Congress Keep the Continental Frigates in Port?

George Washington to John Jay.

Middlebrook, April, 1779

In one of your former letters you intimate, that a free communication of sentiments will not be displeasing to you. If, under this sanction, I should step beyond the line you would wish to draw, and suggest ideas or ask questions which are improper to be answered, you have only to pass them by in silence. I wish you to be convinced that I do not desire to pry into measures the knowledge of which is not necessary for my government as an executive officer, or the premature discovery of which might be prejudicial to plans in contemplation.

After premising this, I beg leave to ask what are the reasons for keeping the continental frigates in port? If it is because hands cannot be obtained to man them on the present encouragement, some other plan ought to be adopted to make them useful. Had not Congress better lend them to commanders of known bravery and capacity for a limited term, at the expiration of which the vessels, if not taken or lost, to revert to the States—they and their crews, in the mean time, enjoying the exclusive benefit of all captures they make, but acting either singly or conjointly under the direction of Congress? If this or a similar plan could be fallen upon, comprehending the whole number, under some common head, a man of ability and authority commissioned to act as commodore or admiral, I think great advantages might result from it. I am not sure but at this moment, by such a collection of the naval force we have, all the British armed vessels and transports at Georgia might be taken or destroyed, and their troops ruined. Upon the present system, our ships are not only very expensive and totally useless in port, but sometimes require a land force to protect them, as happened lately at New-London. . . .

Will Congress suffer the Bermudian vessels, which are said to have arrived at Delaware and Chesapeake Bays, to exchange their salt for flour, as is reported to be their intention? Will they not rather order them to depart immediately? Indulging them with a supply of provisions at this time will be injurious to us in two respects: it will deprive us of what we really stand in need of for ourselves, and will contribute to the support of that swarm of privateers which resort to Bermuda, from whence they infest our coast, and, in a manner, annihilate our trade. Besides these considerations, by withholding a supply, we throw many additional mouths upon the enemy's magazines, and increase proportionately their distress. They will not and cannot let their people starve.

In the last place, though first in importance, I shall ask, is there any thing doing, or that can be done, to restore the credit of our currency? The depreciation of it is got to so alarming a point that a wagon-load of money will scarcely purchase a wagon-load of provision.

—FITZPATRICK, ed., *Writings of Washington*, XIV, 435-437.

3. THE LEE FAMILY IS BEHIND THE BUNGLING OF NAVAL AFFAIRS

John Jay to George Washington.

Philadelphia, 26th April, 1779

The questions contained in your favour of the — April instant are as important as the manner of introducing them is delicate.

While the maritime affairs of the continent continue under the direction of a committee, they will be exposed to all the consequences of want of system, attention and knowledge. The marine committee consists of a delegate from each State. It fluctuates, new members constantly coming in, and old ones going out. Three or four, indeed, have remained in it from the beginning; and few members understand even the state of our naval affairs, or have time or inclination to attend to them.

But why is not this system changed? It is, in my opinion, convenient to the family compact. The commercial committee was equally useless. A proposition was made to appoint a commercial agent for the States under certain regulations. Opposition was made. The ostensible objections were various.

The true reason was its interfering with a certain commercial agent in Europe and his connections.

You will, if I am not greatly mistaken, find Mr. Gerard disposed to be open and communicative. He has acquired an extensive knowledge of our affairs. I have no reason to believe he will use it to our prejudice. There is as much intrigue in this State-house as in the Vatican, but as little secrecy as in a boarding-school. It mortifies me on this occasion to reflect that the rules of Congress on the subject of secrecy, which are far too general, and perhaps for that reason more frequently violated, restrains me from saying twenty things to you which have ceased to be private.

—JAY, *Correspondence and Public Papers,* I, 209-210.

4. RUNNING THE BLOCKADE

John Deshon (a member) to the Navy Board.

Providence, March 9th, 1778
Saturday evening I got to this place

Gentlemen

Yours of the 3rd and 5th instant are now before me. In ansuer to the former, respecting the ship *Warren*, I am happy she so well succeeded in getting out of this river. Every circumstance combined in her favour that she might [get] clear of the enemy. The night was exceeding dark, and there was but little wind untill the crittecal time of passing the greatest danger, when the wind shifted very suddenly into the N.W. and blowd exceeding hard, so that the enemy could not without the greatest difficulty get under sail and persue.

I was at Warrick Neck and up the most part of the night when the *Warren* passed and am very sure it was imposable for Capt. Hopkins to gain the port of N. London, there being so much wind and the weather so severe cold. There where [were] on board the *Warren* about 170 men, manny of which had not a second shift of cloaths; therefore it will be very difficult as well as teadius for Capt. Hopkins to beat this courst at this severe season. The orders given him by me, you have with you, which gives him not the least encouragement to cruise. Nevertheless, should the ship keep out this three weeks, I shall not be in the least uneasy about her, well knowin[g] the men in no condission to beat a winters courst. We have succeeded b[e]yound expectation in geting her out, and I have not the least doubt but she will in due time return with honor to the commander and his company. . . .

—DESHON, "Letter," *R. I. Hist. Soc. Pub.,* New Series, VIII, 214.

5. A PATRIOT ARGUMENT AGAINST BUILDING BIG WARSHIPS

William Ellery to William Vernon.

York Town, March 16th, 1778
I read that part of your letter respecting the seventy-four at Portsmouth, and a paragraph of one I received about the same time and upon the same subject from Mr. Whipple, to the Marine Committee, and it was agreed to

stop the building of her for the present. These huge ships are too costly and unwieldy, and it will require as many men to man one of them as to man three or four frigates. Besides, we cannot with all the naval force we can collect be able to cope with the British Navy. Our great aim should be to destroy the trade of Britain, for which purpose frigates are infinitely better calculated than such large ships.

Mr. Whipple proposes to the Marine Committee to put the timber prepared for the seventy-four into a frigate to mount 30 18-pounders on one deck, and this proposal I believe would be complied with if our finances were not at present very low and the demands of the great departments of war very high. I wish we may be able to finish, man and get to sea, in the course of the next summer, the frigates that are now in hand; but I very much doubt it.

It gave the Marine Committee great satisfaction to find that the *Warren* had got out. We have since heard that she had arrived at Boston, which we hope will prove true. I hope you will get out the *Providence* and *Columbus*. The *Virginia* hath made two fruitless attempts to pass out Chesapeak. She is ordered to make another. There are four or five men of war in that bay; but I cannot think it so difficult to pass by them as it is to pass those in our bay. Our last accounts from Charlestown, So. Carolina, were that Capt. Biddle with three State armed vessels were determined to go over the bar and attack several British vessels of about an equal force with them. I cannot forbear being anxious for the event.

The Marine Committee lately ordered Capt. Barry of the *Effingham* to take the four boats belonging to the frigates which are sunk in the Delaware, and proceed on a cruise upon that river. On the 7th instant two of them—the other two had not then got below the city—joined by five boats, half manned, attacked (near Bombay-hook) and took two of the enemy's transport ships—one mounting six four-pounders, the other two swivels—and also a schooner with eight 4-pounders, twelve 4-pound howitzers and 32 men, properly equipped for an armed vessel. They first boarded the ships, and, learning from them the strength of the schooner, Capt. Barry prudently sent a flag to the schooner, ordering the captain of her to submit, and promising that he and his officers, on compliance, should be allowed their private baggage; whereupon they thought it proper to strike. As the ships were loaded only with forage, Capt. Barry, after stripping, burnt them. The schooner, being a suitable vessel for a cruiser, he is ordered to purchase and employ on the Delaware so long as he thinks it may be safe. She had in [her] a variety of useful and valuable articles.

This gallant action reflects great honour on Capt. Barry, his officers and the crews of those boats. The other two boats have since got down, and in their way took a small sloop, with fresh provisions, bound to the city. I expect every day to hear of their further success. These boats will annoy and injure the enemy more, in my opinion, than both the seventy-fours would, if they were built, equipped and manned—at least upon the Delaware.

—ELLERY, "Letter," *R. I. Hist. Soc. Pub.*, New Series, VIII, 222-224.

6. "Give the Seamen All the Prizes"

John Paul Jones to Robert Morris.

Providence Sloop-of-War,
at Newport, Rhode Island, October 17, 1776

I wrote to you at sea 4th ultimo, by the brigantine *Sea-Nymph*, my second prize. I have taken sixteen sail, manned and sent in eight prizes, and sunk, burned or destroyed the rest. . . .

It is to the last degree distressing to contemplate the state and establishment of our Navy. The common class of mankind are actuated by no nobler principle than that of self-interest. This, and this only, determines all adventurers in privateers, the owners as well as those they employ. And while this is the case, unless the private enrollment of individuals in our Navy is made superior to that in privateers, it never can become respectable, it never will become formidable; and without a respectable Navy, alas America!

In the present critical situation of affairs, human wisdom can suggest no more than one infallible expedient: Inlist the seamen during pleasure and give them all the prizes. What is the paltry emolument of two-thirds of prizes to the finances of this vast continent? If such a poor resource is essential to its independency, in sober sadness we are involved in a woful predicament, and our ruin is fast approaching. The situation of America is new in the annals of mankind; her affairs cry haste, and speed must answer them. Trifles, therefore, ought to be wholly discharged, as being, in the old vulgar proverb, "penny wise and pound foolish." If our enemies, with the best-established and most formidable Navy in the universe, have found it expedient to assign all prizes to the captors, how much more is such policy essential to our infant fleet?

But I need use no arguments to convince you of the necessity of making the emoluments of our Navy equal, if not superior, to theirs. We have had proof that a Navy may be officered almost on any terms; but we are not so sure the officers are equal to their commissions; nor will the Congress ever obtain such certainty until they in their wisdom see proper to appoint a Board of Admiralty competent to determine impartially the respective merits and abilities of their officers, and to superintend, regulate and point out all the motions and operations of the Navy.

—Force, *American Archives*, 5th Series, II, 1105-1106.

7. The Seniority System Blocks Paul Jones's Promotion

Captain James Nicholson to Captain John Barry.

Philadelphia, June 24th 1781

After congratulating you on your safe arrival and success, I shall without any apology relate to you what has been transacting in this quarter relative to rank for this week past. It still hangs over our head and requires every exertion of interest to prevent its taking place. The attempt has been bold and daring and is only equaled by the man who made it.

The Chevalier [John Paul Jones] ever since his arrival in this city has devoted his time, privately, by making personal application to the individual

Members of Congress to give him rank at the head of our Navy, and after interesting (by being an accomplished courtior) every Member who was weak or of his own stamp in his favor, hands into Congress a narrative of his services from the beginning of time, containing the best part of a quire of paper, and attended with a modest petition seting forth the injustice he had done him in the establishment of rank and desire of redress, etc.

This had the desired effect, and he had a committee of Congress, consisting of Gen. Vernon, Mr. Mathews and Mr. Clymer, appointed to enquire into his claim and to make report. They accordingly did and in his favor. Congress was upon the point of taking the report up, and I have too much reason to believe would have gratified the hight of his ambition, had we not by the greatest accident discovered it. This was done by information a Member of Congress gave Mrs. Reade in whose house he lived. He was also on the most familiar terms with myself. So far he had proceeded without the least suspisian on our side.

As soon as I was informed of it, I immediately took my hat and with very little ceremony waited on the President of Congress at his house, and informed what I had heard. He received me politely and told me my suspisians was just. I therefore desired as my right that Congress might delay determining on it untill Capt. Reade and myself, in behalf of our selves and the absent brother officers equally concerned, should have an opportunity of being heard, which he promised me his interest to have done, and that day Capt. Reade and myself threw in our remonstrance to Congress (a copy of mine you have enclosed), the consequence of which was the committee was ordered to reconsider it and to give us notice to attend. We according did and found Capt. Jones without doors in conferance with two of them.

Capt. Jones did not attend. I desired the chairman would send for him. The reason I assigned was that I would say many things in his presence that I would not in his absence. He sent word that he would wait on us, but never came. We found the President and Mr. Mathews predetermined in his favor, but Mr. Clymer otherwise. After pointing out the absurdity of his claim, which proceeded from a brevial from Commodore Hopkins to the command of the sloop *Providence* ... Capts. Whipple, Hallock, yourself and Alexander where [were] captains before him—I say after pointing out this to them, the President appeared to be convinced, but if so in reality I won't pretend to say. We had a good deal of conversation with the committee. Mr Mathews alone seemed his most strenious advocate and in my oppinion behaved obstinate and ungentiel. I said many things pretty severe of the Chevalier's private as well as public carrector, too odious to mention and yet unnoticed.

Upon the whole we acquited ourselves well. It happened five days ago and they have not yet made their report. Should it be in his favor again, I have some reason to believe the honest part, as well as those who had been imposed on from their ignorance about our naval transactions and the method of establishing rank, are now sufficiently alarmed, and should the report be taken up at all, they will not determine in his favor. Your arrival and success came very opportunily and I did not fail to make use of it—I mean outdoors in presence of Capt. Jones and some of his advocated Members, by observing that you had acquit yourself well, which they acknowledged. I then told them they could not do less than make you admiral also. I had not a sentense of reply. It irritated the Chevalier so much that he was obliged to decamp.

I yesterday was informed by a Member of Congress, a friend of mine, that they had received a letter from Bob Morris (the Financier) that he would undertake to fitt out immediately my ship and the seventy-four and if they agreed to it, there would be a necessity for appointing a captain to her immediately, and at the same time asked if I would accept of the command of her. I refused, but at the same time pointed out the necessity of the next senior officer having the offer and so down, and in case none of them would accept untill it came to Chevalier, that then he should have the offer. He seemed convinced from the arguments I made use of of the necessity of this mode as the only one that would give satisfaction and make our Navy of repute. How it will opperate with Congress I cant undertake to determine. . . .

—NICHOLSON, "Letter," *Naval Hist. Soc. Pub.*, I, 125-126.

III. SANDWICH PRESIDES OVER THE MISFORTUNES OF THE BRITISH NAVY

If any one person must shoulder the blame for Britain's unreadiness at sea and the incompetent direction of her naval operations during the Revolution a scapegoat is near at hand. He is the First Lord of the Admiralty in the North ministry, the notorious profligate and rake, John Montagu, Earl of Sandwich. With a mad wife and a spendthrift son, Sandwich might well be pardoned for his long week ends away from home and office.

But all the blame for Britain's naval inadequacies should not be borne by Sandwich. True, he made some bad decisions. From the start of the war he husbanded his naval strength in European waters, fearing war with France, rather than providing full naval support for combined all-out operations that might have smashed the rebellion at the start. Concentrating on military rather than naval operations in America, the British wasted their army in pointless forays into the interior, and failed to use their naval forces to establish a tight blockade on the coast, as Viscount Barrington for one had repeatedly urged. But Lord North was equally to blame. It was Lord North who was so concerned about cutting down the public debt that he was willing to decommission a substantial part of Britain's Navy. Sandwich fought these cuts, but North's economy was bolstered by his and the King's fear of arousing France by building up the Navy to more formidable strength. However, as a symbol of profligacy, corruption and administrative ineptitude the Earl is a far more colorful personage than his cabinet colleague, Lord George Germain, Secretary of State for the American Department, who, despite having been court-martialed for cowardice after the Battle of Minden in the Seven Years' War, was in charge of military operations in North America. Before the war was long under way these two foolish and incompetent directors of operations were at loggerheads.

On April 23, 1779, a motion was put in the House of Lords to remove Sandwich from his direction of the Admiralty. It was defeated, by 78 votes to 39. *Lord North had stepped into the breach with the assertion that a vote of censure against one member of the Cabinet involved the whole, and that the entire cabinet accepted responsibility for Admiralty measures.*

What is most extraordinary is the fact that the debate over this motion was postponed owing to the murder on April 7 of Martha Ray, who had been Sandwich's mistress for sixteen years and had borne him two sons. She was murdered by James Hackman outside Drury Lane Theatre.

In addition to a few excerpts dealing with Sandwich's private and public affairs, there is included in this section a letter denouncing the scandalous corruption that accompanied the outfitting and supplying of ships.

1. The Earl of Sandwich Is Trouting as Usual

David Hume to William Strahan.

Bath, May 10, 1776

... When we passed by Spine Hill near Newbury we found in the inn Lord Denbigh, who was an acquaintance of my fellow traveller. His Lordship informed him that he, Lord Sandwich, Lord Mulgrave, Mr. Banks and two or three ladies of pleasure had passed five or six days there, and intended to pass all this week and the next in the same place; that their chief object was to enjoy the trouting season; that they had been very successful; that Lord Sandwich in particular had caught trouts near twenty inches long, which gave him incredible satisfaction; but that for his part, being a great admirer of sea fish, in which Bath abounded, and hearing that Friday was the great market day for fish, he commissioned my friend to send him up by the London fly a good cargo of soles, John Dories and pipers, which would render their happiness compleat.

I do not remember in all my little or great knowledge of history (according as you and Dr. Johnson can settle between you the degrees of my knowledge) such another instance; and I am sure such a one does not exist: That the First Lord of the Admiralty, who is absolute and uncontrouled master in his department, should, at a time when the fate of the British Empire is in dependance, and in dependance on him, find so much leizure, tranquillity, presence of mind and magnanimity as to have amusement in trouting during three weeks near sixty miles from the scene of business, and during the most critical season of the year. There needs but this single fact to decide the fate of the nation. What an ornament would it be in a future history to open the glorious events of the ensuing year with the narrative of so singular an incident.

—Hill, ed., *Letters of Hume to Strahan*, pp. 324-325.

2. George III Consoles Sandwich on the Murder of His Mistress

April 11, 1779

... I am sorry Lord Sandwich has met with any severe blow of a private nature. I flatter myself this world scarcely contains a man so void of feeling as not to compassionate your situation.

—Barnes & Owen, *Sandwich Papers*, II, 249.

3. Lord North Holds the Cabinet Responsible for the Acts of the Admiralty

Minutes of Debate in the House of Lords.

April 23, 1779

Every expedition, in regard to its destination, object, force and number of ships, is planned by the Cabinet, and is the result of the collective wisdom of all his Majesty's confidential ministers. The First Lord of the Admiralty is only the executive servant of these measures; and if he is not personally a Cabinet minister he is not responsible for the wisdom, the policy, and the propriety of any naval expedition. But if he is in the Cabinet, then he must share in common with the other ministers that proportional division of censure which is attached to him as an individual. In no situation is he more or less responsible to his country than his colleagues from any misconduct which flows from a Cabinet measure.

—Barnes & Owen, *Sandwich Papers*, II, 255-256.

4. "With Such Rapacity, How Can a Nation Support a War?"

Captain W. Young to Charles Middleton, Lord Barham.

Sandwich: Sandy Hook, 15 November, 1780

I have the pleasure to acquaint you that the South Carolina and New York convoys are arrived, and not above one or two missing. This has been the most fortunate supply that has made its appearance since this war took place. I must again recommend it to you to push and urge the admiralty to establish men-of-war for this service; and let them be the uncoppered ships, as the coppered ones are very unfit for convoys to deep-laden victuallers. I most sincerely wish you to attend to this service, as you are the person army and navy look up to, and not the navy board.

I am likewise to acquaint you of the immense neglects of the people at Woolwich Yard in the lading of the storeships for New York. The beds were all stowed in the hatchway, by which means a great part of them are rotten; the whole of the colours destroyed by their putting up the iron cringles for staysails in the casks with them—the iron having been wet when put up has effectually ruined them, so that out of the whole number only a few are serviceable.

The complaints respecting transports are great, and with great justice; those sent out totally unfit for service, the whole under the auspices of Mr. Wilkinson's house. Sir Hugh [Vice-Admiral Sir Hugh Palliser], I do suppose concerned with them as formerly, though you do not perceive it; I find too many proofs here for this information, as well as those which I well knew when in that department myself. While those men interfere and are concerned, the public must be robbed.

Mr. Arbuthnot's secretary follows the example of the great: he loses sight of no opportunity to rob and distress. In my last I gave you an account of such circumstance as the people chose to send me. I am now to inform you of a part of his villainy which I can personally prove, which is the purchase of

LAFAYETTE

After the original by Charles Willson Peale

NATHANAEL GREENE

After the original by Charles Willson Peale

BENJAMIN LINCOLN

After the original by Charles Willson Peale

BARON VON STEUBEN

After the original by Charles Willson Peale

STORMING OF STONY POINT

"March on, carry me into the Fort, and let me die at the head of the column."
—Anthony Wayne

From the original painting by Chappel

fresh beef. He is supplied with it at Sandy Hook at 10d. York currency per pound, and charges the public 1s. sterling per pound; consequently he clears 5d. sterling, or near it, on every pound supplied. I have it from captains in Gardener's Bay, where Mr. Arbuthnot has been ever since our arrival here, that he has supplied the squadron with fresh beef, and on the same principle as at Sandy Hook. With the rapacity of this man of this Navy, and others such as this fellow is, and those in the Army of the same kidney, how can it be supposed that a minister and a nation can support a war? Sir, it is not possible. We must bankrupt, or other methods must be adopted.

—BARHAM, *Letters and Papers*, I, 82-83.

IV. THE NAVAL WAR OFF THE NEW ENGLAND COAST

Holding a military base at Boston and a supply base at Halifax, the British government in the year 1775 was concerned with guarding communications to General Gage's troops, with procuring and transporting supplies needed by the army, with sealing off trade between New England and foreign countries (after July 1 by Parliamentary authorization), and with barring New Englanders from the North Atlantic fisheries (after July 20). The activities of the British fleet in Patriot harbors and offshore were bound to be resented, and the earliest naval engagements were more or less spontaneously ignited, lacking any central planning, direction or official sponsorship on the part of the Patriots. We have already read something of this story in the chapter on the battle for Boston—the ineffectual attacks on Bristol and Falmouth and the general dissatisfaction with the conduct of Admiral Graves.

Several months before the Congress took action to organize a Navy, naval warfare flared up along the New England coast. The action off Machias, in the district of Maine, is generally considered the first naval engagement of the Revolution. Closely related to the battle of Lexington, reports of which reached the Maine area around May 9, the action resulted from the firm resolve of the Patriots to keep a British armed schooner, the Margaretta, from convoying lumber for the use of the King's troops in Boston. A plot was concocted to seize Captain Moore and the other officers of the Margaretta as they were attending church on the Sabbath, but the officers jumped out of the window and escaped to their vessel. Moore fired a few shots at the town and then dropped down about four miles below it. When pursued from shore, he anchored in the bay. Then a New York lad named Jeremiah O'Brien, temporarily residing in Machias, joined forces with a local inhabitant, Joseph Wheaton. Together they boarded one of the sloops being convoyed and moved to the attack. It was spontaneous, planned by no formal Patriot organization. For this reason Machias has been appropriately called the "Lexington of the Sea."

O'Brien's naval career was indeed conspicuously launched. He now fitted out a privateer, captured two armed schooners off the Bay of Fundy, and delivered the prisoners to General Washington at Cambridge. On the general's recommendation O'Brien was appointed by the revolutionary government of Massachusetts to command the two prizes he had seized.

1. The First Naval Hero—Jeremiah O'Brien

Official report of the Machias Committee of Correspondence to the Massachusetts Provincial Congress.

June 14, 1775

. . . On the 2nd instant Capt. Ichabod Jones arrived in the river with two sloops, accompanied with one of the King's tenders. On the 3rd instant a paper was handed about for the people to sign, as a prerequisite to their obtaining any provisions, of which we were in great want. The contents of this paper required the signers to indulge Capt. Jones in carrying lumber to Boston, and to protect him and his property at all events. But, unhappily for him, if not for us, it soon expired after producing effects directly contrary in their nature to those intended.

The next effort, in order to carry those favorite points, was to call a meeting, which was accordingly done. On the 6th the people generally assembled at the place appointed and seemed so averse to the measures proposed that Capt. Jones privately went to the tender and caused her to move up so near the town that her guns would reach the houses, and put springs upon her cables. The people, however, not knowing what was done, and considering themselves nearly as prisoners of war, in the hands of the common enemy (which is our only plea for suffering Capt. Jones to carry any lumber to Boston, since Your Honors conceive it improper), passed a vote that Capt. Jones might proceed in his business as usual without molestation, that they would purchase the provisions he brought into the place and pay him according to contract.

After obtaining this vote Capt. Jones immediately ordered his vessel to the wharf and distributed his provisions among those only who voted in favor of his carrying lumber to Boston. This gave such offence to the aggrieved party that they determined to take Capt. Jones, if possible, and put a final stop to his supplying the King's troops with anything. Accordingly they secretly invited the people of Mispecka and Pleasant River to join them; accordingly a number of them came and, having joined our people in the woods near the settlement, on the 11th they all agreed to take Capt. Jones and Stephen Jones, Esq., in the place of worship, which they attempted, but Capt. Jones made his escape into the woods and does not yet appear. Stephen Jones, Esq., only was taken and remains as yet under guard.

The Captain and Lieutenant of the tender were also in the meeting house and fled to their vessell, hoisted their flag and sent a message on shore to this effect: "That he had express orders to protect Capt. Jones; that he was determined to do his duty whilst he had life; and that if the people presumed to stop Capt. Jones' vessells he would burn the town."

Upon this a party of our men went directly to stripping the sloop that lay at the wharf, and another party went off to take possession of the other sloop which lay below and brought her up nigh a wharf, and anchored in the stream.

The tender did not fire, but weighed her anchors as privately as possible, and in the dusk of the evening fell down and came to within musket shot of the sloop, which obliged our people to slip their cable and run the sloop aground. In the meantime a considerable number of our people went down in boats and canoes, lined the shore directly opposite to the tender, and having demanded her to "surrender to America!" received for answer, "Fire and be damned!" They immediately fired in upon her, which she returned, and a smart engagement ensued. The tender, at last, slipped her cable and fell down to a small sloop, commanded by Capt. Tobey, and lashed herself to her for the remainder of the night.

In the morning of the 12th she took Capt. Tobey out of his vessel for a pilot, and made all the sail they could to get off, as the wind and tide favored; but having carried away her main boom, and meeting with a sloop from the Bay of Fundy, they came to, robbed the sloop of her boom and gaff, took almost all her provisions, together with Mr. Robert Avery of Norwich in Connecticut, and proceeded on their voyage.

Our people, seeing her go off in the morning, determined to follow her. About forty men, armed with guns, swords, axes and pitchforks, went in Capt. Jones's sloop, under the command of Capt. Jeremiah O'Brien; about twenty armed in the same manner, and under the command of Capt. Benj. Foster, went in a small schooner. During the chase our people built them breastworks of pine boards and anything they could find in the vessels that would screen them from the enemy's fire. The tender, upon the first appearance of our people, cut her boats from her stern, and made all the sail she could; but being a very dull sailor, they soon came up with her, and a most obstinate engagement ensued, both sides being determined to conquer or die; but the tender was obliged to yield. Her captain was wounded in the breast with two balls, of which wounds he died next morning. Poor Mr. Avery was killed and one of the marines, and five wounded.

Only one of our men was killed and six wounded, one of which is since dead of his wounds.

The battle was fought at the entrance of our harbour and lasted for near the space of one hour. We have in our possession four double fortifyed three-pounders and fourteen swivels and a number of small arms, which we took with the tender, besides a very small quantity of ammunition, etc.

—MACHIAS COMMITTEE OF CORRESPONDENCE, *Maine Hist. Soc. Coll. and Proc.*, 2nd Series, VI, 129-131.

2. THE BRITISH RAID ON GLOUCESTER

The continued depredations of the British Navy off the New England coast aroused the Patriots to acts of self-defense and retaliation. On August 9, 1775, Captain John Linzee of the sloop-of-war Falcon *chased two schooners bound for the West Indies to Salem. One he captured; the other took refuge in Gloucester harbor. When Linzee entered in pursuit the inhabitants rallied to defend the schooner and fired from shore upon the British boarding party. Linzee in retaliation cannonaded the town, but lost both schooners along with two barges to the defenders. He then quit the harbor and headed for the safety of Nantasket Road.*

The emotionally charged newspaper account of the Gloucester correspondent is largely supported by Captain Linzee's own report to Vice-Admiral Graves, dated August 10. Linzee asserted that his attempt to fire the town failed because "an American part of my complement (who had always been active in our cause) set fire to the powder before it was properly placed." One man was blown up, the Americans then deserted, and further attempts to fire the town failed.

From the *Pennsylvania Packet*.

A correspondent at Gloucester, Cape Ann, has sent the following authentic and particular account of an engagement there, viz:

"Gloucester, Aug. 13.

"On the 9th instant, the *Falcon* sloop of war, Capt. Linzee, hove in sight, and seemed to be in quest of two schooners from the West Indies bound to Salem, one of which he soon brought to, the other taking advantage of a fair wind, put into our harbour; but Linzee, having made a prize of the first, pursued the second into our harbour and brought the first with him. He anchored and sent two barges with fifteen men in each, armed with muskets and swivels; these were attended with a whale boat, in which was the lieutenant and six privates; their orders were to seize the loaded schooner and bring her under the *Falcon*'s bow.

"The militia and other inhabitants were alarmed at this daring attempt and prepared for a vigorous opposition. The barge-men under the command of the lieutenant boarded the schooner at the cabbin windows, which provoked a smart fire from our people on the shore, by which three of the enemy were killed, and the lieutenant wounded in the thigh, who thereupon returned to the man of war. Upon this Linzee sent the other schooner and a small cutter he had to attend him well armed, with orders to fire on the damned rebels wherever they could see them, and that he would in the mean time cannonade the town. He immediately fired a broadside upon the thickest settlements and stood himself with diabolical pleasure to see what havock his cannon might make.

" 'Now,' said he, 'my boys, we will aim at the damned Presbyterian Church. Well, my brave fellows, one shot more and the house of God will fall before you.'

"While he was venting his hellish rage and setting himself as it were against Heaven, the Almighty was on our side: not a ball struck or wounded an individual person, although they went through our houses in almost every direction when filled with women and children; under God, our little party at the water side performed wonders, for they soon made themselves masters of both the schooners, the cutter, the two barges, the boat and every man in them. In the action, which lasted several hours, we lost but one man, two others wounded, one of which is since dead, the other very slightly wounded.

We took of the man of war's men thirty five, several were wounded and one since dead; twenty-four sent to headquarters; the remainder, being impressed from this and neighboring towns, were permitted to return to their friends. Next day, Capt. Linzee warped off with but half his men, never a prize, boat nor tender, except a small skiff the wounded lieutenant returned in. . . ."

—*Pennsylvania Packet*, Aug. 28, 1775.

3. THE DEATH OF CAPTAIN MUGFORD OF MARBLEHEAD

Although the main British fleet had quit Boston harbor with the embarkation of the British army from that town in the spring of 1776, a few vessels stayed in the vicinity of Nantasket Road, and naval skirmishes resulted. In June 1776, General Artemas Ward, left in command by Washington, commissioned Captain James Mugford, and subsequently he was recommissioned by Congress. The account of his heroic death by General Ward, contained in a letter to Washington of May 20, 1776, differs from the following excerpt as regards the fatal injury the naval captain suffered. According to Ward, "he was run through with a lance while he was cutting off the hands of the pirates as they were attempting to board him, and it is said that with his own hands he cut off five pairs of theirs." Among the defenders Mugford alone was killed.

Boston, May 20, 1776

Early last Friday morning the *Franklin* schooner, one of the Continental cruisers, commanded by Captain James Mugford, of Marblehead, fell in with one of the enemy's transport ships from Cork, bound directly into this harbour, the captain not knowing that the place had been evacuated by the British fleet and army. Notwithstanding she appeared to be an armed ship and was in sight of the enemy's men of war lying in Nantasket, Captain Mugford resolutely bore down upon her and took her without opposition. She mounted six carriage-guns, a number of swivels, and had on board eighteen men. The *Franklin*, at that time, had only twenty-one men. Captain Mugford determining to bring her into this harbour, the inhabitants, on leaving their respective places of worship after the forenoon's service (it being the day of the Continental fast), had the pleasure of seeing the most valuable prize taken since the commencement of the war entering the harbour. . . .

The enemy, on board the men of war below, intolerably vexed and chagrined that the above ship should be taken and unloaded in their open view, formed a design of wreaking their vengeance on the gallant Captain Mugford, who took her. The Sunday following Captain Mugford, in company with Captain Cunningham in the *Lady Washington*, a small privateer armed with swivels, blunderbusses and muskets, fell down in order to go out in the bay. The enemy observed their sailing and fitted out a fleet of boats for the purpose of surprising and taking them in the night; and the *Franklin's* running aground in the cut gave them a good opportunity for executing their plan.

The *Lady Washington* came to anchor near Captain Mugford; and between nine and ten o'clock he discovered a number of boats, which he hailed, and received for answer that they were from Boston. He ordered them to keep off, or he would fire upon them. They begged him for God's sake not to fire, for they were going on board him. Captain Mugford instantly fired and was followed by all his men; and cutting his cable, brought his broadside to bear, when he discharged his cannon, loaded with musket-ball, directly in upon them. Before the cannon could be charged a second time, two or three boats were alongside, each of them supposed to have as many men on board as the *Franklin*, which were only twenty-one, including officers.

By the best accounts there were not less than thirteen boats in all, many of them armed with swivels and having on board, at the lowest computation, two hundred men. Captain Mugford and his men plied those alongside so closely with firearms and spears, and with such intrepidity, activity and success that two boats were soon sunk and all the men either killed or drowned. But while the heroick Mugford, with outstretched arms, was righteously dealing death and destruction to our base and unnatural enemies, he received a fatal ball in his body, which in a few minutes put a period to a life from which, had it been spared, his oppressed country would undoubtedly have reaped very eminent advantages.

After our brave men had maintained this unequal contest for about half an hour, the enemy thought proper to retire. The carnage among them must have been great; for, besides the two boat-loads killed and drowned, many were doubtless killed and wounded on board the others. Great execution was done by spears. One man, with that weapon, is positive of having killed nine of the enemy....

—FORCE, *American Archives*, 4th Series, VI, 495-496.

V. A SUBMARINE IN NEW YORK WATERS?

The successful amphibious landing of the British forces on Long Island in August 1776 remains the most brilliant example of joint operations by the British in the entire war. Against the powerful British fleet, the defenders relied on land and island bases, but their artillery proved ineffective. One other resource was called upon to stop the navy—an ingenious submarine which had been invented by David Bushnell in 1775, and was called—from its appearance—the American Turtle. *Bushnell was a Connecticut farm boy with a turn for mechanics, who thought up the submarine and worked it out himself. In 1775 he presented his idea to the Governor and Council of Safety of Connecticut and was authorized by them to go ahead with it. The next year it was ready for action; there was nothing wrong with it in principle, but Bushnell was never able to find a man who could operate it satisfactorily. The submarine was tried in New York waters in 1776-77, and in Philadelphia waters a year later, but in vain. Bushnell later settled in the South where in true Jack-of-all-trades style he taught school and practiced medicine. This account, though written many years after the events it relates, takes on a special authenticity from the fact that the writer was personally acquainted with Ezra Lee, who operated the submarine. The account is addressed to one of the leading American scientists of his generation, Benjamin Silliman, first professor of chemistry and natural history at Yale.*

Charles Griswold to Professor Silliman.

Lyme, Connecticut, February 21st, 1820

It is to be presumed that every person who has paid any attention to the mechanical inventions of this country, or has looked over the history of her Revolutionary War, has heard of the machine invented by David Bushnell for submarine navigation and the destruction of hostile shipping. I have thought that a correct and full account of that novel and original invention would not be unacceptable to the public, and particularly to those devoted to the pursuit of science and the arts.

If the idea of submarine warfare had ever occurred to any one before the epoch of Bushnell's invention, yet it may be safely stated that no ideas but his own ever came to any practical results. To him, I believe, the whole merit of this invention is unanimously agreed to belong.

But such an account as I have mentioned must derive an additional value and an increased interest from the fact that all the information contained in the following pages has been received from the only person in existence possessed of that information, and who was the very same that first embarked in this novel and perilous navigation.

Mr. Ezra Lee, first a sergeant and afterwards an ensign in the Revolutionary Army, a respectable, worthy and elderly citizen of this town, is the person to whom I have alluded. To him was committed the first essay for destroying a hostile ship by submarine explosion, and upon his statement an implicit reliance may be placed.

Considering Bushnell's machine as the first of its kind, I think it will be pronounced to be remarkably complete throughout in its construction, and that such an invention furnishes evidence of those resources and creative powers, which must rank him as a mechanical genius of the first order.

I shall first attend to a description of this machine, and afterwards to a relation of the enterprise in it by Sergeant Lee; confining myself, in each case, strictly to the facts with which he has supplied me.

Bushnell's machine was composed of several pieces of large oak timber, scooped out and fitted together, and its shape my informer compares to that of a round clam. It was bound around thoroughly with iron bands, the seams were corked, and the whole was smeared over with tar, so as to prevent the possibility of the admission of water to the inside.

It was of a capacity to contain one engineer, who might stand or sit, and enjoy sufficient elbow room for its proper management.

The top or head was made of a metallic composition, exactly suited to its body, so as to be water-tight; this opened upon hinges, and formed the entrance to the machine. Six small pieces of thick glass were inserted in this head for the admission of light: in a clear day and clear sea-water, says my informer, he could see to read at the depth of three fathoms. To keep it upright and properly balanced, seven hundred pounds of lead were fastened to its bottom, two hundred pounds of which were so contrived as to be discharged at any moment, to increase the buoyancy of the machine.

But to enable the navigator when under water to rise or sink at pleasure, there were two forcing pumps, by which water could be pressed out at the bottom; and also a spring, by applying the foot to which a passage was formed for the admission of water. If the pumps should get deranged, then resort was had to letting off the lead ballast from the bottom.

The navigator steered by a rudder, the tiller of which passed through the back of the machine at a water joint, and in one side was fixed a small pocket compass, with two pieces of shining wood (sometimes called foxfire) crossed upon its north point, and a single piece upon the last point. In the night when no light entered through the head, this compass thus lighted was all that served to guide the helmsman in his course.

The ingenious inventor also provided a method for determining the depth of water at which the machine might at any time be. This was achieved by means of a glass tube, twelve inches in length and about four in diameter, which was also attached to the side of the machine: this tube enclosed a piece of cork that rose with the descent of the machine and fell with its ascent, and one inch rise of the cork denoted a depth of about one fathom. The principle upon which such a result was produced, and also the mechanical contrivance of this tube, entirely escaped the observation of Mr. Lee, amidst the hurry and constant anxiety attendant upon such a perilous navigation.

But not the least ingenious part of this curious machine was that by which the horizontal motion was communicated to it. This object was effected by means of two oars or paddles, formed precisely like the arms of a wind-mill, which revolved perpendicularly upon an axletree that projected in front; this axletree passed into the machine at a water joint, and was furnished with a crank by which it was turned: the navigator, being seated inside, with one hand laboured at the crank, and with the other steered by the tiller.

The effect of paddles so constructed, and turned in the manner stated by propelling or rather drawing a body after them under water, will readily occur to any one without explanation.

These paddles were but twelve inches long and about four wide. Two smaller paddles of the same description also projected near the head, provided with a crank inside by which the ascent of the machine could be assisted.

By vigorous turning of the crank, says my informer, the machine could be propelled at the rate of about three miles an hour in still water. When beyond the reach of danger, or observation of an enemy, the machine was suffered to float with its head just rising from the water's surface, and while in this situation, air was constantly admitted through three small orifices in the head, which were closed when a descent was commenced.

The efficient part of this engine of devastation, its magazine, remains to be spoken of. This was separate and distinct from the machine. It was shaped like an egg and, like the machine itself, was composed of solid pieces of oak scooped out and in the same manner fitted together, and secured by iron bands, etc. One hundred and thirty pounds of gun powder, a clock, and a gun lock, provided with a good flint that would not miss fire, were the apparatus which it enclosed. This magazine was attached to the back of the machine, a little above the rudder, by means of a screw, one end of which passed quite into the magazine and there operated as a stop upon the movements of the clock, whilst its other end entered the machine. This screw could be withdrawn from the magazine, by which the latter was immediately detached, and the clock commenced going. The clock was set for running twenty or thirty minutes, at the end of which time the lock struck and fired the powder, and in the mean time the adventurer effected his escape.

But the most difficult point of all to be gained was to fasten this magazine to the bottom of a ship. Here a difficulty arose, which, and which alone, as will appear in the ensuing narrative, defeated the successful operations of this warlike apparatus.

Mr. Bushnell's contrivance was this—A very sharp iron screw was made to pass out from the top of the machine, communicating inside by a water joint; it was provided with a crank at its lower end, by which the engineer was to force it into the ship's bottom: this screw was next to be disengaged from the machine, and left adhering to the ship's bottom. A line leading from this screw to the magazine kept the latter in its destined position for blowing up the vessel. . . .

I shall now proceed to the account of the first attempt that was made to destroy a ship of war, all the facts of which, as already stated, I received from the bold adventurer himself.

It was in the month of August 1776, when Admiral Howe lay with a formidable British fleet in New-York bay, a little above the Narrows, and a numerous British force upon Staten Island, commanded by General Howe, threatened annihilation to the troops under Washington, that Mr. Bushnell requested General Parsons of the American army to furnish him with two or three men to learn the navigation of his new machine, with a view of destroying some of the enemy's shipping.

Gen. Parsons immediately sent for Lee, then a sergeant, and two others, who had offered their services to go on board of a fire ship; and on Bushnell's request being made known to them, they enlisted themselves under him for this novel piece of service. The party went up into Long Island Sound with the machine, and made various experiments with it in the different harbors along shore, and after having become pretty thoroughly acquainted with the mode of navigating it, they returned through the Sound; but during their absence, the enemy had got possession of Long Island and Governor's Island. They therefore had the machine conveyed by land across from New-Rochelle to the Hudson River, and afterwards arrived with it at New-York.

The British fleet now lay to the north of Staten-Island, with a large number of transports, and were the objects against which this new mode of warfare was destined to act; the first serene night was fixed upon for the execution of this perilous enterprise, and Sergeant Lee was to be the engineer. After the lapse of a few days, a favorable night arrived, and at 11 o'clock a party embarked in two or three whale boats, with Bushnell's machine in tow. They rowed down as near the fleet as they dared, when Sergeant Lee entered the machine, was cast off, and the boats returned.

Lee now found the ebb tide rather too strong and, before he was aware, had drifted him down past the men of war. He however immediately *got the machine about*, and by hard labour at the crank for the space of five glasses by the ship's bells, or two and a half hours, he arrived under the stern of one of the ships at about slack water. Day had now dawned, and by the light of the moon he could see the people on board, and heard their conversation. This was the moment for diving: he accordingly closed up overhead, let in water, and descended under the ship's bottom.

He now applied the screw, and did all in his power to make it enter, but owing probably in part to the ship's copper, and the want of an adequate pressure, to enable the screw to get a hold upon the bottom, his attempts all failed; at each essay the machine rebounded from the ship's bottom, not having sufficient power to resist the impulse thus given to it.

He next paddled along to a different part of her bottom, but in this manoeuvre he made a deviation, and instantly arose to the water's surface on the east side of the ship, exposed to the increasing light of the morning, and in imminent hazard of being discovered. He immediately made another descent, with a view of making one more trial, but the fast approach of day, which would expose him to the enemy's boats and render his escape difficult, if not impossible, deterred him; and he concluded that the best generalship would be to commence an immediate retreat.

He now had before him a distance of more than four miles to traverse, but the tide was favourable. At Governor's-Island great danger awaited him, for his compass having got out of order, he was under the necessity of looking out from the top of the machine very frequently to ascertain his course, and at best made a very irregular zigzag track.

The soldiers at Governor's-Island espied the machine, and curiosity drew several hundreds upon the parapet to watch its motions. At last a party came down to the beach, shoved off a barge, and rowed towards it. At that moment, Sergeant Lee thought he saw his certain destruction, and as a last act of defence, let go the magazine, expecting that they would seize that likewise, and thus all would be blown to atoms together.

Providence however otherwise directed it: the enemy, after approaching within fifty or sixty yards of the machine, and seeing the magazine detached, began to suspect a *yankee trick*, took alarm and returned to the island.

Approaching the city, he soon made a signal, the boats came to him and brought him safe and sound to the shore. The magazine in the mean time had drifted past Governor's-Island into the East River, where it exploded with tremendous violence, throwing large columns of water and pieces of wood that composed it high into the air. Gen. Putnam, with many officers, stood on the shore spectators of this explosion.

In a few days the American army evacuated New-York, and the machine was taken up the North River. Another attempt was afterwards made by Lee upon a frigate that lay opposite Bloomingdale. His object now was to fasten the magazine to the stern of the ship, close at the water's edge. But while attempting this, the watch discovered him, raised an alarm and compelled him to abandon his enterprise. He then endeavoured to get under the frigate's bottom, but in this he failed, having descended too deep. This terminated his experiments.

—GRISWOLD, "Letter," *Am. Journal Science and Arts,* II, No. 2, 94-101.

VI. THE NAVAL WAR IN FOREIGN WATERS

Late in 1775 Congress put a little squadron under the command of Esek Hopkins, but it was too weak to operate as a fleet. Hopkins carried out a successful raid on Nassau in March 1776, in which a hundred cannon were captured, but thereafter the United States Navy generally operated in single units whenever a captain could slip out to sea through the British cordon off the American coast. The most damaging blows the American fleet struck were not to the British Navy, however, but to the British merchant marine. In fact, by the end of the war, only two of the seventeen frigates commissioned by Congress remained in service. The others had been burned or captured.

By May 1777, the American Commissioners in France were convinced of the need for stationing American warships in European waters. It was natural that their choice for conducting American naval operations from European ports should fall on Lambert Wickes. As the first captain commissioned by Congress to carry a Continental cruiser across the ocean, Wickes had brought Franklin to France on the Reprisal. *Operating from French bases Wickes raided English shipping. But since war had not yet been declared by France against Great Britain, Vergennes felt constrained to deny Wickes the right to outfit war vessels in French ports on the ground that such acts would constitute a flagrant violation of neutrality. Before Vergennes took that stand Wickes as, the humorous if biased account of a* Reprisal *raid reveals, had caused panic among British merchant shippers.*

1. FRANKLIN AND DEANE: ATTACK THE ENEMY IN HIS HOME PORTS!

American Commissioners in France to Committee of Foreign Affairs of the Continental Congress.

May 26, 1777

We have not the least doubt but that two or three of the Continental frigates sent into the German Ocean, with some lesser swift sailing cruisers, might intercept and seize great part of the Baltic and Northern trade, could they be in those seas by the middle of August, at farthest; and the prizes will consist of articles of the utmost consequence to the States. One frigate would be sufficient to destroy the whole of the Greenland whale fishery, or take the Hudson Bay ships returning. . . .

A blow might be struck that would alarm and shake Great Britain and its credit to the centre. The thought may appear bold and extravagant, yet we have seen as extraordinary events within these two years past as that of carrying the war to our enemy's doors. As it appears extravagant, it would be in consequence unexpected by them, and the more easily executed. The burning or plundering of Liverpool, or Glasgow, would do more essential service than a million of treasure and much blood spent on the continent. It would raise our reputation to the highest pitch, and lessen in the same degree that of our enemy's. We are confident it is practicable, and with very little danger, but times may alter with the arrival of the frigates, yet in that case their cruise on this coast bids fairer to be profitable than any other, and they may at least carry back in safety many of the stores wanted, which is a most capital object, should the other be laid aside.

—WHARTON, ed., *Revolutionary Diplomatic Correspondence*, II, 325-326.

2. Lambert Wickes Harries British Merchantmen

Extract of a letter from France, dated March 10, 1777.
Journal of the transactions respecting the Lisbon *packet and four other prizes, after their capture by the* Reprisal, *an American privateer.*

As the curiosity of the public is no doubt a good deal excited to know all that has passed in regard to the five prizes lately brought in by the *Reprisal*, I have endeavoured to procure the most exact information, and the following is an authentic account:

Prizes taken by the Reprisal

Polly and *Nancy*, Kentuluar, from Pool for Cadiz, with about 2000 quintels of dry fish—150 tons.

Hibernia, Jefferson, from Dublin to Lisbon, with wheat and flour—150 tons.

Generous Friends, Duncan, from Orkney to Cadiz, with barley—70 tons.

Swallow packet, with private adventures of the officers, worth 5 or 600 £. (all restored to them)—150 tons.

Betty, Campbell, from Bourdeaux to Londonderry, with 70 tons of wine and brandy—150 tons.

Each captain's private adventure, and all the bedding, cabin furniture, etc., he chose to claim, was restored to him, as were all the seamen's cloaths, except what had been pillaged and stole by the rabble that composed the crew of the *Reprisal*, unknown to Captain Wickes. This must not be attributed to Wickes's own generosity, the captain of the privateer, as I understand his orders from his employers were to that effect. . . .

It is said here (at Paris) that our ambassador, on application at court, was informed that Wickes had been ordered out of port [Port Louis] with his prizes, which (by the bye) he reported as his vessels, forced in by stress of weather; and it is also said, and believed here, that Wickes had found means to elude the orders and was not sailed from L'Orient the 28th ult.

It was also believed that he had found means to make a private sale of all the vessels, and that two of them had actually sailed for L'Orient, but their destination was not known. In case the under-writers should make any objections, on account of the protest not being made out within the limited time, the accounts I have given will show that no time was lost for that purpose. The protests were to be sworn to at the head Admiralty office at Vannes; and the claim to the vessel was to be made then by the captains, after presenting their protests. They all set out for that place the 28th ult. And I have since learned that they arrived the 2d or 3d inst. and part of them are sailed for Jersey, or Guernsey, in their way to England. Captain N—— goes to London and will inform you of any further particulars.

The protests made by the captains of the ships taken and carried into L'Orient by the *Reprisal* mention that vessel as a ship carrying an unknown flag, with thirteen stripes in it and the union at one corner; that when they came on board, they were informed the said vessel was called the *Reprisal*, commanded by Lambert Wickes, who said he had a commission as captain of a man of war from some persons who appear to be a society of people at Philadelphia, calling themselves the Congress; the protests being in French, the words are *une certaine société à Philadelphie, soi-disant le Congrès.*

The packet sailed from Falmouth the 3d of February; she was taken on the 5th, after an engagement of forty minutes. She would by no means have struck so soon, had she not unfortunately taken fire and been for some time in imminent danger of blowing up. The captain and men behaved in the bravest manner; but her force was very unequal, for she carried only eight four-pounders, four two-pounders and some swivels. The privateer carried sixteen six-pounders and ten or twelve swivels, with about three times as many men as the packet. The *Reprisal* had one man killed and two wounded, whereof one was the first lieutenant, who lost an arm. The packet had none killed nor wounded, excepting two sailors scorched with gunpowder, their cartridges having blown up by accident. They were nine days at sea before they could make L'Orient after taking the packet. The passengers and captain of the packet lived in the same manner as Wickes did, and dined at his table. The other captains and inferior officers were also properly treated while on board the privateer.

It appears by another letter that the prizes have been sold at £120,000 French money, the packet excepted, and they are sailed from L'Orient. The privateer is carreening there, but is ordered to depart as soon as possible.

—ALMON, ed., *The Remembrancer for 1776*, Part III, 308-311.

VII. JOHN PAUL JONES

Once war had broken out between France and England the stage was set for far more audacious raids, some of them under the command of that peppery Scotsman John Paul Jones. Paul Jones, as he preferred to be known in America, quickly won a reputation as a ruthless disciplinarian. At least one mutineer was slain by Jones in self-defense, and an incompetent and lazy ship carpenter died when a cat-o'-nine-tails at Jones's direction was too diligently laid on. When, in the course of one of Jones's many cruises, a naval lieutenant named Thomas Simpson "held up to the crew that, being Americans fighting for liberty, the voice of the people should be taken before the captain's orders were obeyed," Jones promptly thrust the exponent of naval democracy into the brig.

Commissioned in December 1775 a lieutenant in the newly organized Continental Navy, Paul Jones quickly distinguished himself by capturing sixteen prizes as commander of the Providence. *By the time of the incident reported below he had already been promoted to a captaincy. This incident occurred on the direct sea lane between the West Indies and London, where Jones had already inflicted punishing blows to British commerce. Next Jones headed for the fishing coast off Nova Scotia, where by the end of a month he was able to report to the Marine Committee of Congress that he had invaded the harbors of Canso and the Island of Madam and effectively destroyed the fisheries at both places, in addition to taking nine ships. "I only left two small schooners and one small brig to convey a number of unfortunate men, not short of three hundred, across the Western Ocean. Had I gone further, I stood chargeable with inhumanity." This expedition was a rehearsal for the daring raids Jones was later to stage along the English coast.*

1. Captain John Paul Jones Reports on His Victories at Sea

To Commodore Esek Hopkins.

Providence, at Sea, in N. Lat. 37° 40′, and W. Long 54°,

September 4, 1776

. . . And now for my success. I sent in a Nantucket whaler by Captain Grinnell, 27th ultimo. She appeared, by the voluntary testimony of the master, mate, etc., to be the property of rank Tories, who had ordered their oil to be carried to the London market, and the amount of it to be shipped out in English goods to Nantucket. Since that time I have been further to the southward, where I brought to a number of French, Spanish and Danish ships, but saw no Englishmen till the 1st current, when I fell in with five sail. One of them being very large, we took her to be either an old East-Indiaman or a Jamaica three-decker; but she proved to be an English frigate, mounting twenty-six guns upon one deck. She sailed fast and pursued us by the wind till, after four hours' chase, the sea running very cross, she got within musket shot of our lee quarter.

As they had continued firing at us from the first without showing colours, I was angry at this low piece of conduct; therefore, ordered ours to be hoisted and began to fire at them. They then hoisted American colours and fired guns to the leeward. But the bait would not take. Having everything prepared, I bore away across his forefoot and set all our light sails at once, so that before her sails were trimmed and steering sails set, I was almost out of reach of grape and soon after out of reach of cannon shot. Our "hair-bredth 'scape," and the saucy manner of making it, must have mortified him not a little. Had he foreseen this motion and been prepared to counteract it, he might have fired several broadsides while we were within pistol shot. He was a bad marksman and did not hit the *Providence* with one of the many shot which he fired.

I met with no other adventure till last night, when I took the brigantine *Sea-Nymph*, bound from Barbadoes for London with a cargo of two hundred and twenty-seven hogsheads of rum, besides oil, sugar, ginger and Madeira wine.

I understand by this brig that the *Andrew Doria* is off Bermuda, and that

Captain Weeks hath given a trimming to an English sloop-of-war off Martinico. I am much afraid that the storeships come out under convoy; for who would have expected to find a frigate with no more than two ships, a brig and a sloop? . . .

—FORCE, *American Archives*, 5th Series, II, 171-172.

2. JONES CARRIES THE WAR TO ENGLAND

As early as April '78 Paul Jones had been instructed by Franklin to raid the English coast. These instructions he carried out in a sensational manner. Commanding the Ranger, *he struck at Whitehaven on the northwest coast. Although he failed to accomplish his main objective—the destruction of Whitehaven's shipping—he did bring the war home to the British with a vengeance. British newspaper accounts reflected their consternation.*

Whitehaven, April 28, 1778: Late last night or early this morning a number of armed men (to the amount of 30) landed at this place by two boats from an American privateer, as appears from one of the people now in custody. Whether he was left through accident or escaped by design is yet uncertain. This much has however been proved: that a little after 3 o'clock this morning he rapped at several doors in Marlborough Street (adjoining one of the piers) and informed them that fire had been set to one of the ships in the harbour; matches were laid in several others; the whole world would be soon in a blaze, and the town also destroyed; that he was one belonging to the privateer, but had escaped for the purpose of saving the town and shipping from further destruction.

An alarm was immediately spread, and his account proved too true. The *Thomson*, Captain Richard Johnson, a new vessel and one of the finest ever built here, was aflame. It was low water, consequently all the shipping in the port was in the most imminent danger and the vessel on which they had begun the diabolical work, lying close to one of the steaths, there was the greatest reason to fear that the flames would, from it, soon be communicated to the town. The scene was too horrible to admit of any further description; we shall therefore only add to this part of this alarming story that, by an uncommon exertion, the fire was extinguished before it reached the rigging of the ship, and thus in a providential manner prevented all the dreadful consequences which might have ensued.

The man who remained on shore was examined by the magistrates, merchants, etc., about eight o'clock this morning. The following is the purport of his affadavit:

"*The Ranger* privateer is commanded by John Paul Jones, fitted out at Piscataqua in New England, mounted 18 six-pounders and 6 swivels, but is pierced for twenty guns. She has on board between 140 and 150 men; sailed from Piscataqua for Brest the 1st of November, 1777, arrived at Nantz the 2nd of December. Took in the passage of two brigs, one commanded by Capt. Richards, the other by Capt. Goldfinch.

"Sailed from Nantz for Quiberon Bay, lay there about three weeks ago in which time she has taken one ship from London (having on board General

Irwin's baggage) and sent her to Brest. She also took and sunk a brig loaden with flax-seed, a schooner with barley and oats, and a sloop from Dublin to London in ballast.

"On Sunday or Monday night, from the intelligence she gained by a fishing boat, she sailed into Belfast Lough, with an intent to attack an armed vessel (the *Drake* sloop of war), stood within half gun shot of her, hailed her, and then stood out again."

David Freeman, the person who was examined and gave the above information, says that the name of the commander is John Paul Jones, the First Lieutenant Thompson Simpson, Second Lieutenant Elisha Hall, Sailing-master David Cullen, Lieutenant of Marines Samuel Willingford.

The above John Paul Jones, alias John Paul, it further appears, served his apprenticeship to the sea in a vessel called the *Friendship*, belonging to this port, was afterwards in the employ of some merchants here, latterly had a brig out of Kirkcudbright, and is well known by many people in this town. David Freeman, it is said, has also declared that the said Paul Jones commanded the party which landed here this morning and was himself on shore.

While this infernal business was transacting, the ship laid to with her head to the northward, distant about two miles, until the boats put off to go on board, which was between three and four o'clock. By this time some of the guns at the Half-moon Battery were loaded, two of which were fired at the boats, but without the desired effect. The boats then fired their signal guns and the ship immediately tacked and stood towards them till they got along aside, and then made sail to the north westward.

The incendiaries had spiked most of the guns of both our batteries; several matches were found on board different vessels, and other combustible matter in different parts of the harbour.

It appears that this infernal plan, unprecedented except in the annals of John the Painter,* was laid at Brest, where for a considerable sum of money *Paul* or *Jones* (the latter is only an addition to his name) engaged to burn the shipping and town of Whitehaven; for which purpose he was convoyed through the channel by a French frigate of 38 guns.

A number of expresses have been dispatched to all the capital sea-ports in the kingdom where any depredations are likely to be made; all strangers in this town are, by an order of the magistrate, to be secured and examined: similar notices have been forwarded through the country, etc., and in short, every caution taken that the present alarming affair could suggest.

The privateer is the same ship which chased the *Hussar* cruiser last week, but the cutter or smack did not belong to her.

They took three people away with them, and staid some time in a public house on the Old Quay.

The *Hussar*, Capt. Gurley, and other vessels are sent to different ports in Ireland express with the news.

There has been almost a continual meeting at Haile's coffee-room to-day; a number of men are raising for the defence of the town by subscription, and

---

* The reader has already made the acquaintance of this notorious saboteur.

the forts, guns, etc., it is expected will now be put into proper condition.
—*London Morning Post and Daily Advertiser,* April 28, 1778.

3. THE CAPTURE OF THE *Drake*

Following hard upon his daring raid on Whitehaven, Paul Jones crossed the Irish sea and struck on the northern coast of Ireland, capturing the sloop-of-war Drake *inside the harbor of Carrickfergus. In his account to Franklin, Jones reported the action as "warm, close and obstinate," and as lasting an hour and four minutes. The enemy called for quarter after her sails and rigging had been cut to ribbons, her masts shattered, and her hull "very much galled." In prisoners and wounded the British lost some forty men; Jones's Ranger suffered three killed and six wounded.*

The chagrined British press attributed the loss of the Drake *to a combination of British naval graft and the fighting spirit of the Americans.*

To the American Commissioners.

May 27, 1778

On the morning of the 24th [April], I was again off Carrickfergus, and would have gone in, had I not seen the *Drake* preparing to come out. It was very moderate, and the *Drake's* boat was sent out to reconnoitre the *Ranger.* As the boat advanced, I kept the ship's stern directly towards her; and though they had a spy-glass in the boat, they came on within hail, and alongside. When the officer came on the quarter deck, he was greatly surprised to find himself a prisoner; although an express had arrived from Whitehaven the night before. I now understood, what I had before imagined, that the *Drake* came out in consequence of this information, with volunteers, against the *Ranger.* The officer told me also, that they had taken up the *Ranger's* anchor. The *Drake* was attended by five small vessels full of people, who were led by curiosity to see an engagement. But when they saw the *Drake's* boat at the *Ranger's* stern, they most wisely put back.

Alarm smokes now appeared in great abundance, extending along on both sides of the channel. The tide was unfavorable, so that the *Drake* worked out but slowly. This obliged me to run down several times, and to lay with courses up, and maintopsail to the mast. At length the *Drake* weathered the point, and having led her out to about mid-channel, I suffered her to come within hail. The *Drake* hoisted English colours, and at the same instant, the American stars were displayed on board the *Ranger.* I expected that preface had been now at an end, but the enemy soon after hailed, demanding what ship it was? I directed the master to answer, "the American Continental ship *Ranger;* that we waited for them and desired that they would come on; the sun was now little more than an hour from setting, it was therefore time to begin." The *Drake* being astern of the *Ranger,* I ordered the helm up, and gave her the first broadside. The action was warm, close and obstinate. It lasted an hour and four minutes, when the enemy called for quarters; her fore and main-topsail yards being both cut away, and down on the cap; the top-gallant yard and mizen-gaff both hanging up and down along the mast; the second ensign which they had hoisted shot away, and hanging on the quarter gallery in the water; the jib shot away, and hanging in the water; her sails and rigging entirely cut to pieces; her masts and yards all wounded, and her hull also very much galled.

I lost only Lieutenant Wallingsford and one seaman, John Dougall, killed, and six wounded; among whom are the gunner, Mr. Falls, and Mr. Powers, a midshipman who lost his arm. One of the wounded, Nathaniel Wills, is since dead; the rest will recover. The loss of the enemy in killed and wounded was far greater. All the prisoners allow that they came out with a number not less than a hundred and sixty men; and many of them affirm that they amounted to a hundred and ninety. The medium may, perhaps, be the most exact account; and by that it will appear that they lost in killed and wounded forty-two men. The captain and lieutenant were among the wounded; the former, having received a musket ball in the head the minute before they called for quarters, lived, and was sensible some time after my people boarded the prize. The lieutenant survived two days. They were buried with the honours due to their rank, and with the respect due to their memory.

The night and almost the whole day after the action being moderate, greatly facilitated the refitting of both ships. A large brigantine was so near the *Drake* in the afternoon that I was obliged to bring her to. She belonged to Whitehaven, and was bound for Norway.

—TAYLOR, *Life and Correspondence of John Paul Jones*, pp. 84-85.

4. THE *Bon Homme Richard* AND THE *Serapis*

The most spectacular episode in the naval annals of the American Revolution was the three-hour battle fought between the old Indiaman, renamed the Bon Homme Richard *in honor of "Poor Richard," the literary pseudonym of the popular American commissioner to France, and the* Serapis, *which occurred on September 23, 1779. After his sensational raids of the spring of that year John Paul Jones put to sea from France in August with a squadron of four vessels, including the* Bon Homme Richard *and the* Alliance, *the latter under the command of the treacherous and unstable French Captain Pierre Landais. Taking a number of prizes, the squadron passed around the north of Scotland, and followed the east coast of England into the North Sea. Jones's crew was motley, his officers were inexperienced Americans. Forced by a gale to postpone a bold plan to seize shipping and extort a ransom from Leith, the port of Edinburgh, Jones made for the open seas and soon sighted a fleet of forty British merchantmen returning from the Baltic under convoy of the* Serapis, *forty-four guns, and the* Countess of Scarborough, *twenty-eight guns. The merchantmen scurried to the safety of the shore batteries, and Paul Jones took on the* Serapis, *although outgunned by forty-four to forty.*

Numerous accounts of that engagement have come down to us, including the reports by both Paul Jones and Captain Richard Pearson, commander of the Serapis. *The two most vivid stories come from the pens of Lieutenant Richard Dale and Midshipman Nathaniel Fanning. The former was stationed on the main deck in command of a battery of 12-pounders and in a comparatively unfavorable position to observe the maneuvers, but he alone reports the immortal reply of Jones to the* Serapis *when asked, "Has your ship struck?" Midshipman Fanning was stationed in the maintop of the ship. The two ac-*

*counts supplement each other extraordinarily well. Fanning's is especially
full on the latter phases of the action. In addition, Jones put down on paper
several accounts of Landais' treachery, which is also corroborated by Lieutenant Henry Lunt in an account originally written in the* Serapis' *log after
the Americans had taken that ship. In his letter to Franklin, Jones spelled out
the charge against Landais. Writing ten days later to Robert Morris, Jones
insisted that "the* Alliance *contributed much to the loss of the* Bon Homme
Richard *by hitting her between wind and water and under the water." Politics saved Landais from a court-martial at this time, but he was not so fortunate on a later occasion. With the connivance of Arthur Lee and certain
French naval officers Landais was left in command of the* Alliance *and made a
summer voyage to America in 1780. During that voyage he behaved like a
man whose mind was unhinged. He was supplanted in command of the ship
after a rising of passengers and officers against him, was court-martialed on
reaching Boston, found guilty, and dismissed from the service.*

A. "I HAVE NOT YET BEGUN TO FIGHT!"

Account by Lieutenant Richard Dale.

On the 23d of September, 1779, being below, was roused by an unusual
noise upon deck. This induced me to go upon deck when I found the men
were swaying up the royal yards, preparatory to making sail for a large fleet
under our lee. I asked the coasting pilot what fleet it was?

He answered, "The Baltic fleet under convoy of the *Serapis* of 44 guns and
the *Countess of Scarborough* of 20 guns."

A general chase then commenced of the *Bon Homme Richard*, the *Vengeance*, the *Pallas* and the *Alliance*, the latter ship being then in sight after a
separation from the squadron of nearly three weeks, but which ship, as usual,
disregarded the private signals of the Commodore. At this time our fleet
headed to the northward with a light breeze, Flamborough Head being about
two leagues distant. At 7 P.M. it was evident the Baltic fleet perceived we
were in chace from the signal of the *Serapis* to the merchantmen to stand in
shore. At the same time the *Serapis* and *Countess of Scarborough* tacked ship
and stood off shore, with the intention of drawing off our attention from the
convoy. When these ships had separated from the convoy about two miles,
they again tacked and stood in shore after the merchantmen.

At about eight, being within hail, the *Serapis* demanded, "What ship is
that?"

He was answered, "I can't hear what you say."

Immediately after, the *Serapis* hailed again, "What ship is that? Answer
immediately, or I shall be under the necessity of firing into you."

At this moment I received orders from Commodore Jones to commence
the action with a broadside, which indeed appeared to be simultaneous on
board both ships. Our position being to windward of the *Serapis* we passed
ahead of her, and the *Serapis* coming up on our larboard quarter, the action
commenced abreast of each other. The *Serapis* soon passed ahead of the *Bon
Homme Richard*, and when he thought he had gained a distance sufficient to
go down athwart the fore foot to rake us, found he had not enough distance,

and that the *Bon Homme Richard* would be aboard him, put his helm a-lee, which brought the two ships on a line, and the *Bon Homme Richard*, having head way, ran her bows into the stern of the *Serapis*.

We had remained in this situation but a few minutes when we were again hailed by the *Serapis*, "Has your ship struck?"

To which Captain Jones answered, "I have not yet begun to fight!"

As we were unable to bring a single gun to bear upon the *Serapis* our topsails were backed, while those of the *Serapis* being filled, the ships separated. The *Serapis* bore short round upon her heel, and her jibboom ran into the mizen rigging of the *Bon Homme Richard*. In this situation the ships were made fast together with a hawser, the bowsprit of the *Serapis* to the mizenmast of the *Bon Homme Richard*, and the action recommenced from the starboard sides of the two ships. With a view of separating the ships, the *Serapis* let go her anchor, which manoeuver brought her head and the stern of the *Bon Homme Richard* to the wind, while the ships lay closely pressed against each other.

A novelty in naval combats was now presented to many witnesses, but to few admirers. The rammers were run into the respective ships to enable the men to load after the lower ports of the *Serapis* had been blown away, to make room for running out their guns, and in this situation the ships remained until between 10 and 11 o'clock P.M., when the engagement terminated by the surrender of the *Serapis*.

From the commencement to the termination of the action there was not a man on board the *Bon Homme Richard* ignorant of the superiority of the *Serapis*, both in weight of metal and in the qualities of the crews. The crew of that ship was picked seamen, and the ship itself had been only a few months off the stocks, whereas the crew of the *Bon Homme Richard* consisted of part Americans, English and French, and a part of Maltese, Portuguese and Malays, these latter contributing by their want of naval skill and knowledge of the English language to depress rather than to elevate a just hope of success in a combat under such circumstances. Neither the consideration of the relative force of the ships, the fact of the blowing up of the gundeck above them by the bursting of two of the 18-pounders, nor the alarm that the ship was sinking, could depress the ardor or change the determination of the brave Captain Jones, his officers and men. Neither the repeated broadsides of the *Alliance*, given with the view of sinking or disabling the *Bon Homme Richard*, the frequent necessity of suspending the combat to extinguish the flames, which several times were within a few inches of the magazine, nor the liberation by the master-at-arms of nearly 500 prisoners, could charge or weaken the purpose of the American commander. At the moment of the liberation of the prisoners, one of them, a commander of a 20-gun ship taken a few days before, passed through the ports on board the *Serapis* and informed Captain Pearson that if he would hold out only a little while longer, the ship alongside would either strike or sink, and that all the prisoners had been released to save their lives. The combat was accordingly continued with renewed ardor by the *Serapis*.

The fire from the tops of the *Bon Homme Richard* was conducted with so much skill and effect as to destroy ultimately every man who appeared upon the quarter deck of the *Serapis*, and induced her commander to order the survivors to go below. Nor even under the shelter of the decks were they more secure. The powder-monkies of the *Serapis*, finding no officer to receive the 18-pound cartridges brought from the magazines, threw them on the main deck and went for more. These cartridges being scattered along the deck and numbers of them broken, it so happened that some of the hand-grenades thrown from the main-yard of the *Bon Homme Richard*, which was directly over the main-hatch of the *Serapis*, fell upon this powder and produced a most awful explosion. The effect was tremendous; more than twenty of the enemy were blown to pieces, and many stood with only the collars of their shirts upon their bodies. In less than an hour afterward, the flag of England, which had been nailed to the mast of the *Serapis*, was struck by Captain Pearson's *own hand*,* as none of his people would venture aloft on this duty; and this too when more than 1500 persons were witnessing the conflict, and the humiliating termination of it, from Scarborough and Flamborough Head.

Upon finding that the flag of the *Serapis* had been struck, I went to Captain Jones and asked whether I might board the *Serapis*, to which he consented, and jumping upon the gun-wale, seized the main-brace pennant and swung myself upon her quarter-deck. Midshipman Mayrant followed with a party of men and was immediately run through the thigh with a boarding pike by some of the enemy stationed in the waist, who were not informed of the surrender of their ship.

I found Captain Pearson standing on the leeward side of the quarter-deck and, addressing myself to him, said, "Sir, I have orders to send you on board the ship alongside." The first lieutenant of the *Serapis* coming up at this moment inquired of Captain Pearson whether the ship alongside had struck to him. To which I replied, "No, Sir, the contrary: he has struck to us."

The lieutenant renewed his inquiry, "Have you struck, Sir?"

"Yes, I have."

The lieutenant replied, "I have nothing more to say," and was about to return below when I informed him he must accompany Captain Pearson on board the ship alongside. He said, "If you will permit me to go below, I will silence the firing of the lower-deck guns."

This request was refused, and with Captain Pearson, he was passed over to the deck of the *Bon Homme Richard*. Orders being sent below to cease firing, the engagement terminated, after a most obstinate contest of three hours and a half.

Upon receiving Captain Pearson on board the *Bon Homme Richard*, Captain Jones gave orders to cut loose the lashings, and directed me to follow him with the *Serapis*. Perceiving the *Bon Homme Richard* leaving the *Serapis*, I sent one of the quartermasters to ascertain whether the wheel-ropes were cut away, supposing something extraordinary must be the matter, as the ship

---

* Captain Pearson subsequently stated: "I found it in vain, and indeed impracticable from the situation we were in, to stand out any longer with the least prospect to success. I therefore struck."

would not pay off, although the head sails were aback, and no after sail; the quartermaster, returning, reported that the wheel-ropes were all well, and the helm hard a-port. Excited by this extraordinary circumstance, I jumped off the binnacle, where I had been sitting, and falling upon the deck, found to my astonishment I had the use of only one of my legs. A splinter of one of the guns had struck and badly wounded my leg without my perceiving the injury until this moment. I was replaced upon the binnacle, when the sailing-master of the *Serapis* coming up to me observed that from my orders he judged I must be ignorant of the ship *being at anchor*. Noticing the second lieutenant of the *Bon Homme Richard*, I directed him to go below and cut away the cable, and follow the *Bon Homme Richard* with the *Serapis*. I was then carried on board the *Bon Homme Richard* to have my wound dressed.

—SHERBURNE, *Life and Character of Jones*, pp. 126-129.

B. CAPTAIN PEARSON CRIES OUT, "QUARTERS, FOR GOD'S SAKE!"

Midshipman Nathaniel Fanning's narrative.

... The battle had now continued about three hours, and as we, in fact, had possession of the *Serapis's* top, which commanded her quarter-deck, upper gun-deck and forecastle, we were well assured that the enemy could not hold out much longer, and were momently expecting that they would strike to us, when the following farcical piece was acted on board our ship.

It seems that a report was at this time circulated among our crew between deck, and was credited among them, that Captain Jones and all his principal officers were slain, the gunners were now the commanders of our ship, that the ship had four or five feet of water in her hold, and that she was then sinking. They therefore advised the gunner to go up on deck, together with the carpenter and master at arms, and beg of the enemy quarters, in order, as they said, to save their lives.

These three men, being thus delegated, mounted the quarter-deck, and bawled out as loud as they could, "Quarters, quarters, for God's sake, quarters! Our ship is sinking!" and immediately got upon the ship's poop with a view of hauling down our colours.

Hearing this in the top, I told my men that the enemy had struck and was crying out for quarters, for I actually thought that the voices of these men sounded as if on board of the enemy; but in this I was soon undeceived. The three poltroons, finding the ensign and ensign-staff gone, they proceeded upon the quarter-deck, and were in the act of hauling down our pennant, still bawling for "quarters!" when I heard our commodore say in a loud voice, "What d——d rascals are them?—Shoot them!—Kill them!" He was upon the forecastle when these fellows first made their appearance upon the quarter-deck where he had just discharged his pistols at some of the enemy. The carpenter and the master-at-arms, hearing Jones's voice, sculked below, and the gunner was attempting to do the same when Jones threw both of his pistols at his head, one of which struck him in the head, fractured his skull and knocked him down at the foot of the gang-way ladder, where he lay till the battle was over.

Both ships now took fire again; and on board of our ship it communicated to and set our main top on fire, which threw us into the greatest consternation imaginable for some time, and it was not without some exertions and difficulty that it was overcome. The water which we had in a tub, in the fore part of the top, was expended without extinguishing the fire. We next had recourse to our clothes, by pulling off our coats and jackets, and then throwing them upon the fire and stamping upon them, which in a short time smothered it. Both crews were also now, as before, busily employed in stopping the progress of the flames, and the firing on both sides ceased.

The enemy now demanded of us if we had struck, as they had heard the three poltroons halloo for quarters. "If you have," said they, "why don't you haul down your pendant?" as they saw our ensign was gone.

"Ay, ay," said Jones, "we'll do that when we can fight no longer, but we shall see yours come down the first; for you must know that Yankees do not haul down their colours till they are fairly beaten."

The combat now recommenced again with more fury if possible than before, on the part of both, and continued for a few minutes, when the cry of fire was again heard on board of both ships. The firing ceased, and both crews were once more employed in extinguishing it, which was soon effected, when the battle was renewed with redoubled vigour, with what cannon we could manage, hand grenadoes, stink pots, etc., but principally, towards the closing scene, with lances and boarding pikes. With these the combatants killed each other through the ship's port holes, which were pretty large; and the guns that had been run out at them becoming useless, as before observed, had been removed out of the way.

At three quarters past 11 P.M. the *Alliance* frigate hove in sight, approached within pistol shot of our stern and began a heavy and well-directed fire into us as well as the enemy, which made some of our officers as well as men believe that she was an English man of war. (The moon at this time, as though ashamed to behold this bloody scene any longer, retired behind a dark cloud.) It was in vain that some of our officers hailed her and desired them not to fire any more; it was in vain they were told they had slain a number of our men; it was in vain also that they were told that the enemy was fairly beaten, and that she must strike her colours within a few minutes. The *Alliance*, I say, notwithstanding all this, kept a position either ahead of us or under our stern, and made a great deal of havock and confusion on board of our ship; and she did not cease firing entirely till the signal of recognisance was displayed in full view on board of our ship; which was three lighted lanthorns ranged in a horizontal line about fifteen feet high, upon the fore, main and mizzen shrouds, upon the larboard side. This was done in order to undeceive the *Alliance*, and which had the desired effect, and the firing from her ceased.

And at thirty-five minutes past 12 at night, a single hand grenado having been thrown by one of our men out of the main top of the enemy, designing it to go among the enemy who were huddled together between her gun decks, it on its way struck on one side of the combings of her upper hatchway,* and rebounding from that, it took a direction and fell between their decks, where it communicated to a quantity of loose powder scattered about the enemy's cannon; and the hand grenado bursting at the same time made a dreadful explosion and blew up about twenty of the enemy.

This closed the scene, and the enemy now in their turn (notwithstanding the gasconading of Capt. Parsons [*sic*]) bawled out "Quarters, quarters, quarters, for God's sake!"

It was, however, some time before the enemy's colours were struck. The captain of the *Serapis* gave repeated orders for one of his crew to ascend the quarter-deck and haul down the English flag, but no one would stir to do it. They told the captain they were afraid of our rifle-men, believing that all our men who were seen with muskets were of that description. The captain of the *Serapis* therefore ascended the quarter-deck, and hauled down the very flag which he had nailed to the flag-staff a little before the commencement of the battle, and which flag he had at that time, in the presence of his principal officers, swore he never would strike to that infamous pirate J. P. Jones.

The enemy's flag being struck, Captain Jones ordered Richard Dale, his first lieutenant, to select out of our crew a number of men and take possession of the prize, which was immediately put in execution. Several of our men (I believe three) were killed by the English on board of the *Serapis* after she had struck to us, for which they afterwards apologized by saying that the men who were guilty of this breach of honour did not know at the time that their own ship had struck her colours.

Thus ended this ever memorable battle, after a continuance of a few minutes more than *four hours*. The officers, headed by the captain of the *Serapis* now came on baord of our ship; the latter (Captain Parsons) enquired for Captain Jones, to whom he was introduced by Mr. Mase, our purser. They met, and the former accosted the latter, in presenting his sword, in this manner: "It is with the greatest reluctance that I am now obliged to resign you this, for it is painful to me, more partciularly at this time, when compelled to deliver up my sword to a man who may be said to fight *with a halter around his neck!*"

Jones, after receiving his sword, made this reply: "Sir, you have fought like a hero, and I make no doubt but your sovereign will reward you in a most ample manner for it."

Captain Parsons then asked Jones what countrymen his crew principally consisted of.

The latter said, "Americans."

"Very well," said the former, "it has been *diamond cut diamond with us.*"

Captain Parsons's officers had, previous to coming on board of our ship,

---

* The hatchways are generally taken off during an action; for this reason, that if anything thrown on board, such as a hand grenado and the like, happens to fall in through the hatchway, it descends down upon the haul-up-deck, where if it bursts it will injure nobody.

delivered their side arms to Lieutenant Dale. Captain Parsons in his conversation with Captain Jones owned that the Americans were equally as brave as the English. The two captains now withdrew into the cabin and there drank a glass or two of wine together. . . .

—FANNING, Narrative, pp. 40-45.

C. "FORBEAR FIRING ON THE *Bon Homme Richard!*"

John Paul Jones to Benjamin Franklin.

On Board the Ship Serapis, at anchor without the Texel,
in Holland, October 3, 1779

. . . At last, at half-past 9 o'clock, the *Alliance* appeared, and I now thought the battle at an end; but, to my utter astonishment, he discharged a broadside full into the stern of the *Bon Homme Richard*. We called to him: "For God's sake to forbear firing into the *Bon Homme Richard!*" Yet he passed along the off side of the ship and continued firing. There was no possibility of his mistaking the enemy's ship for the *Bon Homme Richard*, there being the most essential difference in their appearance and construction; besides, it was then full moonlight, and the sides of the *Bon Homme Richard* were all black, while the sides of the prizes were yellow. Yet, for the greater security, I shewed the signal of our reconnoissance by putting out three lanthorns, one at the head [bow], another at the stern [quarter], and the third in the middle in a horizontal line. Every tongue cried that he was firing into the wrong ship, but nothing availed. He passed round, firing into the *Bon Homme Richard's* head, stern and broadside; and by one of his volleys killed several of my best men and mortally wounded a good officer on the forecastle.

My situation was really deplorable. The *Bon Homme Richard* received various shots under water from the *Alliance*, the leak gained on the pumps, and the fire increased much on board both ships. Some officers persuaded me to strike, of whose courage and good sense I entertain a high opinion. My treacherous master-at-arms let loose all my prisoners without my knowledge, and my prospect became gloomy indeed. I would not, however, give up the point. The enemy's mid-mast began to shake, their firing decreased, ours rather increased, and the British colors were struck at half an hour past 10 o'clock. . . .

Upon the whole, the captain of the *Alliance* has behaved so very ill in every respect that I must complain loudly of his conduct. He pretends that he is authorized to act independent of my command. I have been taught the contrary; but, supposing it to be so, his conduct has been base and unpardonable. . . . Either Captain Landais or myself is highly criminal, and one or the other must be punished. I forbear to take any steps with him until I have the advice and approbation of your excellency. I have been advised by all the officers of the squadron to put M. Landais under arrest; but, as I have postponed it so long, I will bear with him a little longer until the return of my express.

—SHERBURNE, Life and Character of Jones, pp. 116-120.

D. JONES WINS HIS GREATEST VICTORY OVER AGAIN IN LAVISH STYLE

[1808]

Midshipman Captain Nathaniel Fanning's narrative.

About the tenth of December [1779] great preparations were made on board of our ship in consequence of a great number of people of the first character in l'Orient—one prince of the blood royal, and three French admirals, with some ladies of the first quality—having had cards of invitation sent them by Captain Jones inviting them on board of his ship the next day to take dinner with him precisely at 3 o'clock in the afternoon, and also informing the company that Captain Jones would, in the evening of that day, on board of his ship exhibit to them a sham sea fight; and that it should in part represent his battle with the *Serapis*, particularly her tops. . . .

First then, all the boats belonging to our ship were busily employed with their respective crews from the time the approaching scene was known on board (which was the day before it was to take place) at ten o'clock in the morning till about twelve at night of the day on which the company were to dine, in passing to, and coming from the shore, bringing off from thence all the articles wanted. And the reader may rest assured that neither cash nor pains were spared in order that the scene every way should appear magnificent.

In a short time our quarter-deck had the appearance of a lady of qualities' drawing room. Overhead was suspended an elegant awning, the edgings of which were cut in scallops and decorated with a variety of silk roses, tassils, etc., from a little below the awnings. At the sides were hung thin canvass lined with pink coloured silk, and which fell down so as to reach the quarter-deck. These sides were hung with a great variety of French pictures and looking glasses; some of the first had been drawn by one of the most finished artists in France, and many of which were quite indecent, especially to meet the eyes of a virtuous woman. However, in these days they were a part of French etiquette on such an occasion. The quarter-deck of our ship was covered with the most elegant carpet. The plate alone which was made use of on this singular occasion was estimated to be worth two thousand guineas. (For my own part I believe it might have been rated at double that sum.)

French cooks and waiters or servants were brought from the shore to assist in this business, and for nearly twenty hours preceeding the serving up of dinner, we were almost suffocated with garlick and onions, besides a great many other stinking vegetables. A French lady (who was said to be a great *connoiseur* in the art of cookery, and in hanging and arranging pictures in a room where the first companies went to dine) was gallanted on board by Captain Jones the evening before the day on which the company were to dine, and was by him directed to take upon herself the superintendance of the approaching feast.

The next day was ushered in by thirteen guns, and the dressing of the ship with the thirteen stripes, and the colours of all nations who were friendly to the United States. Captain Jones and his officers were all dressed in uniform, with their best bib and band on, and we were directed by Captain Jones to conduct ourselves with propriety and to pay implicit obedience to my *lady superintendent* of the ceremonies.

At a quarter before 3 o'clock in the afternoon the ship's boats (three in number, each having a midshipman who acted for this time as coxswain, and the men who rowed the boats were all neatly dressed in blew broad cloth, with the American and French cockades in their hats) were despatched on shore to bring on board the company. Jones received them as they came up the ship's side, and conducted them to their seats on the quarter deck with a great deal of ease, politeness and good nature.

Dinner was served up at half past 3 P.M. The company did not rise from table till a little after the sun set, when Captain Jones ordered his first lieutenant to cause all hands to be called to quarters, which was done just as the moon was rising. I of course mounted into the main top, which had always been my station as long as I had served under Jones (of which and the men quartered there, I had the command). Orders were given before we mounted into the tops that we must be well supplied with ammunition, blunder busses, muskets, cowhorns, hand grenadoes, etc., the same as if we were now to engage with an enemy; and when the signal was given (which was to be a cannon fired upon the forecastle) . . . the sham fight was to commence.

At 8 o'clock it began, and lasted about an hour and a quarter without any intermission. Such a cracking of great guns, swivels, small arms, cowhorns, blunder busses, etc., such a hissing and popping of hand grenadoes, stink pots, powder flasks was now heard, as they fell into the water alongside, as was never the like in the harbour of l'Orient seen or heard. Some of the ladies were much frightened and the sham fight would have continued longer had it not been that some of them intreated Captain Jones to command the firing to cease. The fight over, a band of music, which had been ordered on board by the commandant, and who had been paraded upon the fore part of the quarter-deck, now played their part, and all was glee and harmony.

At about twelve at night the company took their leave of Captain Jones, and the boats set them safe on shore, in the same order and regularity as they came on board, excepting a few who were landed *half seas over;* these the midshipmen assisted along to their lodgings, and returned on board to give an account to Captain Jones that we saw all the company safe at their respective places of abode.

For several days after this, nothing of any note was to be heard in conversation among the French at l'Orient, in their coffee houses and private dwellings, but Captain Jones's feast and sham fight. Upon the whole, I believe it must have cost himself, as well as the United States, a vast sum of money. There was certainly a great quantity of powder burnt, and an abundance of wine (besides other liquors) drank. The cost of the whole of this entertainment, including the powder, amounted (by an estimate made by the American agent's first clerk, and who it seems paid the cash for sundry bills relative to this business) to 3,027 crown at 6s. 8d. each, Massachusetts currency.

Whether Captain Jones charged the whole or any part of the expense of this business to the United States I never learned.

—FANNING, *Memoirs*, pp. 98-100.

VIII. THE *TRUMBULL* AND THE *WATT*

Next to the clash of the Bon Homme Richard *with the* Serapis, *the naval action fought between the Continental frigate* Trumbull, *commanded by Captain James Nicholson, and the British letter of marque* Watt *was probably the severest sea battle of the war, although inconclusive in its results. It took place some two hundred miles north of Bermuda on June 2, 1780. Nicholson wrote his own account on his return to Boston. His adversary, Captain John Coulthard of the British privateer, gave a somewhat different version, but one which in no way reflected on the fighting stamina of either crew. Gilbert Saltonstall, the captain of the marines aboard the* Trumbull, *observed that "there has not been a more close, obstinate, and bloody engagement since the war began. I hope it won't be treason if I don't except Paul Jones. All things considered we may dispute title with him."*

Nicholson was fortunate on this occasion. On August 8, 1781, the Trumbull *on escort duty to a fleet of 28 merchant ships was forced to strike her colors to the British 32-gun frigate* Iris, *formerly the American frigate* Hancock, *captured off Halifax. The* Iris *was supported by two other British ships. The* Trumbull *was badly manned, partly with British prisoners, and most of the crew disobeyed orders at the height of the engagement. Nicholson carried on the fight as long as possible with a crippled ship and a handful of loyal officers and seamen.*

1. A FIERCE ENCOUNTER WITH A BRITISH LETTER OF MARQUE

Account of James Nicholson, captain of the *Trumbull*.

Boston, June 20, 1780

At half past ten in the morning of June 2d, lat. 35. N., long. 64. W. we discovered a sail from the masthead and immediately handed all our sails, in order to keep ourselves undiscovered until she came nearer to us, she being to windward. At eleven we made her to be a large ship from the deck, coming down about three points upon our quarter. At half-past eleven we thought she hauled a point more a-stern of us. We therefore made sail, and hauled upon a wind towards her, upon which she came right down upon our beams. We then took in all our small sails, hauled the courses up, hove the main-top-sail to the mast, got all clear for action, and waited upon her.

At half past eleven we filled the main-top (the ship being then about gunshot to windward of us) in order to try her sailing; also that by her hauling up after us we might have an opportunity of discovering her broadside. She immediately got her main tack out and stood after us. We then observed she had thirteen ports of a side, exclusive of her briddle ports, and eight or ten on her quarter deck and forecastle.

After a very short exhortation to my people they most chearfully agreed to fight her. At twelve we found we greatly outsailed her and got to windward of her. We therefore determined to take that advantage. Upon her observing our intention she edged away, fired three shot at us and hoisted British colours as a challenge. We immediately wore after her and hoisted British colours also. This we did in order to get peaceably alongside of her, upon which she made us a private signal and upon our not answering it she gave us the first broadside, we then being under British colours and about one hundred yards distant. We immediately hoisted the Continental colours and returned her a broadside, then about eighty yards distance; when a furious and close action commenced and continued for five glasses, no time of which we were more than eighty yards asunder and the greater part of the time not above fifty; at one time our yard-arms were almost enlocked. She set us twice on fire with her wads, as we did her once; she had difficulty in extinguishing her's, being obliged to cut all her larboard quarter nettings away.

At the expiration of the above time my first lieutenant (after consulting and agreeing with the second) came aft to me and desired I would observe the situation of our masts and rigging, which were going over the side; therefore begged I would quit her before that happened; otherwise we should certainly be taken. I therefore most unwillingly left her, by standing on the same course we engaged on; I say unwillingly, as I am confident if our masts would have admitted of our laying half an hour longer alongside of her, she would have struck to us, her fire having almost ceased and her pumps both going. Upon our going ahead of her she steered about four points away from us. When about musquet shot asunder, we lost our main and mizen topmast and in spite of all our efforts we continued losing our masts until we had not one left but the foremast and that very badly wounded and sprung. Before night shut in we saw her lose her maintopmast.

I was in hopes when I left her of being able to renew the action after securing my mast, but upon inquiry found so many of my people killed and wounded, and my ship so much of a wreck in her masts and rigging, that it was impossible. We lost eight killed and thirty one wounded; amongst the former was one lieutenant, one midshipman, one serjeant of marines and one quarter gunner; amongst the latter was one lieutenant, since dead, the captain of marines, the purser, the boatswain, two midshipmen, the cockswain and my clerk. The rest were common men, nine of which in the whole are since dead.

No people shewed more true spirit and gallantry than mine did. I had but one hundred and ninety-nine men when the action commenced, almost the whole of which, exclusive of the officers, were green country lads, many of them not clear of their sea-sickness, and I am well persuaded they suffered more in seeing the masts carried away than they did in the engagement. We plainly perceived the enemy throw many of his men overboard in the action, two in particular which were not quite dead; from the frequent cries of his wounded and the appearance of his hull, I am convinced he must have lost many more men than we did and suffered more in his hull. Our damage was most remarkable and unfortunate in our masts and rigging, which I must again say alone saved him; for the last half hour of the action I momently expected to see his colours down, but am of opinion he persevered from the appearance of our masts.

You will perhaps conclude from the above that she was a British man of war, but I beg leave to assure you that it was not then, nor is it now my opinion; she appeared to me like a French East-Indiaman cut down. She fought a greater number of marines and more men in her tops than we did, the whole of which we either killed or drove below. She dismounted two of our guns and silenced two more; she fought four or six and thirty twelve-pounders, we fought twenty-four twelves and six sixes. I beg leave to assure you that let her be what she would, either letter of marque or privateer, I give you my honour that was I to have my choice tomorrow, I would sooner fight any two-and-thirty-gun frigate they have on the coast of America than to fight that ship over again. Not that I mean to degrade the British men of war, far be it from me, but I think she was more formidable and was better manned than they are in general.

—ALMON, ed., *The Remembrancer*, X, 225-227.

2. "MY MEN BEHAVED LIKE TRUE SONS OF OLD ENGLAND"

June 14, 1780

Account of John Coulthard, captain of the *Watt*.

Saw a large ship under the lee bow, bearing N.W. by W., distant about three or four miles; supposed her to be a rebel vessel bound to France and immediately bore down upon her. When she perceived we were standing for her she hauled up her courses and hove to. We then found her to be a frigate of 34 or 36 guns and full of men and immediately hoisted our colours and fired a gun; she at the same time hoisted Saint George's colours and fired a gun to leeward. We then took her for one of his Majesty's cruizing frigates and intended speaking to her, but as soon as she saw we were getting on her weather quarter, they filled their topsails and stood to the eastward. We then fired five guns to bring her to, but she having a clean bottom and we foul and a cargo in, could not come up with her. Therefore, finding it a folly to chace, fired two guns into her and bore ship to the westward; at the same time she fired one gun at us, loaded with grape shot and round, and bore after us. Perceiving this, we immediately hauled up our courses and hove to for her.

She still kept English colours flying till she came within pistol shot on our weather quarter. She then hauled down English colours and hoisted rebel colours, upon which we instantly gave her three cheers and a broadside. She returned it and we came alongside one another and for above seven glasses engaged yard arm and yard arm. My officers and men behaved like true sons of Old England. While our braces were not shot away, we box hauled our ship four different times and raked her through the stern, shot away her main topmast and main yard and shattered her hull, rigging and sails very much. At last all our braces and rigging were shot away and the two ships lay alongside of one another, right before the wind. She then shot a little ahead of us, got her foresail set and run. We gave her t'other broadside and stood after her. She could only return us two guns. Not having a standing shroud, stay or back-stay, our masts wounded through and through, our hull, rigging and sails cut to pieces, and being very leaky from a number of shot under water, only one pump fit to work, the other having been torn to pieces by a twelve-pound shot, after chasing her for eight hours, lost sight and made the best of our way to this port. We had eleven men killed, two more died the next day, and seventy-nine wounded.

—ALMON, ed., *The Remembrancer*, X, 142-143.

IX. THE *PROTECTOR* AND THE *ADMIRAL DUFF*

In addition to the small and hard-hit Continental Navy, several states raised their own naval forces. These improvised fleets comprised a few deep-sea cruising vessels, but mostly gunboats, barges and other makeshift floating defenses. The chief role of the state forces was to serve as coast defense. An exception to the less formidable ships in the states' naval service was the 26-gun frigate Protector, *launched by Massachusetts in 1779. In one of the fiercest actions of the war the* Protector *on June 9, 1780, sank the 32-gun* Admiral Duff *off the banks of Newfoundland. Luther Little, a midshipman on the Massachusetts frigate, has left a stirring account of this action.*

Narrative of Luther Little.

When the fog lifted, saw large ship to windward under English colors, standing before the wind for us, we being to leeward. Looked as large as a 74. Concluded she was not a frigate. All hands piped to quarters. Hammocks brought and stuffed in the nettings, decks wet and sanded, etc. . . .

We stood on under cruising sail. She tried to go ahead of us and then hove to under fighting sail. We showed English flag. She was preparing for action. We steered down across her stern and hauled up under her lee quarter, breeching our guns aft to bring them to bear. Our first lieutenant hailed from the gangboard. . . .

Our captain [John Foster Williams] ordered broadside and colors changed. She replied with three cheers and a broadside. Being higher, they overshot us, cutting our rigging. A regular fight within pistol range. In a half hour a cannon shot came through our side, killing Mr. Scollay, a midshipman who commanded the fourth 14-pounder from the stern. His brains flew over my face and my gun, which was the third from the stern.

In an hour all their topmen were killed by our marines, sixty in number and all Americans. Our marines killed the man at their wheel, and the ship came down on us, her cat-head staving in our quarter galley. We lashed their jib-boom to our main shrouds. Our marines firing into the port holes kept them from charging. We were ordered to board, but the lashing broke and we were ordered back. Their ship shooting alongside nearly locked our guns and we gave a broadside, which cut away her mizenmast and made great havoc. Saw her sinking and her main topgallant sail on fire, which run down her rigging and caught a hogshead of cartridges under her quarter deck and blew it off.

A charge of grape entered my port hole. One passed between my backbone and windpipe and one through my jaw, lodging in the roof of my mouth and taking off a piece of my tongue, the other through my upper lip, taking away part and all my upper teeth. Was carried to cockpit; my gun was fired only once after. I had fired it nineteen times. Thinking I was mortally wounded, they dressed first those likelier to live. Heard the surgeon say, "He will die."

The *Duff* sunk, on fire, colors flying. Our boats had been injured, but were repaired as well as possible and sent to pick up the swimmers; saved fifty-five, one half wounded. Their first lieutenant confided to me that many were drowned rather than be made captives. Some tried to jump from the boats. Our surgeons amputated limbs of five of them. One was sick with West India fever and had floated out of his hammock between decks. The weather was warm and in less than ten days sixty of our men had it. Among those saved were two American captains and their crews, prisoners on board the *Duff*. One of the American captains told us that Captain [Richard] Stranger [commander of the *Admiral Duff*] had hoped we were a Continental frigate when he first saw us.

—ALLEN, *Naval History of the Revolution*, II, 515-517.

X. THE EXPEDITIONS OF CAPTAIN JOHN BARRY

The Alliance, *which had been under the colorful misdirection of the eccentric Pierre Landais and the legendary John Paul Jones, ended her career with Captain John Barry on the quarter-deck. Barry's most successful cruise started in February 1781, when the* Alliance *sailed from Boston for France, capturing the privateer* Alert *en route. Leaving L'Orient in company with the 40-gun letter of marque* Marquis de Lafayette, *Barry first put down a mutiny ("I believe a ship never put to sea in a worse condition as to seamen," he reported). Then he captured the privateers* Mars *and* Minerva, *and after a hot engagement forced two British brigs, the* Atalanta *and the* Trepassey, *to strike.*

One of the big litigations to clog the docket of the Admiralty Court in Boston and the Court of Appeals in Cases of Capture set up by Congress to handle prize disputes was the issue over the disposition of the captured brig Mars. *A jury in the Boston court awarded the* Alliance *two-thirds of the prize, and gave the remainder to her consort, the French privateer* Marquis de Lafayette. *The French consul insisted on a fifty-fifty split, but this claim was destined to die on appeal. Of special interest in the case are the depositions of the master of the brig* Mars *and of passengers on the* Alliance, *both supporting the claim of Barry and his crew to having played the decisive role in bringing about the capture of the prize.*

To Captain Barry, too, must go the distinction of having fought the last naval action of the war save for some privateering exploits. The Alliance *sailed from L'Orient on December 8, 1782, arrived at Martinique early in January, and found orders to proceed to Havana. Leaving that port in company with the Continental frigate* Duc de Lauzun *he encountered the* Sybille. *John Kessler, mate aboard the* Alliance, *has left us an account of that action.*

1. THE TAKING OF THE PRIZE *Mars*

Deposition of William Ryan, captain of the *Mars*, in *John Barry* v. *Brig Mars.*
August 25, 1781

I, William Ryan, late sailing master of the brigg *Mars* captured by the *Alliance*, a Continental frigate commanded by John Barry, Esq., do testify and declare that said brigg was British property, and that her owners were some of them in England and some in Guernsey, that she was taken the second day of April, a Domini 1781, being then on a cruise in the Bay of Bisca.

When we struck to the *Alliance*, the French ship, called the *Marquis Fayette*, whom I took to be a merchantman, was in sight, to leward, but not within gun-shot, but making towards us, but did not fire at us till about fifteen minutes after we had struck as afore mentioned, which was as soon as he could bring his guns to bear. I did not see any colours flying on the *Marquis* till after we struck and then saw a white flagg. When the *Marquis* came up with me, by the appearance of the ship I took her to be about thirty guns.

Soon after the *Mars* struck, the *Alliance* threw out a signal, which I supposed was for the *Marquis* to take charge of the *Mars* while the *Alliance* went after another vessel, then in sight, because the *Marquis* on the signal sent a number of hands on board the *Mars*, and the *Alliance* then went after said other vessel. It was about an hour after our striking before the *Marquis's* hands came on board the *Mars*, and about ten of said hands remained on board until her arrival in portage. Then with about eighteen or twenty of the *Alliance's* men there were no officers from the *Marquis*. When the *Marquis's* men came on board the *Mars*, they began to plunder immediately and took from me seven half Jo's, and about forty moidores in a purse from the purser of the *Mars*, broke open chests, took all the slops, spy glasses and wearing apparell, which they carried away from the *Mars;* when they took out the men, being about ninety eight in number, and carried [them] on board the *Marquis*.

It is my opinion that the *Marquis* could not have come up with the *Mars,* unless she had been stopped by the *Alliance*, nor could she have taken the *Mars,* if she had come up with her. The *Mars* mounted twenty twelve, two six and sixteen brass five-pounders and had an hundred and twelve men on board. I did not count the *Marquis's* guns, nor know how many men she had on board. I heard our purser say that she had stores on board to the value of three hundred and fifty pounds sterling.

Deposition of Samuel Bradford in *Barry v. Mars.*

I, Samuel Bradford, say that I was a passenger on board the Continental frigate *Alliance*; that a ship called the *Marquiss de la Fayette* loaded with stores for the United States sailed under convoy of said frigate; that on the passage the *Alliance* captured an armed brig called the *Mars*, at which time the *Marquiss de la Fayette* was at the distance of about a mile standing the same course with us; that the *Alliance* hung out a signal for the *Marquiss* to secure the prize, in consequence of which the *Marquiss* came up, took out the prisoners and kept possession of her till Capt. Barry returned, when Capt. B. put on board a prize master, and some sailors belonging to the *Marquiss de la Fayette*. That the *Mars* gave information of having spoke with the preceding day a large ship carrying fifty guns, and that the day after the *Alliance* discovered a large ship. Capt. Barry supposing her to be the ship referred to, ordered the *Marquiss* to haul her wind in order to get out of her way which she readily complied with. Capt. B. then pursued the said ship, which proved to be a Portuguese merchantman. The *Alliance* and *Marquiss* then joined company.

I further testify that the *Alliance* after capturing the *Mars* pursued the brig that was in company with her and captured her likewise. That I heard Mr. Williams of Nantes say that he had chartered the *Marquiss de la Fayette* and in behalf of Dr. Franklin for the United States. That I heard Capt. Barry say when we were bearing down on the Portuguese that should she prove an enemy's ship and superior to himself he would fight her till the *Marquiss* had time to get away. That the *Marquiss* appeared to be mounted with forty guns.

Sworn to in Court August 25, 1781

—Records of the Court of Appeals in Cases of Capture, National Archives.

2. CAPTAIN BARRY FIGHTS THE LAST NAVAL BATTLE OF THE WAR

Account of John Kessler, mate on the *Alliance*.

March 7, 1783

Sailed after taking on board a large quantity of dollars and in company with the Continental ship *Luzerne* of 20 guns, Captain Green, who also had a quantity of dollars on board for Congress. We left the Havana for the United States, after having taken on board between one and two hundred thousand dollars (specie) for Congress.

On the passage one morning when it became light we discovered three frigates right ahead within two leagues of us. The *Alliance* and *Luzerne* hove about and the three frigates gave us chase. The *Alliance* left them and the *Luzerne* fast, and Captain Barry, seeing that they were gaining on the *Luzerne*, we lay by for her to come up. The enemy also immediately lay by. When the *Luzerne* came up Captain Barry told Captain Greene to heave his guns overboard and put before the wind, while the *Alliance* would be kept by the wind that the *Luzerne* might escape. It was not probable that the enemy would attend most to the *Alliance*, and the *Alliance* was out of danger in consequence of her superior sailing. Captain Green threw overboard all his guns but two or three, but instead of bearing away he got on our weather bow. A sail being observed on our weather bow standing towards us, Captain Barry hoisted a signal which was answered, and thereby Captain Barry knew her to be a French 50-gun ship from the Havana, and he concluded to permit the enemy to come up, under the assurance that the French ship would arrive and assist.

Two of the enemy's ships kept at a distance on our weather quarter as if waiting to ascertain about the French ship, while the other was in our wake with topsails only and courses hauled, as was also the case with the *Alliance*. The French ship approaching fast, Captain Barry went from gun to gun on the main deck, cautioning against too much haste and not to fire until the enemy was right abreast. He ordered the main topsail hove to the mast that the enemy (who had already fired a bow gun, the shot of which struck into the cabin of the *Alliance*) might come up as soon as he was abrest, when the action began, and before an half hour her guns were silenced and nothing but musketry was fired from her. She appeared very much injured in her hull. She was of thirty-two guns and appeared very full of men, and after an action of forty-five minutes she sheered off. Our injured was, I think, three killed and eleven wounded (three of whom died of their wounds) and one sail and rigging cut. During all the action the French lay to as well as the enemy's ships.

As soon as the ship which we had engaged hove from us, her consorts joined her and all made sail, after which the French ship came down to us, and Captain Barry asked them why they did not come down during the action. They answered that they thought we might have been taken and the signal known and the action only a sham to decoy him. His foolish idea thus perhaps lost us the three frigates, for Captain Barry's commencing the action was with the full expectation of the French ship joining and thereby not only be able to cope, but in fact subdue part, if not the whole, of them. The French captain proposed, however, giving chase, which was done; but it soon appeared that his ship would not keep up with us, and the chase was given over.

—GRIFFIN, *Commodore John Barry*, pp. 222-224.

CHAPTER TWENTY-FOUR

Privateering

THE REGULAR *Continental Navy never was built up to impressive strength, never engaged in full battle maneuvers, but confined its efforts to convoying ships and to forays upon shipping and single British frigates. These facts, however, do not adequately spell out the offensive power of the Patriots at sea, for the principal naval engagements were fought by privateers, privately owned vessels sailing under licenses (letters of marque) issued by the Continental or state governments. To mount such an offensive was relatively easy. There was a long tradition of privateering in the colonies reaching back to the earliest of the intercolonial wars and burgeoning to impressive strength during the French and Indian War. The fact that fishing off the Great Banks was barred to the Patriots meant that thousands of New England fishermen were unemployed. They preferred privateering to enlisting in the Continental or state naval service, for the rewards were infinitely greater. The profits of privateering went to the owners and the crews, and more than one privateersman became a very rich man as a result of a fortunate cruise. Compared with the rich prizes attainable, the wages of the Continental Navy seemed most unattractive.*

Estimates vary as to the number of ships which were commissioned as privateers, ships often operating but for a single voyage. Congress commissioned some 1,700. But the states probably sent out an even greater number of privateers. Massachusetts alone commissioned 600 vessels, and considerable numbers were commissioned also by Rhode Island, Connecticut, New Hampshire and Delaware, as well as from the Chesapeake and more southerly states. In all, perhaps 2,000 were commissioned by the states. These privateers ranged from under 100 to 500 tons, with as many as 20 guns. The average crew of a privateer was 100 men. Some estimates place the number of seamen engaged in privateering for the Patriots at upwards of 60,000, but these figures doubtless involve a good deal of duplication. Were we to add the total of men aboard privateers to the numbers enlisted in the regular Navy it is probable that the American Navy, public, semipublic and private, drew as many men as the Patriot Army.

As commerce raiders the privateers were far more feared by the British than were the few Continental frigates with their occasional forays. It is estimated that the privateers took in all some 600 prizes worth altogether $18 *million as compared with less than 200 prizes amounting to $6 million credited to the Continental Navy proper. When the Navy dwindled toward the end of the war, privateering expanded in scope and volume.*

It was perhaps not unexpected that Silas Deane and his brother Simeon should have been active in promoting privateering. Shrewd merchants who knew how to combine patriotism and profits, they represented that fraternity of businessmen who combined private interests and public duty. What Simeon Deane wrote about the primacy of Massachusetts was underscored by a letter of James Warren to Samuel Adams of August 15, 1776, in which he wrote:

> *The spirit of privateering prevails here greatly. The success of those that have before engaged in that business has been sufficient to make a whole country privateering mad. Many kinds of West India goods that we used to be told we should suffer for want of, are now plentier and cheaper than I have known them for many years.*

I. BOON OR BANE OF THE REVOLUTIONARY CAUSE?

Privateering offered formidable competition to the Navy, as those responsible for its direction confessed. If seamen were not seduced to join privateering ventures or private voyages, it might be possible, William Vernon of the Eastern Navy Board pointed out to John Adams, to have the Navy make a move in force. Vernon's idea of the ill effects of privateering on the regular Navy were borne out by the letter of William Whipple, New Hampshire's delegate to the Continental Congress, to Josiah Bartlett, a leading New Hampshire Patriot. Some lads like young Andrew Sherburne resisted the lure of privateering and chose the Continental service, but they were a distinct minority in New England.

1. CONNECTICUT MEN ASK CONGRESS FOR PRIVATEERING COMMISSIONS

Simeon Deane to Silas Deane.

Wethersfield, Connecticut, November 27, 1775

I am desired by a number of gentlemen here to ask, thro' your influence, whether the Congress will grant commission to private adventurers to fit out a privateer or privateers to take British property on this coast, or in the West Indies. I observe that the General Assembly of Massachusetts have commissioned armed vessels on their coast, though we are not told what their limitations (if any) are. In case American privateers are to be allowed to take British property in the West Indies, you are sensible that the first opportunity may be very advantageous, and as well disposed of in this Colony as anywhere, especially as the persons now applying are your good friends and would prosecute the affair immediately.

If you think there is a probability of permission from the Congress, pray attempt it and write me in answer per next post, as those persons desirous of adventuring are very impatient to be informed, and any very considerable delay would perhaps put it out of their power to equip in season....

—DEANE, "Correspondence," II, 326.

2. THE LURES OF PRIVATEERING FOR THE LADS OF NEW ENGLAND

Memoirs of Andrew Sherburne.

... Ships were building, prizes taken from the enemy unloading, privateers fitting out, standards waved on the forts and batteries. The exercising of soldiers, the roar of cannon, the sound of martial music and the call for volunteers so infatuated me that I was filled with anxiety to become an actor in the scene of war. My eldest brother, Thomas, had recently returned from a cruise on board the *General Mifflin*, of Boston, Capt. McNeal. This ship had captured thirteen prizes, some of which, however, being of little value, were burnt, some were sold in France, others reached Boston, and their cargoes were divided among the crew of that ship.

On my brother's return, I became more eager to try my fortune at sea. My father, though a high Whig, disapproved the practice of privateering. Merchant vessels, at this period, which ran safe, made great gains, seamen's wages were consequently very high. Through my father's influence Thomas was induced to enter the merchants' service. Though not yet fourteen years of age, like other boys, I imagined myself almost a man. I had intimated to my sister that if my father would not consent that I should go to sea, I would run away and go on board a privateer. My mind became so infatuated with the subject that I talked of it in my sleep, and was overheard by my mother. She communicated what she had heard to my father. My parents were apprehensive that I might wander off and go on board some vessel without their consent. At this period it was not an uncommon thing for lads to come out of the country, step on board a privateer, make a cruise and return home, their friends remaining in entire ignorance of their fate until they heard it from themselves. Others would pack up their clothes, take a cheese and a loaf of bread and steer off for the army. There was a disposition in commanders of privateers and recruiting officers to encourage this spirit of enterprise in young men and boys. ...

The continental ship of war *Ranger*, of eighteen guns, commanded by Thomas Simpson, Esq., was at this time shipping a crew in Portsmouth. This ship had been ordered to join the *Boston* and *Providence* frigates and the *Queen of France* of twenty guns, upon an expedition directed by Congress. My father, having consented that I should go to sea, preferred the service of Congress to privateering. He was acquainted with Capt. Simpson. On board this ship were my two half uncles, Timothy and James Weymouth. Accompanied by my father, I visited the rendezvous of the *Ranger* and shipped as one of her crew. There were probably thirty boys on board this ship. As most of our principal officers belonged to the town, parents preferred this ship as a station for their sons who were about to enter the naval service. Hence most of these boys were from Portsmouth. As privateering was the order of the day, vessels of every description were employed in the business. Men were not wanting who would hazard themselves in vessels of twenty tons or less, manned by ten or fifteen hands. Placing much dependence on the protection of my uncles, I was much elated with my supposed good fortune, which had at last made me a sailor. ...

Boys were employed in waiting on the officers, but in time of action a boy was quartered to each gun to carry cartridges. I was waiter to Mr. Charles Roberts, the boatswain, and was quartered at the third gun from the bow. —SHERBURNE, *Memoirs*, pp. 18-20.

3. THE "PERNICIOUS CONSEQUENCES" OF PRIVATEERING

William Whipple to Dr. Josiah Bartlett, both members of the Continental Congress from New Hampshire.

Portsmouth, N. H., July 12, 1778

... As I am happy in agreeing with you in opinion in general, I should be exceedingly glad if there was a coincidence in our sentiments respecting privateering. I agree with you that the privateers have much distressed the trade of our enemies, but had there been no privateers is it not probable there would have been a much larger number of public ships than has been fitted out, which might have distressed the enemy nearly as much and furnished these states with necessaries on much better terms than they have been supplied by privateers?

However, I will not contend with you about the advantages or disadvantages that have been the consequence of that business. All I wish to convince you of is that [it] is *now* attended with the most pernicious consequences, which there would be no need of my undertaking if you were only to pass three months in this or any other town where the spirit for privateering rages with such violence as it does here. No kind of business can so effectually introduce luxury, extravagance and every kind of dissipation that tend to the distraction of the morals of people. Those who are actually engaged in it soon lose every idea of right and wrong and, for want of an opportunity of gratifying their insatiable avarice with the property of the enemies of their country, will, without the least compunction, seize that of her friends.

Thus far I am sure you would agree with me, had you the opportunity before mentioned of making your observations, but perhaps you may say these are evils attendant on this business to society in general. I will allow that to be the case, but then, it must be allowed, they will operate with more violence in this country, in its present unsettled state, than in a country where all the powers of government can be vigorously exercised. But besides these, there are many other mischiefs that attend this business peculiar to these states in our present circumstances. Some of the towns in this state have been obliged to give 400 dollars bounty (per man) to serve three or four months at Rhode Island, exclusive of what is allowed by the state. This is wholly owing to privateering. The farmers cannot hire a laborer for less than 50 or 40 dollars per month, and in the neighbourhood of this town, 3 or 4 dollars per day, and very difficult to be had at that. This naturally raises the price of provision. Indian corn is not to be purchased under 6 dollars per bushel.

There is at this time 5 privateers fitting out here, which I suppose will take 400 men. These must be by far the greater part countrymen, for the seamen are chiefly gone, and most of them in Halifax gaol. Besides all this, you may depend no public ship will ever be manned while there is a privateer fitting out. The reason is plain. Those people who have the most influence with the seamen think it their interest to discourage the public service, because by that they promote their own interest, viz. privateering. In order to do this effectually, every officer in the public service (I mean in the Navy) is treated with general contempt. A man of any feeling cannot bear this; he, therefore, to avoid these indignities, quits the service and is caressed. By this means all the officers that are worth employing will quit the service, and you'll have the Navy (if you think it worth while to keep up that show) officered by tinkers, shoemakers and horse jockeys, and no gentleman worth employing will accept a commission. This you may depend will soon be the case, unless privateering is discouraged, and the business of the Marine in this department more attended to and conducted with more regularity. In short, it would be better to set fire to the ships now in port than to pretend to fit them for sea, for as matters now are (if I am rightly informed and my authority is very good), the public are at an amazing expense to procure men for privateers, for if they (the public ships) get two men one day, they are sure to lose four the next, who take care to carry off with them the advance pay, etc. . . .

—WHIPPLE, "Letter," *Historical Magazine*, VI, pp. 74-75.

4. "THE INFAMOUS PRACTICE OF SEDUCING" SEAMEN OF THE NAVY

William Vernon to John Adams.

Boston, 17th December, 1778

Since my last, we have lost the brig *Resistance* that was given to Capt. Burke. She was sent out as far as Cape-Cod to look for Count de Estaing's fleet that was expected here after the Rhode Island expedition was given up. Missing of them off Cape-Cod, he stood to the southward. The third day, fell in with Lord How's squadron, who captured him.

We have now in this harbour the Continental ships *Warren*, *Providence*, *Boston*, *Queen of France* and *Dean*, the last full manned and ready to sail. The other ships are in great forwardness, may sail in three weeks, if it was possible to get men, which we shall never be able to accomplish unless some method is taken to prevent desertion, and a stopage of private ships sailing until our ships are manned. The infamous practice of seducing our men to leave their ships, and taking them off at an out-port, with many other base methods, will make it impossible ever to get our ships ready to sail in force, or perhaps otherwise than single ships—from which we cannot expect any great matters. Indeed it hath generally proved fatal.

I wish, I hope and pray for [that] an embargo upon all private property, whether armed or merchant ships, may take place through all the United States, until the fleet is compleatly manned. This is the only method, in my opinion, that can be taken. They elude our utmost efforts at present, and at a most enormous expence. It was truly great before you left us, but you can scarsely form an idea of the increase and groath of the extravagance of the people in their demands for labour and every article for sale, etc. Dissipation has no bounds at present. When or where it will stop, or if a reform will take place, I dare not predict.

—VERNON, "Papers," *R. I. Hist. Soc. Pub.*, New Series, VIII, 255-256.

5. "THE WRETCHES LIVE BY PIRACY"

Admiral Rodney to Philip Stephens, Secretary of the Admiralty.

Sandwich off New York, 28th October 1780

The ships I stationed upon the coast have been very successful against the enemy's privateers and ships of war, eleven having been taken since my arrival, and the others obliged to take shelter in their ports.

By the great number of prisoners taken (which amount to upwards of 1400) the rebels will find it extremely difficult to man the Continental ships of war now in the Delaware and at Boston. Their Lordships by the Gazette Extraordinary, which I have the honor to inclose for their perusal, will perceive to what a low state the rebel Navy is reduced, and I am fully persuaded that if their prisoners are not released it will be of the greatest advantage to the commerce of His Majesty's loyal subjects, and the severest blow that can be given to the rebels, whose chief support arises from the piratical captors they make.

The wretches with which their privateers are manned have no principal whatever; they live by piracy and the plunder of their fellow subjects; when they have been released out of humanity to return to their families and live by honest industry, they forget the mercy that has been shown them, and instantly return to renew their acts of piracy.

Since my arrival here I have allowed none of them to be released, and have given notice that till the seven hundred prisoners their Congress owes are liquidated the rebel sailors will be detained in confinement; as with pleasure I can assure their Lordships that very few of the British seamen are in the possession of the rebels.

The great increase of prisoners and the extreme bad condition of the prison ships rendered it necessary to convert the *Jersey* hospital ship into a prison ship, which I hope will meet with their Lordships approbation, more especially as a naval hospital ship (because unfit for that service) [she was] totally useless, and by converting her into a prison ship has saved a considerable expense to Government. . . .

G. B. RODNEY
—RODNEY, *Letter-books*, I, 54-56.

II. SOME PRIVATEERING ADVENTURES

Privateering held all the ordinary risks of a Continental frigate, and one that was extraordinary. There was always the danger that British naval authorities would treat captured privateers as pirates, especially where the vessel seized was commanded by an American who had lately been English or Scot, or where the crew were largely drawn from these nationalities. Seamen switched from the Continental naval service to privateering, then back to Continental or state service, and a considerable number were captured and confined in British prisons.

Some of the risks that privateers took are typified by the engagement of the Yankee Hero, *recounted in the first excerpt below. While making a run from Newburyport to Boston on June 7, 1776, that privateer, with only a*

third of her complement of men, was attacked by an English frigate. Priva-
teersmen often saw the world from the inside of jails. The narrative of Captain Philip Besom of Marblehead exemplifies the extraordinary risks priva-
teersmen often saw the world from the inside of jails. The narrative of Cap-
Cromwell chartered out of New London, attests to the fact that Colonel Prescott's immortal words at Bunker's Hill soon became the common property of
aspiring naval heroes. Joshua Davis, a Boston seaman who was pressed and
served on six ships aboard the British Navy, gives testimony to the iron discipline imposed by captains of privateers. In this case the captain was a well-
known naval commander, John Manley, who had a series of heartbreaking
adventures of his own and more than his share of hard luck. He had been
obliged to strike the frigate Hancock, and then lost a privateer, the Cumberland, to a British frigate. With other prisoners he escaped from Barbados,
seized a sloop, and finally reached Boston in April 1779, when the story of the
cruise of the Jason begins. One of the sensational engagements of the war
was the capture of the British naval sloop Savage by Captain George Geddes
of the Philadelphia privateer Congress. Captain Charles Stirling, the vanquished commander, recounts that episode. The ship he lost was later recap-
tured by the British frigate Solebay.

1. The Yankee Hero Strikes to the British Frigate Melford

[June 7, 1776]

... After some time, the ship thus getting in the wake of the brig, the wind
again came fresh to the westward, upon which the brig hauled to the wind,
in the best angle for the shore. The ship gave chase and in an hour came up
within half a mile, and began to fire her bowchasers, which the brig only
answered with a swivel, Captain Tracy reserving his whole fire until the
ship, keeping a constant fire, came up within pistol-shot upon his lee-quarter,
when the brig gave her the best return they could make from their main and
quarter-deck guns, swivels and small arms, and after that kept up a constant
fire.

The ship was soon up alongside; and with twelve nine-pounders of a side,
upon one deck, besides forecastle and quarter-deck guns, and with her marines overlooking the brig as high as her leading blocks, kept a continual fire.
After some time the ship hauled her wind so close (which obliged the brig to
do the same) that Captain Tracy was unable to fight his lee guns; upon this he
backed under her stern; but the ship, which sailed much faster and worked as
quick, had the advantage, and brought her broadside again upon him, which
he could not evade, and in this manner they lay not a hundred feet from each
other, yawing to and fro, for an hour and twenty minutes, the privateer's men
valiantly maintaining their quarters against such a superior force.

About this time the ship's foremast guns beginning to slack fire, Captain
Tracy slacked under her stern, and, when clear of the smoke and fire, perceived his rigging to be most shockingly cut—yards flying about without
braces, some of his principal sails shot to rags, and half of his men to appearance dying and wounded. Mr. Main, his First Lieutenant, was among the first
wounded, and Mr. Davis, one of the prize-masters, fell in the last attack.

In this situation they went to work to refit the rigging and to carry the wounded below, the ship having then taken a broad sheer some way off, and none of her guns bearing; but before they could get their yards to rights, which they zealously tried for in hopes still to get clear of the ship, as they were now nearer in shore, or to part from her under the night, she again came up and renewed the attack, which obliged Captain Tracy to have recourse to his guns again, though he still kept some hands aloft to his rigging; but before the brig had again fired two broadsides, Captain Tracy received a wound in his right thigh, and in a few minutes he could not stand. He laid himself over the arm-chest and barricade, determined to keep up the fire, but in a short time, from pain and loss of blood, he was unable to command, growing faint, and they helped him below. As soon as he came to, he found his firing had ceased and his people round him wounded and, not having a surgeon with them, in a most distressed situation, most of them groaning and some expiring.

Struck severely with such a spectacle, Captain Tracy ordered his people to take him up in a chair upon the quarter-deck, and resolved again to attack the ship, which was all this time keeping up her fire; but after getting into the air, he was again so faint that he was for some time unable to speak, and finding no alternative but they must be taken or sunk, for the sake of the brave men that remained he ordered them to strike to the ship (the *Melford,* of twenty-eight guns, John Burr commander).

Thus was this action maintained for upwards of two hours in a low single-decked vessel, with not half the metal the ship had, against an English frigate, whose Navy has been the dread of nations, and by a quarter the number of people in the one as the other. . . .

–Force, *American Archives,* 4th Series, VI, 747-748.

2. A Mutiny, a Daring Escape and the Inside of a French Jail

Captain Philip Besom's narrative of a privateer's life.

In the year 1771, I commenced going to sea, from Marblehead, in the merchant service; and returned from the last voyage, previous to taking any part in the Revolutionary War, immediately after the battle at Concord; at which time, in consequence of an English sloop-of-war being in Marblehead harbor, we proceeded directly to Salem; from which place my father sent the cargo to Andover, where he had removed his family, and left me and one other young man to take care of the vessel. On the 17th of June, 1775, I returned to Marblehead, and, with seventeen more young men, proceeded to Bunker Hill; but, finding it impossible to cross the ferry, returned back to Marblehead.

I then went to Andover and enlisted as a soldier in Captain Abbot's company, which was attached to Colonel Hitchcock's regiment in Roxbury; from which place we were sent to Dorchester Heights, and remained there until the English left Boston.

I then went with my father to Lyndesborough, and remained there until 1777, when I left his house, unknown to any of the family, and went back to Marblehead again, and shipped on board the privateer *Satisfaction* of fourteen guns, Captain John Stevens. We went to sea immediately, and, during that cruise, captured four English ships, one of which carried sixteen guns. On my return from that cruise, I went on board the brig *Fanny*, of fourteen guns, Captain Lee, and captured on the Banks of Newfoundland, after a severe engagement, an English ship of fourteen guns, the captain of which we killed. We destroyed fifteen Newfoundland fishermen, and proceeded to cruise in the channel of England, where we captured a French brig laden with English goods. I was put on board of her as prize-master and succeeded in getting her into Marblehead. The privateer afterwards went on shore in Mount's Bay, and the crew were taken prisoners and sent to Mill Prison.

I then entered on board the ship *Brandywine*, intending to cruise about the shores of Nova Scotia: but, being chased into a harbor by an English sloop-of-war, we were compelled to run our vessel ashore, when one other young man and myself set fire to her and took to the woods in order to make our escape. We travelled about ten miles, then returned to the shore and, finding three whale-boats, took them and succeeded in getting home. I then sailed with Captain St. Barbs from Newburyport for North Carolina. After arriving there, we were blockaded by an English squadron and were obliged to travel home.

I then sailed in the ship *Freemason*, Captain Conway. We captured four vessels. I returned and entered on board the ship *Monmouth* of twenty guns, commanded by Thomas Colyer. We captured four prizes, one of which, loaded with brandy, I was put on board of as prize-master; was taken by an English privateer, and carried to Bristol; from which place I ran away, and succeeded in getting to a town called Kingswood, where I, together with another young man by the name of Thomas Johnson, of Salem, shipped on board an English brig bound to New York. We soon became acquainted with the English sailors, and, after some consultation, agreed to rise upon the officers, take the brig and carry her to Marblehead. When we had sailed as far west as Nantucket Shoals, we did take the brig, and had her in possession two days, when we unfortunately fell in with the English sloop-of-war *Hunter*, bound to New York, with the news of their having destroyed the American squadron at Penobscot. We were retaken, carried to New York in her and put on board a sloop-of-war at Sandy Hook.

News of what we had done was immediately communicated to the commander of the *Russel*, seventy-four—which, together with the Cork fleet, was bound directly to England—[who] gave orders to have the leaders in the affair brought on board his ship, to be tried for their lives. We were then taken out of irons and went to the boat; viz., myself and an Englishman. We were placed in the stern sheets. The boat's crew consisted of six men, commanded by a lieutenant, assisted by a cockswain. The ship lay at a considerable distance, and the sloop in which we were being to the leeward of them and the wind favorable to our design, as we were going to the seventy-four the Englishman knocked the cockswain overboard; I knocked the lieutenant down, took his pistols and dagger from him and, putting the boat before the wind, made for the shore.

As soon as we landed, we obliged the boat's crew to go before us until we reached a house. We told the man residing there that we were refugees and asked for help. He informed us that Colonel Washington was stationed at Middleton, only four miles' distance, with a regiment. We started off for his quarters, and, on arriving, were taken for spies and placed under guard for three days; after which time, I, together with the young man, w[as] set at liberty and proceeded to Amboy, where Lord Stirling was stationed with a brigade; who generously gave us a good dinner, and forty dollars in money to assist us in getting home.

I then sailed in the ship *Aurora*, of twenty guns, Thomas Colyer, master. We took four prizes; had an engagement with two ships and a brig, in which we lost five or six men, and were obliged to retreat and return home. I then sailed for Guadaloupe, mate of a schooner, and, on returning, was taken and carried to Bermuda, but, in consequence of there being no provisions for us, we had the liberty of going at large. Here we found a ship which we rigged for St. George's, but proceeded to a place about opposite on the same island, called Salt Kettle, where I shipped on board a schooner bound to Turk's Island for a cargo of salt for Halifax. We agreed to take the schooner as soon as we arrived on the coast; but, on our passage to Turk's Island, we were obliged to cut away our masts in a gale of wind in order to save the schooner, and we put for Jamaica. When we arrived off Cape François, we took her and carried her in there; but the governor seized the schooner and caused us to be put in prison, where we remained four days, being obliged to beg of strangers part of a subsistence; when it happened that Colonel Thorndike, having arrived there in a letter of marque, was accidentally passing by. I asked of him some trifle. He inquired the cause of my imprisonment. I informed him; and he, together with some American captains, prevailed on the governor, and we were taken from prison, and sent home in a letter of marque.

I then sailed in the privateer *Montgomery*, of fourteen guns—John Carnes, master—from Salem, to cruise on the West-Indies' coast. We took three prizes, fought a ship of sixteen guns, and had seventeen men killed and wounded; after which we captured a schooner for New York. I came home as prize-master of it.

My next cruise was with the same person, John Carnes, in the ship *Porus*. We captured four prizes. I returned home in one, and proceeded immediately to sea in the letter-of-marque ship *Cato*, Captain John Little, for Virginia. She mounted fourteen guns and had a crew of fifty-seven men and boys. We loaded with tobacco and proceeded to sea; but we had scarcely cleared the capes before we fell in with three English privateers—one of which carried sixteen guns; one, fourteen guns; and a sloop, eight guns. We fought them from two to four, P.M., when they attempted to board us; but, the largest of them having lost a considerable part of their crew, we succeeded—after having our foremast a little below the top, and our mizenmast above the top, cut away—in beating them off; and we continued on our voyage to Nantes, in France, where we arrived without any other trouble. On our return home, we made one prize; but, happening to spring a leak, were compelled to stop at St. Andero [?], in Spain, and repair our vessel. We arrived home in March 1783. . . .

—BESOM, "Narrative," *Mass. Hist. Soc. Proc.*, V, 357-360.

3. "Don't Fire Till We Can See the White of Their Eyes"

Timothy Boardman's journal.

April 7th, [1778]: The *Defence* had five men broke out with the small pox.

9th: They lost a man with the small pox.

10th: Exersised cannon and musquetry.

11th: Saw a sail. The *Defence* spoke with her. She was a Frenchman from Bourdeaux bound to the West Indies.

13th: Crossed the tropick, shaved and duck about 60 men.

14th: At four oclock afternoon saw a sail bearing E S E. We gave chase to her and came up with her at 8 o'clock. She was a large French ship. We sent the boat on board of her. She informed us of two English ships which she left sight of at the time we saw her.

15th: At day break we saw two sail bareing SE.S distance 2 leagues. We gave chase under a moderate sail. At 9 oclock P. M. came up with them. They at first shew French colours to decoy us. When we came in about half a mile of her they ups with English colours. We had Continental colours flying. We engaged the ship *Admiral Kepple* as follows. When we came in about 20 rods of her we gave her a bow gun. She soon returned us a stern chaise and then a broad side of grape and round shot.

Capt. [Parker] orders not to fire till we can see the white of their eyes. We got close under their larboard quarter. They began another broad side and then we began and held tuff and tuff for about 2 glasses, and then she struck to us. At the same time the *Defence* engaged the *Cyrus*, who, as the *Kepple* struck, wore round under our stern. We wore ship and gave her a stern chase, at which she immediately struck. The loss on our side was one killed and six wounded, one mortally who soon died. Our ship was hulled nine times with six-pound shott, three of which went through our birth, one of which wounded the boatswains yoeman. The loss on their side was two killed and six wounded. Their larbourd quarter was well filled with shott. One nine-pounder went through her main mast. Imployed in the after-noon takeing out the men and maning the prise. The *Kepple* mounted 20 guns, 18 six-pounders and two wooden ditto with about 45 men; the *Cyrus* mounted 16 six-pounders with 35 men: letters of marque bound from Bristol to Jamaica laden with dry goods, paints, etc.

18th: Capt Day died.

19th: Capt Brown of the ship *Admiral Kepple* and Capt Dike of the *Cyrus*, with three ladies and 8 men, sett off in a long boat for St. Kitts on Captains Parker and Smedleys permition.

20th: Imployed in taking things out of the prize, viz., one chist of Holland, a quantity of hatts and shoes, cheeses, porter and some crockery ware, small arms, pistols, hangers, two brass barrel blunderbusses, a quantity of riggen, etc.

—Boardman, *Log-Book*, pp. 51-53.

4. Captain Manley Finds Privateering as Hazardous as Naval Service

Joshua Davis' narrative.

[1779]

I, Joshua Davis, was born in Boston, in the Commonwealth of Massachusetts, on the 30th of June, 1760. On the 14th of June, 1779, I entered on board of the privateer *Jason*, of 20 guns, commanded by Commodore John Manly, bound on a cruise. About the 25th of the same month, we sailed from Boston to Portsmouth, N. H. in order to take on board Lieutenant Frost and a number of men. We arrived there the next day and, after taking the men on board, put to sea again.

The morning following, the man at the masthead discovered two sail ahead of us. . . . On running nearer them, we supposed them to be enemies, and Lieutenant Thayer advised the captain to heave the ship in stays, to see if they would follow us; to which the captain consented, and we hove the ship about. When they saw this, they hove in stays and gave us chase. We ran back for Portsmouth, and by the time we had got within half a league of the Isle of Shoals, the vessel got within two gun-shot of us.

We perceived a squall coming on to the westward, very fast, and the captain ordered every man to stand by to take in sail. When the squall struck us, it hove us all aback, when we clued down. In ten seconds the wind shifted our sails. In a few seconds more the wind shifted on our starboard quarter and struck us with such force that hove us on our beam ends and carried away our three masts and bowsprit. She immediately righted and the squall went over. The vessels that were in chase of us saw our trouble, hove about, and went off with the squall. We never saw no more of them.

We went to work to strip our masts and to get the sails and rigging on board; when we found one of our men drowned under the foretop-sail. We got up jury-masts and run in between the Isle of Shoals and Portsmouth, where our captain was determined to take our masts in. In a few days Captain Manly went on shore to see to getting the masts on board. While he was gone, Patrick Cruckshanks, our boatswain, Michael Wall, boatswain's mate, and John Graves, captain of the forecastle, went forward and set down on the stump of the bowsprit, and said they would not step the masts in such a wild rodestead, to endanger their lives; but if the ship was taken into the harbour, they would do it with pleasure.

When the captain came on board, he asked Mr. Thayer why the people were not at work, and was told they wished to get into the harbour first.

The captain answered, "I'll harbour them," and stepped up to the sentry at the cabin door, took his cutlass out of his hand, and ran forward, and said, "Boatswain, why do you not go to work?"

He began to tell him the impropriety of getting the masts in where the ship then was, when Captain Manly struck him with the cutlass on the cheek with such force that his teeth were to be seen from the upper part of the jaw to the lower part of the chin.

He next spoke to John Graves, and interrogated, and was answered in a similar manner, when the captain struck him with the cutlass on the head, which cut him so bad that he was obliged ot be sent to the hospital with the boatswain.

The captain then called the other to come down and to go to work. Michael Wall come down to him. The captain made a stroke at him which missed, and while the captain was lifting up the cutlass to strike him again,

Wall gave him a push against the stump of the foremast and ran aft. The captain made after him. Wall ran to the main hatchway and jumped down between decks and hurt himself very much.

The captain then with severe threats ordered the people to go to work. They went to work and stepped the masts, got the topmasts on end, lower yards athwart, top sail yards on the cap, top gallant masts on end, sails bent, running rigging rove, boats on the booms, etc., and all done in the space of 36 hours.

Following the repairs, Manley resumed the cruise. Off Sandy Hook on July 23 the Jason *fell in with two British privateer brigs of sixteen and eighteen guns. Joshua Davis resumes his narrative:*

The enemy hove upon the wind with his larboard tacks on board, run up his courses, hoisted his colours and gave us a broadside. Our captain ordered the sailing master to get the best bower anchor out, so that the bill of it should take into the fore shrouds of the enemy. It was quickly done. The captain ordered the helm hard a-port, which brought us alongside. The anchor caught their fore rigging.

Our captain then said, "Fire away, my boys!"

We then gave them a broadside which tore her off side very much and killed and wounded some of them. The rest all ran below, except their captain who stood on the deck like a man amazed.

Both privateers surrendered and were brought safely into Boston harbor, but off Newfoundland the Jason *was overhauled by a frigate, which cut it to ribbons and forced Manley to take the trumpet and call out for quarters. Manley was sent to Mill Prison, near Plymouth, England, where he remained for more than two years; this was the third and last time he was captured during the war.*

—DAVIS, *Narrative,* pp. 3-12.

5. THE PRIVATEER *Congress* DEFEATS THE NAVAL SLOOP *Savage*

Captain Charles Stirling to Rear Admiral Thomas Graves.

Lancaster, Sept. 23, 1781

It is with the most poignant grief that I acquaint your Excellency of the capture of his Majesty's sloop *Savage,* late under my command, the particulars of which I have the honour to transmit. Early in the morning of the 6th. inst., 10 leagues east of Charles Town, we espied a ship bearing down on us, who, when about four miles distant, hauled her wind to the eastward, shewing, by her appearance, she was an American cruizer. Her force could not be easily distinguished. I therefore gave way to the pleasing idea that she was a privateer, carrying 20 nine-pounders, whom I had intelligence was cruizing off here, and instantly resolved either to bring her to action or oblige her to quit the coast; for which purpose we gave chase, but were prevented continuing it long by her edging down, seemingly determined to engage us.

Conscious of her superiority in sailing and force, this manoeuver coincided with my wishes. I caused the *Savage* to lay by, till we perceived on her nearer approach she was far superior to what we imagined, and that it was necessary to attempt making our escape, without some fortunate shot, in the course of a running fight (which we saw inevitable), admitted our taking advantages and bringing on a more equal conflict. At half past ten she began firing her bow chasers, and at eleven, being close on our quarter, the action commenced with musquetry, which, after a good deal of execution, was followed by a heavy cannonade on both sides.

In an hour's time I had the mortification to see our braces and bowlings shot away, and not a rope left to trim the sail with, notwithstanding every precaution had been taken. However, our fire was so constant and well directed that the enemy did not see our situation, but kept along side of us till accident obliged him to drop astern. The *Savage* was now almost a wreck, her sails, rigging and yards so much cut that it was with the utmost difficulty we could alter our position time enough to avoid being raked, the enemy lying directly athwart our stern for some minutes. This was the only intermission of great guns, but musquetry and pistols still did execution and continued till they opened again, which was not till both ships were almost on board each other, when the battle became more furious than before. Our quarter-deck and forecastle were soon now nearly cleared, scarce a man belonging to either not being killed or wounded, with three guns on our main deck rendered useless.

In this situation, we fought near an hour with only five six-pounders, the fire from each ship's guns scorching the men who opposed them, shot and other implements of war thrown by hand doing execution; when—our mizen-mast being shot away by the board; our main mast tottering, with only three shrouds standing; the ship on fire dangerously; only forty men on duty to oppose the foe, who was attempting to board us in three places; no succour in sight, or possibility of making further resistance—I was necessitated at a quarter before 3 P. M. to surrender to the *Congress*, a private ship of war, belonging to Philadelphia, who carried 215 men and mounted 20 twelve-pounders on her main deck and four sixes above, fourteen of which were fought on one side.

She lost during the action eleven men and had nearly thirty wounded, several of them mortally. Her masts, her sails and rigging were so much damaged that she was obliged to return to port, which partly answered my wishes prior to the action, as great part of the Carolina trade was daily expected on the coast, and this privateer we saw sailed remarkably fast. Three days were employed putting her in a condition to make sail, and five for the *Savage*, who was exceedingly shattered. Indeed it is astonishing more damage was not done, as the weather was fine, the water remarkably smooth, and the ships never thirty yards asunder.

The courage, intrepidity and good behaviour of the officers and ship's company I had the honour to command, deserve the highest commendation and my warmest thanks.

—STIRLING, "Letter," *Annual Register, 1781*, Appendix.

III. CAPTAIN CONYNGHAM STRIKES AT BRITAIN
FROM FRENCH BASES

Some of the most daring and damaging raids upon British shipping were launched by American privateers from French bases. Until her formal entry into the war against Britain, France found these activities a source of some embarrassment. France was willing to aid the United States short of war, but the activities of American privateers operating from her ports was a flagrant violation of her treaty obligation with Great Britain made in 1713 and renewed in 1763, by which she bound herself not to harbor the prizes or privateers of the enemies of Britain, except in real emergencies such as storm or shipwreck, and not to allow private ships of war to be fitted out in her ports. But American privateers, encouraged by Deane and Franklin, constantly fitted out in French ports, and even sold their prizes to French buyers without going through the formality of a condemnation by a French court of admiralty. Vergennes moved to stop these activities only when Lord Stormont, the British ambassador, presented him with a virtual ultimatum. Even then the French embargo was at best temporary. During the year 1777, marine insurance rates in Great Britain rose over twenty per cent, solid testimony to the effectiveness of American privateering. As England stormed and threatened, France backed and filled until she felt the time had come openly to declare war.

The case of Captain Gustavus Conyngham can be technically differentiated from that of Captain Lambert Wickes. The latter had sailed from French ports in a Continental cruiser. The former, though an officer in the Continental Navy, sailed in privateers fitted out in France. His expeditions were partly public and partly private in character. But the British were disinclined to split hairs. Conyngham had been furnished with a blank commission given the American commissioners in France for that purpose and signed by John Hancock as President of Congress. To the British he was not a naval officer but a pirate.

For Conyngham's ventures a lugger was purchased at Dover and sent to Dunkirk, where it was fitted out with armament and crew and named the Surprise. *Conyngham, sailing from Dunkirk, picked up the packet* Prince of Orange *and a brig. His seizures caused an outcry across the Channel. Conyngham was jailed, his lugger confiscated, and his prizes returned. But soon the French ministry, on the intervention of the American commissioners, secured his release. Another vessel, a cutter, was bought and armed for him, partly by private persons, and on the flimsy pretext that he was going on a trading voyage, he sailed on the* Revenge. *This trip was much more successful. Conyngham made several prizes, actually refitted his vessel in an English port, and then eluded the English Navy when his presence became known. Again the British stormed. The French made a characteristic gesture. This time they shipped William Hodge, a Philadelphia merchant and backer of Conyngham, off to the Bastille. After a short time he was released. Silas Deane's account to Congress and Franklin's letter to Ferdinand Grand, a Swiss financier who was close to both the American commissioners and the French government, provide proof, if such were needed, that the American commissioners stood solidly behind Conyngham.*

1. Vergennes Promises the British Ambassador That Privateers Will Not Be Built or Manned in French Ports for Attacks on England

Lord Stormont to Lord Weymouth.

Paris, 16th April, 1777

. . . I then, my Lord, went to a subject of more importance: I mean the French vessels that are to be manned by French soldiers and commanded by American captains. I told him [M. de Vergennes] that it was more necessary for me to repeat what I had said both to his Excellency and the Monsieur de Maurepas upon this very unpleasant subject, as I found that the number of those vessels increased and that instead of four ships, which my first intelligence mentioned, there would be eight or ten. I added, my Lord, that I did not indeed know the names of these ships nor the ports of France from which they were to sail, but that I did know there was such a design, and was certain that there were several American captains now at Paris who expected the command of those ship and were waiting here till they could be got ready. I likewise informed him, my Lord, that according to my last intelligence those ships are designed not only to cruise in our seas but to insult our coast (I have information which says one of the projects is an attack on Glasgow). I ended with saying that we had, to be sure, little to apprehend from such enterprises, but I begged him to consider what an impression the mere attempt must necessarily make—ships built in France for the use of the rebels, manned with French sailors and commanded by American captains, who sail from the ports of France to insult and attempt to ravage the coast of Great Britain.

I spoke to him, my Lord, very strongly but in the politest and most friendly manner, and went all along upon this supposition: that after the mutual assurances that had passed and the public proofs we meant to give of our pacific intentions, everything that had a contrary tendency must be as disagreeable to this Court as it could be to mine. He readily assented to this, said that if there was any such thing in agitation it should be prevented, *qu'on y mettroit ordre*, and that no such attempt ever should be made from the ports of France, and that they never would suffer their sailors to be so employed.

In a word, my Lord, his promises were as fair as I could wish; but I do not expect the performance to be complete. I see but too plainly that my best endeavours will not prevent these secret succours; but still, my Lord, I shall continue them, as they show we are upon the watch and tend to retard and lessen the evil they cannot remove.

—Barnes and Owen, *Private Papers of the Earl of Sandwich*, I, 221-222.

2. "The French Violate the Laws of Nations"

London, July 4, 1777

The following advertisement appeared in all the daily newspapers:

"New Lloyd's Coffee-house, July 3, 1777.

"THE merchants, owners of ships, and insurers, observing that the French, in violation of the laws of nations, have permitted American privateers not only to bring in British ships and cargoes, but also to sell the same in their ports in Europe and the West-Indies, many of which privateers, it is well known, are the property of, and manned by, Frenchmen; and whereas a continuance of such practice must prove ruinous to the commercial interests of this kingdom, the owners of all such ships and cargoes as have been, or may be, taken and sold in any of the ports of France or the West Indies are earnestly intreated to send the particulars thereof to Lord Viscount Weymouth, his Majesty's Secretary of State for the southern department, and also to the Lords of the Admiralty, in order that Administration may be fully apprised of the alarming extent of this growing and destructive evil."

For the Remembrancer

The number of our ships taken by the American and French privateers is truly alarming; and what appears more surprising is that we scarcely ever hear of any of those privateers being taken, but frequently a number of their trading ships. This circumstance to the intelligent English merchant accounts for the mystery, viz., in former wars the first object of administration was to protect our own commerce, then to annoy the enemy's; for which purpose, besides the proper convoys, a number of our own men of war were ordered to cruize in the various tracts and latitudes of *our trade*, which effectually secured it. The residue of our fleet was either employed in squadrons against the enemy, or in single ships in the latitudes of *their trade*, to destroy it. But this wise and safe system has been reversed, for the sake of encouraging a few naval commanders at the expence of the merchants; for our officers are now at liberty, without any regard to the protection of our trade, to cruize in the latitudes of the enemy's where they joyfully succeed in taking some prizes.

—ALMON, ed., *The Remembrancer*, (1777), p. 176.

3. THE THAMES IS CROWDED WITH FRENCH SHIPS

Silas Deane's narrative, read before Congress.

[1778 ?]

From Dunkirk, Mr. Hodge fitted out Captain Conyngham in a cutter, with the design of intercepting a rich packet-boat from Harwich, to destroy some of the transports carrying over the Hessian troops to England, and to cruise in the Northern Ocean. Captain Conyngham captured a packet-boat and, supposing he had intercepted important intelligence, unadvisedly returned into port. He also took a brig on his return. Mr. Hodge came up to Paris with the letters taken in the packet. Orders were sent from the court to restore the two prizes, to detain Captain Conyngham's vessel, and to imprison him and his people. These orders were executed; but these expeditions caused a great sensation to the British commerce; and for the first time since Britain was a maritime power, the River Thames and others of its ports were crowded with French and other ships taking in freight, in order to avoid the risk of having British property captured.

After the alarm had a little subsided, liberty was obtained to send Captain Conyngham and his people out of France in another vessel. To effect this, Mr. Carmichael went with Mr. Hodge to Dunkirk, purchased and fitted out a second vessel well armed against the insults of British cruisers, and ordered Captain Conyngham not to cruise or commit hostilities on the coast of France. Captain Conyngham sailed with the resolution of following his orders, but he had not been long at sea before his people mutinied and obliged him to take prizes. This renewed the alarm in England, occasioned fresh and warm complaints from that side; to silence which, Mr. Hodge was confined in the Bastile for five or six weeks, where he was treated as well as a prisoner could be and suffered in nothing but the confinement, which indeed was sufficiently severe to one of his spirit and feelings.

Captain Conyngham pursued his cruise, sailed round England and Ireland.
—NEESER, *Gustavus Conyngham*, pp. 145-146.

4. CONYNGHAM WILL BE PUNISHED "IF HE HAS BEEN GUILTY OF PIRACY"

Benjamin Franklin to Ferdinand Grand, banker to the American ministers.
Passy, October 14, 1778

I have considered the note you put into my hands containing a complaint of the conduct of Captain Conyngham in the *Revenge* privateer. We have no desire to justify him in any irregularities he may have committed. On the contrary, we are obliged to our friends who give us information of the misconduct of any cruisers, that we may take the occasion of representing the same to our Government, and recommending more effectual provisions for suppressing, punishing, and preventing such practices in future.

By the papers I have the honor to send you enclosed, and which I request you would put into the hands of his excellency Count of Aranda [Spanish Ambassador at Paris], the care of the Congress to avoid giving offense to neutral powers will appear most evident: First, in the commission given to privateers, wherein it appears that sureties are taken of their owners that nothing shall be done by them "inconsistent with the usage and custom of nations," and those sureties are obliged to make good all damages. Courts of admiralty are regularly established in every one of the United States for judging of such matters, to which courts any person injured may apply, and will certainly find redress. Secondly, in the proclamation of Congress, whereby strict orders are given to all officers of armed vessels to pay a sacred regard to the rights of neutral powers and the usage and customs of civilized nations, and a declaration made that if they transgress they shall not be allowed to claim the protection of the States, but shall suffer such punishment as by the usage and custom of nations may be inflicted on them. Lastly, in the particular care taken by Congress to secure the property of some subjects of Portugal (a power that has not been very favorable to us).

All these will show that the States give no countenance to acts of piracy; and if Captain Conyngham has been guilty of that crime he will certainly be punished for it when duly prosecuted, for not only a regard to justice in general, but a strong disposition to cultivate the friendship of Spain, for whose sovereign they have the greatest respect, will induce the Congress to pay great attention to every complaint, public and private, that shall come from thence.

—NEESER, *Gustavus Conyngham*, pp. 146-148.

CHAPTER TWENTY-FIVE

American Diplomats on the Vaunted Scene of Europe

BRINGING FRANCE *into the war was a triumph for American diplomacy, but it was only half the diplomatic battle. American diplomats—never working as a harmonious team—were dispatched to win over Spain, Holland, Prussia and other countries. These countries had stakes in the possible spread of the conflict, and their diplomatic interests did not—as the American plenipotentiaries were to discover to their dismay—coincide with those of the United States. This was notably true of Spain, and, to a varying degree, American diplomats found this to be true in every capital to which they were assigned. As negotiations dragged painfully on, a civil war was metamorphosed into a world war. In 1779 Spain came in on the side of France, rather than on the side of America; the next year England concluded that Holland's violation of neutrality justified a declaration of war. Most of the other nations of Europe formed a League of Armed Neutrality, and England found herself isolated on the diplomatic as on the military front.*

In this chapter we observe the American commissioners in action in Paris, then visit Madrid with Jay, and Amsterdam and Leyden with John Adams. Both diplomats steadfastly defended American interests despite innumerable frustrations. Space does not permit our chronicling the story of Arthur Lee's futile efforts to obtain recognition from the King of Prussia. He received nothing for his pains, but had his confidential papers stolen by the British minister, Hugh Elliott. Arthur's brother, William, was equally unsuccessful in his mission to Vienna. Ralph Izard failed to be received as a commissioner to the Grand Duke of Tuscany, and Francis Dana received no encouragement from Catherine the Great of Russia. Franklin had an apt comment for this futile and humiliating policy of sending missions to countries without any advance indication that such missions would be acceptable. "A virgin state," Franklin dryly observed, "should preserve its virgin character, and not go about suitoring for alliances, but wait with decent dignity for the application of others."

I. THE AMERICAN COMMISSION IS RIDDLED WITH DISSENSION

Unfortunately, the American diplomatic corps was riddled with dissension, and some of the commissioners quickly became the laughingstock of European courts. These indecorous brawls are considered because they had an impact on the course of our diplomacy abroad.

The most notorious of the quarrels was that between Arthur Lee and the hapless Silas Deane. Deane, who came to France in July 1776 as an agent of Congress, was joined in Paris by Arthur Lee and Benjamin Franklin. All three were designated as commissioners to negotiate treaties with European nations. Lee was a trying colleague. Quarrelsome, suspicious, a born trouble-maker, he did not get on with his associates from the start, was disliked intensely and with good reason by the French, and was at least as careless as his colleagues in guarding the secrets of the American mission. Nevertheless, despite his low repute in France, Lee counted on his influential friends in Congress, whom he bombarded with accusations against Deane and Franklin. While Franklin proved invulnerable to attack, Deane was recalled for questioning. The French government, in a gesture of confidence and friendship, sent him back to America on a warship along with the new minister Conrad Gérard. Returning to France in 1780 to adjust his official accounts, Deane deserted the cause of independence and was in communication with Paul Wentworth, a British agent. Letters of Deane advocating peace with Great Britain without independence were published in the New York press, and caused him to be denounced by the Patriots as a renegade. He died abroad, but many years later Congress paid his heirs the sum of $37,000 for expenses incurred by him in carrying out his difficult mission.

Franklin's support of Deane made him the target for attack by Arthur Lee and his faction in Congress. Lee hounded Franklin although he was unable to find anything wrong with his accounts, and made himself a formidable enemy of the French alliance. Arthur Lee's brother William wrote in 1779, "America has struggled to a fine purpose to make a Ben. instead of a Geo. her absolute lord and master."

1. Beaumarchais Explains Lee's Hatred of Deane

March 13, 1778

Secret Memoir to the King's Ministers, sent to the Count de Vergennes.

Mr. Arthur Lee, from his character and his ambition, at first was jealous of Mr. Deane. He has ended by becoming his enemy, as always happens in little minds more concerned to supplant their rivals than to surpass them in merit.

Mr. Lee's connections in England and his two brothers in Congress have since made him a prominent and dangerous man. His design has ever been to choose, as between England and France, the power that would most surely promote his fortunes, and he has frequently declared this at his dissolute suppers.

But to succeed, it was first necessary to dispose of a colleague so formidable, because of his intelligence and patriotism, as Mr. Deane. He has succeeded, by rendering him, in many respects, an object of suspicion to Congress.

Having learned that foreign officers demanding commissions were unfavorably regarded by the American Army, he has put the worst construction upon the conduct of his colleagues who sent them, and the behavior of some Frenchmen, slipping over from our (West Indian) islands, justifying perhaps the aversion with which our officers are regarded in America. Mr. Lee has turned these circumstances to his advantage by maintaining to Congress that Mr. Deane, arbitrarily, and in spite of good advice, is responsible for their presence, as costly as it is unprofitable to the Republic.

Moreover, in order to disavow everything that Mr. Deane has done, advantage has been taken of his earlier instructions, which mentioned only commercial matters, and this is today one of the reasons for his recall.

Another reason is the officious zeal displayed by Mr. Lee in continually writing to Congress that all the merchandise and European supplies furnished through the firm of Hortalez were a present from France to America, and that he had been so informed by M. Hortalez himself. Congress, in consequence, has viewed with much mistrust the prices-current, the requests for payment and for purchases to be made, although these were attested and signed by Mr. Deane, as having been entered into with a business firm, and strictly on condition of returns to be sent as soon as possible. Nothing, then, has been easier than for the adroit Lee to blacken the conduct of Mr. Deane, by representing it as the result of underhand measures, contrived to support demands for money in which he expected to share; and this explains the silence, more than astonishing, that Congress has observed in regard to over ten letters of mine full of details.

At present Mr. Deane, overwhelmed with troubles, finds himself rudely and imperatively recalled, and commanded, moreover, to explain his conduct and to vindicate himself from the imputation of numerous faults not mentioned.

Conscious of injustice, Mr. Deane had resolved not to return until Congress should communicate the charges and complaints against him, unwilling, as he said, to deliver himself to his personal enemies without proofs capable of confuting them. But I have persuaded him to change his resolution.

In order fully to understand this recall at a critical moment it is necessary, if I may be permitted to speak frankly, that others should be persuaded, as I am, that England has much to do with the proceedings of Mr. Lee. It is necessary to realize that he has brought his brother, the alderman, from London, that it is through him he maintains his secret correspondence, and that after I had investigated many theories of the means employed by England to keep perfectly informed of everything done in France, I was the more impressed with the idea that Mr. Lee was a two-edged sword, and that within four days of the arrival of letters recalling Mr. Deane and appointing Mr. Adams, Mr. Lee furtively sent his valet de chambre, who set out the day before yesterday, to London.

Why this mysterious message? How does it happen that what passes at Versailles is always so accurately known in London? In what way was the information of the projected treaty instantly conveyed, and with what intent have strenuous efforts been made to corrupt and bribe me to speak, unless, by giving ground for insinuations, to involve me in Mr. Deane's disgrace, and to ruin me at Versailles while he was being ruined at Philadelphia? The expedition of that valet to London upon the news of Mr. Deane's recall explains everything.

Thus it is clear, in my opinion, that while England sends Commissioners to America, and Mr. Lee's relatives and friends exert themselves to render popular a reconciliation between the two countries, there is at the same time an attempt to destroy by slander the influence or the credit of Mr. Deane and myself—the men known to be the most attached to the policy of an alliance between France and America. . . .

—DEANE, *Papers, N.Y. Hist. Soc. Coll.,* XX, 399-406.

2. FRANKLIN TESTIFIES TO DEANE'S PATRIOTISM AND ABILITY

Benjamin Franklin to Henry Laurens, President of Congress.

Passy, near Paris, March 31, 1778

Sir: My colleague, Mr. Deane, being recalled by Congress, and no reasons given that have yet appeared here, it is apprehended to be the effect of some misrepresentations from an enemy or two at Paris and at Nantes. I have no doubt that he will be able clearly to justify himself; but having lived intimately with him now fifteen months, the greatest part of the time in the same house, and being a constant witness of his public conduct, I cannot omit giving this testimony, though unasked, in his behalf, that I esteem him a faithful, active and able Minister, who, to my knowledge, has done, in various ways, great and important services to his country, whose interests I wish may always be, by everyone in her employ, as much and as effectually promoted. . . .

—FRANKLIN, Letter, *N.Y. Hist. Soc. Coll.,* XX, 445.

3. THE AMERICAN NEGOTIATORS TRADE INSULTS

Arthur Lee to Benjamin Franklin.

Chaillot, April 2, 1778

It was with the utmost surprise that I learned yesterday that M. Gerard was to set out in the evening for America in a public character, and that Mr. Deane was to accompany him, without either you or he having condescended to answer my letter of the preceding day. . . .

I trust, Sir, that you will think with me that I have a right to know your reasons for treating me thus. If you have anything to accuse me of, avow it, and I will answer you. If you have not, why do you act so inconsistently with your duty to the public and injuriously to me? Is the present state of Europe of so little moment to our constituents as not to require our joint consideration, and information to them? Is the character of the Court here, and of the person sent to negotiate with our constituents, of no consequence for them to be appraised of? Is this the example, you, in your superior wisdom, think proper to set, of order, decorum, confidence, and justice?

I trust, too, Sir, that you will not treat this letter, as you have done many others, with the indignity of not answering it. Though I have been silent, I have not felt the less the many affronts of this kind which you have thought proper to offer me. . . .

In reply to Lee's letter of April 2, Franklin prepared two drafts. The first he did not send; nor is it clear that he dispatched the second draft, which we reproduce here.

Benjamin Franklin to Arthur Lee.

Passy, April 4th, 1778

Mr. Deane communicated to me his intention of setting out for America immediately as a secret, which he desired I would mention to nobody. I complied with his request. If he did not think fit to communicate it to you also, it is from him you should demand his reasons. . . .

You ask me why I act so inconsistently with my duty to the public. This is a very heavy charge, sir, which I have not deserved. But it is to the public that I am accountable, and not to you. I have been a servant to many publics, through a long life; have served them with fidelity, and have been honored by their approbation. There is not a single instance of my ever being accused before of acting contrary to their interest or my duty. I shall account to the Congress, when called upon, for this my terrible offence of being silent to you about Mr. Deane's and M. Gerard's departure. And I have no doubt of their equity in acquitting me.

It is true that I have omitted answering some of your letters, particularly your angry ones, in which you, with very magisterial airs, schooled and documented me, as if I had been one of your domestics. I saw in the strongest light the importance of our living in decent civility towards each other, while our great affairs were depending here. I saw your jealous, suspicious, malignant and quarrelsome temper, which was daily manifesting itself against Mr. Deane and almost every other person you had any concern with. I, therefore, passed your affronts in silence, did not answer, but burnt your angry letters, and received you, when I next saw you, with the same civility as if you had never written them. Perhaps I may still pursue the same conduct, and not send you these. I believe I shall not, unless exceedingly pressed by you; for, of all things, I hate altercations. . . .

—Bigelow, ed., *Works of Franklin*, VII, 277, 283.

4. Parties and Divisions Have Pernicious Effects

Diary of John Adams.

April 21, 1778 . . . It is with much grief and concern that I have learned, from my first landing in France, the disputes between the Americans in this kingdom: the animosities between Mr. Deane and Mr. Lee; between Dr. Franklin and Mr. Lee; between Mr. Izard and Dr. Franklin; between Dr. Bancroft and Mr. Lee; between Mr. Carmichael and all. It is a rope of sand. I am at present wholly untainted with these prejudices, and will endeavor to keep myself so. Parties and divisions among the Americans here must have disagreeable, if not pernicious, effects. Mr. Deane seems to have made himself agreeable here to persons of importance and influence, and is gone home in such splendor that I fear there will be altercations in America about him. Dr. Franklin, Mr. Deane and Dr. Bancroft are friends. The Lees and Mr. Izard are friends. Sir James Jay insinuated that Mr. Deane had been at least as attentive to his own interest, in dabbling in the English funds and in trade, and in fitting out privateers, as to the public; and said he would give Mr. Deane fifty thousands pounds for his fortune, and said that Dr. Bancroft too had made a fortune. Mr. McCreery insinuated to me that the Lees were selfish, and that this was a family misfortune.

What shall I say? It is said that Mr. Lee has not the confidence of the ministry, nor of the persons of influence here; that he is suspected of too much affection for England, and of too much intimacy with Lord Shelburne; that he has given offence by an unhappy disposition, and by indiscreet speeches before servants and others, concerning the French nation and government—despising and cursing them. I am sorry for these things, but it is no part of my business to quarrel with anybody without cause; it is no part of my duty to differ with one party or another, or to give offence to anybody; but I must do my duty to the public, let it give offence to whom it will.

The public business has never been methodically conducted. There never was, before I came, a minute book, a letter book or an account book; and it is not possible to obtain a clear idea of our affairs.

Mr. Deane lived expensively, and seems not to have had much order in his business, public or private; but he was active, diligent, subtle and successful, having accomplished the great purpose of his mission to advantage.

—ADAMS, ed., *Works of John Adams*, III, 138-140.

5. THE NEW ENVOY TAKES A POOR VIEW OF HIS PARIS COLLEAGUES

John Adams to James Warren, member of the Navy Board for the Eastern Department.

Passy, December 5, 1778

I wish I could unbosom myself to you, without reserve, concerning the state of our affairs here. But you know the danger. The two passions of ambition and avarice, which have been the bane of liberty, and the curse of human kind in all ages and countries, are not without their influence upon our affairs here. But I fancy the last of the two has done the most mischief. Where the carcas is, there the crows will assemble, and you and I have had too much experience of the greediness with which the Continental Treasury has been aimed at by many, to expect that the coffers of the American banker here would not make some mens mouths water. This appetite for the bankers treasures I take to have been the source of most of the altercations and dissentions that have happened here. Your old friend [Arthur Lee] I take to be a man of honor and integrity, yet, to be very frank, he cannot easily govern his temper, and he has some notions of elegance, rank and dignity that may be carried rather too far. He has been of opinion that the public money has been too freely issued here, and has often opposed. The other [Benjamin Franklin] you knew personally, and that he loves his ease, hates to offend, and seldom gives any opinion untill obliged to do it. I know also, and it is necessary you should be informed, that he is overwhelmed with a correspondence from all quarters, most of them upon trifling subjects, and in a mere trifling style; with unmeaning visits from multitudes of people chiefly from the vanity of having it to say they have seen him.

There is another thing which I am obliged to mention. There are so many private families, ladies, and gentlemen that he visits so often and they are so fond of him that he cannot well avoid it, and so much intercourse with accademicians that all these things together keep his mind in such a constant state of dissipation that if he is left alone here, the public business will suffer in a degree beyond description, provided our affairs are continued upon the present footing.

If indeed you take out of his hands the public treasury, and the direction of the frigates and Continental vessells that are sent here, and all commercial affairs, and intrust them to persons to be appointed by Congress, at Nantes and Bourdeaux, I should think it would be best to leave him here alone, with such a secretary as you can confide in.

But if he is left here alone, even with such a secretary, and all maritime and commercial as well as political affairs and money matters are left in his hands, I am persuaded that France and America both will have reason to repent it. He is not only so indolent that business will be neglected; but you know that altho' he has as determined a soul as any man, yet it is his constant policy never to say Yes or No decidedly but when he cannot avoid it, and it is certain in order to preserve the friendship between the two countries the Minister here must upon some occasions speak freely and without reserve, preserving decency and politeness at the same time. Both he and his colleague [Silas Deane], who is or has been lately with you, were, I am sorry to say, in a constant opposition to your old friend, and this misunderstanding was no secret at court, in the city or in the seaport towns, either to French, English or Americans, and this was carried so far that insinuations, I have been told, have been made at Court against your old friend, not by either of his colleagues that I know of, but by somebody or other, emboldened by and taking advantage of the misunderstanding among the three, that he was too friendly to the English, too much attached to Lord Shelburne, and even that he corresponded with his Lordship and communicated intelligence to him. . . .

The other gentleman [Silas Deane], whom you know, I need not say much of. You know his ambition, you know his desire for making a fortune, of promoting his relations; you also know his art and his enterprize. Such characters are often useful, altho always to be carefully watched and controuled, especially in such a government as ours.

There has been so much said among Americans here and in America about his making a fortune by speculating in English funds and by private trade that it is saying nothing new to mention it. Our countrymen will naturally like to know if it is true, and it will be expected of me that I should say something of it. I assure you I know nothing about it. An intimate friend of his . . . certainly speculated largely in the funds, and some persons suspect that the other was concerned with him. But I know of no proof that he was.

Combinations, associations, copartnerships in trade have been formed here, in which he and his brothers are or have been supposed to be connected, but I know nothing more than you do about them.

But suppposing it was proved that he speculated and traded, the question will arise whether it was justifiable. Neither you nor I should have done it, it is true; but if he did not employ the public money, nor so much of his own time as to neglect the public business, where is the harm? That is the question, and it ought to be remembered that he was here a long time, not as Ambassador, Envoy, Commissioner or Minister, or in any other trust or character from Congress, but merely as an agent for the committees of Commerce and Correspondence. . . .

This letter is not so free as I wish to write to you, but still it is too free to be used without discretion. You will use it accordingly only for the public good. Knowing the animosity that has been in two against one here, which I believe to have been carried to unwarrantable lengths, knowing the inveteracy of many subaltern and collateral characters, which I think is injurious to the individuals as well as the public, and knowing that you have these things, and will have them, in contemplation and much at heart, I have said thus much of my sentiments upon these subjects, which I hope will do no harm.

—*Warren-Adams Letters*, II, 73-77.

6. Adams Is *Persona Non Grata* to Vergennes

A. Adams: the king did nothing until solicited

John Adams to the Count de Vergennes.

Paris, July 27, 1780

Sir: Since my letter of the 21st, and upon reading over again your Excellency's letter to me of the 20th, I observed one expression which I think it my duty to consider more particularly. The expression I have in view is this: "that the King, without having been solicited by the Congress, had taken measures the most efficacious to sustain the American cause."

Upon this part of your letter, I must entreat your Excellency to recollect that the Congress did as long ago as the year 1776, before Dr. Franklin was sent off for France, instruct him, Mr Deane and Mr Lee to solicit the King for six ships of the line, and I have reason to believe that the Congress have been from that moment to this persuaded that this object has been constantly solicited by their Ministers at this Court. . . .

—Sparks, ed., *Diplomatic Correspondence*, V, 301-302.

B. Vergennes: "i did not expect the animadversion . . ."

Count de Vergennes to John Adams.

Versailles, July 29, 1780

I have received the letter, which you did me the honor to write me on the 27th of this month. When I took upon myself to give you a mark of my confidence by informing you of the destination of Messrs De Ternay and Rochambeau, I did not expect the animadversion which you have thought it your duty to make on a passage of my letter of the 20th of this month. To avoid any further discussions of that sort, I think it my duty to inform you that Mr. Franklin being the sole person who has letters of credence to the King from the United States, it is with him only that I ought and can treat of matters which concern them, and particularly of that which is the subject of your observations.

Besides, Sir, I ought to observe to you that the passage in my letter which you thought it your duty to consider more particularly related only to sending the fleet commanded by the Chevalier de Ternay, and had nothing further in view than to convince you that the King did not stand in need of your solicitations to induce him to interest himself in the affairs of the United States.

— SPARKS, ed., *Diplomatic Correspondence*, V, 304-305.

C. VERGENNES: LET CONGRESS JUDGE WHETHER ADAMS IS ENDOWED WITH A CONCILIATING SPIRIT

Count de Vergennes to Benjamin Franklin.

Versailles, July 31, 1780

The character with which you are invested, your wisdom, and the confidence I have in your principles and sentiments, induce me to communicate to you a correspondence which I have had with Mr Adams.

You will find, I think, in the letters of that Plenipotentiary opinions and a turn which do not correspond either with the manner in which I explained myself to him, or with the intimate connexion which subsists between the King and the United States. You will make that use of these pieces which your prudence shall suggest. As to myself, I desire that you will transmit them to Congress, that they may know the line of conduct which Mr Adams pursues with regard to us, and that they may judge whether he is endowed, as Congress no doubt desires, with that conciliating spirit which is necessary for the important and delicate business with which he is intrusted.

— SPARKS, ed., *Diplomatic Correspondence*, V, 305-306.

II. MISSION TO SPAIN

Spain felt that France had been too precipitate in allying herself with America. As Charles III's chief minister, Grimaldi, had said earlier in the war, "The rights of all sovereigns to their respective territories ought to be regarded as sacred, and the example of a rebellion is too dangerous to allow of His Majesty's wishing to assist openly." Floridablanca, who succeeded to Grimaldi's post in 1777, distrusted the United States even more than he feared England. Under pressure from Vergennes Spain finally agreed to the secret Convention of Aranjuez of April 12, 1779. Spain was now ready to go to war alongside of France. The bait was Gibraltar, then in British hands. No commitment was made to fight for the independence of the United States. On June 21 Spain, on the pretext that her mediation efforts had been spurned and her territories attacked, declared war against Great Britain.

From time to time Spain had advanced funds to America. In 1776 a million livres were turned over to Beaumarchais to help finance his operations. Small sums were added in the two years that followed. But Spain was understandably anxious about America's objectives which might conflict with her own interests. She feared that America would wrest control of the Mississippi from her and was concerned about the probable southern and western boundaries of the United States. The southern boundary that the Americans wanted clearly conflicted with Spain's claims to Florida, which she had been forced to cede to Great Britain in 1763. Since Spain soon reconquered West Florida the conflict of interest was serious. Spain claimed that the northern boundary of West Florida ran at the latitude of the mouth of the Yazoo River (about 32° 28'), the boundary which Britain had established in 1764. The United States wanted its southern boundary to lie at 31° north latitude. This was a thorny problem in the peace negotiations and in the postwar years.

To secure recognition of the independence of the United States, an effective military alliance, and the concession to America of the right to navigate the Mississippi to the sea, along with a substantial subsidy or loan, John Jay, the New York lawyer Patriot, was sent as diplomatic representative to Madrid.

John Jay was in Spain from January 1780 to May 1782. Except for a small advance of $174,000, which the United States chose to regard as a loan, Jay secured no satisfaction on any of the points at issue between America and France's ally. He refused to barter the Mississippi for a Spanish alliance. He was prepared to yield, at Congress' urging, the right to navigate the lower Mississippi, but withdrew that concession when Spain did not enter into an alliance with America.

To Floridablanca, Jay was disagreeably insistent. As the Spanish minister put it, "His two chief points were: Spain, recognize our independence; Spain, give us more money." Jay's forthright reactions are found in excerpts from some of his own letters written from Madrid.

1. "THE KING AND THE MINISTRY ARE WARM, THE NATION IS COLD"

John Jay to Samuel Huntington, President of Congress.

Madrid, May 26, 1780

The people in this country are in almost total darkness about us. Scarce any American publications have reached them, nor are they informed of the most recent and important events in that country. The affairs of Stony Point, Paulus Hook, etc., etc., had never been heard of here, except perhaps by the great officers of state, and they could scarcely believe that the Roman Catholic religion was even tolerated there.

There are violent prejudices among them against us. Many of them have even serious doubts of our being civilized, and mention a strange story of a ship driven into Virginia by distress, about thirty years ago, that was plundered by the inhabitants, and some of the crew killed in a manner and under circumstances which, if true, certainly indicate barbarity. The King and Ministry are warm, yet I have reason to believe that the bulk of the nation is cold toward us. They appear to me to like the English, hate the French, and to have prejudices against us.

I mention these things to show in a stronger light the necessity of punctuality in sending me from time to time all American intelligence of importance, and observing such conduct towards Spaniards in general as may tend to impress them with more favourable sentiments of us.

—JAY, *Correspondence and Public Papers*, I, 342-343.

2. SPAIN SETS A HIGH PRICE FOR MEAGER AID

John Jay's account of conferences with Don Diego de Gardoqui, financial intermediary between the Spanish Court and the United States, and with

Del Campo, confidential secretary to the Count de Floridablanca, who in turn was official spokesman for the King in the negotiations.

September 3-4, 1780

In the evening M. Gardoqui . . . paid me a visit and pointedly proposed my offering the navigation of the Mississippi as a consideration for aids.

I told him that object could not come in question in a treaty for a loan of one hundred thousand pounds, and Spain should consider that, to render alliances permanent, they should be so formed as to render it the interest of both parties to observe them; that the Americans, almost to a man, believed that God Almighty had made that river a highway for the people of the upper country to go to the sea by; that this country was extensive and fertile; that the General, many officers, and others of distinction and influence in America were deeply interested in it; that it would rapidly settle, and that the inhabitants would not readily be convinced of the justice of being obliged either to live without foreign commodities and lose the surplus of their productions, or be obliged to transport both over rugged mountains and through an immense wilderness, to and from the sea, when they daily saw a fine river flowing before their doors and offering to save them all that trouble and expense, and that without injury to Spain.

He observed that the present generation would not want this navigation, and that we should leave future ones to manage their own affairs, etc.

The next day, that is, the 4th of September, I met M. Gardoqui at M. Del Campo's. After some unconnected conversation, I observed to M. Del Campo that as all the papers between the Minister and myself had passed through his hands, it was unnecessary to give him any information, except what related to the present state of the bills drawn upon me, which I proceeded to state in a short but particular manner.

He replied by making several strictures on the impropriety of drawing bills without previous notice and consent. He remarked that they might with more propriety have been drawn on France, with whom we were allied, and who were richer than they; that the King must first take care of his own people before he could supply us; that Spain had been brought into the war by our quarrel but received no advantage from us; that they had been told of our readiness to assist in taking Pensacola, etc., but instead of aids, he had heard of nothing but demands from us; that our situation was represented as being deplorable, and that the enemy talked of the submission of some of the States, and of negotiations being on foot for that purpose.

Whether this style proceeded from natural arrogance or was intended to affect my temper, I cannot say. In either case, I thought it most prudent to take no notice of it, but proceed calmly and cautiously, and the more so as this was the first time I had ever conversed with this man. I told him in substance, though more at large, that the assurances given Congress of the friendly disposition of Spain by M. Mirales and others had been confided in and had induced Congress to expect the aids in question. That if this application could be called a demand, it was still the first they had made to my knowledge; that men in arms against the enemies of Spain were serving her as well as themselves, and therefore might without impropriety request her

Gouverneur Morris Papers, Columbia University Library

JAY VIOLATES THE INSTRUCTIONS OF CONGRESS AND IGNORES THE FRENCH MINISTER

Cipher letter of John Jay, a member of the American Peace Commission, to Gouverneur Morris, October 13, 1782

aid; that our separation from Britain was an object important to Spain, and that the success with which we had opposed her whole force for six years showed what the power of both, if under one direction, might be capable of; that I knew nothing of Spain's having been drawn into the war by or for us, and that this was not [to] be found among the reasons she had alleged for it; that an attack on Pensacola could not be expected to be made by troops actually employed in repelling the enemy's assaults from their own doors, and that the principles of self-defence would not permit or justify it; that Spain had much to expect in future from our commerce, and that we should be able as well as willing to pay our debts; that the tales told of our despondency and submission resulted from the policy of the enemy, not from fact, and I believed no more of their private negotiations between America and Britain than I did of there being private negotiations between Spain and Britain for a separate peace, which the Minister assured me was not the case. . . .

He . . . then made some reflections on the proposal of a treaty. We agreed perfectly well that mutual interest should be the basis of it, and I added that the good opinion entertained of the King and nation by America was also a pleasing circumstance. He said, however that might be, America did not seem inclined to gratify Spain in the only point in which she was deeply interested. Here followed much common-place reasoning about the navigation of the Mississippi, of which your Excellency has heretofore heard too much to require a repetition. . . .

—JAY, *Correspondence and Public Papers*, I, 394 ff.

3. JAY REFUSES TO SUPPLICATE

John Jay to the President of Congress.

Madrid, November 6, 1780

. . . On Wednesday afternoon, 30th of August, I waited on the [French] ambassador to know the result of the conversation he had promised to have with the minister on our affairs. He did not appear very glad to see me. . . . He said . . . he hoped things would take a more favorable turn; that to his knowledge the minister had been of late much occupied and perplexed with business; that I should continue to conduct the business smoothly, having always in view the importance of Spain, and remembering that we were as yet only rising States, not firmly established or generally acknowledged, etc., and that he would by all means advise me to write the minister another letter *praying* an audience.

I answered that the object of my coming to Spain was to make *propositions*, not *supplications*, and that I should forbear troubling the minister with further letters till he should be more disposed to attend to them. That I considered America as being, and to continue, independent in *fact*, and that her becoming so in *name* was of no further importance than as it concerned the common cause, in the success of which all the parties were interested; and that I did not imagine Congress would agree to purchase from Spain the acknowledgment of an undeniable fact at the price she demanded for it; that I intended to abide patiently the fate of the bills, and should transmit to Congress an account of all matters relative to them; that I should then write the minister another letter on the subject of the treaty, and if that should be treated with like neglect, or if I should be informed that his Catholic majesty declined going into that measure, I should then consider my business at an end, and proceed to take the necessary measures for returning to America; that I knew my constituents were sincerely desirous of a treaty with Spain, and that their respect for the house of Bourbon, the desire of France signified in the secret article, and the favorable opinion they had imbibed of the Spanish nation were the strongest inducements they had to wish it; that the policy of multiplying treaties with European nations was with me questionable, and might be so with others; that for my own part, I was inclined to think it the interest of America to rest content with the treaty with France, and by avoiding alliances with other nations, remain free from the influence of their disputes and politics; that the situation of the United States, in my opinion, dictated this policy; that I knew it to be their interest, and of course their disposition, to be at peace with all the world; and that I knew too it would be in their power, and I hoped in their inclination, always to defend themselves.

The ambassador was at a stand. After a little pause he said he hoped my mission would have a more agreeable issue. . . .

—WHARTON, *Revolutionary Diplomatic Correspondence*, IV, 130-132.

III. JOHN ADAMS DESCENDS UPON THE DUTCH

Looking back upon his mission to the Netherlands, John Adams wrote Jay in July 1782: "I hope in God that your Spanish negotiation has not wrecked your constitution as my Dutch one has mine. I would not undergo again what I have suffered in body and mind for the fee simple of all their Spice Islands. I love them, however, because with all their faults and under all their disadvantages they have at bottom a strong spirit of Liberty, a sincere affection for America, and a kind of religious veneration for her cause."

Unlike the absolute monarchy of France which flamed with enthusiasm for the American cause, the Dutch republic was apathetic, divided, cautious. In the long run French diplomacy and British naval policy created a more favorable climate of opinion in the Netherlands for the cause of the United States. The Amsterdam shippers and merchants, whose highly profitable contraband trade with America via the Dutch island of St. Eustatius in the West Indies was challenged by the British Navy, put the pressure on the Dutch government, which finally decided to convoy their merchant ships. The British regarded this as a violation of old treaty commitments, and declared war late in 1780. The pretext was the seizure of dispatches that Henry Laurens was carrying when he was captured by the British indicating that the Dutch had been negotiating with the United States. The Dutch Navy was not built up rapidly enough to ward off serious blows upon her commerce inflicted by the British fleet, which wiped out the clandestine trade between the United States and St. Eustatius.

The issue of the freedom of the seas and the rights of neutrals impelled Catherine the Great of Russia to organize, in February 1780, a League of Armed Neutrality, which Denmark, Sweden, the Netherlands, Prussia, Portugal, Austria and the Kingdom of the Two Sicilies joined in the next two years.

Great Britain had to reshape her naval activities and was now diplomatically isolated. It was a triumph for Vergennes that John Adams was quick to exploit.

Adams, who had already done some effective propaganda work for the American cause in Holland, arranged a loan of ten million livres which was guaranteed by France, secured recognition as minister plenipotentiary, and negotiated a substantial loan directly with a consortium of Dutch bankers. He topped it off with a treaty of commerce and friendship, which he signed in October 1782. "One thing, thank God, is certain," Adams wrote to his friend James Warren: "I have planted the American standard at the Hague."

1. THE DUTCH KNOW NOTHING OF THE AMERICAN CAUSE

John Adams to Samuel Huntington.

Amsterdam, September 25, 1780

There are persons in this republic who have been attentive to this war, and who know somewhat of the history of the rise and progress of the United States of America; but it is surprising that the number should be so small. Even in the city of Amsterdam, which is the most attentive to our affairs and the best inclined towards us, there are few persons who do not consider the American resistance as a desultory rage of a few enthusiasts, without order, discipline, law or government. There are scarcely any who have an adequate idea of the numbers, the increasing population or the growing commerce of America.

Upon my arrival here some gentlemen were inquisitive about our governments. I asked if they had seen them in print, and was answered no. Upon this I made it my business to search in all the booksellers' shops for the collection of them which was published in French two or three years ago, but could find only two copies, which I presented to the gentlemen who made the inquiry. Nothing would serve our cause more than having a complete edition of the American constitutions correctly printed in English by order of Congress and sent to Europe, as well as sold in America. The Rhode Island and Connecticut constitutions ought not to be omitted, although they have undergone no alteration; and it would be proper to print the Confederation in the same volume. This work would be read by everybody in Europe who reads English and could obtain it, and some would even learn English for the sake of reading it; it would be translated into every language of Europe, and would fix the opinion of our unconquerability more than anything could, except driving the enemy wholly from the United States.

There has been nobody here of sufficient information and consideration to turn the attention of the public towards our affairs, to communicate from time to time with the public, in a language that is understood, intelligence from America, France, England, etc.; but, on the contrary, there have been persons enough employed and well paid by our enemies to propagate misinformation, misrepresentation and abuse.

The ancient and intimate connection between the houses of Orange and Brunswick, the family alliances and the vast advantages which the princes of Orange have derived from them in erecting, establishing and at last perpetuating the stadtholderate against the inclination of the Republican party, and the reliance which this family still has upon the same connection to support it, have attached the executive power of this government in such a manner to England that nothing but necessity could cause a separation. On the contrary, the Republican party, which has heretofore been conducted by Barnevelt, Grotius, the De Witts and other immortal patriots, have ever leaned towards an alliance with France, because she has ever favored the republican form of government in this nation. All parties, however, agree that England has been ever jealous and envious of the Dutch commerce, and done it great injuries; that this country is more in the power of France, if she were hostile, than of England; and that her trade with France is of vastly greater value than that with England. Yet England has more influence here than France. The Dutch—some of them, at least—now see another commercial and maritime power arising that it is their interest to form an early connection with. All parties here see that it is not their interest that France and Spain should secure too many advantages in America and too great a share of her commerce, and especially in the fisheries in her seas. All parties, too, see that it would be dangerous to the commerce, and even independence, of the United Provinces to have America again under the dominion of England; and the Republicans see, or think they see, that a change in this government and the loss of their liberties would be the consequence of it too.

Amidst all these conflicts of interest and parties and all these speculations the British ambassador, with his swarms of agents, are busily employed in propagating reports, in which they are much assisted by those who are called here stadtholderians, and there has been nobody to contradict or explain anything. This should be the business in part of a minister plenipotentiary. Such a minister, however, would not have it in his power to do it effectually without frequent and constant information from Congress. At present this nation is so ignorant of the strength, resources, commerce and constitution of America; it has so false and exaggerated an imagination of the power of England; it has so many doubts of our final success; so many suspicions of our falling finally into the hands of France and Spain; so many jealousies that France and Spain will abandon us or that we shall abandon them; so many fears of offending the English ministry, the English ambassador, the great mercantile houses that are very profitably employed by both, and, above all, the stadtholder and his friends, that even a loan of money will meet with every obstruction and discouragement possible. These chimeras, and many more, are held up to people here, and influence men's minds and conduct to such a degree that no man dares openly and publicly to disregard them.

—WHARTON, ed., *Revolutionary Diplomatic Correspondence,* IV, 67-69.

2. ADAMS DESCRIBES HIS DIFFICULTIES IN RAISING A DUTCH LOAN

John Adams to the President of Congress.

Leyden, 19 March, 1781

I have experienced since my residence in this republic a great change in the external behavior of several persons of rank, who, upon my first arrival, received me with distinction, but, from the moment of the publication of the papers taken with Mr. Laurens, have been afraid to see me. The nation has indeed been in a violent fermentation and crisis. It is divided in sentiments. There are stadtholderians and republicans; there are proprietors in English funds, and persons immediately engaged in commerce; there are enthusiasts for peace and alliance with France, Spain and America; and there is a third sort who are for adhering in all things to Russia, Sweden and Denmark; some are for acknowledging American independence and entering into treaties of commerce and alliance with her; others start at the idea with horror, as an everlasting impediment to a return to the friendship and alliance with England; some will not augment the Navy without increasing the Army; others will let the Navy be neglected rather than augment the Army.

In this perfect chaos of sentiments and systems, principles and interests, it is no wonder there is a languor, a weakness and irresolution that is vastly dangerous in the present circumstances of affairs. The danger lies not more in the hostile designs and exertions of the English than in the prospect of seditions and commotions among the people, which are every day dreaded and expected. If it were not for a standing Army and troops posted about in several cities, it is probable there would have been popular tumults before now; but everybody that I see appears to me to live in constant fear of mobs and in a great degree of uncertainty whether they will rise in favor of war or against it, in favor of England or against it, in favor of the Prince or of the city of Amsterdam, in favor of America or against it.

I have ventured, in the midst of these critical circumstances, pressed as I am to get money to discharge the bills of exchange which Congress have drawn and I have accepted, to open a loan; but this is looked upon as a very hardy and dangerous measure, which nobody but an American would have risked, and I am obliged to assure Congress that people are as yet so much afraid of being pointed out by the mob or the soldiery as favorers of this loan that I have no hopes at all of succeeding for several months, if ever.

—ADAMS, ed., *Works of John Adams*, VII, 380-381.

CHAPTER TWENTY-SIX

War out of Niagara

THE AMERICAN FRONTIER *of the 1770's stretched in a great broken arc from Maine to Georgia—through northern Vermont, along the borderland of New York, across northern and western Pennsylvania, through Ohio and to Detroit, southward to the Ohio, into the Kentucky country, along the Appalachians down through Virginia and the Carolinas to the frontier of Georgia. It embraced a large part of the American territory, and a substantial part of the American population, and all of it was exposed to Indian depredations. And Indian war was a constant all through the Revolution. Sometimes it was in the background—a threat, a tension, a fear that drove pioneers back to the safety of the settlements; sometimes, as with the Wyoming Valley massacre, it was in the foreground. It began, in a sense, with Lord Dunmore's War in 1774; it did not end until Indians overwhelmed Kentuckians at Blue Licks in August 1782 and Colonel Willett launched an abortive attack on Oswego in February 1783. It played a not unimportant part in the war; it played an important part in the American imagination, in history, story and legend.*

The Indians were everywhere, and most of them were hostile to the Americans. If they were to be involved in the war it was clear that they would fight on the side of the British. The British had the supplies, the articles for trade, the fur-trading posts; the British seemed to be there as their defenders; it was the Americans who were advancing into their hunting grounds. And it was inevitable that the Indians would be caught up in the war. The British could not advance, by land, except through their territory—from Canada, from Niagara, from Detroit, from Georgia—and from the first the two Johnsons and Stuart and General Carleton made use of them.

The use that they made of the Indians, however, was halfhearted, sporadic, and shortsighted. There was no grand strategy; there was no strategy at all. Organized, officered, armed and supplied by the British, the Indians might have been a formidable force; they might even have been a decisive force. It is difficult to see how the Americans could have resisted a co-ordinated series of attacks from the sea and a series of attacks along their frontiers. Had the British struck at Boston, New York and Charleston (as they did) and, at the same time, down the Champlain frontier, the Mohawk frontier, the Susquehanna frontier, the mountainous frontier of the Allegheny-Monongahela, the newly settled frontier of Kentucky, back-country Carolina and Georgia, the impact would have been irresistible. Happily for the Americans the threat of organized Indian warfare never materialized. Some of the Indian tribes were actually friendly to the Americans; others adopted neutrality, at least for a time. And the British had no master plan, nor is there any strong reason to suppose that the Indians would have lent themselves to such a plan.

At that the border warfare went badly for the Americans. There were, to be sure, some bright spots: Clark's conquest of the Northwest, for example, or the punishment of the Cherokee in the South. But most of the news from the frontier was bad news. Tories and Indians wiped out the flourishing settlements along the Susquehanna; ravaged the Mohawk and Schoharie valleys; and made New York borderlands an open wound all through the war. The British reconquered the Northwest; the Indians ravaged Kentucky again and again, and carried the war to the smoking cabins on the Monongahela. At the end of the war the Indians were still unsubdued, and the British controlled most of the territory north of the Ohio.

For all the terror that they spread among the Americans, it is by no means clear that the Indians really helped the British in the war. They were a distraction. They diffused and dissipated British energies. They exacerbated opinion back home and turned many a neutral frontiersman into an implacable enemy. They were not reliable either on a long campaign or in a battle. Properly used they might have changed the fortunes of war; actually all they did was to change the nature of the war, and for the worse.

It is impossible to give here even a sampling of the vast literature dealing with the borderlands during the Revolution. Fighting surged back and forth, winter after winter, on a dozen frontiers; each of these frontier skirmishes took on—in the minds of its participants—a heroic quality, each of them seemed as worthy of annals as the Trojan War or the Crusades. We select for this chapter some accounts that give a history of the most important of the Indian campaigns—the fight for back-country New York. Our next chapter will chronicle the exploits of George Rogers Clark and the battle for Kentucky.

I. BOTH SIDES ENLIST INDIANS

"Everybody" knows that the English were the first to employ Indians. The Great Declaration itself contributes this to history: "He has . . . endeavored to bring on the inhabitants of our frontiers, the merciless Indian Savages, whose known rule of warfare is an undistinguished destruction of all ages, sexes and conditions." Burke denounced the use of Indians, and Chatham exhausted his eloquence in excoriation of so wicked a policy. The consequences that they foresaw were, alas, realized: Wyoming, Cherry Valley, German Flats, Blue Licks were all monuments to the infamy of using the "merciless Indian."

Yet in fact it was the Americans who took the first step in enlisting the Indians. Even before the battle of Lexington the Massachusetts Provincial Congress enlisted the Stockbridge Indians as "minutemen"; not content with this they tried to raise Indian soldiers from Nova Scotia. In May 1775 Congress instructed its Indian commissioners to try to hold the Indians to neu-

trality; if that was not possible, however, they should enlist them on the American side. As we know, it was not possible. Already the two Johnsons— Sir John and Sir Guy—were moving in a gingerly fashion toward using the Indians of the Six Nations, at first for defensive but ultimately for offensive operations. By July 1775 the devout Lord Dartmouth officially sanctioned the employment of Indians; no less than a year later the Continental Congress came out strongly for the same policy. "It is highly expedient," they resolved, "to engage the Indians in the service of the United Colonies," and they even offered bounties for prisoners taken by the Indians.

Both sides, to be sure, tried to tame the savages; both discovered that they could as soon tame the panther or the rattlesnake as tame the Mohawk or the Delaware when he was aroused and on the warpath. Both were to find their Indian allies something of an embarrassment; as the Americans had few Indian allies their embarrassment was ephemeral, but the British suffered severely from an outraged opinion, not only in America but at home as well. We give here, along with some of the letters about enlisting the Indian, Chatham's famous reply to the Earl of Suffolk's speech urging the use of all means "that God and nature had put in our hands."

1. "INDUCE THE SIX NATIONS TO TAKE UP THE HATCHET"

The Earl of Dartmouth to Colonel Guy Johnson.

Whitehall, 24. July 1775

I have already in my letter to you of the 5th inst. hinted that the time might possibly come when the King, relying upon the attachment of his faithful allies, the Six Nations of Indians, might be under the necessity of calling upon them for their aid and assistance in the present state of America.

The unnatural rebellion now raging there calls for every effort to suppress it, and the intelligence His Majesty has received of the Rebells having excited the Indians to take a part, and of their having actually engaged a body of them in arms to support their rebellion, justifies the resolution His Majesty has taken of requiring the assistance of his faithful adherents the Six Nations.

It is therefore His Majesty's pleasure that you do lose no time in taking such steps as may induce them to take up the hatchet against His Majesty's rebellious subjects in America, and to engage them in His Majesty's service upon such plan as shall be suggested to you by General Gage to whom this letter is sent accompanied with a large assortement of goods for presents to them upon this important occasion.

Whether the engaging the Six Nations to take up arms in defence of His Majesty's Government is most likely to be effected by separate negociation with the chiefs or in a general council assembled for that purpose, must be left to your judgement, but at all events as it is a service of very great importance, you will not fail to exert every effort that may tend to accomplish it, and to use the utmost diligence and activity in the execution of the orders I have now the honor to transmit to you.

—O'CALLAGHAN, ed., *Documents Relating to Colonial History of New York*, VIII, 596.

2. GERMAIN ENCOURAGES THE USE OF INDIAN WARRIORS

Lord George Germain to John Stuart, Indian Agent.

Whitehall, 6th November, 1776

. . . I expect with some impatience to hear from you of the success of your negociation with the Creeks and the Choctaws and that you have pre-vailed with them to join the Cherokees who I find have already commenced hostilities against the Rebels in Carolina and Virginia. The Rebel govern-ment in the former province have, I also learn, not only offered considerable rewards for the scalps of those Indians but declared their children of a certain age which may be taken prisoners the slaves of the captors, a measure which I am sure must inflame the enmity of that nation to the highest pitch against them and excite the resentment of all the other Indians in so great a degree that I cannot doubt of your being able under such advantageous circumstances to engage them in a general confederacy against the Rebels in defence of those liberties of which they are so exceedingly jealous and in the full enjoyment of which they have always been protected by the King.

At this distance and before the issue of the campaign to the northward can be known here it is impossible to give you any instructions for the em-ployment of the savages. General Howe will no doubt give you full directions when he has formed his plan of operations against the Southern Colonies. In the mean time as the Cherokees have declared for us they must be supported and it will be your duty to procure them all the aid in your power from the other Indian nations and to supply them with arms and ammunition and other necessaries to enable them to carry on the war. I am not without hopes that Governor Sawyer will find means of assisting them with a detachment of his numerous garrison, and if the well affected inhabitants in the back countries could be collected and embodied to conduct and support the Indians, the Rebels on the sea coast would soon feel the distress from the want of the accustomed supplies, the discontent of the people with the new mode of government would increase with that distress, and resentment against the authors of their calamities would be the necessary consequences.

Inclosed I send you by the King's command printed copies of His Maj-esty's most gracious speech at the opening of the session together with the addresses of both Houses of Parliament to His Majesty in return, which I have the pleasure to acquaint you were passed in both Houses by very great majorities.

—SAUNDERS, ed., *Colonial Records of North Carolina*, X, 893-894.

3. TRYON CALLS FOR BRUTALITY FROM THE INDIANS

Governor William Tryon to William Knox, Secretary of the War Office in London.

New York, 21 April, 1777

I thank you for the favour of your letter of the 14th of January, which gave me much satisfaction in the assurance that my sentiments respecting the present rebellion correspond with those of my superiors. I am exactly of opinion with Colonel La [Corne] St Luc, who says; *Il faut lacher les sauvages contre les misérables Rebels, pour imposer de terreur sur les frontiers; il dit de plus (mais un peu trop pour moi) "qu'il faut brutalizer les affaires"; assurément, il est bien enragé de la mauvais traitement qu'il a reçu de les aveugles peuples*—but not to blunder longer on in a language I know imperfectly, I shall express his other sentiments in the English dialect.

He assured me that upon the opening of the first assembly with the savages in Canada, his feelings would be too poignant at their first interview, as would impose a perfect silence upon him, while tears would run down his cheeks; and that when he should be able to expatiate on the indignities and injuries he had experienced, they would instantly take up the hatchet and resent his affronts. So reciprocal is the affection between the Father and his Children, for such they style each other respectively, and by whom he is as much cherished as was Sir Wm Johnson by the Indians of the Six Nations. These anecdotes you may esteem worthy to communicate.

His Excellency General Sir William Howe has been pleased to appoint me to command the Provincial Corps within this Province with the rank of Major General of the Provincial Forces. This places me behind all the Majors General in this army, though I am an older Colonel than any of them. However, at this crisis a *passé droit* does not weigh so much with me as an opportunity given me to lend a hand to beat down this republican revolt. . . .

—O'CALLAGHAN, ed., *Documents Relating to Colonial History of New York*, VIII, 707-708.

4. CHATHAM: "WE TURN LOOSE THESE SAVAGE HELL-HOUNDS"

Speech of William Pitt, Earl Chatham, delivered in the House of Lords, November 18, 1777.

My lords, I am astonished to hear such principles confessed! I am shocked to hear them avowed in this house, or in this territory! Principles, equally unconstitutional, inhuman, and unchristian!

My lords, I did not intend to have encroached again on your attention; but I cannot repress my indignation. I feel myself impelled by every duty. My lords, we are called upon as members of this house, as men, as Christian men, to protest against such notions standing near the throne, polluting the ear of majesty. "That God and nature put into our hands!" I know not what ideas that lord may entertain of God and nature; but I know that such abominable principles are equally abhorrent to religion and humanity.

What! to attribute the sacred sanction of God and nature to the massacres of the Indian scalping knife? to the cannibal savage, torturing, murdering, roasting and eating; literally, my lords, *eating* the mangled victims of his barbarous battles! Such horrible notions shock every precept of religion, divine or natural, and every generous feeling of humanity. And, my lords, they shock every sentiment of honor; they shock me as a lover of honorable war, and a detester of murderous barbarity.

These abominable principles and this more abominable avowal of them demand the most decisive indignation. I call upon that right reverend bench, those holy ministers of the gospel and pious pastors of our church: I conjure them to join in the holy work and vindicate the religion of their God. I appeal to wisdom and the law of this *learned bench* to defend and support the justice of their country. I call upon the bishops to interpose the unsullied sanctity of their *lawn;* upon the learned judges to interpose the purity of their *ermine*, to save us from this pollution. I call upon the honor of your lordships to reverence the dignity of your ancestors, and to maintain your own. I call upon the spirit and humanity of my country to vindicate the national character. I invoke the genius of the constitution.

From the tapestry that adorns these walls, the immortal ancestor of this noble lord frowns with indignation at the disgrace of his country. In vain he led your victorious fleet against the boasted armada of Spain, in vain he defended and established the honor, the liberties, the religion, the protestant religion of this country, against the arbitrary cruelties of popery and the inquisition, if these more than popish cruelties and inquisitorial practices are let loose among us; to turn forth into our settlements, among our ancient connections, friends and relations, the merciless cannibal, thirsting for the blood of man, woman and child! to send forth the infidel savage—against whom?—against your protestant brethren; to lay waste their country; to desolate their dwellings, and extirpate their race and name, with these horrible hell-hounds of savage warfare!

Spain armed herself with blood-hounds to extirpate the wretched natives of America; and we improve on the human example even of Spanish cruelty. We turn loose these savage hell-hounds against our brethren and countrymen in America, of the same language, laws, liberty and religion, endeared to us by every tie that should sanctify humanity.

My lords, this awful subject, so important to our honor, our constitution and our religion, demands the most solemn and effectual inquiry. And I again call upon your lordships and the united power of the state to examine it thoroughly and decisively, and to stamp upon it an indelible stigma of the public abhorrence. And I again implore those holy prelates of our religion to do away these iniquities from among us. Let them perform a lustration; let them purify this house and this country from this sin.

My lords, I am old and weak and at present unable to say more; but my feelings and indignation were too strong to have said less. I could not have slept this night in my bed nor reposed my head upon my pillow without giving this vent to my eternal abhorrence of such preposterous and enormous principles.

—COBBETT, *Parliamentary History of England*, XIX, 368-370.

5. WASHINGTON: EMPLOY INDIANS WHEN DIVESTED OF SAVAGE CUSTOMS

To the Commissioners of Indian Affairs.

Head Quarters, Valley Forge, March 13, 1778

Gentlemen: You will perceive, by the inclosed Copy of a Resolve of Congress, that I am impowered to employ a body of four hundred Indians, if they can be procured upon proper terms. Divesting them of the Savage customs exercised in their Wars against each other, I think they may be made of excellent use, as scouts and light troops, mixed with our own Parties. I propose to raise about one half the number among the Southern and the remainder

SULLIVAN'S INDIAN CAMPAIGN

among the Northern Indians. I have sent Colo Nathl. Gist, who is well acquainted with the Cherokees and their Allies, to bring as many as he can from thence, and I must depend upon you to employ suitable persons to procure the stipulated number or as near as may be from the Northern tribes. The terms made with them should be such as you think we can comply with, and persons well acquainted with their language, manners and Customs and who have gained an influence over them should accompany them. The Oneidas have manifested the strongest attachment to us throughout this dispute and I therefore suppose, if any can be procured, they will be most numerous. Their Missionary Mr Kirkland seemed to have an uncommon ascendency over that tribe and I should therefore be glad to see him accompany them. If the Indians can be procured, I would choose to have them here by the opening of the Campaign, and therefore they should be engaged as soon as possible as there is not more time between this and the Middle of May than will be necessary to settle the business with them and to March from their Country to the Army. I am not without hopes that this will reach you before the treaty which is to be held, breaks up. If it should, you will have an Opportunity of knowing their sentiments, of which I shall be glad to be informed, as soon as possible. I have the honour, etc.

—FITZPATRICK, ed., *Writings of Washington*, XI, 76-77.

II. WYOMING

A special pathos clings to the Wyoming Massacre, which has been called "the surpassing horror of the Revolution." The Wyoming Valley, along the banks of the beautiful Susquehanna, near present-day Wilkes-Barre, was claimed by the state of Connecticut and had been settled largely from that state. From the time of its original settlement, in 1762, down to the Revolution, these Connecticut Yankees had fought an almost continuous struggle with Indians and Pennsylvanians—and nature—for their cherished lands; even as late as 1775 Pennsylvania militiamen had invaded the valley, only to be driven out. The Wyoming settlements—flourishing towns and farms, with a population of over 2,000—had sent a large portion of their able-bodied men to the Connecticut Line and were all but defenseless. In 1777, after their defeat at Fort Stanwix and Oriskany, Butler's Tory Rangers and their Indian allies planned an attack on these rich settlements. In July 1778 they struck, twelve hundred strong. Against them Colonel Zeb Butler, veteran of the wars with Pennsylvania, could muster only 300 old men and boys. He managed them badly, sallying out from the Forty Fort—which offered some protection—to seek battle in the open. There his forces were ambuscaded and destroyed. Then the Wyoming settlements were put to the torch, and many of the inhabitants killed.

Not long after, the Indian leader Thayendanegea—known as Joseph Brant—struck at the frontier settlement of Cherry Valley, near Otsego Lake, killed or imprisoned most of its inhabitants, including women and children, and burned all its houses. Brant disclaimed responsibility for the barbarities of this massacre, but the frontiersmen held him responsible and regarded him with execration.

We give here two accounts of Wyoming. The first comes from the untutored pen of a carpenter, Richard McGinnis, who fought under the British Colonel John Butler. The second is by the famous American farmer, Hector Saint-John de Crèvecoeur, whose "Letters" are a classic of American literature and history; this essay on the Wyoming Massacre is valuable chiefly for its picture of the refugees from border war.

1. "Loyalty and Order Triumph over Confusion and Treason"

From the Journal of Richard McGinnis, carpenter.

May 2, [*1778*]. We set out for Wioming with about 70 white volunteers and about 300 Indians of different tribes, cheifly Senecas and Delawares. With these nations Col. Butler held frequent counsels. The purport of them was cheifly to deter them if possible from murdering the women and innocent, in consequence of which they agreed not to do it on any pretence whatever, and I must say for my part they did not comit any thing of the kind to my certain knowledge.

In our way through the savage country we many a time had very hungry times. I was under the needsesity of giving an hard doller for 4 small Indian cakes and sometime could not get it [at] all. Many a time I have gone into a wigwam a[nd] waited for the hommany kettle with the greatest impatience to get a trifle and was as often disappointed.

When we came to Tioga there was some familys on their [way] to Niagara that had left their places. I remember I gave a woman an excellent white shirt for 4 quarts of rye meal and was glad to get it. In one word, let it suffice to say I went through every species of distress to serve my King and country in the best manner I possibly could.

From the banks of Tioga we proceeded to the Standing Stone on the Susquehannah, and from thence to Wylucing. This place was formerly inhabited by the Moraving people. We stayed one night.

Next day, being the 28 of June, 1778, we came to a mill belonging to the Rebles. The Savages burnt the mill and took 3 prisoners, two white men and a Negro whom they afterward murdered in their own camp.

About this time we were much distrest for provision, having nothing to subsist on except a little parched corn stamped at the mill above mentioned. The savages found 5 barrels of flour, but little good was it to us. I know I was very glad to scrape the moulded husks from out of the barrels and secure it for a rainy day, which happened the day after. But in the midst of our distress kind Providence was indeed very, very favourable to us. June 30th at night two men, Wintermots by name, hearing of our approach and distress for provision, came to our releif with 14 head of fat cattle. The blessed moment they arrived we set to work and butchered and divided severally amongst us.

The men above mentioned had a fort at Wioming of their own name, which immediately surrendered to the arms of His Majesty our Gracious Sovereign, under the command of Col. John Butler.

Upon this success a flag was sent to 40 Fort and another to Jenkins to surrender. Jenkins Fort complyed immediately, but Forty thought proper to se it out, for a Mr Stewart told the flag—to wit Mr Tourney, a Leiutenat of the Rangers, and John Phillips, fifer of the same—that he never would give it over to Tories and savages but stand it out to the last and defend it to the last extremity. Upon which the flag told him that he was very sorry, and was setting of[f] to delever his answer to Col. John Butler. Stewart, however, invited the flag to take some spirits, as he looked on him to be a good fellow, and which he refused. He then told him—to wit, the flag—that as he had refused the offer, he or they then in possession of 40 Fort would give them spirits enough before night. Mr. Fourney and Phillips returning and delivering their message, Col. Butler ordered a number of Indians to watch their mote and to hold ourselves in constant readiness.

July 3, 1778, 5 o'clock, P.M., they left their strong holds and proceeded up to give us battle. The fort called Wintermot's above mentioned we set on fire to decoy the enemy, they thinking by this that we were fled. But they soon found it a mistake to their sorrow, for we immediately treed ourselves and secured every spot that was any way advantageous to our designs. When the enemy came within sight of us they fell a-blackguarding of us, calling out aloud, "Come out, ye villianous Tories! Come out, if ye dare, and show your heads, if ye durst, to the brave Continental Sons of Liberty!" (Remark, I call them Sons of Sedition, Schism and Rebellion.)

But we came out to their confusion indeed—for the Indians on the right under the command of Col. Butler and their King Quirxhta entirely surrounded the enemy, and the white men under the command of Quiskkal . . . on the left drove and defeated the enemy on every quarter. They fled to the river and many of them even there where [were] pursued by the savages and shared the same fate as those on the land.

The prisoners that we took told us there where [were] 450 men in the battle and after we went to the 40 Fort . . . to destroy it, they protested not above 45 returned. The loss on our side was one Indian killed and two white men wounded. One of the white men, Willson by name, died of his wound, it having mortefeid. The other recovered. Thus did loyalty and good order that day triumph over confusion and treason, the goodness of our cause, aided and assisted by the blessing of Divine Providence, in some measure help to restore the ancient constitution of our mother country, governed by the best of kings. This I must say: Every man behaved with uncommon bravery. They vied each other for glory to se who should do most in supporting the injured cause of our excellent constitution.

With the defeat of the rebles followed a total confiscation of all their property, such as oxen, cows, horses, hogs, sheep and every other thing of that kind. Thus did Rebellion get a severe shock. The Rebles begged of us to restore them something back, but "No," we replyed. "Remember how you served the peaceable subjects of his Majesty at Tankennick. Remember how you took their property and converted it to Reble porpesses, and their persons fell in your hands, you immediately sent them of[f] to prison clean into Connetticut and left their numerous familys in the utmost distress. And be contented, Rebles, that your lives are still spared and that you have not shared the same fate with your sedetious brethren."

This was the argument we made use of to the surviving Rebles of Wioming. But on the whole my heart was affected for the women and children, who came after us, crying and beseeching us that we would leave them a few cows, and we told them it was against the orders of Col. Butler. However, privately we let them have 4 or 5 cows. . . .

—McGinnis, *Journal*, pp. 12-18.

2. CRÈVECOEUR REFLECTS ON THE TRAGEDY OF WYOMING

The assailants formed a body of about eight hundred men who received their arms from Niagara; the whites under the conduct of Colonel Butler, the Indians under that of Brant. After a fatiguing march, they all met at some of the upper towns of the Susquehanna, and while they were refreshing themselves and providing canoes and every other necessary implement, parties were sent out in different parts of the country. Some penetrated to the west branch and did infinite mischief; it was easy to surprise defenceless, isolated families who fell an easy prey to their enemies. Others approached the New England settlements, where the ravages they committed were not less dreadful. Many families were locked up in their houses and consumed with all their furniture. Dreadful scenes were transacted which I know not how to retrace. This was, however, but the prelude of the grand drama. A few weeks afterwards, the whole settlement was alarmed with the news of the main body coming down the river. Many immediately embarked and retired into the more interior parts of Pennsylvania; the rest immediately retired with their wives and children into the stockade they had erected there some time before.

Meanwhile, the enemy landed at Lackawanna or Kingston, the very place where the stockade was erected. Orders were immediately issued by their commanders for the rest of the militia to resort to them. Some of the most contiguous readily obeyed; distance prevented others. Colonel Butler, seeing they had abandoned their dwellings, proposed to them to surrender and quit the country in a limited time. It was refused by the New England people, who resolved to march out and meet them in the open fields. Their number consisted of five hundred and eighty-two. They found the enemy advantageously situated, but much weaker in numbers, as they thought, than had been reported. This encouraged them; they boldly advanced; and the Indians as sagaciously retreated. Thus they were led on to the fatal spot where all at once they found themselves surrounded. Here some of the New England leaders abandoned them to their evil destiny. Surprised as they were at this bad omen, they still kept their ground and vigorously defended themselves until the Indians, sure of their prey, worked up by the appearance of success to that degree of frenzy which they call courage, dropped their guns and rushed on them with the tomahawk and the spear. The cruel treatment they expected to receive from the wrathful Indians and offended countrymen animated them for a while. They received this first onset with the most undaunted courage, but, the enemy falling upon them with a redoubled fury and on all sides, they broke and immediately looked for safety in flight.

Part of them plunged themselves into the river with the hopes of reaching across, and on this element a new scene was exhibited not less terrible than that which had preceded it. The enemy, flushed with the intoxication of success and victory, pursued them with the most astonishing celerity, and, being naked, had very great advantage over a people encumbered with clothes. This, united with their superiority in the art of swimming, enabled them to overtake most of these unfortunate fugitives, who perished in the river pierced with the lances of the Indians. Thirty-three were so happy as to reach the opposite shores, and for a long time afterwards the carcasses of their companions, become offensive, floated and infested the banks of the Susquehanna as low as Shamokin. The other party, who had taken their flight towards their forts, were all either taken or killed. It is said that those who were then made prisoners were tied to small trees and burnt the evening of the same day.

The body of the aged people, the women and children who were enclosed in the stockade, distinctly could hear and see this dreadful onset, the last scenes of which had been transacted close to the very gates. What a situation these unfortunate people were in! Each wife, each father, each mother could easily distinguish each husband and son as they fell. But in so great, so universal a calamity, when each expected to meet the same fate, perhaps they did not feel so keenly for the deplorable end of their friends and relations. Of what powerful materials must the human heart be composed, which could hold together at so awful a crisis! This bloody scene was no sooner over than a new one arose of a very similar nature. They had scarcely finished scalping the numerous victims which lay on the ground when these fierce conquerors demanded the immediate entrance to the fort. It was submissively granted. Above a hundred of them, decorated with all the dreadful ornaments of plumes and colour of war, with fierce animated eyes, presented themselves and rushed with impetuosity into the middle of the area, armed with tomahawks made of brass with an edge of steel. Tears relieved some; involuntary cries disburdened the oppression of others, a general shriek among the women was immediately heard all around.

What a spectacle this would have exhibited to the eyes of humanity: hundreds of women and children, now widows and orphans, in the most humble attitude, with pale, dejected countenances, sitting on the few bundles they had brought with them; keeping their little unconscious children as close to them as possible; hiding by a mechanical instinct the babies of their breasts; numbers of aged fathers oppressed with the unutterable sorrow; all pale, all trembling, and sinking under the deepest consternation, were looking towards the door—that door through which so many of their friends had just passed, alas! never more to return. Everyone at this awful moment measured his future punishment by the degree of revenge which he supposed to animate the breast of his enemy. The self-accusing consciences of some painted to them each approaching minute as replete with the most terrible fate. Many there were who, recollecting how in the hour of oppression they had insulted their countrymen and the natives, bitterly wept with remorse; others were animated with the fiercest rage. What a scene an eminent painter might have copied from that striking exhibition, if it had been a place where a painter could have calmly sat with the palette in his hands! How easily he might have gathered the strongest expressions of sorrow, consternation, despondency, and despair, by taking from each countenance some strong feature of affright, of terror, and dismay, as it appeared delineated on each face! In how many different modes these passions must have painted themselves according as each individual's temper, ardent or phlegmatic habit, hurried or retarded the circulation of the blood, lengthened or contracted the muscles of his physiognomy!

But now a scene of unexpected humanity ensues. . . . Happily these fierce people, satisfied with the death of those who had opposed them in arms, treated the defenceless ones, the woman and children, with a degree of humanity almost hitherto unparalleled.

In the meantime the loud and repeated war-shouts began to be re-echoed from all parts; the flames of conflagrated houses and barns soon announced to the other little towns the certainty of their country's defeat; these were the first marks of the enemies' triumph. A general devastation ensued, but not such as we read of in the Old Testament where we find men, women, children, and cattle equally devoted to the same blind rage. All the stock, horses, sheep, etc., that could be gathered in the space of a week, were driven to the Indian towns by a party which was detached on purpose. The other little stockades, hearing of the surrender of their capital, opened their gates and submitted to the conquerors. They were all immediately ordered to paint their faces with red, this being the symbol established then, which was to preserve peace and tranquillity while the two parties were mingled together.

Thus perished in one fatal day most of the buildings, improvements, mills, bridges, etc., which had been erected there with so much cost and industry. Thus were dissolved the foundations of a settlement begun at such a distance from the metropolis, disputed by a potent province; the beginning of which had been stained with blood shed in their primitive altercations. Thus the ill-judged policy of these ignorant people and the general calamities of the times overtook them and extirpated them even out of that wilderness which they had come twelve years before to possess and embellish. Thus the grand contest entered into by these colonies with the mother-country has spread everywhere, even from the sea-shores to the last cottages of the frontiers. This most diffusive calamity, on this fatal spot in particular, has despoiled of their goods, chattels, and lands, upwards of forty-five hundred souls, among whom not a third part was ever guilty of any national crime. Yet they suffered every extent of punishment as if they had participated in the political iniquity which was attributed to the leaders of this unfortunate settlement. . . .

The complete destruction of these extended settlements was now the next achievement which remained to be done, in order to finish their rude triumph, but it could not be the work of a few days. Houses, barns, mills, grain, everything combustible to conflagrate; cattle, horses, and stock of every kind to gather; this work demanded a considerable time. The collective industry of twelve years could not well be supposed, in so great an extent, to require in its destruction less than twelve days. . . .

For a considerable time the roads through the settled country were full of these unhappy fugitives, each company slowly returning towards those counties from which they had formerly emigrated. Some others, still more unfortunate than others, were wholly left alone with their children, obliged to carry through that long and fatiguing march the infants of their breasts, now no longer replenished as before with an exuberant milk. Some of them were reduced to the cruel necessity of loading the ablest of them with the little food they were permitted to carry. Many of these young victims were seen bare-headed, bare-footed, shedding tears at every step, oppressed with fatigues too great for their tender age to bear; afflicted with every species of misery, with hunger, with bleeding feet, every now and then surrounding their mother as exhausted as themselves. "Mammy, where are we going? Where is Father? Why don't we go home?"

"Poor innocents, don't you know that the King's Indians have killed him and have burnt our house and all we had? Your Uncle Simon will perhaps give us some bread."

Hundreds were seen in this deplorable condition, yet thinking themselves happy that they had safely passed through the great wilderness, the dangers of which had so much increased the misfortunes of their situation. Here you might see a poor starved horse as weak and emaciated as themselves, given them perhaps by the enemy as a last boon. The poor beast was loaded with a scanty feather-bed serving as a saddle which was fastened on him with withes and bark. On it sat a wretched mother with a child at her breast, another on her lap, and two more placed behind her, all broiling in the sun; accompanied in this pilgrimage of tribulation by the rest of the family creeping slowly along; leading at a great distance behind a heifer once wild and frolicsome but now tamed by want and hunger; a cow, perhaps, with hollow flanks and projecting ribs closed the train; these were the scanty remains of greater opulence. Such was the mournful procession, which for a number of weeks announced to the country through which they passed the sad disaster which had befallen them. The generous farmers sent their wagons to collect as many as they could find, and convey them to the neighbouring county, where the same kindness was repeated. Such was their situation, while the carcasses of their friends were left behind to feed the wolves of that wilderness on which they had so long toiled, and which they had come to improve.

—CRÈVECOEUR, *Sketches of 18th Century America*, pp. 197-206.

III. THE AMERICANS STRIKE BACK: THE SULLIVAN EXPEDITION

The Wyoming and Cherry Valley massacres, together with sporadic attacks on American settlements in the Mohawk and Schoharie valleys, spread terror all through the New York and Pennsylvania borderlands. Unless the Americans were to abandon this hard-won ground to the Tories and their Indian allies—and such an abandonment would have serious military consequences for the Hudson Valley—they would have to mount a counteroffensive against the Six Nations. In the spring of 1779 Washington planned the strategy of such a counteroffensive; when General Gates refused command, it was given to General Sullivan. The plan called for a three-pronged invasion of the Indian country. One column, under Sullivan, was to move up the Susquehanna to the New York border; another, under General James Clinton, was to strike across the Mohawk Valley, down Otsego Lake, and down the Susquehanna; a third, under Colonel Daniel Brodhead, was to advance from Pittsburgh up the Allegheny into the Indian country.

During the summer of 1779 this complicated plan was carried through with qualified success. Clinton—brother to Governor George and father to Governor De Witt Clinton—made his way along the Mohawk, down to Lake Otsego; there he built a dam, then broke it and floated downstream on the swollen waters to join Sullivan, who had come up from Easton, Pennsylvania. Brodhead, as we shall see, invaded from the west but did not join forces with the eastern armies. Altogether Sullivan commanded about 4,000 fighting men, probably the largest of frontier armies during the Revolution. During August he built a fort at Tioga, near the New York boundary. Late that month the combined forces moved out on the offensive; on the twenty-sixth they met an army of Indians and Tories, shattered them, and drove them from the field. They then proceeded systematically to lay waste the country of the Seneca, the Cayuga and the Onondaga, cutting down orchards, burning the standing grain, destroying the Indian "castles." But though the Indians were forced to flee to Niagara and to depend on the bounty of the British, their power was unbroken and they were able to resume the offensive the following year.

Few Revolutionary expeditions were so fully recorded as this one; almost every officer, it seems, kept a journal or a diary. We give here excerpts from three of these journals, and a letter from General Clinton to his brother. Of Lieutenant Barton little is known except that he was from New Jersey. So, too, was Lieutenant—afterwards Major—Erkuries Beatty. Only twenty years old at the time of the Sullivan expedition, he was already a veteran; he had fought at White Plains, Brandywine and Germantown, and suffered through Valley Forge; he was in on the surrender at Yorktown, and stayed on in the army after the war until 1793—one of our earliest professional soldiers. Major Fogg—a graduate of Harvard College and a student in the office of the famous Theophilus Parsons—like Beatty, fought through the whole war; later he achieved some minor prominence in New Hampshire politics.

1. General Sullivan Spreads Terror along the Border

From the Journal of Lieutenant William Barton.

Tuesday, June 8th, 1779.—Took leave of my friends and set out to join the regiment at Wyoming: arrived at Easton the same evening where I found the second and third Jersey regiments and one company of our regiment which was left behind to take care of the baggage belonging to it, and was the next day to proceed with it on horses to Wyoming. . . .

[*July*] *31st.*—The army marched at 12 o'clock, after signals being given by a discharge of cannon from the fort, which were immediately answered from the boats, which carried all the artillery and stores, excepting some kegs of flour, which were carried on horses—Gen. Hand, having previously advanced about one mile, being appointed to the light corps on this expedition. The whole proceeded, only our regiment, which composed the rear guard, having in charge stragglers, cattle, etc., which occasioned us to march very slow. After a tedious march, came to some cleared fields one mile distant from Lackawannah, then 11 P.M. . . . .

[*August*] *26th.*—At half past 12 P.M. began our march with several pieces of cannon, which caused us to move very slowly, as we had formed a hollow square, in which the pack horses and cattle were all driven together with the cannon. This day received information that Col. Broadhead, with six hundred troops, was within forty miles of the Senakee [Seneca] castle, and had destroyed almost one whole tribe of Indians by strategem; he painted his men like Indians, with cutting their hair, etc. We this day likewise received intelligence of Count De Estaing's victory over the British fleet, and having taken the island of St. Vincents. This day marched about four miles and encamped at 5 P.M. near a large flat, on the north-east side of Cahuga Creek. This day's march through a level land, but very poor, excepting the flats, which are good, grown up with grass of great height.

Sunday, 29th.—Proceeded very slowly two miles, occasioned by the roughness of the way, which we had to clear for the artillery, baggage, etc., to pass. Here we halted for one hour and a half, until the artillery, etc., should raise a difficult height, at which time an advanced party of our riflemen discovered the enemy throwing up some works on the other side of a morass, and a difficult place through which we had to pass. It appears this was intended for an ambuscade, it being on a small height, where some logs, etc., were laid up, covered with green bushes; which extended half a mile. On the right was a small town which they had destroyed themselves, making use of the timber, etc., in the above works. After the ground was well reconnoitered, the artillery was advanced on their left. At the same time Gen'l Poor with his brigade was endeavoring to gain their rear around their left; Gen'l Hand's brigade was following in rear of Poor. Our brigade was kept as a reserve, as also Gen'l Clinton's, until their rear should be gained; but they having a party posted on a very considerable height, over which our right flank had to pass, we were discovered by them.

Previous to this, some shells and round shot were thrown among them in their works, which caused them to give several yells, and doubtless intimidated them much. But at this discovery they gave a most hideous yell and quit their works, endeavoring to prevent Gen'l Poor's ascending the height by a loose scattering fire; but our troops, pressing forward with much vigor, made them give way, leaving their dead behind (amounting to eleven or twelve), which were scalped immediately. We likewise took one white man, who appeared to be dead, and was stripped, when an officer came up and examined him, said he was not wounded, gave him a stroke and bade him get up; he immediately rose up and implored mercy, and was kept a prisoner some time. In the evening a Negro was taken. Their number wounded not known. Two or three of ours killed, and thirty-four or five wounded. Among the latter Major Titcomb, Capt. Cloise, and Lt. Allis.

At half after three the firing ceased, and the army proceeded one mile and a half to a considerable town consisting of about twenty huts. The number of the enemy uncertain, but from the best intelligence from the prisoners, the whites were about two hundred, the Indians five. They were commanded by Butler and Brant, who had been waiting some days for our approach. It appears their expectations were great, from their numbers, situation, etc. The prisoners likewise inform us they had been kept on an allowance of seven ears of corn per day each although there is a very great abundance of corn, beans, potatoes, squashes, etc., for several miles on the creek, upon which our whole army has subsisted for days. We had nevertheless to destroy some hundred bushels. Here was found a deal of plunder of theirs, such as blankets, brass kettles, etc.

Monday [September] 13th.—At half past four, morning, proceeded one mile and a half; came to a considerable town, Canesaah, consisting of from sixteen to twenty huts, and halted for the troops to get some refreshment and to build a bridge across a creek; meantime a party of twenty-six men, commanded by Lt. Boyd, was sent out to a town about six miles for discovery, at which place he arrived without molestation. Here an Indian was killed and scalped by his party. He then dispatched two men to inform us what had happened; after they had gone two miles they saw five Indians. They immediately ran back and told the lieutenant what they had seen, who marched on to the place with all speed, when he discovered some few of them who retreated; he pursued and killed one of them. The men then went to scalp him, which caused some dispute who should have it; at the same instant the enemy rose up from their ambuscade, when the action commenced, but they being much superior in numbers, caused him and one or two others to surrender, though not until the rest were all killed and got off.

About the same time, Capt. Lodge, surveyor of the road, with a small party, was discovered about one mile beyond, where the party was building a bridge. They were fired on by the Indians and one of his men wounded. The rest ran off and were pursued so closely that one of them drew out his tomahawk and was close on the heels of one of our men, when a sentinel from the party at the bridge fired at the Indian, which caused them all to run off. Major Poor immediately pushed on, hearing the firing, and found the knapsacks, etc., of the Indians, who had all run off on his approach.

At two o'clock the bridge being completed, we marched on to a town, Casawavalatetah, where we arrived about dark, in expectation of an attack, and encamped. Land continuing very fertile; at both of these places was a large quantity of corn; at the former we did not destroy all.

Tuesday, 14th.—Early in the morning was ordered to destroy the corn, which we did by throwing the ears into the creek, which runs close to the town and is a branch of the Canisee [Genesee] River, which empties into the Lake Ontario about fourteen miles hence. At 2 P.M. marched and crossed the creek, and forded the main branch of Canisee, and proceeded four miles down to the Chenisee castle, where we arrived about four P.M. At this place was Lieut. Boyd and one soldier found, with their heads cut off; the Lieutenants head lay near his body; his body appeared to have been whipped and pierced in many different places. The others head was not found. A great part of his body was skinned, leaving the ribs bare.

Wednesday, 15th.—The whole army employed until 3 o'clock in gathering the corn, and burning it in their huts, which were in number about eighty or a hundred, and much the largest quantity of corn I have yet seen in any one place since I have been out. Here came in a white woman with a young child, who was almost starved, having made her escape two or three nights before from the enemy. She informs us they were in great confusion, the Indians some times agreeing to treat with us, but it was made void by Butler and Johnson, who promised to supply them with provisions. One of the Indians at this cocked his gun and was about to shoot Johnson, but was prevented. This woman was taken from Wyoming in '77, where her husband was killed. At half past two P.M. we began our march for returning, and proceeded as far as the fording place of the creek, crossed onto, encamping near the town Casawavalatetah. This place very rich and good. Distance from here to Niagaree said to be about eighty miles, whither the Indians carry all their furs, etc., for sale. They go and return in canoes in five or six days.

Thursday, 23rd.—Proceeded to Catharine town, at which place we arrived at twelve o'clock, finding the old squaw here which was left as we went up, with a paper that had many lines of Indian wrote underneath, a protection that was given her by the general, the contents of which I did not hear. We likewise found the corpse of a squaw who appeared to have been shot three or four days, which lay in a mud hole; supposed to have came there since our departure to take care of the old brute. Who killed her I cannot ascertain, but it is generally believed to be three men of ours who were sent up from Tioga express a few days before. At our departure from here the General ordered there should be left a keg of pork and some biscuit, etc., for the old creature to subsist on, although it was so scare an article that no officer under the rank of a field officer had tasted any since leaving Tioga, and a very scant allowance of half a pound of poor beef and a like quantity of flour.

Proceeded at two o'clock about three miles through a swamp of exceeding bad road for the pioneers to repair them and halted for the army's arrival, which was at five o'clock P.M., on a small flat of cleared ground, and encamped. Distance of day's march from 16 to 18 miles. This evening we, the advance guard, had orders to march at reveille for the purpose of having the roads repaired through a most notorious swamp of five miles, and appearance of rain, which would render the swamp almost impassable.

Sunday, 26th.—Still remained at Fort Reed. In the morning there was a detachment of three hundred men ordered to be sent up the river Kihuga [Cayuga] for the purpos of destroying a town or two, but was defered by reason of rain coming. At one in the afternoon the detachment under Col. Durbin, that came down the south of the Kihuga lake, arrived with two squaws, and inform us they burnt three or four towns. They likewise say they found one Indian and one other squaw, the latter so old as not to be able to be brought off; the Indian man young but decrepid to such a degree that he could not walk. I have since heard it said, the Colonel left one house standing for them to stay in, and would not suffer them to be hurt, but some of the soldiers taking an opportunity when not observed set the house on fire, after securing and making the door fast. The troops having got in motion and marched some distance, the house was consumed together with the savages, in spite of all exertions.

Monday, 27th.—The morning clear. The detachment yesterday detained by rain has gone out with an addition of two hundred men more, and divided into two parties, one under the command of Col. Courtland, and the other under Col. D'Hart; one going up the north side, and the other the south of the Kihuga Creek. In the evening the detachments came in, after destroying a considerable quantity of corn, etc.

Tuesday, 28th.—The same detachment again sent out an account of a small party being sent farther up, who say there is a large quantity of corn yet standing on the creek. About ten o'clock A.M. the detachment under Col. Butler came in from the north of Kihuga Lake, who say they have destroyed vast quantities of corn and several very considerable of their towns. . . .

—Cook, ed., *Journals of Expedition of Sullivan*, pp. 3-13.

2. GENERAL SULLIVAN SMASHES BRANT AT NEWTOWN

James Clinton to George Clinton.

New Town 5 miles above Chemung, August 30, 1779

Dear Brother, I have just time to inform you that the army under Genl. Sullivan arrived on this ground yesterday evening, in perfect helth and spirits. On Thursday last the 26th we left Tioga, but being incumbered with a train of artillery and waggons and the roads being very bad, owing to an heavy rain the preceeding day, together with other circumstances attending the first day's movements, we did not march more than three miles and encamped. Friday we proceeded on our march about eight o'clock in the morning, but my brigade, which formed the rear or second line of the army, had not marched from their ground more than two miles before the infantry in front halted at a narrow defile formed by the jutting out of the mountain to the river. This defile which was near half a mile in length and would at first sight have been judged impassible, particularly to artillery, etc., detain the army so long that it was near ten o'clock at night before the rear of the main body, consisting of Poor's and Maxwell's brigades, had passed. As it was then dark, and as the cattle had not yet passed it, I judged it most proper not to attempt it that night, but marched back about a mile and encamped on tolerable good ground. Saturday I decamped and joined the army at Chemung about twelve o'clock. This town, which is about twelve miles from Tioga, had been destroyed by Genl. Sullivan immediately on his arrival at Tioga, together with a large quantity of corn, beans, etc., preserving only one field, consisting of about forty acres, for the use of the army on their arrival, and which they effectually consumed and destroyed.

Altho we had every reason to expect the enemy would have attempted to prevent our progress and retard our march, from the amaizing advantages Nature had liberally furnished them with, yet they never gave us the least opposition, or ever made their appearance, except a small party who fired upon and killed and wounded a few of Genl. Hand's advanced guard on the former attempt to destroy the settlement.

Sunday the army was put in motion about nine o'clock with the greatest circumspection and caution. Our scouts had brought intelligence the preceeding evening that the enemy were discovered at about five miles distance, supposed to be at or near New Town, and from the magnitude of their fires appeared to be in considerable force; that the sound of their axes were heard distinctly, which induced us to believe they intended either to throw up works or obstruct the march of the army, untill they could form a plan to attack our flanks or rear.

This in fact appeared to be their intention, and if we had proceeded as they expected, in all probability we should have been very severely handled. About ten o'clock a scattering fire commenced between some of their scouts and a few of our rifle men and volunteers, when the former gave way, and the latter proceeded untill they plainly discovered their works which were very extensive, tho' not impregnable. As our design was not to drive them, but to surround or bring them to a fair open action, the army halted, and a council being called, it was concluded that the artillery, supported by Genl. Hand with the infantry and rifle corps, should commence the action, previously allowing sufficient time for Poor's and my brigade to gain their right flank, while Maxwell's and the covering party under Col. Ogden might gain their left.

About one o'clock Col. Proctor commenced a very warm cannonade upon their works, which continued near two hours, in which time we attempted to compleat our march upon their flanks, but from the very thick swamps and rough country thro' which we were to pass we were in some measure prevented. The enemy, finding their situation in their lines rather uncomfortable and finding we did not intend to storm them, abandoned them some time before the infantry discouvered it, and immediately proceeded to join the remaining half of their force who were posted on a hill, and attack our right flank as we expected. Genl. Poor who was near a quarter of a mile on the left of my front, had assended a considerable mountain about half way, which was very steep, when he discouvered them and received their fire accompanied by the war whoop, but tho' his troops were considerably fatigued with ascending the mountain under their heavy packs, yet they pushed up in the face of their fire, driving them from tree to tree untill they fled with the utmost precipitation, leaving their pack and blankets behind them, etc. in order to take off their dead and wounded, which must be very considerable as they left nine Indians on the field whom they could not carry off. My brigade, which had just reached the foot of the hill when the firing commenced, pushed up with such ardor that many of them almost fainted and fell down with excessive heat and fatigue, for the ground was so steep that no person could ride up.

During the action which lasted from the first to the last near six hours, we had three privates killed and forty wounded, among whom were three officers, Major Titcomb, Capt. Clause and Lt. McCauly, who is since dead of his wounds; there are few of the wounded dangerous.

The enemy's loss must be considerable; nine of them were found dead on the field, and many of them must have been wounded, as they were tracked some three miles by the blood, while others were seen sent off in canoes.

After the action we descended the hill, and encamped on a most beautiful plain, where we refreshed ourselves after the fatigues of the day, which were neither few nor small.

Monday this day, eight hundred men have been employed in destroying all the corn, etc., etc., etc., about the town, which is by far the finest I ever saw in my life; upwards of six thousand bushells have been cut down and piled up, the more effectually to destroy it. And such is the spirit of the troops that they have requested the General to put them upon half allowance of bread and beef, as long as they can supply themselves with corn and beans, in order that they may lengthen out the campaign and the more effectually to compleat the business they were sent upon, so that we have the strongest assurances to hope that under the smiles of Heaven we shall be able to work out a lasting blessing to our country.

I had almost forgot to tell you that we took two prisoners, a Negro and a Torie, one Hoghtailer from the Helder Barrack, who inform us that the enemy's force consisted of about two hundred and fifty white men, comanded by Col. and Capt. Butler, and about five hundred Indians commanded by Brandt; that they had eat nothing but corn for eight days past, except a small proportion of five small cattle; that before the corn was fit to roast they fed upon herbs and roots which they found in the woods.

We shall send off our wounded down to Tioga in boats brought up with provisions, but we have not five sick men in the whole army.

I beg you will receive this scrawl, as rough as the country thro' which we march, without reflecting on the accuracy of my aid de camp, who would have transcribed it, but the express is waiting with the utmost impatience. I am with perfect esteem, dear Brother, Yours sincerely,

JAMES CLINTON
—CLINTON, *Public Papers*, V, 224-228.

3. "THE NESTS ARE DESTROYED BUT THE BIRDS ARE STILL ON THE WING"

Account of Jeremiah Fogg, major with General Sullivan.

[*September*] *30th, 1779.* Arrived at Tioga about 3 o'clock, where we were saluted by thirteen cannon from the fort. From hence we have water carriage to Wyoming, a most fortunate affair as our horses are worn down and our men are naked.

Although we are, now, one hundred and twenty miles from peaceful inhabitants, yet we consider ourselves at home, and the expedition ended; having fulfilled the expectations of our country by beating the enemies and penetrating and destroying their whole country. The undertaking was great and the task arduous. The multiplicity of disappointments, occasioning a long delay at the beginning, foreboded a partial, if not a total frustration of our design; but the unbounded ambition and perseverance of our commander and army led him to the full execution contrary to our most sanguine expectations.

The army marched from Tioga, with twenty pounds of beef and twenty seven pounds of flour per man, with which they marched twenty days out through an enemy's country yet unexplored with five pieces of artillery; having a road to clear, through swamps and over mountains a hundred and fifty miles; after having marched three hundred from their winter quarters; a cruel, subtle and desultory foe to contend with; void of hospital stores and conveniences for the sick and wounded; scarcely able to move for want of means of transportation. One battle, at the extent of our route, must have been attended with consequences such as nothing but the event itself could ascerain; yet a march of three hundred miles was performed, a battle was fought and a whole country desolated in thirty days.

But let us not arrogate too much, for "The battle is not to the strong" is a proverb fully verified in this expedition; the special hand and smiles of Providence being so apparently manifested that he who views the scene with indifference is worse than an infidel. The dimest eye must observe through the whole a succession of most unfortunate events. The very evils that at first predicted a defeat were a chain of causes in our favor. (I mean our delay.) Had we marched when we wished we could not have had a general engagement; for a great scarcity amounting almost to a famine the preceding year had prevented their embodying until the growth of the present crop, and we must therefore have been harassed daily by small parties much to our disadvantage. The artillery, which at first seemed a clog and totally useless, served a noble purpose. The action being general, their total rout together with the thunder of our artillery impressed them with such a terrific idea of our importance that a universal panic struck both the sachem and the warrior, each finding full employment in removing his little ones from threatening danger.

The place of action was likewise remarkable, having water carriage for our wounded. Not a single gun was fired for eighty miles on our march out, or an Indian seen on our return. Then we expected the greatest harassment—a hundred might have saved half their country by retarding us until our provisions were spent; and a like number hanging on our rear in the return would have occasioned the loss of much baggage and taught us an Indian dance. Their corn and vegetables were half our support, which we should have been deprived of had our march been earlier. And to say no more, the extraordinary continuance of fair weather has infinitely facilitated our expectations, having never been detained a single day, nor has there been an hour's rain since the thirtieth day of August.

The question will naturally arise, What have you to show for your exploits? Where are your prisoners? To which I reply that the rags and emaciated bodies of our soldiers must speak for our fatigue, and when the querist will point out a mode to tame a partridge, or the expediency of hunting wild turkeys with light horse, I will show them our prisoners. The nests are destroyed, but the birds are still on the wing.

—Cook, ed., *Journals of Expedition of Sullivan*, p. 101.

4. THE AMERICANS CARRY FIRE AND SWORD TO THE ONONDAGA

From the Journal of Erkuries Beatty, lieutenant with General Sullivan.

Kanadasgo. Wednesday 8th. This morning came out orders that the men was to remain here all day and for the men to clean their pieces likewise, for all the sick, lame, etc., to return to Tyoga properly officered. After 10 oclock Major Parr with the rifle corps and the cohoun was going up the lake to a little town called Kushay to destroy it. I with a number of others went volunteers and got there about 12 o'clock, found it about 8 miles from camp and the town opposite to where we lay two nights ago. The town consisted of about 15 houses tolerable well built and all together we got here 5 horses and a great number of potatoes, apples, peaches, cucumbers, watermelons, fowls, etc., and found a great quantity of corn here which we went about to destroy, after burning the houses, but our party being to[o] small Major Parr sent for a reinforcement to camp. We all lay under a bark hutt to night or shed. I believe the Indians had left it the same time they left Kanadasago. It lies on the banks of the lake, very prettyly situated, which is 4 miles wide here.

Tuesday 14th. The whole army was under arms this morning an hour before day and remained so till sunrise; about 7 oclock fatigue parties was sent out to destroy corn, which was there in great abundance, and beans. About 12 o'clock we marched, crossed over the branch of the Jinasee River and came upon a very beautiful flat of great extent growing up with wild grass higher in some places than our heads. We marched on this flat 2 mile and crossed the Jinesee River, which is about as big as the Tyoga but very crooked. Left the flats and marched thro the woods 3 mile and arrived at Chenesee Town, which is the largest we have yet seen; it lies in a crook of the river on extraordinary good land, about 70 houses, very compact and very well built, and about the same number of out houses in cornfields, etc. On entering the town we found the body of Lt. Boyd and another rifle man in a most terrible mangled condition. They was both stripped naked and their heads cut off, and the flesh of Lt. Boyds head was intirely taken of[f] and his eyes punched out. The other mans hed was not there. They was stabed, I supose, in 40 diferent places in the body with a spear and great gashes cut in their flesh with knifes, and Lt. Boyds privates was nearly cut of[f] and hanging down, his finger and toe nails was bruised of[f], and the dogs had eat part of their shoulders away; likewise a knife was sticking in Lt. Boyds body. They was imediately buried with the honour of war.

Wensday 15th. The whole army went out this morning 6 oclock to destroy corn and was out till 12 o'clock. There was here the greatest quantity of corn and beans here of any of the towns. Some of it we husked and threw in the river; the rest we carried to the houses and burned; the whole we totally destroyed. About 10 o'clock we received orders to begin our march home, which we did leaving the towns in flames. To day there was a white woman and child came in to us but I believe brought no intelligence of consequence. Marched over the Chenesee River and encamped after dark on the edge of the flats nigh to Cossawauloughly town.

Thursday 16th. The whole army was out this morning cutting corn which we left as we was going. Our brigade crossed the river to cut, which we did, and I believe there was a great quantity destroyed and some houses burnt. Marched of[f] about 10 o'clock in the following line of march: an advance guard of 100 men in front, Genl. Clintons brigade following in 4 columns, the other troops marching as usual, Genl. Hands brigade fetching up the rear, 2 pieces of artillery in the rear of him and the rifle men in the rear of the whole, the cohoun with the advance guard. Capt. Henderson with 60 men went in front of the army to bury the dead, and just as we came up he was a-going to bury 14 bodies in a most terrible mangled condition. They was buryed with the honour of war. Encamped to night at Adjutse. . . .

Tuesday 28th. This morning all the sick was ordered to go down in boats to Tiogo, and the lame to ride down the worst horses. The same detachment that was up the Tyoga yesterday was ordered up again to day and a very large comand was ordered to go down the Tyoga to destroy corn. Just as our detachment paraded Col. Butlers command came in and informed us that they had destroyed on the east side of the Cauga Lake three capital towns and a great number of scattering houses and destroyed a very great quantity of corn. The houses, I am informed, was much larger and better built than any we have yet seen, and it was a very old sittled country as they had great number of apple and peach trees which they likewise cut down. Our detachment marched up the Tyoga 5 miles above where we was yesterday and burnt 2 or 3 houses and destroyed a little corn on each side of the river. A little before night I went up the river about 5 mile farther but found no corn and returned, where we found them encamped in one of the corn fields but had no tents.

—Cook, ed., *Journals of Expedition of Sullivan*, pp. 30-35.

IV. THE AMERICANS STRIKE BACK: THE BRODHEAD EXPEDITION

The western Pennsylvania frontier was the scene of intermittent warfare all through the Revolution. Sparsely settled, it offered no substantial population on which to draw for defense, and a good many men of fighting age had joined the armies of the East, or those which George Rogers Clark from time to time recruited. The Allegheny frontier was exposed to attack by the Seneca from the north, by the Shawnee and the Miami from the west. In 1778 the Scots Highlander, Lachlan McIntosh of Charleston, was given command of the Western Department with headquarters at Pittsburgh. He did little but quarrel with his subordinates, and in the spring of 1779 he was directed to turn the command over to Daniel Brodhead. Brodhead was almost equally quarrelsome, but did display some energy. With some 600 men he advanced up the Allegheny to the New York border, through country "almost impassable by reason of the stupendous heights and frightful declivities," scattered a slight Indian opposition, burned Indian villages and fields of standing grain, and then returned to Fort Pitt—a march of 400 miles in 33 days without the loss of a man, something of a record in the Revolution.

We give here a letter from General McIntosh describing conditions on the Pennsylvania frontier, an account of the Brodhead expedition, and a report of a council meeting with the Wyandots—more commonly known as Hurons —of the Ohio country.

1. "Things Have Taken a Turn Much for the Worse"

General Lachlan McIntosh to George Washington.

March 12, 1779

The emigration down the Ohio from this quarter I fear will depopulate it altogether, unless I have orders to put a timely stop to it immediately. It is thought that near one half of what remain here will go down to Kentucky, the Falls or the Illinois, as they say themselves, this spring. Their design of securing land is so great, notwithstanding the danger of this country, they will go, etc.

I am sorry to inform you that, contrary to my expectations, things have taken a turn here much for the worse since I wrote you the 13th of January. The 30th of that month I received an express from Col. Gibson, informing me that one Simon Girty, a renegade among many others from this place, got a small party of Mingoes, a name by which the Six Nations, or rather Seneca Tribe, is known among the Western Indians, and waylaid Capt. Clark of the 8th Pennsylvania Regiment with a seargent and 14 privates, about three miles this side of Fort Laurens, as they were returning after escorting a few supplies from that post, and made Clark retreat to the fort again after killing two and taking one of his men with his saddle bags and all his letters.

Upon hearing this unexpected intelligence, I immediately sent for Cols. Crawford and Brodhead to advise with them upon the best method of supplying that garrison with provisions, of which it was very short, and we had barely horses enough fit for service to transport a sufficient quantity of flour over the mountains for our daily consumption, and scarce of forage for them, altho' they were most worn down. It was, therefore, thought most eligible upon that and other accounts to send a supply by water up Muskingum River by Maj. Taylor, who was charged with that duty. . . .

The 26th of February a scalping party killed and carried off 18 persons, men, women and children, upon the branches of Turtle Creek, 20 miles east of this, upon the Pennsylvania road, which was the first mischief done in the settlements since I marched for Tuscarawas, and made me apprehensive now that the savages were all inimically inclined, and struck the inhabitants of Westmoreland with such a panick that a great part of them were moving away. While I was endeavoring to rouse the militia, and contriving by their assistance to retaliate and make an excursion to some Mingo Towns upon the branches of Alleghany River who were supposed to have done the mischief, a messenger came to me the 3d of March instant, who slipt out of Fort Laurens in the night of Sunday the 28th February—by whom Col. Gibson would not venture to write—and informed me that on the morning of Tuesday, the 23d February, a waggoner who was sent out of the fort for the horses to draw wood, and 18 men to guard him, were fired upon, and all killed and scalped in sight of the fort, which the messenger left invested and besieged by a number of Wyandotts, Chippewas, Delawares, etc.; and in the last account I had from them, which made me very unhappy, as they were so short of provision, and out of my power to supply them with any quantity, or, if I had it, with men for an escort, since Major Taylor went, who I thought now was inevitably lost; and if I had both, there were no horses to carry it, or forage to feed them, without which they cannot subsist at this season.

In this extreme emergency and difficulty, I earnestly requested the lieutenants of the several countys on this side of the mountains to collect all of the men, horses, provisions and forage they could at any price and repair to Beaver Creek [Fort McIntosh] on Monday next, the 15th instant, in order to march on that or the next day to Tuscarawas; and if they would not be prevailed on to turn out, I was determined with such of the Continental troops as are able [to] march, and all the provisions we have, at all events to go to the relief of Fort Laurens; upon the support of which I think the salvation of this part of the country depends.

I have yet no intelligence from the country that I can depend on. Some say the people will turn out on this occasion with their horses; others, that mischievous persons influenced by our disgusted staff are discouraging them as much as possible. But I am now happily relieved by the arrival of Major Taylor here, who returned with 100 men and 200 kegs of flour. He was six days going up about 20 miles of Musking[um] River, the waters were so high and stream so rapid; and as he had above 130 miles more to go, he judged it impossible to relieve Col. Gibson in time, and therefore returned, having lost two of his men sent to flank him upon the shore, who were killed and scalpt by some warriors coming down Muskingum River, and I have my doubts of our only pretended friends, the Delawares of Cooshocking, as none other are settled upon that water.

I have the honor to enclose you the last return from Col. Brodhead at Beaver Creek. . . .

—KELLOGG, *Frontier Advance*, 240-242.

2. COLONEL BRODHEAD SPREADS DESOLATION ALONG THE ALLEGHENY

Pittsburgh, September 16, 1779

Colonel Brodhead, who commanded a party from Fort Pitt, has penetrated the Indian country, lying on the Alleghany River, one hundred and eighty miles, burnt ten of the Mingo, Munsey and Seneca towns in that quarter, containing one hundred and sixty-five houses, and destroyed all the fields of corn, computed to be five hundred acres, with the only loss on our side three men slightly wounded. Forty-three of their warriors were met by Lieutenant Harding and an advance party of twenty-two men, who attacked the savages and routed them, killed five on the spot and took all their canoes and blankets.

A gentleman who attended Colonel Brodhead, gives the following particular account of the expedition:—The many savage barbarities and horrid depredations committed by the Seneca and Munsey nations upon the western frontiers had determined Colonel Brodhead, as the most effectual way to prevent such hostilities in future, and revenge the past, to carry the war into their own country and strike a decisive blow at their towns.

On the 11th of August, our little army, consisting of only six hundred and five rank and file, marched from Pittsburg with one month's provision. At Mahoning, fifteen miles above the Old Kittanning, we were detained four days by the excessive rains, from whence (leaving the river, which flows in a thousand manners) we proceeded by a blind path leading to Cuscushing, through a country almost impassable by reason of the stupendous heights and frightful declivities, with a continued range of craggy hills, overspread with fallen timber, thorns and underwood; here and there an intervening valley, whose deep, impenetrable gloom has always been impervious to the piercing rays of the warmest sun. As Cuscushing (which is fifteen miles above Venango) we crossed the Alleghany and continued our route upon its banks. But here our march was rendered still more difficult by the mountains, which jutted close upon the river, forming a continued narrow defile, allowing us only the breadth of an Indian path to march upon.

In the midst of these defiles, our advanced party, consisting of fifteen white men and eight Delawares, discovered between thirty and forty warriors land-ing from their canoes, who, having also seen part of our troops, immediately stripped themselves and prepared for action. Lieutenant Harding, who com-manded our advance, disposed his men in a semi-circular form, and began the attack with such irresistible fury, tomahawk in hand, that the savages could not long sustain the charge, but fled with the utmost horror and precipitation, some plunging themselves into the river, and others, favored by the thickness of the bushes, made their escape on the main, leaving five dead on the field, without any loss on our side except three men slightly wounded.

Upon the first alarm, supposing it to be more serious, the army was arranged for fight; both officers and men, enraged at their former cruelties, animated by the calmness, resolution and intrepidity of the commandant, showed the utmost ardor to engage; and had the action been general, we had every pros-pect of the most ample success from a brave commander at the head of brave men.

Continuing our march, we arrived the same day at Buchan, where, leaving our baggage, stores, etc., under a guard, we proceeded to their towns with the utmost despatch, which we found at the distance of about twenty miles further, with extensive cornfields on both sides of the river, and deserted by the inhabitants on our approach. Eight towns we set in flames and committed their pagod and war posts to the river. The corn, amounting in the whole to near six hundred acres, was our next object, which in three days we cut down and piled into heaps, without the least interruption from the enemy.

Upon our return, we several times crossed a creek about ten miles above Venango, remarkable for an oily liquid which oozes from the sides and bottom of the channel and the adjacent springs, much resembling British oil, and if applied to woolen cloth, burns in an instant.

After burning the old towns of Conauwago and Mahusquachinkocken, we arrived at Pittsburg, the fourteenth instant, with the scalps we had taken and three thousand dollars' worth of plunder; having, in the course of thirty-three days, completed a march of near four hundred miles, through a country the Indians had hitherto thought impenetrable by us, and considered as a sufficient barrier for the security of their towns; and, indeed, nothing but the absolute necessity of such a measure and a noble sprit of enterprise could be a sufficient inducement to undertake so arduous a task and encounter those difficulties and obstacles which require the most consummate fortitude to surmount.

—MOORE, *Diary of the American Revolution*, II, 216-219.

3. THE WYANDOT TREAT FOR PEACE BUT BRODHEAD IS NOT CONTENT

A. THE WYANDOTS' SPEECH TO COLONEL DANIEL BRODHEAD, HEADQUARTERS, PITTSBURGH, SEPTEMBER 17, 1779

The Speech of Doonyontat, the Wyandot Chief, to Maghingwe Keeshuch:
Brother, listen to me!
Brother, it grieves me to see you with the tears in your eyes. I know it is the fault of the English.

DEATH OF PULASKI AT SAVANNAH

BATTLE OF KING'S MOUNTAIN

Brother, I wipe away all those tears, and smooth down your hair, which the English and the folly of my young men has ruffled.

Now, *my brother*, I have wiped away all the stains from your clothes, and smoothed them where my young men had ruffled them, so that you may now put on your hat, and sit with that ease and composure which you would desire.

(Four strings of white wampum)

Brother, listen to the Huron Chiefs!

Brother, I see you all bloody by the English and my young men. I now wipe away all those stains and make you clean.

Brother, I see your heart twisted, and neck and throat turned to the one side, with the grief and vexation which my young men have caused, all which disagreeable sensations I now remove, and restore you to your former tranquillity, so that now you may breathe with ease, and enjoy the benefit of your food and nourishment.

Brother, your ears appear to be stopped, so that you cannot listen to your brothers when they talk of friendship. That deafness I now remove, and all stoppage from your ears, that you may listen to the friendly speeches of your brothers, and they may sink deep into your heart.

(Seven strings of white wampum)

Brother, listen to me!

When I look around me, I see the bones of our nephews lie scattered and unburied.

Brother, I gather up the bones of all our young men on both sides, in this dispute, without any distinction of party.

Brother, I have now gathered up all the bones of our relations on both sides, and will bury them in a large deep grave, and smooth it over so that there shall not be the least sign of bones, or any thing to raise any grief or anger in our minds hereafter.

Brother, I have now buried the bones of all our and your relations very deep. You very well know that there are some of your flesh and blood in our hands prisoners: I assure you that you shall see them all safe and well.

(Eight strings of white wampum)

Brother, I now look up to where our Maker is, and think there is still some darkness over our heads, so that God can hardly see us, on account of the evil doings of the King over the great waters. All these thick clouds, which have [been] raised on account of that bad King, I now entirely remove, that God may look and see in our treaty of friendship, and be a witness to the truth and sincerity of our intentions.

(Four strings of white wampum)

Brother, As God puts all our hearts right, I now give thanks to God Almighty, to the chief men of the Americans, to my old father the King of France, and to you, Brother, that we can now talk together on friendly terms, and speak our sentiments without interruption.

(Four strings of black and white wampum)

Brother, you knew me before you saw me and that I had not drawn away my hand from yours, as I sent word last year by Captain White Eyes.

Brother, I look up to Heaven, and call God Almighty to witness to the truth of what I say, and that it really comes from my heart.

Brother, I now tell you that I have forever thrown off my Father the English, and will never give him any assistance; and there are some amongst all the nations that think the same things that I do, and I wish they would all think so. . . .

Brother, I now take a firmer hold of your hand than before, and beg that you will take pity upon other nations who are my friends, and if any of them should incline to take hold of your hand, I request that you would comply and receive them into friendship.

(A black belt of eleven rows)

Brother, listen! I tell you to be cautious, as I think you intend to strike the man near to where I sit [the chief refers to an anticipated attack upon Detroit by the American forces], not to go the nighest way to where he is, lest you frighten the owners of the lands who are living through the country between this and that place.

Brother, you now listen to me, and one favour I beg of you is that when you drive away your enemies you will allow me to continue in possession of my property, which if you grant will rejoice me.

Brother, I would advise you, when you strike the man near where I sit, to go by water, as it will be the easiest and best way.

Brother, if you intend to strike, one way is to go up the Allegheny and by Prisquille; another way is to go down this river and up the Wabash.

Brother, the reason why I mentioned the road up the river is that there will be no danger of your being discovered until you are close upon them, but on the road down the river you will be spied.

Brother, now I have told you the way by Prisquille, and that it is the boundary between us and your enemies; if you go by Wabash your friends will not be surprised.

Brother, you must not think that what I have said is only my own thoughts, but the opinion of all the Huron Chiefs, and I speak in behalf of them all. If you grant what favours I have asked of you, all our friends and relations will be thankful and glad as far as they can hear all round.

Brother, the reason why I have pointed out these two roads is that when we hear you are in one of them we will know your intentions without further notice, and the Huron Chiefs desired me particularly to mention it that they may meet you in your walk, and tell you what they have done, who are your enemies and who are your friends, and I in their name request a pair of colors to shew we have joined in friendship. . . .

(Fourteen strings of black wampum)

B. COLONEL DANIEL BRODHEAD'S SPEECH TO DOONYONTAT,
THE WYANDOT CHIEF, SEPTEMBER 18TH, 1779

Maghingwe Keeshuch to Doonyontat, principal chief of the Wyandots
Brother, yesterday I had the pleasure to hear you speak. But when I had heard

all, and you had taken no notice of what I mentioned to you before against the English, I could not tell what to think.

Brother, the Chiefs of the Wyondats have lived too long with the English to see things as they ought to do. They must have expected when they were councilling that the Chief they sent to this council fire would find the Americans asleep. But the sun which the Great Spirit has set to light this island discovers to me that they are much mistaken.

(Four strings of white and black wampum)

Brother, I will tell you why they are mistaken: they must have thought that it was an easy matter to satisfy us, after doing all the mischief they could. They must have heard that the English were getting weaker and the Americans stronger, and that a few flattering words would, with giving up our prisoners, secure to them their lives, the lives of their women and children, and their lands and the wicked Shawnese who have so often embrued their hands in the blood of the Americans; and that in my military operations they had a right to mark out the road I should march on.

(Six strings of white and black wampum)

Brother, I, however, thank you for wiping away the blood and burying the bones of our young men, and for casting off that bad father the King of Britain over the great lake. . . .

(Three strings of white wampum)

Brother, I will now tell you what I conceive to be right, and I will leave it to all the world to judge it. I think the Nations you mention and wish me to receive into friendship, ought to send hostages to me. As I said before, unless they have killed and taken as many from the English and their allies as they have killed and taken from the Americans, and return whatever they have stolen from their brothers, together with their flesh and blood, and on every occasion join us against their enemies—upon these terms, which are just, they and their posterity may live in peace and enjoy their property without disturbance from their brethren of this island, so long as the sun shines or the waters run.

(A black belt—rows)

Brother, I have now spoke from my heart. I am a warrior as well as a councillor; my words are few, but what I say I will perform. And I must tell you that if the Nations will not do justice, they will not be able, after the English are driven from this island, to enjoy peace or property.

(Four strings black wampum)

Brother, when I go to war, I will take my choice of roads; if I meet my friends I shall be glad to see them, and if I meet my enemies I shall be ready to fight them.

Brother, you told you had not yet spoken to the Shawnese. You likewise say that you had not yet let slip my hand; if so, why did you not speak to them? They have heard their grandfathers the Delawares, and they have heard me. I sent them a good talk, but they threw it into the fire.

Now, *Brother*, I must tell you that I cannot now prevent the Shawnese being struck. Col. Clark, I hear, is gone against them and will strike them before I

can send to him to call him back; but if the Shawnese do what is right, as I
have told you, they should enjoy peace and property. This belt confirms my
words.

(A white and black belt—rows)
—KELLOGG, ed., *Frontier Retreat*, 67-72.

V. THE FINAL CAMPAIGNS ALONG THE NEW YORK
BORDERLANDS

*Sullivan's expedition had checked but not defeated the Tories and their
Indian allies, and there were still two more years of war along the battered
New York frontier. In April 1780 Brant destroyed the little village of Har-
persfield and attacked the Schoharie forts. The next month Sir John Johnson
came down the Champlain, destroyed Johnstown, and swept on to the Mohawk Valley settlements. The American reaction was feeble, and in August
the British renewed their assault, burning Canajoharie, on the Mohawk, and
once again ravaging Schoharie. In September Johnson collected a formidable
force at Montreal, ferried them across to Oswego, and marched on Unadilla
on the upper Susquehanna; here he joined forces with Brant, and together
they ravaged at will the Mohawk and Schoharie valleys. Finally the Americans
collected a force under General Robert Van Rensselaer, advanced on the
enemy and dispersed him, but Van Rensselaer lacked the resolution to pursue
the defeated foe, and the campaign was, once again, inconclusive. The following spring, 1781, Brant and Johnson and Walter Butler were once again on
the warpath, spreading death and destruction almost at will. Not until the
fall did the Americans strike back with any effectiveness. Then Governor
Clinton called on that sturdy frontier fighter, Colonel Marinus Willett, to
save the border. Willett met the enemy at Johnstown, defeated them, and
pursued them relentlessly to the gates of Oswego.*

1. AN INCONCLUSIVE FIGHT AT CANAJOHARIE

A. "THE ENEMY HAVE BURNT THE WHOLE OF SCHOHARY"

Lieutenant Colonel V. Veeder to General Robert Van Rensselaer.

Lower Fort Schohary, October 17, 1780

Dear Sir, The enemy have burnt the whole of Schohary; the first fire was
discovered about the middle fort 8 o'clock this morning; they passed by this
post on both sides at 4 o'clock this afternoon; they took the whole of their
booty and moved down to Harmen Sitneys; they have fired two swivel shoots
thro' the roof of the church. I have sent three scouts to make some discoveries
about the middle fort at different times this day, and none have as yet returned;
no express has arrived at this post from either fort; by what we have seen of
the enemy we suppose their force to be between 5 or 600, mostly regulars and
Tories.

—CLINTON, *Public Papers*, VI, 303.

B. GENERAL VAN RENSSELAER IS APPREHENSIVE

Robert Van Rensselaer to Governor George Clinton.

> Canajoharie opposite Frey's, October 18, 1780

Sir, this morning about nine I arrived so near the enemy's rear as to afford me a prospect of engaging them before noon. They have, however, by the celerity of their movements effected their escape to Stone Arabia, part of which is now in flames and the whole will probably share the same fate before I can possibly support the distressed inhabitants. I intend to ford the river immediately and march in quest of them, but harrassed and fatigued as my force is by a long march, I am apprehensive I shall not be able to pursue them with that dispatch which is necessary to overtake them. No exertion, however, shall be wanting on my part to effect it. . . .

> —CLINTON, *Public Papers*, VI, 319.

C. "SIR JOHN JOHNSON HAS BEEN PUT TO ROUT"

General Philip Schuyler to Governor George Clinton.

> Saratoga, October 20, 1780

Dear Sir: Your Excellency's favor of yesterday morning from Caghnawaga I had the pleasure to receive at five in the afternoon. I am happy to learn that Sir John Johnson has been overtaken and put to rout; when your letter arrived, we had about 150 men at Fort Edward and as many more had arrived here about ten in the morning; those at Fort Edward without any beef, and those here with none but what I could furnish them; all my cattle fit for the knife are already killed and I have sent to try and collect some more, but I fear a supply will arrive too late to push a party in pursuit of the enemy who were at Ballstown. I have, however, sent to Fort Edward on the subject, but with little hopes that any will move from thence. One of the enemies party, who stole into the country and was taken, informs that Major Carlton intended to remain at Tyconderoga and to push for White Creek as soon as the militia should be retired; the prisoner calls himself an ensign and came from New York in August last. Another villain is gone past here, who corroborates the account as some tories advice with whom he lodged.

The panic that has seized the people is incredible; with all my efforts I cannot prevent numbers from deserting their habitations, and I very much apprehend that the whole will move, unless the militia will remain above until a permanent relieve can be procured. I am, D'r Sir, most sincerely your Excellency's Obed: Hu. Serv't.

> —CLINTON, *Public Papers*, VI, 324-325.

D. ONCE AGAIN SIR JOHN AND BRANT ESCAPE

Governor George Clinton to George Washington.

> Pokeepsie, October 30, 1780

Dear Sir, My last letter was dated at Albany and communicated the disagreeable intelligence of the destruction of Schoharie and part of Balls Town, about 12 miles northeast of Schenectady, since which I have not been able to write to Your Excellency. As I then proposed, I immediately left Albany in order to take the necessary measures for checking further incursions of the enemy. On my arrival at Schenectady I was advised that the different parties of the enemy at Schoharie and Balls Town had left those places, the former moving towards the Mohawk River and the latter shaping their course towards Sacondaga.

Genl. Van Rensselaer, who had arrived at Schenectady before me, at the head of about four or five hundred militia and with orders to act according to emergencies, on receiving this intelligence immediately moved up the river in hopes of being able to gain their front, but this proved impracticable as their route was much shorter and their troops more enured to marching; they reached the river at the confluence of the Schoharie Kill about six miles ahead of him, and recommenced in that fertile country their devastations by burning the houses and with marks of the greatest barbarity destroying every thing in their way.

Under these circumstances I was exceedingly perplexed. The militia under Genl. Rensselaer were inferior in number to that of the enemy. The few I had with me were too far in the rear to sustain them and not much could be expected from the militia of the country through which the enemy passed, their whole attention being engaged in the preservation of their families, and the levies were necessarily very much dispersed at the different posts to cover the frontier settlements against the incursions of small parties. Genl. Rensselaer, however, continued to move on and, being soon after joined by Col. DuBois with between 3 and 400 levies and 60 of the Oneida Indians, pursued the enemy with vigor; he came up with them and attacked them at Fox Mills (26 miles from where the enemy first struck the river) about sunset. After a considerable resistance they gave way and fled with precipitation, leaving behind them their baggage, provisions and a brass three-pounder with its ammunition.

The night came on too soon for us to avail ourselves of all the advantages which we had reason to promise ourselves from this action. The enemy took advantage of passing the river at a ford a little above where they again collected and renewed their march up the river with great celerity, and it became necessary for our troops, who had marched upwards of 30 miles without halting, to retire from the ground to refresh themselves. The pursuit was, however, renewed early in the morning and the enemy so closely pushed as to prevent their doing any farther mischief.

The morning after the action, I arrived with the militia under my immediate command, but they were so beat out with fatigue, having marched at least 50 miles in less than 24 hours, as to be unable to proceed any farther. I, therefore, left them and put myself at the head of the advanced troops and continued the pursuit till within about 15 miles of Oneida, and if we could possibly have procured provision to have enabled us to have persisted one or two days longer, there is little doubt that we might have succeeded, at least so far as to have scattered their main body and made many prisoners, but there was no supplies but such as I was obliged to take from the inhabitants on our route and these was inadequate and the collection of them attended with delay, nor could the pack horses, with the small quantities procured in this disagreeable manner, overtake us in so rapid a march through a perfect wilderness. I was, therefore, oblidged, tho' reluctantly, to return, most of the troops having been near two days utterly destitute and unable to proceed. Sir John, Brandt and Butler, immediately after the action at Fox Mills, left their troops and, with a party of Indians on horseback, struck across the country and went towards Oneida, taking their wounded with them. We discovered where they joined their main body again near the waters of the Susquehanna about six miles on this side where we quitted the pursuit. Brandt was wounded through the foot. . . .

The losses we have sustained by these different incursions of the enemy will be most severely felt; they have destroyed, on a moderate computation, 200 dwellings and 150,000 bushels of wheat, with a proportion of other grain and forage. The enemy to the northward continue in the neighborhood of Crown Point, and the inhabitants, in consequence of their apprehensions of danger, are removing from the northern parts of the state. . . .

—CLINTON, *Public Papers*, VI, 351-354.

2. COLONEL WILLETT DRIVES THE BRITISH FROM NEW YORK

Colonel Marinus Willett to Major General Stirling.

26 October, 1781

Major Ross, commanding officer at Bucks Island, with about 450 men left that place in batteaux and proceeded to Oneida Lake, where they left their boats, some provisions and about 20 lame men to take care of them, and proceeded from thence by the way of Cherry Valley to the Mohawk River, and made their first appearance at the place opposite to Anthony's Nose, from whence they proceeded to Warrens Bush and its vicinity and destroyed upwards of 20 farm houses with out houses, great quantity of grain and killed two persons; after that they crossed the Mohawk River at a fording place about 20 miles above this place and proceeded in order to Sir William's [Johnson] Hall, where they arrived about one quarter of an hour before Col. Willet with his body, who had crossed the river about 6 miles higher and marched also for the same place. Col. Willet commenced an action with the British which was much in his favor, had not some of his troops which covered a field piece gave way, which was the loss of the piece and ammunition cart, which in a little while after he bravely recovered; the enemy had, however, stripped the cart of all its ammunition. The evening coming on put an end to the action; part of Col. Willets men, however, passed the hall all night. The enemy retreated about 6 miles back into the woods, where the last account just now comes leaves them. About thirty British have been taken during the action and in the morning before the action commenced yesterday in the afternoon.

Col. Willett went in pursuit of them this morning with a force about equal to theirs. An account is also come to hand (altho not official) that a party is sent from Fort Herkimer to destroy their boats and provisions. There are 7 of the enemy found dead on the field of action this morning, and 3 of ours; between thirty and 40 wounded on both sides.

—CLINTON, *Public Papers*, VII, 443-444.

3. The Death of Captain Walter Butler

Colonel Marinus Willett to Governor George Clinton.

Fort Rensselaer, 2nd November, 1781

Dear Sir, I am just returned from a most fatiguing pursuit of the enemy, and tho it has not been in my power to take or kill the whole of the detachment that lately made their appearance in this quarter, yet I flatter myself they are little better off, as those that are not among the killed and taken are in a famising situation, scattered throughout the wilderness on the rout to Buck Island, where any of them that may arrive will have tales of horror only to relate.

After the affair at Johnstown, which happened on the 25th ultimo, and which would at once have proved fatal to them had the right wing of the small number of troops I had engaged behaved half as well as the left, the enemy took to the wilderness and, finding it out of their power to pass us so as to get to the Oneida Creek where they had left their boats, they directed their rout towards Buck Island, keeping far back in the wilderness. This determined me to cut across from the German Flatts in order to intercept them on that rout. Accordingly, on the evening of the 28th, having furnished near 400 men and sixty Indians, who had just joined me, with four days and a half provisions, which was all I could procure, I crossed the Mohawk from Fort Herkimer and incamped in the woods.

The 29th we marched north upwards of twenty miles in a snow storm, and at eight oclock A.M. of the 30th we fell in with the enemy, who, without making any resistance worth mentioning, fled from that time until night. We pursued them closely and warmly as possible. Nor did they ever attempt to check us in our advance except at one difficult ford in Canada Creek, where they lost several of their men. Amongst those killed at that place was Walter Butler, the person who commanded the massacre at Cherry Valley in November 1778. He was called Major, but by the commission found in his pocket appears to be no more than a captain.

A number of prisoners have been taken and many were killed in our intercourse with those gentry.

To pursue them any farther was thought improper; many of the troops as well as the Indians had laid aside their blankets and provisions in order to pursue with greater ease. And in the evening we find ourselves at least twenty miles from those packs. The woods was strewed with the packs of the enemy; provision they had none. The few horses they had amongst them when we first fell in with them, they were obliged to leave; except five, which were sent a considerable way in front, with some of their wounded and a few prisoners. Their flight was performed in an Indian file upon a constant trott, and one man's being knocked in the head or falling off into the woods never stoped the progress of his neighbour. Not even the fall of their favorite Butler could attract their attention so much as to induce them to take even the money or anything else out of his pocket, altho he was not dead when found by one of our Indians, who finished his business for him and got a considerable booty.

Strange as it may appear, yet it is true, that notwithstanding the enemy had been four days with only half a pound of horseflesh for each man per day, yet they did not halt from the time we began to pursue them untill they had proceeded more than thirty miles (and they continued their rout a considerable part of the night). In this situation to the compassion of a starving wilderness, we left them in a fair way of receiving a punishment better suited to their merit than a musquet ball, a tomahawk or captivity. . . .

—CLINTON, Public Papers, VII, 472-474.

CHAPTER TWENTY-SEVEN

The Conquest of the Old Northwest

MANY OF *the American colonies had claims to lands west of the Appalachians; none of these claims was so well established, or so extensive, as those of Virginia which ran "westward and northward from sea to sea." First the Proclamation Line of 1763 and next the Quebec Act of 1774 challenged colonial claims to the land north of the Ohio. At the time of the outbreak of the war British control over the vast area west of Niagara and south of the Great Lakes was pretty well established. Niagara was one center of British power, Detroit another, and Michilimackinac a third; these were designed to give the British control of the fur trade, of the Indians, and of the water system of the West.*

With the Revolution Virginia—and to a lesser extent other American states—revived their claims to the West. Kentucky had been explored from Virginia as early as the 1750's, but it was not until 1774 that James Harrod planted the first permanent settlement, at Harrodsburg; the next year saw the establishment of Boonesborough and St. Asaph—named after the Anglican bishop so friendly to the American cause.

From the beginning Kentucky was on the defensive, open to raids by the Indians, chiefly those north of the Ohio—and to attack by the British. There is little doubt that the feeble frontier settlements would have been overwhelmed had it not been for the foresight and energy of one man, George Rogers Clark. It was Clark who saved Kentucky; it was Clark who "conquered" the Northwest—that it did not stay conquered was not his fault. No other chapter in the history of the Revolution is so dominated by one man as is this chapter of the struggle for the Northwest. Only 23 when the war broke out, Clark had already had a long experience as surveyor and Indian fighter, and as a leader of those who wanted to see Kentucky part of Virginia, and not a proprietary colony. In 1776 Clark went east to Williamsburg to enlist support for the defense of Kentucky, and was partially successful. During the following year he came to realize that the only effective defense was offense, and conceived the grandiose plan of saving Kentucky by conquering the Northwest—Vincennes, Detroit and Michilimackinac. This plan too he presented to the Virginia authorities, who responded with approval though not with help. Jefferson, for one, saw that a conquest of the Northwest "would have an important bearing ultimately in establishing our western boundary." In any event Clark was commissioned colonel in the Virginia forces, authorized to raise seven companies, and to conquer the northwest—for Virginia.

How Clark carried out this mission is one of the most familiar—and most heroic—chapters in the history of the Revolution; we have given here some of the essential accounts. With less than 200 men he floated down the Ohio to Ft. Massac, below Louisville, marched overland to Kaskaskia and captured it without a struggle. Cahokia surrendered, and so did Vincennes, and the American flag waved over the Northwest. That winter however Governor Hamilton swept down from Detroit with an army of 1,000 Indians and regulars and took over Vincennes. Clark's reconquest of Vincennes, in mid-winter of 1779, remains, with Arnold's march on Quebec, the most heroic episode of the war; unlike Arnold's march it ended not in frustration but in triumph.

Just as the war along the New York border dragged on for two years after Sullivan's expedition, so the war in the Illinois country, Ohio and Kentucky, dragged on to the bitter end. After his victory at Vincennes, Clark was almost continuously on the defensive. He met a British threat to the Spanish outpost in St. Louis in 1780; he hurried back to Kentucky and into Ohio to deal with a serious attack under Colonel Bird; in 1781 he tried to mount an offensive against Detroit but instead was forced to parry a series of attacks on Kentucky. The worst of these attacks came in 1782 while Clark was busy with the defenses at Fort Nelson near the Falls of the Ohio. A band of Pennsylvanians had massacred, in cold blood, the Christian Indians of Gnaddenhütten; this appalling act aroused the Indians of the Ohio country to new energies and new furies. First they defeated a small expedition under Colonel Crawford, subjecting him to fiendish tortures; then in July they invaded Kentucky, besieged Bryant's Station, and, at the battle of Blue Licks (August 19, 1782), inflicted one of the worst defeats of the war on the Kentucky frontiersmen. Clark mounted a counteroffensive into Ohio, with limited success.

Did Clark win the Northwest? This is, in a sense, a trick question. He did conquer the Northwest, but could not hold it. Yet at the close of the war Kentucky was in American hands, and so, too, much of the territory of Ohio and Illinois, while St. Louis was controlled by the Spaniards—who had even thrust one expedition all the way to southern Michigan! Whether the treaty of peace ratified what Clark had achieved, whether it ratified only what he was supposed to have achieved, or whether it recognized merely the inevitable, we are not called on to decide. However clouded the years from 1780 to 1783, nothing can dim Clark's great achievements of 1778 and 1779.

I. KASKASKIA AND VINCENNES: THE FIRST CONQUEST

These three documents tell their own story, and require neither explanation nor elaboration. Two of them are from the vigorous pen of Clark himself—the appeal to Governor Patrick Henry, and the account, written a year later to the Virginian George Mason, of the first conquest of the Illinois country. The third comes from Governor Hamilton. Poor Hamilton had, then and later, a bad reputation. Known as "the hair-buyer" he was execrated throughout the borderlands, and when he was captured and sent to Virginia, Jefferson refused to exchange him or release him on parole because of his reputation for wickedness. He was probably neither better nor worse than other British and American officers dealing with Indians, and it is interesting to note that he himself was horrified at what he regarded as barbarous conduct by Clark!

From George Rogers Clark   Courtesy of the University of Chicago Press
by James A. James

THE NORTHWEST

1. KASKASKIA "WOULD GIVE US THE COMMAND OF THE TWO GREAT RIVERS"

Colonel George Rogers Clark to Governor Patrick Henry, summer or fall of 1777.

According to promise I haste to give you a description of the town of Kus-kuskies, and my plan for taking of it. It is situated 30 leagues above the mouth of the Ohio, on a river of its own name, five miles from its mouth and two miles east of the Mississippi. On the west side of the Mississippi 3 miles from Kuskuskies is the village of Mozier [Misere—Ste. Genevieve] belonging to the Spaniards. The town of Kuskuskies contains about one hundred families of French and English and carry on an extensive trade with the Indians; and they have a considerable number of Negroes that bear arms and are chiefly employed in managing their farms that lay around the town, and send a considerable quantity of flour and other commodities to New Orleans. The houses are framed and very good, with a small but elegant stone fort situated [but a little distance from] the centre of the town. The Mississippi is undermining a part of Fort Chartress; the garrison was removed to this place, which greatly added to its wealth; but on the commencement of the present war, the troops [were] called off to re-inforce Detroit, which is about three hundred miles from it—leaving the fort and all its stores in care of one Roseblack [Roche-blave] as commandant of the place, with instructions to influence as many Indians as possible to invade the Colonies, and to supply Detroit with provisions, a considerable quantity of which goes by the way of the Waubash River, and have but a short land carriage to the waters of the [Maumee].
. . . The fort, which stands a small distance below the town is built of stockading about ten feet high, with blockhouses at each corner, with several pieces of cannon mounted—powder, ball and other necessary stores without [any] guard or a single soldier. Roseblock, who has acted as governor, by large presents engaged the Waubash Indians to invade the frontiers of Kentucky; was daily treating with other nations, giving large presents and offering them great rewards for scalps. The principal inhabitants are entirely against the American cause, and look on us as notorious rebels that ought to be subdued at any rate; but I don't doubt but after being acquainted with the cause they would become good friends to it.

The remote situation of this town on the back of several of the Western Nations; their being well supplied with goods on the Mississippi, enables them to furnish the different nations, and by presents will keep up a strict friendship with the Indians; and undoubtedly will keep all the nations that lay under their influence at war with us during the present contest, without they are induced to submission; they will be able to interrupt any communication that we should want to hold up and down the Mississippi, without a strong guard; having plenty of swivels they might, and I dont doubt but would keep armed boats for the purpose of taking our property. On the contrary, if it was in our possession it would distress the garrison at Detroit for provisions, it would fling the command of the two great rivers into our hands, which would enable us to get supplies of goods from the Spaniards, and to carry on a trade with the Indians. . . .

I am sensible that the case stands thus—that [we must] either take the town of Kuskuskies, or in less than twelve month send an army against the Indians on Wabash, which will cost ten times as much, and not be of half the service.
—CLARK PAPERS, *Ill. State Hist. Lib. Coll.*, VIII, 30-32.

2. THE AMERICANS CAPTURE KASKASKIA

George Rogers Clark to George Mason.

November 19, 1779

I set out from Red Stone the 12th of May, 1778, leaving the country in great confusion, much distressed by the Indians. General Hand, pleased with my intentions, furnished me with every necessary I wanted, and the — of May I arrived at the Canoweay (Kanawha) to the joy of the garrison, as they were very weak and had the day before been attacted by a large body of Indians. Being joined by Capt. Oharrads company on his way to the Osark, after spending a day or two we set out and had a very pleasant voyage to the Falls of Ohio, having sent expresses to the stations on Kentucky from the mouth of the river for Capt. Smith to join me immediately, as I made no doubt but that he was wateing for me. But you may easily guess at my mortification on being informed that he had not arrived; that all his men had been stopt by the incessant labours of the populace, except part of a company that had arrived under the command of one Capt. Delland, some on their march being threatened to be put in prison if they did not return. This information made me as desperate as I was before determined.

Reflecting on the information that I had of some of my greatest opponents censureing the Governour for his conduct, as they thought, ordering me for the protection of Kentucky only; that and some other secret impulses occationed me in spite of all council to risque the expedition to convince them of their error, until that moment secret to the principal officers I had. I was sensible of the impression it would have on many to be taken near a thousand [miles] from the body of their country to attact a people five times their number, and merciless tribes of Indians, their allies and determined enemies to us.

I knew that my case was desperate, but the more I reflected on my weakness the more I was pleased with the enterprise. Joined by a few of the Kentuckians, under Col. Montgomery, to stop the desertion I knew would ensue on troops knowing their destination, I had encamped on a small island in the middle of the Falls, kept strict guard on the boats, but Lieutenant Hutchings of Dillards Company contrived to make his escape with his party after being refused leave to return. Luckely a few of his men was taken the next day by a party sent after them. On this island I first began to discipline my little army, knowing that to be the most essential point towards success. Most of them determined to follow me. The rest seeing no probability of making their escape, I soon got that subbordination as I could wish for. About twenty families that had followed me much against my inclination I found now to be of service to me in guarding a block house that I had erected on the island to secure my provisions.

I got every thing in readiness on the 26th of June, set off from the Falls, double manned our oars and proceeded day and night until we run into the mouth of the Tenesse River. The fourth day landed on an island to prepare ourselves for a march by land. A few hours after we took a boat of hunters but eight days from Kaskaskias; before I would suffer them to answer any person a question after their taking the oath of allegiance, I examined them particularly. They were Englishmen, and appeared to be in our interest; their intiligence was not favourable; they asked leave to go on the expedition. granted it, . . .

In the evening of the same day I run my boats into a small creek about one mile above the old Fort Missack, reposed ourselves for the night, and in the morning took a rout to the northwest and had a very fatigueing journey for about fifty miles, until we came into those level plains that is frequent throughout this extensive country. As I knew my success depended on secrecy, I was much afraid of being discovered in these meadows, as we might be seen in many places for several miles. Nothing extraordinary happened dureing our route excepting my guide loosing himself and not being able, as we judged by his confusion, of giving a just acccount of himself; it put the whole troops in the greatest confusion.

I never in my life felt such a flow of rage—to be wandering in a country where every nation of Indians could raise three or four times our number, and a certain loss of our enterprise by the enemie's getting timely notice. I could not bear the thoughts of returning; in short every idea of the sort served to put me in that passion that I did not master for some time; but in a short time after our circumstance had a better appearance, for I was in a moment determined to put the guide to death if he did not find his way that evening. He begged that I would not be hard with him, that he could find the path that evening; he accordingly took his course and in two hours got within his knowledge.

On the evening of the 4th of July we got within three miles of the town Kaskaskias, having a river of the same name to cross to the town. After making ourselves ready for anything that might happen, we marched after night to a farm that was on the same side of the river about a mile above the town, took the family prisoners, and found plenty of boats to cross in; and in two hours transported ourselves to the other shore with the greatest silence.

I learned that they had some suspician of being attacted and had made some preparations, keeping out spies, but they, making no discoveries, had got off their guard. I immediately divided my little army into two divisions, ordered one to surround the town, with the other I broke into the fort, secured the Governour Mr. Rochblave, in 15 minutes had every street secured, sent runners through the town ordering the people on the pane of death to keep close to their houses, which they observed and before daylight had the whole disarmed; nothing could excell the confusion these people seemed to be in, being taught to expect nothing but savage treatment from the Americans. Giving all for lost, their lives were all they could dare beg for, which they did with the greatest fervancy; they were willing to be slaves to save their families. I told them it did not suit me to give an answer at that time. They repared to their houses, trembling as if they were led to execution; my principal would not suffer me to distress such a number of people, except through policy it was necessary. A little reflection convinced me that it was my interest to attach them to me, according to my first plan; for the town of Cohos [Cahokia] and St. Vincents [Vincennes] and the numerous tribes of Indians attached to the French was yet to influence, for I was too weak to treat them any other way. . . .

As soon as they were a little moderated they told me that they had always been kept in the dark as to the dispute between America and Britain; that they had never heard any thing before but what was prejuditial and tended to insence them against the Americans, that they were now convinced that it was a cause they ought to espouse; that they should be happy of an oppertunity to convince me of their zeal, and think themselves the happyest people in the world if they were united with the Americans. . . .

The priest that had lately come from Canada had made himself a little acquainted with our dispute; contrary to the principal of his brother in Canada was rather prejudiced in favour of us. He asked if I would give him liberty to perform his duty in his church. I told him that I had nothing to do with churches more than to defend them from insult; that by the laws of the state his religion had as great previledges as any other. This seemed to compleat their happiness. They returned to their families, and in a few minutes the scean of mourning and destress was turned to an excess of joy, nothing else seen nor heard—addorning the streets with flowers and pavilians of different colours, compleating their happiness by singing, etc.

In meantime I prepared a detachment on horseback, under Capt. Bowman, to make a descent on Cohos, about sixty miles up the country. The inhabitants told me that one of their townsmen was enough to put me in possession of that place by carrying the good news that the people would rejoice. However, I did not altogether chuse to trust them, dispatched the captain, attended by a considerable number of the inhabitants, who got into the middle of the town before they were discovered; the French gentlemen calling aloud to the people to submit to their happier fate, which they did with very little hesitation. . . .

—Clark Papers, *Ill. State Hist. Lib. Coll.*, VIII, 117-123.

3. Governor Hamilton and Indian Allies Recapture Vincennes

Report of Lieutenant Governor Henry Hamilton to the British authorities, July 6, 1781.

On the 7th of October, 1778, the various necessaries for a winter movement of 600 miles being provided, by the activity and goodwill of Captains Lernoult and Grant, the latter of whom had attended to everything afloat, and by the assistance of Major Hay and Mr. Fleming, the Commissary, we struck our tents and embarked with one field peece which was all could be spared from the garrison.

One single person, he an Indian, was affected with liquor.

We proceeded a little way down the river and encamped. I should observe, once for all, that camp duty was as strictly attended to as the slender knowledge I possessed would admit, and that the guards, picketts and advanced centries were regularly visited from the setting the watch, which was usually at sunset till broad daylight, that the boats were loaded, manned, and arranged in such a way as to be perfectly secured within our centries every night; that the Indians encamped and decamped as regularly as could be wished, and that among them not a single instance of drunkenness or quarrelling occurred for 72 days, nor the least repining at the fatigues of the journey, or the hardships of the season. Their customs in war, their ceremonies on the way, and what passed in the meetings with various tribes, with the speeches, are entered upon my diary, and may be of service to persons who wish to be acquainted with their forms, without an attention to which no hearty assistance is to be expected from them.

On the 9th a snowstorm having subsided, it was debated whether or not we should hazard the passage of the lake from the mouth of Detroit River to that of the Miamis, but considering the advanced season, and that contrary winds or the freezing of the lake would frustrate our design, I determined to make the push. The traverse is of 36 miles and it was noon before the swell on the lake was fallen sufficiently. . . .

On the 24th we arrived at the Miamis town after the usual fatigues attending such a navigation, the water being remarkably low. Here we met several tribes of the Indians previously summoned to meet here, and held several conferences, made them presents, and dispatched messengers to the Shawanese, as well as the nations on our route, inviting them to join us, or at least watch the motions of the Rebels upon the frontiers; for which purpose I sent them amunition.

Having passed the portage of nine miles, we arrived at one of the sources of the Ouabache called the petite Riviere, . . .

In our progress down the Ouabache difficulties encreased, the setting in of the frost lowered the river, the floating ice cut the men as they worked in the water to haul the boats over shoals and rocks, our batteau were damaged, and to be repeatedly unloaded, calked and payd, 97,000 lbs. of provisions and stores to be carried by the men, in which the Indians assisted chearfully, when the boats were to be lightened. It was sometimes a day's work to get the distance of half a league. It was necessary to stop frequently at the Indian villages, to have conferences with them, furnish them with necessarys, and engage a few to accompany us. At length we got into a good depth of water, a fall of rain having raised the river. This advantage was succeeded by fresh difficultys, the frost becoming so intense as to freeze the river quite across. However by hard labour we made our way, and now approaching within a few days' journey of St. Vincennes, our reconnoitring party brought in a lieutenant and three men, sent from Fort Sackville to gain intelligence.

Major Hay was detached with orders to fall down the river and send to the principal inhabitants of St. Vincennes, acquainting them that unless they quitted the Rebels and laid down their arms, there was no mercy for them. Some chiefs accompanied him to conciliate the Peankashaa Indians residing at St. Vincennes, and to show the French what they might expect if they pretended to resist. Major Hay secured the arms, ammunition and spiritous liquors as soon as the inhabitants laid down their arms, and the officer who commanded in the fort (Captain Helm), being deserted by the officers and men who to the number of 70 had formed his garrison and were in pay of the Congress, surrendered his wretched fort on the very day of our arrival, being the 17th of December 1778. Thus we employed 71 days in coming only six hundred miles, which is to be attributed to the extraordinary difficulties of the way owing to an uncommon drought, the severity of the season, and the inevitable delays at the Indian villages. . . .

—Clark Papers, Ill. State Hist. Lib. Coll., VIII, 178-181.

II. THE CAPTURE OF VINCENNES

Here is the heart of the story, the most splendid chapter in the history of the early West, and one of the illustrious chapters in the history of the Revolution, the subject of more song, story, poetry and painting than almost any other episode except Valley Forge. Once again we draw on Clark's famous letter to George Mason and, for the British side of the story, on the journal kept by Colonel Hamilton.

1. CLARK IS "RESOLVED TO RISQUE THE WHOLE ON A SINGLE BATTLE"

George Rogers Clark to Governor Patrick Henry.

Kaskaskias, February 3, 1779

As it is now near twelve months since I have had the least inteligence from you, I almost despair of any relief sent to me. I have, for many months past, had reports of an army marching against DeTroit, but no certainty.

A late menuver of the famous hair buyer general, Henry Hamilton, Esq., Lieut. Governor of DeTroit, hath allarmed us much. On the 16th of December last he, with a body of six hundred men, composed of regulars, French voluntier and Indians, took possession of St. Vincent on the Waubach, what few men that composed the garison not being able to make the least defence. He is influancing all the Indians he possibly can to join him. I learn that those that have treated with me have as yet refused his offers. I have for some time expected an attact from him. He has blockd up the Ohio River with a party [of] French and Indians.

Yesterday I fortunately got every peace of inteligence that I could wish for, by a Spanish gentleman that made his escape from Mr. Hamilton. No attact to be made on the garison at Kaskaskias until the spring . . . passage is too difficult at present. . . . Both presents and speaches sent to all the nations south of the Ohio amediately to meet at a great council at the mouth of the Tennesse River to lay the best plans for cuting of[f] the Rebels at Illinois and Kentucky, and the Grand Kite and his nation living at Post St Vincent told Mr. Hamilton that he and his people was Big Knives and would not give their hands any more to the English, for he would shortly see his Father that was at Kaskaskias. . . . They are very busy in repairing the fort, which will shortly be very strong; one brass six-pounder, two iron four-pounders and two swivels mounted in the bastians, plenty of amunition and provisions and all kinds of warlike stores, making preparation for the reduction of the Illenois, and has no suspition of a visit from the Americans. This was Mr. Hamilton circumstance when Mr. Vigo left him.

Being sensible that without a reinforcement, which at present I have hardly a right to expect, that I shall be obliged to give up this cuntrey to Mr. Hamilton without a turn of fortune in my favour, I am resolved to take the advantage of his present situation and risque the whole on a single battle. I shall set out in a few days with all the force I can raise of my own troops and a few militia that I can depend on, whole [amounting] to only one hundred, of which —— goes on board a small g[alley sent] out some time ago. . . . This boat is to make her way good if possible and take her station ten leagues below St. Vincens. I shall march across by land my self with the rest of my boys. The principal persons that follow me on this forlorn hope is Capt. Joseph Bowman, John Williams, Edward Worthing[ton], Richard M Carty, and François Charlovielle, Lieuts. Richard Brashears, Abraham Chaplin, John Jerault and John Bayley, and several other brave subalterns.

You must be sensible of the feeling that I have for those brave officers and soldiers that are determined to share my fate, let it be what it will. I know the case is desperate but, Sir, we must either quit the cuntrey or attact mr. Hamilton. No time is to be lost. Was I shoer of a reinforcement I should not attempt it. Who knows what fortune will do for us? Great things have been affected by a few men well conducted. Perhaps we may be fortunate. We have this consolation: that our cause is just, and that our cuntrey will be greatful. . . .

—Clark Papers, *Ill. State Hist. Lib. Coll.*, VIII, 97-100.

2. Clark Describes the Capture of Vincennes

George Rogers Clark to George Mason.

November 19, 1779

By the 4th day of [February] I got every thing compleat and on the 5th I marched, being joined by two volunteer companys of the principal young men of of the Illinois commanded by Capt. McCarthy and Francis Charlaville. Those of the troops was Capts. Bowman and William Worthingtons of the Light Horse. We were conducted out of the town by the inhabitants: and Mr. Jeboth [Gibault] the priest, who, after a very suitable discourse to the purpose, gave us all absolution, and we set out on a forlorn hope indeed; for our whole party with the boats crew consisted of only a little upwards of two hundred. I cannot account for it but I still had inward assurance of success; and never could, when weighing every circumstance, doubt it: but I had some secret check.

We had now a rout before us of two hundred and forty miles in length, through, I suppose, one of the most beautiful country in the world; but at this time in many parts flowing with water and exceeding bad marching. My greatest care was to divert the men as much as possible in order to keep up their spirits.

The first obstruction of any consequence that I met with was on the 13th arriveing at the two Little Wabachces. Although three miles asunder they now make but one, the flowed water between them being at least three feet deep, and in many places four, being near five miles to the opposite hills. The shallowest place, except about one hundred yards, was three feet.

This would have been enough to have stopped any set of men that was not in the same temper that we was, but in three days we contrived to cross by building a large canoe, ferried across the two channels, the rest of the way we waded; building scaffolds at each to lodge our baggage on until the horses crossed to take them. It rained nearly a third of our march, but we never halted for it.

In the evening of the 17th we got to the low lands of the River Umbara [Embarras] which we found deep in water, it being nine miles to St. Vincents which stood on the east side of the Wabache and every foot of the way covered with deep water. We marched down the little river in order to gain the banks of the main, which we did in about three leagues, made a small canoe and sent an express to meet the boat and hurry it up. From the spot we now lay on was about ten miles to town, and every foot of the way put together that was not three feet and upwards under water would not have made the length of two miles and a half, and not a mouthful of provision. To have waited for our boat, if possible to avoid it, would have been impolitic.

If I was sensible that you would let no person see this relation, I would give you a detail of our suffering for four days in crossing those waters, and the manner it was done, as I am sure that you would credit it; but it is too incredible for any person to believe except those that are as well acquainted with me as you are, or had experienced something similar to it. I hope you will escuse me until I have the pleasure of seeing you personally.

But to our inexpressible joy in the evening of the 23d we got safe on terra firma within half a league of the fort, covered by a small grove of trees, had a full view of the wished for spot. (I should have crossed at a greater distance from the town but the White River comeing in jest below us we were affraid of getting too near it). We had already taken some prisoners that was coming from the town. Laying in this grove some time to dry our clothes by the sun, we took another prisoner known to be a friend, by which we got all the intiligence we wished for, but would not suffer him to see our troops except a few.

A thousand ideas flashed in my head at this moment. I found that Governor Hamilton was able to defend himself for a considerable time, but knew that he was not able to turn out of the fort; that if the seige continued long a superior number might come against us, as I knew there was a party of English not far above the river, that, if they found out our numbers, might raise the disaffected savages and harass us. I resolved to appear as darring as possible, that the enemy might conceive by our behaviour that we were very numerous and probably discourage them.

I immediately wrote to the inhabitants in general, informing them where I was and what I determined to do, desireing the friends to the States to keep close in their houses, those in the British interest to repair to the fort and fight for their King: otherways there should be no mercy shewn them etc., etc. Sending the compliments of several officers that was known to be expected to reinforce me to several gentlemen of the town, I dispatched the prisoner off with this letter, waiting until near sunset, giving him time to get near the town before we marched.

As it was an open plain from the wood that covered us, I marched time enough to be seen from the town before dark, but, taking advantage of the land, disposed the lines in such a manner that nothing but the pavilions could be seen, having as many of them as would be sufficient for a thousand men, which was observed by the inhabitants, who had just received my letter, counted the different colours and judged our number accordingly. But I was careful to give them no oppertunity of seeing our troops before dark, which it would be before we could arrive. . . .

I detached Lieut. Bayley and party to attact the fort at a certain signal, and took possession of the posts of the town with the main body. The garrison had so little suspicion of what was to happen that they did not believe the fireing was from an enemy until a man was wounded through the ports (which hapned the third or fourth shot), expecting it to be some drunken Indians. The fireing commenced on both sides very warm. A second division joined the first. A considerable number of British Indians made their escape out of town. The Kickepous and Peankeshaws to the amount of about one hundred that was in town immediately armed themselves in our favour and marched to attact the fort. I thanked the chief for his intended service, told him the ill consequence of our people being mingled in the dark; that they might lay in their quarters until light. He approved of it and sent off his troops, appeared to be much elivated himself and staid with me giving all the information he could. (I knew him to be a friend.) The artillery from the fort played briskly but did no execution. The garrisson was intirely surrounded within eighty and a hundred yards behind houses, palings and ditches, etc., etc. . . .

In a few hours I found my prize sure, certain of taking every man that I could have wished for, being the whole of those that incited the Indians to war. All my past sufferings vanished. Never was a man more happy. It wanted no encouragement from any officer to inflame our troops with a martial spirit. The knowledge of the person they attacted and the thoughts of their massecred friends was sufficient. I knew that I could not afford to loose men and took the greatest care of them that I possibly could; at the same time encouraged them to be daring, but prudent. Every place near the fort that could cover them was crowded, and a very heavy firing during the night. Having flung up a considerable intrenchment before the gate where I intended to plant my artillery when arrived. . . . The firing again commenced, a number of the inhabitants joining the troops and behaved exceeding well in general. . . .

About eight o'clock in the morning I ordered the fireing to cease and sent a flag into the garrisson with a hard bill, recommended Mr. Hamilton to surrender his garrisson and severe threats if he should destroy any letters, etc. He returned an answer to this purpose: that the garrisson was not disposed to be awed into any thing unbecomeing British soldiers. The attact was renewed with greater vigour than ever and continued for about two hours. I was determined to listen to no terms whatever until I was in possession of the fort; and only ment to keep them in action with part of my troops, while I was making necessary preparations with the other (neglected calling on any of the inhabitants for assistants although they wished for it).

A flag appeard from the fort with a proposition from Mr. Hamilton for three days cessation—a desire of a conference with me immediately; that if I should make any difficulty of comeing into the fort, he would meet me at the gate. I at first had no notion of listening to any thing he had to say as I could only consider himself and officers as murderers and intended to treat them as such. But after some deliberation I sent Mr. Hamilton my compliments and beged leave to inform him that I should agree to no other terms than his surrendering himself and garrison prisoners at discretion; but if he was desirous of a conference with me I would meet him at the church.

We accordingly met, he offered to surrender, but we could not agree upon terms. He received such treatment on this conference as a man of his known barbarity deserved. I would not come upon terms with him, recommended to him to defend himself with spirit and bravery, that it was the only thing that would induce me to treat him and his garrisson with lenity in case I stormed it, which he might expect. He asked me what more I could require than the offers he had already made. I told him (which was really the truth) that I wanted a sufficient excuse to put all the Indians and partisans to death, as the greatest part of those villians was then with him. All his propositions was refused. He asked me if nothing would do but fighting. I knew of nothing else. He then begged me to stay until he should return to the garrisson and consult his officers. Being indiferent about him and wanted a few moments for my troops to refresh themselves, I told him that the firing should not commence until such an hour, that during that time he was at liberty to pass with safety.

Some time before, a party of warriers sent by Mr. Hamilton against Kentucky had taken two prisoners, [and] was discovered by the Kickebues who gave information of them. A party was immediately detached to meet them, which hapned in the Commons. They conceived our troops to be a party sent by Mr. Hamilton to conduct them in—an honour commonly paid them. I was highly pleased to see each party hooping, hollowing and striking each others breasts as they approached in the open fields. Each seemed to try to out do the other in the greatest signs of joy. The poor devils never discovered their mistake until it was too late for many of them to escape. Six of them was made prisoners, two of them scalped, and the rest so wounded, as we afterwards learnt, but one lived.

I had now a fair oppertunity of making an impression on the Indians that I could have wished for: that of convincing them that Governour Hamilton could not give them that protection that he had made them to belive he could. In some measure to insence the Indians against him for not exerting himself to save their friends, [I] ordered the prisoners to be tomahawked in the face of the garrisson. It had the effect that I expected. Insted of making their friends inviterate against us, they upbraided the English parties in not trying to save their friends, and gave them to understand that they believed them to be liers and no warriers.

A remarkable circumstance hapned that I think worthy our notice: An old

French gentleman of the name of St. Croix, Lieut. of Capt. McCarty's volunteers from Cohos, had but one son, who headed these Indians and was made prisoner. The question was put whether the white man should be saved. I ordered them to put him to death, through indignation which did not extend to the savages. For fear he would make his escape, his father drew his sword and stood by him in order to run him through in case he should stir; being painted could not know him. The wretch, on seeing the executioners tomahawk raise to give the fatal stroke, raised his eyes as if making his last addresses to Heaven, cried out, "O, save me!" The father knew his son's voice. You may easily guess of the adgetation and behaviour of these two persons comeing to the knowledg of each other at so critical a moment. I had so little mercy for such murderers, and so valuable an oppertunity for an example, knowing there would be the greatest selicitations made to save him, that I immediately absconded myself; but by the warmest selicitations from his father who had behaved so exceedingly well in our service, and some of the officers, I granted his life on certain conditions.

Mr. Hamilton and myself again met. He produced certain Articles which was refused; but towards the close of the evening I sent him . . . Articles . . . which was agreed to and fulfilled.

The next day knowing that Governour Hamilton had sent a party of men up the Ouabach to [c]ome for stores that he had left there which must be on the return, I waited about twelve hours for the arival of the galley to intercept them, but, fearing their getting intiligence, dispatched Capt. Helms with a party in armed boats who supprised and made prisoners of forty, among which was Dejeane, Grand Judge of Detroit, with a large packet from Detroit and seven boats load of provisions, Indian goods, etc.

Never was a person more mortified than I was at this time to see so fair an oppertunity to push a victory: Detroit lost for want of a few men.
—Clark Papers, *Ill. State Hist. Lib. Coll.*, VIII, 139-146.

3. HAMILTON OWNS THE MORTIFICATION OF SURRENDER TO CLARK

[*Feb. 22nd, 1779*] Roll calling was just over, when we were surprized by the firing of small arms. This I attributed to some drunken frolic of the inhabitants, but going upon the parade heard the balls sing; still I could not conceive otherways than that some drunken people were amusing themselves.

Shortly after Serjeant Chapman of the King's Regiment was reported to be mortally wounded, but it proved only a contusion, a metal button having saved his life, a shot from a rifled piece having struck him opposite the pit of the stomach. The men had been ordered before this to stand to their arms; they were now sent to occupy the blockhouses and platforms, with orders not to fire till they could be at a certainty of doing it to purpose, and to be very managing of their ammunition.

It was now near dark and the fire increasing we were not at a loss to conclude our opponents were those whose fires had been discovered. In course as three sides of the fort were fired upon, we despaired of our reconnoirting party being able to return to us. The firing continued all night on both sides, but without any effect from us, the enemy having the cover of the church, the churchyard fence, houses, barns, all within muskett shot. We dislodged those at the church by a few discharges of a 3-pounder from the blockhouse, but had little chance of doing any execution against riflemen under cover. It was very practicable to have burned the village, but there were too many reasons against it which I shall take occasion to mention.

The situation of the fort had no one advantage but its neighbourhood to the river.

Our surgeon, who had been in the village when the firing began, finding the fort invested, made a push for the gate and narrowly escaped having several shot fired at him, one of which went thro' his legging. He told us that when the first shots were fired the woman at whose house he was cried out, "There is Colonel Clarke. [He] is arrived from the Ilinois with 500 men."

We had 1 serjt., one matross and 2 men wounded, which were brought into the officers quarters, not being able to bear the cold of the night, for we were obliged to put out the fires in the huts, as the light gave advantage to the riflemen who could see men pass in the fort, and the picketting not being all lined we were much exposed. We worked hard to remedy this defect with what spare picketts and plank we had.

About 4 o'clock in the morning the fire slackened, and a little before sunrise I lay down, when some one came in and told me they were scaling the stockades. Running out hastily and expecting to find the enemy attempting to get over the stockades [I] was agreeably surprized to find Captain La Mothe's party had made a fortunate push, and did actually get over with their arms in their hands, tho' the picketts were perpendicular and eleven feet high. . . .

23d. The firing recommenced on both sides after sunrise. We cleared the houses next the fort by a few cannon shot from the blockhouses, but this did not prevent our having two men wounded thro the loopholes, and one walking across the parade. This last was one of La Mothe's, and I could not find that those of his company had acted with spirit from the first. On the contrary the men of the Kings Regiment behaved with the greatest alacrity, and even exposed themselves more than I wished.

At eleven this morning one of the captains of militia of St. Vincennes advanced towards the fort gate with a flag of truce and being admitted delivered me a letter from Colonel Clarke which was expressed in the following terms—

"St. Vincennes Feby. 23d.

"Sir

"I expect you shall immediately surrender yourself with your garrison prisoners at discretion. If any of the stores be destroyed or any letters or papers burned, you may expect no mercy, for by Heavens you shall be treated as a murtherer—

"I am Sir your humble servant

"*Lt. Govr. Hamilton*   GEORGE ROGERS CLARKE"

The following answer was returned—

"Lieutenant Governor Hamilton acquaints Colonel Clarke that neither he or his garrison are to be prevailed on by threats to act in a manner unbecoming the character of British subjects.

"Fort Sackville, 23d Feby., 1779"

Having called the officers together I read them Col. Clarke's letter, with the answer, and told them I was determined if they and the men were of my mind to hold out to the last, rather than to trust to or accept Colonel Clarkes proposition.

They all declared themselves willing to second me.

The men were then assembled on the parade, when I read the letter and answer in English and French, telling them it was the determination of the officers, as well as my own, to defend the Kings colours to the last extremity rather than yield to such ignominious terms.

The English to a man declared they would stand to the last for the honour of their country, and as they expressed it, would stick to me as the shirt on my back.

Then they cried "God save King George!" and gave three huzzas.

The French hung their heads, and their serjeants first turned round and muttered with their men. Some said it was hard they should fight against their own friends and relations who they could see had joined the Americans and fired against the fort.

This was indeed fact, for as I found afterwards Bosseron had secreted powder with which he had supplyed Colonel Clarke on his arrival, and made an offer of his services with 75 men of the militia of St. Vincennes.

Finding one half of my little garrison thus indisposed, and that with so small a number as were well affected it would be absurd to think of holding out, that to retain the French was to depend on traitors, and to turn them out must give additional confidence to our Enemies, I determined from that moment to accept honorable terms if I could procure them. I first consulted with the officers and then communicated to the English the necessity of a surrender, assuring them at the same time that no consideration whatever should induce me to accept any but honorable terms.

They seemed very unwilling to listen to anything of the kind, but as it was obvious we were not in a condition to make any essential resistance, that we were 600 miles distant from any relief, that duty must fall too heavy on our small numbers now reduced one half by the treachery or cowardice or both of our Canadian volunteers, that we had already a fifth of our trusty Englishmen wounded, and wretched accommodations for them, they agreed to act as I judged best.

The men having had no rest the preceding night I divided the garrison into two watches, and sent one watch to rest. . . .

About two in the afternoon the party of Indians which had gone towards the Falls of Ohio returned, and advancing over the common to the fort, seeing the English flag flying and not knowing that we were attacked, discharged their pieces. 'Tis usual with them to fire three vollies on their approach to a fort or a town, as a salute; this is practiced also among themselves.

This party was in all but 15 or 16 men, of whom were the two sergeants of Volunteers.

Col. Clarke, being informed of their arrival, sent off 70 men to attack them, who fired on these people unprepared for such a salute, killed one, wounded two and made 5 of the rest prisoners, taking them to the village.

On their arrival, they were placed in the street opposite the Fort Gate, where these poor wretches were to be sacrificed—one of them, a young Indian about 18 years of age, the son of Pontiach, was saved at the intercession of one Macarty, a Captain of Col. Clarkes banditti, who said he had formerly owed his life to the Indian's father.

One of the others was tomahawked either by Clarke or one of his officers. The other three, foreseeing their fate, began to sing their death song, and were butcherd in succession, tho at the very time a flag of truce was hanging out at the fort and the firing had ceased on both sides. A young chief of the Ottawa nation called Macutte Mong, one of these last, having received the fatal stroke of a tomahawk in the head, took it out and gave it again into the hands of his executioner, who repeated the stroke a second and third time, after which the miserable being, not entirely deprived of life, was dragged to the river and thrown in with the rope about his neck, where he ended his life and tortures. This horrid scene was transacted in the open street, and before the door of a house where I afterward was quartered, the master of which related to me the above particulars. The blood of the victims was still visible for days afterwards, a testimony of the courage and humanity of Colonel Clarke.

When the prisoners were brought in, Bosseron, the villain already mentioned, levelled his piece at Serjeant [Sanscrainte], whose father (who had come with Clarke from the Illinois) at that instant stepping up, raised the muzzle and obtained his son's life by applying to Col. Clarke.

Serjeant Robert was saved by his sister's interceding. The flag of truce had been hung out on the occasion of my sending a messenger to Col. Clarke that I would treat with him about the surrender of the fort on honorable terms if he would come to a parly, and that I would talk with him on the subject in the fort, passing my word for his security. He sent word he would talk with me on the parade. We were each to bring a person to be present at our interview.

In consequence I met him on the parade outside the fort. He had just come from his Indian tryumph all bloody and sweating—seated himself on the edge of one of the batteaus that had some rainwater in it, and while he washed his hands and face still reeking from the human sacrifice in which he had acted as chief priest, he told me with great exultation how he had been employed. The soldiers in the fort, having some suspicion of treachery, were got into the blockhouse next to us with their pieces loaded and kept a watchfull eye on us during our conversation. The Colonel proceeded to tell me that it was in vain to think of persisting in the defence of the fort, that his cannon would be up in a few hours, that he knew to a man who of my people I could depend upon, with every other circumstance of my situation, and that if from a spirit of obstinacy I persevered while there was no prospect of relief, and should stand an assault, that not a single man should be spared.

I replyed that tho my numbers were small I could depend on them.

He said he knew the reverse, that there were but 35 or 36 that were really staunch and that I could depend on, and that 'twas folly to think of making a defence against such unequal numbers; that if I surrenderd at discretion and trusted to his generosity, I should have better treatment than if I articled for terms.

My answer was, "Then, Sir, I shall abide the consequences, for I never will take a step so disgracefull and unprecedented while I have ammunition and provision."

"You will" (said he) "be answerable for the lives lost by your obstinacy."

I said my men had declared they would die with arms in their hands rather than surrender at discretion.

The officer who was with him said he wished we should come to some composition rather than that blood should be spilt.

I said that I would accept such terms as should consist with my honor and duty—that as I knew what I might pretend to, it would take but little time to draw up articles.

He said he would think upon it and return in half an hour.

He returned accordingly with Captain Bowman, one of his officers, and I met him with Major Hay. We resumed our conversation. He seemed as determined as before. I then said further discourse was in vain. I would return to the fort, and to prevent mistakes the firing should not recommence till an hour after our parting, that each side might be prepared. I then gave him my hand, saying we might part as gentlemen tho not as friends. I had gone but a little way when Major Hay and Captain Bowman called me back, the subject was resumed, and Colonel Clarke agreed to my sending terms which he should assent to or reject, according as he should find their tenor. They were sent that same evening, C. Clarke made his answer, and I agreed to the conditions, having first assembled the officers and exposed to them the necessity of the step.

The men were next called together and I convinced them that the King's service could not derive any advantage from our holding out. . . .

The poltronnerie and treachery of our French Volunteers who made half our number, with the certainty of the St. Vincennes men having joined Col. Clarke, and the miserable state of our wounded men, all conspired to make me adopt the disagreeable terms of capitulation which are refered to. . . .

The mortification, disappointment and indignation I felt may possibly be conceived if all the considerations are taken together which suggested themselves in turn. Our views of prosecuting any design against the enemy totally overturned—the being captives to an unprincipled motley banditti and the being betrayed and sacrificed by those very people who owed the preservation of their lives and properties to us, and who had so lately at the foot of the altar called God to witness their sincerity and loyalty.

—HAMILTON, Journal, pp. 130-139.

III. THE FIGHT FOR ST. LOUIS

From the beginning Spain had made some feeble gestures of aid toward the American cause. As early as 1776 New Orleans was supplying the Western-ers with guns, powder, medicines and other supplies—mostly bought by and on the credit of Oliver Pollock, an American merchant in New Orleans. When Bernardo de Gálvez became governor aid to the Americans was in-creased, and Clark profited greatly by supplies forwarded from New Orleans by Pollock. In the summer of 1779 Spain formally joined the war against Britain. She had little interest in American independence, but a substantial interest in conquering British outposts in the West; in quick succession Baton Rouge, Natchez, Mobile and Pensacola fell to the Spaniards. Far to the north, Governor Sinclair of Michilimackinac decided to counterattack, and launched an expedition whose first objective was St. Louis and whose ultimate objective was New Orleans. British incompetence, the unreliability of Indian allies, the presence of Clark at Kaskaskia, and Spanish resolution frustrated this expedi-tion. The following year the Spaniards launched a counterexpedition towards Detroit which reached Fort St. Joseph in what is now southern Michigan.

1. The Hesse Expedition down the Mississippi Is Launched

Patrick Sinclair to Governor Frederick Haldimand of Canada.

Michilimackinac, 17 February, 1780

Sir,—Since my letter of the 15th instant the arrival of an Indian chief per-sonally acquainted with me, affords me an opportunity, earlier than I expected, of ordering Mr. Hesse, a trader and a man of character (formerly in the 60th Regiment) to assemble the Minomines, Puants, Sacks and Rhenards in the neighborhood and to take post at the portage of the Ouisconsing's and Foxes Rivers, there to collect all the canoes and corn in the country, for his own and for the use of the nations higher up, who will be ordered to join him at the confluence of the Rivers Mississippi and Ouisconseing. Mr. Hesse is ordered not to move from his first stand until I send him instructions by Serjeant [J. F.] Phillips of the 8th Regiment, who will set out from this on the 10th of March with a very noted Chief Machiquawish and his band of Indians. For want of a cypher and to assist the serjeant, I am unwillingly obliged to send a private of the Kings Regiment, a Highlander writing in that language, to the Brigadier.

The reduction of Pencour by surprise, from the easy admission of Indians at that place and from assault from those without, having for its defence, as reported, only 20 men and 20 brass cannon, will be less difficult than holding it afterwards. To gain both these ends the rich furr trade of the Missouri River, the injuries done to the traders who formerly attempted to partake of it, and the large property they may expect in the place will contribute.

The Scious shall go with all dispatch as low down as the Natchez, and as many intermediate attacks as possible shall be made. We will endeavor a sys-tem and connection in directing their operations to the service in view.

I have only to add that I am with the greatest respect, Sir, Your Excellency's most obedient and most humble servant

PATK SINCLAIR

Lt Govr of Michilimackinac

—SINCLAIR, "Letter," *Wis. State Hist. Soc. Coll.*, XI, 147-148.

2. THE SPANIARDS REPULSE CAPTAIN HESSE'S ATTACK ON ST. LOUIS

Martin Navarro to José de Galvez, member of the Council of the Indies under Charles III.

August 18, 1780

Your Excellency—While we were under the belief that the English had been falsely charged with the atrocities committed in North America upon persons of all classes in that continent by the hands of the various savage tribes who followed their banners, there was given a most amazing proof of the fact by Captain Esse [Hesse] at the head of three hundred regular troops and nine hundred savages which left not the least doubt that this nation, having forgotten how to make war according to the system practiced in Europe, does not desire to be false in America to the title with which an author of ability has characterized it.

Captain Don Fernando de Leyba of the infantry regiment of Luisiana was commandant at the post of San Luis de Ylinoises; and having received information that a body of one thousand two hundred men, composed partly of savages and partly of troops, was being drawn up for an attack upon the town under the orders of Captain Esse, he fortified it as well as its open situation permitted. He built at the expense of the inhabitants a wooden tower at one of the ends of the town, overlooking it, and placed therein five cannon. In addition to these he had some cannon with which he defended the two intrenchments that he threw up at the other two extreme points. These were manned by twenty-nine veteran soldiers and two hundred and eighty-one countrymen.

The enemy arrived May twenty-sixth at one o'clock in the afternoon, and began the attack upon the post from the north side, expecting to meet no opposition; but they found themselves unexpectedly repulsed by the militia which guarded it. A vigorous fire was kept up on both sides, so that by the service done by the cannon on the tower where the aforesaid commander was, the defenders at least succeeded in keeping off a band of villains who if they had not opportunely been met by this bold opposition on our part would not have left a trace of our settlements. There were also to be heard the confusion and the lamentable cries of the women and children who had been shut up in the house of the commandant, defended by twenty men under the lieutenant of infantry, Don Francisco Cartabona; the dolorous echoes of which seemed to inspire in the besieged an extraordinary valor and spirit, for they urgently demanded to be permitted to make a sally.

The enemy at last, seeing that their force was useless against such resistance, scattered about over the country, where they found several farmers who with their slaves were occupied in the labors of the field. If these hungry wolves had contented themselves with destroying the crops, if they had killed all the cattle which they could not take with them this act would have been looked upon as a consequence of war, but when the learned world [*mundo filosofico*] shall know that this desperate band slaked their thirst in the blood of innocent victims, and sacrificed to their fury all whom they found, cruelly destroying them and committing the greatest atrocities upon some poor people who had no other arms than those of the good faith in which they lived, the English nation from now on may add to its glorious conquests in the present war that of having barbarously inflicted by the hands of the base instruments of cruelty the most bitter torments which tyranny has invented. The number dead, wounded and prisoners is detailed in the report and information is constantly looked for as to the end of the prisoners, which is believed to be as unfortunate as that of their companions, perhaps more so. . . .

—NAVARRO, "Letter," *Wis. State Hist. Soc. Coll.,* XVIII, 406-408.

IV. KENTUCKY: WAR TO THE BITTER END

The attack on St. Louis was part of a large British plan for the conquest of the trans-Appalachian West. This plan called for an attack on New Orleans out of Pensacola, a drive down the Illinois River, and an invasion of Kentucky from Detroit. Only the last of these materialized. Early in May 1780—just as Hesse was approaching St. Louis—Captain Bird set out from Detroit with a force of some 1,200 Indians and whites, made his way along the Maumee and Miami rivers, and struck into Kentucky. His was the first British expedition to carry artillery, and with this he speedily reduced two Kentucky forts, Ruddle and Martin's Station. Then, laden with plunder, he withdrew. Already Clark had hurried down to Kentucky to organize a counterattack. By August he was ready; with an army of 1,000 men he moved into the Ohio country, burned the Shawnee village of Chillicothe, marched on the Indians at Piqua, on the Big Miami, and defeated them there.

The year 1781 was relatively quiet on the Kentucky frontier, except for attacks by Joseph Brant, veteran of the New York borderland wars. Early in 1782, however, the massacre, by Patriot militia from the Monongahela, of the peaceable Delawares at Gnadenhütten in Ohio set the whole frontier a-flame. The Delawares at once took to the warpath. They joined with the Shawnee and the Wyandots to destroy Colonel Crawford's expedition on the Sandusky. Then a segment of these Indian forces crossed the Ohio, besieged Bryant's Station and, in August, defeated a Kentucky force of some 200 at the battle of Blue Licks. Thereafter the Kentucky frontier was exposed. Clark counterattacked, destroyed Chillicothe for a second time, and gave Kentucky a breathing spell. Happily for the frontiersmen the end of the war put an end to their fighting and their trials.

1. CLARK REPORTS ON HIS CHASTISEMENT OF THE SHAWNEE

Colonel George Rogers Clark to Governor Thomas Jefferson.

Louisville, August 22, 1780

By every possible exertion, and the aid of Col. Slaughter's corps, we completed the number of 1000, with which we crossed the river at the mouth of

Licking on the first day of August, and began our march on the 2d. Having a road to cut for the artillery to pass, for 70 miles, it was the 6th before we reached the first town, which we found vacated, and the greatest part of their effects carried off. The general conduct of the Indians, on our march, and many other corroborating circumstances, proved their design of leading us on to their own ground and time of action. After destroying the crops and buildings of Chillecauthy, we began our march for the Picaway settlements, on the waters of the Big Miami, the Indians keeping runners continually before our advanced guards. At half past two in the evening of the 8th, we arrived in sight of the town and forts, a plain of half a mile in width lying between us. I had an opportunity of viewing the situation and motion of the enemy near their works.

I had scarcely time to make those dispositions necessary before the action commenced on our left wing, and in a few minutes became almost general, with a savage fierceness on both sides. The confidence the enemy had of their own strength and certain victory, or the want of generalship, occasioned several neglects, by which those advantages were taken that proved the ruin of their army, being flanked two or three different times, drove from hill to hill in a circuitous direction for upwards of a mile and a half; at last took shelter in their strongholds and woods adjacent, when the firing ceased for about half an hour, until necessary preparations were made for dislodging them. A heavy firing again commenced, and continued severe until dark, by which time the enemy were totally routed. The cannon playing too briskly on their works they could afford them no shelter. Our loss was about 14 killed and thirteen wounded; theirs at least triple that number. They carried off their dead during the night, except 12 or 14 that lay too near our lines for them to venture. This would have been a decisive stroke to the Indians, if unfortunately the right wing of our army had not been rendered useless for some time by an uncommon chain of rocks that they could not pass, by which means part of the enemy escaped through the ground they were ordered to occupy.

By a French prisoner we got the next morning we learn that the Indians had been preparing for our reception ten days, moving their families and effects: That the morning before our arrival, they were 300 warriors, Shawanese, Mingoes, Wyandots and Delawares. Several reinforcements coming that day, he did not know their numbers; that they were sure of destroying the whole of us; that the greatest part of the prisoners taken by Byrd were carried to Detroit, where there were only 200 regulars, having no provisions except green corn and vegetables. Our whole store at first setting out being only 300 bushels of corn, and 1500 of flour; having done the Shawanese all the mischief in our power, after destroying Picawey settlements, I returned to this post, having marched in the whole 480 miles in 31 days. We destroyed upwards of 800 acres of corn, besides great quantities of vegetables, a considerable proportion of which appear to have been cultivated by white men, I suppose for the purpose of supporting war parties from Detroit. I could wish to have had a small store of provisions to have enabled us to have laid waste part of the Delaware settlements, and falling in at Pittsburg, but the excessive heat and weak diet shew the impropriety of such a step. Nothing could excel the few regulars and Kentuckians, that composed this little army in bravery and implicit obedience to orders; each company vying with the other who should be the most subordinate.

—CLARK PAPERS, *Ill. State Hist. Lib. Coll.*, VIII, 451-453.

2. GNADENHÜTTEN: "THEY SANG HYMNS TILL THE TOMAHAWKS STRUCK"

Diary of David Zeisberger, Moravian missionary to the Delawares.

March 7, 1782. The militia, some 200 in number, as we hear, came first to Gnadenhütten. A mile from town they met young Schebosh in the bush, whom they at once killed and scalped, and, near the houses, two friendly Indians, not belonging to us, but who had gone there with our people from Sandusky, among whom were several other friends who perished likewise. Our Indians were mostly on the plantations and saw the militia come, but no one thought of fleeing, for they suspected no ill. The militia came to them and bade them come into town, telling them no harm should befall them. They trusted and went, but were all bound, the men being put into one house, the women into another.

The Mohican, Abraham, who for some time had been bad in heart, when he saw that his end was near, made an open confession before his brethren, and said: "Dear brethren, according to appearances we shall all very soon come to the Saviour, for as it seems they have so resolved about us. You know I am a bad man, that I have much troubled the Saviour and the brethren, and have not behaved as becomes a believer, yet to him I belong, bad as I am; he will forgive us all and not reject me; to the end I shall hold fast to him and not leave him."

Then they began to sing hymns and spoke words of encouragement and consolation one to another until they were all slain, and the above mentioned Abraham was the first to be led out, but the others were killed in the house. The sisters also afterwards met the same fate, who also sang hymns together. Christina, the Mohican, who well understood German and English, fell upon her knees before the captain, begging for life, but got for answer that he could not help her. Two well-grown boys, who saw the whole thing and escaped, gave this information. One of these lay under the heaps of slain and was scalped, but finally came to himself and found opportunity to escape. The same did Jacob, Rachel's son, who was wonderfully rescued. For they came close upon him suddenly outside the town, so that he thought they must have seen him, but he crept into a thicket and escaped their hands. . . . He went a long way about and observed what went on.

John Martin went at once to Salem when the militia came, and thus knew nothing about how the brethren in Gnadenhütten fared. He told them there the militia were in Gnadenhütten, whereupon they all resolved not to flee, but John Martin took with himself two brethren and turned back to Gnadenhütten, and told them there were still more Indians in Salem, but he did not know [how] it had gone with them in Gnadenhütten. A part of the militia went there on the 8th with a couple of Indians, who had come to Salem and brought the brethren away, after they had first taken away their arms, and when they came to Gnadenhütten, before they led them over the stream, they bound them, took even their knives from them. The brethren and the sisters alike were bound, led into town, and slain. They made our Indians bring all their hidden goods out of the bush, and then took them away; they had to tell them where in the bush the bees were, help get the honey out; other things also they had to do for them before they were killed. Prisoners said that the militia themselves acknowledged and confessed they had been good Indians. They prayed and sang until the tomahawks struck into their heads. The boy who was scalped and got away said the blood flowed in streams in the house. They burned the dead bodies, together with the houses, which they set on fire.

–ZEISBERGER, *Diary, Hist. and Phil. Soc. of Ohio Pub.*, New Series, II, 79-81.

3. KENTUCKY IS ONCE AGAIN DRENCHED IN BLOOD

A. THREATENED WITH "ANARCHY, CONFUSION AND DESTRUCTION"

John Floyd to John May.

April 8, 1782

Dear Sir, The savages began their hostilities early in February, and are constantly ravaging the most interior parts of the country, which makes it impossible for any one settlement to assist another. Even the populous parts of Lincoln are infested, and from the number of horses already taken off by them, it is notorious to every capacity that their design is to disable the inhabitants from removing untill their present intended campaign from Detroit against Fort Nelson can be carried into effect. This design is communicated to us thro' three different channels, and so well authenticated that it can not be doubted; and the conduct of the enemy ever since last fall coincides exactly with the information.

One fourth of the militia is called for by Genl Clark for the purpose of fortifying the fort against a siege; but from the immediate danger in which every one conceives his own family, the authority of militia officers at such a distance from Government growing every day weaker and weaker, and the new invented ideas of a separate State, calculated on purpose for disaffection and an evasion of duty, are so many causes to retard this necessary business, and seems to threaten us on all sides with anarchy, confusion, and I may add destruction.

But even to suppose that the works can be completed before the arrival of the enemy, it is then impossible that Genl Clark with the inconsiderable number of troops he now has can defend it; and a dependence on militia scattered over three extensive counties under the circumstances before mentioned, is depending upon a very great uncertainty; especially when the enemy have all the advantages of a heavy current from high up the Miamia to the very place of their destination. They can float from the mouth of that river to the falls in less than thirty hours. And to suppose that our spies should discover their approach as high up as Miamia, it will then take eight days at least before we can be collected if we were under the strictest military subordination. Should no reinforcements arrive in May, and if Genl Clark be obliged to evacuate his post rather than suffer such a quantity of military stores to fall into the hands of the enemy, and the whole Indian army let loose among the scattered inhabitants unprepared to receive them, what must be the consequence? Is it not evident that the whole must fall a sacrifice?

As a means of averting the storm which is gathering against us, and preventing those fatal consequences, your immediate interposition with the legislative body and with the Governor and Council is now called for by every inhabitant of Jefferson County. This is our last effort; and your exertions on this occasion may possibly save our families from the hands of merciless savages.

You are sensible from your own knowledge of this Western country that no place can be better calculated for the purpose of carrying on the Indian war against (if I may use the expression) the interior frontiers of this State than the Falls of the Ohio. Its situation is exactly centrical to the Northern, Southern, and Western tribes. The distance to Holston, Clinch, New River, Green Brier, etc., very trifling. Their supplies already here provided, and the communication to the British posts in Canady very safe and easy. I would further observe that if this country must be laid waste, which nothing but an early reinforcement or an accident can prevent, those settlements above mentioned must once more experience the disadvantages of a savage war, and must contend with more than ten times the number which have heretofore visited their borders. One who is unacquainted with the true situation of this county, and also with me, might probably conclude that those reflections might proceed from timidity. But you are acquainted with both and can judge whether it is so or not.

Our whole strength at this time is three hundred and seventy men, and who, according to the best calculations I can make, have about eight hundred and fifty helpless women and children to take care of, and very generally deprived of every possible means of removing back to the settlement.

This is at present as just a state of this county as I am able to give you, only I omitted to mention that this number of men were exclusive of the small remains of the Illinoise Regement. Who am, Dear Sir, with much respect your very hble Servt.   Jn Floyd

— Clark Papers, *Ill. State Hist. Lib. Coll.*, XIX, 54-56.

B. COLONEL CRAWFORD IS TORTURED TO DEATH

William Croghan to William Davies.

Fort Pitt, July 6th, 1782

Dear Colonel: . . . Gen. Irvine commands at this post, where he has so few Continental troops (about 200 for duty) that 'tis not in his power to go from the garrison against the Indians, who are daily committing murders through this country. The Pennsylvania militia formed an expedition against the Indians about three months ago; but instead of going against the enemies of the country, they turned their thoughts on a robbing, plundering, murdering scheme, on our well known friends, the Moravian Indians, all of whom they met in the most cool and deliberate manner (after living with them apparently in a friendly manner for three days), men, women and children, in all ninety three, tomahawked, scalped and burned, except one boy, who after being scalped made his escape to the Delaware Indians (relations of the Moravians) who have ever since been exceeding cruel to all prisoners they have taken.

About six weeks ago, 500 volunteers of this country, commanded by (our old) Colonel William Crawford, went on an expedition against the Indian towns . . . the men behaved amiss (were cowardly) no more than about 100 having fought the Indians, who came out from their towns to meet them . . . the firing continued at long shot with rifles for near two days. . . . The second evening our party broke off and retreated in the most disorderly manner. . . . Colonel Crawford and a few others, finding the men would pay no attention to orders, were going on coolly in the rear, leaving the road in case the Indians should pursue, until the second day when they thought they might venture on the road, but before they had marched two miles, a body of Indians fell in between them and the rear of the party, and took them prisoners.

We had no certainty of this unhappy affair until yesterday, when Doctor Knight, who was taken with Crawford, came into the garrison in the most deplorable condition man could be in and be alive. He says that the second day after they were taken, they were carried to an Indian town, stripped and then blacked, and made to march through the Indians, when men, women and children beat them with clubs, sticks, fists, etc., in the most cruel manner.

Col. Crawford and the Doctor were confined together all night; the next day they were taken out, blacked again, and their hands tied behind their backs, when Col. Crawford was led by a long rope to a high stake, to the top of which the rope about the colonel was tied; all around the stake a great quantity of red hot coals were laid, on which the poor colonel was obliged to walk barefoot, and at the same time the Indians firing squibs of powder at him, while others poked burning sticks on every part of his body; thus they continued torturing him for about two hours, when he begged of Simon Girty, a white renegade who was standing by, to shoot him, when the fellow said, "Don't you see I have no gun?"

Some little time after they scalped him, and struck him on the bare scull several times with sticks. Being now nearly exhausted, he lay down on the burning embers, when the squaws put shovels full of coals on his body, which, dying as he was, made him move and creep a little. The Doctor was obliged to stand by and see the cruelty performed. When the Colonel was scalped, they slapped the scalp over the Doctor's face, saying, "This is your great captain's scalp; to-morrow we will serve you so."

The Doctor was to be served in the same manner in another town some distance off; and on his way to this place of torment he passed by where Col. Crawford's dead body had been dragged and burned, and saw his bones. The Doctor was guarded by but one Indian, who seemed pretty kind to him; on the way the Indian wanted a fire made, and untied the Doctor, ordering him to make it. The Doctor appeared willing to obey, and was collecting wood till he got a good chunk in his hand, with which he gave the Indian so severe a blow as levelled him; the Indian sprang up, but seeing the Doctor seize his gun, he ran away; the Doctor could not get the gun off, otherwise would have shot the Indian. He steered through the woods, and arrived here the twenty first day after he left the Indian, having no clothes. The gun being wood bound, he left it after carrying it a few days.

For the twenty one days, and two or three more while he had been under sentence of death, he never ate anything but such vegetables as the woods afforded. None of the prisoners were put to death but those that fell into the hands of the Delawares, who say they will shew no mercy to any white man, as they would shew none to their friends and relations, the religious Moravians. I believe I have not told you that the whole of the five hundred who went out with Crawford returned, except about fifty. Colonel Harrison and Mr. William Crawford, relatives of Col. Crawford, were likewise taken prisoners, but fortunately fell into the hands of the Shawnees, who did not kill their prisoners.

–Clark Papers, *Ill. State Hist. Lib. Coll.*, XIX, 71-73.

C. "THE DIREFUL CATASTROPHY OF BLUE LICKS"

Andrew Steele to Benjamin Harrison, Governor of Virginia.

August 26, 1782

Sir: Through the continued series of a seven years vicessitude, nothing has happened so alarming, fatal and injurious to the interest of the Kanetuckians of particular and all its votaries in general, as the present concatination of hostilities, wherewith I am now to acquaint your Excellency.

The fifteenth of this inst. Bryan's Station was besieged by a number of Indians, whereof I am not able to form a just estimate. The attack continued warm for about thirty hours, during which period the enemy burned several exterior houses, killed three of our men and made large depredations on the neat stock and crop. They then retired, leaving three of their savage party dead on the ground, besides a number of circumstantially so.

The seventeenth, we were reinforced from Lincoln with one hundred and fifty horse men, commanded by Lieut. Col. Stephen Trigg, and joined by a few of the Fayette commanded by Colo. Jno. Todd, who composed an army of one hundred and eighty two. We followed them to the Lower Blue Licks, where ended the direfull catastrophy—in short we were defeated, with the loss of seventy five men, among whom fell our two commanders with many others officers and soldiers of distinguished bravery. To express the feelings of the inhabitants of both the counties at this ruefull scene of hitherto unparalelled barbarities barre all words and cuts description short.

The twenty fifth, five hundred of the Lincoln Militia commanded by Col. Benjamin Logan (who hitherto had neither been consulted, nor solicited to our assistance) marched to the battle ground in expectation of a second engagement, but the enemy had marched several days before. From the order of their march, with many other accruing circumstances, their number was supposed to be nearly six hundred.

Forty seven of our brave Kanetuckians were found in the field, the matchless massacraed victims of their unprecedented cruelty. We are led to conceive that none were captivated, from the number found at the crossing of the creek tied and butchered with knives and spears.

Labouring under these distressing circumstances we rely on your goodness (actuated from a principle of universal benevolence which is the distinguishing characteristic of the truly great and noble soul) that we will not only become subjects of your commiseration, but of your patronage and protection also. The ballance stands upon an equilibrium and one stroke more will cause it to preponderate to our irretrievable wo, and terminate in the intire break of our country, if your Excellency is not concerned in our immediate safety.

The author of this narrative is a person in a private sphere of life and hopes that your forgiving candour will induce you to not only pardon the intrusion, but the many inaccuracies that may appear through the whole of this illiterate and undigested detail, as it comes from a wel-wisher to Ameriacn liberty and your Excellency's most obed't H'ble Servt.

—Clark Papers, *Ill. State Hist. Lib. Coll.*, XIX, 96-97.

CHAPTER TWENTY-EIGHT

The Redcoats Carry the War to the South

Throughout *the war the British demonstrated wonderful incapacity to evolve an over-all strategy to crush the rebellion. They first moved against New England, regarded as the prime instigator of sedition. When that move failed, they transferred their main operations to the Middle States. Here again they failed to co-ordinate their efforts in a plan to conquer New York, and frittered away time and expense on a second campaign to subdue Pennsylvania.*

The story of the campaigns in the South reflects the same lack of capacity to evolve a unified plan and to muster all the resources of the empire behind it. Even in the early period of the war the South attracted British military planners because it was regarded as a stronghold of loyalism. There was some justification for this view. The Scottish Highlanders, many of whom were centered in the Cape Fear country of North Carolina, possessed a romantic attachment to the Stuart Pretenders which in the crisis was transmuted into a stanch loyalty to George III. In the back country of North and South Carolina were persons of motley national origins, although mostly Scotch-Irish and German, who had long-standing grievances against local government. Setting themselves up in defiance of the courts, they called themselves Regulators, and forced the royal governor, William Tryon, to defeat them on the field of battle in 1771. Many left North Carolina and went into Tennessee, where they became chiefly Patriots, but those who stayed were more incensed at the seaboard planters and wealthy merchants than at the royal government. Although they were mostly Presbyterians, and the ministry of that denomination was overwhelmingly Patriot, these settlers constituted a stronghold of loyalism.

A checkerboard of sectional divisions made large parts of the lower South a political no man's land. In these areas partisan bands flourished. They were commanded by such inspired leaders as Francis Marion, the "Swamp Fox," who joined lightning action with humane restraint; Thomas Sumter, the "Carolina Game Cock," a bold and imperious fighter who was often too self-centered to fit into the general strategy of larger forces; and Andrew Pickens, a dour but vigorous elder of the Presbyterian Church. The troops they commanded were irregulars and varied in numbers from a handful to hundreds. Sometimes they were ragged and ill-armed. Sometimes they descended upon their foes as uniformed dragoons and acted in concert with the Continental troops. In large measure they kept Patriot resistance alive until substantial Continental forces could be spared for the South.

THE CHARLESTON EXPEDITION

In addition to attempting to put down the Patriot movement in Virginia and North Carolina the British organized an expedition against the Southern colonies generally. An intercepted letter of December 23, 1775, from Lord George Germain to Governor Robert Eden of Maryland, reveals that a fleet and seven regiments were to proceed to North Carolina, and then "either to South Carolina or Virginia as circumstances . . . shall permit." The expedition sailed from Cork on February 13, 1776, under the command of Admiral Sir Peter Parker. The crushing defeat of the Loyalists at Moore's Creek Bridge persuaded the British command to direct the expedition to Charleston, the most important port south of Philadelphia. Early in June two ships of the line and six frigates brought seven regiments of regulars from Britain under Lord Cornwallis, who was joined by Sir Henry Clinton, to command the land operations. Accompanying this force was a regiment made up of units lately evacuated from Boston.

The defense of the harbor was entrusted by the Carolinians to Colonel William Moultrie, whose brother John was an ardent Tory. Breastworks were hurriedly thrown up around the town, but the major effort was devoted to preventing access of the fleet. The entry into the harbor was controlled by fortifications on two islands, Fort Johnson on James Island, which had been seized by provincial troops in September of '75 and held since then, and, opposite it, Sullivan's Island, on whose southern shore the principal fortifications were now constructed. A square redoubt was originally planned, but at the time of the British attack only the front wall toward the sea was completed. The side walls had been built to a height of only seven feet, and the rear was virtually open and undefended. General Charles Lee, who had been given a separate command in the South, arrogantly argued that Sullivan's Island was a "slaughter pen" and should be abandoned. But fortunately Rutledge and Moultrie did not yield.

The defenders were helped by an unforeseeable event—the grounding of three British ships of war on the shoals. Had not this occurred the three ships could have attacked the undefended rear of the fort. The British navy hardly covered itself with glory. Neither did the army. Sullivan's Island could have been taken from the rear by a successful landing from Long Island, a short distance away. There Clinton had put his forces. But when Clinton tried the crossing, the resistance was so furious that his halfhearted efforts at an amphibious operation were abandoned, to the immense annoyance of the British navy and to his own "unspeakable mortification." He discovered that the channel separating the two islands was not a mere eighteen inches, as he had been told, "but nowhere shallower at low water than seven feet." He had neither sufficient boats nor derring-do to accomplish his mission. A battered navy turned tail and headed north to New York.

1. MOULTRIE AND LEE PREPARE TO DEFEND CHARLESTON

Memoirs of Colonel William Moultrie of South Carolina.

May 31, 1776, expresses were sent to the President from Christ-church Parish, informing him that a large fleet of British vessels were seen off Dewee's Island, about twenty miles to the northward of the bar; and on the *first of June* they displayed about fifty sail before the town, on the out side of our bar. The sight of these vessels alarmed us very much—all was hurry and confusion, the President with his council busy in sending expresses to every part of the country to hasten down the militia; men running about the town looking for horses, carriages and boats to send their families into the country; and as they were going out through the town gates to go into the country, they met the militia from the country marching into town. Traverses were made in the principal streets; fleches thrown up at every place where troops could land; military works going on every where, the lead taken from the windows of the churches and dwelling houses to cast into musket balls, and every preparation to receive an attack which was expected in a few days.

June 4. General Lee arrived from the northward and took the command of the troops; his presence gave us great spirits, as he was known to be an able, brave and experienced officer, though hasty and rough in his manners, which the officers could not reconcile themselves to at first: it was thought by many that his coming among us was equal to a reinforcement of 1000 men, and I believe it was, because he taught us to think lightly of the enemy, and gave a spur to all our actions. After Gen. Lee had waited upon the President and talked with him upon his plan of defence, he hurried about to view the different works and give orders for such things to be done as he thought necessary. He was every day and every hour of the day on horse back, or in boats viewing our situation and directing small works to be thrown up at different places.

When he came to Sullivan's Island, he did not like that post at all; he said there was no way to retreat, that the garrison would be sacrificed; nay, he called it a "slaughter pen," and wished to withdraw the garrison and give up the post, but President Rutledge insisted that it should not be given up. Then Gen. Lee said it was "absolutely necessary to have a bridge of boats for a retreat"; but boats enough could not be had, the distance over being at least a mile. Then a bridge was constructed of empty hogsheads buoyed at certain distances, and two planks from hogshead to hogshead; but this would not answer, because when Col. Clark was coming over from Haddrell's with a detachment of 200 men, before they were half on it sunk so low that they were obliged to return.

Gen. Lee's whole thoughts were taken up with the post on Sullivan's Island; all his letters to me shew how anxious he was at not having a bridge for a retreat. For my part, I never was uneasy on not having a retreat because I never imagined that the enemy could force me to that necessity; I always considered myself as able to defend that post against the enemy. I had upwards of 300 riflemen, under Col. Thompson, of his regiment, Col. Clark, with 200 North-Carolina regulars, Col. Horry, with 200 South-Carolina, and the Racoon

Company of riflemen, 50 militia at the point of the island behind the sand hills and myrtle bushes; I had also a small battery with one 18-pounder, and one brass field-piece, 6-pounder, at the same place, which entirely commanded the landing and could begin to fire upon them at 7 or 800 yards before they could attempt to land. This would have disconcerted them very much. Besides, had they made their landing good, the riflemen would have hung upon their flanks for three miles as they marched along the beach, and not above fifty yards from them.

Col. Thompson had orders that if they could not stand the enemy they were to throw themselves into the fort, by which I should have had upwards of 1000 men in a large strong fort, and Gen. Armstrong in my rear with 1500 men, not more than one mile and a half off, with a small arm of the sea between us, that he could have crossed a body of men in boats to my assistance. This was exactly my situation. I therefore felt myself perfectly easy because I never calculated upon Sir Henry Clinton's numbers to be more than 3000 men. As to the men-of-war, we should have taken very little notice of them if the army had attacked us.

Gen. Lee one day on a visit to the fort, took me aside and said, "Col. Moultrie, do you think you can maintain this post?"

I answered him, "Yes, I think I can."

That was all that passed on the subject between us.

Another time Capt. Lamperer, a brave and experienced seaman, who had been master of a man-of-war and captain of a very respectable privateer many years ago, visited me at the fort after the British ships came over our bar; while we were walking on the platform looking at the fleet, he said to me: "Well, Colonel, what do you think of it now?"

I replied that "we should beat them."

"Sir," said he, "when those ships" (pointing to the men-of-war) "come to lay along side of your fort, they will knock it down in half an hour," (and that was the opinion of all the sailors).

"Then," I said, "we will lay behind the ruins and prevent their men from landing."

—MOULTRIE, *Memoirs*, I, 140-144.

2. THE BATTERIES OF CHARLESTON REPEL THE BRITISH NAVY

Letter of a surgeon with the British fleet.

July 9, 1776

We left Cape-Fear on the 27th of May, and anchored the same evening off the bar. The camp was struck at the same time, and the troops embarked the same evening on board the several transports. All our motions were so languid and so innervate that it was the 9th of June before the *Bristol* and *Pigot* passed the bar of Charlestown; the *Bristol* in passing struck, which alarmed us all exceedingly; but, as it wanted two hours of high water, she soon floated again. The *Prince of Piedmont*, a victualling ship, was totally lost on the north breakers of the bar. General Clinton and Lord Cornwallis were both on board when she struck; but as the weather was very fine, they were not in the least danger.

By our delays we gave the people every opportunity they could have asked for to extend their lines, etc.: they were not idle—every hour gave us astonishing proofs of their industry. As we anchored at one league distance from Sullivan's Island, we could see all that was going on with the help of our glasses. The fort of this island is exceedingly strong (or rather the battery); it is built of palm trees and earth, and on it are mounted eighteen of the lower deck guns of the *Foudroyant:* I never could distinguish more than seventeen; others imagined they could see nineteen—however, that is immaterial.

The signal for attacking was made by Sir Peter Parker on the 27th of June; but the wind coming suddenly to the northward, the ships were obliged again to anchor. The troops have been encamped on Long-Island since the 15th, and it was intended that General Clinton should pass the neck that divides Long-Island from Sullivan's Island, and attack by land while Sir Peter attacked by sea. General Lee had made such a disposition of masked batteries, troops, etc., that it is the opinion of all the officers of the Army whom I have heard mention this circumstance, that if our troops had attacked, they must have been cut off; but this assertion does not satisfy the Navy, for they certainly expected great assistance from the Army. Excuse this necessary digression.

On the morning of the 28th, the wind proved favourable; it was a clear fine day, but very sultry. The *Thunder,* bomb, began the attack at half past eleven by throwing shells while the ships were advancing. The ships that advanced to attack the battery were the *Bristol* and *Experiment*, two fifty-gun ships; the *Solebay*, *Active*, *Acteon* and *Syren*, of twenty-eight guns; the *Sphinx*, of twenty, and the *Friendship*, an armed ship of twenty-eight guns. With this force what might not have been expected?

Unfortunately the bomb was placed at such a distance that she was not of the least service. This Colonel James, the principal engineer, immediately perceived; to remedy which inconvenience, an additional quantity of powder was added to each mortar: the consequences were the breaking down the beds and totally disabling her for the rest of the day.

The *Bristol* and *Experiment* have suffered most incredibly: the former very early had the spring of her cable shot away—of course she lay end on to the battery and was raked fore and aft; she lost upwards of one hundred men killed and wounded. Captain Morris, who commanded her, lost his arm; the worthy man, however, died a week after on board the *Pigot*. Perhaps an instance of such slaughter cannot be produced; twice the quarter-deck was cleared of every person except Sir Peter, and he was slightly wounded. She had nine thirty-two-pound shot in her mainmast, which is so much damaged as to be obliged to be shortened; the mizzen had seven thirty-two-pound shot and was obliged, being much shattered, to be entirely cut away.

It is impossible to pretend to describe what our shipping have suffered. Captain Scott, of the *Experiment*, lost his right arm, and the ship suffered exceedingly; she had much the same number killed and wounded as the *Bristol*. Our situation was rendered very disagreeable by the *Acteon*, *Syren* and *Sphinx* running foul of each other, and getting on shore on the middle ground. The *Sphinx* disengaged herself by cutting way her bowsprit; and, as it was not yet flood-tide, the *Sphinx* and *Syren* fortunately warped off. The *Acteon* was burnt next morning by Captain Atkins, to prevent her falling into the hands of the Provincials, as fine a new frigate as I ever saw.

Our ships, after laying nine hours before the battery, were obliged to retire with great loss. The Provincials reserved their fire until the shipping were advanced within point-blank shot; their artillery was surprisingly well served, it is said, under the command of a Mr. Masson and DeBrahm; it was slow, but decisive indeed; they were very cool, and took great care not to fire except their guns were exceedingly well directed. But there was a time when the battery appeared to be silenced for more than an hour; the Navy say, had the troops been ready to land at this time, they could have taken possession. How that is I will not pretend to say. I will rather suppose it; but the fire became exceedingly severe when it was renewed again, and did amazing execution after the battery had been supposed to have beeen silenced.

This will not be believed when it is first reported in England. I can scarcely believe what I myself saw on that day—a day to me one of the most distressing of my life. The Navy, on this occasion, have behaved with the usual coolness and intrepidity; one would have imagined that no battery could have resisted their incessant fire.

—FORCE, ed., *American Archives*, 4th Series, VI, 1209n.-1210n.

3. "Never Did Men Fight More Bravely"

Memoirs of Colonel William Moultrie.

On the morning of the 28th of June [1776], I paid a visit to our advance-guard (on horseback three miles to the eastward of our fort.) While I was there, I saw a number of the enemy's boats in motion, at the back of Long-Island, as if they intended a descent upon our advanced post; at the same time I saw the men-of-war loose their topsails. I hurried back to the fort as fast as possible; when I got there the ships were already under sail. I immediately ordered the long roll to beat, and officers and men to their posts. We had scarcely manned our guns when the following ships of war came sailing up, as if in confidence of victory. As soon as they came within the reach of our guns, we began to fire. They were soon a-breast of the fort . . . let go their anchors, with springs upon their cables, and begun their attack most furiously about 10 o'clock A. M. and continued a brisk fire till about 8 o'clock P. M.

The ships were:

The *Bristol*, of 50 guns, Commodore Sir Peter Parker: the captain had his arm shot off, 44 men killed and 30 wounded.

The *Experiment*, 50 guns: the captain lost his arm, 57 men killed and 30 wounded.

The *Active*, 28 guns: 1 lieutenant killed, 1 man wounded.

The Sole-Bay, 28 guns: 2 killed, 3 or 4 wounded.

The *Syren*, 28 guns.

The *Acteon*, 28 guns: burnt; 1 lieutenant killed.

The *Sphinx*, 28 guns: lost her bowsprit.

The *Friendship*, 26 guns; an armed vessel taken into service.

The *Thunder*, bomb, had the beds of her mortar soon disabled; she threw her shells in a very good direction; most of them fell within the fort, but we had a morass in the middle that swallowed them up instantly, and those that fell in the sand and in and about the fort were immediately buried so that very few of them bursted amongst us. At one time the Commodore's ship swung round with her stern to the fort, which drew the fire of all the guns that could bear upon her: we supposed he had had the springs of her cables cut away. The words that passed along the platform by officers and men were: "Mind the Commodore! Mind the two fifty-gun ships!" Most all the attention was paid to the two fifty-gun ships, especially the Commodore, who, I dare say, was not at all obliged to us for our particular attention to him; the killed and wounded on board those two fifty-gun ships confirms what I say.

During the action Gen. Lee paid us a visit through a heavy line of fire and pointed two or three guns himself; then said to me, "Colonel, I see you are doing very well here. You have no occasion for me. I will go up to town again," and left us.

When I received information of Gen. Lee's approach to the fort, I sent Lieut. Marion from off the platform, with 8 or 10 men, to unbar the gateway. Our gate not being finished, the gateway was barricaded with pieces of timber 8 or 10 inches square, which required 3 or 4 men to remove each piece. The men in the ships' tops, seeing those men run from the platform, concluded "we were quitting the fort," as some author mentions. Another says, "We hung up a man in the fort at the time of the action." That action was taken from this circumstance: when the action begun (it being a warm day), some of the men took off their coats and threw them upon the top of the merlons. I saw a shot take one of them and throw it into a small tree behind the platform. It was noticed by our men and they cried out, "Look at the coat!"

Never did men fight more bravely, and never were men more cool; their only distress was the want of powder; we had not more than 28 rounds, for 26 guns, 18 and 26-pounders, when we begun the action; and a little after, 500 pounds from town and 200 pounds from Captain Tufft's schooner lying at the back of the fort.

There cannot be a doubt but that, if we had had as much powder as we could have expended in the time, the men-of-war must have struck their colors or they would certainly have been sunk, because they could not retreat, as the wind and tide were against them; and if they had proceeded up to town, they would have been in a much worse situation. They could not make any impression on our fort, built of palmetto logs and filled in with earth. Our merlons were 16 feet thick and high enough to cover the men from the fire of the tops. The men that we had killed and wounded received their shots mostly through the embrasures.

An author, who published in 1779, says, "The guns were at one time so long silenced that it was thought the fort was abandoned; it seems extraordinary that a detachment of land forces were not in readiness on board of the transports, or boats, to profit of such an occasion."

The guns being so long silent was owing to the scarcity of powder which we had in the fort, and to a report that was brought to me "that the English troops were landed between the advance-guard and the fort." It was upon this information that I ordered the guns to cease firing, or to fire very slow upon the shipping; that we should reserve our powder for the musketry to defend ourselves against the land forces, there being a scarcity of powder at this time.

At one time, 3 or 4 of the men-of-war's broadsides struck the fort at the same instant, which gave the merlons such a tremor that I was apprehensive that a few more such would tumble them down. During the action three of the men-of-war, in going round to our west curtain, got entangled together, by which the *Acteon* frigate went on shore on the middle ground; the *Sphinx* lost her bow-sprit; and the *Syren* cleared herself without any damage; had these three ships effected their purpose, they would have enfiladed us in such a manner as to have driven us from our guns. It being a very hot day, we were served along the platform with grog in fire-buckets, which we partook of very heartily: I never had a more agreeable draught than that which I took out of one of those buckets at the time. It may be very easily conceived what heat and thirst a man must feel in this climate, to be upon a platform on the 28th June, amidst 20 or 30 heavy pieces of cannon in one continual blaze and roar, and clouds of smoke curling over his head for hours together; it was a very honourable situation, but a very unpleasant one.

During the action thousands of our fellow-citizens were looking on with anxious hopes and fears, some of whom had their fathers, brothers and husbands in the battle; whose hearts must have been pierced at every broad-side. After some time our flag was shot away; their hopes were then gone, and they gave up all for lost, supposing that we had struck our flag, and had given up the fort! Sergeant Jasper, perceiving that the flag was shot away and had fallen without the fort, jumped from one of the embrasures and brought it up through a heavy fire, fixed it upon a spunge-staff, and planted it upon the ramparts again. Our flag once more waving in the air revived the drooping spirits of our friends; and they continued looking on till night had closed the scene and hid us from their view; only the appearance of a heavy storm, with continual flashes and peals like thunder. At night when we came to our slow firing (the ammunition being nearly quite gone) we could hear the shot very distinctly strike the ships.

At length the British gave up the conflict. The ships slipt their cables and dropped down with the tide, and out of the reach of our guns. When the firing had ceased, our friends for a time were again in an unhappy suspense, not knowing our fate till they received an account by a dispatch boat, which I sent up to town to acquaint them that the British ships had retired and that we were victorious.

Early the next morning was presented to our view the *Acteon* frigate hard and fast aground at about 400 yards distance. We gave her a few shot, which she returned, but they soon set fire to her and quitted her. Capt. Jacob Milligan and others went in some of our boats, boarded her while she was on fire, and pointed 2 or 3 guns at the Commodore and fired them; then brought off the ship's bell and other articles, and had scarcely left her when she blew up, and from the explosion issued a grand pillar of smoke, which soon expanded itself at the top and, to appearance, formed the figure of a palmetto tree; the ship immediately burst into a great blaze that continued till she burnt down to the water's edge.

—MOULTRIE, *Memoirs*, I, 174-181.

4. SERGEANT JASPER RAISES THE FLAG OVER FORT MOULTRIE

Major Barnard Elliott of South Carolina to his wife.

Charleston, June 29, 1776

As soon as I got to my battery after leaving you, we took up several places on the inside of the cabin, upon which were brass screws, all bespattered with blood, and other ornaments of the man-of-war. The firing continued till near 10 o'clock, and I have the pleasure to inform you that we have lost but ten men and twenty-two wounded. Dr. Faysseaux came up this morning with the latter. He tells me that Richard Baker, our nephew, behaved gallantly, as did all the officers and men.

The expression of a Sergeant McDaniel, after a cannon ball had taken off his shoulder and scouped out his stomach, is worth recording in the annals of America: "Fight on, my brave boys; don't let liberty expire with me today!"

Young, the barber, an old artillery man, who lately enlisted as sergeant, has lost a leg. Several arms are shot away. Not an officer is wounded.

My old grenadier, Serj. Jasper, upon the shot carrying away the flag-staff, called out to Col. Moultrie: "Colonel, don't let us fight without our flag!"

"What can you do?" replied the Colonel. "The staff is broke."

"Then, sir," said he, "I'll fix it to a halbert and place it on the merlon of the bastion next to the enemy," which he did, through the thickest fire.

General Lee crossed from Haddrell's to Sullivan's in the heat of the cannonade and was at the fort. His letter to the President says he never saw but one cannonade equal to this, though he has seen many; nor did he ever see officers and men behave better, nor could any in the world exceed them.

A fine sight from our cupola. I wish you and Rinchey were here to look at it, viz.: One of the finest of the enemy's frigates was all in a blaze, and has been burning two hours. She is one of the two that got on shore on the middle ground, which they, not being able to get off, have burnt. A bowsprit was shot away yesterday afternoon; part of her rigging came up with the tide— also, several yards of the masts.

The *Bristol*, of 50 guns, the *Roebuck*, of 44 guns, and the *Syren*, of 28, were the three ships that lay nearest the fort. The distance, though it appeared great from our cupola, did not exceed 400 yards. Six men-of-war engaged. Col. Moultrie has sent up for ammunition. The President told me he had sent to Dorchester for 2000 lbs. The fort was three-quarters of an hour yesterday without powder.

I think you and Rinchey may come down with safety to-day, and if they should renew the attack in the afternoon, you may stay till Johnston's Fort is engaged. Now, my dear wife, let us not forget to whom we are indebted for this success against our enemy. Let us return God thanks for it. It is He that does all for us. He inspires our officers and men with courage, and shields their heads in the day of battle. He is the wonderful God of victory.

—GIBBES, *Documentary History of the American Revolution*, II, 6-7.

5. A REVOLUTIONARY FALSTAFF COMES TO GRIEF

A New War Song
by Sir Peter Parker
1777

(Tune: "Well Met, Brother Tar")

My Lords, with your leave
An account I will give
That deserves to be written in meter;
For the Rebels and I
Have been pretty nigh—
Faith! almost too nigh for Sir Peter.

With much labour and toil
Unto Sullivan's Isle
I came fierce as Falstaff or Pistol,
But the Yankees (od rot 'em)—
I could not get at 'em—
Most terribly mauled my poor *Bristol*.

Bold Clinton by land
Did quietly stand
While I made a thundering clatter;
But the channel was deep,
So he could only peep
And not venture over the water.

De'il take 'em; their shot
Came so swift and so hot,
And the cowardly dogs stood so stiff, sirs,
That I put ship about
And was glad to get out,
Or they would not have left me a skiff, sirs!

Now bold as a Turk
I proceed to New York
Where with Clinton and Howe you may find me.
I've the wind in my tail,
And am hoisting my sail,
To leave Sullivan's Island behind me.

But, my lords, do not fear
For before the next year,
(Altho' a small island could fret us),
The Continent whole
We shall take, by my soul,
If the cowardly Yankee will let us.

—MOORE, ed., *Songs and Ballads*, p. 135.

CHAPTER TWENTY-NINE

The Second Campaign to Conquer the South

FOLLOWING *the withdrawal of the British army from Philadelphia, Clinton was ordered to dispatch troops to Georgia or Florida and to attempt what was optimistically expected to be the "comparatively easy" conquest of South Carolina. That long-drawn-out campaign was a seesaw affair, marked by ups and downs for both sides, advance and retreat, siege and countersiege, the capitulation of towns and garrisons, the disastrous rout of the Patriots in the field, only to be succeeded by a total capitulation of the main British army in the South.*

First the British won Georgia, and despite partisan resistance held it against the Patriots. Then came the fall of Charleston, not only the worst defeat which the Americans suffered in the Revolution, but the worst defeat in American military history until Bataan. Now the Carolinas lay open to Cornwallis; what with the collapse of American finances, and the treason of Arnold, the Patriot cause seemed desperate that summer of 1780. But once again—as in New England and in the Middle States—British plans miscarried. Heat, disease, swamps and space combined with guerrillas and partisans to frustrate and then to defeat the invaders. Loyalists were numerous, but weakened the British by their excesses and their independence. Though the incompetent Gates was disastrously defeated at Camden, partisans and regulars combined to overwhelm the Loyalists at King's Mountain. The British did not know it, but that was the turn of the tide.

I. THE FALL OF SAVANNAH

The campaign against the South was outlined by Germain to Clinton as early as March 8, 1778, but it took time for the fleet and armies to get moving. A force from Florida under Brigadier General Augustine Prevost pushed up north to reinforce the main attack against Savannah, which was assigned to Lieutenant Colonel Archibald Campbell. Campbell's fleet of transports and war vessels arrived at the mouth of the Savannah River at the end of December, 1778.

Campbell's amphibious expedition was opposed by a small American army in the South under General Robert Howe. Against a hard-pressed attack the Savannah defenses proved untenable. A Negro guided Campbell's men through the wooded swamps guarded by Howe's forces and gained their rear. Attacked from front and rear, the Americans broke in confusion. Many were

From The American Revolution   *Courtesy of Harper & Brothers*
by John Richard Alden

*drowned in the rice swamps in their headlong flight. The American losses
were immensely heavy for such small forces—83 killed or drowned, 453
captured, against British casualties of three killed, ten wounded. Following
the fall of Savannah, Sunbury and Augusta were taken, and the royal government, including a royal legislature, re-established. Howe was cleared by a*

court of inquiry, but his reputation was permanently damaged. As "Light-Horse Harry" Lee put it, "never was a victory of such magnitude so completely gained, with so little loss."

1. Britain Launches a New Move in the South

Lord George Germain to Sir Henry Clinton.

March 8, 1778

. . . Could a small corps be detached at the same time to land at Cape Fear and make an impression on North Carolina, it is not doubted that large numbers of the inhabitants would flock to the King's standard, and that His Majesty's Government would be restored in that province also. But your own knowledge of those provinces, and the information you can collect from the naval and military officers that have been upon service there, will enable you to give the officer to whom you may entrust the command better instructions than I can pretend to point out to you at this distance. I will therefore only further observe to you that the conquest of these provinces is considered by the King as an object of great importance in the scale of the war, as their possession might be easily maintained, and thereby a very valuable branch of commerce would be restored to this country and the rebels deprived of a principal resource for the support of their foreign credit, and of paying for the supplies they stand in need of, as the product of these provinces make a considerable part of their remittances to Europe.

While these operations are carrying on, every diversion should be made in the provinces of Virginia and Maryland that the remaining troops which can be spared for the offensive service, in conjunction with the fleet, will admit of. The great number of deep inlets and navigable rivers in these provinces expose them in a peculiar manner to naval attacks, and must require a large force to be kept on foot for their protection, and disable them from giving any assistance to the Carolinas. The seizing or destroying their shipping would also be attended with the important consequence of preventing the Congress from availing themselves, as they have done, of their staple commodity, tobacco, on which, and the rice and indigo of Carolina and Georgia, they entirely depend for making remittances to Europe.

Should the success we may reasonably hope for attend these enterprizes, it might not be too much to expect that all America to the south of the Susquehannah would return to their allegiance, and in the case of so happy an event, the northern provinces might be left to their own feelings and distress to bring them back to their duty, and the operations against them confined to the cutting off all their supplies and blocking up their ports. . . .

—Gr. Brit. Hist. Mss. Comm., *Stopford-Sackville Manuscripts*, II, 99.

2. "Come and Take It!"—Fort Morris Dares the British Invaders

Colonel L. V. Fuser of the British Army to Colonel John McIntosh of the Continental Army, commanding at Fort Morris in Georgia.

November 25, 1778

Sir:—You cannot be ignorant that four armies are in motion to reduce this Province. The one is always under the guns of your fort, and may be joined when I think proper, by Colonel Prevost, who is now at the Medway meeting-house. The resistance you can or intend to make will only bring destruction upon this country. On the contrary, if you will deliver me the fort which you command, lay down your arms, and remain neuter until the fate of America is determined, you shall, as well as all the inhabitants of this parish, remain in peaceable possession of your property. Your answer, which I expect in an hour's time, will determine the fate of this country, whether it is to be laid in ashes, or remain as above proposed.

I am, sir, your most obedient, etc.,

L. V. Fuser

P.S.—Since this letter was closed, some of your people have been firing scattering shot about the line. I am to inform you that if a stop is not put to such irregular proceedings, I shall burn a house for every shot so fired.

McIntosh's reply.

Fort Morris, November 25, 1778

Sir:—We acknowledge we are not ignorant that your army is in motion to endeavour to reduce this State. We believe it entirely chimerical that Colonel Prevost is at the meeting-house; but should it be so, we are in no degree apprehensive of danger from a junction of his army with yours. We have no property compared with the object we contend for that we value a rush, and would rather perish in a vigorous defence than accept your proposals. We, sir, are fighting the battles of America, and therefore disdain to remain neutral till its fate is determined. As to surrendering the fort, receive this laconic reply, *"Come and take it!"* Major Lane, whom I send with this letter, is directed to satisfy you with respect to the irregular, loose firing mentioned on the back of your letter.

I have the honour to be,

Sir, your most obedient serv't,

John McIntosh,

Colonel of Continental Troops

—White, *Historical Collections of Georgia*, pp. 525-526.

3. The Maneuver That Led to the Fall of Savannah

Lieutenant Colonel Archibald Campbell to Lord George Germain.

Savannah, January 16, 1779

In consequence of Sir Henry Clinton's orders to proceed to Georgia with His Majesty's Seventy-first Regiment of Foot, two battalions of Hessians, four battalions of Provincials and a detachment of the Royal Artillery, I have the honor to acquaint your lordship of our having sailed from the Hook on the 27th of November, 1778, escorted by a squadron of His Majesty's ships of war under the command of Commodore Parker; and of the arrival of the whole fleet off the island of Tybee on the 23rd of December thereafter, two horse-sloops excepted.

Having no intelligence that could be depended upon with respect to the military force of Georgia or the disposition formed for its defence, Sir James Baird's Highland company of light-infantry, in two flat-boats, with Lieutenant

Clark of the Navy, was dispatched in the night of the 25th to seize any of the inhabitants they might find on the banks of Wilmington Creek. Two men were procured by this means, by whom we learned the most satisfactory intelligence concerning the state of matters at Savannah, and which settled the Commodore and I in the resolution of landing the troops the next evening at the plantation of one Gerridoe, an important post. This post was the first practicable landing-place on the Savannah River; the whole country between it and Tybee being a continued tract of deep marsh, intersected by the creeks of St. Augustine and Tybee, of considerable extent, and other cuts of water, impassable for troops at any time of the tide.

The *Vigilant*, man-of-war, with the *Comet*, galley, the *Keppel*, armed brig, and the *Greenwich*, armed sloop, followed by the transports in the divisions, in the order established for a descent, proceeded up the river with the tide at noon; about 4 o'clock in the evening the *Vigilant* opened the reach to Gerridoe's plantation and was cannonaded by two rebel galleys, who retired before any of their bullets had reached her: a single shot from the *Vigilant* quickened their retreat.

The tide and evening being too far spent, and many of the transports having grounded at the distance of five or six miles below Gerridoe's plantation, the descent was indispensably delayed till next morning. The first division of the troops, consisting of all the light-infantry of the army, the New York Volunteers and first battalion of the Seventy-first under the command of Lieutenant-colonel Maitland, were landed at break of day on the river-dam, in front of Gerridoe's plantation, from whence a narrow causeway of six hundred yards in length, with a ditch on each side, led through a rice-swamp directly to Gerridoe's house, which stood upon a bluff of thirty feet in height above the level of the rice-swamps.

The light-infantry, under Captain Cameron, having first reached the shore, were formed and led briskly forward to the bluff, where a body of fifty rebels were posted, and from whom they received a smart fire of musketry, but the Highlanders, rushing on with their usual impetuosity, gave them no time to repeat it: they drove them instantly to the woods and happily secured a landing for the rest of the army. Captain Cameron, a spirited and most valuable officer, with two Highlanders, were killed on this occasion, and five Highlanders wounded.

Upon the reconnoitering the environs of Gerridoe's plantation, I discovered the rebel army, under Major-general Robert Howe, drawn up about half a mile east of the town of Savannah, with several pieces of cannon in their front. The first division of troops, together with one company of the second battalion of the Seventy-first, the first battalion of Delancey's, the Wellworth, and part of the Weissenbach regiment of Hessians, being landed, I thought it expedient, having the day before me, to go in quest of the enemy rather than give them an opportunity of retiring unmolested.

A company of the second battalion of the Seventy-first, together with the first battalion of Delancey's, were accordingly left to cover the landing-place, and the troops marched for the town of Savannah.

The troops reached the open country near Tatnal's plantation before three o'clock in the evening and halted in the great road about two hundred paces short of the gate leading to Governor Wright's plantation, the light-infantry excepted, who were ordered to form immediately upon our right of the road, along the rails leading to Governor Wright's plantation.

The enemy were drawn up across the road at the distance of eight hundred yards from this gateway. One half, consisting of Thompson's and Eugee's [Huger's] regiments of Carolina troops, were formed under Colonel Eugee, with their left obliquely to the great road leading to Savannah, their right to a wooded swamp, covered by the houses of Tatnal's plantation, in which they had placed some riflemen. The other half of their regular troops, consisting of part of the first, second, third and fourth battalions of the Georgia brigade, was formed under Colonel Elbert, with their right to the road and their left to the rice-swamps of Governor Wright's plantation, with the fort of Savannah Bluff behind their left wing, in the style of second flank; the town of Savannah, round which they had the remains of an old line of intrenchment, covered their rear. One piece of cannon was planted on the right of their line, one upon the left, and two pieces occupied the traverse, across the great road, in the centre of their line. About one hundred paces in front of this traverse, at a critical spot between two swamps, a trench was cut across the road, and about one hundred yards in front of this trench, a marshy rivulet ran almost parallel the whole extent of their front, the bridge of which was burned down to interrupt the passage and retard our progress.

I could discover from the movements of the enemy that they wished and expected an attack upon their left, and I was desirous of cherishing that opinion.

Having accidentally fallen in with a Negro who knew a private path through the wooded swamp upon the enemy's right, I ordered the first battalion of the Seventy-first to form on our right of the road and move up to the rear of the light-infantry, whilst I drew off that corps to the right as if I meant to extend my front to that quarter, where a happy fall of ground favored the concealment of this manoeuvre, and increased the jealousy of the enemy with regard to their left. Sir James Baird had directions to convey the light-infantry in this hollow ground quite to the rear and penetrate the wooded swamp upon our left, with a view to get round by the new barracks into the rear of the enemy's right flank. The New York volunteers, under Colonel Trumbull, were ordered to support him.

During the course of this movement, our artillery were formed in a field on our left of the road, concealed from the enemy by a swell of ground in front, to which I meant to run them up for action when the signal was made to engage, and from whence I could either bear advantageously upon the right of the rebel line, as it was then formed, or cannonade any body of troops in flank which they might detach into the wood to retard the progress of the light-infantry.

The regiment of Wellworth was formed upon the left of the artillery, and the enemy continued to amuse themselves with their cannon without any return upon our part till it was visible that Sir James Baird and the light-infantry had fairly got round upon their rear. On this occasion I commanded the line to move briskly forward. The well-directed artillery of the line, the rapid advance of the Seventy-first Regiment and the forward countenance of the Hessian regiment of Wellworth instantly dispersed the enemy.

A body of the militia of Georgia, posted at the new barracks with some pieces of cannon to cover the road from Great Ogeeche, were at this juncture routed, with the loss of their artillery, by the light-infantry under Sir James Baird, when the scattered troops of the Carolina and Georgia brigades ran across the plain in his front. This officer with his usual gallantry dashed the light-infantry on their flank and terminated the fate of the day with brilliant success.

Thirty-eight officers of different distinctions, and four hundred and fifteen non-commissioned officers and privates, one stand of colors, forty-eight pieces of cannon, twenty-three mortars, ninety-four barrels of powder, the fort with all its stores, agreeable to the inclosed return, and, in short, the capital of Georgia, the shipping in the harbor, with a large quantity of provisions, fell into our possession before it was dark, without any other loss on our side than that of Captain Peter Campbell, a gallant officer of Skinner's light-infantry, and two privates killed, one sergeant and nine privates wounded. Eighty-three of the enemy were found dead on the Common, and eleven wounded. By the accounts received from their prisoners, thirty lost their lives in the swamp, endeavoring to make their escape.

—DAWSON, *Battles of the United States*, I, 477-479.

II. ADVANCE AND REPULSE IN GEORGIA

General Lincoln, dispatched by Congress to take command in the South, pushed down from Charleston toward Savannah. He encamped at Purrysburg opposite Prevost, who was across the river on the Georgia side. Morale was high but the numbers of Patriot soldiers were too few to mount an attack. Nevertheless in quick succession two victories were scored against the British—at Beaufort and at Kettle Creek. Moultrie marched a force from Purrysburg over to Beaufort where they came to grips with the British. The American victory was the more astonishing since the Patriots fought on open ground while the British fought from bushes and swamp which they had quickly seized: a reversal of the usual military pattern of the Revolutionary War.

Kettle Creek was a fight between Tories and militiamen. The former, chiefly Scotsmen, were marching from North Carolina to join up with Tory partisans in back-country Georgia. Colonel Pickens caught the Tories by surprise at Kettle Creek, where they were engaged in slaughtering a herd of stolen cattle. Attacked from both wings and in the center, the British force broke and scattered. Seventy of the prisoners were condemned to death, all but five pardoned. These, the ringleaders, were hanged.

From his camp at Purrysburg Lincoln now seized the initiative. He sent one force to the eastern bank of the Savannah River opposite Augusta, another to the Black Swamp, and a third to Briar Creek south of Augusta. This last force was under the command of General John Ashe and comprised some 1,400 North Carolina militia and a handful of Continentals. As the Patriot forces converged on Augusta, Campbell evacuated that frontier town and set his own troops in motion for the return to Savannah. Ashe followed in pursuit. Campbell crossed Briar Creek and destroyed the bridge over it. Then Ashe came up and set to work to rebuild it. This encouraged Campbell to send a detachment under Colonel Mark Prevost, younger brother of the commander, to make a wide turning movement, cross the creek above Ashe's camp and attack him from the rear. When that attack came, the militia fled. The Patriots suffered 400 casualties against 16 for the British. Six hundred others ran home. In all, only 400 ever got back to Lincoln, who had lost one third of his army. Briar Creek showed that the militia were still not consistently reliable under fire and spelled finis to Lincoln's campaign to recapture Georgia at that time.

1. "Let Not Economy Border Too Much upon Parsimony"

William Moultrie to C. C. Pinckney, President of the Senate of South Carolina.

Purisburgh [Purrysburg] January 10, 1779

I challenge you to open a correspondence between Charlestown and our camp. If you accept I shall expect to hear from you, and shall continue to write you and give you the earliest and best intelligence that comes in my way; and shall hope you will answer me accordingly.

We are (I mean the Continentals) encamped at Purisburgh, the N. Carolinians on the road leading to this place, about two miles from us. Our numbers are about 500 privates (Continentals), and the North-Carolinians about 1200 of all ranks. We are all in good spirits and ready to receive the enemy, but are not strong enough to pay them the first visit. From all the intelligence we can get, their numbers on the opposite side of the river to us amount to about 1500 and they occupy all the posts near us over which we could possibly pass; besides our men are undisciplined and many unarmed. I hope Richardson and others will soon join us. I think we should have 5,000 men before we cross the river, as we shall get immediately into action.

I hope we shall drive those gentry on board their vessels. We hear their drums beat every morning from our out posts; nay, hear their sentinels cough. I have no idea of the enemy coming over to us; their principal aim seems to be, until they can strengthen themselves from the back parts of these two southern states, then perhaps they may endeavor to push us from hence. I hope our countrymen turn out cheerfully; if they do not, I fear the war will be long and serious and brought into our own state, which will be very unfortunate.

A late instance I have had before my eyes: the poor women and children and Negroes of Georgia, many thousands of whom I saw on my journey to this place (a spectacle that even moved the hearts of the soldiers), travelling to they knew not where.

I fear we have lost Sunberry and two gallies that took shelter under that battery last Thursday or Friday, as we heard a very heavy cannonade from that quarter. The officer commanding had about 120 Continentals and some inhabitants within the fort, refused to evacuate the post; notwithstanding his receiving positive orders for that purpose, he Don Quixote-like thought he was strong enough to withstand the whole force the British had in Georgia, for which I think he deserved to be hanged.

We have the *Congress* and *Lee,* gallies, a ten-gun sloop and two schooners now lying under this bluff (they pushed up here to get out of the way of the British). They may be of some service to cover our crossing, should it be expedient to land below this place, or to establish any post on the other side of the river. I believe they cannot go much higher than where they now are.

As it is absolutely necessary to keep open the communication between this place and Charlestown, I wish you would think of some way, either legislatively or otherwise, to keep the roads and bridges in good order; they are now wearing away fast, notwithstanding we have had so much dry weather; how will they be when the rains set in, as they seem to begin to day? For God's sake, let not your legislative or executive economy border too much upon parsimony! Be generous to your militia. Allow them every thing necessary to take the field. It is now time to open your purse strings. Our country is in danger. Be more bountiful than you have been hitherto in this present administration. Have the modesty to allow that very few of you have the least idea of what is necessary for an army, and grant what the officers shall ask for that purpose. They are certainly the best judges.

Excuse me for this digression, but I cannot help being warmed, when I think how ill the officers of this state have been treated, in being refused almost every necessary they applied for; and had not Gen. Lincoln arrived here as he did, with the money, we should not have been able to take the field at this time, and our country might have been lost. I shall say no more on this head, as my warmth might carry me too far. . . .

—MOULTRIE, *Memoirs,* I, 258-261.

2. AT BEAUFORT A REVERSAL OF THE USUAL WAY OF FIGHTING

William Moultrie to General Benjamin Lincoln.

Beaufort, February 4, 1779

I wrote you a few days ago from Gen. Bull's, when I was there. The militia requested me to cross the river with them, which I readily consented to. The next morning, after leaving a proper guard to our camp, we began to cross the ferry and got near three hundred over by sun set. We immediately marched off and continued till we got within one mile of Beaufort. Here I rested the troops a few hours and then proceeded to the town which we entered at sun rise next morning.

Having ordered the troops into quarters and reposed myself a little, I rode down to view the fort with Gen. Bull and two or three other gentlemen. We had scarce been a moment there when an express arrived informing that the enemy were in full march for Beaufort and not more than five miles off; upon this I requested Gen. Bull to ride on to town and have the men turned out. I followed immediately and found them all paraded, and had another account that the enemy were coming very fast.

I then moved off the troops in order to meet them and, having marched

two miles, was again informed they were within four miles of us. I then proceeded very slowly, looking for a proper piece of ground to form upon. Having soon found a very advantageous spot, I continued there, waiting an hour
for the enemy, and was then informed that they had, after halting awhile,
altered their march and were going towards our ferry. I followed them and
had gone about three miles when I learnt that they were upon their return
from the ferry, in full march towards us, and not more than one mile distant.
Having sent my aid, Mr. Kinlock, to reconnoitre and bring me a particular
account, he soon returned and informed me they were just at hand. I hastened
our march to gain a swamp which was near; but finding the enemy had already
got possession of the ground I intended to occupy, I halted at about two hundred yards distance from the enemy and drew up the troops to the right and
left of the road, with two field-pieces (6-pounders) in the centre, and one
small piece (2-pounder) on the right in the wood. On the enemy's near
approach, I ordered Capt. Thomas Heyward to begin with the two field-
pieces, and advanced my right and left wings nearer the swamp, and then the
firing became pretty general.

This action was reversed from the usual way of fighting between the
British and Americans: they taking to the bushes and we remaining upon the
open ground. After some little time, finding our men too much exposed to
the enemy's fire, I ordered them to take trees. About three quarters of an
hour after the action began, I heard a general cry through the line of "No
more cartridges"; and was also informed by Captains Heyward and Rutledge
that the ammunition for the field-pieces was almost expended, after firing
about forty rounds from each piece. Upon this I ordered the field-pieces to be
drawn off very slowly, and their right and left wings to keep pace with the
artillery to cover their flanks, which was done in tolerable order for undisciplined troops. The enemy had beat their retreat before we began to move,
but we had little or no ammunition and could not of consequence pursue.
They retreated so hastily as to leave an officer, one sergeant and three privates
wounded in a house near the action, and their dead lying on the field. . . .

It makes me happy to assure you that our militia have that spirit which
they have always been allowed to possess. Nothing but discipline is wanting
to make them good troops. The Charlestown artillery behaved gallantly;
they stood to their pieces like veterans and served them well, until I was
constrained to order them to retire in consequence of their ammunition being
nearly expended. I had in the action only nine Continental troops: Capt. De
Treville, two officers, and six privates, with one brass two-pounder and only
fifteen rounds. I must, in justice to them, say, that they behaved well.

                                        —MOULTRIE, *Memoirs*, I, 291-295.

3. The Disastrous Repulse at Briar Creek

General John Ashe of North Carolina to Governor Caswell of North Carolina.
                                        Camp, Zubley's Ferry, March 17, 1779
I should have wrote you long since, had I had time or opportunity, but we
have been constantly marching since we left Elizabeth—from thence to

Charlestown, to Purisburg, to Augusta—to prevent the enemies' crossing into this State and making a junction with the disaffected (which are numerous) of this and our State.

The night of our arrival opposite to Augusta, the enemy encamped and made a precipitate retreat down the Savannah River (tho' double our number), from an information that my command amounted to eleven thousand, when in fact it did not exceed twelve hundred. I halted at this place, considering it an important pass to the State of South Carolina, till directed by General Lincoln to cross the river and march down to a place called Bryer Creek, the bridge of which the enemy had burnt down on their retreat. The creek makes out of the Savannah River, on the Georgia side, about sixty miles below Augusta, runs at right angles from the river about half a mile back of the river swamp, and then runs almost parallel with the river, so that forty miles up the river it is but ten miles distant, the swamp of the river being generally three miles wide, and on the creek a deep swamp, eight miles above the bridge a mill, and several fords between the bridge and mill, and also above.

Here we reached on the 27th ulto., and halted till the 3rd instant, expecting to be reinforced with such of the Georgia militia as were well affected, about one hundred and thirty Georgia Continentals, horse and some of the militia from South Carolina, and General Rutherford's brigade—none of which, except two hundred and seven horse from South Carolina, one hundred and fifty only of which were fit for duty, joined us. Genl. Rutherford, with part of his brigade, had reached Matthew's Bluff, about five miles above, with the river between, and Col. Marbury, of the Georgia horse, lay a few miles above on Bryer Creek, so that I had with me only Genl. Bryan's brigade, consisting of nine hundred men; Lieut. Col. Lytle's light infantry of about two hundred fit for duty; about seventy Georgia Continental troops (the South Carolina light horse being sent over the creek to reconnoitre); one four-pound brass field-piece, and two iron two-pound swivels, mounted as field-pieces. From these are to be deducted near a hundred waggoners and carters, which were always returned as soldiers in Gen. Bryan's brigade, with a guard of 50 men that had been sent to guard the baggage across the river, about eight miles above us (which had fortunately been effected a few minutes before the enemy appeared), and fifty on a fatigue party, to make bridges and clear the road (about three miles above us) to the river for General Rutherford's brigade and two brass field-pieces that had been sent from head quarters to Matthews' Bluff.

In this situation, without a possibility of retreat, I had advice of the enemy being about eight miles above, in full march toward us. We immediately beat to arms, formed the troops into two lines and served them with cartridges, which they could not prudently have been served with sooner, as they had several times received cartridges which had been destroyed and lost for want of cartouch boxes. We marched out of lines to meet the enemy, some carrying their cartridges under their arms, others in the bosoms of their shirts, and some tied up in the corners of their hunting shirts. Having advanced about a quarter of a mile from our encampment, I saw the enemy on a quick march, in force amounting, as I have since been informed, to eighteen hundred regulars. Several hundred Georgia and Florida scouts, with four or five hundred horse (by some said to be nine hundred), formed in three columns, with several field-pieces called grasshoppers. When they came within one hundred and fifty yards of us, they then displayed their columns to the right and left to form a line.

It was now that the Georgia Continentals and Col. Perkins' regiment, which formed the right of our first line, began their fire. The Georgia Continentals, under Genl. Elbert who acted as colonel, after two or three rounds advanced without orders a few steps beyond the line and moved to the left in front of the regiment from the district of New Bern, which much impeded their firing. By this movement and that of the Edenton regiment, which had been obliged to move a little to the right, there was a vacancy in the line. At this instant of time the Halifax regiment, which was upon the left of the second line, broke and took to flight without firing a gun. The Wilmington (except a small part under the command of Lieut. Col. Young, who were advancing in their line to the right to prevent being flanked, and fired two or three rounds) and the New Bern regiments followed their example. The Edenton regiment continued for two or three discharges longer, when they gave way and took to flight, just as Lieut. Col. Lytle, with his light infantry and a brass field-piece (which had been posted at the bridge about a mile and a half from the field), came up. As he saw the impossibility of the troops being rallied, and that it would be only exposing his small corps to no purpose, he moved off in order in the rear of the fugitives, reserving his fire. The Georgia Continentals still continued in action some little time longer, till their General surrendered himself a prisoner.

When I found the second line had given way, I rode across from the rear of Perkins' regiment and the Georgians, where I had taken post for a better observation of the movement of the enemy, to the rear of the fugitives, and called to the officers to rally their men, which I was in expectation might be done while there was an opposition made by the first line, but by the time I had wheeled my horse and got a few paces on my return, I saw the Edenton regiment break and take to flight. I then used my utmost exertions to get in front of the fugitives for half a mile or three-quarters, in order to rally them; in which I was assisted by Col. Perkins, Lieut. Cols. Young and Williams, Majors Blount and Doherty, with some few others, who exerted themselves on this occasion, when, finding it impossible, and that if I proceeded much further I must unavoidably fall into the hands of the enemy, I wheeled to the left into the river swamp and made my escape to Matthews' Bluff, which I had crossed on my return from Genl. Lincoln the preceding day—a place unknown to the troops, about four miles up the swamp—accompanied by Majors Pointer and McIlhean and one light horseman, swimming several lagoons on our horses.

I imagined most of the troops would have been either killed or taken, as they had very little further to fly before the broken bridge at Bryer Creek must stop them; but by a lucky halt which the enemy made for a few moments at the place of our encampment, they made their escape down the creek and thro' the river swamp, many of which swam the river, some crossed on rafts which they made, and others were fetched across in canoes, which were ordered down from Matthews' Bluff; so that we have only one hundred and fifty missing, upwards of fifty of which, we hear, crossed the river above and returned into our State. . . .

The little attention paid to orders, both by officers and soldiers, the several mutinies of the Halifax regiment, and desertions from the brigade, and Genl. Bryan's unhappy temper, from my march from Elizabeth to Bryer Creek, have rendered my command very disagreeable; and since the action, his conduct has been such as will forever render him contemptible to me; of which I shall inform you when I have the pleasure of seeing you, which I hope will be ere long. Let it suffice that at present I only add that he has, by himself and his tools, endeavored to propagate a report that I was both a traitor and coward, on which I have procured a court of inquiry to be held. . . .

—*North Carolina State Records*, XIV, 39-43.

III. PREVOST'S CHARLESTON EXPEDITION

Lincoln still kept the initiative despite the reverse at Briar Creek. On April 23 he marched up the Savannah River to cross near Augusta and cut off supplies to the British from the west. He left Moultrie with a thousand men at Purrysburg and Black Swamp to guard Savannah. Realizing Moultrie's weakness, Prevost crossed the Savannah and drove up toward Charleston. Moultrie retreated before him, delaying the advance by rear-guard skirmishes.

When Prevost reached Charleston he found it more formidable than he had anticipated. The neck of land between Charleston and the mainland was now fortified, and the city had received reinforcements under Count Casimir Pulaski. Nevertheless, to hold off the attack, Moultrie, at Governor Rutledge's request, entered into negotiations with the British. To everyone's surprise Rutledge offered to have the state remain neutral, a far cry from the heroic resistance back in '76. Prevost insisted on unconditional surrender. The approach of a relief force under Lincoln persuaded the British commander to pull out while he still had the chance. He withdrew through the islands along the coast, establishing a strong force on the mainland at Stono Ferry, where he could secure the navigation of the Stono River and protect the retreat to Georgia. As the South Carolina militia were beginning to drift homeward and the terms of the Virginia and North Carolina militia would expire in a few days, a Council of War determined to attack the Stono Ferry. A force under Moultrie arrived before the works just after daybreak, but his numbers were inadequate. The Highlanders stood up against a bayonet attack until all but eleven of them had fallen. The British were able to retreat safely to Savannah, hopping from island to island.

The Prevost expedition was accompanied by enormous looting by the British troops. Many of the slaves who flocked to the British army were sold off to the West Indies. But pillage was to become a minor phase of the fratricidal slaughter that now flared up in the Carolinas and Georgia as war's terrors spread throughout the lower South.

MOULTRIE DECIDES: "WE WILL FIGHT IT OUT"

About 3 o'clock in the morning [of May 11, 1779], it being still very dark, I heard some person inquiring for me. I rode up and was then told the governor wanted to see me; upon which I rode up to him. He then took me aside and asked me "whether we had not best have a parly with the enemy, and whether we were able to resist their force"; and asked about our numbers.

I assured him that they were upwards of 2,200 men.

He replied, "he did not think we had more than 1,800 men; and that the enemy's force, as he was informed, was 7 or 8,000 men at least; and should they force the lines, a great number of the citizens would be put to death." He represented to me the horrors of a storm: he told me that the state's engineer (Col. Senf) had represented to him the lines to be in a very weak state. After some conversation, he proposed to me the sending out a flag, to know what terms we could obtain.

I told him I thought we could stand against the enemy, that I did not think they could force the lines, and that I did not chuse to send a flag in my name, but if he chose it and would call the council together, I would send any message. They requested me to send the following, which was delivered by Mr. Kinlock:

"Gen. Moultrie, perceiving from the motions of your army that your intention is to besiege the town, would be glad to know on what terms you would be disposed to grant a capitulation, should he be inclined to capitulate."

About 11 o'clock, A.M., the following letter was sent in from the enemy:

"Sir,

"The humane treatment which the inhabitants of Georgia and this province have hitherto received will, I flatter myself, induce you to accept of the offers of peace and protection which I now make by the orders of Gen. Prevost; the evils and horrors attending the event of a storm (which cannot fail to be successful) are too evident not to induce a man of human feelings to do all in his power to prevent it: you may depend that every attention shall be paid, and every necessary measure be adopted, to prevent disorders; and that such of the inhabitants who may not chuse to receive the generous offers of peace and protection may be received as prisoners of war, and their fate decided by that of the rest of the colonies.

"Four hours shall be allowed for an answer; after which your silence, or the detention of the bearer of this, will be deemed a positive refusal.

"I have the honor to be, etc.,

"J. M. PREVOST,

"Col. commanding the advance,

"Camp at Ashley-Ferry.

"May 11th, 1779

"Brig. Gen. Moultrie, or the commanding officer in Charlestown."

On my receiving this letter, I showed it to the governor, who immediately summoned his council to meet at his own house, and requested I would go with them and bring Count Paulaski with me. Col. Laurens was also sent for. And I sent to Col. Cambray, the engineer, to work upon the left of our lines as fast as possible, because that part was very incomplete, and also ordered the bringing up the ammunition from town to the lines, as a number of the men had not more than three rounds the preceeding night. They had come in but the night before from the country. We scarcely had time to furnish them with arms and ammunition when the enemy were at our gates.

On the meeting of the council, the letter was read to them; they argued the matter of giving up the town amongst themselves. Gen. Count Paulaski and myself advised them not to give up the town, that we had men enough to beat the enemy; and so did Col. Laurens. They then asked me our number, which I gave the governor an account of, corps by corps, and which he took down on the back of the letter sent to me from Col. Prevost. They amounted to 3,180 at the lowest computation. I had mentioned more, in some of the corps, but it would not be allowed me: the governor was sure there must be some mistake in the returns; that he did not think we had more than 2,500 men on the lines. . . .

A gentleman who had been reconnoitreing with a party of horse about Ponpon Bridge and Parker's-ferry was asked his opinion respecting the number of the enemy; he gave them to the governor, corps by corps, according to the information he had received; which account was taken down by the governor on the back of the same letter from Col. Prevost and [totaled 3,620 men]. . . .

The gentleman also said that he was informed that besides those already taken down, there were a great many tories from North and South-Carolina and Georgia that had joined them.

I then replied to him, "that I believed they could not have more than 1,000, at most."

He said, "he could not tell."

During this business at the governor's house Captain Dunbar, of the Second Regiment, came in great haste to acquaint me that Gen. Prevost had observed our working on the lines during the passing of the flags, and that if I did not immediately desist, he would march his troops in. I sent orders to stop the working, and urged the governor and council to conclude upon something, as the time was growing very short, and that I wanted to be at the lines. At length they resolved I should send the following message:

"Charlestown, May 12th, 1779.

"Sir,

"I cannot possibly agree to so dishonorable a proposal as is contained in your favor of yesterday; but if you will appoint an officer to confer on terms, I will send one to meet him, at such time and place as you fix on.

"I have the honor to be, etc.
"William Moultrie.

"Brig. Gen. Prevost."

On my retreat from Black-swamp, Colonel Senf, from the governor's camp, Orangeburgh, joined me at Ponpon Bridge with the Racoon Company, commanded by Captain John Allston, of about fifty men on horseback. I ordered the stores at the borough to be burnt, with a quantity of rice that was in them, to prevent its falling into the enemy's hands, and the bridge to be destroyed; I also ordered Colonel Senf, with his men, to keep in my rear, and to burn all boats and bridges and throw every obstruction in the enemy's way to retard their march. They were the last corps that came into the town before the gates were shut.

When the question was carried for giving up the town upon a neutrality, I will not say who was for the question, but this I well remember, that Mr. John Edwards, one of the privy council, a worthy citizen and a very respectable merchant of Charlestown, was so affected as to weep, and said, "What, are we to give up the town at last?"

The governor and council adjourned to Colonel Beekman's tent on the lines at the gate. I sent for Colonel John Laurens from his house, to request the favor he would carry a message from the governor and council to General Prevost; but when he knew the purport, he begged to be excused from carrying such a message, that it was much against his inclination; that he would do any thing to serve his country; but he could not think of carrying such a message as that.

I then sent for Colonel M'Intosh and requested he would go with Colonel Roger Smith, who was called on by the governor, with the message. They both begged I would excuse them; hoped and requested I would get some other person. I however pressed them into a compliance; which message was as follows:

"To propose a neutrality during the war between Great-Britain and America, and the question whether the state shall belong to Great-Britain or remain one of the United States be determined by the treaty of peace between those two powers."

Colonel Prevost was appointed one of the commissioners to confer with Colonel M'Intosh and Colonel Smith, and they held their conference a quarter of a mile from our gate. We could see them from our lines. Upon the above proposal being made, Colonel Prevost answered, "that they did not come in a legislative capacity, but if Colonel Smith pleased, he would show the proposal to the general." Upon meeting them a second time, at 12 o'clock, Colonel Prevost said, "he had nothing to do with the governor, that his business was with General Moultrie, and as the garrison was in arms, they must surrender prisoners of war." ...

Upon this the governor and council looked very grave and stedfastly on each other and on me, not knowing what I would say. After a little pause, I said to the governor and council, "Gentlemen, you see how the matter stands. The point is this: Am I to deliver you up prisoners of war or not?"

Some replied "yes."

BATTLE OF THE WAXHAWS

COLONELS WASHINGTON AND TARLETON CLASH AFTER THE BATTLE OF COWPENS

I then said, "I am determined not to deliver you up prisoners of war. *We will fight it out!*"

Upon my saying this, Colonel Laurens, who was in the tent, jumped up and said, "Thank God! we are upon our legs again"; and as I was coming out of the tent, General Gadsden and Mr. Ferguson, two of the council who were against giving up the town, followed me and said, "Act according to your own judgment, and we will support you."

I immediately ordered the flag to be waved from the gate, which was a signal agreed upon should the conference be at an end. They did not perceive our flag wave; they therefore continued with theirs flying some time longer, upon which I sent out Mr. Kinlock to inform them "that I was very sorry they should be detained so long, that our flag had been waved some time ago, and that all conference was at an end." After which I hurried on in preparing every thing for our defence.

In justice to the citizens, they knew nothing of what was going forward in the council. They all seemed firm, calm, and determined to stand to the lines and defend their country.

The next morning at day-light, to the great joy of the citizens, it was cried out along the line, "The enemy is gone." There is no doubt they must have begun their retreat with their main body immediately after the conference was at an end, leaving some of their light troops to make a show before our lines, to divert us from treading too close upon their rear, and to move themselves off under the cover of the night. Early next morning, not seeing any of them, it was conjectured they were gone; and Count Paulaski went out on horseback and made two or three circuits at full speed; and not discovering any of them, returned in and made his reports, and then collected the cavalry and followed; but they had crossed Ashley River before he got there. I had given orders to him to endeavor to find out where Gen. Lincoln was, with his army. . . .

On the 14th I received the following letter from Gen. Lincoln:

"May 10th, 1779, 4 o'clock, P.M.
"Dear Sir,
"I just now received your favor of the 8th. . . . We are making and shall continue to make every exertion for the relief of Charlestown. The baggage will be left. . . . The inability of the men only will put a period to our daily marches. . . . I am unhappy to inform you that the 1,000 horse you mention are decreased to less than 150, a number scarcely sufficient for our front and flank guards and the other necessary duties of camp. . . . Pray stimulate your people to every exertion for the defence of the town, until the troops here can arrive. Our men are full of spirits; I think they will do honor to themselves, and render service to the public. . . . *Do not give up, or suffer the people to despair.*

"I am, etc.
"B. Lincoln

"Brig. Gen. Moultrie."

A copy of this letter was taken by the British on the 11th near our lines, which we suppose obliged them to retreat so precipitately, as they found Gen. Lincoln was on his march downwards with about 4,000 men, and had they staid two or three days longer on the town-neck, they would have been in a very unpleasant situation between two fires; and if they had retreated the same way back, they would have met Gen. Lincoln's army. They therefore filed off to the left and went on the islands.

—MOULTRIE, *Memoirs*, I, 426-437.

IV. THE FRANCO-AMERICAN EXPEDITION
TO RECAPTURE SAVANNAH

The withdrawal of Prevost from the outskirts of Charleston resulted in the initiative once more passing to the Patriots. The operations of Admiral d'Estaing against the British West Indies served to check militant moves by the British in the lower South. Governor Rutledge of South Carolina and General Lincoln were convinced now that, with the co-operation of the French fleet, Georgia might be regained to the Patriot cause. The main body of D'Estaing's fleet, consisting of 22 ships of the line and 11 frigates, arrived off the approaches to Savannah on September 8, 1779. The British sent a call for help by fast ship to Sir Henry Clinton in New York, and planned to employ their own vessels of war either to retire up the river or defend the entry to the harbor. Slave labor was employed to improve the town's fortifications. Two vessels of war and four transports were sunk in the channel, blocking it up. The combined Franco-American attacking forces numbered 5,000, along with General Pulaski's Legion, as against 3,200 defenders.

Savannah was the Charleston story again, but in reverse. D'Estaing called on the garrison to surrender. Prevost stalled for time. Under cover of the truce until the following day Colonel Maitland's forces from Port Royal, after a remarkable march, reached the town in safety, and, thus reinforced, Prevost refused to surrender. Several bombardments did some damage to the town, but not to the British military installations. D'Estaing decided that unless the town could be taken by storm, he would discontinue the siege. The assault took place on October 9, preceded by a heavy bombardment. But plans misfired: some troops got lost in a swamp and were exposed to heavy enemy fire; others, betrayed by a deserter, were hard hit by both direct fire from the redoubt and cross fire from the works on the right and an armed ship in the river. Some of the attackers scaled the ramparts, and a bloody fight ensued, until they were forced to give way and a retreat was ordered. Count Pulaski, having dashed forward to charge the rear of the enemy's line, was struck by a small cannon ball and mortally wounded. The allied casualties exceeded 800; the British were hardly more than 150.

Admiral d'Estaing had had enough. As a French officer put it, "Our situation had become terrible and disheartening." On October 20 the French returned to their fleet, and the ships proceeded to leave on different missions. The Americans recrossed the river. Thus ended the campaign of 1779.

SIEGE OF SAVANNAH

Numerous ironical ballads commemorated the Franco-American rout at Savannah, and British and Tories rejoiced that another allied operation in which D'Estaing played a central role was a fiasco.

> *To Charleston with fear*
> *The rebels repair;*
> *D'Estaing scampers back to his boats, sir,*
> *Each blaming the other,*
> *Each cursing his brother,*
> *And—may they cut each other's throats, sir!*

1. BAD WEATHER DELAYS D'ESTAING'S LANDING OPERATIONS

Journal of an anonymous French naval officer with the fleet.

[September 8-18, 1779].

Wednesday, the eighth of September, we made the coast of Florida [should be Georgia]. That evening the fleet anchored within three leagues of the lighthouse at the entrance of the Savannah River in New Georgia. Of all their former possessions in this quarter of the South, the English held only Savannah and Saint Augustine. . . .

We took possession of such small craft as attempted to escape from us along the coast. The general wished to debark his troops that night, but found that the place where he proposed to land them, and which with twenty-five men he had himself reconnoitered, was an island. He then determined to place all his troops, forming a corps of about four thousand men, including eight hundred free mulattoes taken and enlisted in the colony of Saint Domingo, on board six ships entrusted to the command of M. de la Motte-Piquet, with instructions to proceed six leagues further south to the River Saint Mary, and there disembark. He was to carry with him nearly all the long-boats of the vessels left at the first anchorage. The Chevalier du Rumain was ordered to enter the river with his frigate, and two store ships armed with 18-pounder guns, and as many lighters as possible, and advance as near the city as was practicable. The frigates were engaged in guarding the various passes. *Le Sagittaire* and *le Fier Rodrigue* blockaded Port Royal.

Having made these dispositions M. d'Estaing, on the 11th of September, accompanied the six ships of M. de la Motte-Piquet, leaving the command of the fleet to the Count de Broves. He anchored that evening at the mouth of the Saint Mary and, during the night, debarked with fifteen hundred men, each soldier, in obedience to his orders, carrying provisions and water for three days.

The rowboats having accomplished this first landing were desirous of returning to the ships that they might bring the remainder of the troops. Some of the longboats and canoes which, despite the bad weather, obstinately determined to leave the river in obedience to the positive instructions of the general, who knew not the difficulties which confronted them, perished. . . .

The bad weather lasted until the 18th. It was impossible to continue the disembarkation. Not even a canoe could be sent ashore. Nearly all the vessels, moored on the open coast, were forced to set sail and go far out to sea to escape destruction.

For six days Count d'Estaing remained on shore, with fifteen hundred men having only their guns, some rounds of ammunition and three days rations, destitute of tents and baggage, exposed to a constant rain, and near enough to the enemy to apprehend an attack each instant. Fortunately the enemy was ignorant of the situation of our troops.

At last the weather permitted us to finish the debarkation; and Count d'Estaing, without losing a moment, advanced upon the enemy whom he found entrenched below the city of Savannah. With the few troops under his command he could not attack with hope of success. Many have thought he should, under the circumstances, have then re-embarked. It is certain, had he done so, he would have followed a wiser plan, for his entire fleet was lying exposed upon the coast. But this is judgment after event. M. d'Estaing could rely on the co-operation of the Americans. Major General Prevost seemed inclined to surrender. In a conference he announced that he would, to save his honor, make an apparent defense; but Colonel Meklen [Maitland], who with seven hundred men threw himself into the place by way of Saint Augustine Creek, changed all at once these pacific dispositions.

—JONES, ed., *Siege of Savannah*, pp. 58-60.

2. SAVANNAH'S CIVILIANS BEAR THE BRUNT OF THE BOMBARDMENT

Loyalist Chief Justice Anthony Stokes of Georgia to his wife.

November 9, 1779

The French and Americans had invested the town, and the French had intrenched themselves up to the chin, about two hundred yards from our lines, some time before their artillery and ammunition came up from their ships; and as a slight cannonade had passed over, many began to flatter themselves that the enemy would go away without any further effects. But in this they found themselves much mistaken; for at midnight of the third of October, when all the woman and children were asleep, the French opened a battery of nine mortars and kept up a very heavy bombardment for an hour and a half, in which time those who counted the shells found that they fired one hundred, which were chiefly directed to the town.

I heard one of the shells whistle over my quarters, and presently afterwards I got up and dressed myself; and as our neighborhood seemed to be in the line of fire, I went out with a view to go to the eastward, out of the way; but a shell that seemed to be falling near me, rather puzzled me how to keep clear of it, and I returned to the house not a little alarmed. I then proceeded to the westward, and then the shells seemed to fall all around. There I soon joined a number of gentlemen who had left their houses on account of the bombardment and, like me, were retiring from the line of fire to Yammacraw. Here we stayed till between one and two in the morning, when the bombardment ceased. Fortunately for us, there was no cannonade at the same time, and in the night shells are so discernible that they are more easily avoided than in the day.

Being indisposed, I had not slept a wink from my going to bed at nine till the bombardment began at twelve; and before I returned again, it was near three in the morning, when from fatigue I soon fell asleep; but at five I was awakened with a very heavy cannonade from a French frigate to the north of the town, and with a bombardment which soon hurried me out of bed; and before I could get my clothes on, an eighteen-pounder entered the house, stuck in the middle partition, and drove the plastering all about. We who were in the house now found ourselves in a cross fire; and notwithstanding the rum in the cellar, we thought it less dangerous to descend there than to continue in the house, as the fall of a shell into the cellar was not so probable as the being killed in the house with a cannon ball; for the cellar being under ground, a shot in its usual direction would not reach us.

The cellar was so full of rum and provisions that Mrs. Cooper, the Negroes and myself could hardly creep in; and after we had descended into it, some shot struck the house, and one passed through the kitchen, from which the Negroes had then lately come down; and had they not luckily moved away, it is probable that several of them would have been killed. Whilst we were in the cellar, two shells burst not far from the door, and many others fell in the neighborhood all around us. In this situation a number of us continued in a damp cellar, until the cannonade and bombardment almost ceased, for the French to cool their artillery; and then we ascended to breakfast.

As the cannonade and bombardment were chiefly directed to the town, no mischief was done in the lines that I heard of; but a Mr. Pollard, deputy barrack-master, was killed by a shell in that house on the bay which was formerly inhabited by Mr. Moss; and the daughter of one Thomson was almost shot in two by a cannon ball, at the house next to where Mr. Elliott lived. I am told there were other lives lost, but I have not heard the particulars.

Fortunately for us, after breakfast the town adjutant's wife and myself went over to Captain Knowles, who is agent for the transports, and to whose cellar Mr. Prevost, the general's lady and several gentlemen and ladies had retired for security. This house was directly opposite to my quarters, and about thirty or forty feet distant. The general's lady and Captain Knowles invited us to stay there, which invitation we accepted, and we continued in the cellar, with several others, as agreeably as the situation of matters would admit of, until three o'clock on Tuesday morning.

During the whole of this time the French kept up a brisk cannonade and bombardment, the shot frequently struck near us, and the shells fell on each side of us with so much violence that in their fall they shook the ground, and many of them burst with a great explosion. On Monday night we heard a shot strike my quarters, and in the morning we found an eighteen-pounder had entered the house and fallen near the head of my Negro, Dick, who providentially received no hurt.

The guns seemed to approach on each side, and about three o'clock on Wednesday morning a shell whistled close by Captain Knowles' house. Soon afterwards another came nearer and seemed to strike my quarters, and I thought I heard the cry of people in distress. We all jumped up, and before I could dress myself, my quarters were so much in flames that I could not venture further than the door, for fear of an explosion from the rum. George and Jemmy were over with me in Captain Knowles' cellar; the others were at my quarters. George ran over before me, and fortunately for me drew out of the flames the two black trunks with some of my apparel, etc., that I brought out with me, and then removed them over to Captain Knowles' passage, which was all the property I saved, except a little black trunk that was put into one of the large ones by accident; for I momently expected that the explosion of the rum would blow up the house and kill every one near it; and as soon as the French observed the flames, they kept up a very heavy cannonade and bombardment and pointed their fire to that object to prevent any person approaching to extinguish the flames.

I retired to Captain Knowles', where, in vain, I called out for some Negroes to help me to save my two trunks, for I expected that Captain Knowles' house, and the commodore's next to it, would be destroyed. No Negro came to my assistance, and I was informed that mine, who slept at the quarters, being frightened at the shell, had ran away; but unfortunately that information was not true. Being in the direction of the French fire, I was every moment in danger of being smashed to pieces with a shell, or shot in two with a cannon ball; and as each of the trunks were too large for me to carry off, I thought it safer to abandon them and retire to a place of safety than to run the risk of losing my life as well as my property.

I had some distance to go before I got out of the line of fire, and I did not know the way under Savannah Bluff, where I should have been safe from cannon balls; and, therefore, whenever I came to the opening of a street, I watched the flashes of the mortars and guns, and pushed on until I came under cover of a house; and when I got to the common and heard the whistling of a shot or shell, I fell on my face. But the stopping under cover of a house was no security, for the shot went through many houses; and Thomson's daughter was killed at the side opposite to that where the shot entered. . . .

The appearance of the town afforded a melancholy prospect, for there was hardly a house which had not been shot through, and some of them were almost destroyed. Ambrose, Wright and Stute's, in which we lived, had upwards of fifty shot that went through each of them, as I am informed; and old Mr. Habersham's house, in which Major Prevost lived, was almost destroyed with shot and shells. In the streets and on the common there was a number of large holes made in the ground by the shells, so that it was not without some difficulty the chair got on; and in the church and Mr. Jones' house I observed that the shells came in at the roof and went through to the ground; and a number of other houses suffered by shells. The troops in the lines were much safer from the bombardment than the people in town. . . .

In short, the situation of Savannah was at one time deplorable. A small garrison in an extensive country was surrounded on the land by a powerful enemy, and its seacoast blocked up by one of the strongest fleets that ever visited America. There was not a single spot where the women and children could be put in safety; and the numerous desertions daily weakened that force which was at first inadequate to man such extensive lines; but the situation of the ground would not permit the able engineer to narrow them. However, with the assistance of God, British valor surmounted every difficulty.

—MOORE, *Diary of the American Revolution*, II, 224-228.

3. THE STORMING OF SAVANNAH: PULASKI IS KILLED

Account of Major Thomas Pinckney of the South Carolina militia.

On that day [October 8] we were ordered to parade near the left of the line at 1 o'clock of the next morning, where we were to be joined by the French, and to march to the attack in the following order: The French troops were to be divided into three columns, the American into two, the heads of which were to be posted in a line, with proper intervals at the edge of the wood adjoining the open space of five or six hundred yards between it and the enemy's line, and at 4 o'clock in the morning, a little before daylight, the whole was, on a signal being given, to rush forward and attack the redoubts and batteries opposed to their front. The American column of the right, which adjoined the French, were to be preceded by Pulaski, with his cavalry and the cavalry of South Carolina, and were to follow the French until they approach[ed] the edge of the wood, when they were to break off and take their position. . . .

A faint attack by the South Carolina militia and Georgians, under Brigadier General Huger, was ordered to be made on the enemy's left; but, instead of the French troops being paraded so as to march off at 4 o'clock, it was near four before the head of that column reached our front. The whole army then marched towards the skirt of the wood in one long column and, as they approached the open space, were to break off into the different columns, as ordered for the attack. But by the time the first French column had arrived at the open space, the day had fairly broke, when Count d'Estaing, without waiting until the other columns had arrived at their position, placed himself at the head of his first column and rushed forward to the attack. But this body was so severely galled by the grape-shot from the batteries as they advanced, and by both grape-shot and musketry when they reached the abbatis, that, in spite of the effort of the officers, the column got into confusion and broke away to their left toward the wood in that direction; the second and the third French columns shared successively the same fate, having the additional discouragement of seeing, as they marched to the attack, the repulse and loss of their comrades who had preceded them.

Count Pulaski, who, with the cavalry, preceded the right column of the Americans, proceeded gallantly until stopped by the abbatis, and before he could force through it, received his mortal wound. In the mean time, Colonel Laurens at the head of the light infantry, followed by the 2d South Carolina Regiment and 1st Battalion Charleston Militia, attacked the Spring Hill Redoubt, got into the ditch and planted the colours of the 2d Regiment on the berm, but the parapet was too high for them to scale it under so heavy a fire, and after much slaughter they were driven out of the ditch. When General Pulaski was about to be removed from the field, Colonel D. Horry, to whom the command of the cavalry devolved, asked what were his directions. He answered, "Follow my lancers to whom I have given my order of attack." But the lancers were so severely galled by the enemy's fire that they also inclined off to the left, and were followed by all the cavalry breaking through the American column, who were attacking the Spring Hill Redoubt.

By this time the 2d American column headed by Gen. M'Intosh, to which I was attached, arrived at the foot of the Spring Hill Redoubt, and such a scene of confusion as there appeared is not often equalled. Col. Laurens had been separated from that part of his command that had not entered the Spring Hill ditch by the cavalry, who had borne it before them into the swamp to the left, and when we marched up, inquired *if we had seen them.* Count d'Estaing was wounded in the arm, and endeavouring to rally his men, a few of whom with a drummer he had collected. General M'Intosh did not speak French, but desired me to inform the commander-in-chief that his column was fresh, and that he wished his directions, where, under present circumstances, he should make the attack. The Count ordered that we should move more to the left, and by no means to interfere with the troops he was endeavoring to rally; in pursuing this direction we were thrown too much to the left, and before we could reach Spring Hill Redoubt, we had to pass through Yamacraw Swamp, then wet and boggy, with the galley at the mouth annoying our left flank with grape-shot.

While struggling through this morass, the firing slacked, and it was reported that the whole army had retired. I was sent by General M'Intosh to look out from the Spring Hill, where I found not an assailant standing. On reporting this to the general, he ordered a retreat, which was effected without much loss, notwithstanding the heavy fire of grape-shot with which we were followed.

The loss of both armies in killed and wounded amounted to 637 French and 457 Americans, 1100. The Irish Brigade in the French service and our 2d Regiment particularly distinguished themselves and suffered most. The loss of the British amounted only to fifty-five.

Thus was this fine body of troops sacrificed by the imprudence of the French general, who, being of superior grade, commanded the whole. If the French troops had left their encampment in time for the different corps to have reached their positions, and the whole attacked together, the prospect of success would have been infinitely better, though even then it would have been very doubtful on account of the strength of the enemy's line, which was well supplied by artillery. But if Count d'Estaing had reflected a moment, he must have known that attacking with a single column, before the rest of the army could have reached their position, was exposing the army to be beaten in detail. In fact the enemy, who were to be assailed at once on a considerable part of their front, finding themselves only attacked at one point, very deliberately concentrated their whole fire on the assailing column, and that was repeated as fast as the different corps were brought up to the attack.

General Lincoln had the command of the reserve and covered the retreat; if he had led the attack, I think the event could not have been so disastrous, and I am warranted in this opinion by the attack he made on the enemy's lines at Stono, where, when he found how strongly the enemy were entrenched, although his light infantry, on both flanks, had gained some advantage, withdrew the troops without any considerable loss.

—Hough, *Siege of Savannah*, pp. 164-170.

V. THE FALL OF CHARLESTON

The next phase of the British effort to conquer the South revealed that the British had finally learned something from their previous and relatively ineffectual moves. If there was to be a conquest it could be achieved only by a move in force. Sir Henry Clinton, a cautious man at all times, felt that his move against Charleston was being made without sufficient superiority over the combined defenders. But the armada Clinton dispatched was indeed formidable. Having recalled to New York the 3,000 men stationed at Newport, he was able to spare 3,500 British, Hessian and Tory soldiers for the Charleston expedition. Along with crews numbering 5,000, this large force sailed on December 26, 1779, in a fleet of 90 transports under Admiral Arbuthnot's command.

Clinton's expedition almost came to grief on the high seas. The voyage was stormy, horses perished, stores were damaged, and the fleet dispersed. It was not until February 11, 1780, that the fleet finally entered Edisto Inlet and

Americans. ▦▦▦
British ▬▬
A. Wilkin's Battery, 16 Guns
B. Gibb's Battery, 9 Guns
C. Ferguson's Battery, 5 Guns
D. Old Magazine, 5 Guns
E. Citadel, 66 Guns
F. Where garrison laid down
   arms
G. Gadsden's Wharf, 7 Guns
H. Old Indian Wharf, 5 Guns
I. Governor's Bridge, 3 Guns
J. 4 Guns
K. Darrell's, 7 Guns
* Redoubts
Vessels behind Boom
L'Aventure, 24 Guns
Boston, 32 Guns
LePolaque, 16 Guns
Ranger, 20 Guns
Providence, 32 Guns
Five Galleys

SIEGE OF CHARLESTON

*landed troops on Johns Island, thirty miles south of Charleston. That city's
defenses had been allowed to fall into shocking disrepair. The forts on Sullivan's and James islands were no longer tenable and there was no artillery defense against an attacking fleet entering the harbor. The city was connected
with the mainland by a narrow isthmus known as the Neck, partially fortified
in 1779. Clinton's customary cautious advance gave the Americans time to
work on the town's fortifications. The Neck was cut across by a canal, behind
which breastworks and redoubts were raised, a redoubt was erected at the
town's southern extremity, and a line of small forts hastily put up along the
Cooper and Ashley sides.*

    *Charleston was Long Island all over again except that the retreat of the
besieged was cut off—an important difference. The disaster which befell the
Patriot defenders must be placed at the door of their commander, General
Lincoln. Although he stationed cavalry detachments at Monck's Corner near
the head of the Cooper River, some thirty miles north of Charleston, to keep
open his communication with the northern part of the state, he drew all other
available troops into the town, and thus committed his army to a fatal trap.
His forces numbering 3,600 were reinforced by 1,500 Virginia and North
Carolina Continentals. But Clinton also called on his huge garrison in New
York for more men, until he had built up his attacking force, excluding seamen, to 10,000.*

In the cavalry sorties in the vicinity of Charleston Southerners came to know and fear a new luminary on the British military horizon, the twenty-five-year-old Lieutenant Colonel Banastre Tarleton, commandant of the green-uniformed British Legion, a Tory cavalry outfit. "Bloody" Tarleton was to become a synonym for ruthless warfare. His surprise attack upon General Huger's cavalry at Moncks' Corner tightened the escape corridor from Charleston. The arrival of reinforcements from New York enabled Clinton to send a force into the last open stretch of ground between the Cooper and the sea. The American army was bottled up.

Lieutenant Governor Christopher Gadsden and his Council pleaded with Lincoln not to abandon the town, yet the longer he stayed on, the more perilous became his position and the greater the danger to the town itself. Finally, the civilians could endure the siege no longer. The capitulation came on May 12 and was the largest single American loss of the war.

Under the British surrender terms, the Continental troops were to be prisoners of war, but the militia and armed civilians were allowed to go home on parole. With colors cased and drums beating a Turkish march—not a British one as Lincoln had requested—the Patriot defenders marched out and piled their arms beside the Citadel, a redoubt in the center of the lines.

For Charleston it was all over, but in the rest of the South the real war was just beginning.

1. The Perilous Voyage of the British Transports

Diary of Captain Johann Hinrichs of the Hessian Jäger Corps.

Jan. 3, [1780]. Today was no better than yesterday; in fact, it was worse. Left to the fury of wave and wind, we drifted southward with helm lashed and before one sail, the wind being westerly. Of the entire fleet we saw this morning only one man-of-war and seventeen sail. It may be safely said that the most strenuous campaign cannot be as trying as such a voyage; for (1) one cannot prepare a decent meal; (2) one takes every morsel with the greatest difficulty and discomfort; (3) one enjoys not a moment of sleep because of the fearful rolling and noise, which is worse in the cabin than in any other place in the ship. Nevertheless, so far we have all been well and in good spirits, although somewhat weakened.

Jan. 4. Last night was no better than the previous night, nor was the day any better— if anything, it was worse. It was so gloomy and dark that we lost sight of the fleet during the night. Hence, in spite of the abominable weather, we set four sails at eight o'clock in the morning. Toward noon we rejoined the fleet and then lay to again. The wind was NW. and we drifted SW. Of the entire fleet only forty-eight ships were together; but among the missing were the *Russell*, the *Renown* and the *Robust*, which presumably were with the greater part of the missing ships. The absence of the *Renown* allowed us to hope that the *Anna* transport, which was carrying Captain von Hanger's company of chasseurs and had lost her mainmast and mizzenmast in the first storm, was still afloat and the chasseurs alive, for she had been taken in tow by the *Renown* after the first storm.

Jan. 5. This morning we sailed for a few hours, but then the storm began to rage again so violently that toward noon it was necessary to lash the helm again and furl all sails except one. The entire day and night one could see and hear nothing but the flags and shots of ships in distress. However, no one could go to their assistance. At noon our ship, too, sprung a leak below the cabin, near the helm. But it was easily stopped since one could get to it without trouble. The wind was NW. and we stood SW. . . .

Jan. 8. The wind was as violent as before, and from yesterday noon until noon today it was SW. The ship drifted WSW. In the afternoon we caught a shark. It weighed about two hundred pounds and measured nine feet and two and one-half inches from head to tail. I kept a piece of its skin, which is so sharp that it can be used as a fine saw in a mechanic's shop. . . .

Jan 9. Up to midnight last night we had a SW. storm; about twelve o'clock in the night the wind was WSW., and around ten o'clock in the morning it was N. by W. The helm was unlashed, and we made nine miles W. by N. before two in the afternoon. At two o'clock the wind veered to the north and the storm abated. During the night there was a calm.

Jan. 10. At seven o'clock in the morning we again raised the top-yard and set all mainsails. We were fifty-five ships. Around ten o'clock there came a gentle breeze from S. by W., before which we stood W. by N. In a short time the sea had become so calm and looked so innocent that one could almost come to love this treacherous element. We were especially happy because not a single jäger had become ill, and flattered ourselves that we would be able to land within a few days; however, at two o'clock in the afternoon the wind veered to W.

Jan. 11. This morning we had a head wind (SW.), and every inch we moved we went farther from our destinaton. We plied from S. to N. and from N. to S. In the afternoon there was a little mutiny among the crew, who complained to the ship's master about their rations. But everything was adjusted. . . .

Jan. 13. Everything the same! Still a westerly wind! We cruised up and down. Terrible weather! Snow, rain, hail, storm, foaming waves and bitter cold! Toward noon the *Judith* transport, carrying fascines and engineers, hoisted a flag of distress. She had sprung a leak and, furthermore, had lost all her yards. She approached the flagship and obtained assistance. Toward evening it cleared up, but the blue horizon was a foreboding of severe cold. During the night the wind veered somewhat to N., so that it was about NW. We stood WSW. and were hoping for the wind to shift still more to the north. With such hopes we slept fairly well, especially since the ship did not roll as much as usual, for snow and rain had beaten down the waves somewhat.

Jan 14. However, we had hoped in vain; the wind remained the same, backing even more to the westward in the morning. We cruised up and down. The weather was rather good, but there was no indication of any change of wind in spite of the fact that the moon entered the first quarter in the afternoon.

—UHLENDORF, ed., *Siege of Charleston*, pp. 117-125.

2. The British and Hessians Land in the Rear of the Defenders

Diary of Captain Johann Hinrichs.

Feb. 11. Because of our extremely long voyage and because of severe storms and the scattering of many of our ships, the enemy no longer seriously thought that we would still land in South Carolina. They were, furthermore, confused by our stay at Tybee, by certain orders given publicly at headquarters for the purpose of deceiving them, and by the movements of the regiments under the command of General Paterson, who had already actually advanced toward Purysburg. The enemy were looking for development near Beaufort, their troops having advanced as far as Ponpon. Thus we were able to land unmolested on Johns Island in the enemy's rear.

Feb 11 [*1780*]. This afternoon the light infantry, the British grenadiers and two companies of Hessian grenadiers began the disembarkation. Rain and darkness prevented us from following. . . .

The landing place was Simmons Point on Simmons Island, unmarked by name on any map. It is a part of Johns Island, desolate and salty, and full of cabbage trees. The landing was effected under the direction of Captain Elphinstone of the *Perseus*, who had demolished a battery here two years ago and had roamed all over Johns Island. The Commanding General and Lord Cornwallis were at the head of the light infantry. They advanced as far as Simmons' house and bridge, the generals remaining with the men as they marched through the woods in swamp and rain.

Feb. 12. While we and the rest of the troops were landing, the light infantry advanced as far as Wilson's house and the British grenadiers to within three miles of Simmons' house. The latter was used as headquarters, and the two Hessian grenadier companies remained there. Our landing was effected in good enough time, although we had to go two miles in boats; but the march to headquarters was the more arduous. A column making its way through a wilderness of deep sand, marshland, and impenetrable woods where human feet had never trod! Even Elphinstone, our guide, led us two miles out of our way. Sometimes we had to struggle, singly or two abreast, through marsh and woodland for half a mile. What a land to wage war in! Toward afternoon we arrived at headquarters, advanced another one and one-half miles and made camp on the left of the road, close to the Bohicket River. At our right was the 33rd Regiment, and next to it were the Hessian grenadiers.

We were encamped twenty-two miles from James Chapel, one and one-half miles from Simmons' bridge and twenty-five miles from Charleston.

—Uhlendorf, ed., *Siege of Charleston*, pp. 179-183.

3. The Desperate Position of the Defenders

Lieutenant-Colonel John Laurens of the Continental Army to George Washington.

Charleston, March 14, 1780

The enemy's present disposition of his force, and all his late operations, indicate a design to attack Charleston by a siege in form. To complete the investiture, he must introduce his ships of war into the harbour. That it is his intention appears from his fixing buoys on the bar, barricading his ships' waists, and anchoring them in a station where they may embrace the first favorable spring tides to enter. His transports and store-ships have removed from Edisto up Stono River, where they lie contiguous to Wappoo Cut, which is the water communication from thence to Ashley River. At a point of the mainland, formed by the issuing of the former in the latter, he raised, in the course of a night, the 11th instant, a battery of six embrasures. This situation, naturally advantageous, he will probably render very strong and establish in it his deposit of military stores and provisions. He then may either force a passage over Ashley River or turn it by a circuitous march, fortify a camp on the Neck and open his trenches. The best communication between his magazines and camp will be across Ashley River, from a bluff marked Bull in your large map.

Your Excellency will have learnt that the Commodore and all his officers renounce the idea of defending the passage of the bar; they declare it impracticable for the frigates to lie in a proper position for that purpose. The government has neglected to provide floating batteries, which might have been stationed there; so that it has been agreed, as the next best plan, to form a line of battle in such a manner as to make a cross-fire with Fort Moultrie, a shoal called the Middle Grounds being on the right of the ships, and the fort advanced on the left. As it would be the enemy's policy, with a leading wind and tide, to pass the fire of the fort and run aboard of our ships, the Commodore is contriving an obstruction which he thinks will check their progress and allow time for the full effect of our fire.

The impracticability of defending the bar, in the first instance, appears to me a great diminution of our means of defence. We must not only have a greater number of shipping below, and consequently withdraw them from flanking the enemy's approaches on the Neck, but are subject to the chances of a combat, which, in the other case, were out of the question. The Commodore has destroyed one set of the enemy's buoys, and I hope he will cut away such as may have been since put down, and order the galleys to give all possible annoyance to the enemy's ships in the act of entering.

The attention of the engineers has been distracted by different demonstrations on the part of the enemy, and they have not perfected the line across Charleston Neck. Henceforward I hope they will confine themselves solely to completing it, and then proceed to the construction of some interior inclosed works, to prolong the defence.

As the enemy is determined to proceed by regular approaches, all his operations are submitted to calculation, and he can determine with mathematical precision that with such and such means, in a given time, he will accomplish his end. Our safety, then, must depend upon the seasonable arrival of such re-enforcements as will oblige him to raise the siege. The Virginia line is much more remote than we could have thought it would have been at this moment. Your Excellency, in person, might rescue us all. Virginia and North Carolina would follow you. The glory of foiling the enemy in his last great effort and terminating the war ought to be reserved for you. Whatever fortune attends us, I shall, to my latest moments, feel that veneration and attachment which I always had for your Excellency.

—SPARKS, *Correspondence of the American Revolution*, II, 413-415.

4. A Coup at Monck's Corner Narrows the Escape Outlet

Lieutenant-Colonel Banastre Tarleton's account.

The Americans had joined a body of militia to three regiments of Continental cavalry, and the command of the whole was intrusted to Brigadier-General Huger. This corps hold possession of the forks and passes of Cooper River, and maintained a communication with Charles Town, by which supplies of men, arms, ammunition and provision might be conveyed to the garrison during the siege, and by which the Continental troops might escape after the defences were destroyed. Sir Henry Clinton was thoroughly sensible of the inconveniencies that might arise from this situation of the enemy's light troops; and being lately relieved by a detachment of sailors and mariners from the charge of Fort Johnson, he directed his attention to disloge them from their position. As soon as he received intelligence of the arrival of a number of waggons, loaded with arms, ammunition and clothing, from the northward, he selected a detachment of one thousand four hundred men, whom he committed to Lieutenant-Colonel Webster, with orders to counteract the designs of the Americans, and to break in upon the remaining communications of Charles Town.

On the 12th of April, Lieutenant-Colonel Tarleton, being reinforced at the quarter house by Major Ferguson's corps of marksmen, advanced to Goose Creek. Colonel Webster arrived on the following day at the same place, with the 33d and 64th Regiments of infantry. Tarleton again moved on in the evening, with his own and Ferguson's corps, toward Monk's Corner . . . in order, if possible, to surprise the Americans encamped at that place.

An attack in the night was judged most advisable, as it would render the superiority of the enemy's cavalry useless, and would, perhaps, present a favourable opportunity of getting possession of Biggin Bridge, on Cooper River, without much loss to the assailants. Profound silence was observed on the march. At some distance from Goose Creek, a Negro was secured by the advanced guard, who discovered him attempting to leave the road. A letter was taken from his pocket, written by an officer in General Huger's camp the afternoon of that day, and which he was charged to convey to the neighbourhood of Charles Town. The contents of the letter, which was opened at a house not far distant, and the Negro's intelligence, purchased for a few dollars, proved lucky incidents at this period.

Lieutenant-Colonel Tarleton's information relative to the situation of the enemy was now complete. It was evident that the American cavalry had posted themselves in front of the Cooper River, and that the militia were placed in a meeting house which commanded the bridge, and were distributed on the opposite bank. At three o'clock in the morning, the advanced guard of dragoons and mounted infantry, supported by the remainder of the legion and Ferguson's corps, approached the American post. A watch word was immediately communicated to the officers and soldiers, which was closely followed by an order to charge the enemy's grand guard on the main road, there being no other avenue open, owing to the swamps upon the flanks, and to pursue them into their camp.

The order was executed with the greatest promptitude and success. The Americans were completely surprised. Major Vernier, of Pulaski's legion, and some other officers and men who attempted to defend themselves were killed or wounded. General Huger, Colonels Washington and Jamieson, with many officers and men, fled on foot to the swamps close to their encampment, where, being concealed by the darkness, they effected their escape. Four hundred horses belonging to officers and dragoons, with their arms and appointments (a valuable acquisition for the British cavalry in their present state), fell into the hands of the victors; about one hundred officers, dragoons and hussars, together with fifty wagons loaded with arms, clothing and ammunition, shared the same fate.

Without loss of time, Major Cochrane was ordered to force the bridge and the meeting house with the infantry of the British legion. He charged the militia with fixed bayonets, got possession of the pass and dispersed every thing that opposed him.

In the attack at Monk's Corner, and at Biggin Bridge, the British had one officer and two men wounded, with five horses killed and wounded. This signal instance of military advantage may be partly attributed to the judgement and address with which this expedition was planned and executed, and partly to the injudicious conduct of the American commander, who, besides making a false disposition of his corps by placing his cavalry in front of the bridge during the night and his infantry in the rear, neglected sending patroles in front of his videttes; which omission equally enabled the British to make a surprise and prevented the Americans recovering from the confusion attending an unexpected attack.

When the news of this success reached Colonel Webster, he commenced his march for Biggin Bridge with the two British regiments under his command, as there were other difficulties to be surmounted before the general's plan was fully accomplished. On his arrival at Monk's Corner, he detached Lieutenant-Colonel Tarleton to seize the boats and take possession of Bonneau's Ferry—a necessary, but easy operation, whilst the country felt the influence of the late unexpected defeat. This passage over another branch of Cooper River was secured, and by the subsequent movement of the King's troops into the district of St. Thomas, Charles Town became completely invested.

—TARLETON, *History of Campaigns in the Southern Provinces*, pp. 15-18.

5. A SCOTTISH OFFICER DESCRIBES THE BOMBARDMENT OF CHARLESTON

Journal of Lieutenant John Peebles of the Royal Highland Regiment.

Thursday, 13th April, 1780. After 12 days work in compleating the first paralel which stands opposed the enemy line from six to eight hundred yards distance and which consists of six works numbered from the right and a battery in front of No. 5 and a line of approach advanced from thence. The three batteries opened this morning between 8 and 9 o'clock with above 20 pieces of cannon (mostly 24-pounders), 2 howitzers, a mortar and some cohorns, and kept up a tolerable fire during the day, which brought a warm return from the enemy. We set the town on fire at 3 different times, 2 places with shells carcases or red hot shot, but they soon put it out again, and the General gave orders himself to the artillery officers not to set the town on fire again. This day's firing has dismounted several of the enemy's guns and toward evening they were almost silent. An artillery man lost an arm and an assistant killed by one of our own guns hanging fire and going off when they put in the spunge. A man of the 37th Light Infantry had his backside shot away looking for balls. The working party last night advanced the aproach and made a traverse on it, but the moonlight increasing makes the nights very short for working.

Found five deserters came in last night who say Mr. Lincoln is determined to defend the place to the last. . . .

Sunday, 16th April, fair weather and warm. Went to the trenches last night, and was sent to occupy the intrenchment at the head of the sap with 130 men. A working party came there of 200 and lengthened the trench a good way to the left and carried out the sap about 20 yards in front ending with a traverse. They left off about 3 o'clock in the morning and went home. Soon after 50 Yagers came there who were posted along the banquet before day, ready to take a shot when they could see, and we stood to our arms till near sunrise—firing from both sides in the course of the night as usual. The rebels throw their shells better than we do, but did no harm. The night very light being almost full moon. When it was fair daylight the Yagers began to fire at any body they could see about the enemy's works, which are above 300 yards distant yet. They returned the fire from some marksmen in a trench without their line of works, but to very little purpose on both sides. The Yagers think they killed one, and the rebels killed one of our party, a light infantry man of the 16th shot in the eye.

Our batterys kept up a superior fire all day, the rebels having but a few guns on their left that fire, and only two or three little mortars on their right. The Yagers went off in the evening and I was releived 'tween 8 and 9. A rebel galley came in the afternoon near the hospital and fired a good many shot, one of which went thro' the house, but a small gun was brought down and drove her off. . . .

Monday, 17th April, warm weather and little wind about N.E. A good deal of firing last night, 4 or 5 wounded. The working party carried out another sap in front of No. 2 about as far advanced as that to the left. The fire from the batteries kept up as usual. We sent a dead 13-inch shell into the town yesterday to let them see what we have, but the beds of the 2 large mortars are both insufficient.

I hear the navy have made a battery at the mouth of Wapoo from whence they fire into the town when the fancy strikes them.

Some frigates and armed sloops are ready to come up Cooper River when the wind serves; two flag staffs set up at the foot of the garden at Lord Cornwallis' quarters for signals for them.

Dined with Lordship today, who is always very civil to me.

—PEEBLES, *Journal*, pp. 1-4.

6. CHARLESTON IN ITS EXTREMITY

From General William Moultrie's journal.

Monday, [April] 24th, [1780]. A party composed of three hundred men, Virginians and South-Carolinians, under the command of Lieutenant Colonel Henderson, made a sortie upon the enemy's approaches opposite the advance redoubts at day light. They were completely surprised, and lost about fifteen or twenty men killed with the bayonet, besides twelve persons brought off, seven of whom were wounded. Captain Moultrie killed and two men wounded on our side. The enemy attempted to support their guards from the trenches, but on receiving rounds of grape, made their retreat. The prisoners report their party to have beeen commanded by Major Hall of the 71st Regiment, but no officers were to be found. Colonel Parker killed about eight o'clock, looking over the parapet; two privates killed and seven wounded. The greatest part of the 1st South-Carolina Regiment came into garrison this morning, with Colonel C. Pinckney from Fort Moultrie.

Tuesday, 25th. Between twelve and one this morning, a heavy fire of cannon and musketry commenced from our advanced redoubt and the right of the lines, occasioned, as it was said, by the enemy's advancing in column. It is certain they gave several huzzas, but whether they were out of their trenches it is not clear. They kept up a very heavy and incessant fire with musketry for thirty minutes. The enemy threw several light balls into town. Two o'clock P. M. Lord Cornwallis at Mount-Pleasant.

Wednesday, 26th. The *Lord George Germaine* and a sloop joined the enemy's fleet. The enemy were very quiet all day and last night. We suppose they are bringing cannon into their third parallel. They are strengthening their approaches. Lord Cornwallis took possession of Mount-Pleasant yesterday. Brigadier General du Portail arrived from Philadelphia. The garrison ordered to be served with the usual quantity of provision, a plentiful supply having been received. One killed, Captain Goodwin of the Third South-Carolina Battalion, and one private wounded.

On General du Portail declaring that the works were not tenable, a council was again called upon for an evacuation, and to withdraw privately with the Continental troops. When the citizens were informed upon what the council were deliberating, some of them came into council and expressed themselves very warmly, and declared to General Lincoln that if he attempted to withdraw the troops and leave the citizens, they would cut up his boats and open the gates to the enemy. This put a stop to all thoughts of an evacuation of the troops, and nothing was left for us but to make the best terms we could.

—MOULTRIE, *Memoirs*, II, 78-80.

7. THE LAST AMERICAN SORTIE IS REPULSED

Diary of Captain Johann Hinrichs.

[*April 24, 1780*]. I was ordered by Major General Leslie at three o'clock this morning to take thirty men and occupy the left of the advanced work, while Lieutenant von Winzingeroda with thirty jägers was to proceed to the right. When I arrived at the part thrown up last night, I had my jägers halt, while I myself and two men inspected the work, for I was aware of our light way of building and knew that we were right under the enemy's outer works. There was not a single traverse in a trench four hundred paces long. I went as far as the enemy's gatework. But as day was breaking, the enemy sent two enfilading shots from their left front redoubt into our trench, one of them enfilading *en flanc* down the entire trench as far as the sap, while the other, *en revers*, struck the back of the parapet a hundred paces this side of the gatework.

I had my two jägers halt at the end of the trench to watch the gatework while I ran back to the British grenadiers in the second parallel. I brought one noncommissioned officer and twelve men (of the grenadier company of the 42nd Regiment) and had a traverse made approximately in the center of the trench. General Leslie came and was surprised that no infantry was here yet. He thanked me for my labors. In the meantime I had my jägers fetch sandbags and lay them on the parapet. While in the trench, which was barely six feet deep where I stood, I heard a loud yelling in the center, *i.e.* in the space that was still between the right and the left section of the third parallel. At the same moment the double post I had left standing above fired, and the workmen on the other side of the traverse came running over crying, "D— me, the rebels are there!"

I jumped on the parapet and when I saw the enemy, who were already pressing upon our right wing from a barrier situated at their left-wing front redoubt and were also rushing out of the gatework, I had my workmen seize their muskets, withdrew the two jägers this side of the traverse, and opened a continuous fire along the unoccupied part of the parallel as far as the gatework. The enemy, having penetrated our right wing, were already more than fifty paces behind us, partly between the third and second parallels. I ordered some jägers and Corporal Rübenkönig behind the traverse and had them fire behind the trench across the plain. Now our second parallel began to fire. This made many bullets fall in our rear. But when the second parallel pressed forward on our right wing, the enemy withdrew, leaving twenty muskets behind. But they covered their retreat with so excessive a shower of canisters which were loaded with old burst shells, broken shovels, pickaxes, hatchets, flat-irons, pistol barrels, broken locks, etc., etc. (these pieces we found in our trench), and so enfiladed us at the same time from the front redoubt of their left wing (fifteen balls were embedded in the traverse I had thrown up) that one could hardly hear another close beside him.

It was still dark, and the smoke of the powder was so thick that one could not tell friend from enemy. Since I could not know that the enemy had withdrawn, I jumped on the parapet and had my jägers and grenadiers keep up such a hot fire along the trench and upon their embrasures that after half an hour's cannonade the enemy's batteries were silent. A deserter told us in the evening that Colonel Parker and several artillerymen were killed in an embrasure. I suffered no loss except one Englishman slightly wounded with a bayonet. The entire parapet where I stood with my men was razed more than one foot by the enemy's battery. What luck!

Our right wing, where Lieutenant von Winzingeroda was stationed with thirty jägers and twenty-five light infantry, did not get off so well. One light-infantryman was killed, five wounded; two jägers had bayonet wounds and three, one of whom had a bullet wound in the abdomen, were taken prisoners. They were compelled to repair to the second parallel because through the negligence of the English the enemy was upon them too quickly, and without support they could not make a stand with discharged rifles against bayonets.

From Captain Lawson of the artillery I had borrowed two pieces resembling cohorns, taken on the *Delaware* frigate, which he had changed into swivels. They were made of brass and had a chamber. They served me splendidly today, for my jägers had no more cartridges. (At ten o'clock fifteen fresh men and two companies of light infantry came to support me.) These Lawsons, as I shall call them, threw a hand grenade 1,800 feet. I also fired 100-bullet canisters, 3-pound case shot, and one-half-pound bogy shot, firing in the course of the day 130 shots. The enemy tried to silence me with cannon, a sign that our fire was effective. However, I moved from one place to another with my pieces and sometimes fired three to four 100-bullet canisters into the enemy's embrasures. During the night this part of the parallel, which was pretty well shot to pieces, was repaired again and provided with several traverses. Likewise, a new sap was begun on the left wing of the left section of the third parallel.

The signal that the enemy was making a sortie along the whole line was a threefold "Hurray!" on our side—a fatal signal, indeed! About twenty to thirty of the enemy were seen at the gatework. Our nearest infantry post on guard gave the signal and fired. Everyone repeated the signal; the workmen ran back; the second parallel saw them coming, heard the "Hurray!" believed they were enemies, and fired. Within a short time there was a tremendous fire of musketry, cannon and shell on both sides. It was two o'clock in the morning before everyone realized that it was a mistake. We had an officer killed (71st) and more than fifty [men] killed and wounded. Besides, our working parties could accomplish little or nothing during the night.

—Uhlendorf, ed., *Siege of Charleston*, pp. 259-265.

8. "Our Last Great Effort—It Availed Us Nothing"

Memoirs of General William Moultrie.

"May 9th, 1780

"Sir,

"No other motives but those of forbearance and compassion induced us to renew offers of terms you certainly had no claim to. The alterations you propose are all utterly inadmissable; hostilities will in consequence commence afresh at eight o'clock.

"H. CLINTON, M. ARBUTHNOT

"Maj. Gen. Lincoln"

After receiving the above letter, we remained near an hour silent, all calm and ready, each waiting for the other to begin. At length we fired the first gun and immediately followed a tremendous cannonade, and the mortars from both sides threw out an immense number of shells. It was a glorious sight to see them like meteors crossing each other and bursting in the air; it appeared as if the stars were tumbling down. The fire was incessant almost the whole night; cannon-balls whizzing and shells hissing continually amongst us; ammunition chests and temporary magazines blowing up; great guns bursting, and wounded men groaning along the lines. It was a dreadful night! It was our last great effort, but it availed us nothing. After this our military ardor was much abated. We began to cool, and we cooled gradually, and on the eleventh of May we capitulated, and in the morning of the twelfth we marched out and gave up the town.

"To Sir Henry Clinton.

"Charlestown, May 11th, 1780
"Sir,

"The same motives of humanity which inclined you to propose articles of capitulation to this garrison induced me to offer those I had the honor of sending you on the 8th inst. They then appeared to me such as I might proffer, and you receive, with honor to both parties. Your exceptions to them, as they principally concerned the militia and citizens, I then conceived were such as could not be concurred with; but a recent application from those people, wherein they express a willingness to comply with them, and a wish on my part to lessen as much as may be the distresses of war to individuals, lead me now to offer you my acceptance of them.

"I have the honor to be, etc.

"B. LINCOLN."
—MOULTRIE, *Memoirs*, II, 96-97.

9. POWDER STORE BLOWS UP DURING THE CAPITULATION

Memoirs of General William Moultrie.

About eleven o'clock A.M. on the twelfth of May, we marched out between 1500 and 1600 Continental troops (leaving five or six hundred sick and wounded in the hospitals) without the horn-work, on the left, and piled our arms. The officers marched the men back to the barracks, where a British guard was placed over them. The British then asked where our second division was? They were told these were all the Continentals we had, except the sick and wounded. They were astonished, and said we had made a gallant defence.

Captain Rochfort had marched in with a detachment of the artillery to receive the returns of our artillery stores. While we were in the horn-work together in conversation, he said, "Sir, you have made a gallant defence, but you had a great many rascals among you "(and mentioned names) "who came out every night and gave us information of what was passing in your garrison."

The militia marched out the same day and delivered up their arms at the same place; the Continental officers went into town to their quarters, where they remained a few days to collect their baggage and signed their paroles, then were sent over to Haddrell's Point. The militia remained in Charleston. The next day the militia were ordered to parade near Lynch's pasture and to bring all their arms with them, guns, swords, pistols, etc., and those that did not strictly comply were threatened with having the grenadiers turned in among them. This threat brought out the aged, the timid, the disaffected and the infirm, many of them who had never appeared during the whole siege, which swelled the number of militia prisoners to, at least, three times the number of men we ever had upon duty.

I saw the column march out and was surprised to see it so large; but many of them we had excused from age and infirmities; however, they would do to enrol on a conqueror's list. When the British received their arms, they put them in waggons and carried them to a store-house, where we had deposited our fixed ammunition (about 4,000 pounds) and although they were informed by some of our officers that the arms were loaded, and several of them went off before the explosion took place, yet in taking them out of the waggons they threw them so carelessly into the store that some at last set fire to the powder, which blew up the whole guard of fifty men and many others that were standing by; their carcasses, legs and arms were seen in the air and scattered over several parts of the town. One man was dashed with violence against the steeple of the new independent church, which was at a great distance from the explosion, and left the marks of his body there for several days. The houses in the town received a great shock, and the window sashes rattled as if they would tumble out of the frames. . . .

The British were very much alarmed at the explosion; all the troops were turned out under arms and formed: they could not tell what was the matter. Some of the British and Hessian officers supposed it was designed by us. I was abused and taken up by a Hessian officer (whose guard was at Broughton's battery). He was very angry and said to me, "You, General Moultrie, you rebels have done this on purpose, as they did at New-York"; and ordered his guard to take me a prisoner into a house near, and placed a sentry at the door, where a number of us were confined; but I soon got a note over a back way to General Leslie, acquainting him of my situation, upon which he immediately sent one of his aids to me with an apology, that my confinement was contrary to orders, and ordered the sentry from the doors.

After a little time the alarm subsided. They went back and stopped the progress of the fire.

—MOULTRIE, *Memoirs*, II, 108-111.

VI. THE MASSACRE AT THE WAXHAWS

After the fall of Charleston the British sought to extinguish the flame of insurrection throughout the state. Learning that a force of 300 men from Virginia under the command of Colonel Buford had reversed their course toward Charleston on news of the capitulation, had retired toward Hillsborough, and then had temporarily halted near the Waxhaw Creek, about nine miles from Lancaster Courthouse, Cornwallis detached a mixed force of dragoons, but mainly men from the Loyal Legion under Tarleton, to intercept them. When hot weather proved fatal to his horses, the indomitable Tarleton had others seized in their places and drew close to Buford. Then he sent forth an emissary, enjoining the Americans to surrender and magnifying the numbers of their pursuers. "If you are rash enough to reject the terms," Tarleton informed the Americans, "the blood be upon your head."

"I reject your proposals," Buford wrote, "and shall defend myself to the last extremity."

This literary exchange proved prophetic. Although only 300 yards separated the forces, Tarleton was astonished to hear the American officers shouting to their men to hold their fire until the dragoons were within ten paces. The Americans soon asked for quarter, and Buford hoisted the white flag. However, on the pretext that he was shot at during the negotiations, Tarleton allowed his dragoons to plunge their bayonets into men who had surrendered and to carry out a massacre which for sheer savagery was unmatched in the entire war. From this atrocity was born the American battle cry of "Tarleton's quarter!" As "Light-Horse Harry" Lee put it, "This bloody day only wanted the war dance and the roasting fire to have placed it first in the records of torture and death in the West."

South Carolina was now firmly in British hands. Clinton's work was done, and he returned to New York, leaving the rest of the Southern campaign in the hands of Lord Cornwallis.

1. TARLETON'S DRAGOONS GAVE "THE HORRID YELLS OF DEMONS"

Dr. Robert Brownsfield to William D. James.

. . . In a short time Tarleton's bugle was heard, and a furious attack was made on the rear guard, commanded by Lieut. Pearson. Not a man escaped. Poor Pearson was inhumanely mangled on the face as he lay on his back. His nose and lip were bisected obliquely; several of his teeth were broken out in the upper jaw, and the under completely divided on each side. These wounds were inflicted after he had fallen, with several others on his head, shoulders and arms. As a just tribute to the honour and Job-like patience of poor Pearson, it ought to be mentioned that he lay for five weeks without uttering a single groan. His only nourishment was milk, drawn from a bottle through a quill. During that period he was totally deprived of speech, nor could he articulate distinctly after his wounds were healed.

This attack gave Buford the first confirmation of Tarleton's declaration by his flag. Unfortunately he was then compelled to prepare for action, on ground which presented no impediment to the full action of cavalry. Tarleton, having arranged his infantry in the centre and his cavalry on the wings, advanced to the charge with the horrid yells of infuriated demons. They were received with firmness and completely checked, until the cavalry were gaining the rear.

Buford, now perceiving that further resistance was hopeless, ordered a flag to be hoisted and the arms to be grounded, expecting the usual treatment sanctioned by civilized warfare. This, however, made no part of Tarleton's creed. His ostensible pretext for the relentless barbarity that ensued was that his horse was killed under him just as the flag was raised. He affected to believe that this was done afterwards, and imputed it to treachery on the part of Buford; but, in reality, a safe opportunity was presented to gratify that thirst for blood which marked his character in every conjuncture that promised probable impunity to himself. Ensign Cruit, who advanced the flag, was instantly cut down.

Viewing this as an earnest of what they were to expect, a resumption of their arms was attempted, to sell their lives as dearly as possible; but before this was fully effected, Tarleton with his cruel myrmidons was in the midst of them, when commenced a scene of indiscriminate carnage never surpassed by the ruthless atrocities of the most barbarous savages.

The demand for quarters, seldom refused to a vanquished foe, was at once found to be in vain; not a man was spared, and it was the concurrent testimony of all the survivors that for fifteen minutes after every man was prostrate they went over the ground plunging their bayonets into every one that exhibited any signs of life, and in some instances, where several had fallen one over the other, these monsters were seen to throw off on the point of the bayonet the uppermost, to come at those beneath.

Capt. Carter, who commanded the artillery and who led the van, continued his march without bringing his guns into action; this conduct excited suspicions unfavourable to the character of Carter, and these were strengthened by his being paroled on the ground, and his whole company without insult or injury being made prisoners of war. Whether he was called to account for his conduct, I have never learnt. These excepted, the only survivors of this tragic scene were Capts. Stokes, Lawson and Hoard, Lieuts. Pearson and Jamison, and Ensign Cruit. . . .

Capt. John Stokes . . . received twenty-three wounds, and as he never for a moment lost his recollection, he often repeated to me the manner and order in which they were inflicted.

Early in the sanguinary conflict he was attacked by a dragoon, who aimed many deadly blows at his head, all of which by the dextrous use of the small sword he easily parried; when another on the right, by one stroke, cut off his right hand through the metacarpal bones. He was then assailed by both, and instinctively attempted to defend his head with his left arm until the forefinger was cut off, and the arm hacked in eight or ten places from the wrist to the shoulder. His head was then laid open almost the whole length of the crown to the eye brows. After he fell he received several cuts on the face and shoulders. A soldier, passing on in the work of death, asked if he expected quarters. Stokes answered, "I have not, nor do I mean to ask quarters. Finish me as soon as possible." He then transfixed him twice with his bayonet. Another asked the same question and received the same answer, and he also thrust his bayonet twice through his body.

Stokes had his eye fixed on a wounded British officer sitting at some distance, when a serjeant came up who addressed him with apparent humanity and offered him protection from further injury at the risk of his life.

"All I ask," said Stokes, "is to be laid by that officer that I may die in his presence."

While performing this generous office the humane serjeant was twice obliged to lay him down and stand over him to defend him against the fury of his comrades. Doctor Stapleton, Tarleton's surgeon, . . . was then dressing the wounds of the officer. Stokes, who lay bleeding in every pore, asked him to do something for his wounds, which he scornfully and inhumanely refused until peremptorily ordered by the more humane officer, and even then only filled the wounds with rough tow, the particles of which could not be separated from the brain for several days.

. . . Shortly after the adoption of the constitution of the United States, he [Stokes] was promoted to the bench in the Federal Court—married Miss Pearson—and settled on the Yadkin River, where the county is called Stokes, after his name.

—JAMES, *Marion*, Appendix, 1-7.

2. TARLETON ATTRIBUTES HIS VICTORY TO THE MISTAKES OF BUFORD
[written in 1787]

By pressing horses on the road, the light troops arrived the next day May 28, at Camden, when Lieutenant-Colonel Tarleton gained intelligence that Colonel Buford had quitted Rugely's mills on the 26th, and that he was marching with great diligence to join a corps then upon the road from Salisbury to Charlotte town in North Carolina.

This information strongly manifested that no time was to be lost, and that a vigorous effort was the only resource to prevent the junction of the two American corps. At two o'clock in the morning, the British troops being tolerably refreshed continued their pursuit. They reached Rugeley's by day light, where they learned that the Continentals were retreating above twenty miles in their front, towards the Catawba settlement, to meet their reinforcement. At this period, Tarleton might have contented himself with following them at his leisure to the boundary line of South Carolina, and from thence have returned upon his footsteps to join the main army, satisfied with pursuing the troops of Congress out of the province; but animated by the alacrity which he discovered both in the officers and men to undergo all hardships, he put his detachment in motion, after adopting a stratagem to delay the march of the enemy. Captain Kinlock, of the legion, was employed to carry a summons to the American commander, which, by magnifying the number of the British, might intimidate him into submission, or at least delay him whilst he deliberated on an answer. Colonel Buford, after detaining the flag for some time, without halting his march, returned a defiance. By this time many of the British cavalry and mounted infantry were totally worn out and dropped successively into the rear; the horses of the three-pounder were likewise unable to proceed. In this dilemma, Lieutenant-Colonel Tarleton found himself not far distant from the enemy, and, though not in a suitable condition for action, he determined as soon as possible to attack, there being no other expedient to stop their progress and prevent their being reinforced the next morning. The only circumstance favourable to the British light troops at this hour was the known inferiority of the Continental cavalry, who could not harass their retreat to Earl Cornwallis's army, in case they were repulsed by the infantry.

At three o'clock in the afternoon, on the confines of South Carolina, the advanced guard of the British charged a serjeant and four men of the American light dragoons and made them prisoners in the rear of their infantry. This event happening under the eyes of the two commanders, they respectively prepared their troops for action. Colonel Buford's force consisted of three hundred and eighty Continental infantry of the Virginia line, a detachment of Washington's cavalry, and two six-pounders. He chose his post in an open wood, to the right of the road. He formed his infantry in one line, with a small reserve. He placed his colours in the center, and he ordered his cannon, baggage and waggons to continue their march.

Lieutenant-Colonel Tarleton made his arrangement for the attack with all possible expedition. He confided his right wing, which was composed of sixty dragoons and nearly as many mounted infantry, to Major Cochrane, desiring him to dismount the latter to gall the enemy's flank, before he moved against their front with his cavalry. Captains Corbet and Kinlock were directed, with the 17th Dragoons and part of the legion, to charge the center of the Americans, whilst Lieutenant-Colonel Tarleton, with thirty chosen horse and some infantry, assaulted their right flank and reserve. This particular situation the commanding officer selected for himself, that he might discover the effect of the other attacks. The dragoons, the mounted infantry, and three-pounder in the rear, as they could come up with their tired horses, were ordered to form something like a reserve, opposite to the enemy's center, upon a small eminence that commanded the road; which disposition afforded the British light troops an object to rally to, in case of a repulse, and made no inconsiderable impression on the minds of their opponents.

The disposition being completed without any fire from the enemy, though within three hundred yards of their front, the cavalry advanced to the charge. On their arrival within fifty paces, the Continental infantry presented, when Tarleton was surprised to hear their officers command them to retain their fire till the British cavalry were nearer. This forbearance in not firing before the dragoons were within ten yards of the object of their attack, prevented their falling into confusion on the charge, and likewise deprived the Americans of the farther use of their ammunition. Some officers, men and horses suffered by this fire; but the battalion was totally broken, and slaughter was commenced before Lieutenant-Colonel Tarleton could remount another horse, the one with which he led his dragoons being overturned by the volley.

Thus in a few minutes ended an affair which might have had a very different termination. The British troops had two officers killed, one wounded; three privates killed, thirteen wounded; and thirty-one horses killed and wounded. The loss of officers and men was great on the part of the Americans, owing to the dragoons so effectually breaking the infantry, and to a report amongst the cavalry that they had lost their commanding officer, which stimulated the soldiers to a vindictive asperity not easily restrained. Upwards of one hundred officers and men were killed on the spot; three colours, two six-pounders and above two hundred prisoners, with a number of waggons containing two royals, quantities of new clothing, other military stores and camp equipage, fell into the possession of the victors.

The complete success of this attack may, in great measure, be ascribed to the mistakes committed by the American commander. If he had halted the waggons as soon as he found the British troops pressing his rear, and formed them into a kind of redoubt for the protection of his cannon and infantry against the assault of the cavalry, in all probability he either would not have been attacked or by such a disposition he might have foiled the attempt. The British troops, in both cases, would have been obliged to abandon the pursuit, as the country in the neighborhood could not immediately have supplied them with forage or provisions; and the Continentals might have decamped in the night, to join their reinforcement. Colonel Buford also committed a material error in ordering the infantry to retain their fire till the British dragoons were quite close; which, when given, had little effect either upon the minds or bodies of the assailants, in comparison with the execution that might be expected from a successive fire of platoons or divisions, commenced at the distance of three or four hundred paces.

—TARLETON, *History of Campaigns in the Southern Provinces,* pp. 29-33.

3. SOUTH CAROLINA RESOLVES TO FIGHT ON

President John Rutledge of South Carolina to Governor Abner Nash of North Carolina.

Camden, May 24, 1780

I could not obtain a copy of the Articles of Capitulation at Charles Town untill yesterday. Inclosed you will receive it. Last Saturday the enemy took post, with a considerable force, at Dupree's Ferry on Santee River, which they began to cross that day on their march to George Town, whither they had sent some vessels from Charles Town. They are certainly in possession of George Town, which was not defensible. Genl. Caswell, who lay a little below Lanier's Ferry with the North Carolina Brigade and the Virginia Continentals under Col. Buford, had luckily retreated this way before the enemy got to that ferry, and thereby prevented their cutting off his retreat, which was probably their first scheme.

Those troops are now under command of Brigadier Gen. Huger, about 15 miles below this place, and will be here to-day; his future motions will be directed by the camp and force of the enemy. Sorry I am to say, his force is altogether inadequate to any offensive operations. The enemy, according to advices received last night were, the evening before, at Black Mingo, but whether their intention was to take a circuit by way of the Hanging Rock Road in order to get in the rear of our troops, or to proceed for your state, is as yet uncertain. The next movement they make will demonstrate which of these points is their objects. Parties are gone to reconnoitre; however, I think it advisable not to wait their return, but to give you the foregoing intelligence and what follows as early as possible, especially as I have charged the bearer to collect what intelligence he can as he proceeds, and to communicate it to you

We have no certain account what the force above mentioned is, or by whom commanded, but it is said to be considerable, and under Lord Cornwallis. It is evident that the conquest of North as well as South Carolina is the enemy's plan. The time for which they endeavour to enlist men is untill those countries can be conquered, and a junction with them at Cross Creek will probably be attempted with the body above mentioned, who have with them a large Highland regiment. I have good reason to believe that they will send vessels (some perhaps with troops) to possess your rivers, and the towns on them, and it is probable that they will establish at Brunswick and Wilmington magazines of provisions. They may send hither great quantities of rice from the lower part of our State. They can hardly expect, I apprehend, to penetrate far into your back country unless they depend more than I hope they can with good grounds on the disaffection of your people, but I presume they will extend their camp along, and at some distance from the sea.

I hope, indeed, that their progress will be soon checked, tho' their numbers are really great; but surely Virginia will now be roused, and the forces of your State, in conjunction with the Virginians, and (supported, as I hope you will be, powerfully by Congress) will make the enemy repent of their audacity in attempting a conquest your way. Can't account for the backwardness of the troops ordered hither by Congress and Virginia, and for our want of intelligence respecting them. I still hope, however, that a combination of forces and better fortune than our late experience will soon oblige the enemy to head back their steps, and that, altho' there is no hope of regaining Charles Town except by treaty, the country will be preserved, and North Carolina, and even Georgia, be retained in the Union; for surely our brethren and allies will never give up the independence of either of those States or suffer such valuable territories to be lopped off.

I request the favour of you to forward the inclosed per express immediately to the governor of Virginia. Whether attempts will be made by the enemy on our back country (except by Tories and Indians) is still uncertain. If they send up a regular force, I am convinced they will be joined by numbers, and many will fall a sacrifice to the resentment of our domestic or internal enemies. But if regular troops are not sent up, I think our people will manage the disaffected and keep them from doing any considerable mischief. However, I expect no other service from the militia; they are so apprehensive of their families being killed (and their properties destroyed) by the Tories and Indians, who daily threaten hostilities while they are absent from their districts, that I believe it will be impracticable to keep any number worth mentioning on duty when the army are at any distance from their homes. If I can get them to embody in their own districts and keep the country quiet, it is really as much as I expect they will do at present and until troops arrive from the northward, but even this depends on the enemy's not sending up regular forces to take post in the back parts of the State; for if they do the disaffected will certainly flock to them, and those who are not disaffected will either abscond if they can or, which is more probable, be taken prisoners without arms, in which case they will expect to be treated as others are who have been taken under similar circumstances, in being dismissed on their parole, a piece of policy which the enemy have adopted with respect to our militia for obvious reasons.

This is a melancholy but a faithful representation of our affairs at this period. However, we must not despair. I still hope for great and speedy success from our brethren to animate and support our people and for a reverse of our late bad fortune, but immediate and the greatest exertions of the Northern States are indispensable to prevent the desolation and ruin of this State and Georgia, and the enemy's obtaining (what they flatter themselves with securing shortly) the three southernmost States, too valuable a prize ever to be given up by them.

—*North Carolina State Records*, XIV, 821-824.

VII. PATRIOTS WHIP TORIES AT RAMSOUR'S MILL

Although partisan bands were to render his interior position in South Carolina insecure, Cornwallis felt that his hold on the province was strong enough to justify pushing north into North Carolina, once the hot weather had abated. But a restless Tory in North Carolina jumped the gun. John Moore gathered some 1,300 Tories and encamped them near Ramsour's Mill, in Lincoln County, North Carolina. Colonel Locke and 400 of the North Carolina militia arrived at daybreak of June 20 to within a mile of the enemy. The Tory camp was thrown into disorder by the forward move of the Whig horsemen. Some Tories stood their ground, fired down the hill, and pursued the retreating horsemen, only to fall into a trap as the Whig infantry opened fire. A Patriot move on the Tories' right flank forced them to fall back toward the summit of the hill and over its brow. Hemmed in between two fires, they finally managed to withdraw in small parties. The Whig casualties were unusually heavy, 150 killed and wounded out of the 250 that saw action. The Tories had casualties of 150.

The remarkable fact about Ramsour's Mill is that the Whigs did not act as a unit. The officers made decisions as representatives of the men, and each officer, once the action started, was on his own. The battle proved a crushing loss of face for the Tories in that section of the state.

Account of General Joseph Graham of North Carolina, written in 1820.

The Tories were encamped on a hill three hundred yards east of Ramsour's Mill, and half a mile north of the present flourishing village of Lincolnton. The ridge stretched nearly to the east on the south side of the mill pond, and the road leading to the Tuckasege ford, by the mill, crosses the point of the ridge in a north-western direction. The Tories occupied an excellent position on a summit of the ridge; their right on the road fronting the south. The ridge has a very gentle slope, and was then interspersed with only a few trees, and the fire of the Tories had full rake in front for more than two hundred yards. The foot of the hill was bounded by a glade, the side of which was covered with bushes. The road passed the western end of the glade, at right angles; opposite the centre of the line and on the road a fence extended from the glade to a point opposite the right of the line. The picket guard, twelve in number, were stationed on the road, two hundred and fifty yards south of the glade, and six hundred yards from the encampment.

The companies of Captains Falls, M'Dowell and Brandon being mounted, the other [Whig] troops under Colonel Locke were arranged in the road, two deep, behind them and, without any other organization or orders, they were marched to battle. When the horsemen came within sight of the picket, they plainly perceived that their approach had not been anticipated. The picket fired and fled towards their camp. The horsemen pursued, and turning to the right out of the road, they rode up within thirty steps of the line and fired at the Tories, who, being in confusion, had not completely formed their line; but seeing only a few men assailing them, they quickly recovered from their panic and poured in a destructive fire, which obliged the horsemen to retreat. They retreated in disorder, passing through the infantry, who were advancing; several of the infantry joined them and never came into action. At a convenient distance the greater part of the horsemen rallied and, returning to the fight, exerted themselves with spirit during its continuance. The infantry hurried to keep near the horsemen in pursuit of the picket, and their movements being very irregular, their files were opened six or eight steps, and when the front approached the Tories, the rear was eighty poles back.

The Tories, seeing the effect of their fire, came down the hill a little distance and were in fair view. The infantry of the Whigs kept the road to the point between the glade and the corner of the fence, opposite the centre of the Tories. Here the action was renewed; the front fired several times before the rear came up. The Tories being on their left, they deployed to the right in front of the glade and came into action without order or system. In some places they were crowded together in each other's way; in other places there were none. As the rear came up, they occupied those places, and the line gradually extending, the action became general and obstinate on both sides. In a few minutes the Tories began to retire to their position on the top of the ridge, and soon fell back a little behind the ridge to shelter part of their bodies from the fire of the Whigs who were fairly exposed to their fire. In this situation their fire became very destructive, so that the Whigs fell back to the bushes near the glade, and the Tories, leaving their safe position, pursued them half way down the ridge.

At this moment Capt. Harden led a party of Whigs into the field, and, under cover of the fence, kept up a galling fire on the right flank of the Tories; and some of the Whigs, discovering that the ground on the right was more favorable to protect them from the fire of the Tories, obliqued in that direction towards the east end of the glade. This movement gave their line the proper extension. They continued to oblique until they turned the left flank of the Tories; and the contest being well maintained in the centre, the Tories began to retreat up the ridge. They found part of their position occupied by the Whigs. In that quarter the action became close, and the parties mixed together in two instances, and having no bayonets, they struck at each other with the butts of their guns. In this strange contest, several of the Tories were taken prisoners, and others, divesting themselves of their mark of distinction (which was a twig of green pine top stuck in their hats), intermixed with the Whigs, and all being in their common dress, they escaped unnoticed.

The Tories, finding the left of their position in possession of the Whigs, and their centre being closely pressed, retreated down the ridge toward the mill, exposed to the fire of the centre and of Captain Harden's company behind the fences. The Whigs pursued until they got entire possession of the ridge, when they perceived to their astonishment that the Tories had collected in force on the other side of the creek, beyond the mill. They expected the fight would be renewed and attempted to form a line; but only eighty-six men could be paraded. Some were scattered during the action, others were attending to their wounded friends, and, after repeated efforts, not more than one hundred and ten could be collected.

In this perilous situation of things it was resolved that Major Wilson and Captain William Alexander of Rowan should hasten to General Rutherford and urge him to press forward to their assistance. Rutherford had marched early in the morning and, at the distance of six or seven miles from Ramsour's, was met by Wilson and Alexander. Major Davie's cavalry was started at full gallop, and Colonel Davidson's infantry were ordered to hasten on with all possible speed. At the end of two miles they were met by others from the battle, who informed them that the Tories had retreated. The march was continued, and the troops arrived on the ground two hours after the battle had closed. The dead and most of the wounded were still lying where they fell.

As soon as the action began, those of the Tories who had no arms, and several who had, retreated across the creek. They were joined by others when they were first beaten back up the ridge, and by two hundred that were well-armed, who had arrived two days before from Lower Creek, in Burke County, under Captains Whiston and Murray. Col. Moore and Major Welch soon joined them, and those of the Tories who continued the fight to the last crossed the creek and joined them as soon as the Whigs got possession of the ridge. Believing that they were completely beaten, they formed a stratagem to secure their retreat. About the time that Wilson and Alexander were dispatched to General Rutherford, they sent in a flag under a pretence of proposing a suspension of hostilities, to make arrangements for taking care of the wounded and burying the dead. To prevent the flag-officer from perceiving their small number, Major James Rutherford and another officer were ordered to meet him a short distance from the line. The proposition being made, Maj. Rutherford demanded that the Tories should surrender as prisoners within ten minutes, and then the arrangements should be made that were requested.

In the meantime, Moore and Welsh gave orders that such of their men as were on foot, or had inferior horses, should move off singly as fast as they could; and when the flag returned, not more than fifty returned. They immediately fled. Moore with thirty men reached the British army at Camden, when he was threatened with a trial by a court-martial for disobedience of orders, in attempting to embody the royalists before the time appointed by the commander-in-chief. He was treated with disrespect by the British officers, and held in a state of disagreeable suspense; but it was at length deemed impolitic to order him before a court-martial.

As there was no organization of either party, nor regular returns made after the action, the loss could not be ascertained with correctness. Fifty-six lay dead on the side of the ridge where the heat of the action prevailed; many lay scattered on the flanks and over the ridge toward the mill. It is believed that seventy were killed, and that the loss on each side was equal. About an hundred men on each side were wounded, and fifty Tories were taken prisoners. The men had no uniform and it could not be told to which party many of the dead belonged. Most of the Whigs wore a piece of white paper on their hats in front, and many of the men on each side being excellent riflemen, this paper was a mark at which the Tories often fired, and several of the Whigs were shot in the head. The trees behind which both Whigs and Tories occasionally took shelter were grazed by the balls; and one tree in particular on the left of the Tory line, at the root of which two brothers lay dead, was grazed by three balls on one side and by two on the other.

In this battle neighbors, near relations and personal friends fought against each other, and as the smoke would from time to time blow off, they would recognize each other. In the evening, and on the next day, the relations and friends of the dead and wounded came in, and a scene was witnessed truly afflicting to the feelings of humanity.

After the action commenced, scarcely any orders were given by the officers. They fought like common soldiers and animated their men by their example, and they suffered severely. Captains Fall, Dobon, Smith, Bowman and Armstrong were killed, and Captains Houston and M'Kissick wounded. Of the Tories Captains Cumberland, Murray and Worlick were killed, and Captain Carpenter wounded. Few either of the officers or men had ever been in battle before.

—MURPHEY, *Papers*, II, 222-226.

VIII. PILLAGE AND CIVIL WAR FLAME IN SOUTH CAROLINA

The British and Tory invaders quickly earned an unenviable reputation for pillage, looting, and disrespect toward women. Patriot ladies whose husbands were prisoners of war or were away with the partisan bands showed remarkable courage in standing up to British and Tory looting parties. In fact, much smuggling of supplies from Charleston to the partisans in the interior was carried on by Patriot ladies.

The main forces on which the South Carolina Patriots counted to keep

The Unfortunate DEATH of MAJOR ANDRE

(Adjutant General to the English Army) at Head Quarters in New York, Oct.r 2. 1780, who was found within the American Lines in the character of a Spy.

Engraving by John Goldar, 1783

the British off balance were the partisans under such leaders as Thomas Sumter and Francis Marion. The former moved at the end of July 1780 against a detachment of British troops stationed at Rocky Mount, a high point on the western bank of the Catawba River, thirty miles from Camden. The loghouse fortifications were defended by Tories commanded by Lieutenant Colonel Turnbull. Apprised by other Tories of the approach of Sumter, Turnbull was ready. Three times the Americans charged but, lacking artillery, they were unable to penetrate the defenses of felled trees.

About a week later Sumter joined with Major William Davie in an attack on an open camp of the enemy at Hanging Rock, about twelve miles from Rocky Mount. After stout resistance this encampment fell to the attackers, who then proceeded to plunder the stores and get drunk. Seeing the confusion among the victors, the enemy rallied, formed themselves into a square and held off the Patriots until reinforcements forced Sumter with his plunder-laden troops to quit the field. One of the most obstinately fought engagements of the war, Hanging Rock was a fight between Patriots and Tories—not a single British soldier participated. However, on August 18 Tarleton surprised Sumter's encampment at Fishing Creek, about two miles from its junction with the Catawba and forced the surviving defenders to precipitous flight and to abandon the booty gained in previous engagements.

1. The Redcoats Strip Patriot Women of Their Jewels

Letter from Eliza Wilkinson.

Yonge's Island

Well, now comes the day of terror—the 3d of June [1780]. (I shall never love the anniversary of that day.) In the morning, fifteen or sixteen horsemen rode up to the house. We were greatly terrified, thinking them the enemy, but from their behavior were agreeably deceived and found them friends. They sat a while on their horses, talking to us; and then rode off, except two, who tarried a minute or two longer and then followed the rest, who had nearly reached the gate. One of them said two must needs jump a ditch—to show his activity I suppose; for he might as well, and better, have gone in the road. However, he got a sad fall; we saw him, and sent a boy to tell him, if he was hurt, to come up to the house, and we would endeavor to do something for him. He and his companion accordingly came up; he looked very pale and bled much; his gun somehow in the fall had given him a bad wound behind the ear, from whence the blood flowed down his neck and bosom plentifully. We were greatly alarmed on seeing him in this situation, and had gathered around him, some with one thing, some with another, in order to give him assistance.

We were very busy examining the wound when a Negro girl ran in, exclaiming, "O! the King's people are coming! It must be them, for they are all in red!" Upon this cry, the two men that were with us snatched up their guns, mounted their horses and made off, but had not got many yards from the house before the enemy discharged a pistol at them. Terrified almost to death as I was, I was still anxious for my friends' safety. I tremblingly flew to the window, to see if the shot had proved fatal, when, seeing them both safe, "Thank heaven," said I, "they've got off without hurt!"

I'd hardly uttered this when I heard the horses of the inhuman Britons coming in such a furious manner that they seemed to tear up the earth, and the riders at the same time bellowing out the most horrid curses imaginable, oaths and imprecations, which chilled my whole frame. Surely, thought I, such horrid language denotes nothing less than death; but I'd no time for thought. They were up to the house—entered with drawn swords and pistols in their hands. Indeed, they rushed in, in the most furious manner, crying out, "Where're these women rebels?" (pretty language to ladies from the *once famed Britons!*). That was the first salutation!

The moment they espied us, off went our caps (I always heard say none but women pulled caps!). And for what, think you? Why, only to get a paltry stone and wax pin, which kept them on our heads; at the same time uttering the most abusive language imaginable, and making as if they'd hew us to pieces with their swords. But it's not in my power to describe the scene. It was terrible to the last degree; and, what augmented it, they had several armed Negroes with them, who threatened and abused us greatly. They then began to plunder the house of every thing they thought valuable or worth taking; our trunks were split to pieces, and each man, pitiful wretch, crammed his bosom with the contents, which were our apparel, etc., etc., etc.

I ventured to speak to the inhuman monster who had my clothes. I represented to him the times were such we could not replace what they'd taken from us, and begged him to spare me only a suit or two; but I got nothing but a hearty curse for my pains; nay, so far was his callous heart from relenting that, casting his eyes towards my shoes, "I want them buckles," said he, and immediately knelt at my feet to take them out, which, while he was busy about, a brother villain, whose enormous mouth extended from ear to ear, bawled out, "Shares there! I say, shares!" So they divided my buckles between them.

The other wretches were employed in the same manner; they took my sister's ear-rings from her ears; hers, and Miss Samuells's buckles. They demanded her ring from her finger. She pleaded for it, told them it was her wedding ring, and begged they'd let her keep it. But they still demanded it, and, presenting a pistol at her, swore if she did not deliver it immediately, they'd fire. She gave it to them, and, after bundling up all their booty, they mounted their horses. But such despicable figures! Each wretch's bosom stuffed so full they appeared to be all afflicted with some dropsical disorder. Had a party of rebels (as they called us) appeared, we should soon have seen their circumference lessen. . . .

—WILKINSON, *Letters*, pp. 27-30.

2. ROCKY MOUNT AND HANGING ROCK: "NO PRISONERS COULD BE TAKEN"

Recollections of Colonel William R. Davie.

Colonels Sumpter and Neal with a number of the South Carolina Refugees and Col. Irwin with 300 of the Mecklenburg Militia rendezvoused near Major Davie's camp about the last of July, and a council was immediately held by the officers to fix upon a proper object to strike at while this volunteer force was collected. Rocky-Mount and the Hanging-Rock presented themselves as not only the most important at the time but lying within their reach and strength; and it was finally agreed that Col. Sumpter should march with the Refugees and the North Carolinians under Col. Irwin to the attack of Rocky-Mount, while Major Davie made a diversion to engage the attention of the corps at the Hanging-Rock, and their detachments marched the same evening.

The defences of Rocky-Mount consisted of two log houses calculated for defense, and a loop-holed building, the whole secured by a strong abbatis. The situation was considerably elevated, and surrounded with cleared grounds. Col. Sumpter arrived before this place early the next day. Some small parties of rifle men were advanced under the cover of rocks and trees and kept up a fire under the houses. Several corps of this detachment marched repeatedly thro' the old field to the attack with great intrepidity, but were repulsed by the heavy fire of the garrison. Various stratagems were employed in vain to set the buildings on fire, and having no artillery they were obliged to give over the attempt of taking the place. . . . The retreat was effected without interception.

Major Davie's detachment consisted of 40 mounted rifle-men and about that number of dragoons, and considering himself obliged to alarm the enemy in their camp at all events the same day, he approached the Hanging Rock about 1 o'clock, and fortunately while he was reconoitering their position to fix upon the point of attack, he received information that three companies of their mounted infantry, returning from some excursion, had halted at a farmer's house, situated in full view of the camp. The house was placed in the point of a right angle made by a lane of staked and ridered fence, the one end of which opened to the enemy's encampment, the other terminated in the woods. The major advanced on that next to the woods, and as the rifle-men were not distinguishable from the Loyalists, they were sent round to the other end of the lane with orders, on gaining it, to rush forward and fire on the enemy. The dragoons were divided so that one half could occupy the lane while the other half entered the field. This disposition was made with such promptitude that the attention or suspicion of the enemy was never excited. The rifle company . . . passed the camp sentries without being challenged, dismounted in the lane and gave the enemy a well-directed fire.

The astonished Loyalists fled instantly the other way, and were immediately charged by the dragoons in full gallop and driven back in great confusion. On meeting again the fire of the infantry, they all rushed impetuously against the angle of the fence where in a moment they were surrounded by the dragoons who had entered the field and literally cut them to pieces. As this was done under the eye of the whole British camp, no prisoners could be safely taken, which may apologize for the slaughter that took place on this occasion. They took sixty valuable horses with their furniture and one hundred muskets and rifles; the whole camp beat to arms but the business was done and the detachment out of their reach before they recovered from their consternation.

—Davie-Weems Collection, No. 2540.

IX. AT CAMDEN GATES'S NORTHERN LAURELS
TURN TO SOUTHERN WILLOWS

Although Nathanael Greene was Washington's personal choice to take command of the Southern troops after Lincoln's capture, and although in fact Major General Johann de Kalb, who fancied the title "Baron de Kalb," was already in the South with a force of Virginia and North Carolina Continentals, Congress had other ideas. It named the victor of Saratoga to that critical post. "Take care lest your Northern laurels turn to Southern willows," Charles Lee warned Gates.

Gates had no illusions about either his army or his situation, but he was shockingly unintelligent in handling his problems. Writing to Governor Jefferson on July 19, he deplored the "multiplied and increasing wants" of his command. Lack of meat and corn "must eventually break up our camp," he asserted. Furthermore, little if any assistance could be expected from the inhabitants, as the area was now swarming with Tories.

Gates's defeat can be laid to a series of inexplicable errors. He ignored well-informed advice to follow a circuitous route from North Carolina to Camden by way of Salisbury and Charlotte, which would have taken his army through fruitful and friendly country, and chose instead a route 50 miles shorter through wilderness and swampland, one of the most belligerently Tory regions in the South. He forced his men, starved and ill though many of them were, to march 18 miles a day. Yet his army was doubled by the addition of 2,000 North Carolina militia, and on paper he had a tremendous numerical superiority over the forces he was opposing. Lord Rawdon of Bunker's Hill fame concentrated his troops at Camden to check the American advance, and called on Cornwallis for reinforcements.

Gates weakened his army by detaching some 400 regulars and sending them to Sumter, and by dispatching Marion on a meaningless mission when in fact he should have held every man and called all the irregulars to his colors. At the least, if he had to spare men it should have been his militia, not his trained troops. To compound his difficulties, Gates tried to send back to Charlotte his heavy baggage and the women and children camp followers, but there was no transportation for the former, and the women and children clung to their protectors.

Then, over the protests of his own staff, he called for a night march. "I will breakfast tomorrow in Camden with Lord Cornwallis at my table," tradition has him say. Not having rum available, he issued a gill of molasses to each man, along with a ration of half-cooked meat and corn meal. The gastronomical disturbances that followed debilitated a substantial part of his troops.

By coincidence, Cornwallis also decided on a night march to surprise the Patriots, and the two armies came upon each other to their mutual surprise. Cornwallis carefully disposed his men and waited until daylight. Then Gates made another mistake. He had his untried militia on the left and center change position just as the armies were on the point of engaging. The British light infantry saw the opportunity and charged. A stampede followed. The militia

FIRST POSITION

Americans ▥
British ▮

Smallwood
1st Maryland

Retreat to Rugeley's Mills

Retreat

Retreat

G a t e s

Armand

Gist
2 Md.   Del.

Caswell
N.C. Militia

Va. Militia

Stevens

Kalb

S W A M P

ADVANCE   ADVANCE

S
W
A
M
P

N.C. Vol.

Bryan

Brit.
Legion

Irish
Vol.

33rd   23rd   Lt.Infy.

Webster

Rawdon

Cornwallis

71st.   71st.

Tarleton

Saunders   Cr.

TO CAMDEN WAXHAW ROAD

SECOND POSITION

TO RUGELEY'S MILLS

WAXHAW ROAD

Tarleton

Smallwood

Lt.Inf.

S W A M P

N.C.Mil.

23rd

Col.Dixon

33rd

Original Line

Del.

71st

1 Vol.   Webster

N.C. Vol.

Bryan

Brit.
Legion

Kalb

Md.

71st

Irish
Vol.

Lord Rawdon

CAMDEN

*threw away their arms and fled precipitately. De Kalb gallantly stood his
ground and was mortally wounded, and only a handful of regular troops—the
stalwart Maryland and Delaware regiments—were left to resist the British. A
combined charge of cavalry and foot broke up these last defenses. The Patriot
army was routed, dispersed, disintegrated and dissolved. As John Marshall
aptly described it, "Never was a victory more complete, or a defeat more
total."*

*Camden spelled finis to the military career of Horatio Gates. But the general
did accomplish one remarkable feat that day. Fleeing with his militia on
the fastest horse in the army, he did not stop until he reached Charlotte that
night, sixty miles from the battlefield.*

1. Gates Takes His Starving Army by the Wrong Road to Camden

Narrative of Colonel Otho Williams of the Continental Army, an Adjutant
General with Gates's troops.   [1780]

General Gates, who had so fortunately terminated the career of General
Burgoyne in the north, was appointed to command the southern army immediately after the reduction of Charleston. His arrival on the 25th of July was
a relief to DeKalb, who, condescendingly, took command of the Maryland
division, which included the regiment of Delaware. Besides these two corps,
the army consisted only of a small legionary corps, which formed a junction
with them a few days before, under the command of Colonel Armand, being
about sixty cavalry and as many infantry; and Lieutenant Colonel Carrington's detachment of three companies of artillery, which had joined in Virginia.

General Gates was received with respectful ceremony; the baron ordered
a Continental salute from the little park of artillery—which was performed on
the entrance into camp of his successor, who made his acknowledgments to
the baron for his great politeness, approved his standing orders, and, as if
actuated by a spirit of great activity and enterprise, ordered the troops to hold
themselves in readiness *to march at a moment's warning*. The latter order was
a matter of great astonishment to those who knew the real situation of the
troops. But all difficulties were removed by the general's assurances that
plentiful supplies of *rum* and *rations* were on the route, and would overtake
them in a day or two—assurances that certainly were too fallacious, and that
never were verified.

All were in motion, however, early in the morning of the 27th of July,
and the general took the route over Buffalo Ford, leading towards the enemy's
advanced post on Lynch's Creek, on the road to Camden, leaving two brass
field-pieces and some baggage for want of horses. Colonel Williams, presuming on the friendship of the general, ventured to expostulate with him upon
the seeming precipitate and inconsiderate step he was taking. He represented
that the country through which he was about to march was by nature barren,
abounding with sandy plains, intersected by swamps, and very thinly inhabited; that the little provisions and forage which were produced on the
banks of its few small streams were exhausted, or taken away by the enemy,
and by the hordes of banditti (called Tories) which had retired from what they

called the persecution of the rebels, and who would certainly distress his army, small as it was, by removing what little might remain out of his way.

On the other hand, the colonel represented that a route about north west would cross the Pee Dee River some where about where it loses the name of Yadkin, and would lead to the little town of Salisbury in the midst of a fertile country and inhabited by a people zealous in the cause of America. That the most active and intelligent officers had contemplated this route with pleasure, not only as it promised a more plentiful supply of provisions, but because the sick, the women and children, and the wounded, in case of disaster, might have an asylum provided for them at Salisbury or Charlotte, where they would remain in security, because the militia of the counties of Mecklenburgh and Roan, in which these villages stand, were staunch friends. The idea of establishing a laboratory for the repair of arms at a secure place was also suggested as necessary—the security of convoys of stores from the northward, by the upper route—the advantage of turning the left of the enemy's out-posts even by a circuitous route—that of approaching the most considerable of these posts (Camden) with the River Wateree on our right, and our friends on our backs—and some other considerations were suggested. And, that they might the more forcibly impress the general's mind, a short note was presented to him, concisely intimating the same opinion and referring to the best informed gentlemen under his command.

General Gates said he would confer with the *general officers* when the troops should halt at noon. Whether any conference took place or not, the writer don't know.

After a short halt at noon, when the men were refreshed upon the *scraps* in their *knapsacks*, the march was resumed. The country exceeded the representation that had been made of it—scarcely had it emerged from a state of sterile nature—the few rude attempts at improvement that were to be found were most of them abandoned by the owners and plundered by the neighbours. Every one, in this uncivilized part of the country, was flying from his home and joining in parties under adventurers who pretended to yield them protection until the British army should appear—which they seemed confidently to expect. The distresses of the soldiery daily increased—they were told that the banks of the Pee Dee River were extremely fertile—and so indeed they were; but the preceding crop of corn (the principal article of produce) was exhausted, and the new grain, although luxuriant and fine, was unfit for use. Many of the soldiery, urged by necessity, plucked the green ears and boiled them with the lean beef, which was collected in the woods, made for themselves a repast, not unpalatable to be sure, but which was attended with painful effects. Green peaches also were substituted for bread and had similar consequences. Some of the officers, aware of the risk of eating such vegetables, and in such a state, with poor fresh beef and without salt, restrained themselves from taking any thing but the beef itself, boiled or roasted. It occurred to some that the hair powder which remained in their bags would thicken soup, and it was actually applied.

The troops, notwithstanding their disappointment in not being overtaken by a supply of *rum* and provisions, were again amused with promises, and gave early proofs of that patient submission, inflexible fortitude and undeviating integrity which they afterwards more eminently displayed.

On the 3d day of August the little army crossed Pee Dee River in batteaus at Mask's Ferry, and were met on the southern bank by Lieutenant Colonel Porterfield, an officer of merit, who, after the disaster at Charleston, retired with a small detachment and found means of subsisting himself and his men in Carolina until the present time.

Colonel Marion, a gentleman of South Carolina, had been with the army a few days, attended by a very few followers, distinguished by small black leather caps and the wretchedness of their attire; their number did not exceed twenty men and boys, some white, some black, and all mounted, but most of them miserably equipped; their appearance was in fact so burlesque that it was with much difficulty the diversion of the regular soldiery was restrained by the officers; and the general himself was glad of an opportunity of detaching Colonel Marion, at his own instance, towards the interior of South Carolina, with orders to watch the motions of the enemy and furnish intelligence.

These trifling circumstances are remembered in these notes to show from what contemptible beginnings a good capacity will rise to distinction. The history of the war in South Carolina will recognize Marion as a brave partisan, if only the actions of the two last year's campaigns are recorded.

The expectation, founded on assurances, of finding a plentiful supply of provisions at May's Mill induced the troops again to obey the order to march with cheerfulness; but being again disappointed, fatigued and almost famished, their patience began to forsake them, their looks began to be vindictive; mutiny was ready to manifest itself, and the most unhappy consequences were to be apprehended; when the regimental officers, by mixing among the men and remonstrating with them, appeased murmurs, for which, unhappily, there was too much cause. The officers, however, by appealing to their own empty canteens and mess cases, satisfied the privates that all suffered alike; and, exhorting them to exercise the same fortitude of which the officers gave them the example, assured them that the best means of extricating them from the present distress should be immediately adopted; that if the supplies expected by the general did not arrive very soon, detachments should go from each corps in all directions to pick up what grain might possibly be found in the country and bring it to the mill.

Fortunately, a small quantity of Indian corn was immediately brought into camp—the mill was set to work, and as soon as a mess of meal was ground it was delivered out to the men; and so, in rotation, they were all served in the course of a few hours—more poor cattle were sacrificed—the camp kettles were all engaged—the men were busy but silent until they had each taken his repast; and then all was again content, cheerfulness and mirth. It was as astonishing as it was pleasing to observe the transition. . . .

Dangerous as deceptions had been, it was still thought expedient to flatter the expectation of the soldiery with an abundance of provisions, so soon as a junction could be formed with the militia; therefore, after collecting all the corn which was to be found in the neighbourhood of May's Mill, and huckstering all the meal that could be spared from our present necessities, the march was resumed towards Camden.

—JOHNSON, *Life of Greene*, I, 486-488, 489.

2. THE PANIC-STRICKEN MILITIA FLEE WITHOUT FIRING A SHOT

Narrative of Colonel Otho Williams.

It has been observed that the direct march of the American army towards Camden and the prospect of considerable re-enforcements of militia had induced the commanding officer, Lord Rawdon, to collect there all the forces under his direction. And it is certain that the seeming confidence of the American general had inspired him with apprehensions for his principal post. Lord Cornwallis, at Charlestown, was constantly advised of the posture of affairs in the interior of the country; and, confident that Lord Rawdon could not long resist the forces that might, and probably would, be opposed to him, in a very short time resolved to march himself, with a considerable re-enforcement, to Camden. He arrived on [August] 14th and had the discernment at once to perceive that delay would render that situation dangerous, even to his whole force; the disaffection from his late assumed, arbitrary and vindictive power having become general through all the country above General Gates' line of march, as well as to the eastward of Santee and to the westward of Wateree Rivers. He, therefore, took the resolution of attacking the new constituted American army in their open irregular encampment at Clermont. Both armies, ignorant of each other's intentions, moved about the same hour of the same night and, approaching each other, met about half way between their respective encampments at midnight.

The first revelation of this new and unexpected scene was occasioned by a smart, mutual salutation of small arms between the advanced guards. Some of the cavalry of Armand's legion were wounded, retreated and threw the whole corps into disorder; which, recoiling suddenly on the front of the column of infantry, disordered the First Maryland Brigade and occasioned a general consternation through the whole line of the army. The light infantry under Porterfield, however, executed their orders gallantly; and the enemy, no less astonished than ourselves, seemed to acquiesce in a sudden suspension of hostilities.

Some prisoners were taken on both sides. From one of these, the deputy adjutant general of the American army extorted information respecting the situation and numbers of the enemy. He informed that Lord Cornwallis commanded in person about three thousand regular British troops, which were in line of march, about five or six hundred yards in front. Order was soon restored in the corps of infantry in the American army, and the officers were employed in forming a front line of battle when the deputy adjutant general communicated to General Gates the information which he had from the prisoner. The general's astonishment could not be concealed. He ordered the deputy adjutant general to call another council of war. All the general officers immediately assembled in the rear of the line. The unwelcome news was communicated to them.

General Gates said, "Gentlemen, what is best to be done?"

All were mute for a few moments, when the gallant Stevens exclaimed, "Gentlemen, is it not too late *now* to do any thing but fight?"

No other advice was offered, and the general desired the gentlemen would repair to their respective commands.

The Baron de Kalb's opinion may be inferred from the following fact: When the deputy adjutant general went to call him to council, he first told him what had been discovered. "Well," said the baron, "and has the general given you orders to retreat the army?" The baron, however, did not oppose the suggestion of General Stevens, and every measure that ensued was preparatory for action.

Lieutenant Colonel Porterfield, in whose bravery and judicious conduct great dependence was placed, received in the first rencontre a mortal wound (as it long afterwards proved) and was obliged to retire. His infantry bravely kept the ground in front; and the American army were formed in the following order: The Maryland division, including the Delawares, on the right—the North Carolina militia in the center—and the Virginia militia on the left. It happened that each flank was covered by a marsh, so near as to admit the removing of the First Maryland Brigade to form a second line, about two hundred yards in the rear of the first. The artillery was removed from the center of the brigades and placed in the center of the front line; and the North Carolina militia (light infantry) under Major Armstrong, which had retreated at the first rencontre, was ordered to cover a small interval between the left wing and the swampy grounds on that quarter.

Frequent skirmishes happened during the night between the advanced parties—which served to discover the relative situations of the two armies—and as a prelude to what was to take place in the morning.

At dawn of day (on the morning of the 16th of August) the enemy appeared in front, advancing in column. Captain Singleton, who commanded some pieces of artillery, observed to Colonel Williams that he plainly perceived the ground of the British uniform at about two hundred yards in front. The deputy adjutant general immediately ordered Captain Singleton to open his battery, and then rode to the general, who was in the rear of the second line, and informed him of the cause of the firing which he heard. He also observed to the general that the enemy seemed to be displaying their column by the right; the nature of the ground favored this conjecture, for yet nothing was clear.

The general seemed disposed to wait events—he gave no orders. The deputy adjutant general observed that if the enemy, in the act of displaying, were briskly attacked by General Stevens' brigade, which was already in line of battle, the effect might be fortunate, and first impressions were important.

"Sir," said the general, "that's right—let it be done."

This was the last order that the deputy adjutant general received. He hastened to General Stevens, who instantly advanced with his brigade, apparently in fine spirits. The right wing of the enemy was soon discovered *in line* —it was too late to attack them displaying. Nevertheless, the business of the day could no longer be deferred. The deputy adjutant general requested General Stevens to let him have forty or fifty privates, volunteers, who would run forward of the brigade and commence the attack. They were led forward within forty or fifty yards of the enemy, and ordered to take trees and keep up as brisk a fire as possible. The desired effect of this expedient, to extort the enemy's fire at some distance in order to the rendering it less terrible to the militia, was not gained.

General Stevens, observing the enemy to rush on, put his men in mind of their bayonets; but the impetuosity with which they advanced, *firing* and *huzzaing,* threw the whole body of the militia into such a panic that they generally threw down their *loaded* arms and fled in the utmost consternation. The unworthy example of the Virginians was almost instantly followed by the North Carolinians; only a small part of the brigade commanded by Brigadier General Gregory made a short pause. A part of Dixon's regiment of that brigade, next in the line to the Second Maryland Brigade, fired two or three rounds of cartridge. But a great majority of the militia (at least two-thirds of the army) fled without firing a shot. The writer avers it of his own knowledge, having seen and observed every part of the army, from left to right, during the action.

He who has never seen the effect of a panic upon a multitude can have but an imperfect idea of such a thing. The best disciplined troops have been enervated and made cowards by it. Armies have been routed by it, even where no enemy appeared to furnish an excuse. Like electricity, it operates instantaneously—like sympathy, it is irresistible where it touches. But, in the present instance, its action was not universal. The regular troops, who had the keen edge of sensibility rubbed off by strict discipline and hard service, saw the confusion with but little emotion. They engaged seriously in the affair; and, notwithstanding some irregulartiy, which was created by the militia breaking pell mell through the second line, order was restored there—time enough to give the enemy a severe check, which abated the fury of their assault and obliged them to assume a more deliberate manner of acting. The Second Maryland Brigade, including the battalion of Delawares, on the right, were engaged with the enemy's left, which they opposed with very great firmness. They even advanced upon them and had taken a number of prisoners when their companions of the First Brigade (which formed the second line), being greatly outflanked and charged by superior numbers, were obliged to give ground.

At this critical moment the regimental officers of the latter brigade, reluctant to leave the field without orders, inquired for their commanding officer (Brigadier General Smallwood) who, however, was not to be found. Notwithstanding, Colonel Gunby, Major Anderson and a number of other brave officers, assisted by the deputy adjutant general and Major Jones, one of Smallwood's aids, rallied the brigade and renewed the contest. Again they were obliged to give way, and were again rallied. The Second Brigade were still warmly engaged. The distance between the two brigades did not exceed two hundred yards, their opposite flanks being nearly upon a line perpendicular to their front.

At this eventful juncture, the deputy adjutant general, anxious that the communication between them should be preserved, and wishing that, in the almost certain event of a retreat, some order might be sustained by them, hastened from the First to the Second Brigade, which he found precisely in the same circumstances. He called upon his own regiment (the 6th Maryland) not to fly, and was answered by the Lieutenant Colonel, Ford, who said, "They have done all that can be expected of them. We are outnumbered and outflanked. See the enemy charge with bayonets!"

The enemy having collected their corps and directing their whole force against these two devoted brigades, a tremendous fire of musketry was for some time kept up on both sides with equal perseverance and obstinacy, until Lord Cornwallis, perceiving there was no cavalry opposed to him, pushed forward his dragoons, and his infantry charging at the same moment with fixed bayonets put an end to the contest.

His victory was complete. All the artillery and a very great number of prisoners fell into his hands. Many fine fellows lay on the field, and the rout of the remainder was entire. Not even a company retired in any order. Every one escaped as he could. If in this affair the militia fled too soon, the regulars may be thought almost as blamable for remaining too long on the field, especially after all hope of victory must have been despaired of. Let the commandants of the brigades answer for themselves. Allow the same privilege to the officers of the corps comprising those brigades, and they will say that they never received orders to retreat, nor any order from any *general* officer, from the commencement of the action until it became desperate. The brave Major General, the Baron de Kalb, fought on foot with the Second Brigade and fell, mortally wounded, into the hands of the enemy, who stripped him even of his shirt: a fate which probably was avoided by other generals only by an opportune retreat.

The torrent of unarmed militia bore away with it Generals Gates, Caswell and a number of others, who *soon* saw that all was lost. General Gates at first conceived a hope that he might rally, at Clermont, a sufficient number to cover the retreat of the regulars; but the farther they fled the more they were dispersed, and the generals soon found themselves abandoned by all but their aids. Lieutenant Colonel Senf, who had been on the expedition with Colonel Sumpter, returned and, overtaking General Gates, informed him of their complete success—that the enemy's redoubt on Wateree, opposite to Camden, was first reduced, and the convoy of stores, etc., from Charleston was decoyed and became prize to the American party almost without resistance. That upwards of one hundred prisoners and forty loaded waggons were in the hands of the party, who had sustained very little loss; but the general could avail himself nothing of this trifling advantage. The detachment under Sumpter was on the opposite side of the Wateree, marching off as speedily as might be to secure their booty—for the course of the firing in the morning indicated unfavorable news from the army.

The militia, the general saw, were in air, and the regulars, he feared, were no more. The dreadful thunder of artillery and musketry had ceased, and none of his friends appeared. There was no existing corps with which the victorious detachment might unite, and the Americans had no post in the rear. He, therefore, sent orders to Sumpter to retire in the best manner he could; and proceeded himself with General Caswell towards Charlotte, an open village on a plain, about sixty miles from the fatal scene of action. The Virginians, who knew nothing of the country they were in, involuntarily reversed the route they came, and fled, most of them, to Hillsborough. General Stevens pursued them, and halted there as many as were not sufficiently refreshed before his arrival to pursue their way home. Their terms of service, however, being very short, and no prospect presenting itself to afford another proof of their courage, General Stevens soon afterwards discharged them.

The North Carolina militia fled different ways, as their hopes led or their fears drove them. Most of them, preferring the shortest way home, scattered through the wilderness which lies between Wateree and Pee Dee rivers, and thence towards Roanoke. Whatever these might have suffered from the disaffected, they probably were not worse off than those who retired the way they came; wherein they met many of their insidious friends, armed and advancing to join the American army; but, learning its fate from the refugees, they acted decidedly in concert with the victors, and, captivating some, plundering others and maltreating all the fugitives they met, returned, exultingly, home. They even added taunts to their perfidy. One of a party who robbed Brigadier General Butler of his sword consoled him by saying, "You'll have no further use of it."

The regular troops, it has been observed, were the last to quit the field. Every corps was broken and dispersed; even the boggs and brush, which in some measure served to screen them from their furious pursuers, separated them from one another. Major Anderson was the only officer who fortunately rallied, as he retreated, a few men of different companies, and whose prudence and firmness afforded protection to those who joined his party on the rout. . . .

The general order for moving off the heavy baggage, etc., to Waxaws was not put in execution, as directed to be done on the preceding evening. The whole of it, consequently, fell into the hands of the enemy, as well as all that which followed the army except the waggons of the Generals Gates and De Kalb; which, being furnished with the stoutest horses, fortunately escaped under the protection of a small quarter guard. Other waggons also had got out of danger from the enemy; but the cries of the women and the wounded in the rear and the consternation of the flying troops so alarmed some of the waggoners that they cut out their teams and, taking each a horse, left the rest for the next that should come. Others were obliged to give up their horses to assist in carrying off the wounded, and the whole road, for many miles, was strewed with signals of distress, confusion and dismay.

What added not a little to this calamitous scene was the conduct of Armand's Legion. They were principally foreigners, and some of them, probably, not unaccustomed to such scenes. Whether it was owing to the disgust of the colonel at general orders, or the cowardice of his men, is not with the writer to determine; but certain it is, the Legion did not take any part in the action of the 16th. They retired early and in disorder, and were seen plundering the baggage of the army on their retreat. One of them cut Captain Lemar, of the Maryland infantry, over the hand for attempting to reclaim his own portmanteau, which the fellow was taking out of the waggon. Captain Lemar was unarmed, having broke his sword in action, and was obliged to submit both to the loss and to the insult. The tent covers were thrown off the waggons, generally, and the baggage exposed, so that one might take what suited him to carry off. General Caswell's mess waggon afforded the best refreshment; very unexpectedly to the writer, he there found a pipe of good Madeira, broached, and surrounded by a number of soldiers, whose appearance led him to inquire what engaged their attention. He acknowledges that in this instance he shared in the booty and took a draught of wine, which was the only refreshment he had received that day.

—JOHNSON, Life of Greene, I, 494-498.

3. "STRAYED, DESERTED, OR STOLEN—A WHOLE ARMY"

September 15, 1780

REWARD

STRAYED, DESERTED, OR STOLEN, from the subscriber, on the 16th of August last, near Camden, in the State of South Carolina, a whole ARMY, consisting of horse, foot and dragoons, to the amount of near TEN THOUSAND (as has been said) with all their baggage, artillery, wagons and camp equipage. The subscriber has very strong suspicions, from information received from his aid de camp, that a certain CHARLES, EARL CORNWALLIS, was principally concerned in carrying off the said ARMY with their baggage, etc. Any person or persons, civil or military, who will give information, whether to the subscriber, or to Charles Thompson, Esq., Secretary to the Continental Congress, where the said ARMY is, so that they may be recovered and rallied again, shall be entitled to demand from the Treasurer of the United States the sum of

THREE MILLION OF PAPER DOLLARS

as soon as they can be spared from the public funds, and

ANOTHER MILLION

for apprehending the person principally concerned in taking the said ARMY off. Proper passes will be granted by the President of the Congress to such persons as incline to go in search of the said ARMY. And as a further encouragement, no deduction will be made from the above reward on account of any of the Militia (who composed the said ARMY) not being found or heard of, as no dependence can be placed on their services, and nothing but the most speedy flight can ever save their Commander.

HORATIO GATES, M. G.
and late Commander in Chief of the Southern Army, August 30, 1780
—Rivington's Royal Gazette, Sept. 17, 1780.

4. "For God's Sake, Send Greene!"

Alexander Hamilton to James Duane.

September 6, 1780

. . . What think you of the conduct of this great man? I am his enemy personally, for unjust and unprovoked attacks upon my charatcer; therefore what I saw of him ought to be received as from an enemy, and have no more weight than as it is consistent with fact and common sense. But did ever any one hear of such a disposition or such a flight? His best troops placed on the side strongest by nature, his worst on that weakest by nature, and his attack made with these. 'Tis impossible to give a more complete picture of military absurdity. It is equally against the maxims of war and common sense. We see the consequences. His left ran away, and left his right uncovered. His right wing turned on the left has in all probability been cut off. Though, in truth, the general seems to have known very little what became of his army. Had he placed his militia on his right, supported by the morass, and his Continental troops on his left, where it seems he was most vulnerable, his right would have been more secure, and his left would have opposed the enemy; and instead of going backward when he ordered to attack, would have gone forward. The reverse of what has happened might have happened.

But was there ever an instance of a general running away, as Gates has done, from his whole army? And was there ever so precipitate a flight? One hundred and eighty miles in three days and a half. It does admirable credit to the activity of a man at his time of life. But it disgraces the general and the soldier. I have always believed him to be very far short of a Hector or a Ulysses. All the world, I think, will begin to agree with me.

But what will be done by Congress? Will he be changed or not? If he is changed, for God's sake overcome prejudice, and send Greene. You know my opinion of him. I stake my reputation on the events, give him but fair play.

But, above all things, let us have, without delay, a vigorous government, and a well constituted army for the war.

—Morris, *Hamilton and the Founding of the Nation*, pp. 38, 39.

X. THE PATRIOT CAUSE LOOKS UP: KING'S MOUNTAIN

Having routed Gates and scattered Sumter's forces, Cornwallis moved from Camden on September 8, 1780, pressing a full-scale invasion into North Carolina. Three parallel forces moved northward—Cornwallis, with the main body of his army; Tarleton at the head of the British Legion and light infantry; and still farther westward, Major Ferguson and his Tory command. Colonel Davie, at the head of such fragments of American troops as he could command, fell back; then on the night of September 20 he surprised the hated British Legion at the plantation of one of his own officers, Captain Wahab, near Charlotte, inflicted severe casualties upon them and retired with his booty. Knowing that Wahab was with the attackers, the enemy burned the plantation to the ground as soon as Davie's forces retired.

If Gates found his route to Camden infested with hostile Tories, the score was evened when Cornwallis made Charlotte, North Carolina, his temporary

KING'S MOUNTAIN

headquarters. *That area was a stronghold of die-hard Patriot resistance. Under Davie the Patriots put up a brilliant defense. The British finally took Charlotte with substantial losses in an affair where the British Legion scarcely covered itself with glory. Cornwallis found that communication with Camden was difficult to maintain and that foraging parties ran into crack-shot guerrilla forces that played havoc with morale.*

Major Ferguson's Tories were assigned to move along the foothills and cover Cornwallis' left flank. At the suggestion of Colonel Isaac Shelby measures were taken for co-operative action by partisan leaders to cut off Ferguson's forces. Accordingly, forces under Colonels Charles McDowell, John Sevier, Isaac Shelby and William Campbell assembled at Watauga on September 25 and were joined by Colonel Benjamin Cleveland. Learning of the approach of this force, Ferguson first sought to retreat to the Catawba, then was forced to take a stand on King's Mountain, a mile and a half south of the North Carolina boundary line. This narrow stony ridge was about 500 yards in length, some 70 to 120 yards in width, and averaged 100 feet in height above the ravines surrounding it. Atop this level summit Ferguson "defied God Almighty and all the rebels out of Hell to overcome him." The Americans attacked the enemy in front and on his left flank simultaneously, and within five minutes followed with an attack on the enemy's right flank. It was a complete envelopment. Ferguson was killed after desperate resistance and at the moment when he had cut down the Patriot Colonel Williams. Then the largely Tory force surrendered, with losses of 400 killed and wounded, and 700 captured, to Patriot casualties of 88. Scores of prisoners were shot after they surrendered and a dozen hanged by way of reprisal for the British having executed several deserters who had taken up arms against them.

For undisciplined and largely inexperienced troops King's Mountain was an exhilarating achievement. It was also a stunning blow to Cornwallis and imperiled his position in North Carolina. He was forced to pull back across the state line to Winnsborough. King's Mountain once and for all destroyed Tory influence in North Carolina.

1. The Hated British Legion Is Surprised at the Waxhaws

Recollections of Colonel William R. Davie.

The camp of Lord Cornwallis extended along the north side of the Waxhaw Creek, and the 71st Regiment was posted in the rear about half a mile on the south side in a parallel line. The Catawba River in some measure covered their left flank and the Loyalists and light troops encamped on their right and already began to spread havoc and destruction.

Throughout the neighbouring country Col. Davie had procured information of their situation and formed a design to attack them; for this purpose he marched [September 20] with his own corps and Major Davidson's rifle men, making together one hundred and fifty men, with intention to fall on their quarters in the night, hoping by these means to check, if not entirely disperse, these lawless marauders. After taking a considerable circuit to avoid the patroles of the enemy, about 2 o'clock in the morning he turned Lord Cornwallis' right flank and approached a plantation where the Tories were said to be encamped; but on examining the ground [it] was found they had changed their position a few days before. Two other places were reconoitered in consequence of advice received in the night from terrified or disaffected people. At the last of these certain information was procured that they had retired within the flanks of the British army to the plantation of a Capt. Wahab, which was overlooked by the camp of the 71st Regiment, and that they might amount to three or four hundred mounted infantry. This partizan [Davie], unwilling to lose his object, reached Wahab's as the sun was rising. The moment was fortunate. The British party were going on command, their sentries were all called in, and about sixty of them with a party of the British Legion were mounted near the house which stood about the middle of a lane, covered on the same side by a corn field cultivated to the very door.

A company of infantry were detached thro' the corn with orders to take possession of the houses and immediately fire on the enemy. The cavalry were sent round the corn field with directions to gain the other end of the lane and charge the foe as soon as the fire commenced at the houses, while the Colonel advanced to receive them with about forty riflemen. The houses were briskly attacked, and the cavalry charged at the same moment. The enemy, being completely surprised, had no time to form and crowded in great disorder to the other end of the lane, when a well-reserved fire from the rifle men drove them back upon the cavalry and infantry who were now drawn up at the houses, and by whom they were instantly attacked. Thus pushed vigorously on all sides, they fluctuated some moments under the impressions of terror and dismay and then bore down the fences and fled in full speed. The Colonel's situation was too hazardous to risque any time in pursuit; the horses and arms were ordered to be collected, and in a few minutes the infantry were all mounted and the surplus horses secured. . . .

The British left fifteen or 20 dead on the field and had about forty wounded; they were surprised, pushed off their reflection and made no resistance, so that only one man of the Americans was wounded and that by mistake; being unwarily separated in the pursuit and having no regimentals, he was not distinguishable from the enemy. The British commanding officer, out of pique or a mistaken and cruel policy, immediately ordered the improvements of the plantation to be set on fire, and the houses, barns and fences were all laid in ashes, although there were three families of women and children living there at the time.

The proprietor, Capt. Wahab, was a volunteer with Colonel Davie and had been exiled some time from his family, and his wife and children were unavoidably in the midst of the action. "These were moments which try men's souls." They gathered round him in tears of joy and distraction, the enemy advanced, and he could only embrace them, and in a few minutes afterwards, turning his eyes back towards his all, as the detachment moved off, he had the mortification to see their only hope of subsistence wrapt in flames. This barbarous practice was uniformly enacted by the British officers in the Southern States. However casual the rencounter might be, when it happened at a plantation, their remaining in possession of the ground was always marked by committing the houses to the flames.

The Colonel, expecting to attack the enemy in the night, had given orders to take no prisoners. These orders in the hurry of the morning were not revoked. This circumstance, the vicinity of the British quarters and the danger of pursuit satisfactorily account for no prisoners being taken. He brought off ninety-six horses with their furniture, and one hundred and twenty stand of arms, and arrived at his camp the same afternoon, having performed a march of sixty miles in less than twenty-four hours, notwithstanding the time employed in seeking and beating the enemy.

—Davie-Weems Collection, No. 2540.

2. Banastre Tarleton Finds Charlotte a Hornets' Nest

Account written in 1787.

Charlotte town afforded some conveniences, blended with great disadvantages. The mills in its neighbourhood were supposed of sufficient consequence to render it for the present an eligible position and, in future, a necessary post when the army advanced. But the aptness of its intermediate situation between Camden and Salisbury and the quantity of its mills did not counterbalance its defects. The town and environs abounded with inveterate enemies. The plantations in the neighbourhood were small and uncultivated;

the roads narrow and crossed in every direction; and the whole face of the country covered with close and thick woods. In addition to these disadvantages, no estimation could be made of the sentiments of half of the inhabitants of North Carolina, whilst the royal army remained at Charlotte town.

It was evident, and it had been frequently mentioned to the King's officers, that the counties of Mecklenburg and Rohan were more hostile to England than any other in America. The vigilance and animosity of these surrounding districts checked the exertions of the well-affected, and totally destroyed all communication between the King's troops and the Loyalists in the other parts of the province. No British commander could obtain any information in that position which would facilitate his designs or guide his future conduct. Every report concerning the measures of the governor and assembly would undoubtedly be ambiguous; accounts of the preparations of the militia could only be vague and uncertain; and all intelligence of the real force and movements of the Continentals must be totally unattainable.

The foraging parties were every day harassed by the inhabitants, who did not remain at home to receive payment for the produce of their plantations, but generally fired from covert places to annoy the British detachments. Ineffectual attempts were made upon convoys coming from Camden and the intermediate post at Blair's mill; but individuals with expresses were frequently murdered. An attack was directed against the picket at Polk's mill, two miles from the town. The Americans were gallantly received by Lieutenant Guyon, of the 23d Regiment; and the fire of his party from a loop-hold building adjoining the mill repulsed the assailants. Notwithstanding the different checks and losses sustained by the militia of the district, they continued their hostilities with unwearied perseverance; and the British troops were so effectually blockaded in their present position that very few, out of a great number of messengers, could reach Charlotte town in the beginning of October, to give intelligence of Ferguson's situation.

—TARLETON, *History of Campaigns in the Southern Provinces*, pp. 162-164.

3. FERGUSON VOWS "HE NEVER WOULD YIELD TO DAMNED BANDITTI"

Account of Colonel Isaac Shelby of North Carolina.

In September 1780 Maj. Ferguson, who was one of the best and most enterprising of the British officers in America, had succeeded in raising a large body of Tories, who, with his own corps of regulars, constituted an effective force of eleven hundred and twenty-five men. With a view of cutting off Col. Clarke, of Georgia, who had recently made a demonstration against Augusta, which was then in the hands of the British, Ferguson had marched near the Blue Ridge and had taken post at Gilbert Town, which is situated but a few miles from the mountains. Whilst there he discharged a Patriot, who had been taken prisoner on his parole, and directed him to tell Col. Shelby (who had become obnoxious to the British and Tories from the affair at Musgrove's Mill) that if Shelby did not surrender he (Ferguson) would come over the mountains and put him to death, and burn his whole county.

It required no further taunt to rouse the patriotic indignation of Col. Shelby. He determined to make an effort to raise a force, in connection with other officers, which should surprise and defeat Ferguson. With this object in view, he went to a horse race near where Jonesborough has since been built, to see Sevier and others. Shelby and Sevier there resolved that if Col. Campbell would join them they would raise all the force they could and attack Ferguson; and if this was not practicable they would co-operate with any corps of the army of the United States with which they might meet. If they failed and the country was overrun and subdued by the British, they would then take water and go down to the Spaniards in Louisiana.

Col. Campbell was notified of their determination, and a place of rendezvous in the mountains appointed east of Jonesborough. At the time appointed, September 25th, Campbell joined them, and their united force numbered about one thousand riflemen. They crossed the mountains on the 27th in a ravine and fell in, accidentally, with Col. Cleveland, of North Carolina, who had under his command about four hundred men.

The force having been raised by officers of equal rank, and being without any higher officer entitled to command the whole corps, there was a general want of organization and arrangement. It was then determined that a board of officers should convene each night and decide on the plan of operations for the next day; and further, that one of the officers should see those orders executed as officer of the day, until they should otherwise conclude. Shelby proposed that Col. Campbell should act as officer of the day. Campbell took him aside and requested Shelby to withdraw his name and consent to serve himself. Shelby replied that he was himself the youngest Colonel present from his State, that he had served that year under several of the officers who were present and who might take offence if he commanded; that Gen. McDowell, who was with them, was too slow an officer for his views and the enterprise in which they were engaged, and added that as he ranked Campbell, yet as Campbell was the only officer from Virginia, if he (Shelby) pressed his appointment no one would object. Col Campbell felt the force of this reasoning and consented to serve, and was appointed to the command as officer of the day.

The force of the detachment was still considered insufficient to attack Ferguson, as his strength was not known. It was agreed that an express be sent to invite Gen. Morgan or Gen. Davidson to take the command. Gen. McDowell tendered his serviecs for this purpose and started on his mission. Before proceeding far he fell in with Col. Williams, of South Carolina, who was at the head of from two to three hundred refugees. Gen. McDowell advised them where the patriot force was encamped. They joined the army and thus made a muster roll of about sixteen hundred men.

The board of officers determined to march upon Ferguson. In the meantime two or three of their men had deserted after their first rendezvous, and had gone to Ferguson and advised him of the intended attack. The army marched to Gilbert Town and found that Ferguson had left it several days before, having taken the route towards Fort Ninety-Six.

Finding that Ferguson was retreating, and learning what was his real strength, it was determined on Thursday night the 5th of October, to make a desperate effort to overtake him before he should reach any British post or receive any further reinforcements. Accordingly, they selected all who had good horses, who numbered about nine hundred and ten, and started the next morning in pursuit of Ferguson as soon as they could see.

Ferguson, after marching a short distance towards Ninety-Six, had filed off to the left toward Cornwallis. His pursuers never stopped until late in the afternoon, when they reached the Cowpens. There they halted, shot down some beeves, ate their suppers and fed their horses. This done, the line of march was resumed and continued through the whole night, amidst an excessively hard rain. In the morning Shelby ascertained that Campbell had taken a wrong road in the night and had separated from him. Men were posted off in all directions and Campbell's corps found and put in the right road. They then crossed Broad River and continued their pursuit until twelve o'clock, the 7th of October. The rain continued to fall so heavily that Campbell, Sevier and Cleveland concluded to halt, and rode up to Shelby to inform him of their determination. Shelby replied: "I will not stop till night, if I follow Ferguson into Cornwallis' lines!" Without replying, the other colonels turned off to their respective commands and continued the march. They had proceeded but a mile when they learned that Ferguson was only seven miles from them at King's Mountain.

Ferguson, finding that he could not elude the rapid pursuit of the mounted mountaineers, had marched to King's Mountain, which he considered a strong post, and which he had reached the night previous. The mountain, or ridge, was a quarter of a mile long, and so confident was Ferguson in the strength of his position that he declared the Almighty could not drive him from it.

When the patriots came near the mountain they halted, tied all their loose baggage to their saddles, fastened their horses and left them under charge of a few men, and then prepared for an immediate attack. About 3 o'clock the patriot force was led to the attack in four columns. Col Campbell commanded the right centre column, Col. Shelby the left centre, Col. Sevier the right flank column, and Col. Cleveland the left flank. As they came to the foot of the mountain, the right centre and right flank columns deployed to the right, and the left centre and left flank columns to the left, and thus surrounding the mountain they marched up, commencing the action on all sides.

Ferguson did all that an officer could do under the circumstances. His men, too, fought bravely. But his position, which he thought impregnable against any force the Patriots could raise, was really a disadvantage to him. The summit was bare, whilst the sides of the mountain was covered with trees. Ferguson's men were drawn up in close column on the summit and thus presented fair marks for the mountaineers, who approached them under cover of the trees. As either column would approach the summit, Ferguson would order out a charge with fixed bayonet, which was always successful, for the riflemen retreated before the charging column slowly, still firing as they retired. When Ferguson's men returned to regain their position on the mountain, the patriots would again rally and pursue them. In one of these charges Shelby's column was considerably broken; he rode back and rallied his men, and when the enemy retired to the summit he pressed on his men and reached the summit whilst Ferguson was directing a charge against Cleveland.

Col. Sevier reached the summit about the same time with Shelby. They

The Spirit of 'Seventy-Six

united and drove back the enemy to one end of the ridge. Cleveland's and Campbell's columns were still pressing forward and firing as they came up. The slaughter of the enemy was great, and it was evident that further resistance would be unavailing. Still Ferguson's proud heart could not think of surrender. He swore "he never would yield to such a d——d banditti," and rushed from his men, sword in hand, and cut away until his sword was broken and he was shot down. His men, seeing their leader fall, immediately surrendered. The British loss, in killed and prisoners, was eleven hundred and five. Ferguson's morning report showed a force of eleven hundred and twenty-five. A more total defeat was not practicable. Our loss was about forty killed. Amongst them we had to mourn the death of Col. Williams, a most gallant and efficient officer. The battle lasted one hour.

—*North Carolina State Records*, XV, 105-108.

4. THE FACE OF THE MOUNTAIN IS STREWN WITH THE BODIES OF TORIES

Account of Ensign Robert Campbell of North Carolina.

Ferguson, finding that he must inevitably be overtaken, chose his ground and waited for the attack on King's Mountain. On the 7th of October, in the afternoon, after a forced march of forty-five miles on that day and the night before, the volunteers came up with him. The forenoon of the day was wet, but they were fortunate enough to come on him undiscovered and took his pickets, they not having it in their power to give an alarm. They were soon formed in such order as to attack the enemy on all sides. The Washington and Sullivan regiments were formed in the front and on the right flank; the North and South Carolina troops, under Cols. Williams, Sevier, Cleveland, Lacey and Brandon, on the left. The two armies being in full view, the centre of the one nearly opposite the centre of the other, the British main guard posted nearly half-way down the mountain, the commanding officer gave the word of command to raise the Indian war-whoop and charge. In a moment King's Mountain resounded with their shouts, and on the first fire the guard retreated, leaving some of their men to crimson the earth. The British beat to arms and immediately formed on top of the mountain behind a chain of rocks that appeared impregnable, and had their wagons drawn up on their flank across the end of the mountain, by which they made a strong breast work.

Thus concealed, the American army advanced to the charge. In ten or fifteen mintues the wings came round, and the action became general.

The enemy annoyed our troops very much from their advantageous position. Col. Shelby, being previously ordered to reconnoitre their position, observing their situation and what a destructive fire was kept up from behind those rocks, ordered Robert Campbell . . . to advance and post themselves opposite to the rocks and near to the enemy, and then return to assist in bringing up the men in order, who had been charged with the bayonet. These orders were punctually obeyed, and they kept up such a galling fire as to compel Ferguson to order a company of regulars to face them, with a view to cover his men that were posted behind the rocks.

At this time a considerable fire was drawn to this side of the mountain by the repulse of those on the other, and the Loyalists not being permitted

1142

to leave their post. This scene was not of long duration, for it was the brave Virginia volunteers and those under Col. Shelby, on their attempting rapidly to ascend the mountain, that were charged with the bayonet. They obstinately stood until some of them were thrust through the body, and having nothing but their rifles by which to defend themselves, they were forced to retreat. They were soon rallied by their gallant commanders, Campbell, Shelby and other brave officers, and by a constant and well-directed fire of their rifles drove them back in their turn, strewing the face of the mountain with their assailants, and kept advancing until they drove them from some of their posts.

Ferguson, being heavily pressed on all sides, ordered Capt. DePeyster to reinforce some of the extreme post with a full company of British regulars. He marched, but to his astonishment, when he arrived at the place of destination, he had almost no men, being exposed in that short distance to the constant fire of their rifles. He then ordered his cavalry to mount, but to no purpose. As quick as they were mounted they were taken down by some bold marksman. Being driven to desperation by such a scene of misfortune, Col. Ferguson endeavored to make his escape, and, with two colonels of the Loyalists, mounted his horse and charged on that part of the line which was defended by the party who had been ordered round the mountain by Col. Shelby where it appeared too weak to resist them. But as soon as he got to the line he fell, and the other two officers, attempting to retreat, soon shared the same fate.

It was about this time that Col. Campbell advanced in front of his men and climbed over a steep rock close by the enemy's lines to get a view of their situation, and saw that they were retreating from behind the rocks that were near to him.

As soon as Capt. DePeyster observed that Col. Ferguson was killed, he raised a flag and called for quarters. It was soon taken out of his hand by one of the officers on horse back and raised so high that it could be seen by our line, and the firing immediately ceased. The Loyalists, at the time of their surrender, were driven into a crowd, and being closely surrounded, they could not have made any further resistance.

In this sharp action, one hundred and fifty of Col. Ferguson's party were killed, and something over that number were wounded. Eight hundred and ten, of whom one hundred were British regulars, surrendered themselves prisoners, and one thousand five hundred stand of arms were taken. The loss of the American army on this occasion amounted to thirty killed and something over fifty wounded, among whom were a number of brave officers. Col. Williams, who has been so much lamented, was shot through the body, near the close of the action, in making an attempt to charge upon Ferguson. He lived long enough to hear of the surrender of the British army. He then said, "I die contented, since we have gained the victory," and expired.

—North Carolina State Records, XV, 101-103.

5. A Nervous Recruit Describes the Charge in the Center

Account of James P. Collins.

The enemy was posted on a high, steep and rugged ridge—very difficult of access. . . . The plan was to surround the mountain and attack them on all sides, if possible. In order to do this, the left had to march under the fire of the enemy to gain the position assigned to them on the stream on the right of the enemy, while the right was to take possession of the other stream. In doing this they were not exposed, the cliff being so steep as to cover them completely.

Each leader made a short speech in his own way to his men, desiring every coward to be off immediately. Here I confess I would willingly have been excused, for my feelings were not the most pleasant. This may be attributed to my youth, not being quite seventeen years of age—but I could not well swallow the appellation of coward. I looked around. Every man's countenance seemed to change. Well, thought I, fate is fate; every man's fate is before him and he has to run it out. . . .

We were soon in motion, every man throwing four or five balls in his mouth to prevent thirst, also to be in readiness to reload quick. The shot of the enemy soon began to pass over us like hail. The first shock was quickly over, and for my own part, I was soon in profuse sweat. My lot happened to be in the center, where the severest part of the battle was fought. We soon attempted to climb the hill, but were fiercely charged upon and forced to fall back to our first position. We tried a second time, but met the same fate; the fight then seemed to become more furious. Their leader, Ferguson, came in full view, within rifle shot as if to encourage his men, who by this time were falling very fast. He soon disappeared. We took to the hill a third time; the enemy gave way.

When we had gotten near the top, some of our leaders roared out, "Hurrah, my brave fellows! Advance! They are crying for quarter."

By this time, the right and left had gained the top of the cliff; the enemy was completely hemmed in on all sides, and no chance of escaping—besides, their leader had fallen. They soon threw down their arms and surrendered. After the fight was over, the situation of the poor Tories appeared to be really pitiable; the dead lay in heaps on all sides, while the groans of the wounded were heard in every direction. I could not help turning away from the scene before me with horror and, though exulting in victory, could not refrain from shedding tears. . . .

On examining the dead body of their great chief, it appeared that almost fifty rifles must have been leveled at him at the same time; seven rifle balls had passed through his body, both of his arms were broken, and his hat and clothing were literally shot to pieces. Their great elevation above us had proved their ruin. They overshot us altogether, scarce touching a man, except those on horseback, while every rifle from below seemed to have the desired effect. . . .

Next morning, which was Sunday, the scene became really distressing; the wives and children of the poor Tories came in, in great numbers. Their husbands, fathers and brothers lay dead in heaps, while others lay wounded or dying—a melancholy sight indeed! while numbers of the survivors were doomed to abide the sentence of a court martial, and several were actually hanged. . . .

We proceeded to bury the dead, but it was badly done. They were thrown into convenient piles and covered with old logs, the bark of old trees, and rocks; yet not so as to secure them from becoming a prey to the beasts of the forest or the vultures of the air; and the wolves became so plenty that it was dangerous for any one to be out at night, for several miles around; also, the hogs in the neighborhood gathered in to the place to devour the flesh of men, inasmuch as numbers chose to live on little meat rather than eat their hogs, though they were fat. Half of the dogs in the country were said to be mad and were put to death. I saw, myself, in passing the place a few weeks after, all parts of the human frame lying scattered in every direction. . . .

    —Collins, *Autobiography of a Revolutionary Soldier*, pp. 259-261.

CHAPTER THIRTY

The Turn of the Tide

ON OCTOBER 14, 1780, *the same day that Shelby and Campbell annihilated the Tories at King's Mountain, General Nathanael Greene was named to succeed Gates in the Southern command. Greene did not reach the field until December. In the meantime Cornwallis' forces in South Carolina were continually and effectively harassed by partisans, notably the small bands skillfully and daringly led by Frances Marion and Thomas Sumter, the latter increasingly independent of direction. More and more Cornwallis counted on Tarleton to cope with the guerrillas. Even the affair at Blackstock's in which Tarleton suffered ten casualties to every one suffered by Sumter was magnified by the Green Dragoon into a victory, and as such was accepted by Cornwallis.*

Outnumbered by Cornwallis three to two, and operating in a theater terribly wracked by war, pillage and discord, Greene wisely concentrated first on guerrilla tactics, developing on a more comprehensive scale the tactics of the Carolina partisans. He detached some of his own forces and placed them under Morgan, one of the few military geniuses the war produced, who had now come out of self-imposed retirement. Morgan was sent to harass the British outposts in the western part of South Carolina, and Greene moved to the north-central part of the state to support the American partisans. The disaster Morgan inflicted upon the British at Cowpens ended the legend of Tarleton's invincibility.

Now Cornwallis became the pursuer. Too late to catch Morgan, he tried to corner Greene, pressing him north into Virginia, only to fall back on Hillsborough for support. Guilford Courthouse was a costly technical victory for Cornwallis, who momentarily kept the field but had his army terribly mauled by Greene's men. The British commander now gave up all thought of capturing Greene, moved to the coast, and finally quit North Carolina for a new theater of action in Virginia, where to all intents and purposes he brought the curtain down on the war.

I. PARTISAN WARFARE TAKES ITS TOLL

1. "DAMN IT, BOYS, YOU . . . YOU KNOW WHAT I MEAN! GO ON!"

Memoirs of Captain Tarleton Brown of South Carolina.

Overtaking General Marion at Kingstree, Black River, S. C., we immediately united with his troops. Marion's route lay then between the Santee and Little Pedee rivers; and being desirous to intercept and defeat Col. Watts, who was then marching at the head of 400 men between Camden and Georgetown, every arrangement and preparation was made to carry into execution his design. All things being now ready, Watts appeared in sight at the head of his large force, and as they marched down the road with great show and magnificence (hoping, no doubt, to terrify and conquer the country), they spied us; at which time, the British horse sallied forth to surround us.

Marion, with his characteristic shrewdness and sagacity, discovered their manoeuvres, anticipated their object and retreated to the woods, some four or five hundred yards, and prepared for them. In a few moments they came dashing up, expecting to find us all in confusion and disorder, but to their astonishment we were ready for the attack, and perceiving this, they called a halt, at which time Marion and Horry ordered a charge. Col. Horry stammered badly, and on this occasion he leaned forward, spurred his horse, waved his sword and ran fifty or sixty yards, endeavoring to utter the word *charge*, and finding he could not, bawled out, *"Damn it, boys, you . . . you know what I mean. Go on!"*

We were then doing what we could, pressing with all rapidity to the strife, and before the British could get back to the main body we slew a goodly number of them. Being eager to do all the damage we could, we pursued the fellows very close to the line of their main body, and as soon as they got in, Watts began to thunder his cannon at us, and to tear down the limbs and branches of the trees, which fell about us like hail, but did no other damage than to wound one of our men, Natt. Hutson, and one horse slightly. Marion, now finding his force, which consisted only of two hundred men (though sterling to a man, brave, fearless and patriotic), was too small to give Watts open battle, guarded the bridges and swamps in his route, and annoyed and killed his men as they passed.

For prudence sake, Marion never encamped over two nights in one place, unless at a safe distance from the enemy. He generally commenced the line of march about sun-set, continuing through the greater part of the night. By this policy he was enabled effectually to defeat the plans of the British and to strengthen his languishing cause. For while the one army was encamping and resting in calm and listless security, not dreaming of danger, the other, taking advantage of opportunity and advancing through the sable curtains of the night unobserved, often effectually vanquished and routed their foes. It was from the craftiness and ingenuity of Marion, the celerity with which he moved from post to post, that his enemies gave to him the significant appellation of the "Swamp Fox." Upon him depended almost solely the success of the provincial army of South Carolina, and the sequel has proven how well he performed the trust reposed in him. His genuine love of country and liberty, and his unwearied vigilance and invincible fortitude, coupled with the eminent success which attended him through his brilliant career, has endeared him to the hearts of his countrymen, and the memory of his deeds of valor shall never slumber so long as there is a Carolinian to speak his panegyric.

The heavy rains which prevailed at this time and inundated the country to a considerable extent, proved very favorable to Marion. He now sent a detachment of seventy men, myself one of the number, across the Santee, to attack the enemy stationed at Scott's Lake and Monk's Corner. We crossed the river at night in a small boat, commanded by Captains James and John Postell, dividing our force into two companies, each consisting of thirty-five men. Capt. James Postell took one company and proceeded to Scott's Lake, but ascertaining the strength of the enemy and finding the place too well fortified to warrant an attack, he abandoned the project and returned again to the river, and awaited the arrival of Capt. John Postell, who, in the meantime, had marched with the other company to Monk's Corner. It was my good fortune to accompany the latter.

Just about the break of day we charged upon the enemy. Our appearance was so sudden and unexpected that they had not time even to fire a single gun. We took thirty-three prisoners, found twenty-odd hogsheads of old spirits and a large supply of provisions. The former we destroyed, but returned with the latter and our prisoners to the army on Santee. The news of our attack on Monk's Corner having reached the enemy at Scott's Lake, they forthwith marched to their assistance, but arrived too late to extend any. We had captured their comrades, bursted their hogsheads of spirits, gathered their provisions and decamped before their arrival. Capt. James Postell, being apprised of their march to assist their friends at Monk's Corner, returned to the fort, set fire to it and burned it level to the ground.

—BROWN, *Memoirs*, pp. 34-38.

2. NATHANAEL GREENE ASSUMES COMMAND IN THE SOUTH

Nathanael Greene to Catherine Greene.

[October, 1780]

My dear Angel

What I have been dreading has come to pass. His Excellency General Washington by an order of Congress has appointed me to the command of the Southern Army, Gen. Gates being recalled to undergo an examination into his conduct. This is so foreign from my wishes that I am distressed exceedingly: especially as I have just received your letter of the 2d of this month where you describe your distress and sufferings in such a feeling manner as melts my soul into the deepest distress.

I have been pleasing my self with the agreeable prospect of spending the winter here with you; and the moment I was appointed to the command I sent off Mr Hubbard to bring you to camp. But alas, before we can have the happiness of meeting, I am ordered away to another quarter. How unfriendly is war to domestic happiness! . . .

—GREENE, "Letter," *R. I. Hist. Soc. Coll.*, XX, 106.

3. ONLY TARLETON IS ABLE TO COPE WITH THE PARTISANS

Lord Cornwallis to Sir Henry Clinton.

Camp at Wynnesborough, December 3, 1780

Wynnesborough, my present position, is an healthy spot, well situated to protect the greatest part of the northern frontier and to assist Camden and Ninety-Six. The militia of the latter, on which alone we could place the smallest dependence, was so totally disheartened by the defeat of Ferguson that of that whole district we could with difficulty assemble one hundred, and even those, I am convinced, would not have made the smallest resistance if they had been attacked. I determined to remain at this place until an answer arrived from Gen. Leslie, on which my plan for the winter has to depend, and to use every possible means of putting the Province into a state of defence, which I found to be absolutely necessary, whether my campaign was offensive or defensive.

Bad as the state of our affairs was on the northern frontier, the eastern part was much worse. Col. Tynes, who commanded the militia of the High Hills of Santee, and who was posted on Black River, was surprized and taken, and his men lost all their arms. Col. Marion had so wrought on the minds of the people, partly by the terror of his threats and cruelty of his punishments, and partly by the promise of plunder, that there was scarce an inhabitant between the Santee and Pedee that was not in arms against us. Some parties had even crossed the Santee and carried terror to the gates of Charles-town. My first object was to reinstate matters in that quarter, without which Camden could receive no supplies. I therefore sent Tarleton, who pursued Marion for several days, obliged his corps to take to the swamps, and by convincing the inhabitants there was a power superior to Marion who could likewise reward and punish, so far checked the insurrection that the greatest part of them have not dared openly to appear in arms against us since his expedition. . . .

Major Wemyss, who had just passed Broad River at Brierly's Ferry, came to me on the seventh of last month and told me that he had information that Sumpter had moved to Moore's Hill, within five miles of Fishdam Ford and about twenty-five miles from the place where the 63d then lay; that he had accurate accounts of his position and good guides, and that he made no doubt of being able to surprize and rout him. As the defeating of so daring and troublesome a man as Sumpter, and dispersing such a banditti, was a great object, I consented to his making the trial on the 9th at daybreak, and gave him forty of the dragoons which Tarleton had left with me, desiring him, however, neither to put them in the front nor to make any use of them during the night.

Major Wemyss marched so early and so fast on the night of the 8th that he arrived at Moore's Hill soon after midnight. He then had information that Sumpter had marched that evening to Fishdam Ford, where he lay with his rear close to Broad River on a low piece of ground. The Major immediately proceeded to attack him in his new position, and succeeded so well as to get into his camp whilst the men were all sleeping round the fires; but as Major Wemyss rode into the camp at the head of the dragoons and the 63d followed them on horseback, the enemy's arms were not secured, and some of them recovering from the first alarm got their rifles and with the first fire wounded Major Wemyss in several places and put the cavalry into disorder. The 63d then dismounted and killed and wounded about seventy of the rebels, drove several over the river and dispersed the rest. The command, however, devolving on a very young officer who neither knew the ground nor Major Wemyss's plan, nor the strength of the enemy, some few of which kept firing from the wood on our people who remained in the enemy's camp and who were probably discovered by their fires, our troops came away before daybreak, leaving

Major Wemyss and 22 sergeants and rank and file at a house close to the field of action. In the morning those who were left with a flag of truce with the wounded found that the enemy were all gone, but on some of their scouting parties discovering that our people had likewise retired, Sumpter returned and took Major Wemyss's parole for himself and the wounded soldiers. Major Wemyss is gone to Charleston and is in a fair way of recovery.

The enemy on this event cried "Victory," and the whole country came in fast to join Sumpter, who passed the Broad River and joined Branan, Clarke, etc. I detached Major McArthur with the 1st Battalion of the 71st and the 63d Regiment, after having sent my aid-de-camp, Lieut. Money, to take the command of it, to Brierly's Ferry on Broad River, in order to cover our mills and to give some check to the enemy's march to Ninety-Six. At the same time I recalled Lieut. Col. Tarleton from the Low Country. Tarleton was so fortunate as to pass not only the Wateree but the Broad River without Gen. Sumpter's being apprised of it, who, having increased his corps to one thousand, had passed the Ennoree and was on the point of attacking our hundred militia at Williams's house, fifteen miles from Ninety-Six, and where I believe he would not have met with much resistance.

Lt. Col. Tarleton would have surprized him on the south of Ennoree had not a deserter of the 63d given notice of his march. He, however, cut to pieces his rear guard in passing that river, and pursued his main body with such rapidity that he could not safely pass the Tyger and was obliged to halt on a very strong position at a place called Black Stocks, close to it. Tarleton had with him only his cavalry and the 63d mounted, his infantry and 3-pounder being several miles behind. The enemy, not being able to retreat with safety, and being informed of Tarleton's approach and want of infantry by a woman who passed him on the march and contrived by a nearer road to get to them, were encouraged by their great superiority of numbers and began to fire on the 63d, who were dismounted. Lt. Col. Tarleton, to save them from considerable loss, was obliged to attack, altho' at some hazard, and drove the enemy, with loss, over the river. Sumpter was dangerously wounded, three of their colonels killed, and about 120 men killed, wounded or taken. On our side about 50 were killed and wounded. Lieuts. Gibson and Cope, of the 63d, were amongst the former, and my aid-de-camp, Lieut. Money, who was a most promising officer, died of his wounds a few days after.

Lt. Col. Tarleton, as soon as he had taken care of his wounded, pursued and dispersed the remaining part of Sumpter's corps, and then, having assembled some militia under Mr. Cunningham, whom I appointed Brig. General of the Militia of that district, and who has by far the greatest influence in that country, he returned to the Broad River, where he at present remains, as well as Major McArthur, in the neighborhood of Brierley's Ferry.

It is not easy for Lt. Col. Tarleton to add to the reputation he has acquired in this Province, but the defeating 1,000 men posted on very strong ground and occupying log houses with 190 cavalry and 80 infantry is a proof of that spirit and those talents which must render the most essential services to his country. . . .

—*North Carolina State Records*, XV, 303-306.

4. Governor Rutledge Indicts Tarleton for Barbarity

Governor John Rutledge to South Carolina's delegates in the Continental Congress.

December 8, 1780

It is really melancholy to see the desolate condition of Mr. Hill's plantation in the New Acquisition: all his fine iron-works, mills, dwelling-houses and buildings of every kind, even his Negro-houses, reduced to ashes, and his wife and children in a little log hut. I was shocked to see the ragged, shabby condition of our brave and virtuous men, who would not remain in the power of the enemy but have taken to arms.

This, however, is but a faint description of the sufferings of our country, for it is beyond a doubt the enemy have hanged many of our people, who from fear and the impracticability of removing had given paroles, and from attachment to our side joined it. Nay, Tarleton has since the action at Black-stocks hung one Johnson, a magistrate of respectable character. They have also burnt a prodigious number of houses, and turned a vast many women, formerly of affluent and easy fortunes, with their chilldren, almost naked into the woods.

Tarleton, at the house of General Richardson, exceeded his usual barbarity; for, having dined in his house, he not only burnt it afterwards, but having driven into the barns a number of cattle, hogs and poultry, he consumed them, together with the barn and the corn in it, in one general blaze. This was done because he pretended to believe that the poor old general was with the Rebel army, though had he opened his grave before the door, he might have seen the contrary. Colonel Charles Cotesworth Pinckney's family was turned out of his house.

In short, the enemy seem determined, if they can, to break every man's spirit, if they cannot ruin him. Engagements of capitulations and proclamations are no security against their oppressions and cruelties.

—Moultrie, *Memoirs*, II, 239-240.

5. Greene's Troops Are "Wretched Beyond Description"

Nathanael Greene to Joseph Reed of Pennsylvania.

Camp on the Pedee, January 9, 1781

I intended to have written you before, but I have been so employed since I left Philadelphia that I have been obliged to deny myself the pleasure of writing to my friends, to attend to the more immemdiate duties of my department. On my journey I visited the Maryland and Virginia Assemblies and laid before them the state of this army, and urged the necessity of an immediate support. They both promised to do everything in their power, but such was their poverty, even in their capitals, that they could not furnish forage for my horses. I have also written to the States of Delaware and North Carolina, neither of which have taken any measures yet for giving effectual aid to this army. I left General Gist in Maryland, and Baron Steuben in Virginia, to forward the recruits and supplies. Measures are taking in Virginia which promise us some aid, though very trifling to what they ought to give and what our state requires. All the way through the country as I passed, I found the people engaged in matters of interest and in pursuit of pleasure, almost regardless of their danger, public credit totally lost, and every man excusing himself from giving the least aid to Government, from an apprehension that they would get no return for any advance. This afforded but a dull prospect, nor has it mended since my arrival.

I overtook the army at Charlotte, to which place General Gates had advanced. The appearance of the troops was wretched beyond description, and their distress, on account of provisions, was little less than their sufferings for want of clothing and other necessaries. General Gates had lost the confidence of the officers, and the troops all their discipline, and [they have been] so addicted to plundering that they were a terror to the inhabitants. The general and I met upon very good terms, and parted so. The old gentleman was in great distress, having but just heard of the death of his son before my arrival. . . .

The wants of this army are so numerous and various that the shortest way of telling you is to inform you that we have nothing, as General du Portail can inform you from his own observation. The great departments of the army had nobody at the head of them fit to provide in a country like this for a sergeant's party. I have got Colonel Carrington to accept of the Quartermaster-General's department, and am in hopes of getting a good man at the head of the commissaries, without which I foresee we must starve. I am endeavouring to bring everything into order and perfect our arrangements as much as possible, but it is all an up-hill business.

The loss of our army in Charleston and the defeat of General Gates has been the cause of keeping such vast shoals of militia on foot, who, like the locusts of Egypt, have eaten up everything, and the expense has beeen so enormous that it has ruined the currency of the State. It is my opinion there is no one thing upon the Continent that wants regulating so much as the right which the States exercise of keeping what militia on foot they please at the Continental expense. I am persuaded North Carolina has militia enough to swallow up all the revenues of America, especially under their imperfect arrangements, where every man draws and wastes as much as he pleases.

The country is so extensive and the powers of government so weak that everybody does as he pleases. The inhabitants are much divided in their political sentiments, and the Whigs and Tories pursue each other with little less than savage fury. The back-country people are bold and daring in their make, but the people upon the sea-shore are sickly and but indifferent militia. The ruin of the State is inevitable if there are such large bodies of militia kept on foot. No army can subsist in the country long if the ravages continue. Indeed, unless this army is better supported than I see any prospect of, the country is lost beyond redemption, for it is impossible for the people to struggle much longer under their present difficulties. There appears a foolish pride in the representation of things from this quarter; the strength and resources of the country are far overrated, and those who are engaged in this business, to indulge their pride, will sacrifice their country. The inhabitants are beginning to move off in great bodies, and unless a firmer barrier can be formed, this quarter will be all depopulated.

We are living upon charity and subsist by daily collections. Indian meal and beef is our common diet, and not a drop of spirits have we had with us since I came to the army. An army naked and subsisted in this manner, and not more than one-third equal to the enemy in numbers, will make but a poor fight, especially as one has beeen accustomed to victory and the other to flight. It is difficult to give spirits to troops that have nothing to animate them.

I have been obliged to take an entire new position with the army. General Morgan is upon Broad River with a little flying army, and Colonel Washington since his arrival there has defeated a party of Tories, the particulars of which I beg leave to refer you to the President of Congress for. This camp I mean as a camp of repose, for the purpose of repairing our wagons, recruiting our horses and disciplining the troops. . . .

—Reed, *Life and Correspondence of Reed*, II, 334-336.

II. COWPENS, THE PATRIOTS' BEST-FOUGHT BATTLE

Morgan and Greene were now 140 miles apart, the former in the western part of South Carolina, the latter operating with the guerrillas in the north-central part of the state. Cornwallis detached Tarleton to handle Morgan while he readied himself to take on Greene.

On January 16, 1781, Morgan, with 1,000 men, including reinforcements under Colonel Andrew Pickens, was informed by his scouts that Tarleton, with a mixed force of 1,100 regulars and Tories, was but a day's march away. Should Morgan retreat, he knew his militia would vanish. A withdrawal across the unfordable Broad River meant dangerous delay, as he lacked boats. Should he fight, his troops might panic again as at Camden. He decided to stand and fight.

Morgan made his stand in a level clearing known as the Cowpens, once a pasture for backwoods cattle. The Broad River cut off all retreat for his men. The night before, he went among the militia, for whom he had reserved a conspicuous role, and encouraged them, telling them that "the 'Old Wagoner' would crack his whip over Ben in the morning, as sure as he lived." He exhorted them to fire two volleys, after which they could retire. There was no sleep for Morgan that night.

Morgan acted in a very unorthodox way. In the front line he placed his raw militia. Behind them on slightly rising land were the Continentals and some seasoned Virginia militiamen under Lieutenant Colonel John Eager Howard. They were ordered to hold their ground at all cost. Farther to the rear on a low ridge, sheltered from British fire, he placed his cavalry under Lieutenant Colonel Washington.

To Tarleton Cowpens seemed a perfect setup for the standard tactics of a frontal bayonet attack, before which the militia had always run. When the British approached to within 100 yards of the Americans they were met by the first volleys. The sharpshooting militiamen heeded Morgan's exhortation, "Look for the epaulets! Pick off the epaulets!" They fired twice with lethal effect, then moved around to the American left toward the low ridge in the rear. The British line now lunged forward and attacked the second line. To

FIRST POSITION

BROAD RIVER

PICKENS' MILITIA REFORMED

WASHINGTON'S CAVALRY

MORGAN'S CONTINENTALS

PICKENS' MILITIA

SKIRMISH LINE

ATTACK

TARLETON

FINAL POSITION

BROAD RIVER

WASHINGTON'S CAVALRY

PICKENS' MILITIA

MORGAN'S CONTINENTALS

SURRENDER

SURRENDER

TARLETON

WASHINGTON

FLIGHT

FLIGHT

▥ Americans
■ British

COWPENS

bring the battle to a swift ending Tarleton ordered his reserves to advance on the extreme left of his line, and the cavalry, still farther to the left, to turn the right flank of the American line. To counter this threat, Howard ordered his right flank company to change its front and form at right angles with the main body. Instead, in the confusion the men fell back. Then, Morgan, keeping his head at the most critical moment of the battle, ordered the entire line to pull back, too. Sensing victory, Tarleton's men rushed forward impetuously, wildly, and in complete disorder.

Now was Morgan's great opportunity. He ordered the line to halt and face about. Howard had his men charge the enemy with bayonets, and Washington prevented Tarleton's dragoons from covering his retreat. The British surrendered en masse. Their casualties were 100 killed, 200 wounded, 600 prisoners. The Patriots lost 12 killed, 60 wounded. With a corporal's guard Tarleton escaped, but not before a colorful hand-to-hand saber encounter with Colonel Washington.

Morgan's masterly battle strategy was used by Greene at Guilford Courthouse and Eutaw Springs, but in neither case was the execution so precise nor were the results so successful. The British never forgot Cowpens. "The late affair almost broke my heart," Cornwallis confessed to Lord Rawdon. Tarleton preserved his fiery impetuosity throughout the rest of the campaign, but the ghost of Cowpens continued to haunt him on his return to England. There his most acid critic, Lieutenant Mackenzie of the 71st Regiment of Highlanders, who was wounded at Cowpens, published a series of attacks upon Tarleton's conduct of the battle. Tarleton was charged with putting his troops into battle immediately after a night march and with advancing his line before it had been properly formed. In one of his most savage letters, published in the London Morning Chronicle *on August 9, 1782, Mackenzie asserted:*

> *You got yourself and the party completely ambuscaded, completely surrounded, upon all sides, by Mr. Morgan's rifle men. What was the consequence? The two detachments of British were made prisoners after a great slaughter was made among them, your legion dragoons were so broke by galling fire of rifle shot that your charging was in vain, till prudence, on your side, with about twenty more who were well mounted, made your retreat good, by leaving the remains of the poor blended legion in the hands of Mr. Morgan, who I must say, though an enemy, showed great masterly abilities in this manoever.*

Thus fell, at one blow, all the Provincial Legion, with about three hundred veterans!

1. CORNWALLIS ORDERS TARLETON TO PUSH MORGAN "TO THE UTMOST"

Winnsborough, January 2, 1781

Dear Tarleton: I sent Haldane to you last night to desire you would pass Broad River with the Legion and the first battalion of the 71st as soon as possible. If Morgan is still at Williams's, or any where within your reach, I should wish you to push him to the utmost. I have not heard, except from McArthur, of his having cannon, nor would I believe it, unless he has it from very good authority. It is, however, possible, and Ninety-six is of so much consequence that no time is to be lost.

Yours sincerely,
Cornwallis

Let me know if you think that the moving the whole, or any part, of my corps can be of use.

—Tarleton, *History of Campaigns in the Southern Provinces*, p. 244.

2. Morgan Exults: "One More Fire and the Day Is Ours!"

Account of James P. Collins.

. . . About sunrise on the 17th of January, 1781, the enemy came in full view. The sight, to me at least, seemed somewhat imposing. They halted for a short time, and then advanced rapidly as if certain of victory. The militia under Pickins and Moffitt was posted on the right of the regulars some distance in advance, while Washington's cavalry was stationed in the rear. We gave the enemy one fire; when they charged us with their bayonets, we gave way and retreated for our horses. Tarleton's cavalry pursued us. "Now," thought I, "my hide is in the loft."

Just as we got to our horses, they overtook us and began to make a few hacks at some, however without doing much injury. They, in their haste, had pretty much scattered, perhaps thinking they would have another Fishing Creek frolic, but in a few moments Col. Washington's cavalry was among them like a whirlwind, and the poor fellows began to keel from their horses without being able to remount. The shock was so sudden and violent they could not stand it and immediately betook themselves to flight. There was no time to rally, and they appeared to be as hard to stop as a drove of wild Choctaw steers going to a Pennsylvania market. In a few moments the clashing of swords was out of hearing and quickly out of sight.

By this time both lines of the infantry were warmly engaged and we, being relieved from the pursuit of the enemy, began to rally and prepare to redeem our credit, when Morgan rode up in front and, waving his sword, cried out, "Form, form, my brave fellows! Give them one more fire and the day is ours. Old Morgan was never beaten."

We then advanced briskly and gained the right flank of the enemy, and they, being hard pressed in front by Howard and falling very fast, could not stand it long. They began to throw down their arms and surrender themselves prisoners of war. The whole army, except Tarleton and his horsemen, fell into the hands of Morgan, together with all the baggage. . . .

—Collins, *Autobiography of a Revolutionary Soldier*, pp. 264-265.

3. Howard's Retreating Troops Face About and Charge the Enemy

Lieutenant Colonel John Eager Howard's account.

. . . Seeing my right flank was exposed to the enemy, I attempted to change the front of Wallace's company (Virginia regulars); in doing it, some confusion ensued, and first a part, and then the whole of the company commenced a retreat. The officers along the line seeing this, and supposing that orders had been given for a retreat, faced their men about and moved off. Morgan, who had mostly been with the militia, quickly rode up to me and expressed apprehensions of the event; but I soon removed his fears by pointing to the line and observing that men were not beaten who retreated in that order. He then ordered me to keep with the men until we came to the rising ground near Washington's horse; and he rode forward to fix on the most proper place for us to halt and face about.

In a minute we had a perfect line. The enemy were now very near us. Our men commenced a very destructive fire, which they little expected, and a few rounds occasioned great disorder in their ranks. While in this confusion, I ordered a charge with the bayonet, which order was obeyed with great alacrity. As the line advanced, I observed their artillery a short distance in front and called to Captain Ewing, who was near me, to take it. Captain Anderson (now General Anderson, of Montgomery County, Maryland), hearing the order, also pushed for the same object, and both being emulous for the prize, kept pace until near the first piece, when Anderson, by placing the end of his spontoon forward into the ground, made a long leap which brought him upon the gun and gave him the honor of the prize.

. . . In the pursuit I was led towards the right, in among the 71st, who were broken into squads, and as I called to them to surrender, they laid down their arms, and the officers delivered up their swords. Captain Duncanson, of the 71st Grenadiers, gave me his sword and stood by me. Upon getting on my horse, I found him pulling at my saddle, and he nearly unhorsed me. I expressed my displeasure and asked him what he was about. The explanation was that they had orders to give no quarter, and they did not expect any; and as my men were coming up, he was afraid they would use him ill. I admitted his excuse and put him into the care of a sergeant. . . .

—LEE, *Campaign of 1781 in the Carolinas*, pp. 97n-98n.

4. "AND ALL THEIR MUSIC ARE OURS"—MORGAN SUMS UP COWPENS

General Daniel Morgan to Nathanael Greene.

Camp near Cain Creek, January 19, 1781

The troops I have the honor to command have been so fortunate as to obtain a complete victory over a detachment from the British army, commanded by Lieut. Col. Tarleton. The action happened on the 17th inst., about sunrise, at the Cowpens. It, perhaps, would be well to remark, for the honor of the American arms, that although the progress of this corps was marked with burning and devastation, and although they waged the most cruel warfare, not a man was killed, wounded or even insulted after he surrendered. Had not Britons during this contest received so many lessons of humanity, I should flatter myself that this might teach them a little. But I fear they are incorrigible.

To give you a just idea of our operations, it will be necessary to inform you that on the 14th inst., having received certain intelligence that Lord Cornwallis and Lieut. Col. Tarleton were both in motion, and that their movements clearly indicated their intentions of dislodging me, I abandoned my encampment on Grindall's Ford on the Pacolet, and on the 16th, in the eve-

ning, took possession of a post about seven miles from the Cherokee Ford on
Broad River. My former position subjected me at once to the operations of
Cornwallis and Tarleton, and in case of a defeat, my retreat might easily have
been cut off. My situation at the Cowpens enabled me to improve any advantages I might gain, and to provide better for my own security should I be
unfortunate. These reasons induced me to take this post, at the risk of its
wearing the face of a retreat.

I received regular intelligence of the enemy's movements from the time
they were first in motion. On the evening of the 16th inst., they took possession of the ground I had removed from in the morning, distant from the scene
of action about twelve miles. An hour before daylight one of my scouts returned and informed me that Lieut. Col. Tarleton had advanced within five
miles of our camp. On this information, I hastened to form as good a disposition as circumstances would admit, and from the alacrity of the troops we
were soon prepared to receive him.

The light infantry, commanded by Lieut. Col. Howard, and the Virginia
militia, under the command of Maj. Triplett, were formed on a rising ground
and extended a line in front. The third regiment of dragoons, under Lieut.
Col. Washington, were posted at such a distance in their rear as not to be subjected to the line of fire directed at them, and to be so near as to be able to
charge the enemy should they be broken. The volunteers of North Carolina,
South Carolina and Georgia, under the command of the brave and valuable
Col. Pickens, were situated to guard the flanks. Maj. McDowell, of the North
Carolina volunteers, was posted on the right flank in front of the line, one
hundred and fifty yards; and Maj. Cunningham, of the Georgia volunteers, on
the left, at the same distance in front. Cols. Brannon and Thomas, of the
South Carolinians, were posted in the right of Maj. McDowell, and Cols. Hays
and McCall, of the same corps, on the left of Maj. Cunningham. Capts. Tate
and Buchanan, with the Augusta riflemen, to support the right of the line.

The enemy drew up in single line of battle, four hundred yards in front of
our advanced corps. The first battalion of the 71st Regiment was opposed to
our right, the 7th Regiment to our left, the infantry of the Legion to our
centre, the light companies on their flanks. In front moved two pieces of
artillery. Lieut. Col. Tarleton, with his cavalry, was posted in the rear of his
line.

The disposition of battle being thus formed, small parties of riflemen were
detached to skirmish with the enemy, upon which their whole line moved on
with the greatest impetuosity, shouting as they advanced. McDowell and
Cunningham gave them a heavy and galling fire and retreated to the regiments
intended for their support. The whole of Col. Pickens's command then kept
up a fire by regiments, retreating agreeably to their orders. When the enemy
advanced to our line, they received a well-directed and incessant fire. But
their numbers being superior to ours, they gained our flanks, which obliged
us to change our position. We retired in good order about fifty paces, formed,
advanced on the enemy and gave them a fortunate volley, which threw them
into disorder. Lieut. Col. Howard, observing this, gave orders for the line to
charge bayonets, which was done with such address that they fled with the

utmost precipitation, leaving their fieldpieces in our possession. We pushed our advantage so effectually that they never had an opportunity of rallying, had their intentions been ever so good.

Lieut. Col. Washington, having been informed that Tarleton was cutting down our riflemen on the left, pushed forward and charged them with such firmness that instead of attempting to recover the fate of the day, which one would have expected from an officer of his splendid character, [they] broke and fled.

The enemy's whole force were now bent solely in providing for their safety in flight—the list of their killed, wounded and prisoners will inform you with what effect. Tarleton, with the small remains of his cavalry and a few scattering infantry he had mounted on his wagon-horses, made their escape. He was pursued twenty-four miles, but, owing to our having taken a wrong trail at first, we never could overtake him.

As I was obliged to move off of the field of action in the morning to secure the prisoners, I cannot be so accurate as to the killed and wounded of the enemy as I could wish. From the reports of an officer whom I sent to view the ground, there were one hundred non-commissioned officers and privates and ten commissioned officers killed and two hundred rank and file wounded. We have now in our possession five hundred and two non-commissioned officers and privates prisoners, independent of the wounded, and the militia are taking up stragglers continually. Twenty-nine commissioned officers have fell into our hands.* Their rank, etc., you will see by an enclosed list. The officers I have paroled; the privates I am conveying by the safest route to Salisbury.

Two standards, two fieldpieces, thirty-five wagons, a travelling forge and all their music are ours. Their baggage, which was immense, they have in a great measure destroyed.

Our loss is inconsiderable, which the enclosed return will evince. I have not been able to ascertain Col. Pickens' loss, but know it to be very small.

From our force being composed of such a variety of corps, a wrong judgment may be formed of our numbers. We fought only eight hundred men, two-thirds of which were militia. The British, with their baggage-guard, were not less than one thousand one hundred and fifty, and these veteran troops. Their own officers confess that they fought one thousand and thirty-seven.

Such was the inferiority of our numbers that our success must be attributed to the justice of our cause and the bravery of our troops. My wishes would induce me to mention the name of every sentinel in the corps I have the honor to command. In justice to the bravery and good conduct of the officers, I have taken the liberty to enclose you a list of their names, from a conviction that you will be pleased to introduce such characters to the world. . . .

—GRAHAM, *Life of Morgan*, pp. 467-470.

---

* In a postscript Morgan lists the American losses at 12 killed, 60 wounded; the British killed—10 commissioned officers and over a hundred enlisted men, with 200 British wounded, and 27 officers and more than 500 enlisted men prisoners. In addition to the booty listed in the letter, he adds 800 stand of arms and over 100 dragoon horses.

III. THE HUNTER BECOMES THE HUNTED:
GUILFORD COURTHOUSE

Cornwallis now prepared to avenge Cowpens. Having lost his light troops in that battle, he transformed his whole force into light troops by destroying superfluous baggage, most wagons, all his tents, all provisions except what his men could carry, and even had his rum casks stove in. To his soldiers this was the cruelest blow of all. He was now stripped down for sprinting.

Greene, outnumbered three to two, kept ahead of his pursuer, conducting a masterly retreat. He crossed the Catawba, the Yadkin, the Deep River and finally the Dan. As Alexander Hamilton said: "To have effected a retreat in the face of so ardent a pursuit, through so great an extent of country, through a country offering every obstacle, affording scarcely any resource; with troops destitute of every thing, who a great part of the way left the vestiges of their march in their own blood—to have done all this, I say, without loss of any kind, may, without exaggeration, be denominated a masterpiece of military skill and exertion."

In crossing the Dan, Greene took with him all the boats to the farther shore. Cornwallis had lost the race. Having rashly destroyed his supplies, the British commander was now forced to get closer to his supply base. He reversed his course and returned to Hillsboro. Greene, on receiving small reinforcements from Virginia, recrossed the Dan, took post in the vicinity of the British army and harassed their communication with the country. For three weeks Greene eluded the action that Cornwallis sought, and the massacre by Pickens' men of a body of 400 Tories under Colonel John Pyle on their way to the British army ended all hope of Loyalist reinforcements for Cornwallis. The Tories, now indifferent or terror-stricken, were a bitter disappointment to Cornwallis.

When Greene outnumbered the enemy he prepared to give battle. On March 14, 1781, he went into camp near Guilford Courthouse. He planned the battle after the pattern of Cowpens. He put the raw North Carolina militia in the center, and followed Morgan's advice to put picked troops in their rear "to shoot down the first man that runs." The first line was reinforced by a second, 300 yards back, and that in turn by a last line along the courthouse hill back another 550 yards. Greene gave the militia the privilege of withdrawing after firing two rounds. They fired their two volleys and rushed pell-mell to the rear. Still Greene might have destroyed the British had he been willing to throw his cavalry upon the disordered ranks of the enemy, but he was reluctant to risk his whole army on the fate of this attack. Instead, he withdrew after Cornwallis, in a desperate expedient, opened fire with grapeshot which killed both British and Americans. Cornwallis kept the field but he lost one fourth of his army, along with some of his finest officers. In his dispatches home he claimed the victory, but, as Charles James Fox put it, "Another such victory would destroy the British army."

Now the two commanders faced major decisions. Should each go after the other for a final showdown? Cornwallis felt he could not risk a stand in the interior any longer, and three days later pulled up stakes for Wilmington

GUILFORD COURTHOUSE

on the coast. Greene might have pursued him, but he prudently recognized that Virginia could look to Washington for military assistance, and therefore made the crucial decision to move southward and reconquer South Carolina and Georgia. Hamilton compared that decision to "Scipio leaving Hannibal in Italy, to overcome him at Carthage!" Cornwallis felt that it would be unwise to pursue him. Writing to Clinton on April 23, 1781, he confessed: "My present undertaking sits heavy on my mind. I have experienced the distresses and dangers of marching some hundreds of miles, in a country chiefly hostile, without one active or useful friend; without intelligence, and without communication with any part of the country." Virginia, and a chance to recoup some of his reverses, beckoned, and he quit the soil of the Carolinas for the last time.

1. Nathanael Greene Retreats to the Dan

Lewis Morris, Jr., of the Continental Army to his father, General Lewis Morris.

Halifax Court House, Virginia, February 19, 1781

You can be no stranger to the weakness and embarrassments of this army. My letters must have long since informed you. You will hear of Tarleton's fortunate defeat, and perhaps conclude in your sanguine moments that the destruction of the British army must follow; but before this can reach you, you will hear of Lord Cornwallis' rapid movement and of our retreat through North Carolina. This will be very alarming to those at a distance, and no doubt censured as a very unmilitary step; but the man who is to defend the liberties of his country, and is charged with the command of an army, ought not to regard the popular prejudice or the censures and opinion of the ignorant and disappointed. I am convinced it was dictated by necessity and conducted with the strictest military propriety.

The army was evidently the object of the enemy, and while we can keep that together the country never can be conquered—disperse it, and the people are subjugated. An action in Carolina, circumstanced as we were, certainly would have involved us in this predicament. The General was well aware of the consequences—to prevent which he was under the necessity of retiring—and he was closely pressed by a much superior army and incumbered with an immense deal of baggage and stores. The retreat was performed without any loss—not even a broken waggon to show that we were hurried—and, what makes it the more brilliant, the enemy had burned all their baggage and pursued us perfectly light.

The militia in Carolina gave us no assistance. They were more intent upon saving their property by flight than by embodying to protect it.

The enemy are encamped on the other side of Dan River and are collecting provisions for a ten days' march. It is the general opinion that they will not pursue us any farther, but file off for Hallifax and Newbern in Carolina. If so we shall recross the Dan and press upon their rear. The army has recovered from its fatigue, and the militia of Virginia are turning out in great numbers. We shall move as light as they are, and may engage them partially without hazarding a general action. We have a superior body of cavalry, and the militia may go on without any apprehension, and if we can but turn the tide against them I am confident a very considerable part of the soldiers will desert.

—Morris, "Letters," *N. Y. Hist. Soc. Coll.*, VIII, 480-481.

2. "The Battle Was Long, Obstinate and Bloody"

Nathanael Greene to President Joseph Reed of Pennsylvania.

Camp near the Iron Works, March 18, 1781

. . . Our force was so small and Lord Cornwallis's movements were so rapid that we got no reinforcements of militia, and therefore were obliged to retire out of the State, upon which the spirits of the people sunk, and almost all classes of the inhabitants gave themselves up for lost. They would not believe themselves in danger until they found ruin at their doors. The foolish prejudice of the formidableness of the militia being a sufficient barrier against any attempts of the enemy prevented the Legislature from making any exertions equal to their critical and dangerous situation. Experience has convinced them of their false security.

It is astonishing to me how these people could place such a confidence in a militia scattered over the face of the whole earth, and generally destitute of everything necessary to their own defence. The militia in the back country are formidable, the others are not, and all are very ungovernable and difficult to keep together. As they have generally come out, twenty thousand might be in motion, and not five hundred in the field.

After crossing the Dan and collecting a few Virginia militia, finding the enemy had erected their standard at Hillsborough and the people began to flock to it from all quarters, either for protection or to engage in their service, I determined to recross at all hazards, and it was very fortunate that I did, otherwise Lord Cornwallis would have got several thousand recruits. Seven companies were enlisted in one day. Our situation was desperate at the time we recrossed the Dan; our numbers were much inferior to the enemy, and we were without ammunition, provisions or stores of any kind, the whole having retired over the Stanton River. However, I thought it was best to put on a good face and make the most of appearances. Lieutenant Colonel Lee's falling in with the Tories upon the Haw almost put a total stop to their recruiting service.

Our numbers were, doubtless, greatly magnified, and pushing on boldly towards Hillsborough led Lord Cornwallis into a belief that I meant to attack him wherever I could find him. The case was widely different. It was certain I could not fight him in a general action without almost certain ruin. To skirmish with him was my only chance. Those happened daily, and the enemy suffered considerably; but our militia coming out principally upon the footing of volunteers, they fell off daily after every skirmish and went home to tell the news. In this situation, with an inferior force, I kept constantly in the neighbourhood of Lord Cornwallis until the 6th, when he made a rapid push at our Light Infantry, commanded by Colonel Williams, who very judiciously avoided the blow. This manoeuvre of the enemy obliged me to change my position. Indeed, I rarely ever lay more than two days in a place. The country, being much of a wilderness, obliged the enemy to guard carefully against a surprise and rendered it difficult to surprise us. We had few wagons with us— no baggage, and only tents enough to secure our arms in case of a wasting rain.

Here has been the field for the exercise of genius and an opportunity to practise all the great and little arts of war. Fortunately, we have blundered through without meeting with any capital misfortune. On the 11th of this month I formed a junction, at the High Rock Ford, with a considerable body of Virginia and North Carolina militia, and with a Virginia regiment of eighteen months' men. Our force being now much more considerable than it had been and upon a more permanent footing, I took the determination of

giving the enemy battle without loss of time and made the necessary dispositions accordingly.

The battle was fought at or near Guilford Court-House, the very place
from whence we began our retreat after the Light Infantry joined the army
from the Pedee. The battle was long, obstinate and bloody. We were obliged
to give up the ground and lost our artillery, but the enemy have been so
soundly beaten that they dare not move towards us since the action, notwithstanding we lay within ten miles of him for two days. Except the ground and
the artillery, they have gained no advantage. On the contrary, they are little
short of being ruined. The enemy's loss in killed and wounded cannot be less
than between six and seven hundred, perhaps more.

Victory was long doubtful, and had the North Carolina militia done their
duty, it was certain. They had the most advantageous position I ever saw, and
left it without making scarcely the shadow of opposition. Their general and
field officers exerted themselves, but the men would not stand. Many threw
away their arms and fled with the utmost precipitation, even before a gun was
fired at them. The Virginia militia behaved nobly and annoyed the enemy
greatly. The horse, at different times in the course of the day, performed
wonders. Indeed, the horse is our great safeguard, and without them the
militia could not keep the field in this country. . . . Never did an army labour
under so many disadvantages as this; but the fortitude and patience of the
officers and soldiery rise superior to all difficulties. We have little to eat, less
to drink, and lodge in the woods in the midst of smoke. Indeed, our fatigue
is excessive. I was so much overcome night before last that I fainted.

Our army is in good spirits, but the militia are leaving us in great numbers
to return home to kiss their wives and sweethearts.

I have never felt an easy moment since the enemy crossed the Catawba
until since the defeat of the 15th, but now I am perfectly easy, being persuaded it is out of the enemy's power to do us any great injury. Indeed, I
think they will retire as soon as they can get off their wounded. My love to
your family and all friends. . . .

— REED, *Life and Correspondence of Reed*, II, 348-351.

3. "COME ON, BRAVE FUZILEERS!"—WEBSTER RALLIES THE BRITISH
[1809]

Journal of Sergeant R. Lamb of the Royal Welsh Fusiliers.

. . . After the brigade formed across the open ground, the colonel rode
on to the front and gave the word, "*Charge!*" Instantly the movement was
made, in excellent order, in a smart run, with arms charged. When arrived
within forty yards of the enemy's line, it was perceived that their whole force
had their arms presented and resting on a rail fence, the common partitions in
America. They were taking aim with the nicest precision. . . . At this awful
period a general pause took place; both parties surveyed each other for the
moment with the most anxious suspense. . . . Colonel Webster rode forward
in the front of the 23d Regiment and said with more than even his usual
commanding voice (which was well known to his brigade), "Come on, my
brave Fuzileers!" This operated like an inspiring voice; they rushed forward

amidst the enemy's fire; dreadful was the havoc on both sides. At last the Americans gave way, and the brigade advanced to the attack of their second line. Here the conflict became still more fierce. . . .

I saw Lord Cornwallis riding across the clear ground. His Lordship was mounted on a dragoon's horse (his own having been shot); the saddle-bags were under the creature's belly, which much retarded his progress, owing to the vast quantity of underwood that was spread over the ground; His Lordship was evidently unconscious of his danger. I immediately laid hold of the bridle of his horse and turned his head. I then mentioned to him that if His Lordship had pursued the same direction, he would have been surrounded by the enemy and, perhaps, cut to pieces or captured. I continued to run along side of the horse, keeping the bridle in my hand, until His Lordship gained the 23d Regiment, which was at that time drawn up in the skirt of the woods.

—LAMB, *Journal of Occurrences*, pp. 361-362.

4. "LIGHT-HORSE HARRY" LEE ATTEMPTS TO RALLY THE FUGITIVES

Memoirs of Henry Lee.

Lieutenant Colonel Webster took his part with his usual ability, moving upon the Virginia militia, who were not so advantageously posted as their comrades of North Carolina, yet gave every indication of maintaining their ground with obstinacy. Stevens, to give efficacy to this temper, and stung with the recollection of their inglorious flight in the battle of Camden, had placed a line of sentinels in his rear with orders to shoot every man that flinched. When the enemy came within long shot, the American line, by order, began to fire. Undismayed, the British continued to advance and, having reached a proper distance, discharged their pieces and rent the air with shouts.

To our infinite distress and mortification, the North Carolina militia took to flight, a few only of Eaton's brigade excepted, who clung to the militia under Clarke, which, with the legion, manfully maintained their ground. Every effort was made by the Generals Butler and Eaton, assisted by . . . many of the officers of every grade, to stop this unaccountable panic, for not a man of the corps had been killed or even wounded. Lieutenant Colonel Lee joined in the attempt to rally the fugitives, threatening to fall upon them with his cavalry. All was vain—so thoroughly confounded were these unhappy men that, throwing away arms, knapsacks and even canteens, they rushed like a torrent headlong through the woods.

Gunby, being left free by Webster's recession, wheeled to his left upon Stuart, who was pursuing the flying Second Regiment. Here the action was well fought, each corps manfully struggling for victory, when Lieutenant Colonel Washington, who had, upon the discomfiture of the Virginia militia, placed himself upon the flank of the Continentals agreeably to the order of battle, pressed forward with his cavalry.

Stuart beginning to give ground, Washington fell upon him sword in hand, followed by Howard with fixed bayonets, now commanding the regiment in consequence of Gunby being dismounted. This combined operation was irresistible. Stuart fell by the sword of Captain Smith, of the First Regiment, . . . his battalion driven back with slaughter, its remains being saved by the British artillery, which, to stop the ardent pursuit of Washington and Howard, opened upon friends as well as foes; for Cornwallis, seeing the vigorous advance of these two officers, determined to arrest their progress, though every ball levelled at them must pass through the flying guards. Checked by this cannonade, and discovering one regiment passing from the woods on the enemy's right across the road, and another advancing in front, Howard, believing himself to be out of support, retired, followed by Washington. . . .

The night succeeding this day of blood was rainy, dark and cold; the dead unburied, the wounded unsheltered, the groans of the dying and the shrieks of the living shed a deeper shade over the gloom of nature. The victorious troops, without tents and without food, participated in sufferings which they could not believe.*

The ensuing morning was spent in performing the last offices to the dead and in providing comfort for the wounded. In executing these sad duties, the British general regarded with equal attention friends and foes. As soon as this service was over Lord Cornwallis put his army in motion for New Garden, where his rear guard, with his baggage, met him. All his wounded incapable of moving (about seventy in number) he left to the humanity of General Greene.

                                                                    —LEE, *Memoirs*, I, 343-359.

5. THE VIRGINIA MILITIA RAN "LIKE A FLOCK OF SHEEP"

Major St. George Tucker of the Virginia militia to his wife.

                                                          Laura Town, March 18, 1781

When the cannonade ceased, orders were given for Holcombe's regiment and the regiment on the right of him to advance and annoy the enemy's left flank. While we were advancing to execute this order, the British had advanced, and, having turned the flank of Col. Mumford's regiment—in which Skipwith commanded as major, we discovered them in our rear. This threw the militia into such confusion that, without attending in the least to their officers who endeavored to halt them and make them face about and engage the enemy, Holcombe's regiment and ours instantly broke off without firing a single gun and dispersed like a flock of sheep frightened by dogs. With infinite labor Beverley and myself rallied about sixty or seventy of our men and brought them to the charge. Holcombe was not so successful. He could not rally a man though assisted by John Woodson, who acted very gallantly. With the few men which we had collected we at several times sustained an irregular kind of skirmishing with the British, and were once successful enough to drive a party for a very small distance. On the ground we passed over I think I saw about eight or ten men killed and wounded. During the battle I was forced to ride over a British officer lying at the root of a tree. One of our soldiers gave him a dram as he was expiring and bade him die like a

---

* Having no tents, and the houses being few, many of both armies were necessarily exposed to the deluge of rain, which fell during the night; and it was said that not less than fifty died before morning.

brave man. How different this conduct from that of the barbarians he had commanded! . . .

The Virginia militia had the honor to receive Gen. Greene's thanks for their conduct. Some were undoubtedly entitled to them, while others ought to blush that they were undeservedly included in the number of those who were supposed to have behaved well. . . . I believe the rest of the Virginia militia behaved better than Holcombe's regiment and ours. The surprise at finding the enemy in their rear I believe contributed to the disgraceful manner in which they fled at first. But it is not a little to the honor of those who rallied that they fired away fifteen or eighteen rounds—and some twenty rounds—a man, after being put into such disorder. Such instances of the militia rallying and fighting well are not very common, I am told. Perhaps it is more honorable than making a good stand at first, and then quitting the field in disorder. . . .

—TUCKER, "The Southern Campaign," *Magazine of American History*, VII, 40-42.

6. "I AM DETERMINED TO CARRY THE WAR INTO SOUTH CAROLINA"

Nathanael Greene to George Washington.

Head-quarters at Colonel Ramsay's, on Deep River, March 29, 1781

The regular troops will be late in the field in the southern States, if they are raised at all. Virginia, from the unequal operation of the law for drafting, is not likely to get many soldiers. Maryland, as late as the 13th of this month, had not got a man, nor is there a man raised in North Carolina, or the least prospect of it. In this situation, remote from reinforcements, inferior to the enemy in number, and no prospect of support, I am at a loss what is best to be done. If the enemy fall down towards Wilmington, they will be in a position where it would be impossible for us to injure them if we had a force.

In this critical and distressing situation, I am determined to carry the war immediately into South Carolina. The enemy will be obliged to follow us or give up their posts in that State. If the former takes place it will draw the war out of this State and give it an opportunity to raise its proportion of men. If they leave their posts to fall, they must lose more than they can gain here. If we continue in this State, the enemy will hold their possessions in both. All things considered, I think the movement is warranted by the soundest reasons, both political and military. The manoeuvre will be critical and dangerous, and the troops exposed to every hardship. But as I share it with them, I hope they will bear up under it with that magnanimity which has already supported them, and for which they deserve everything of their country.

I expect to be ready to march in about five days, and have written to General Sumter to collect the militia to aid the operations. I am persuaded the movement will be unexpected to the enemy, and I intend it shall be as little known as possible. Our baggage and stores not with the army, I shall order by the route of the Saura Towns and Shallow Ford to Charlotte. By having them in the upper country we shall always have a safe retreat, and from those inhabitants we may expect the greatest support. I shall take every measure to

avoid a misfortune, but necessity obliges me to commit myself to chance; and
I trust my friends will do justice to my reputation if any accident attends me.

—GREENE, *Life of Greene*, III, 213-214.

7. CORNWALLIS PLANS TO MAKE THE CHESAPEAKE "THE SEAT OF WAR"

Lord Cornwallis to Sir Henry Clinton.

Camp near Wilmington, April 10, 1781

The fatigue of the troops and the great number of wounded put it out of
my power to pursue beyond the Reedy Fork in the afternoon of the action;
and the want of provisions and all kinds of necessaries for the soldiers made
it equally impossible to follow the blow next day. I, therefore, issued the inclosed Proclamation, and, having remained two days on the field of battle,
marched to Bell's-Mill on Deep-River, near part of the country where the
greatest number of our friends were supposed to reside. Many of the inhabitants rode into camp, shook me by the hand, said they were glad to see us and
to hear that we had beat Greene, and then rode home again; for I could not
get 100 men in all the Regulators' country to stay with us, even as militia.

With a third of my army sick and wounded, which I was obliged to carry
in waggons or on horseback, the remainder without shoes and worn down
with fatigue, I thought it was time to look for some place of rest and refitment.
I, therefore, by easy marches, taking care to pass through all the settlements
that had been described to me as most friendly, proceeded to Cross-Creek.
On my arrival there, I found, to my great mortification and contrary to all
former accounts, that it was impossible to procure any considerable quantity
of provisions, and that there was not four days forage within twenty miles.
The navigation of Cape Fear River, with the hopes of which I had been flattered, was totally impracticable, the distance from Wilmington by water
being 150 miles, the breadth of the river seldom exceeding one hundred yards,
the banks generally high, and the inhabitants on each side almost universally
hostile. Under these circumstances I determined to move immediately to
Wilmington. By this measure the Highlanders have not had so much time as
the people of the upper country to prove the sincerity of their former professions of friendship. But, tho' appearances are rather more favourable among
them, I confess they are not equal to my expectations. . . .

I am now employed in disposing of the sick and wounded, and in procuring supplies of all kinds, to put the troops into a proper state to take the field.
I am, likewise, impatiently looking out for the expected reinforcement from
Europe, part of which will be indispensibly necessary to enable me either to
act offensively or even to maintain myself in the upper parts of the country,
where alone I can hope to preserve the troops from the fatal sickness which
so nearly ruined the army last autumn.

I am very anxious to receive Your Excellency's commands, being as yet
totally in the dark as to the intended operations of the summer. I cannot help
expressing my wishes that the Chesapeak may become the seat of war, even
(if necessary) at the expence of abandoning New-York; untill Virginia is in
a manner subdued, our hold of the Carolinas must be difficult, if not precari-

ous. The rivers of Virginia are advantageous to an invading army, but North-Carolina is, of all the provinces in America, the most difficult to attack (unless material assistance could be got from the inhabitants, the contrary of which I have suffiicently experienced) on account of its great extent, of the numberless rivers and creeks, and the total want of interior navigation.

—Stevens, ed., *Clinton-Cornwallis Controversy*, I, 395-399.

IV. THE PARTISAN ROLE IN THE RECONQUEST OF SOUTH CAROLINA

The campaign for regaining South Carolina moved quickly into high gear. In the short space of two months all the interior posts were reduced and the state in large measure brought once more under Patriot control. In that achievement no inconsiderable part was played by Francis Marion, who, in co-operation with "Light-Horse Harry" Lee, began systematically to cut Rawdon's tenuous communication line between Camden and Charleston. The task of investing Augusta and Ninety-Six was assigned to Pickens, and Greene moved directly against Camden.

This was civil war and it was ugly. Each side accused the other of carrying on inhuman warfare. Colonel John Watson of the British Army charged that Sumter's men fired upon prisoners. "The houses of desolate widows have been laid waste," he declared, and "innocent and neutral persons murdered by partisans." But he in turn defended under "the law of nations" the hanging of Patriot militiamen who had been placed on parole after the Charleston capitulation and then had taken up arms once more. The Whig case was presented by Captain Tarleton Brown of South Carolina, who recorded in his Memoirs *numerous instances where the Tories killed aged and harmless persons in cold blood.*

Both sides were equally guilty. As Andrew Jackson, a youthful participant, later put it, "In the long run, I am afraid the Whigs did not lose many points in the game of hanging, shooting and flogging. They had great provocation, but upon calm reflection I feel bound to say that they took full advantage of it."

But the main objective of each side was to kill fighting men. In this kind of merciless guerrilla warfare Jackson had his first brush with the enemy. He reminisced about his role in the Revolution to a number of his friends. According to one account, he was, along with his brother Robert, a member of a company of some forty Whigs assembled at the Waxhaw meetinghouse. The defenders were deceived by a ruse, as the British surprised the Patriots by placing a body of Tories, wearing the dress of the country, in advance of the Redcoats. Eleven were taken prisoner, the rest scattered. Young Andrew was trapped by Tory intelligence at the home of a Patriot fighter. The dragoons smashed the furnishings to pieces. The British officer in command ordered Jackson to clean his high jackboots.

Jackson replied, "Sir, I am a prisoner of war, and claim to be treated as such."

The officer smashed his sword down on the boy's head, but Andrew broke the force of the blow with his left hand. He carried to his grave two wounds —a deep gash on his head, another on his hand. He would not soon forget the British.

1. Young Andrew Jackson Refuses to Clean an Officer's Boots

His experience as a Revolutionary soldier, as reported to Francis P. Blair.

[Spring, 1781]

I witnessed two battles, Hanging Rock and Hobkirk's Hill, but did not participate in either. I was in one skirmish—that of Sands House—and there they caught me, along with my brother Robert and my cousin, Tom Crawford. A lieutenant of Tarleton's Light Dragoons tried to make me clean his boots and cut my arm with his sabre when I refused. After that they kept me in jail at Camden about two months, starved me nearly to death and gave me the small-pox. Finally my mother succeeded in persuading them to release Robert and me on account of our extreme youth and illness. Then Robert died of the small-pox and I barely escaped death. When it left me I was a skeleton—not quite six feet long and a little over six inches thick! It took me all the rest of that year [1781] to recover my strength and get flesh enough to hide my bones. By that time Cornwallis had surrendered and the war was practically over in our part of the country.

I was never regularly enlisted, being only fourteen when the war practically ended. Whenever I took the field it was with Colonel Davie, who never put me in the ranks, but used me as a mounted orderly or messenger, for which I was well fitted, being a good rider and knowing all the roads in that region. The only weapons I had were a pistol that Colonel Davie gave me and a small fowling-piece that my Uncle Crawford lent to me. This was a light gun and would kick like sixty when loaded with a three-quarter-ounce ball or with nine buckshot. But it was a smart little gun and would carry the ball almost as true as a rifle fifteen or twenty rods, and threw the buckshot spitefully at close quarters—which was the way I used it in the defence of Captain Sands's house, where I was captured.

I was as sorry about losing the gun there as about the loss of my own liberty, because Uncle Crawford set great store by the gun, which he had brought with him from the old country; and, besides, it was the finest in that whole region. Not long afterward—while I was still in the Camden jail or stockade—some of Colonel Davie's men under Lieutenant Curriton captured a squad of Tories, one of whom had that gun in his possession, together with my pistol that Colonel Davie had given to me. This Tory's name was Mulford. The gun and pistol cost him his life. Davie's men regarded his possession of them as prima facie evidence that he had been a member of the party that captured Captain Sands's house, sacked and burned it and insulted the womenfolks of his family. He pleaded that he was not there; that he had bought the gun and pistol from another Tory. Davie's men told him it would do him no good to add lying to his other crimes, hanged him forthwith and afterward restored the gun and pistol to their proper owners.

The Tories also got the horse I had when captured. He was a three-year-old colt—fine fellow—belonging to Captain Sands himself. He was hid in the woods when they attacked the house, but they [the Tories] found him the next morning. This colt was also retaken about six weeks afterward. The Tory who had him was not hanged, because he had been shot through the stomach before he surrendered and was already dying.

Take it altogether, I saw and heard a good deal of war in those days, but did nothing toward it myself worth mention.

—BUELL, *History of Jackson*, I, 51-53.

2. ONE OF MARION'S SWAMP FOXES

Narrative of Paul Hamilton of the South Carolina militia.

Having remained sometime with Marion, I availed myself of an opportunity that offered of returning homeward with Col. Harden, who had fled from the Parish of Prince William to Marion's camp and, assembling about 70 followers, determined to return southward and, by stirring up his friends who had submitted to the enemy, to cover that part of our country. Him I joined as a volunteer, having previously received, while with Marion, a letter from my good mother with a supply of money and clothes, most wonderfully conveyed to me through the country then overrun by the enemy. With Harden I approached Jacksonboro, and hearing that my mother was then at the plantation of my deceased Grandfather Branford, two miles off, I with leave quitted the party, galloped off to the plantation opposite (then Dupont's, now Jacob Walter's), where, finding a small canoe which I ordered a Negro man to enter, I threw thereon my arms, and on my horse swam the river.

Arriving near the house I was informed that my grandfather's widow was then in a most dreadful state with small pox, which I had not had, and that my mother had that morning gone to her house at Wiltown. . . . To avoid the infection of small pox I had remained at the fence of the plantation near the swamp, where I met the best of mothers.

What our meeting was I cannot describe. Neither had for minutes the power of utterance. At length a flood of tears on her part enabled her to break silence, when such affectionate expressions were poured out as I can never forget, nor the warmth of that maternal embrace in which I was clasped to her aching bosom, after an absence of 12 months lacking 6 days, during which she had received but one letter from me and had often heard of my having been killed. I remained with her for two hours. I then left her with her blessing on my head, and an assurance that I would shortly again see her. She presented me with some clothing which she had prepared for me; these she had tied up hastily in a pillow case, and I tucked them behind my saddle, a circumstance which had well nigh cost me my life that very night.

On regaining my party we proceeded southwardly, and at midnight encountered a body of British cavalry near Saltketcher Bridge. The onset was in our favor, but, Harden being but an indifferent commander, we were defeated and in the rout I suffered a hard pursuit, in which my pursuers were guided by the whiteness of the pillow case that contained the clothes behind me. A good horse and some presence of mind at last secured me from pursuit. Our whole party was dispersed, and about 15 severely wounded with the sabre. In two days we were again collected and retorted this defeat by surprising and making prisoners of part of this cavalry at Pocataligo, among them their Colonel Fenwicke and other officers.

This success led to the surrender of the British Fort Balfour, at the above place, under the ramparts almost of which this surprise was made. I must, as I am writing of myself, be allowed to be somewhat particular as to this little, but handsome military exploit. Colonel Harden, knowing that we had some staunch friends who had been compelled to enter and garrison the fort, thought that if he could destroy the cavalry, he might induce a surrender of the remainder of the garrison, which were militia, and perhaps one half of them friendly to the American cause; some of whom were men of considerable influence and weight. He therefore drew near the fort and with the effective force he had remaining formed an ambuscade. Twelve well-mounted young men, of whom I was one, named as Light Horsemen, were selected and ordered to decoy the cavalry out.

With this view we moved on briskly and openly toward Von Bitter's Tavern, which stood almost a quarter of a mile from the fort and in full view. While approaching we discovered that some of the enemy were at the tavern, on which we darted forward and captured as follows: Col Fenwicke, Lieut. Bond, a sergeant and 15 privates of the cavalry with Lieut. Col. Lechmere of the British militia. Lechmere was taken as he ran within 100 yards of the fort, and brought off by one of our young men named Green. Our prisoners had come out on foot to the tavern to regale themselves [and], having only their swords, made no attempt to resist. They were hurried off to the ambuscade and delivered. After which, reinforced by eight more swordsmen, we returned, 20 in number, to the tavern, drew up in the adjoining pasture, offered battle to the British cavalry whose number we had reduced now to about our standard, a part of their force having been previously detached to Charleston immediately after we had been defeated by them at Saltketchie. The cavalry made a show of advancing to the charge, but finding us firm they turned about and were insulted by us as they retired to the fort.

Col. Harden now came up with the remainder of his force. Leaving the servants and baggage just partly in view to keep up the appearance of a reserve, Major Harden, the brother of the colonel, was now sent to summon the fort to surrender with threats of an assault if refused. I accompanied the major. We were met by Major De Veaux (after Col. DeVeaux who took the Bahamas from Spain) at so short a distance from the fort that we could recognize countenances and exchanged an occasional nod with some of the garrison.

At first the answer through Major DeVeaux was a refusal from Col. Kitsall, who commanded the fort, to surrender, on which I was desired by Major Harden to communicate to his brother this answer. The colonel inquired of me if we could distinguish any of our friends in the fort. I replied that Major Harden had recognized Cols. Stafford and Davis and Mr. Thomas Hutson, with none of whom I had any acquaintance, but that I thought that I discovered some confusion and clamour in the fort. On which the colonel, his countenance brightening, formed his men in column and ordered them to prepare for immediate action.

This done, he turned to me and said, "Go to Major Harden and say to him that I allowed ten minutes to Col. Kitsall to consider of a surrender, after which, if he refuses, you are both to return immediately to me and, by God, I will be in the fort!"

The major communicated this to Major De Veaux with whom he had been chatting with great familiarity, being acquaintances and closely related by blood. The latter went in and delivered this last message to Col. Kitsall, who, having discovered a division among his militia, agreed to lay down his arms.

Thus was Fort Balfour, which had for some months completely bridled that part of the country, surrendered without a shot. The garrison consisted of 92 militia, about 25 regulars, cavalry well mounted and equipped and uniformed as Light Dragoons. In the fort we found an abundance of provisions, some muskets and a six-pound cannon, with a good supply of ammunition for it.

—HAMILTON, "Extracts from a Private Manuscript,"
Year Book of Charleston, 1898, pp. 315-320.

3. GREENE PRAISES MARION'S "COURAGE, ADDRESS AND MANAGEMENT"

Nathanael Greene to Francis Marion.

Camp before Camden, April 24, 1781

Your favour of the 21st has just come to hand. When I consider how much you have done and suffered, and under what disadvantages you have maintained your ground, I am at a loss which to admire most, your courage and fortitude or your address and management. Certain it is no man has a better claim to the public thanks or is more generally admired than you are. History affords no instance wherein an officer has kept possession of a country under so many disadvantages as you have. Surrounded on every side with a superior force, hunted from every quarter with veteran troops, you have found means to elude all their attempts, and to keep alive the expiring hopes of an oppressed militia, when all succour seemed to be cut off. To fight the enemy bravely with a prospect of victory is nothing; but to fight with intrepidity under the constant impression of a defeat, and inspire irregular troops to do it, is a talent peculiar to yourself.

Nothing will give me greater pleasure than to do justice to your merit, and I shall miss no opportunity of declaring to Congress, the Commander-in-chief of the American Army and to the world in general the great sense I have of your merit and services.

I thank you for the measures you have taken to furnish us with provisions, and for the intelligence you communicate. A field piece is coming to your assistance, which I hope will enable you and Col. Lee to get possession of the fort [Watson]. With the artillery you will receive 100 lbs. powder and 400 lbs. lead. I wish my present stock would enable me to send you a larger supply, but it will not, having sent you near half we have. I have reason to believe the enemy have evacuated their post upon the Congarees; and if there is no object very important on the other side of the river, it is my wish you should move upon this, in order to enable us to invest Camden to more advantage, the garrison of which, I have good reason to believe, is short of provisions.

Retreat for 2 Miles

MILES TO SAUNDERS CR.
ROAD TO SALISBURY

Militia

Gen'l Greene
Reserve   ← Col. Washington

Light Infantry

Hobkirk's Hill

Col. Williams
Gunby   Ford
Maryland   Irish Vol.
Dragoons

Brig. Gen'l Huger
Lt. Col. Campbell   Lt. Col. Hawes

N.Y. Dragoons
63rd Reg't   Capt. Kirkwood

Virginia Brigade

The King's
Americans
Benson   Morgan
American   Lord Rawdon
Picket
Convalescents

British ▨▨ Americans
☐ Original Column of attack
▨ Formation for assault
◧ Final Position
▥ American 1st Position
▥ American 2nd Position

Col.
Washington

*Thickets with
few trees*

1 ¾ MILES FROM CAMDEN TO HILL
WAXHAW ROAD TO CAMDEN

HOBKIRK'S HILL

I have this moment got intelligence that Lord Cornwallis crossed the Cape Fear River last week, in order to begin his march towards this State. I beg you to take measures to discover his route and approach. Col. Horry's attack upon a party of Watson's does him great honour.

—GIBBES, ed., *Documentary History of the Revolution*, III, 58-59.

V. HOBKIRK'S HILL, THE SECOND BATTLE OF CAMDEN

The element of surprise was lacking in Greene's advance on Camden, as Rawdon was informed of his approach. Facing a chain of strong redoubts which protected the town, Greene decided to fall back to Hobkirk's Hill, a high ridge overlooking Camden and about a mile from it. He hoped to lure the enemy out of their fortified position, and his expectations were gratified when, on the morning of April 25, Rawdon sallied from the town at the head of 900 men. Against him Greene could count on 1,400, nearly four fifths of them Continentals.

The battle plan was a modified version of Cowpens. Greene borrowed from Cornwallis' desperate tactics at Guilford Courthouse. When the enemy advanced on a narrow front, Greene had his two center regiments draw aside, uncovered his guns and opened fire with canister and grape, throwing the enemy into momentary confusion. Then the center regiments charged with the bayonet, and the flank regiments tried to effect a double envelopment, with Washington's cavalry sweeping around to get at the British rear.

Unlike Guilford Courthouse, the weak link in Greene's battle plan proved to be not the raw militia but the battle-hardened Continentals, in this case Colonel John Gunby's 1st Maryland Regiment. They paused to fire a volley instead of pushing on with the bayonet. A captain was shot. His men faltered. Confusion spread. Gunby ordered the whole regiment to retire to the foot of the hill and re-form there. The British seized on the opportunity and plunged forward. Then the 5th Maryland broke, and panic hit the 4th Virginia. Now the guns were in danger and they were saved only by the timely arrival of Washington's dragoons. But Washington, in the course of his encirclement, had cluttered up his forces with a horde of noncombatant prisoners, surgeons, commissaries, quartermasters and the like. This made it necessary for him to abandon the attack on the enemy's rear, and he got back just in time to save the artillery. Greene retreated in good order. Washington's cavalry charged the British down the hill and forced them to withdraw into town. Rawdon actually suffered slightly heavier casualties, about 270 to 234 for the Americans.

For this setback Gunby was the scapegoat. "Gunby was the sole cause of the defeat," Greene wrote Joseph Reed. "I found him much more blameable afterwards than I represented him in my public letters." But the quick thinking of Rawdon and the brilliant fighting of the Grenadier Guards had saved the day for the British. Greene took the repulse philosophically. He wrote to Luzerne, the French envoy, "We fight, get beat, rise, and fight again."

1. Defeat Is Snatched from the Jaws of Victory

Nathanael Greene to Samuel Huntington, President of Congress.

April 25, 1781

I had the honour to write to Your Excellency the 2d instant, April, to inform you that we were encamped before Camden, having found it impossible to attempt to storm the town with any hopes of success; and having no other alternative but to take such a position as should induce the enemy to sally from their works. To this end we posted ourselves on an eminence about a mile from the town, near the high road leading to Wacsaws. It was covered with woods, and flanked on the left by an impassable swamp. The ground between this place and the town is covered by a thick wood and shrubbery. In this situation we remained constantly on the watch and ready for action at a moment's warning.

On the morning of the 25th, about eleven o'clock, our advanced pickets received the first fire from the enemy and returned it warmly. The line was formed in an instant. General Huger's brigade to the right; Colonel Williams' Maryland brigade to the left; the artillery in the center; Colonel Read, with some militia, formed a kind of second line; Captain Kirkwood, with the light infantry, was posted in our front, and when the enemy advanced, he was soon engaged with them, and both he and his men behaved with a great deal of bravery; nor did the pickets under Captains Morgan and Benson act with less courage or regularity.

Observing that the enemy advanced with but few men abreast, I ordered Lieut.-Col. Ford, with the 2d Maryland Regiment, to flank them on the left, while Lieut.-Col. Campbell was to do the same on the right. Colonel Gunby, with the 1st Maryland Regiment, and Lieut.-Col. Hawes, with the 2d Virginia Regiment, received orders at the same time to descend from the eminence and attack in front; and I sent Lieut.-Col. Washington at the same time to double the right flank and attack the rear of the enemy.

The whole line was soon in action in the midst of a very smart fire, as well from our small arms as from our artillery, which, under the command of Colonel Harrison, kept playing upon the front of the enemy, who began to give way on all sides, and their left absolutely to retreat; when, unfortunately, two companies on the right of the 1st Maryland Regiment were entirely thrown into disorder; and, by another stroke of fortune, Colonel Gunby ordered the rest of the regiment, which was advancing, to take a new position towards the rear, where the two companies were rallying. This movement gave the whole regiment an idea of a retreat, which soon spread through the 2d Regiment, which retreated accordingly. They both rallied afterwards, but it was too late. The enemy had gained the eminence, silenced the artillery and obliged us to draw it off.

The 2d Virginia Regiment having descended the eminence a little, and having its flank left naked by the retreat of the Marylanders, the enemy immediately doubled upon them and attacked them both on the flank and in front. Colonel Campbell's regiment was thrown into confusion, and had retreated a little. I therefore thought it necessary for Colonel Hawes to retreat also. The troops rallied more than once; but the disorder was too general and had struck too deep for one to think of recovering the fortune of the day, which promised us at the onset the most complete victory; for Colonel Washington, on his way to double and attack in the rear, found the enemy, both horse and foot, retreating with precipitation towards the town, and made upwards of two hundred of them prisoners, together with ten or fifteen officers, before he perceived that our troops had abandoned the field of battle. The colonel, upon this occasion, and indeed his whole corps acquired no inconsiderable share of honour.

We then retreated two or three miles from the scene of action without any loss of artillery, waggons or provisions, having taken the precaution to send away our baggage at the beginning of the action. The enemy have suffered very considerably; our forces were nearly equal in number; but such were the dispositions that I had made that, if we had succeeded, the whole of the enemy's army must have fallen into our hands, as well as the town of Camden. . . .

—TARLETON, *History of Campaigns in the Southern Provinces*, pp. 482-484.

2. "A Single Word Turned the Fate of the Day"

Samuel Mathis to General W. R. Davie.

[Camden], June 26, 1819

The British when they first attacked near the spring pressed directly forward and succeeded in turning our left. Their left had displayed towards our right and under cover of thick woods and could scarcely be seen except by our pickets until they began to rise the hill (which is about 150 or 60 yards from bottom to top). The cavalry had reached the great road and advanced in close order and slow step up the hill directly in front of our cannon which had just arrived and opened on them in the road. A well-directed fire with cannister and grape did great execution and soon cleared the road so that all their doctors were sent to take care of the wounded. Washington's cavalry coming up at this moment completed the route [*sic*] of the York Volunteers, took all the British doctors or surgeons and a great many others (alas! too many) prisoners; more than one third of Washington's men were incumbered with prisoners, who hindered their acting when necessary.

Here the battle was equal or rather in our favor, and only *one* word, a single *word*, and that only because it was spoken out of season, turned the fate of the day.

Our left was somewhat turned or yielding, then our Col. (Ford) was wounded, but the men were neither killed nor prisoners. The left of the British, at least their cavalry, were routed, many killed and many prisoners. Lord Rawdon, hearing the cannon and seeing his horse dispersed, was stunned beyond measure, . . . and, galloping up to the scene of disaster, was quickly surrounded by Washington's horse and his sword demanded. One of his aids received a severe wound from the sword of a dragoon.

Lord Rawdon is a man of uncommon address. This was a critical moment. Altho' our left was giving way, yet Gen. Huger on our right was gaining ground and was beginning to advance upon the enemy and Col. Gunby's regiment of brave soldiers, veterans of the Maryland line, had all got to their arms, were well formed and in good order, but too impatient waiting the word of command. Some of them had begun to fire in violation of orders and, seeing the British infantry coming up the hill in front of them, Col. Gunby suffered them to come up within a few paces and then ordered his men to charge without firing. Those near him, hearing the word, first rushed forward, whereby the regiment was moving forward in the form of a bow. Col. Gunby ordered a "halt" until the wings should become straight: this turned the fate of the day. Previously being ordered not to fire and now ordered to *halt*, while the British were coming up with charged bayonets, before the colonel could be understood and repeat the charge, the enemy were in among them and made them give way.

Lord Rawdon was surrounded near the head of this regiment and saw the scene and also that some of his cavalry had rallied and with infantry were coming to his relief, while he very politely bowed and seemed to acquiesce with the demand of the dragoons around him, pretended that his sword was hard to get out of the scabbard, feigned to endeavor to draw or unhook it for the surrender required, until the party that took him were attacked and had to fly.

. . . The scene was quickly changed. Washington's dragoons were now attacked by horse and foot, and the very prisoners that they had mounted behind them seized the arms of their captors and overcame them. Gen. Green now ordered a retreat and pushed on Washington's cavalry to Saunders' Creek, which lay 4 miles in the rear, to halt the troops and stop the straglers should there be any either from the militia or regulars attempting to make off. In this he succeeded, carrying off with him all the British surgeons and several officers.

As above mentioned the artillery had just come up . . . and now, seeing a general retreat of the American army, attempted to get off through the woods without going out into and along the road. They soon got . . . entangled among the trees and could not get along, but cut their horses and fled, leaving the limbers of both pieces of cannon in the woods where they were found by the British and taken.

Under these circumstances Gen. G[reene] galloped up to Capt. John Smith and ordered him to fall into the rear and save the cannon. Smith instantly came and found the artillery men hauling off the pieces with the drag-ropes; he and his men laid hold and off they went in a trot, but had not gone far until he discovered that the British cavalry were in pursuit. He formed his men across the road, gave them a full fire at a short distance and fled with the guns as before. This volley checked the horses and threw many of the riders; but they after some time remounted and pushed on again. Smith formed his men, gave them another fire with the same effect, and proceeded as before. This he repeated several times until they had got two or three miles from the field of action. Here one of Smith's men fired or his gun went off by accident before the word was given, which produced a scattering fire, on which the cavalry rushed in among them and cut them all to pieces. They fought like bull-dogs and were all killed or taken. This took up some time, during which the artillery escaped.

—MATHIS, Letter, *American Historical Record*, II, 106-109.

VI. THE FALL OF THE BRITISH OUTPOSTS

Even as the Patriots were repulsed at Hobkirk's Hill the British outposts between Camden and Charleston were beginning to fall. On April 22 Lee and Marion invested Fort Watson near Vance's Ferry in the Sumter District. Since the attackers had neither artillery nor entrenching tools, they worked out an ingenious device of building a wooden tower higher than the walls of the fort. The idea is credited to Colonel Hezekiah Maham of South Carolina and was thereafter known as a "Maham tower." From atop the tower riflemen poured a lethal barrage into the stockade. Meanwhile the troops breached the wall and compelled the garrison to surrender.

A different device was used on May 12 in the siege of Fort Motte, located on the south bank of the Congaree some 33 miles below Columbia. Marion had flaming arrows shot into the main structure of the fort, setting it afire. The day before, Orangeburg fell to Sumter, and Augusta was taken by Lee and Pickens on May 22. Again a Maham tower contributed to the downfall of that post. On the same day Greene began the siege of Ninety-Six, actually 96 miles from the old frontier fort of Prince George on the Keowee River. Its commander was the New York Tory, Lieutenant Colonel John Harris Cruger. Here Kosciusko's parallel approaches, the Maham tower some 40 feet in height, and fire arrows seemed to spell inevitable doom for the stubborn defenders, until Rawdon, who had marched from Charleston in relief, saved the day. The incorrigible and truculent Sumter violated Greene's orders to keep in Rawdon's front and failed to intercept the British commander. As Morgan had discovered earlier, Sumter was now a liability. Again a setback for Greene, and again a scapegoat. But soon after, Georgetown fell to Marion, and on July 3 Ninety-Six was abandoned by the British.

Writing toward the end of July from a camp at "High Hills Santee," Lewis Morris, Jr., reported the evacuation by Cruger of Ninety-Six, the junction of his Tories with Lord Rawdon at Orangeburg, and Rawdon's own return to Charleston, thoroughly worn out from his exertions. "Light-Horse Harry" Lee took prisoners as close as six miles from Charleston, causing panic in that town. "Let me observe," Morris added, "that we are now in full possession of all the upper country in this state as well as Georgia, and that, though the enemy have lately received a reinforcement of at least two thousand men, they have been obliged to act upon the defensive by a little army, scarcely one third of their number."

1. FORT MOTTE: A PATRIOT LADY AIDS THE BURNING OF HER HOUSE

Memoirs of "Light-Horse Harry" Lee.

[*May 6-11, 1781*]. This post [Fort Motte] was the principal depot of the convoys from Charleston to Cambden, and sometimes of those destined for Fort Granby and Ninety-Six. A large new mansion house, belonging to Mrs. Motte, situated on a high and commanding hill, had been selected for this establishment. It was surrounded with a deep trench, along the interior margin of which was raised a strong and lofty parapet. To this post had been regularly assigned an adequate garrison of about one hundred and fifty men, which was now accidentally increased by a small detachment of dragoons. . . . Captain M'Pherson commanded, an officer highly and deservedly respected.

Opposite to Fort Motte, to the north, stood another hill, where Mrs. Motte, having been dismissed from her mansion, resided in the old farmhouse. On this height Lieut. Col. Lee with his corps took post, while Brigadier Marion occupied the eastern declivity of the ridge on which the fort stood.

Very soon the fort was completely invested; and the six-pounder was mounted on a battery erected in Marion's quarter for the purpose of raking the northern face of the enemy's parapet, against which Lee was preparing to advance. M'Pherson was unprovided with artillery and depended for safety upon timely relief, not doubting its arrival before the assailant could push his preparations to maturity.

. . . The works advanced with rapidity. Such was their forwardness on the 10th that it was determined to summon the commandant.

A. Spring
B. Stockade Fort
C. Jail, fortified
D. Court House
E. Star Redoubt
F. Mine

G. American Camps
H. Stockade.
I. Covered way from
    Stockade to Fort
K. Abatis

NINETY-SIX

A flag was accordingly despatched to Captain M'Pherson, stating to him with truth our relative situation. . . . The captain replied that, disregarding consequences, he should continue to resist to the last moment in his power. The retreat of Rawdon was known in the evening to the besiegers; and in the course of the night a courier arrived from General Greene confirming that event, urging redoubled activity. . . .

The large mansion in the centre of the encircling trench left but a few yards of the ground within the enemy's works uncovered: burning the house must force their surrender.

. . . Orders were instantly issued to prepare bows and arrows, with missive combustible matter. This measure was reluctantly adopted, for the destruction of private property was repugnant to the principles which swayed the two commandants.

. . . Taking the first opportunity which offered the next morning, Lieut. Col. Lee imparted to Mrs. Motte the intended measure, lamenting the sad necessity and assuring her of the deep regret which the unavoidable act excited in his and every breast.

With the smile of complacency this exemplary lady listened to the embarrassed officer and gave instant relief to his agitated feelings by declaring that she was gratified with the opportunity of contributing to the good of her country. . . . Shortly after, seeing accidentally the bows and arrows which had been prepared, she sent for the lieutenant colonel, and presenting him with a bow and its apparatus imported from India, she requested his substitution of these, as probably better adapted for the object than those we had provided. . . .

It was now about noon, and the rays of the scorching sun had prepared the shingle roof for the projected conflagration. . . . The first arrow struck and communicated its fire; a second was shot at another quarter of the roof, and a third at a third quarter; this last also took effect, and, like the first, soon kindled a blaze. M'Pherson ordered a party to repair to the loft of the house and by knocking off the shingles to stop the flames. This was soon perceived, and Captain Finley was directed to open his battery, raking the loft from end to end.

The fire of our six-pounder, posted close to one of the gable ends of the house, soon drove the soldiers down; and no other effort to stop the flames being practicable, M'Pherson hung out the white flag.

. . . Powerfully as the present occasion called for punishment, and rightfully as it might have been inflicted, not a drop of blood was shed, nor any part of the enemy's baggage taken. M'Pherson and his officers accompanied their captors to Mrs. Motte's and partook with them in a sumptuous dinner, soothing in the sweets of social intercourse the ire which the preceding conflict had engendered.

—LEE, *Memoirs*, II, 73-80.

2. RAWDON TO THE RESCUE—THE TORY DEFENSE OF NINETY-SIX

Narrative of Roderick Mackenzie of the British Army.

When the advanced corps of the enemy appeared, upon the 21st of May, the works were far from being finished; even the platforms in the Star were not in a condition to receive guns.

The whole American army, amounting to upwards of four thousand men, with a respectable park of field artillery, encamped in a wood within cannon shot of the village. Flushed with success from the reduction of a number of the British posts, they, with a contemptuousness to the garrison of Ninety Six to this day unexplained, in the night between the 21st and 22d threw up two works, at no greater distance than seventy paces from the Star. General Greene did not even condescend to summon the place. Whether he meant to assault and reduce it by a *coup de main*, or designed these works for places of arms, is another point as yet undetermined. It can hardly be conceived that his engineer, Koziusco, a foreign adventurer whom *they* created a Count of Poland, would break ground and begin a sap within so small a distance of a regular fortification, if he had intended its reduction by the common mode of approaches.

By eleven o'clock in the morning of the 22d of May, the platform in the salient angle of the Star nearest to the Americans was completed and mounted with guns to fire *en barbet*. These, with incessant platoons of musquetry, played on the works constructed by the enemy the preceding night, under cover of which thirty men, marching in Indian-file, entered them and put every man they could reach to the bayonet. This party was immediately followed by another of the loyal militia, who, in an instant, levelled those works and loaded a number of Negroes with the entrenching tools of the Americans. Though General Greene put his whole army in motion to support the advanced corps, they were intirely routed before he could effect his design. The handful of brave men that performed this service retired into the Star without any loss, excepting that of the officer who led them, Lieutenant Roney. He was mortally wounded, and died the following night, much esteemed and justly lamented.

From such a check the American commander began to entertain a respectable idea of the troops with whom he had to contend. On the night of the 23d the Americans again broke ground, but at the distance of four hundred paces from the Star and behind a ravine. They here began two saps, erected block batteries to cover them, and appointed two brigades for their support. Sorties by small parties were made during the night to interrupt the enemy and retard their approaches. These were occasionally continued for the rest of the siege, notwithstanding which, by incessant labour and the numbers employed, the besiegers had completed a second parallel by the 3d of June, when, for the first time, they beat the chamade and their adjutant general advanced with a flag of truce, desiring to speak to the commandant.

Lieutenant Stelle, the officer on duty who met him, observed that it was unusual for commanding officers to receive and answer flags of truce in person, but that if he had any thing to communicate to Lieutenant Colonel Cruger, it should be forwarded. The American officer then produced a paper, signed by himself, setting forth, with the highest eulogiums, the invincible gallantry of their troops; enumerating their recent conquests "upon the Congaree, the Wateree and the Santee"; declaring that the garrison had every thing to hope from their generosity, and to fear from their resentment; making the commandant *personally* responsible for a fruitless resistance, and demanding an immediate and unconditional surrender to the army of the United States of America. He farther protested that this summons should not be repeated, nor any flag of truce hereafter received, without it conveyed the preliminary proposals for a capitulation.

The commandant directed an officer to inform the person who brought this extraordinary paper that Ninety Six was committed to his charge, and that both duty and inclination pointed to the propriety of defending it to the last extremity. He added that the promises and threats of General Greene were alike indifferent to him.

The truce therefore ceased; the enemy immediately opened four batteries, commenced a heavy cross fire which enfiladed some of the works, and continued this cannonade at intervals for several days, at the same time pushing a sap against the Star and advancing batteries. One of these constructed of fascines and gabions, at no greater distance than thirty-five paces from the abbatis, was elevated forty feet from the earth; upon it a number of riflemen were stationed, who, as they overlooked the British works, did great execution. The garrison crowned their parapet with sand-bags, leaving apertures through which the loyal militia fired their rifles with good effect. African arrows were thrown by the besiegers on the roofs of the British barracks to set them on fire, but this design was immediately counteracted by Lieut. Col. Cruger, who directed all the buildings to be unroofed, an order which, though it exposed both officers and men to the bad effects of the night air, so pernicious in this climate, was obeyed with an alacrity that nothing but their confidence in him could inspire.

With the intention to burn the rifle battery of the assailants, attempts were made to heat shot, but these were frustrated for want of furnaces. The besieged therefore in the Star being no longer able to continue with the cannon on the platforms in the day time, they were dismounted and used only in the night.

On the 8th of June, the garrison had the mortification to see that of Augusta marched by them prisoners of war. Though the gallantry displayed by Lieutenant Colonel Brown in its defence would have excited admiration in a generous foe, Colonel Lee, by whom they were taken, enjoyed the gratification of a little mind in exhibiting them before Ninety Six, with a British standard reversed, drums beating and fifes playing, to ridicule their situation. This pitiful recourse had an effect quite contrary to that which it was intended to produce. The soldiers were easily convinced by their officers that death was preferable to captivity with such an enemy. Having enjoyed this triumph, Colonel Lee, with his corps called the Legion, next sat down to reduce the stockade upon the left, which preserved a communication with the water; his approaches, however, commenced at a respectful distance, and his advances by sap were conducted with extreme caution, while the operations of General Greene were directed against the Star.

On the evening of the 9th of June, in the apprehension that something extraordinary was carrying on in the enemy's works, two sallies, with strong parties, were made. One of these, entering their trenches upon the right and penetrating to a battery of four guns, were prevented from destroying them for want of spikes and hammers. They here discovered the mouth of a mine, designed to be carried under a curtain of the Star, upon springing of which the breach was to be entered by the American army, sword in hand. The other division that marched upon the left fell in with the covering party of the besiegers, a number of whom were put to the bayonet, and the officer who commanded them brought in prisoner. Both divisions returned to the garrison with little loss, though it was impossible for that of the enemy not to have been considerable. Never did luckless wight receive a more inglorious wound, upon any occasion, than Count Koziusco did on this—it was in that part which Hudibras has constituted the seat of honour, and was given just as this engineer was examining the mine which he had projected!

Colonel Lee continued his approaches to the stockade upon the left, before which his corps suffered greatly. On the 12th of June, in a paroxysm of temerity and folly, he directed a serjeant and six men, at eleven o'clock in the forenoon, to advance with lighted combustibles and set fire to the abbatis of the work which he had invested. Not one of them returned to upbraid him with his rashness, and he was the first to solicit a truce to bury the bodies of the men he had so scandalously sacrificed. Having now redoubled his efforts and mounted a number of cannon which followed him from Augusta, he completely enfiladed this work by a triangular fire and by the 17th of June rendered it untenable. It was evacuated in the night without loss and taken possession of by the enemy.

The sufferings of the garrison were now extreme. With infinite labour a well was dug in the Star, but water was not to be obtained, and the only means of procuring this necessary element in a torrid climate in the month of June was to send out naked Negroes, who brought a scanty supply from within pistol shot of the American pickets, their bodies not being distinguishable in the night from the fallen trees with which the place abounded.

Far from despondence in this extremity, Lieutenant Colonel Cruger encouraged the troops, in the hope of relief from the arrival of an army before the enemy, though already advanced in their third parallel, could possibly reach the ditch. From the treatment of their fellow soldiers captured at Augusta, he painted to them, in the strongest colours, the mortifying consequences of a surrender; but, if they continued their defence, he had not the least doubt of their having the honour of brightening the future prospects of the royal army in those provinces.

Whilst the commandant was using these endeavours, an American Loyalist, in open day, under the fire of the enemy, rode through their pickets and delivered a verbal message from Lord Rawdon: "That he had passed Orangeburg and was in full march to raise the siege." The name of *Rawdon* inflamed every breast with additional vigour. They declared they would wait patiently for the assailants and meet them even in the ditch. How well they kept their word the transactions of the 18th will shew.

On the morning of this day the third parallel of the besiegers was completed; they turned the abbatis, drew out the pickets and brought forward two trenches within six feet of the ditch of the Star. General Greene, well informed of the advance of Lord Rawdon and knowing that the garrison was equally apprised of it, determined upon a general assault, which he commenced at noon.

Their forlorn hopes, in two divisions, made a lodgement in the ditch and were followed by strong parties with grappling hooks to draw down the sandbags, and tools to reduce the parapet. The riflemen, posted upon their elevated battery, picked off every British soldier that appeared, while the Virginian and Maryland lines fired by platoons from their trenches. The right flank of the enemy was exposed to the fire of a three-pounder, as well as to that of the block houses in the village, and Major Green with the troops in the Star waited with coolness to receive them on the parapet with bayonets and spears. The attack continued, but the main body of the Americans could

Independence National Historical Park Collection

GENERAL DANIEL MORGAN

After the original by Charles Willson Peale

Emmet Collection, New York Public Library

CORNWALLIS

m a painting by John Singleton Copley (engraving by G. Stodart)

Courtesy of the Metropolitan Museum of Art

TARLETON

Engraving by J. R. Smith, after Sir Joshua Reynolds, c. 1782

THE BRITISH LION ENGAGING FOUR POWERS

A contemporary British cartoon depicting Britain at war with America, France, Spain and the Netherlands not be brought forward to the assault; they were contented with supporting the parties in the ditch by an incessant fire from the lines.

At length the garrison became impatient. Two parties, under Captain Campbell of the New Jersey Volunteers and Captain French of Delancey's, issued from the sally port in the rear of the Star. They entered the ditch, divided their men and advanced, pushing their bayonets till they met each other. This was an effort of gallantry that the Americans could not have expected. General Greene, from one of the advanced batteries, with astonishment beheld two parties, consisting only of thirty men each, sallying into a ditch, charging and carrying every thing before them, though exposed to the fire of a whole army. It was an exertion of officers leading troops ardent in the cause of their sovereign, and steeled with the remembrance of injuries which they and their connections had so often received from the subverters of law and good government.

The Americans covered their shame in the trenches, nor was it till the next day that they recollected themselves so far as to ask permission to bury their dead. The groans also of their wounded assailed their ears and called aloud for that relief which ought to have been much earlier administered.

General Greene raised the siege upon the evening of the 19th, and on the morning of the 21st the army under Lord Rawdon made its appearance.
—MACKENZIE, *Strictures on Tarleton's History*, pp. 146-160.

VII. EUTAW SPRINGS

The last big battle in the lower South took place at Eutaw Springs, South Carolina, on September 8, 1781; like most of Greene's battles, it was indecisive. Rawdon had left the British army in the field under the command of Lieutenant Colonel Alexander Stewart, who was encamped on the west side of the Congaree near its junction with the Wataree. Greene was 16 miles north in the High Hills of Santee, but the two rivers between them were so flooded as to make it necessary for him to make a wide circuit of 70 miles to get close to Stewart.

Having cut off all intelligence to the enemy, Greene was able to approach Eutaw Springs without Stewart's knowledge. The Americans outnumbered the British 2,400 to 2,000. Each side claimed deserters from the other. As Greene put it, "At the close of the war, we fought the enemy with British soldiers; and they fought us with those of America."

Greene once again used the Cowpens pattern. In the center he placed the North Carolina militia, with the South Carolina militia on either side. He posted cavalry on either flank—on the right under Lee, on the left under Wade Hampton. In the second line he placed his regulars, with Washington's cavalry and Kirkwood's light infantry held in reserve. The militia stood up manfully, firing 17 rounds before showing any signs of weakening. When that happened the second line came up and drove the enemy back, while Lee's infantry wheeled upon the British left and Howard led the Marylanders in hand-to-hand combat with the British right. The British fell back in disorder. Now Stewart called on his grenadiers and light infantry under Major Majoribanks, who had been concealed by a dense thicket of blackjack. Washington

EUTAW SPRINGS

charged Majoribanks, had his own horse shot down, and half of his corps killed or wounded. He himself was captured. But Kirkwood's troops charged into the thicket and forced Majoribanks down into a ravine. The rest of the British army was in full retreat.

Suddenly the discipline of the Virginia and Maryland Continentals cracked. Naked, starved and thirsty, they halted in the British camp, fell upon the spoils of victory and drank themselves into a state of intoxication. Majoribanks, seizing the opportunity, sallied out into the field, swept down upon the disorganized plunderers and drove them into the woods.

Three hours of bloody fighting in intense heat was enough for both sides. Greene withdrew his men to the shelter of the woods. Stewart held the field for the night, but retired toward Monck's Corner the next day. The American casualties were almost one fourth of all who participated, 522 of all ranks; the British, 866, or two fifths of their forces, including Majoribanks, who died of his wounds. With his army decimated, Stewart found it necessary to withdraw to the vicinity of Charleston and the protection of the British warships. Both sides claimed victory.

Otho Williams' fascinating account of the battle was probably written long after the event and contains addenda furnished by other participants. Williams himself, Greene's adjutant general, was a Marylander who had fought *through the entire war from the siege of Boston, Fort Washington and Monmouth to Camden and King's Mountain.*

Greene lost Eutaw Springs as he had numerous other battles, but, save for Wilmington, N.C., and Charleston and Savannah, he had won the entire lower South.

1. The Conduct of the Militia "Would Have Graced Veterans"

Account furnished by Colonel Otho Williams of the Continental Army, with additions by Colonels W. Hampton, Polk, Howard and Watt.

At about two hundred yards west of the Eutaw Springs, Stewart had drawn up his troops in one line, extending from the Eutaw Creek beyond the main Congaree road. The Eutaw Creek effectually covered his right, and his left, which was, in the military language, in air, was supported by Coffin's cavalry and a respectable detachment of infantry, held in reserve at a convenient distance in the rear of the left under cover of the wood.

The ground on which the British army was drawn up was altogether in wood; but, at a small distance in the rear of this line, was a cleared field extending west, south and east from the dwelling house and bounded north by the creek formed by the Eutaw Springs, which is bold and has a high bank thickly bordered with brush and low wood. From the house to this bank extended a garden enclosed with palisadoes, and the windows of the house, which was two-stories high with garret rooms, commanded the whole circumjacent fields. The house was of brick and abundantly strong to resist small arms, and surrounded with various offices of wood; one particularly, a barn of some size, lay to the southeast a small distance from the principal building. In the open ground, to the south and west of the house, was the British encampment, the tents of which were left standing. . . .

The superiority of his enemy in cavalry made it necessary that Col. Stewart should cast his eye to the Eutaw house for retreat and support. To that, therefore, he directed the attention of Major Sheridan, with orders, upon the first symptoms of misfortune, to throw himself into it and cover the army from the upper windows. On his right also, he had made a similar provision against the possibility of his lines being compelled to give ground. In the thickets which border the creek, Major Majoribanks, with three hundred of his best troops, was posted, with instructions to watch the flank of the enemy, if ever it should be open to attack. This command had assumed a position having some obliquity to the main line, forming with an obtuse angle. The artillery of the enemy was also posted in the main road.

As soon as the skirmishing parties were cleared away from between the two armies, a steady and desperate conflict ensued. That between the artillery of the first line and that of the enemy was bloody and obstinate in the extreme; nor did the American artillery relax for a moment from firing or advancing, until both pieces were dismounted and disabled. One of the enemy's four-pounders had shared the same fate, and the carnage on both sides had been equal and severe.

Nor had the militia been wanting in gallantry and perseverance. It was with equal astonishment that both the second line and the enemy contemplated these men steadily and without faltering advance with shouts and exhortations into the hottest of the enemy's fire, unaffected by the continual fall of their comrades around them. Gen. Greene, to express his admiration of the firmness exhibited on this occasion by the militia, says of them, in a letter to Steuben, "Such conduct would have graced the veterans of the great king of Prussia." But it was impossible that this could endure long, for these men were, all this time, receiving the fire of double their number; their artillery was demolished, and that of the enemy still vomiting destruction on their ranks. They at length began to hesitate.

Governor Rutledge, who was anxiously attending the event of this battle a few miles in the rear, wrote to the South Carolina delegates that the militia fired seventeen rounds before they retired. That distrust of their own immediate commanders which militia are too apt to be affected with never produced an emotion where Marion and Pickens commanded.

Gen. Sumner was then ordered to support them. This was done with the utmost promptness, and the battle again raged with redoubled fury. In speaking of General Sumner's command, Gen. Greene observes "that he was at a loss which most to admire, the gallantry of the officers or the good conduct of the men."

On the advance of Gen. Sumner's command, Col. Stewart had brought up the infantry of his reserve into line on his left, and the struggle was obstinately maintained between fresh troops on both sides.

From the first commencement of the action, the infantry of the American covering parties, on the right and left, had been steadily engaged. The cavalry of the Legion, by being on the American right, had been enabled to withdraw into the woods and attend on its infantry, without being at all exposed to the enemy's fire. But the State troops under Henderson had been in the most exposed situation on the field. The American right, with the addition of the Legion infantry, had extended beyond the British left. But the American left fell far short of the British right; and the consequence was that the State troops were exposed to the oblique fire of a large proportion of the British right, and particularly of the battalion commanded by Majoribanks.

Never was the constancy of a party of men more severely tried. Henderson solicited permission to charge them and extricate himself from their galling fire, but his protection could not be spared from the artillery or the militia. At length he received a wound which disabled him from keeping his horse, and a momentary hesitation in his troops was produced by the shock. The exertions of Col. Wade Hampton, who succeeded to the command, aided by those of Col. Polk and Middleton, proved successful in restoring them to confidence and order, and they resumed their station in perfect tranquility.

In the mean time things were assuming important changes along the front line. Sumner's brigade, after sustaining for some time a fire superior to their own in the ratio of the greater numbers opposed to them, at length yielded and fell back. The British left, elated at the prospect, sprang forward as to certain conquest, and their line became deranged. This was exactly the incident for which the American commander was anxiously watching, and the next moment produced the movement for availing himself of it. Col. Williams now remained in command of the second line. "Let Williams advance and sweep the field with his bayonets" was the order delivered to a gentleman of medical staff, who acted the surgeon, the aid and the soldier indifferently, as occasion required.

Never was order obeyed with more alacrity. The two brigades received it with a shout. Emulous to wipe away the recollections of Hobkirk's Hill, they advanced with a spirit expressive of the impatience with which they had hitherto been passive spectators of the action. When approached within forty yards of the enemy, the Virginians delivered a destructive fire, and the whole second line, with trailed arms and an animated pace, advanced to the charge. Until this period their progress had been in the midst of showers of grape, and under a stream of fire from the line opposed to them. But eye-witnesses have asserted that the roll of the drum and the shouts which followed it drew every eye upon them alone; and a momentary pause in the action, a suspension by mutual consent, appeared to withdraw both armies from a sense of personal danger to fix their attention upon this impending conflict. It may well be supposed with what breathless expectation the Southern commander hung upon a movement on which all his hopes depended. Had it failed, he must have retired under cover of his cavalry.

Under the approach of the second line, the advanced left of the British army had commenced a retrograde movement in some disorder. This was confirmed by the good conduct of Col. Lee. The Legion infantry had steadily maintained its order in its position on the extreme right; and the advance of the British left having exposed its flank, the Legion infantry were promptly wheeled and poured in upon them a destructive enfilading fire; then joining in the charge, the British left wing was thrown into irretrievable disorder. But their centre and right still remained, greatly outnumbering the assailing party and awaiting the impending charge with unshaken constancy.

If the two lines on this occasion did not actually come to the mutual thrust of the bayonet, it must be acknowledged that no troops ever came nearer. They are said to have been so near that their bayonets clashed and the officers sprang at each other with their swords, before the enemy actually broke away.

But the scales of victory, fortunately for man, are never long in equipoise on these occasions.

In this instance, the left of the British centre appear to have been pressed upon and forced back by their own fugitives, and began to give way from left to right. At that moment, the Marylanders delivered their fire, and along their whole front the enemy yielded.

The shouts of victory resounded through the American line, affording a gleam of consolation to many a brave man bleeding and expiring on the field. Among these was the gallant Campbell, who received a ball in the breast during this onset.

The victory was now deemed certain, but many joined in the shouts of victory who were still destined to bleed. The carnage among the Americans had but commenced; it was in the effort to prevent the enemy from rallying and to cut him off from the brick house, which was all that remained to compel the army to surrender, that their great loss was sustained.

A pursuing army is always impeded by the effort that is necessary to maintain its own order, while, whether from terror, for safety or for rallying, the speed of the fugitive is unrestrained. Hence, cavalry are the military means for rendering disorder irretrievable. It is obvious that at this point of time the Legion cavalry might have been turned upon the British left with very great effect. Their position was highly favorable to such a movement, and their infantry was close up with the enemy to afford support. Why this was not done has never been explained. We can only conjecture that it was prevented by one or both of two causes known to have existed on that day. Col. Lee was generally absent from it during the action and bestowing his attention upon the progress of his infantry; and Captain Coffin was in that quarter, attending on the retreat of the British left. Coffin's force was, probably, superior to that of Lee in cavalry; whether so superior as to justify the latter's not attempting the charge in the presence of the British cavalry, although supported by that of his own infantry, could only have been decided by the attempt.

At this stage of the battle, Majoribanks still stood firm in the thickets that covered him; and, as the British line extended considerably beyond the American left, their extreme right still manifested a reluctance to retire; and as their left had first given way and yielded now without resistance, the two armies performed together a half wheel, which brought them into the open ground towards the front of the house.

Gen. Greene now saw that Majoribanks must be dislodged or the Maryland flank would soon be exposed to his fire and the conflict in that quarter renewed under his protection. Therefore, orders were dispatched to Washington to pass the American left and charge the enemy's right. The order was promptly obeyed and, galloping through the woods, Washington was soon in action. Had he had the good fortune to have taken on Kirkwood's infantry behind his men, all would have gone well; to have been detained by their march would have been inconsistent with his general feeling.

Col. Hampton, at the same time, received orders to co-operate with Col. Washington; and the rapid movement which he made to the creek, in order to fall in upon Washington's left, probably hastened the forward movement of the latter. On reaching the front of Majoribanks, and before Hampton had joined him, Washington attempted a charge, but it was impossible for his cavalry to penetrate the thicket. He then discovered that there was an interval between the British right and the creek, by which he was in hopes to succeed in gaining their rear. With this view, he ordered his troop to wheel by sections to the left, and thus brought nearly all his officers next to the enemy, while he attempted to pass their front. A deadly and well-directed fire, delivered at that instant, wounded or brought to the ground many of his men and horses, and every officer except two.

The field of battle was, at this instant, rich in the dreadful scenery which disfigures such a picture. On the left, Washington's cavalry routed and flying, horses plunging as they died or coursing the field without their riders, while the enemy with poised bayonet issued from the thicket upon the wounded or unhorsed rider. In the fore-ground, Hampton covering and collecting the scattered cavalry, while Kirkwood, with his bayonets, rushed furiously to revenge their fall, and a road strewed with the bodies of men and horses, and the fragments of dismounted artillery. Beyond these, a scene of indescribable confusion, viewed over the whole American line advancing rapidly and in order. And, on the right, Henderson borne off in the arms of his soldiers, and Campbell sustained in his saddle by a brave son, who had sought glory at his father's side.

Nothing could exceed the consternation spread at this time through the British ground of encampment. Every thing was given up for lost; the commissaries destroyed their stores; the numerous retainers of the army, mostly Loyalists and deserters, who dreaded falling into the hands of the Americans, leaping on the first horse they could command, crowded the roads and spread alarm to the very gates of Charleston. The stores on the road were set fire to, and the road itself obstructed by the felling of trees, for miles, across it.

Lieut. Gordon and Cornet Simmons were the only two of Washington's officers who could return into action. The colonel himself had his horse shot under him, and his life saved by the interposition of a British officer. The melancholy group of wounded men and officers, who soon presented themselves to the general's view, convinced him of the severity of his misfortune; but he had not yet been made acquainted with the full extent of it.

The survivors of Washington's command, being rallied, united themselves to Hampton's, and were again led up to the charge upon Majoribanks, but without success. That officer was then retiring before Kirkwood, still holding to the thickets and making for a new position, with his rear to the creek and his left resting on the palisadoed garden. By this time Sheridan had thrown himself into the house, and some of the routed companies from the left had made good their retreat into the picketted garden, from the intervals of which they could direct their fire with security and effect. The whole British line was now flying before the American bayonet. The latter pressed closely upon their heels, made many prisoners, and might have cut off the retreat of the rest, or entered pell-mell with them into the house, but for one of these occurrences which have often snatched victory from the grasp of a pursuing enemy.

The retreat of the British army lay directly through their encampment, where the tents were all standing and presented many objects to tempt a thirsty, naked and fatigued soldiery to acts of insubordination. Nor was the concealment afforded by the tents at this time a trivial consideration, for the fire from the windows of the house was galling and destructive, and no cover from it was anywhere to be found except among the tents or behind the building to the left of the front of the house.

Here it was that the American line got into irretrievable confusion. When their officers had proceeded beyond the encampment, they found themselves nearly abandoned by their soldiers, and the sole marks for the party who now poured their fire from the windows of the house. . . .

Everything now combined to blast the prospects of the American commander. The fire from the house showered down destruction upon the American officers; and the men, unconscious or unmindful of consequences, perhaps thinking the victory secure and, bent on the immediate fruition of its advantages, dispersing among the tents, fastened upon the liquors and refreshments they afforded, and became utterly unmanageable.

Majoribanks and Coffin, watchful of every advantage, now made simultaneous movements—the former from his thicket on the left, and the latter from the wood on the right of the American line. Gen. Greene soon perceived the evil that threatened him, and not doubting but his infantry, whose disorderly conduct he was not yet made acquainted with, would immediately dispose of Majoribanks, dispatched Capt. Pendleton with orders for the Legion cavalry to fall upon Coffin and repulse him. . . .

Major Eggleston . . . made the attack without success. . . .

By this time Gen. Greene, being made acquainted with the extent of his misfortune, ordered a retreat.

Coffin, who certainly proved himself a brave and active officer on this day, had no sooner repulsed the Legion cavalry than he hastened on to charge the rear of the Americans, now dispersed among the tents. Col. Hampton had been ordered up to the road to cover the retreat, at the same time the order was issued to effect it, and now charged upon Coffin with a vigour that was not to be resisted. Coffin met him with firmness, and a sharp conflict, hand to hand, was for a while maintained. But Coffin was obliged to retire, and in the ardour of pursuit the American cavalry approached so near Majoribanks and the picketted garden as to receive from them a fatally destructive fire. Col. Polk, who commanded Hampton's left and was, of consequence, directly under its influence, describes it by declaring "that he thought every man killed but himself." Col. Hampton then rallied his scattered cavalry and resumed his station in the border of the wood. But before this could be effected, Majoribanks had taken advantage of the opening made by his fire to perform another gallant action, which was decisive of the fortune of the day.

The artillery of the second line had followed on, as rapidly as it could, upon the track of the pursuit, and, together with two six-pounders abandoned by the enemy in their flight, had been brought up to batter the houses. Unfortunately, in the ardour to discharge a pressing duty, the pieces had been run into the open field, so near as to be commanded by the fire from the house. The pieces had scarcely opened their fire when the pressing danger which threatened the party in the house and, consequently, the whole army, drew all the fire from the windows upon the artillerists, and it very soon killed or disabled nearly the whole of them. And Majoribanks was no sooner disembarrassed of Hampton's cavalry than he sallied into the field, siezed the pieces and hurried them under the cover of the house. Then being re-inforced by parties from the garden and the house, he charged among the Americans, now dispersed among the tents, and drove them before him. The American army, however, soon rallied, after reaching the cover of the wood, and their enemy was too much crippled to venture beyond the cover of the house. . . .

Both parties claimed, on this occasion, a complete victory; but there is no difficulty in deciding the question between them upon the plainest principles. The British army was chased from the field at the point of the bayonet and took refuge in a fortress; the Americans were repulsed from that fortress. And, but for the demoralizing effect of possessing themselves of the British tents, the cover of the barn presented the means of forcing or firing the house with certainty and reducing the whole to submission.

—GIBBES, ed., *Documentary History of the American Revolution*, III, 147-157.

2. "AT EUTAW SPRINGS THE VALIANT DIED"

TO THE MEMORY OF THE
BRAVE AMERICANS
UNDER GENERAL GREENE, IN SOUTH CAROLINA, WHO
FELL IN THE ACTION OF SEPTEMBER 8, 1781

By Philip Freneau

At Eutaw Springs the valiant died;
 Their limbs with dust are covered o'er—
Weep on, ye springs, your tearful tide;
 How many heroes are no more!

If in this wreck of ruin, they
 Can yet be thought to claim a tear,
O smite your gentle breast and say
 The friends of freedom slumber here!

Thou, who shalt trace this bloody plain,
 If goodness rules thy generous breast,
Sigh for the wasted rural reign;
 Sigh for the shepherds, sunk to rest!

Stranger, their humble graves adorn;
 You too may fall and ask a tear;
'Tis not the beauty of the morn
 That proves the evening shall be clear.

They saw their injured country's woe:
 The flaming town, the wasted field;
Then rushed to meet the insulting foe ;
 They took the spear—but left the shield.

Led by thy conquering genius, Greene,
 The Britons they compelled to fly;
None distant viewed the fatal plain,
 None grieved, in such a cause to die—

But, like the Parthian, famed of old,
 Who, flying, still their arrows threw,
These routed Britons, full as bold,
 Retreated, and retreating slew.

Now rest in peace, our patriot band;
    Though far from nature's limits thrown,
We trust they find a happier land,
    A brighter sunshine of their own.
                —FRENEAU, *Poems*, II, 70-71.

CHAPTER THIRTY-ONE

Virginia

VIRGINIA ALONE *of Southern states had long been spared the heavy ravages of war. True, Dunmore had left a heritage of hate, and Norfolk had been burned, but, until the spring of '79, the Old Dominion had been relatively free of conflict. Then, in May 1779, a naval expedition under Vice-Admiral Sir George Collier seized Portsmouth without opposition, took a few other coastal towns, looted neighboring plantations, and destroyed or carried away many ships and 3,000 hogsheads of tobacco.*

Among the subjects on which Clinton and Cornwallis could not agree was the importance of Virginia in over-all strategy. Cornwallis felt that Virginia's seizure would end the war. He wanted Clinton to abandon New York and concentrate all his forces there. Ever cautious, and afraid of unknown risks, Clinton refused to do this, but as 1780 came to a close he sent a large detachmen to Virginia under the renegade Benedict Arnold, now a British brigadier general. To Arnold's force he attached Colonels Dundas and Simcoe, and instructed Arnold to be guided by this pair "in every important measure."

Washington had long before warned Governor Jefferson that Virginia must prepare to defend itself. But Jefferson was strangely inert. Virginia was apathetic and its governor had no talent for leadership in a war emergency. The defense was a travesty. Arnold sailed up the James and disembarked his men at Westover, 25 miles below Richmond, marched his forces entirely unopposed to Richmond and entered that town on January 5, 1781.

The defending militiamen fled without firing a shot. Arnold then sent Simcoe and his Tory Rangers up the river to Westham, where they destroyed an iron foundry and gunpowder factory, along with public records sent there for safekeeping. After burning many buildings in Richmond, Arnold returned down-river. En route Von Steuben, who commanded the Patriot forces in Virginia, caught up with him, but what might have been a successful ambush turned into a rout for the Americans, who fled in disorder. After inflicting these damaging blows, Arnold, with few losses of his own men, encamped for the winter at Portsmouth. Jefferson was unable to lay his hands on "this greatest of all traitors." In the spring of '81 Arnold was superseded in command by Major-General William Phillips.

I. GENERAL ARNOLD INVADES VIRGINIA

1. VIRGINIA MUST DEFEND HERSELF

George Washington to Governor Thomas Jefferson.

Headquarters, Ramapo, N. J., June 29, 1780

I have been honored with two of your Excellency's favors both of the 11th inclosing an extract of a letter from Governor Rutlege.

I cannot but feel most sensibly affected by several parts of your Excellency's letter. The successive misfortunes to the Southward, the progress of the enemy, and the great deficiency in military stores give rise to the most serious reflections, while our situation in this quarter precludes every hope of affording you further assistance. What from the system of short inlistments, and [the unfortunate] delays in filling up our battalions the army in this place, is reduced to a mere handful of men, and left as it were at the mercy of a formidable enemy, subject to see the honor and dignity of the States daily insulted without the power either to prevent it or to retaliate. Under these circumstances your Excellency will perceive how utterly impossible it is to go further in succors than what is already sent. To oppose our Southern misfortunes and surmount our difficulties our principal dependence must be on the means we have left us in your quarter. And it is some consolation amidst all our distresses that these are more than adequate to remove them; and to recover what we have lost that it is only necessary these be properly directed.

—FITZPATRICK, ed., *Writings of Washington*, XIX, 97-98.

2. RICHMOND'S FALL AND THE DESTRUCTION OF THE WESTHAM FOUNDRY

Military journal of Lieutenant Colonel J. G. Simcoe of the Queen's Rangers.

The troops under Gen. Arnold being embarked, he issued an order on the 20th of December [1780] against depredations in the country where the expedition was bound to, and in the most forcible terms and strongest manner called upon the officers to second his intentions and the Commander in Chief's orders in this respect. The expedition sailed from Sandy Hook on the 21st of December and arrived in the Chesapeake, but in a dispersed manner, on the 30th: several ships were missing.

General Arnold, without waiting for them, was enabled, by the fortunate capture which the advance frigate under Capt. Evans had made of some small American vessels, to push up the James River, and this was done with incomparable activity and despatch, the whole detachment showing an energy and alacrity that could not be surpassed. The enemy had a battery at Hood's Point, and there was as yet no certainty whether or not it was defended by an enclosed work. The vessels anchored near it late in the evening of the 3d of January; one of them, in which was Capt. Murray of the Queen's Rangers, not perceiving the signal for anchoring, was fired at. Upon the first shot the skipper and his people left the deck; when Capt. Murray seized the helm and, the soldiers assisting him, he passed by the fort without any damage from its fire and anchored above it.

Gen. Arnold ordered Lt. Col. Simcoe to land with one hundred and thirty of the Queen's Rangers and the light infantry and grenadiers of the 80th Regiment: the landing was effected silently and apparently with secrecy about a mile from the battery, and a circuit was made to surprise its garrison. In the mean time the fleet was fired upon, but ineffectually on account of its distance. On the detachment's approach through bypaths to Hood's, the flank companies of the 80th were ordered to file from the rear and to proceed rapidly to the battery, while the Rangers were ready to support them or to receive any enemy who might possibly be on their march from the adjacent country. Major Gordon on his approach found the battery totally abandoned; the concerted signal was made, and the fleet anchored near it. . . .

On the arrival at Westover, the troops were immediately disembarked. At first, from the reports of the country of the force that was assembling to defend Richmond, Gen. Arnold hesitated whether he should proceed thither or not, his positive injunctions being not to undertake any enterprise that had much risk in it; but Lt. Colonels Dundas and Simcoe concurring that one day's march might be made with perfect security, and that by this means more perfect information might be obtained, the troops were immediately put in motion and proceeded towards Richmond, where the enemy was understood to have very considerable magazines. It was above thirty miles from Westover; several transports had not arrived, and Gen. Arnold's force did not amount to eight hundred men.

On the second day's march, whilst a bridge was replacing over a creek, the advanced guard only having passed over, some of the enemy's militia, who had destroyed it the evening before and were to assemble with others to defend it, were deceived by the dress of the Rangers and came to Lt. Col. Simcoe, who immediately reprimanded them for not coming sooner, held conversation with them and then sent them prisoners to General Arnold.

Within seven miles of Richmond a patrole of the enemy appeared, who, on being discovered, fled at full speed. The Queen's Rangers, whose horses were in a miserable condition from the voyage, could not pursue them.

Soon after Lt. Col. Simcoe halted, having received the clearest information that a road, made passable by wood carts, led through the thickets to the rear of the heights on which the town of Richmond was placed, where they terminated in a plain, although they were almost inaccessible by the common road. On giving this information to Gen. Arnold, he said it was not worth while to quit the road, as the enemy would not fight. On approaching the town, Gen. Arnold ordered the troops to march as open and to make as great an appearance as possible; and the ground was so favourable that a more skilfull enemy than those who were now reconnoitering would have imagined the numbers to have been double.

The enemy at Richmond appeared drawn up on the heights to the number of two or three hundred men. The road passed through a wood at the bottom of these heights, and then ran between them and the river into the lower town. Lt. Col. Simcoe was ordered to dislodge them. He mounted the hill in small bodies, stretching away to the right, so as to threaten the enemy with a design to outflank them; and as they filed off, in appearance to secure their flank, he directly ascended with his cavalry, where it was so steep that they were obliged to dismount and lead their horses. Luckily the enemy made no resistance, nor did they fire, but, on the cavalry's arrival on the summit, retreated to the woods in great confusion.

There was a party of horsemen in the lower town watching the motion of Lt. Col. Dundas, who, the heights being gained, was now entering it. Lt. Col. Simcoe pushed on with the cavalry unnoticed by the enemy in the lower town till such time as he began to descend almost in their rear, when an impassable creek stopped him and gave the enemy time to escape to the top of another hill beyond the town. Having crossed over lower down, he ascended the hill, using such conversation and words towards them as might prevent their inclination to retreat. However, when the Rangers were arrived within twenty yards of the summit, the enemy, greatly superior in numbers, but made up of militia, spectators, some with and some without arms, galloped off. They were immediately pursued, but without the least regularity. . . .

On Lt. Col. Simcoe's return, he met with orders from Gen. Arnold to march to the foundery at Westham, six miles from Richmond, and to destroy it. The flank companies of the 80th, under Major Gordon, were sent as a reinforcement. With these and his corps he proceeded to the foundery. The trunnions of many pieces of iron cannon were struck off, a quantity of small arms and a great variety of military stores were destroyed. Upon consultation with the artillery officer, it was thought better to destroy the magazine than to blow it up. This fatiguing business was effected by carrying the powder down the cliffs and pouring it into the water. The warehouses and mills were then set on fire, and many explosions happened in different parts of the buildings, which might have been hazardous had it been relied on that all the powder was regularly deposited in one magazine; and the foundery, which was a very complete one, was totally destroyed.

It was night before the troops returned to Richmond. The provisions which had been made for them were now to be cooked. Fatigued with the march, the men in general went to sleep. Some of them got into private houses and there obtained rum. . . .

—Simcoe, *Military Journal*, pp. 159-165.

3. "Rather They Had Burnt My House and Ruined the Plantation"

One of the embarrassing incidents of the war took place in April 1781, when a British sloop-of-war paid a visit to Washington's plantation and seized 17 Negro slaves, of whom six were later recovered. To prevent further reprisals, Lund Washington, the general's plantation manager, furnished the British with refreshments. When Lafayette, who had been detailed to Virginia, called this to Washington's attention, the latter was quick to repudiate the action.

A. lafayette to george washington

Alexandria, Virginia, April 23, 1781

Great happiness is derived from friendship, and I do particularly experience it in the attachment which unites me to you. But friendship has its duties, and the man that likes you the best will be the forwardest in letting you know every thing where you can be concerned.

When the ennemy came to your house many Negroes deserted to them. This piece of news did not affect me much as I little value those concerns but you cannot conceive how unhappy I have been to hear that Mr. Lund Washington went on board the ennemy's vessels and consented to give them provisions. This being done by the gentleman who in some measure represents you at your house will certainly have a bad effect, and contrasts with spirited answers from some neighbours that had their houses burnt accordingly.

You will do what you think proper about it, my dear General, but, as your friend, it was my duty *confidentially* to mention the circumstances.

With the help of some waggons and horses we got in two days from the camp near Baltimore to this place. We halted yesterday, and having made a small bargain for a few shoes are marching to Frederis Burg. No official account from Philips, but I am told they are removing stores from Richmond and Petersburg. I am surprised no body writes to me, and hope soon to receive intelligences.

Our men are in high spirits. Their honor having been interested in this affair, they have made it a point to come with us, and discontents as well as desertion are entirely out of fashion.

Requesting my best respects to be presented to Mrs. Washington and compliments to the family.

—GOTTSCHALK, ed., *Letters of Lafayette to Washington*, pp. 187-188.

B. GEORGE WASHINGTON TO LUND WASHINGTON

New Windsor, April 30, 1781

Your letter of the 18th. came to me by the last Post. I am very sorry to hear of your loss; I am a little sorry to hear of my own; but that which gives me most concern, is, that you should go on board the enemys Vessels, and furnish them with refreshments. It would have been a less painful circumstance to me, to have heard, that in consequence of your non-compliance with their request, they had burnt my House, and laid the Plantation in ruins. You ought to have considered yourself as my representative, and should have reflected on the bad example of communicating with the enemy, and making a voluntary offer of refreshments to them with a view to prevent a conflagration.

It was not in your power, I acknowledge, to prevent them from sending a flag on shore, and you did right to meet it; but you should, in the same instant that the business of it was unfolded, have declared, explicitly, that it was improper for you to yield to the request; after which, if they had proceeded to help themselves, *by force*, you could but have submitted (and being unprovided for defence) this was to be prefered to a feeble opposition which only serves as a pretext to burn and destroy.

I am thoroughly perswaded that you acted from your best judgment; and believe, that your desire to preserve my property, and rescue the buildings from impending danger, were your governing motives. But to go on board their Vessels; carry them refreshments; commune with a parcel of plundering

Scoundrels, and request a favor by asking the surrender of my Negroes, was exceedingly ill-judged, and 'tis to be feared, will be unhappy in its consequences, as it will be a precedent for others, and may become a subject of animadversion.

I have no doubt of the enemys intention to prosecute the plundering plan they have begun. And, unless a stop can be put to it by the arrival of a superior naval force, I have as little doubt of its ending in the loss of all my Negroes, and in the destruction of my Houses; but I am prepared for the event, under the prospect of which, if you could deposit, in safety, at some convenient distance from the Water, the most valuable and least bulky articles, it might be consistent with policy and prudence, and a means of preserving them for use hereafter. Such, and so many things as are necessary for common, and present use must be retained and run their chance through the firy trial of this summer.

Mrs. Washington joins me in best and affectionate regard for you, Mrs. Washington and Milly Posey; and does most sincerely regret your loss. I do not know what Negroes they may have left you; and as I have observed before, I do not know what number they will have left me by the time they have done; but this I am sure of, that you shall never want assistance, while it is in my power to afford it.

—FITZPATRICK, ed., *Writings of Washington*, XXII, 14-15.

II. THE FATEFUL SQUABBLE BETWEEN CLINTON AND CORNWALLIS

The correspondence between the two military rivals, Cornwallis and Clinton, leaves the impression that the former was obsessed with the importance of Virginia in over-all British strategy. He insisted on an all-out campaign to reduce that province. Clinton operated with his customary caution. Fearing an attack in force on New York, Clinton was reluctant to reinforce Cornwallis; in fact, he requested that Cornwallis send back most of his army. If a move away from New York were to be made, Clinton preferred Philadelphia or Rhode Island, neither of which made military sense.

As letters went back and forth between the commanders, Cornwallis, who had quit Wilmington, North Carolina, and reached Virginia shortly after the middle of May, at once engaged in a wild-goose chase after Lafayette. Clinton's compromise proposal that Cornwallis hold a post on the Chesapeake with a small force and send back 3,000 troops to New York was intolerable to the Earl. He at once ordered an evacuation from the province. Clinton, alarmed, countermanded this order and categorically insisted in a letter Cornwallis received on July 8 that the latter take over a post and hold it, with his whole army if necessary. Cornwallis picked Yorktown, but Clinton's failure to throw in more support gave Cornwallis an "out" for his defeat. A postwar battle of words was fought in England between the two generals.

Both British armies were now on the defensive. Each had refused to fortify the other, and as they squabbled the British Navy for the time lost command of the sea. A breakdown of command contributed in no unimportant measure to the British disaster at Yorktown.

1. CORNWALLIS OBJECTS TO BEING KEPT TOTALLY IN THE DARK

To Sir Henry Clinton.

Camp near Wilmington, April 10, 1781

. . . I am very anxious to receive your Excellency's commands, being as yet totally in the dark as to the intended operations of the summer. I cannot help expressing my wishes that the Chesapeak may become the seat of war, even (if necessary) at the expense of abandoning New York. Until Virginia is in a manner subdued, our hold of the Carolinas must be difficult, if not precarious. The rivers in Virginia are advantageous to an invading army; but North Carolina is of all the provinces in America the most difficult to attack (unless material assistance could be got from the inhabitants, the contrary of which I have sufficiently experienced), on account of its great extent, of the numberless rivers and creeks, and the total want of interior navigation.

—Ross, ed., *Correspondence of Cornwallis*, I, 86-87.

2. CORNWALLIS: "I AM QUITE TIRED OF MARCHING ABOUT THE COUNTRY"

To Major General William Phillips.

Camp near Wilmington, April 10, 1781

I have had a most difficult and dangerous campaign and was obliged to fight a battle 200 miles from any communication against an enemy seven times my number. The fate of it was long doubtful. We had not a regiment or corps that did not at some time give way; it ended however happily, in our completely routing the enemy and taking their cannon. The idea of our friends rising in any number and to any purpose totally failed, as I expected, and here I am, getting rid of my wounded and refitting my troops at Wilmington. I last night heard of the naval action,* and your arrival in the Chesapeak. Now, my dear friend, what is our plan? Without one we cannot succeed, and I assure you that I am quite tired of marching about the country in quest of adventures. If we mean an offensive war in America, we must abandon New York and bring our whole force into Virginia; we then have a stake to fight for, and a successful battle may give us America. If our plan is defensive, mixed with desultory expeditions, let us quit the Carolinas (which cannot be held defensively while Virginia can be so easily armed against us) and stick to our salt pork at New York, sending now and then a detachment to steal tobacco, etc.

I daily expect three regiments from Ireland. Leaving one of them at Charlestown, with the addition of the other two and the flank companies I can come by land to you; but whether after we have joined we shall have a sufficient force for a war of conquest, I should think very doubtful. By a war of conquest, I mean, to possess the country sufficiently to overturn the Rebel government, and to establish a militia and some kind of mixed authority of our own. If no reinforcement comes, and that I am obliged to march with my present force to the upper frontiers of South Carolina, my situation will be truly distressing. If I was to embark from hence, the loss of the upper posts

---

* The engagement off the Chesapeake between Arbuthnot and Destouches is discussed in section III following.

in South Carolina would be inevitable. I have as yet received no orders. If the reinforcements arrive, I must move from hence, where the men will be sickly and the horses starved. If I am sure that you are to remain in the Chesapeak, perhaps I may come directly to you.

It is very difficult to get any letters conveyed by land on account of the vigilance and severity of the Rebel government. I believe all mine to General Arnold miscarried, and I did not receive one from him.

—Ross, ed., *Correspondence of Cornwallis*, I, 87-88.

3. Cornwallis Urges a Virginia Offensive and Favors Yorktown

To Sir Henry Clinton.

Byrd's Plantation, North of James River, May 26, 1781

. . . I shall now proceed to dislodge La Fayette from Richmond, and with my light troops to destroy any magazines or stores in the neighbourhood which may have been collected either for his use or for General Greene's army. From thence I purpose to move to the Neck at Williamsburgh, which is represented as healthy and where some subsistence may be procured, and keep myself unengaged from operations which might interfere with your plan for the campaign, untill I have the satisfaction of hearing from you. I hope I shall then have an opportunity to receive better information than has hitherto been in my power to procure, relative to a proper harbour and place of arms.

At present I am inclined to think well of York. The objections to Portsmouth are that it cannot be made strong without an army to defend it, that it is remarkably unhealthy, and can give no protection to a ship of the line. Wayne has not yet joined La Fayette, nor can I positively learn where he is, nor what is his force. Greene's cavalry are said to be coming this way, but I have no certain accounts of it. . . .

One maxim appears to me to be absolutely necessary for the safe and honourable conduct of this war, which is, that we should have as few posts as possible, and that wherever the King's troops are, they should be in respectable force. By the vigorous exertions of the present governors of America, large bodies of men are soon collected, and I have too often observed that when a storm threatens, our friends disappear. . . .

I shall take the liberty of repeating that if offensive war is intended, Virginia appears to me to be the only Province in which it can be carried on, and in which there is a stake. But to reduce the Province and keep possession of the country, a considerable army would be necessary, for with a small force the business would probably terminate unfavourably, tho' the beginning might be successfull. In case it is thought expedient and a proper army for the attempt can be formed, I hope your Excellency will do me the justice to believe that I neither wish nor expect to have the command of it, leaving you at New York on the defensive. Such sentiments are so far from my heart that I can with great truth assure you that few things could give me greater pleasure than being relieved by your presence from a situation of so much anxiety and responsibility.

—Stevens, ed., *Clinton-Cornwallis Controversy*, I, 488-490.

III. LAFAYETTE TO THE RESCUE

Learning that the British had reinforced Arnold with 2,000 men under General Phillips, Washington dispatched Lafayette and three regiments of light infantry to the defense of Virginia. He was to be reinforced by the French fleet under Admiral Destouches and 1,200 French soldiers. The first part of the project went according to plan. Lafayette marched from Peekskill to the Head of Elk, thence over water to Annapolis. The young French nobleman borrowed from the merchants of Baltimore on his private credit to purchase clothing and other necessities for the army. The second part of the plan did not come off. Admiral Arbuthnot worsted Destouches off the Chesapeake on March 16, and the French fleet returned to Newport.

Lafayette's position was indeed serious, as, in addition to Arnold's force, he now had to face Phillips' reinforcements numbering some 2,600 men. For additional help Lafayette could count merely upon Von Steuben's force of Virginia Continentals and some untrained militia units. Even before Lafayette's arrival, Phillips, after skirmishing with Von Steuben's troops, took Petersburg and destroyed all the vessels lying in the river. One participant, Lieutenant Daniel Trabue, thought the Virginia militia fought surprisingly well in this engagement. But further setbacks faced the defenders. They were forced to scuttle a naval force they had collected on the James with a view to co-operating with the French fleet against Portsmouth. At length the arrival of Lafayette at Richmond caused Phillips to pull his troops down-river.

Meantime, Clinton ordered the British army in Virginia to co-operate with Cornwallis when he began his movement north from Wilmington in April 1781. Arnold attempted now to turn Lafayette's left flank and get into his rear. Lafayette, recognizing that his forces were too small to risk an engagement against the British army, further reinforced on May 20 by Cornwallis' arrival with some 1,500 troops, retired to the interior. Early in June, Tarleton with 250 cavalrymen sped to Charlottesville and caught several members of the state legislature before they could make their escape. Jefferson, whose term of office had expired but who was still acting as governor, pulled out in time, but he did not join the legislature in their flight over the Blue Ridge Mountains to Staunton. Technically Tarleton put an end to Jefferson's term as the state's chief executive. Captain Francis J. Brooke of the Continental Army reports how the American soldiers were panic-stricken on the approach of Tarleton's forces.

In the face of mounting reinforcements for Lafayette, Cornwallis pulled his troops from the interior toward the Chesapeake to establish closer relations with Clinton in New York. Lafayette hung doggedly onto his rear. After some confused skirmishing near Williamsburg, where Cornwallis was encamped, the British general began moving his army across the James to reach Portsmouth. Before the crossing of the river was completed the British were set upon by Anthony Wayne's men, but repulsed the Americans in sharp but inconclusive fighting. Cornwallis, now assuming a defensive posture, failed to counterattack Lafayette's forces, but instead seized Yorktown and Glou-

cester across the York River and proceeded to fortify them. The trap was soon ready to be sprung.

1. "I Am Determined to Scarmish, but Not to Engage Too Far"

Lafayette to George Washington.

Richmond, May 24, 1781

My official letter, a copy of which I send to Congress, will let you know the situation of affairs in this quarter. I ardently wish my conduct may meet with your approbation. Had I followed the first impulsion of my temper, I would have risked some thing more. But I have been guarding against my own warmth, and this consideration, that a general defeat, which with such a proportion of militia must be expected, would involve this State and our affairs into ruin, has rendered me extremely cautious in my movements. Indeed, I am more embarassed to move, more crippled in my projects than we have been in the Northern States.

Had the Pennsylvanians arrived before Lord Cornwallis I was determined to attack the ennemy and have no doubt but what we would have been successfull. Their unaccountable delay cannot be too much lamented, and will make an immense difference to the fate of this compaign. Should they have arrived time enough to support me in the reception of Lord Cornwallis's first stroke, I would still have thought it well enough. But from an answer of General Waïne received this day and dated the 19th I am affraid that in this moment they have hardly left York town.

Public stores and private property being removed from Richmond, this place is a less important object. I don't believe it would be prudent to expose the troops for the sake of a few houses most of which are empty. But I am wavering betwen two inconveniences. Was I to fight a battle, I'll be cut to pieces, the militia dispersed, and the arms lost. Was I to decline fighting, the country would think herself given up. I am therefore determined to scarmish, but not to engage too far, and particularly to take care against their immense and excellent body of horse whom the militia fears like they would so many wild beasts. . . .

Was I any ways equal to the ennemy, I would be extremely happy in my present command. But I am not strong enough even to get beaten. Governement in this state has no energy, and laws have no force. But I hope this assembly will put matters up on a better footing. I had great deal of trouble to put the departements in a tolerable train. Our expenses were enormous, and yet we can get nothing. Arrangements for the present seem to put on a better face but for this superiority of the ennemy which will chase us where they please. They can over run the country, and untill the Pennsylvanians arrive we are next to nothing in point of opposition to so large a force. This country begins to be as familiar to me as Tappan and Bergen. Our soldiers are hitherto very healthy and I have turned doctor to regulate their diet.

Adieu, my dear General. Let me hear some times from you. Your letters are a great happiness to your affectionate friend.

—Gottschalk, ed., *Letters of Lafayette to Washington*, pp. 197-199.

2. "Cornwallis Is the Scourge"

Richard Henry Lee to Arthur Lee.

Epping Forest, June 4, 1781

... The enemies design seems to be by great distress and much delusion to bring over the minds of the people. It must be confessed that they have the fairest opportunity, for we have no press in the country, we have received next to no assistance from our sister States or from our ally, whilst our veteran regulars have been all sacrificed in the common cause, and a considerable part of our force, being the greatest part of Gen. Green's strength, now in S. Carolina.

The people feel their pressures, find themselves abandoned, and they are exposed to the infinite acts and fraud of our enemies and of our internal Tories. The consequences may be very unpleasing to sound and sensible Whiggism. Shew this to Col. Bland and it will surely rouse him to exert all his powers in Congress to procure us assistance and that which may be effectual. The enemy affect to leave harmless the poor and they take everything from those they call the rich. Tis said that 2 or 3000 Negroes march in their train, that every kind of stock which they cannot remove they destroy—eating up the green wheat and by destroying of the fences expose to destruction the other growing grains. They have burnt a great number of warehouses full of tobacco and they are now pressing on to the large ones on Rappahanock and Potomac rivers and the valuable iron works in our northern parts.

The fine horses on James River have furnished them with a numerous and powerful cavalry—'tis said to consist of 800. I hope that these afflictions are intended to do away some of our overcharge of wickedness, and that we shall be relieved in due season.

Cornwallis is the scourge—and a severe one he is. The doings of more than a year in the South are undoing very fast, whilst they rush to throw ruin into other parts.

I have got your keys from Richmond. Half of our militia is this day to be drafted for the Marquis, but how to get at him I know not, as the enemy are between us and him.

—Ballagh, ed., *Letters of R. H. Lee*, II, 229-231.

3. Tarleton Recalls His Raid on Charlottesville

At this period, the superiority of the army and the great superiority of the light troops were such as to have enabled the British to traverse the country without apprehension or difficulty, either to destroy stores and tobacco in the neighbourhood of the rivers or to undertake more important expeditions. While the main body was in Hanover County and the Marquis de la Fayette lay between them and Fredericksburg, Earl Cornwallis had clear intelligence of the meeting of the governor and assembly at Charlotteville, under the protection of a guard, in order to vote taxes for the exigencies of government, to concert measures for the augmentation of the eighteen-months men, or state troops, and to issue commands for a large draft of militia. At the same time he obtained information that Baron Steuben was gone to Point of Fork, which is situated at the extremity of James River between the Fluvanna and Rivanna, with the eighteen-months men, to cover a Continental store, consisting of cannon, small arms and accoutrements.

To frustrate these intentions, and to distress the Americans by breaking up the assembly at Charlotteville and by taking or destroying the arms and other stores at Point of Fork, his Lordship employed Lieutenant-Colonel Tarleton on the former expedition, as most distant and on that account more within the reach of cavalry, whilst he committed the latter enterprize to the execution of Lieutenant-Colonel Simcoe, with the yagers, the infantry and the hussars of the rangers. It was designed that these blows should, as near as circumstances would permit, be struck at the same moment; that Tarleton, after completing his business, should retire down the Rivanna to give assistance to Simcoe, if he failed in his first attempt, and that both should afterwards join the army, which would in the mean time file to the left through Goochland County and approach the Point of Fork.

Lieutenant-Colonel Tarleton, with one hundred and eighty dragoons, supported by Captain Champagne of the 23d Regiment and seventy mounted infantry, left the army in the beginning of June and proceeded between the North and South Anna. The heat of the weather obliged him to refresh his men and horses in the middle of the day. He pressed forwards in the afternoon, halted at eleven near Louisa Courthouse, and remained on a plentiful plantation till two o'clock in the morning, at which time he again resumed his march. Before dawn he fell in with twelve waggons that were on their journey under a weak guard from the upper parts of Virginia and Maryland, with arms and clothing for the Continental troops in South Carolina. The waggons and stores were burnt, that no time might be lost or diminution of force made by giving them an escort.

Soon after daybreak, some of the principal gentlemen of Virginia, who had fled to the borders of the mountains for security, were taken out of their beds. Part were paroled and left with their families, while others who were suspected to be more hostile in their sentiments were carried off. In the neighbourhood of Dr. Walker's, a member of the Continental Congress was made prisoner, and the British light troops, after a halt of half an hour to refresh the horses, moved on toward Charlotteville. Various were the accounts on the road concerning this place and the force it contained. Lieutenant-Colonel Tarleton imagined that a march of seventy miles in twenty-four hours, with the caution he had used, might, perhaps, give him the advantage of a surprise, and concluded that an additional celerity to the object of his destination would undoubtedly prevent a formidable resistance. He therefore approached the Rivanna, which runs at the foot of the hill on which the town is situated, with all possible expedition. The advanced dragoons reported that the ford was guarded. An attack was nevertheless ordered. The cavalry charged through the water with very little loss and routed the detachment posted at that place.

As soon as one hundred cavalry had passed the water, Lieutenant-Colonel Tarleton directed them to charge into the town, to continue the confusion of the Americans and to apprehend, if possible, the governor and assembly.

Seven members of assembly were secured; a Brigadier-General Scott and several officers and men were killed, wounded or taken. The attempt to secure Mr. Jefferson was ineffectual; he discovered the British dragoons from his house, which stands on the point of a mountain, before they could approach him, and he provided for his personal liberty by a precipitate retreat.

A great quantity of stores were found in Charlotteville and the neighbourhood. One thousand new firelocks that had been manufactured at Fredericksburg were broken. Upwards of four hundred barrels of powder were destroyed. Several hogsheads of tobacco and some Continental clothing and accoutrements shared the same fate. The next morning the British were joined by about twenty men, who, being soldiers of the Saratoga army, had been dispersed throughout the district and allowed to work in the vicinity of the barracks, where they had been originally imprisoned. Many more would probably have joined their countrymen if Lieutenant-Colonel Tarleton had been at liberty to remain at Charlotteville a few days; but his duty pointed out the propriety of returning the same afternoon with his corps and the prisoners down the Rivanna towards the Point of Fork.

The gentlemen taken on this expedition were treated with kindness and liberality. In different conversations with Lieutenant-Colonel Tarleton on the state of public affairs, they generally and separately avowed that if England could prevent the intended co-operation of the French fleet and army with the American forces during the ensuing autumn, both Congress and the country would gladly dissolve the French alliance and enter into treaty with Great Britain. These sentiments were communicated to Earl Cornwallis, who, doubtless, made them known to the commander in chief for the information of the admiral in the West-Indies and the minister in England. The captives of distinction, both civil and military, were restrained by their promise not to quit the camps or line of march of the light troops till they joined the army.
—TARLETON, *History of Campaigns in the Southern Provinces,* pp. 302-306.

4. CORNWALLIS BOASTS, "THE BOY CANNOT ESCAPE ME"

Memoirs of Lafayette.

Lord Cornwallis, when he commenced the pursuit of Lafayette, had written a letter, which was intercepted, in which he made use of this expression: *The boy cannot escape me.* He flattered himself with terminating, by that one blow, the war in the whole southern part of the United States, for it would have been easy for him afterwards to take possession of Baltimore and march towards Philadelphia. He beheld in this manner the failure of the principal part of his plan, and retreated towards Richmond, whilst Lafayette, who had been joined in his new station by a corps of riflemen as well as by some militia, received notice beforehand to proceed forward on a certain day, and followed, step by step, the English general, without, however, risking an engagement with a force so superior to his own. His corps gradually increased. Lord Cornwallis thought proper to evacuate Richmond; Lafayette followed him, and ordered Colonel Butler to attack his rear guard near Williamsburg. Some manoeuvre took place on that side, of which the principal object on Lafayette's part was to convince Lord Cornwallis that his force was more considerable than it was in reality. The English evacuated Williamsburg and passed over James River to James Island.

A warm action took place between the English army and the advance guard, whom Lafayette had ordered to the attack whilst they were crossing the river. Lord Cornwallis had stationed the first troops on the other side, to give the appearance as if the greatest number of the troops had already passed over the river. Although every person was unanimous in asserting that this was the case, Lafayette himself suspected the deception and quitted his detachment to make observations upon a tongue of land from whence he could more easily view the passage of the enemy. A cannon, exposed doubtless intentionally, tempted General Wayne, a brave and enterprising officer.

Lafayette found, on his return, the advance guard engaged in action with a very superior force. He withdrew it, however, (after a short but extremely warm conflict), in good order and without receiving a check. The report was spread that he had had a horse killed under him, but it was merely the one that was led by his aide. The English army pursued its route to Portsmouth; it then returned by water to take its station at Yorktown and Gloucester upon the York River. A garrison still remained at Portsmouth. Lafayette made some demonstrations of attack, and that garrison united itself to the body of the army at Yorktown.

Lafayette was extremely desirous that the English army should unite at that very spot. Such had been the aim of all his movements, ever since a slight increase of force had permitted him to think of any other thing than of retiring without being destroyed and of saving the magazines. He knew that a French fleet was to arrive from the islands upon the American coast. His principal object had been to force Lord Cornwallis to withdraw towards the sea-shore, and then entangle him in such a manner in the rivers that there should remain no possibility of a retreat. The English, on the contrary, fancied themselves in a very good position, as they were possessors of a seaport by which they could receive succours from New York and communicate with the different parts of the coast. An accidental, but a very fortunate circumstance increased their security.

Whilst Lafayette, full of hope, was writing to General Washington that he foresaw he could push Lord Cornwallis into a situation in which it would be easy for him, with some assistance from the navy, to cut off his retreat, the general, who had always thought that Lafayette would be very fortunate if he could save Virginia without being cut up himself, spoke to him of his project of attack against New York, granting him permission to come and take part in it, if he wished it, but representing how useful it was to the Virginian army that he should remain at its head. The two letters passed each other; the one written by Lafayette arrived safely, and Washington prepared beforehand to take advantage of the situation of Lord Cornwallis. Gen. Washington's letter was intercepted, and the English, upon seeing that confidential communication, never doubted for a moment but the real intention of the Americans was to attack New York. Their own security at Yorktown was therefore complete.

—LAFAYETTE, *Memoirs, Correspondence and Manuscripts,* pp. 263-267.

CHAPTER THIRTY-TWO

Yorktown: Washington's Vindication

THE FINAL *British disaster of the American Revolution may be attributed to a variety of causes: to Cornwallis' unwise selection of an encampment which could be cut off by superior sea power; to the triangular division of command among Clinton, Cornwallis and Germain, which compounded the confusion; to the timidity of the British naval commanders and the aggressiveness of a French admiral; and, most of all, to the flexibility of Washington's strategy, his ability to seize a grand opportunity when it came within his grasp.*

It is hardly necessary to add that without the support of the French land and sea forces the victory at Yorktown could not have been achieved. That support had been long in coming. The bulk of the French army reached Newport in July 1780 after Sir Henry Clinton had evacuated his garrison from Rhode Island. The French forces were commanded by the Comte de Rochambeau, a fifty-five-year-old veteran of the Seven Years' War, tactful, dignified and astute. Without naval support, however, those forces might not have proved decisive. Previous French naval expeditions had been maddeningly futile. Lafayette, who played a central role in the Yorktown campaign, put his finger on the problem when he wrote Vergennes in January 1781 that naval superiority was the key to final victory. In the spring of '81 a powerful fleet commanded by the Comte de Grasse sailed from Brest for the West Indies. A giant of a man, energetic and enthusiastic, De Grasse had been directed to come to the American coast in July and August, relieve the smaller French fleet at Newport, and for a limited period act in co-operation with the French and American armies.

I. WASHINGTON'S STRATEGY LOOKS TO THE CHESAPEAKE

The original plan for combined operations was mapped out by Washington and Rochambeau at a conference held at Wethersfield, Connecticut, on May 21, 1781. There the American commander secured Rochambeau's reluctant consent to a joint attack against New York supported by the French West Indian fleet under De Grasse. Rochambeau left De Grasse free either to sail to New York or to operate against the British army in Virginia. The French army moved from Rhode Island and joined Washington's above New York early in July.

A number of events caused Washington to scrap this plan. Skirmishing at the outposts of New York City revealed that it would be bitterly contested.

Furthermore, De Grasse, taking advantage of the latitude in Rochambeau's instructions, decided to go to the Chesapeake rather than New York. It appears from Allen McLane's unpublished journal that he visited De Grasse in the West Indies and persuaded him of the advantages of sailing to Chesapeake Bay. On August 14 a letter from De Grasse reached Washington with news that he was sailing in force from the West Indies for the Chesapeake and that he could not remain longer than October, at which time it would be necessary for him to be on his station again. This ruled out a New York campaign and suggested to Washington the advisability of sending all the combined Franco-American forces that he could spare to Virginia. On August 17 Washington wrote De Grasse: "It has been judged expedient to turn our attention towards the South."

The new plan was carried out in greatest secrecy not only in order that Clinton would not be apprised of it, but also to prevent Admiral Graves, with his fleet in New York and Newport, from joining Sir Samuel Hood and, by occupying the Chesapeake, keeping open communications between Cornwallis and Clinton. Clinton seems to have assumed that the first movements of Washington's forces were aimed at Staten Island or Sandy Hook to cover the entrance of the French fleet into New York harbor. It was not until the main American army had crossed the Delaware that Washington's real objective became obvious. The Franco-American forces moved southward with speed. At Head of Elk they were brought down to Williamsburg by French transports provided by De Grasse. By September 25 the last detachments arrived on the scene and joined Lafayette's forces. The Franco-Americans now enjoyed an overwhelming military superiority of more than two to one over the defenders. Against Cornwallis' 7,500 troops, and an additional several hundred Loyalists, the combined Franco-American armies besieging Yorktown numbered 5,700 Continentals, 3,100 militia, and 7,000 French troops.

When Admirals Graves and Hood reached the Chesapeake they found that De Grasse had already entered that bay and blockaded the mouths of the James and the York. De Grasse went out and engaged the British fleets, and in his absence Admiral de Barras arrived from Newport with additional French ships. The combined naval forces proved too strong for the timid British fleet, which withdrew to New York. Cornwallis' doom was sealed.

1. Naval Superiority Will Decide the War

Lafayette to the Count de Vergennes.

New Windsor on the North River, January 20, 1781

The first copy of this letter will be delivered to you by Lieutenant-Colonel Laurens, aide-de-camp to General Washington, who is charged by Congress with a private mission. Permit me to recommend to you this officer as a man who, by his integrity, frankness and patriotism, must be extremely acceptable to Government.

According to the instructions of Congress, he will place before you the actual state of our affairs, which demand, I think more than ever, the most serious attention. As to the opinions which I may allow myself to express, sir,

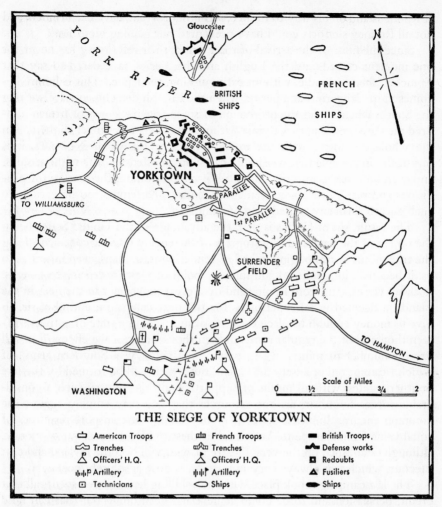

THE SIEGE OF YORKTOWN

🗁 American Troops	🕮 French Troops	▪ British Troops,
🗁 Trenches	🕮 Trenches	◂▪ Defense works
𝝙 Officers' H.Q.	𝝙 Officers' H.Q.	▣ Redoubts
╷╷╷P Artillery	╷╷╷ Artillery	▲ Fusiliers
▣ Technicians	◯ Ships	◖ Ships

From The Encyclopedia of American History   *Courtesy of Harper & Brothers*
by Richard B. Morris

they entirely correspond with those I have hitherto expressed, and the very slight alterations observable in them have been occasioned by a change of time, prejudice and circumstances.

With a naval inferiority it is impossible to make war in America. It is that which prevents us from attacking any point that might be carried with two or three thousand men. It is that which reduces us to defensive operations, as dangerous as they are humiliating. The English are conscious of this truth, and all their movements prove how much they desire to retain the empire of the sea. The harbours, the country and all the resources it offers appear to invite us to send thither a naval force. If we had possessed but a maritime superiority this spring, much might have been achieved with the army that M. de Rochambeau brought with him, and it would not have been necessary to have awaited the division he announced to us. If M. de Guichen [the French admiral whose squadron had been in the West Indies] had stopped at Rhode Island on his way to France, Arbuthnot would have been ruined, and not all Rodney's efforts could have prevented our gaining victories.

Since the hour of the arrival of the French, their inferiority has never for one moment ceased, and the English and the Tories have dared to say that France wished to kindle, without extinguishing, the flame. This calumny becomes more dangerous at a period when the English detachments are wasting the South; when, under the protection of some frigates, corps of fifteen hundred men are repairing to Virginia without our being able to get to them. On the whole continent, with the exception of the islands of Newport, it is physically impossible that we should carry on an offensive war without ships, and even on those islands the difficulty of transportation, the scarcity of provisions and many other inconveniences render all attempts too precarious to enable us to form any settled plan of campaign.

The result, sir, of all this is that, the advantage of the United States being the object of the war, and the progress of the enemy on that continent being the true means of prolonging it, and of rendering it, perhaps, even injurious to us, it becomes, in a political and military point of view, necessary to give us, both by vessels sent from France and by a great movement in the fleet in the islands, a decided naval superiority for the next campaign; and also, sir, to give us money enough to place the American forces in a state of activity: fifteen thousand of the regular army and ten thousand or, if we choose it, a still greater number of militia in this part of the country; a Southern army, of which I cannot tell precisely the extent, but which will be formed by the five Southern states, with all means of supporting in this country such a considerable force. Such, sir, are the resources that you may employ against the common enemy. Immense sums of money could not transport resources of equal value from Europe to America, but these, without a succour of money, although established on the very theatre of war, will become useless; and that succour, which was always very important, is now absolutely necessary.

The last campaign took place without a shilling having been spent; all that credit, persuasion and force could achieve has been done—but that can hold out no longer. That miracle, of which I believe no similar example can be found, cannot be renewed, and our exertions having been made to obtain an army for the war, we must depend on you to enable us to make use of it.

From my peculiar situation, sir, and from what it has enabled me to know and see, I think it is my duty to call your attention to the American soldiers, and on the part they must take in the operations of the next campaign. The Continental troops have as much courage and real discipline as those that are opposed to them. They are more inured to privation, more patient than Europeans, who, on these two points, cannot be compared to them. They have several officers of great merit, without mentioning those who have served during the last wars, and from their own talents have acquired knowledge intuitively; they have been formed by the daily experience of several campaigns, in which, the armies being small and the country a rugged one, all the battalions of the line were obliged to serve as advance-guards and light troops. The recruits whom we are expecting, and who only bear, in truth, the name of recruits, have frequently fought battles in the same regiments which they are now re-entering, and have seen more gun-shots than three-fourths of the European soldiers. As to the militia, they are only armed peasants, who have occasionally fought, and who are not deficient in ardour and discipline, but whose services would be most useful in the labours of a siege. . . .

The English having had sufficient time to think of all the naval points, the attacks of next year will be anything rather than surprises, and our forces must increase in proportion to their precautions. I could have wished that there had been some French troops, and my confidence in the decrease of prejudice has been even greater than that of Congress, General Washington or your minister at that time. The advance-guard of the Count de Rochambeau, although inactive itself from want of ships, by its presence alone has rendered an essential service to Amercia: if it had not arrived, the campaign would have been a ruinous one. When I consider the present state of feeling, my notion, as I have had the honour of telling you before, would be to send hither, for the expedition of New York, a division of about ten thousand Frenchmen. . . .

—LAFAYETTE, *Memoirs, Correspondence and Manuscripts*, pp. 373-379.

2. THE AMERICAN PLAN TO ATTACK NEW YORK IS ABANDONED

Diary of George Washington.

[*August 1st, 1781*]. By this date all my Boats were ready, viz—one hundred New ones at Albany (constructed under the direction of Gen. Schuyler) and the like number at Wappings Creek by the Quarter Master General; besides old ones which have been repaired. My heavy Ordnance and Stores from the Eastward had also come on to the North River and every thing would have been in perfect readiness to commence the operation against New York, if the States had furnished their quotas of men agreeably to my requisitions; but so far have they been from complying with these that of the first not more than half the number asked of them have joined the Army, and of 6200 of the latter pointedly and continuously called for to be with the army by the 15th of last Month, only 176 had arrived from Connecticut, independant of about 300 State Troops under the Command of Gen. Waterbury, which had been on the lines before we took the field, and two Companies of York levies (about 80 Man) under similar circumstances.

Thus circumstanced, and having little more than general assurances of getting the succours called for and energetic Laws and Resolves energetically executed, to depend upon, with little appearance of their fulfilment, I could scarce see a ground upon which to continue my preparations against New York; especially as there was much reason to believe that part (at least) of the Troops in Virginia were recalled to reinforce New York, and therefore I turned my views more seriously (than I had before done) to an operation to the Southward and, in consequence, sent to make inquiry, indirectly, of the principal Merchants to the Eastward what number, and what time, Transports could be provided to convey a force to the Southward if it should be found necessary to change our plan and similar application was made in a direct way to Mr. Morris (Financier) to discover what number could be had by the 20th. of this month at Philadelphia, or in Chesapeak bay. At the same time General Knox was requested to turn his thoughts to this business and make every necessary arrangement for it in his own mind, estimating the ordnance and Stores which would be wanting and how many of them could be obtained without a transport of them from the North River. Measures were also taken to deposit the Salt provisions in such places as to be Water-born; more than these, while there remained a hope of Count de Grasse's bringing a land force with him, and that the States might yet put us in circumstances to prosecute the original plan, could not be done without unfolding matters too plainly to the enemy and enabling them thereby to counteract our Schemes.

—FITZPATRICK, ed., *Diaries of Washington*, II, 248-250.

3. "OUR SITUATION REMINDS ME OF SOME THEATRICAL EXHIBITION"

Journal of Dr. James Thacher, attending the Continental Army.

[*Aug. 15th, 1781*]—General orders are now issued for the army to prepare for a movement at a moment's notice. The real object of the allied armies in the present campaign has become a subject of much speculation. Ostensibly an investment of the city of New York is in contemplation—preparations in all quarters for some months past indicate this to be the object of our combined operations. The capture of this place would be a decisive stroke, and from the moment such event takes place, the English must renounce all hopes of subjugating the United States. But New York is well fortified both by land and water and garrisoned by the best troops of Great Britain. The success of a siege must depend entirely on the arrival and coöperation of a superior French fleet. The enemy have a garrison on Staten Island, which is separated from Long Island only by a strait of two miles wide. The capture of this garrison would be a brilliant affair and would essentially facilitate our operations against New York.

General Washington and Count Rochambeau have crossed the North River, and it is supposed for the purpose of reconnoitering the enemy's posts from the Jersey shore. A field for an extensive encampment has been marked out on the Jersey side, and a number of ovens have been erected and fuel provided for the purpose of baking bread for the army. From these combined circumstances we are led to conclude that a part of our besieging force is to occupy that ground. But General Washington possesses a capacious mind, full of resources, and he resolves and matures his great plans and designs under an impenetrable veil of secrecy, and while we repose the fullest confidence in our chief, our own opinions must be founded only on doubtful conjectures. The royal army at New York have received a reinforcement of three thousand Germans from Europe.

20th.—According to orders, we commenced our line of march yesterday, a party of pioneers being sent forward to clear the road towards King's-bridge, and we expected immediately to follow in that direction; but an army is a machine whose motions are directed by its chief. When the troops were paraded for the march, they were ordered to the right about, and, making a retrograde movement up the side of the North River, we have reached King's-ferry and are preparing to cross the Hudson at this ferry. Our allies are in our rear, and it is probable we are destined to occupy the ground on the Jersey side.

21st.—Colonel Laurens has arrived at head-quarters on his way from Boston to Philadelphia. This gentleman is the son of Mr. Henry Laurens, our ambassador to Holland, who is now confined in the Tower of London. We have the pleasing information that he has brought with him from France a large sum of specie for the United States. He reports that the different powers of continental Europe are friendly to the cause in which we are engaged.

Our situation reminds me of some theatrical exhibition, where the interest and expectations of the spectators are continually increasing, and where curiosity is wrought to the highest point. Our destination has been for some time matter of perplexing doubt and uncertainty; bets have run high on one side that we were to occupy the ground marked out on the Jersey shore, to aid in the siege of New York, and on the other, that we are stealing a march on the enemy and are actually destined to Virginia in pursuit of the army under Lord Cornwallis.

We crossed at King's-ferry, 21st instant, and encamped at Haverstraw. A number of batteaux, mounted on carriages, have followed in our train, supposed for the purpose of conveying the troops over to Staten Island.

22d.—Resumed our line of march, passing rapidly through Paramus, Acquackanack, Springfield and Princeton. We have now passed all the enemy's posts and are pursuing our route with increasing rapidity towards Philadelphia; wagons have been prepared to carry the soldiers' packs, that they may press forward with greater facility. Our destination can no longer be a secret. The British army under Lord Cornwallis is unquestionably the object of our present expedition. It is now rumored that a French fleet may soon be expected to arrive in Chesapeake Bay, to coöperate with the allied army in that quarter. The great secret respecting our late preparations and movements can now be explained. It was a judiciously concerted stratagem, calculated to menace and alarm Sir Henry Clinton for the safety of the garrison of New York and induce him to recall a part of his troops from Virginia for his own defence; or, perhaps, keeping an eye on the city, to attempt its capture, provided that by the arrival of a French fleet favorable circumstances should present. The deception has proved completely successful; a part of Cornwallis' troops are reported to have returned to New York. His Excellency General Washington, having succeeded in a masterly piece of *generalship*, has now the satisfaction of leaving his adversary to ruminate on his own mortifying situation, and to anticipate the perilous fate which awaits his friend Lord Cornwallis in a different quarter. Major General Heath is left commander-in-chief of our army in the vicinity of New York and the highlands, and the menacing aspect of an attack on New York will be continued till time and circumstances shall remove the delusive veil from the eyes of Sir Henry Clinton, when it will probably be too late to afford succour to Lord Cornwallis.

To our officers, the inactivity of the royal army in New York is truly unaccountable: they might, without risking a great deal, harass our army on its march and subject us to irreparable injury; but the royalists are more dexterous in availing themselves of treachery and insurrection than in effecting valorous achievements.

In passing through Princeton but little time was allowed me to visit the college. This once celebrated seminary is now destitute of students, and the business of education is entirely suspended in consequence of the constant bustle and vicissitudes of war. The little village of Princeton is beautifully situated, and the college edifice is of stone, four stories high, and lighted by twenty-five windows in front in each story. It has suffered considerable injury in being occupied alternately by the soldiers of the two contending armies.

Trenton, where we are now encamped for the night, is a much more considerable village, and more advantageously situated, on the north-eastern bank of the Delaware, twenty-seven miles above Philadelphia. This is the town which General Washington has rendered famous to the latest times by a victory in which he so happily displayed the resources of his genius in the severe winter of 1776. Great indeed must be the resources of that man who can render himself the most formidable to an enemy when apparently he is the most destitute of power.

General Washington and Count Rochambeau having proceeded to Virginia by land, Major-General Lincoln takes the command of our troops, and the Baron de Viomenil those of the French.

—THACHER, *Military Journal*, pp. 268-271.

4. THE ADVANCE ON YORKTOWN: "WHAT IS BECOME OF DE GRASSE?"

George Washington to Lafayette.

Head Quarters, Philadelphia, September 2, 1781

. . . Calculating upon the regular force under your immediate Orders, the Militia which have already been called for and may be expected in the field; the whole of the French Army, and the American Corps now marching with Major Gen Lincoln from the Northward in addition to the land Forces expected on board the Fleet; I flatter myself we shall not experience any considerable difficulties from the want of Men to carry our most favourite Projects into execution. The means for prosecuting a Seige with rapidity, energy, and success, and of supplying the Troops while they are engaged in that service (as they are more precarious) have been and still continue to be the great objects of my concern and attention.

Heavy Cannon, Ordnance Stores and Ammunition to a pretty large Amount, are now forwarding. General Knox, in whose immediate province these Arrangements are, who knows our whole resources, is making every exertion to furnish a competent supply, and will be on the spot to remedy every deficiency, as far as the circumstances will possibly admit.

Having also, from the first moment, been extremely anxious respecting the *Supplies* of the Army (in which, I comprehended not only Provisions of the Bread and Meat kind etc. but also Forage and the means of transportation) I had written pressingly to the Governors of Maryland and Virginia on that subject previous to the receipt of your favor of the 21st of August. I have since reiterated my Entreaties, and enforced in the strongest terms I was capable of using, the Requisitions for Specific Supplies made by Congress, and now again called for by the Superintendent of Finance from the States of Jersey, Delaware, and Maryland, and as to the supplies of Pennsylvania, we

THE HORSE AMERICA THROWING HIS MASTER

A British cartoon, 1779

SURRENDER AT YORKTOWN

are to look for them, from the Financier himself. I hope and trust the efforts of these States and of Virginia will be uncommonly great and proportionate to the Magnitude of the object before us.

In Order to introduce some kind of System and Method in our Supplies, to know with certainty what may be depended upon, and to put the business in the best possible train of execution, I shall send forward the Heads of Departments as soon as their presence can be dispensed with. I have spoken to the Surgeon General respecting Hospital Stores and Medicines, all that can be done will be done in that department.

As to Cloathing I am sorry to inform you, little is to be expected, except in the Article of Shoes, of which a full supply will be sent on.

In my progress to the Southward, I shall take care, as far as practicable, to make all the Arrangements necessary for the Operation in view, and to impress the Executives, with an idea of the absolute necessity of furnishing their quotas of Supplies regularly, as we have no other resources to rely upon for the support of the Army, and especially, as I am very apprehensive, that a quantity of 1500 Barrels of salted Provisions which I had ordered to be shipped under Convoy of the Count de Barras, did not arrive in time for that purpose.

But my dear Marquis, I am distressed beyond expression, to know what is become of the Count de Grasse, and for fear the English Fleet, by occupying the Chesapeake (towards which my last accounts say they were steering) should frustrate all our flattering prospects in that quarter. I am also not a little solicitous for the Count de Barras, who was to have sailed from Rhode Island on the 23d Ulto. and from whom I have heard nothing since that time. Of many contingencies we will hope for the most propitious events.

Should the retreat of Lord Cornwallis by water, be cut off by the arrival of either of the French Fleets, I am persuaded you will do all in your power to prevent his escape by land. May that great felicity be reserved for you!

You See, how critically important the present Moment is: for my own part I am determined still to persist, with unremitting ardour in my present Plan, unless some inevitable and insuperable obstacles are thrown in our way.

Adieu my Dear Marquis! If you get any thing New from any quarter, send it I pray you *on the Spur of Speed*, for I am almost all impatience and anxiety.

—FITZPATRICK, ed., *Writings of Washington*, XXIII, 75-77.

5. "SUCH A TORRENT OF GOOD NEWS"

Colonel St. George Tucker of the Virginia militia to his wife.

Williamsburg, September 5, 1781

. . . Hear then, my Fanny, from me what perhaps you have not heard yet from good authority. About the middle of last week twenty-nine ships of the line and four frigates arrived in our bay, with four thousand land forces sent to our assistance by Louis the Great. Besides these there are three thousand marines to be landed in case of an emergency. Of the fleet there are ten sixty-fours; eighteen seventy-fours, and one ship of an hundred and ten guns! A fleet of twelve sail of the line has arrived in the West Indies to keep the enemy still employed in that quarter. Of the troops, three thousand five hundred landed at James Town three days ago and are now on their march to this city. Five hundred are left on board to land at York River. The fleet lies from Lynnhaven bay to the mouth of York River, and some, *we are informed*, have proceeded within two or three miles of the town. The British fleet still lies at York, and their land forces are now in the town.

The Count de Grasse, by a flag, declared to the admiral or the commodore of the British fleet that he would put every man to the sword who should fall into his hands if the fleet was destroyed. *This from report.* Lord Rawdon is actually a prisoner on board the French fleet, having been taken on his way to London with all his plunder. Gov. Bull of Charlestown is in the like predicament.

Our troops lie from four miles beyond this town to near James Town; so that Cornwallis is as effectually hemmed in as our troops were in Charlestown. Our force may now be reckoned to be eight thousand men—of which six thousand are regulars—exclusive of the marines whom I mentioned above.

Nor is this all, for, to my great surprise and pleasure, I was this morning informed from undoubted authority that General Washington is at the Head of Elk with five thousand troops, which are to be embarked from thence in transports sent there for that purpose, of which the Marquis last night received official accounts from General Washington in a letter dated at Chatham.

I have not yet done. The French fleet of ten line-of-battle ships, which lay at Rhode Island, are now actually on the way hither, and are daily expected. Whether the Count de Rochambeau, with his troops, is on board, I know not, nor, indeed, is it very material, I conceive.

If after such a torrent of good news I could wish to add another article, it would be that Lord Cornwallis, with his whole army, were in our possession. But this I hope, in that providence to which I prostrate myself with grateful adoration for the present happy aspect of our affairs, will be the subject of some future letter; or that I may, to the happiness of seeing you again, add that of being able to give you the first notice of so important and so happy an event.

My paper would blush to contain matters of lesser moment after what I have written.

—TUCKER, "Letter," *Magazine of American History*, VII, 210.

6. "WE HAVE GOT HIM HANDSOMELY IN A PUDDING BAG"

General George Weedon of Virginia to Nathanael Greene.

Fredericksburg, September 5, 1781

The business with his Lordship in this State will very soon be at an end, for suppose you know e'er this that we have got him handsomly in a pudding bag with 5000 land forces and about 60 ships including transports.

Count de Grasse took possession of Chesapeak the 1st instant. Cornwallis with his whole force is in York. Four 32-gunn ships have entered York River, and others have secured James River. Gen. De St. [illegible] with 3000 men are landing to reinforce the Marquis and 3000 more are on their march from the northward. His Excellency Gen. Washington it is supposed will pay this armament a visit. Precautions are taken to prevent his Lordship from sliping over York River to plague you again, and if our stars dont most wonderfully deceive us, we shall shortly do his business.

You have stood beating like [illegible]. I have often shuddered for you but, knowing a little of your persevering disposition, have frequently said, "Never fear, the more danger the more honor. I will be bound for my old friend Green notwithstanding this little rebuff." And the event shews it. The success of your operations exceeds the most sanguine expectations, and you not coming into Lord Cornwallis's bate by trapsing after him to Virginia but pursueing the serpent in the South was a most masterly stroke. Please to remember I recommended it to you in the worst of our times here; and urged the propriety of leting us suffer rather than not eradicate the poison in that quarter. I well knew the line you would adopt, and only mentioned it to show you that I thought as you did, and nothing has gained you more real eclat than your wise disposition of the troops.

Our new governor is a military man and I promise you nothing will be wanting (that government can satisfy) to facilitate our plans. . . .

. . . Count de Grasse has 27 line-of-battle ships and six frigates besides the Rhode Island fleet, and I think, my dear fellow, there is little risque of our ever being the juniors at sea again. Indeed I hope to see us all set off for South Carolina the moment we do the business here. . . .

I am all on fire. By the Great God of War, I think we may all hand up our swords by the last of the year in perfect peace and security! When I first set down to write intended (if the fever wan't too severe) to have taken you first to the Marquis and Count de Grasse, looking into affairs there, to have whisked you over into the State of New York, nay to have dined you with Gen. W[ashington] and Count Rochambeau; then just touching at the West Indies, to have introduced you to Hyder Alley Khan in the East, and then to have delivered [you] safe over to the guards at High Hills of Santee. But this being a work too much for a sick man, let it suffice to tell you our affairs in all this quarter continue to flourish.

—Weedon, Letter, Morgan Library.

II. DE GRASSE'S NAVAL VICTORY

On September 1, the day the British became aware of the true objectives of the American march southward, Graves and Hood cleared Sandy Hook to intercept De Grasse's West Indian fleet and Barras's supporting squadron which had left Newport three days earlier. De Grasse won the race to the Chesapeake. French cruisers took up positions in the James River to prevent Cornwallis from crossing and escaping to the south. Others sealed off the mouth of the York. The remainder of the main fleet kept watch at the mouth of the Chesapeake. Contact with the British fleet was made on September 5. Outnumbered by 24 heavy ships of the French to 19 of their own, the British allowed themselves to be hopelessly outmaneuvered as well. With his own fleet running in formation before the wind, Graves might have smashed the French fleet before it cleared Cape Henry, and again when the French van became separated from the center and rear. Graves failed to exploit his opportunities, and according to his junior, Sir Samuel Hood, the defeat of the British was the result of Graves's tactical blunders. The action was indecisive. By the time Graves considered renewing it, De Grasse had been reinforced by Barras, and the combined French fleets blocked passage to Chesapeake Bay. Abandoning the issue, Graves returned to New York and left Cornwallis to his fate. "We cannot succour him, nor venture to keep the sea any longer," Graves wrote Lord Sandwich on September 14.

1. DE GRASSE DRIVES OFF THE ENGLISH RESCUE FLEET

Journal of an anonymous French naval officer with the fleet of Admiral de Grasse.

... On the evening of the same day [September 2, 1781], M. du Portail, a French officer, dispatched by Generals Washington and Rochambeau, announced the departure of the squadron of Count de Barras, escorting the artillery and munitions necessary for the projected siege; he was also directed to ask the assistance of the light vessels of the fleet, to enable the army, on arriving at Baltimore, to come down the Elk by water. The admiral, in the absence of his boats, ordered the vessels of his fleet under 64's to prepare for this service. They were ready to sail September 5th, when the enemy's fleet was signaled.

It had been necessary to post ships-of-the-line at the mouth of the James and York to blockade by sea Lord Cornwallis's army and all the transports attached to his army; these had to be left at their stations; thus the fleet, reduced to twenty-four vessels, had orders to form, at noon, a line in order of swiftness, the tide favoring it at that hour. This movement was executed with such precision and boldness, in spite of the absence of the best-drilled part of the crew, that the enemy, doubtless taken by surprise, at once wore so as to be on the same tack as the French fleet. It had the cape E. and E. N. E.; in this position, being to leeward, it awaited the enemy's attack.

The issue of the expedition, the vacancy left by the crews employed in the debarkation, the fear of getting too far from the mouths of the York and James rivers, and the fear lest the English fleet, by its known superior sailing, should succeed in getting between these mouths and the French fleet, all obliged it to keep on the defensive. The enemy held the weather gage in excess. Their balls did not come near enough to the French to receive a reply. There was no appearance that the combat would become very warm, but the winds ordered otherwise; they shifted till they came to the northeast and forced the English to attack.

The two vans having come so close as to be almost within pistol shot, the fire was long well sustained, and the affair seemed about to be decisive, when Admiral Hood made a signal to the English rear division, which he commanded, to bear down on the French rear. The admiral witnessed this movement with pleasure and prepared to tack his whole fleet together, bearing N. N. W., which would inevitably have thrown the English line into confusion, but Admiral Graves anticipated him and signaled his whole fleet to keep the wind. The heads of the two fleets gradually fell off in consequence of this new order of the English admiral, and the fire ceased at 6½, P. M.

The French fleet passed the night in the presence of the enemy in line of battle, the fires in all the vessels lighted. These signs of victory were not belied in the morning, for we perceived by the sailing of the English that they had suffered greatly; so that during the night of the 9th-10th, they had to blow up the *Terrible*, 64, themselves, and another put into the Hook in a most wretched plight.

The two fleets, in sight of each other, spent the 6th of September in repairing, favored by the calm or rather by the feeble north wind that continued till 4 o'clock. The wind then came from the southwest, and the French availed themselves of it to approach the enemy. It was too late to engage again, and they lay that night as the preceding.

On the 7th of September at daybreak, the French fleet veered and tacked together to attack the head of the enemy's line; he made his van take the opposite tack; as the second English vessel wore, the French van had orders to use all efforts against the enemy; but the English fleet wore and formed a line of battle behind the last vessel. This movement withdrew the English from the French, who, to sail along the enemy's line, were unable to come up except by edging away while the English had studding sails. The variable winds and storms that sprang up in every direction then separated the two fleets.

On the 8th of September the wind was very fresh, and the fleets kept far apart. The English held the north, and it was precisely from this direction that the French expected the squadron of M. de Barras from Newport. It was very essential to gain the weather gage of the enemy, to prevent his revenging himself upon that squadron, composed of only seven ships of the line and one of 50; it escorted all the siege artillery, an object of vital importance. The fleet sailed northward, and at 6 P. M., the enemy lay N. N. W., and N. W. The weather gage thus gained, the French fleet hoped to preserve it to engage in the morning; but the enemy's fleet instantly wore. At 8 P. M., it made signals, and it was thought that they wished to try to get into Chesapeake Bay before us, the more so as on the 6th two frigates detached from the English fleet had entered at full sail.

While the fleets were observing each other, the wind fell during the night, and in the morning, September 9th, a squadron was discovered, though its flag could not be distinguished. The French fleet bore down on it in line of battle, but lost sight of it during the day. It was the squadron of M. de Barras, which anchored on the 10th in Chesapeake Bay. On the same day the French fleet, no longer discovering anything, took its route for the same bay, where it anchored the 11th; two English frigates, the *Iris* and *Richmond*, those detached from the enemy's fleet on the 6th, were taken as they were getting out to rejoin it, by the *Aigrette* and *Diligente*, which were chasing in front of the fleet. They paid dearly for the petty advantage of cutting the buoys which the fleet had left at the anchorage, on hoisting sail September 5.

—SHEA, ed., *Operations of the French Fleet*, pp. 154-158.

2. CLINTON IS "PREPARED TO HEAR THE WORST"

All this time [early in September 1781] I was so confident of our naval strength and Lord Cornwallis' capacity for retaining his post, at least as long as his provisions lasted, that I kept 5000 select troops ready in transports for joining him the instant I should hear that Admiral Graves had cleared the Chesapeake of the enemy's ships and a safe passage was opened for their going thither. For several experienced, sensible officers of rank who had lately left His Lordship at Yorktown were clearly of opinion, which they delivered in council, *that the position he was in might be defended with the troops he then had against twenty thousand assailants for at least three weeks after opened trenches.* And indeed the plans of the ground about Yorktown taken by both English and French officers, which I have since seen, seem strongly to favor this opinion and show that it was not ill founded, as they all represent the exterior position which Lord Cornwallis first occupied to be a space of ground somewhat higher than that round it, between *two impracticable ravines* ascending from the river and not four hundred yards asunder at their extremity, and commanding not only the approaches from the country but, as Mr. Washington expresses it in his letter to Congress, in a near advance all the rest of His Lordship's works in front of the town.

But, when I received the admiral's letter of the 9th of September favoring me with an account of his action on the 5th, I confess my faith in our naval superiority began to waver. However, as I flattered myself (and the admiral still believed it) that Barras' squadron composed part of the French fleet on that day, I was still inclined to hope that Admiral Digby's arrival, which was hourly expected, and the addition of the *Prudent* and the *Robust*, which were now refitted, would soon turn the scale in our favor and enable me to join His Lordship with such a body of troops as might not only dissipate every appearance of danger, but even procure some decisive advantage over the enemy.

This very unpleasant state of doubt, indecision and hope continued until the 23d, when the arrival of Lord Cornwallis' letter of the 16th and 17th of September informed us that Barras' squadron had not been in the action of the 5th, and that his junction with the Count de Grasse augmented the French fleet to thirty-six sail of the line. So unexpected a naval superiority on the side of the enemy—which far exceeded everything we had in prospect—was not a little alarming, and seemed to call for more than common exertion to evade the impending ruin. I consequently solicited an immediate conference in full council with the flag officers of the fleet (which had arrived at Sandy Hook on the 19th), when it was unanimously resolved that above 5000 troops should be embarked in the King's ships as soon as they could be refitted, and every possible effort made to form a junction with the army at Yorktown. A letter was consequently dispatched to Earl Cornwallis, with the approbation of the council, to inform him of their resolution *and that there was every reason to hope we should start from New York about the 5th of October,* to which I had an opportunity of adding that Admiral Digby was just arrived with three ships of the line.

But I must confess that, after I was thus fully apprised of the enemy's strength and informed by the admiral of the crippled condition of his fleet, I should not have been greatly displeased to have heard that Lord Cornwallis had made his escape to Carolina with everything he could take with him. For I could not well comprehend the meaning of His Lordship's declaration in his letter of the 16th that, *if he had no hopes of relief*, he would rather risk an action than defend his half-finished works, but [that], as I said Admiral Digby was hourly expected and *promised every exertion* to assist him, he did not think himself justifiable in putting the fate of the war on so desperate an attempt—as, upon recurring to the letters His Lordship referred to, I could not find that I had promised in them any exertions but *my own*, which I told him must depend upon Admiral Graves' success against De Grasse. But, the admiral's efforts having failed, and it appearing from His Lordship's postscript of the 17th that he knew the French ships of the line then investing his post were at least one-third in number more than we had any probability of even after Admiral Digby should join us, it was manifest His Lordship *could have no hopes of relief*.

Wherefore I was convinced, by his desiring me to *be prepared to hear the worst*, that upon this intelligence His Lordship had resumed his first idea of forcing his way through the enemy before Mr. Washington's junction with Lafayette, and retiring to the southward. But I happened to be single in this opinion, as all the other general officers in council judged the expression *worst* to mean something more serious than *retreat* arising from the unfinished state of His Lordship's works. It was accordingly proposed to their consideration whether a movement into Jersey, threatening Philadelphia, might not be made, provided it could be done without the risk of impeding the principal object we had in view, which was an attempt to join His Lordship in York River. But the general officers were unanimously of opinion that no delay whatsoever should be hazarded as long as we had any reason to expect the fleet would be ready to receive us. And indeed I readily concurred with this opinion, from my being perfectly convinced that nothing but a direct move to the Chesapeake and our being able, after forcing the French fleet, to effect a junction with His Lordship could be now of the least use toward saving the posts of York and Gloucester, or even a part of Lord Cornwallis' army.

—CLINTON, *The American Rebellion*, pp. 337-340.

III. THE SIEGE

Cornwallis occupied Yorktown and Gloucester, on the opposite shore, and pushed through an elaborate system of fortifications. Promptly on their arrival at Williamsburg between September 14 and 24 the allied forces took up siege positions before Yorktown, the Americans moving into a camp on the right and the French on the left, together forming a semicircle around Cornwallis' defenses. Across the river on the Gloucester shore the Duc de Lauzun hemmed in Tarleton. A great artillery barrage opened up on October 9, when Washington touched off the first cannon shot. The climax was reached with the storming by bayonet of two British redoubts near the river, Nos. 9 and 10. The French, under Lieutenant Colonel, the Count Guillaume de Deux-Ponts, were ordered to seize the former redoubt; the American assigned to lead the attack on No. 10 was Alexander Hamilton. Both officers executed their assignments brilliantly, Hamilton with comparatively light casualties.

Cornwallis still had one desperate chance—a night passage of his troops by water to Gloucester and a break-through northward. But a sudden storm forced him to abandon the project. Although he still had considerable ammunition, the British commander felt that there was no way out now but surrender.

It was not until October 17 that Clinton, with his usual timidity and indecision, dispatched a fleet to relieve Cornwallis. Before then Washington was obliged to use powerful arguments to keep De Grasse at his station in the Chesapeake. By the time the British fleet reached Cape Charles a schooner informed the commanders that Cornwallis had surrendered.

1. "Cornwallis May Now Tremble for His Fate"

Colonel St. George Tucker to his wife.

Williamsburg, September 15, 1781

I wrote you yesterday that General Washington had not yet arrived. About four o'clock in the afternoon his approach was announced. He had passed our camp—which is now in the rear of the whole army—before we had time to parade the militia. The French line had just time to form. The Continentals had more leisure. He approached without any pomp or parade, attended only by a few horsemen and his own servants. The Count de Rochambeau and Gen. Hand, with one or two more officers, were with him. I met him as I was endeavoring to get to camp from town in order to parade the brigade; but he had already passed it. To my great surprise he recognized my features and spoke to me immediately by name. Gen. Nelson, the Marquis, etc., rode up immediately after. Never was more joy painted in any countenances than theirs. The Marquis rode up with precipitation, clasped the General in his arms and embraced him with an ardor not easily described.

The whole army and all the town were presently in motion. The General—at the request of the Marquis de St. Simon—rode through the French lines. The troops were paraded for the purpose and cut a most splendid figure. He then visited the Continental line. As he entered the camp the cannon from the park of artillery and from every brigade announced the happy event. His train by this time was much increased; and men, women and children seemed to vie with each other in demonstrations of joy and eagerness to see their beloved countryman. His quarters are at Mr. Wythe's [George Wythe, signer of the Declaration of Independence] house. Aunt Betty has the honor of the Count de Rochambeau to lodge at her house.

We are all alive and so sanguine in our hopes that nothing can be conceived more different than the countenances of the same men at this time and on the first of June.

The troops which were to attend the General are coming down the bay; a part—if not all—being already embarked at the Head of Elk.

Cornwallis may now tremble for his fate, for nothing but some extraordinary interposition of his guardian angels seems capable of saving him and his whole army from captivity. . . .

—Tucker, "The Southern Campaign," *Magazine of American History,* VII, 212-213.

2. WASHINGTON BEGS DE GRASSE TO STAY IN THE CHESAPEAKE

George Washington to Comte de Grasse.

Williamsburg, September 25, 1781

I cannot conceal from your Excellency the painful anxiety under which I have laboured since the receipt of the letter with which you honored me on the 23d inst.

The naval movements which Your Excellency states there as possible considering the intelligence communicated to you by the baron de Clossen, make it incumbent upon me to represent the consequences that wd arise from them, and to urge a perseverance in the plan already agreed upon. Give me leave in the first place to repeat to Yr Excellency that the enterprise against York under the protection of your Ships is as certain as any military operation can be rendered by a decisive superiority of strength and means; that it is in fact reducible to calculation, and that the surrender of the british Garrison will be so important in itself and its consequences, that it must necessarily go a great way towards terminating the war, and securing the invaluable objects of it to the Allies.

Your Excellency's departure from the Chesapeake by affordg an opening for the succour of York, which the enemy wd instantly avail himself of, would frustrate these brilliant prospects, and the consequence would be not only the disgrace and loss of renouncing an enterprise, upon which the fairest expectations of the Allies have been founded, after the most expensive preparations and uncommon exertions and fatigues; but the disbanding perhaps the whole Army for want of provisions.

The present Theatre of the War is totally deficient in means of land transportation, being intersected by large rivers, and the whole dependance for interior communication being upon small Vessels. The Country has been much exhausted besides by the ravages of the enemy and the subsistence of our own Army; that our supplies can only be drawn from a distance and under cover of a fleet Mistress of the Chesapeake.

I most earnestly entreat Your Excellency farther to consider that if the present opportunity shd be missed; that if you shld withdraw your maritime force from the position agreed upon, that no future day can restore us a similar occasion for striking a decisive blow; that the british will be indefatigable in strengthening their most important maritime points, and that the epoch of an honorable peace will be more remote than ever.

The confidence with which I feel myself inspired by the energy of character and the naval talents which so eminently distinguish Yr Excellency leaves me no doubt that upon a consideration of the consequences which must follow your departure from the Chesapeake, that Yr Excellency will determine upon the possible measure which the dearest interests of the common cause wd dictate.

I had invariably flattered myself from the accounts given me by skilful mariners, that Your Excellys position, moored in the Chesapeake might be made so respectable, as to bid defiance to any attempt on the pt of the british fleet, at the same time that it wd support the operations of a siege, secure the transportation of our supplies by water and oeconomise the most precious time by facilitating the debarkation of our heavy Artillery and stores conveniently to the trenches in York River. It is to be observed that the strength of the enemy's reinforcement announced under Admiral Digby as we have the intelligence from the british, may not only be exaggerated, but altogether a finesse, and supposing the account consistent with truth: their total force it was hoped wd. not put them in condition to attack with any prospect of success.

If the stationary position which had been agreed upon should be found utterly impracticable, there is an alternative which however inferior considered relatively to the support and facility of our land operations would save our affairs from ruin; this is to cruise with Your Excellency's fleet within view of the capes, so as effectually to prevent the entrance of any british Vessels.

Upon the whole, I shd. esteem myself deficient in my duty to the common cause of France and America, if I did not persevere in entreating Yr. Excellency to resume the plans that have been so happily arranged, and if invincible maritime reasons prevent, I depend as a last resource upon Your Excellency's pursuing the alternative above mentioned and rendering the Chesapeake inaccessible to any Enemys Vessel.

However the British Admiral may manoeuvre and endeavour to divert Yr Excellency from the object in view, I can hardly admit a belief that it can be his serious intention to engage in a general action with a Fleet whose force will be superior supposing the most flattering accounts for the British to be true; past experience having taught them to engage with caution even upon equal terms, and forced from them acknowledgements, which prove the respect with which they have been inspired.

Let me add Sir that even a momentary absence of the french fleet may expose us to the loss of the british Garrison at York as in the present state of affairs Ld Cornwallis might effect the evacuation with the loss of his Artillery and baggage and such a sacrifice of men as his object would evidently justify.

The Marquis de la fayette who does me the honor to bear this to Yr Excellency will explain many peculiarities of our situation which could not well be comprised in a letter; his candour and abilities are well known to Yr Excellency and entitle him to the fullest confidence in treating the most important interests. I have earnestly requested him not to proceed any farther than the Cape for fear of accidents shd Yr. Excellency have put to sea; in this case he will dispatch a Letter to Yr Excellency in addition to this. I have the honor etc.

—Fitzpatrick, ed., *Writings of Washington,* XXIII, 136-139.

3. The Duc de Lauzun Proves That Tarleton Is Not Irresistible

Memoirs of Armand-Louis de Gontaut, Duc de Lauzun, French cavalry officer under General de Choisy.

Just as we reached the Gloucester plain [on October 3, 1781] some

Virginia state dragoons came up in great fright and told us that they had seen
the English dragoons out and that for fear of accident they had hurried to us
at full speed without stopping to see anything more. I went forward to learn
what I could. I saw a very pretty woman at the door of a little farmhouse
on the high road; I went up to her and questioned her; she told me that Colonel
Tarleton had left her house a moment before; that he was very eager to shake
hands with the French Duke. I assured her that I had come on purpose to
gratify him. She seemed very sorry for me, judging from experience, I suppose, that Tarleton was irresistible; the American troops seemed to be of the
same opinion.

I was not a hundred steps from the house when I heard pistol shots from
my advance guard. I hurried forward at full speed to find a piece of ground
where I could form a line of battle. As I arrived I saw the English cavalry in
force three times my own; I charged it without halting; we met hand to hand.
Tarleton saw me and rode towards me with pistol raised. We were about to
fight single-handed between the two troops when his horse was thrown by
one of his own dragoons pursued by one of my lancers. I rode up to him to
capture him; a troop of English dragoons rode in between us and covered his
retreat; he left his horse with me. He charged me twice without breaking
my line; I charged the third time, overthrew a part of his cavalry and drove
him within the entrenchment of Gloucester. He lost an officer, some fifty
men, and I took quite a number of prisoners.

—LAUZUN, "Memoirs," *Magazine of American History*, VI, 53.

4. THE SIEGE BEGINS

Journal of Colonel Jonathan Trumbull, secretary to George Washington.

[*September*] *28*. A most wonderful and very observable coincidence of
favorable circumstances having concentered our various and extended preparations, the army commences its march from Williamsburg and approaches
within two miles of York Town. The enemy on our approach make some
shew of opposition from their cavalry, but upon our bringing up some field
pieces and making a few shot, they retire, and we take a quiet position for
the night.

The General and family sleep in the field without any other covering than
the canopy of the heavens and the small spreading branches of a tree, which
will probably be rendered venerable from this circumstance for a length of
time to come. Previous to this movement the enemies post at Glocester on the
opposite side of York River had been invested by a body of militia under the
command of Gen. Wedon, the French Legion of the Duke de Lauzun, and
a body of French troops from the fleet all under the command of Brig. Gen.
De Choisey. By the approach of the main body, and lying of the French ships
in the mouth of the river, the enemy were now completely invested, except
by water above the town, where they are yet open, and their boats are troublesome up the river for some distance. To close them on this side the General
has proposed it to the admiral to run some ships above the town and to take
their station there.

[*September*] *29*. The American troops take their station in the front of the enemies works, extend from the left of Pigeon Quarter to Moor's Mill on Wormley's Creek, near the river.

The French troops occupy the left of the Americans and extend to the river above the town. No opposition this day except a few shots from the extream works, and small firing from their jagers and our rifle men.

[*September*] *30*. In the morning it is discovered that the enemy have evacuated all their exterior works, and retired to their interior defence near the town. We immediately take possession of Pigeon Quarter and hill, and of the enemies' redoubts, and find ourselves very unexpectedly upon very advantageous ground, commanding their line of works in near approach. Scarce a gun fired this day. At night our troops begin to throw up some works and to take advantage of the enemies' evacuated labours.

Colonel Scammel,* being officer of the day, is cruelly wounded and taken prisoner while reconnoitering.

—TRUMBULL, "Journal," *Mass. Hist. Soc. Proc.*, XIV, 334-335.

5. ADVANCE OF THE SIEGEWORKS

Entries for October 2 and 4-9, 1781, in the journal of Colonel Richard Butler, and for October 3 and 7 in the diary of James Duncan, both of the Pennsylvania Line.

[Butler] *October 2d*.—The fire of the enemy more severe this morning; about 10 o'clock, A.M. they brought up two 18-pounders in addition to what they brought yesterday. They fired severely all day; the shot expended amounted to 351 between sun-rise and sun-set. Wayne's brigade ordered to camp for convenience, but still the covering party till sun-set. The fire of the enemy continued all night. About 10 o'clock, P.M., a heavy firing of the ships in the bay. I reconnoitered the post at Gloster and the shipping, which I compute at 10 sail; the Gloster post not strong—I think, by the size of the camp, 1,000 men; their works not regular, they have one good water battery on the York side; I observed a good work close by the bank with four embrasures, the ground very good for approaches. In general our works go on slow, the heavy artillery hard to get up; not one piece of cannon as yet fired at them. Indeed, I discover very plainly that we are young soldiers in a siege; however, we are determined to benefit ourselves by experience; one virtue we possess, that is perseverance. . . .

[Duncan] *October 3*.—Last night four men of our regiment, detached with the first brigade, were unfortunately killed (on covering party) by one ball; one of the men belonged to my own company (Smith), a loss I shall ever regret, as he was, without exception, one of the finest men in the army. A militia man this day, possessed of more bravery and [*sic*] prudence, stood constantly on the parapet and d——d his soul if he would dodge for the buggers. He had escaped longer than could have been expected, and, growing fool-hardy, brandished his spade at every ball that was fired, till, unfortunately, a ball came and put an end to his capers. . . .

---

* Later information revealed that Alexander Scammell had been shot in the back by a British soldier after he surrendered, and died of his wounds.

[Butler] *October 4th.*—Very little firing all day. Wayne and Colonel Butler went to reconnoiter on the York River side, the enemy very busy forming new works. Two deserters from the enemy, who report that Cornwallis' army is very sickly, to the amount of 2000 men in the hospital, and that the troops had scarce ground to live on, their shipping in a very naked state and their cavalry very scarce of forage. 2000 French marines landed on Gloster side from Count de Grasse at 9 o'clock P.M. A smart firing of small arms, which brought a very heavy cannonade all night.

[Butler] *October 5th.*—Cannonading all morning. Our part increases fast, and things go on well. To-day about 4 o'clock P.M., Corporal Organ, a brave and honest soldier, was unfortunately killed by a cannon shot; a great deal of firing through the night. Pennsylvania and Maryland Militia for gabion making to-morrow. Confirmation of General Green's success came to the Commander-in-Chief.

[Butler] *October 6th.*—Pennsylvania and some other troops went to gabion making; finished a great number and carried them to the right near the York River, 400 paces from the enemy. The first parallel and other works being laid out by the engineer; a body of troops ordered under Generals Lincoln, Wayne and Clinton to break ground and form works, the materials being got ready and brought previously to the spot. The enemy kept up a severe cannonade all night; it began on the left of the allied army, who lost some men killed and one officer and several men wounded; their intention was to possess the enemy's advanced redoubt on the York River, but one of the dragoons having deserted, the enemy discovered the intention, which caused the enemy to keep up an (almost) incessant fire that way through the night; the allied army, finding the enemy too well apprized, contented themselves with going on with their work. The American part of the army on duty made great progress in forming lines and batteries without the loss of a man.

[Butler] *October 7th.*—The whole continued at work, notwithstanding the enemies fire through the whole day and night. About day light, a very sharp fire of small arms commenced, succeeded by artillery; they go on well, and our loss as yet very trifling; indeed the siege appears to be no more than an experimental movement.

[Duncan] *October 7th.*— . . . The trenches were this day to be enlivened with drums beating and colors flying, and this honor was conferred on our division of light infantry. . . . Immediately upon our arrival the colors were planted on the parapet with this motto: *Manus haec inimica tyrannis.* Our next maneuver was rather extraordinary. We were ordered to mount the bank, front the enemy, and there by word of command go through all the ceremony of soldiery, ordering and grounding our arms; and although the enemy had been firing a little before, they did not now give us a single shot. I suppose their astonishment at our conduct must have prevented them, for I can assign no other reason. Colonel Hamilton gave these orders, and although I esteem him one of the first officers in the American army, must beg leave in this instance to think he wantonly exposed the lives of his men. . . .

[Butler] *October 8th, 1781.*—The division of Steuben for the trenches to-day. This is composed of the Virginia, Maryland and Pennsylvania troops.

The enemy continued to cannonade, mounted at 12 o'clock. The enemy kept hard at work, and fired incessantly on our fatigue parties, who really wrought hard and completed one large battery on our extreme right, on the bank of the river, on which three 29-pounders, three 18-pounders, two 10-inch mortars and two 8-inch howitzers were mounted. The Marquis de St. Simon had a battery completed on the extreme left, of eight 18 and 12-pounders, two 10-inch mortars and two 8-inch howitzers, both which batteries were made ready to open at the same instant. A very fine battery of twelve 32, 24, and 18-pounders, six 10-inch mortars and six 8-inch howitzers was forwarded, with small batteries on the right and left of this grand centre battery. The enemy seem embarrassed, confused and indeterminate; their fire seems feeble to what might be expected; their works, too, are not formed on any regular plan, but thrown up in a hurry occasionally, and although we have not as yet fired one shot from a piece of artillery, they are as cautious as if the heaviest fire was kept up.

[Butler] *October 9th.*—Relieved by Major General Lincoln's division. This day, at 3 o'clock, P.M., the batteries of Lamb and the Marquis de St. Simon opened with great elegance and were quickly followed. The Commander-in-Chief paid the allies the compliment of firing first. The shot and shells flew incessantly through the night, dismounted the guns of the enemy and destroyed many of their embrasures.

—BUTLER, "Journal," *Historical Magazine*, VIII, 107-108; DUNCAN, "Diary," *Pennsylvania Archives*, 2d Ser., XV, 748-752.

6. WASHINGTON UP FRONT WITH THE SAPPERS AND MINERS

Narrative of Sergeant James Sullivan Martin, from Connecticut.

We now began to make preparations for laying close siege to the enemy. We had holed him and nothing remained but to dig him out. Accordingly, after taking every precaution to prevent his escape, settled our guards, provided fascines and gabions, made platforms for the batteries, to be laid down when needed, brought on our battering pieces, ammunition, etc., on the fifth of October we began to put our plans into execution.

One third part of all the troops were put in requisition to be employed in opening the trenches. A third part of our sappers and miners were ordered out this night to assist the engineers in laying out the works. It was a very dark and rainy night. However, we repaired to the place and began by following the engineers and laying laths of pine wood end to end upon the line marked out by the officers for the trenches. We had not proceeded far in the business before the engineers ordered us to desist and remain where we were, and be sure not to straggle a foot from the spot while they were absent from us.

In a few minutes after their departure, there came a man alone to us, having on a surtout, as we conjectured (it being exceeding dark), and inquired for the engineers. We now began to be a little jealous for our safety, being alone and without arms, and within forty rods of the British trenches. The stranger inquired what troops we were; talked familiarly with us a few minutes, when, being informed which way the officers had gone, he went off in the same direction, after strictly charging us, in case we should be taken prisoners, not to discover to the enemy what troops we were. We were obliged to him for his kind advice, but we considered ourselves as standing in no great need of it; for we knew as well as he did that sappers and miners were allowed no quarters, at least are entitled to none by the laws of warfare, and of course should take care, if taken and the enemy did not find us out, not to betray our own secret.

In a short time the engineers returned and the aforementioned stranger with them; they discoursed together sometime, when, by the officers often calling him "Your Excellency," we discovered that it was Gen. Washington. Had we dared, we might have cautioned him for exposing himself so carelessly to danger at such a time, and doubtless he would have taken it in good part if we had. But nothing ill happened to either him or ourselves.

It coming on to rain hard, we were ordered back to our tents, and nothing more was done that night. The next night, which was the sixth of October, the same men were ordered to the lines that had been there the night before. We this night completed laying out the works. The troops of the line were there ready with entrenching tools and began to entrench, after General Washington had struck a few blows with a pickaxe, a mere ceremony, that it might be said, "Gen. Washington with his own hands first broke ground at the siege of Yorktown." The ground was sandy and soft, and the men employed that night eat no "idle bread" (and I question if they eat any other), so that by daylight they had covered themselves from danger from the enemy's shot, who, it appeared, never mistrusted that we were so near them the whole night, their attention being directed to another quarter. There was upon the right of their works a marsh; our people had sent to the western side of this marsh a detachment to make a number of fires, by which, and our men often passing before the fires, the British were led to imagine that we were about some secret mischief there, and consquently directed their whole fire to that quarter, while we were entrenching literally under their noses.

As soon as it was day they perceived their mistake and began to fire where they ought to have done sooner. They brought out a fieldpiece or two without their trenches and discharged several shots at the men who were at work erecting a bomb-battery; but their shot had no effect and they soon gave it over. They had a large bull-dog, and every time they fired he would follow their shots across our trenches. Our officers wished to catch him and oblige him to carry a message from them into the town to his masters, but he looked too formidable for any of us to encounter.

I do not remember, exactly, the number of days we were employed before we got our batteries in readiness to open upon the enemy, but think it was not more than two or three. The French, who were upon our left, had completed their batteries a few hours before us, but were not allowed to discharge their pieces till the American batteries were ready. Our commanding battery was on the near bank of the river and contained ten heavy guns; the next was a bomb-battery of three large mortars; and so on through the whole line; the whole number, American and French, was ninety-two cannon, mortars and howitzers. Our flagstaff was in the ten-gun battery, upon the right of the whole.

I was in the trenches the day that the batteries were to be opened; all were upon the tiptoe of expectation and impatience to see the signal given to open the whole line of batteries, which was to be the hoisting of the American flag in the ten-gun battery. About noon the much-wished-for signal went up. I confess I felt a secret pride swell my heart when I saw the "star-spangled banner" waving majestically in the very faces of our implacable adversaries; it appeared like an omen of success to our enterprize, and so it proved in reality. A simultaneous discharge of all the guns in the line followed, the French troops accompanying it with "Huzza for the Americans!"

It was said that the first shell sent from our batteries entered an elegant house, formerly owned or occupied by the Secretary of State under the British government, and burnt directly over a table surrounded by a large party of British officers at dinner, killing and wounding a number of them;—this was a warm day to the British.

—MARTIN(?), *Narrative of a Revolutionary Soldier*, pp. 166-169.

7. AN ARMY SURGEON DESCRIBES THE GREAT CANNONADE

Journal of Dr. James Thacher.

From the 10th to the 15th [of October 1781], a tremendous and incessant firing from the American and French batteries is kept up, and the enemy return the fire, but with little effect. A red-hot shell from the French battery set fire to the *Charon*, a British 44-gun ship, and two or three smaller vessels at anchor in the river, which were consumed in the night. From the bank of the river I had a fine view of this splendid conflagration. The ships were enwrapped in a torrent of fire, which, spreading with vivid brightness among the combustible rigging, and running with amazing rapidity to the tops of the several masts, while all around was thunder and lightning from our numerous cannon and mortars, and in the darkness of night, presented one of the most sublime and magnificient spectacles which can be imagined. Some of our shells, overreaching the town, are seen to fall into the river and, bursting, throw up columns of water like the spouting of the monsters of the deep.

We have now made further approaches to the town by throwing up a second parallel line and batteries within about three hundred yards; this was effected in the night, and at day-light the enemy were roused to the greatest exertions; the engines of war have raged with redoubled fury and destruction on both sides, no cessation day or night. The French had two officers wounded and fifteen men killed and wounded, and among the Americans, two or three were wounded. I assisted in amputating a man's thigh.

The siege is daily becoming more and more formidable and alarming, and his lordship must view his situation as extremely critical, if not desperate. Being in the trenches every other night and day, I have a fine opportunity of witnessing the sublime and stupendous scene which is continually exhibiting. The bombshells from the besiegers and the besieged are incessantly crossing each others' path in the air. They are clearly visible in the form of a black ball in the day, but in the night they appear like a fiery meteor with a blazing tail, most beautifully brilliant, ascending majestically from the mortar to a certain altitude and gradually descending to the spot where they are destined to execute their work of destruction.

It is astonishing with what accuracy an experienced gunner will make his calculations, that a shell shall fall within a few feet of a given point, and burst at the precise time, though at a great distance. When a shell falls, it whirls round, burrows, and excavates the earth to a considerable extent and, bursting, makes dreadful havoc around. I have more than once witnessed fragments of the mangled bodies and limbs of the British soldiers thrown into the air by the bursting of our shells; and by one from the enemy, Captain White, of the Seventh Massachusetts Regiment, and one soldier were killed and another wounded near where I was standing. About twelve or fourteen men have been killed or wounded within twenty-four hours. I attended at the hospital, amputated a man's arm and assisted in dressing a number of wounds.

The enemy having two redoubts, about three hundred yards in front of their principal works, which enfiladed our intrenchment and impeded our approaches, it was resolved to take possession of them both by assault. The one on the left of the British garrison, bordering on the banks of the river, was assigned to our brigade of light-infantry, under the command of the Marquis de la Fayette. The advanced corps was led on by the intrepid Colonel Hamilton, who had commanded a regiment of light-infantry during the campaign, and assisted by Colonel Gimat.

The assault commenced at eight o'clock in the evening, and the assailants bravely entered the fort with the point of the bayonet without firing a single gun. We suffered the loss of eight men killed and about thirty wounded, among whom Colonel Gimat received a slight wound in his foot, and Major Gibbs, of his excellency's guard, and two other officers were slightly wounded. Major Campbell, who commanded in the fort, was wounded and taken prisoner, with about thirty soldiers; the remainder made their escape. I was desired to visit the wounded in the fort even before the balls had ceased whistling about my ears, and saw a sergeant and eight men dead in the ditch. A captain of our infantry, belonging to New Hampshire, threatened to take the life of Major Campbell to avenge the death of his favorite, Colonel Shammel; but Colonel Hamilton interposed, and not a man was killed after he ceased to resist.

During the assault, the British kept up an incessant firing of cannon and musketry from their whole line. His Excellency General Washington, Generals Lincoln and Knox, with their aids, having dismounted, were standing in an exposed situation waiting the result.

Colonel Cobb, one of General Washington's aids, solicitous for his safety, said to His Excellency, "Sir, you are too much exposed here. Had you not better step a little back?"

"Colonel Cobb," replied His Excellency, "if you are afraid, you have liberty to step back."

The other redoubt on the right of the British lines was assaulted at the same time by a detachment of the French, commanded by the gallant Baron de Viomenil. Such was the ardor displayed by the assailants that all resistance was soon overcome, though at the expense of nearly one hundred men killed and wounded. Of the defenders of the redoubt, eighteen were killed, and one captain and two subaltern officers and forty-two rank and file captured.

Our second parallel line was immediately connected with the two redoubts now taken from the enemy, and some new batteries were thrown up in front of our second parallel line, with a covert way and angling work approaching to less than three hundred yards of their principal forts. These will soon be mantled with cannon and mortars, and when their horrid thundering commences, it must convince his lordship that his post is not invincible, and that submission must soon be his only alternative. Our artillery-men, by the exactness of their aim, make every discharge take effect, so that many of the enemy's guns are entirely silenced, and their works are almost in ruins.

—THACHER, *Military Journal*, pp. 283-286.

8. FATAL DELAY OF THE SECOND BRITISH RELIEF EXPEDITION

Rear Admiral Samuel Hood of the British Navy to George Jackson of the Admiralty.

The *Barfleur* at Sandy Hook, October 14, 1781

On the 24th of last month I attended a consultation of generals and admirals at Sir H. Clinton's, when it was agreed to attempt by the united efforts of army and navy to relieve Lord Cornwallis in the Chesapeake, and I proposed to have three or four fireships immediately prepared, with which the enemy's fleet may possibly be deranged and thrown into some confusion, and thereby give a favourable opening for pushing through it. This was approved, and upwards of 5,000 troops are to be embarked in the King's ships.

While this business was under deliberation, word was brought that Rear-Admiral Digby with the *Canada* and *Lion* were off the Bar. . . . I thank God the disabled ships are now ready, and but for an accident of the *Alcides* driving on board the *Shrewsbury* and carrying away her bowsprit and foreyard, I imagine all the ships would have been here this day; but I hope and trust they will be down tomorrow, and that we shall be moving the day after if the wind will permit. Every moment, my dear Jackson, is precious; and I flattered myself when we came in that we should ere this have been in the Chesapeake, but the repairs of the squadron have gone on unaccountably tedious, which has filled me with apprehension that we shall be too late to give relief to Lord Cornwallis. I pray God grant my fears may prove abortive!

It would, in my humble opinion, have been a most fortunate event had Mr. Graves gone off to Jamaica upon Mr. Digby's arrival as commander-in-chief by commission, and I am persuaded you will think so too, when I relate one circumstance only. On the 7th I received a letter from Mr. Graves, desiring I would meet the flag officers and some captains upon a consultation on board the *London* at ten o'clock the next morning, and acquaint Captain Cornwallis and Captain Reynolds that their company was desired also. Soon after we were assembled, Mr. Graves proposed, and wished to reduce to writing, the following question: "Whether it was practicable to relieve Lord Cornwallis in the Chesapeake?" This astonished me exceedingly, as it seemed plainly to indicate a design of having difficulties started against attempting what the generals and admirals had *most unanimously* agreed to and given under their hands on the 24th of last month, and occasioned my replying immediately that it appeared to me a very unnecessary and improper question, as it had been already maturely discussed and determined upon to be attempted with all the expedition possible; that my opinion had been very strong and pointed (which I was ready to give in writing with my name to it); that an attempt under every risk should be made to force a junction with the troops the commander-in-chief [Sir Thomas Graves] embarks in his Majesty's fleet with the army under General Earl Cornwallis at York; and admitting that junction to be made without much loss, and the provisions landed, I was also of opinion the first favourable opportunity should be embraced of attacking the French fleet, though I own to you I think very meanly of the ability of the present commanding officer. I know he is a *cunning* man, he may be a good theoretical man, but he is certainly a bad practical one, and most clearly proved himself on the 5th of last month to be unequal to the conducting of a great squadron.

If it shall please the Almighty to give success to the arms of his Majesty in the business we are going upon, I think we shall stand a-tiptoe. The *Torbay* and *Prince William* arrived on the 13th, a noble acquisition, and makes my heart bound with joy. Why the *Chatham* is not with us also is matter of astonishment to me.

[P. S.] I trust you will bear in mind that I write to you most *confidentially*. *Desperate* cases require *bold* remedies.

—GRAVES, *Papers*, pp. 116-118.

9. "THE LAST HOPE OF THE BRITISH ARMY"

By Lieutenant Colonel Banastre Tarleton.

A retreat by Gloucester was the only expedient that now presented itself to avert the mortification of a surrender or the destruction of a storm. Though this plan appeared less practicable than when first proposed, and was adopted at this crisis as the last resource, it yet afforded some hopes of success. In the evening [October 16] Earl Cornwallis sent Lord Chewton to Gloucester, with explicit directions for Lieutenant-Colonel Tarleton to prepare some artillery and other requisites from his garrison to accompany the British troops with which his lordship designed to attack Brigadier de Choisy before daybreak, and afterwards retreat through the country. The guards of cavalry and infantry at Tarleton's post were immediately augmented, and many officers were advanced as sentries, to prevent any intelligence being conveyed to the enemy. All the commanding officers of regiments were afterwards acquainted with the intended project, that their corps might be completely assembled and equipped. The spare horses of the garrison were ordered to parade for the benefit of the infantry, and the necessary artillery and waggons were prepared. A number of sailors and soldiers were dispatched with boats from Gloucester, to assist the troops in passing the river.

Earl Cornwallis sent off the first embarkation before eleven o'clock that night, consisting of the light infantry, great part of the brigade of guards, and the 23d Regiment, and purposed himself to pass with the second, when he had finished a letter to General Washington, calculated to excite the humanity of that officer towards the sick, the wounded and the detachment that would be left to capitulate. Much of the small craft had been damaged during the siege; yet it was computed that three trips would be sufficient to convey over all the troops that were necessary for the expedition.

The whole of the first division arrived before midnight, and part of the second had embarked, when a squall, attended with rain, scattered the boats and impeded their return to Gloucester. About two o'clock in the morning the weather began to moderate, when orders were brought to the commanding officers of the corps that had passed, to re-cross the water. As the boats were all on the York side the river, in order to bring over the troops, it required some time to row them to Gloucester, to carry back the infantry of the first embarkation; but soon after daybreak they returned under the fire of the enemy's batteries to Earl Cornwallis, at York town.

Thus expired the last hope of the British army.

—TARLETON, *History of Campaigns in the Southern Provinces*, pp. 396-400.

10. "I HAVE THE MORTIFICATION TO INFORM YOUR EXCELLENCY"

Lord Cornwallis to Sir Henry Clinton.

Yorktown, October 20, 1781

I have the mortification to inform your Excellency that I have been forced to give up the posts of York and Gloucester, and to surrender the troops under my command, by capitulation on the 19th inst. as prisoners of war to the combined forces of America and France.

I never saw this post in a very favourable light, but when I found I was to be attacked in it in so unprepared a state, by so powerful an army and artillery, nothing but the hopes of relief would have induced me to attempt its defence; for I would either have endeavoured to escape to New-York, by rapid marches from the Gloucester side, immediately on the arrival of General Washington's troops at Williamsburgh, or I would notwithstanding the disparity of numbers have attacked them in the open field, where it might have been just possible that fortune would have favoured the gallantry of the handful of troops under my command. But being assured by your Excellency's letters that every possible means would be tried by the navy and army to relieve us, I could not think myself at liberty to venture upon either of those desperate attempts; therefore, after remaining for two days in a strong position in front of this place, in hopes of being attacked, upon observing that the enemy were taking measures which could not fail of turning my left flank in a short time, and receiving on the second evening your letter of the 24th of September informing that the relief would sail about the 5th of October, I withdrew within the works on the night of the 29th of September, hoping by the labour and firmness of the soldiers to protract the defence until you could arrive. Every thing was to be expected from the spirit of the troops, but every disadvantage attended their labour, as the works were to be continued under the enemy's fire, and our stock of intrenching tools, which did not much exceed four hundred when we began to work in the latter end of August, was now much diminished.

The enemy broke ground on the night of the 30th and constructed on that night, and the two following days and nights, two redoubts, which, with some works that had belonged to our outward position, occupied a gorge between two creeks or ravines, which come from the river on each side of the town.

On the night of the 6th of October they made their first parallel, extending from its right on the river to a deep ravine on the left, nearly opposite to the center of this place and embracing our whole left at the distance of six hundred yards. Having perfected this parallel, their batteries opened on the evening of the 9th against our left, and other batteries fired at the same time against a redoubt advanced over the creek upon our right and defended by about one hundred and twenty men of the 23d Regiment and marines, who maintained that post with uncommon gallantry. The fire continued incessant from heavy cannon and from mortars and howitzes, throwing shells from eight to sixteen inches, until all our guns on the left were silenced, our work much damaged, and our loss of men considerable.

On the night of the 11th they began their second parallel, about three hundred yards nearer to us. The troops being much weakened by sickness as well as by the fire of the besiegers, and observing that the enemy had not only secured their flanks but proceeded in every respect with the utmost regularity and caution, I could not venture so large sorties as to hope from them any considerable effect; but otherwise I did every thing in my power to interrupt this work, by opening new embrazures for guns and keeping up a constant fire with all the howitzes and small mortars that we could man.

On the evening of the 14th, they assaulted and carried two redoubts that had been advanced about three hundred yards for the purpose of delaying their approaches and covering our left flank, and during the night included them in their second parallel, on which they continued to work with the utmost exertion.

Being perfectly sensible that our works could not stand many hours after the opening of the batteries of that parallel, we not only continued a constant fire with all our mortars and every gun that could be brought to bear upon it, but a little before daybreak on the morning of the 16th I ordered a sortie of about three hundred and fifty men under the direction of Lieutenant-Colonel Abercrombie to attack two batteries, which appeared to be in the greatest forwardness, and to spike the guns. A detachment of guards with the Eightieth Company of Grenadiers, under the command of Lieutenant-Colonel Lake attacked the one, and one of light infantry under the command of Major Armstrong attacked the other, and both succeeded by forcing the redoubts that covered them, spiking eleven guns, and killing or wounding about one hundred of the French troops, who had the guard of that part of the trenches, and with little loss on our side. This action, though extremely honourable to the officers and soldiers who executed it, proved of little public advantage, for the cannon, having been spiked in a hurry, were soon rendered fit for service again, and before dark the whole parallel and batteries appeared to be nearly complete.

At this time we knew that there was no part of the whole front attacked on which we could show a single gun, and our shells were nearly expended; I therefore had only to chuse between preparing to surrender next day or endeavouring to get off with the greatest part of the troops, and I determined to attempt the latter, reflecting that though it should prove unsuccessful in its immediate object, it might at least delay the enemy in the prosecution of further enterprizes. Sixteen large boats were prepared, and upon other pretexts were ordered to be in readiness to receive troops precisely at ten o'clock. With these I hoped to pass the infantry during the night, abandoning our baggage, and leaving a detachment to capitulate for the town's people and the sick and wounded; on which subject a letter was ready to be delivered to General Washington.

After making my arrangements with the utmost secrecy, the light infantry, greatest part of the Guards and part of the Twenty-Third Regiment landed at Gloucester; but at this critical moment the weather, from being moderate and calm, changed to a most violent storm of wind and rain and drove all the boats, some of which had troops on board, down the river. It was soon evident that the intended passage was impracticable, and the absence of the boats rendered it equally impossible to bring back the troops that had passed; which I had ordered about two in the morning. In this situation, with my little force divided, the enemy's batteries opened at daybreak. The passage between this place and Gloucester was much exposed, but the boats having now returned, they were ordered to bring back the troops that had passed during the night, and they joined us in the forenoon without much loss.

Our works in the mean time were going to ruin, and not having been able to strengthen them by abbatis, nor in any other manner but by a slight fraizing which the enemy's artillery were demolishing wherever they fired, my opinion entirely coincided with that of the engineer and principal officers of the army, that they were in many places assailable in the forenoon, and that by the continuence of the same fire for a few hours longer, they would be in such a state as to render it desperate with our numbers to attempt to maintain them. We at that time could not fire a single gun. Only one eight-inch and little more than an hundred cohorn shells remained. A diversion by the French ships of war that lay at the mouth of York River was to be expected. Our numbers had been diminished by the enemy's fire, but particularly by sickness, and the strength and spirits of those in the works were much exhausted by the fatigue of constant watching and unremitting duty.

Under all these circumstances, I thought it would have been wanton and inhuman to the last degree to sacrifice the lives of this small body of gallant soldiers, who had ever behaved with so much fidelity and courage, by exposing them to an assault, which from the numbers and precautions of the enemy could not fail to succeed. I therefore proposed to capitulate.

—Stevens, ed., *Clinton-Cornwallis Controversy*, II, 205-213.

IV. CORNWALLIS SURRENDERS

Once Cornwallis decided to surrender he had no alternative but to accept Washington's terms. These were, on the whole, both just and generous. The British army was to surrender to the Americans; the navy to the French. Officers were to retain their side arms and private property; soldiers to be kept in

Virginia, Maryland or Pennsylvania; Cornwallis and some other officers per-
mitted to return home on parole. The ceremony itself was to take place on
October 19:

> The garrison of York will march out to a place to be appointed in front
> of the posts, at two o'clock precisely, with shouldered arms, colours cased,
> and drums beating a British or German march. They are then to ground
> their arms, and return to their encampments, where they will remain until
> they are dispatched to the places of their destinations. Two works on the
> Gloucester side will be delivered at one o'clock to a detachment of French
> and American troops appointed to possess them. The garrison will march
> out at three o'clock in the afternoon; the cavalry with their swords drawn,
> trumpets sounding, and the infantry in the manner prescribed for the gar-
> rison of York. They are likewise to return to their encampments until
> they can be finally marched off.

As Cornwallis was not equal to making his surrender in person, his second
in command, General Charles O'Hara, officiated; Washington's second in
command, General Lincoln, received O'Hara's sword.

A New Jersey officer reported that "the British officers in general behaved
like boys who had been whipped at school. Some bit their lips; some pouted;
others cried. Their round, broad-brimmed hats were well-adapted to the oc-
casion, hiding those faces they were ashamed to show."

1. "An Ardent Desire to Spare the Further Effusion of Blood"

A. CORNWALLIS TO WASHINGTON, OCTOBER 17, 1781

I propose a cessation of hostilities for twenty-four hours, and that two
officers may be appointed by each side, to meet at Mr. Moore's house, to settle
terms for the surrender of the posts of York and Gloucester.

B. WASHINGTON TO CORNWALLIS, OCTOBER 17

I have had the Honor of receiving Your Lordship's Letter of this Date.
An Ardent Desire to spare the further Effusion of Blood, will readily incline me to listen to such Terms for the Surrender of your Posts and Garrisons
at York and Gloucester, as are admissible.

I wish previous to the Meeting of Commissioners, that your Lordship's
proposals in writing, may be sent to the American Lines: for which Purpose,
a Suspension of Hostilities during two Hours from the Delivery of this Letter
will be granted.

C. CORNWALLIS TO WASHINGTON, OCTOBER 17

I have this moment been honoured with your Excellency's letter, dated
this day.

The time limited for sending my answer will not admit of entering into
the detail of articles; but the basis of my proposals will be, that the garrisons of
York and Gloucester shall be prisoners of war, with the customary honours.
And, for the conveniency of the individuals which I have the honour to command, that the British shall be sent to Britain, and the Germans to Germany,

under engagement not to serve against France, America, or their allies, until released or regularly exchanged. That all arms and public stores shall be delivered up to you; but that the usual indulgence of side-arms to officers, and of retaining private property, shall be granted to officers and soldiers, and that the interest of several individuals, in civil capacities and connected with us, shall be attended to.

If your Excellency thinks that a continuance of the suspensions of hostilities will be necessary, to transmit your answer, I shall have no objection to the hour that you may propose.

D. WASHINGTON TO CORNWALLIS, OCTOBER 18

To avoid unnecessary Discussions and Delays, I shall at Once, in Answer to your Lordship's Letter of Yesterday, declare the general Basis upon which a Definitive Treaty and Capitulation must take place.

The Garrisons of York and Gloucester, including the Seamen, as you propose, will be received Prisoners of War. The Condition annexed, of sending the British and German Troops to the parts of Europe to which they respectively belong, is inadmissible. Instead of this, they will be marched to such parts of the Country as can most conveniently provide for their Subsistence; and the Benevolent Treatment of Prisoners, which is invariably observed by the Americans, will be extended to them. The same honors will be granted to the Surrendering Army as were granted to the Garrison of Charles town.

The Shipping and Boats in the two Harbours, with all their Guns, Stores, Tackling, Furniture and Apparel, shall be delivered in their present State to an Officer of the Navy, appointed to take possession of them.

The Artillery, Arms, Accoutrements, Military Chest and Public Stores of every Denomination, shall be delivered unimpaired to the Heads of Departments, to which they respectively belong.

The Officers shall be indulged in retaining their Side Arms, and the Officers and Soldiers may preserve their Baggage and Effects, with this Reserve, that Property taken in the Country, will be reclaimed.

With Regard to the Individuals in civil Capacities, whose Interests Your Lordship wishes may be attended to, until they are more particularly described, nothing definitive can be settled.

I have to add, that I expect the Sick and Wounded will be supplied with their own Hospital Stores, and be attended by British Surgeons, particularly charged with the Care of them.

Your Lordship will be pleased to signify your Determination either to accept or reject the Proposals now offered, in the Course of Two Hours from the Delivery of this Letter, that Commissioners may be appointed to digest the Articles of Capitulation, or a Renewal of Hostilities may take place.

E. CORNWALLIS TO WASHINGTON, OCTOBER 18

I agree to open a treaty of capitulation upon the basis of the garrisons of York and Gloucester, including seamen, being prisoners of war, without annexing the condition of their being sent to Europe; but I expect to receive a compensation in the articles of capitulation for the surrender of Gloucester in its present state of defence.

I shall, in particular, desire, that the *Bonetta* sloop of war may be left entirely at my disposal, from the hour that the capitulation is signed, to receive an aid-de-camp to carry my dispatches to Sir Henry Clinton. Such soldiers as I may think proper to send as passengers in her, to be manned with fifty men of her own crew, and to be permitted to sail without examination, when my dispatches are ready: engaging, on my part, that the ship shall be brought back and delivered to you, if she escapes the dangers of the sea, that the crew and soldiers shall be accounted for in future exchanges, that she shall carry off no officer without your consent, nor public property of any kind; and I shall likewise desire, that the traders and inhabitants may preserve their property, and that no person may be punished or molested for having joined the British troops.

If you choose to proceed to negociation on these grounds, I shall appoint two field officers of my army to meet two officers from you, at any time and place that you think proper, to digest the articles of capitulation.

—JOHNSTON, *The Yorktown Campaign*, pp. 185-187.

2. "THIS IS TO US A MOST GLORIOUS DAY"

Journal of Dr. James Thacher.

[*October*] *19th.*—This is to us a most glorious day, but to the English, one of bitter chagrin and disappointment. Preparations are now making to receive as captives that vindictive, haughty commander and that victorious army, who, by their robberies and murders, have so long been a scourge to our brethren of the Southern states. Being on horseback, I anticipate a full share of satisfaction in viewing the various movements in the interesting scene.

The stipulated terms of capitulation are similar to those granted to General Lincoln at Charleston the last year. The captive troops are to march out with shouldered arms, colors cased and drums beating a British or German march, and to ground their arms at a place assigned for the purpose. The officers are allowed their side-arms and private property, and the generals and such officers as desire it are to go on parole to England or New York. The marines and seamen of the king's ships are prisoners of war to the navy of France; and the land forces to the United States. All military and artillery stores to be delivered up unimpaired. The royal prisoners to be sent into the interior of Virginia, Maryland and Pennsylvania in regiments, to have rations allowed them equal to the American soldiers, and to have their officers near them. Lord Cornwallis to man and despatch the *Bonetta* sloop-of-war with despatches to Sir Henry Clinton at New York without being searched, the vessel to be returned and the hands accounted for.

At about twelve o'clock, the combined army was arranged and drawn up in two lines extending more than a mile in length. The Americans were drawn up in a line on the right side of the road, and the French occupied the left. At the head of the former, the great American commander, mounted on his noble courser, took his station, attended by his aids. At the head of the latter was posted the excellent Count Rochambeau and his suite. The French troops, in complete uniform, displayed a martial and noble appearance; their bands of music, of which the timbrel formed a part, is a delightful novelty and produced while marching to the ground a most enchanting effect. The Americans, though not all in uniform, nor their dress so neat, yet exhibited an erect, soldierly air, and every countenance beamed with satisfaction and joy. The concourse of spectators from the country was prodigious, in point of numbers was probably equal to the military, but universal silence and order prevailed.

It was about two o'clock when the captive army advanced through the line formed for their reception. Every eye was prepared to gaze on Lord Cornwallis, the object of peculiar interest and solicitude; but he disappointed our anxious expectations; pretending indisposition, he made General O'Hara his substitute as the leader of his army. This officer was followed by the conquered troops in a slow and solemn step, with shouldered arms, colors cased and drums beating a British march. Having arrived at the head of the line, General O'Hara, elegantly mounted, advanced to his excellency the commander-in-chief, taking off his hat, and apologized for the non-appearance of Earl Cornwallis. With his usual dignity and politeness, his excellency pointed to Major-General Lincoln for directions, by whom the British army was conducted into a spacious field, where it was intended they should ground their arms.

The royal troops, while marching through the line formed by the allied army, exhibited a decent and neat appearance, as respects arms and clothing, for their commander opened his store and directed every soldier to be furnished with a new suit complete, prior to the capitulation. But in their line of march we remarked a disorderly and unsoldierly conduct, their step was irregular, and their ranks frequently broken.

But it was in the field, when they came to the last act of the drama, that the spirit and pride of the British soldier was put to the severest test: here their mortification could not be concealed. Some of the platoon officers appeared to be exceedingly chagrined when giving the word "*ground arms,*" and I am a witness that they performed this duty in a very unofficer-like manner; and that many of the soldiers manifested a *sullen temper,* throwing their arms on the pile with violence, as if determined to render them useless. This irregularity, however, was checked by the authority of General Lincoln. After having grounded their arms and divested themselves of their accoutrements, the captive troops were conducted back to Yorktown and guarded by our troops till they could be removed to the place of their destination.

The British troops that were stationed at Gloucester surrendered at the same time and in the same manner to the command of the Duke de Luzerne [Lauzun].

This must be a very interesting and gratifying transaction to General Lincoln, who, having himself been obliged to surrender an army to a haughty foe the last year, has now assigned him the pleasing duty of giving laws to a conquered army in return, and of reflecting that the terms which were imposed on him are adopted as a basis of the surrender in the present instance. It is a very gratifying circumstance that every degree of harmony, confidence and friendly intercourse subsisted between the American and French troops during the campaign—no contest, except an emulous spirit to excel in exploits and enterprise against the common enemy, and a desire to be celebrated in the annals of history for an ardent love of great and heroic actions.

We are not to be surprised that the pride of the British officers is humbled on this occasion, as they have always entertained an exalted opinion of their own miltiary prowess and affected to view the Americans as a contemptible, undisciplined rabble. But there is no display of magnanimity when a great commander shrinks from the inevitable misfortunes of war; and when it is considered that Lord Cornwallis has frequently appeared in splendid triumph at the head of his army, by which he is almost *adored,* we conceive it incumbent on him cheerfully to participate in their misfortunes and degradations, however humiliating; but it is said he gives himself up entirely to vexation and despair.

—THACHER, *Military Journal,* pp. 288-290.

3. LORD NORTH: "OH GOD! IT IS ALL OVER"

Memoirs of Sir Nathaniel Wraxall, who was in London in 1781.

[*November 1781*]. During the whole month of November, the concurring accounts which were transmitted to Government, enumerating Lord Cornwallis's embarrassments and the positions taken by the enemy, augmented the anxiety of the Cabinet. Lord George Germain in particular, conscious that on the prosperous or adverse termination of that expedition must depend the fate of the American contest, his own stay in office, as well as probably the duration of the Ministry, felt, and even expressed to his friends, the strongest uneasiness on the subject. The meeting of Parliament meanwhile stood fixed for the 27th of November.

On Sunday the 25th about noon, official intelligence of the surrender of the British forces at Yorktown arrived from Falmouth at Lord George Germain's house in Pall-Mall. Lord Walsingham, who, previous to his father Sir William de Grey's elevation to the peerage, had been Under-Secretary of State in that department, and who was selected to second the address in the House of Peers on the subsequent Tuesday, happened to be there when the messenger brought the news. Without communicating it to any other person, Lord George, for the purpose of dispatch, immediately got with him into a hackney-coach and drove to Lord Stormont's residence in Portland Place. Having imparted to him the disastrous information and taken him into the carriage, they instantly proceeded to the Chancellor's house in Great Russell Street, Bloomsbury, whom they found at home, when after a short consultation, they determined to lay it themselves in person before Lord North.

He had not received any intimation of the event when they arrived at his door in Downing Street between one and two o'clock. The First Minister's firmness, and even his presence of mind, which had withstood the [Gordon] riots of 1780, gave way for a short time under this awful disaster. I asked Lord George afterwards how he took the communication when made to him. "As he would have taken a ball in his breast," replied Lord George. For he opened his arms, exclaiming wildly, as he paced up and down the apartment during a few minutes, "O God! it is all over!"—words which he repeated many times under emotions of the deepest consternation and distress.

When the first agitation of their minds had subsided, the four Ministers discussed the question whether or not it might be expedient to prorogue Parliament for a few days; but as scarcely an interval of forty-eight hours remained before the appointed time of assembling, and as many members of both Houses were already either arrived in London or on the road, that proposition was abandoned. It became, however, indispensable to alter and almost to model anew the King's speech, which had been already drawn up and completely prepared for delivery from the throne. This alteration was therefore made without delay, and at the same time Lord George Germain, as Secretary for the American Department, sent off a dispatch to his Majesty, who was then at Kew, acquainting him with the melancholy termination of Lord Cornwallis's expedition. Some hours having elapsed before these different but necessary acts of business could take place, the Ministers separated, and Lord George Germain repaired to his office in Whitehall. There he found a confirmation of the intelligence, which arrived about two hours after the first communication, having been transmitted from Dover, to which place it was forwarded from Calais with the French account of the same event.

I dined on that day at Lord George's, and though the information which had reached London in the course of the morning from two different quarters was of a nature not to admit of long concealment, yet it had not been communicated either to me or to any individual of the company (as it might have been through the channel of common report), when I got to Pall-Mall between five and six o'clock. Lord Walsingham, who likewise dined there, was the only guest that had become acquainted with the fact. The party, nine in number, sat down to table. Lord George appeared serious, though he manifested no discomposure. Before the dinner was finished, one of his servants delivered him a letter, brought back by the messenger who had been dispatched to the King.

Lord George opened and perused it, then looking at Lord Walsingham, to whom he exclusively directed his observation, "The King writes," said he, "just as he always does, except that I observe he has omitted to mark the hour and the minute of his writing with his usual precision."

This remark, though calculated to awaken some interest, excited no comment; and while the ladies, Lord George's three daughters, remained in the room we repressed our curiosity. But they had no sooner withdrawn than, Lord George having acquainted us that from Paris information had just arrived of the old Count de Maurepas, First Minister, lying at the point of death, "It would grieve me," said I, "to finish my career, however far advanced in years, were I First Minister of France, before I had witnessed the termination of this great contest between England and America."

"He has survived to witness that event," replied Lord George with some agitation.

Utterly unsuspicious as I was of the fact which had happened beyond the Atlantic, I conceived him to allude to the indecisive naval action fought at the mouth of the Chesapeake early in the preceding month of September between

Admiral Graves and Count de Grasse: an engagement which in its results might prove most injurious to Lord Cornwallis.

Under this impression, "My meaning," said I, "is that if I were the Count de Maurepas, I should wish to live long enough to behold the final issue of the war in Virginia."

"He has survived to witness it completely," answered Lord George. "The army has surrendered, and you may peruse the particulars of the capitulation in that paper," taking at the same time one from his pocket, which he delivered into my hand not without visible emotion.

By his permission I read it aloud, while the company listened in profound silence. We then discussed its contents as affecting the Ministry, the country and the war. It must be confessed that they were calculated to diffuse a gloom over the most convivial society, and that they opened a wide field for political speculation.

After perusing the account of Lord Cornwallis's surrender at Yorktown, it was impossible not to feel a lively curiosity to know how the King had received the intelligence, as well as how he had expressed himself in his note to Lord George Germain on the first communication of so painful an event. He gratified our wish by reading it to us, observing, at the same time, that it did the highest honour to his Majesty's fortitude, firmness and consistency of character. The words made an impression on my memory which the lapse of more than thirty years has not erased, and I shall here commemorate its tenor as serving to show how that prince felt and wrote under one of the most afflicting as well as humiliating occurrences of his reign. The billet ran nearly to this effect:

"I have received with sentiments of the deepest concern the communication which Lord George Germain has made me of the unfortunate result of the operations in Virginia. I particularly lament it on account of the consequences connected with it and the difficulties which it may produce in carrying on the public business or in repairing such a misfortune. But I trust that neither Lord George Germain nor any member of the Cabinet will suppose that it makes the smallest alteration in those principles of my conduct which have directed me in past time and which will always continue to animate me under every event in the prosecution of the present contest."

Not a sentiment of despondency or of despair was to be found in the letter, the very handwriting of which indicated composure of mind. Whatever opinion we may entertain relative to the practicability of reducing America to obedience by force of arms at the end of 1781, we must admit that no sovereign could manifest more calmness, dignity or self-command than George III displayed in this reply.

—WRAXALL, *Historical and Posthumous Memoirs*, II, 137-142.

4. "THE WORLD TURNED UPSIDE DOWN"

One of the minor mysteries of the ceremonies revolves around the particular piece of music the British band played when the troops marched out to surrender. *Under the terms of the capitulation they were not permitted to play an American or French tune but limited to British or German ones. Dr. Thacher and "Light-Horse Harry" Lee say it was a British march. St. George Tucker tells us that the British drummers beat "a slow march," and at retreat the previous evening played the tune of "Welcome, Brother Debtor." There is some evidence that more than drummers participated, that a full band played. That is what John Conrad Doehla reported.*

Not long after Yorktown the tradition became well entrenched that the tune actually played here, as at the very beginning of the war on Colonel Leslie's retreat from Salem Bridge was, appropriately enough, "The World Turned Upside Down, or The Old Woman Taught Wisdom," quite a different version from the earlier English ballad of the same title. Later, when the words were printed on a music sheet, they were adapted to the English tune, Derry Down.

The version which has the strongest support in tradition and which because of its appropriateness we would like to believe was played appeared in the Gentleman's *Magazine of 1766, beginning "Goody Bull and her daughter fell out." But a case has been made for an imaginative but frothy bit, which was more amusing if less pertinent. It ran something like this:*

> *If buttercups buzzed after the bee,*
> *If boats were on land, churches on sea,*
> *If ponies rode men and grass ate the cows,*
> *And cats should be chased to holes by the mouse,*
> *If the mamas sold their babies to the gypsies for half a crown;*
> *Summer were spring and the t'other way round,*
> *Then all the world would be upside down.*

Regardless of which tune the British played, Yorktown inspired one of the most amazing ballads of the Revolution. Throughout the land Americans sang a tune which began thus:

> *Cornwallis led a country dance,*
> *The like was never seen, sir.*
> *Much retrograde and much advance,*
> *And all with General Greene, sir.*

But the dance comes to a surprising finale as the Americans and the French draw their net around their enemy ever tighter:

> *Now hand in hand they circle round*
> *This ever-dancing pair, sir:*
> *Their gentle movements soon confound*
> *The earl as they draw near, sir.*

> *His music soon forgets to play—*
> *His feet can no more move, sir,*
> *And all his bands now curse the day*
> *They jiggéd to our shore, sir.*

Now Tories all, what can ye say?
Come—is not this a griper,
That while your hopes are danced away,
'Tis you must pay the piper?

"THE WORLD TURNED UPSIDE DOWN"

Goody Bull and her daughter together fell out.
Both squabbled, and wrangled, and made a damned rout,
But the cause of the quarrel remains to be told.
Then lend both your ears, and a tale I'll unfold.

The old lady, it seems, took a freak in her head
That her daughter, grown woman, might earn her own bread:
Self-applauding her scheme, she was ready to dance;
But we're often too sanguine in what we advance.

For mark the event: thus by fortune we're crossed,
Nor should people reckon without their good host;
The daughter was sulky, and wouldn't come to,
And pray, what in this case could the old woman do?

In vain did the matron hold forth in the cause
That the young one was able; her duty, the laws;
Ingratitude vile, disobedience far worse;
But she might e'en as well sung psalms to a horse.

Young, froward and sullen, and vain of her beauty,
She tartly replied that she knew well her duty,
That other folks' children were kept by their friends,
And that some folks loved people but for their own ends.

"Zounds, neighbor!" quoth Pitt, "what the devil's the matter?
A man cannot rest in his house for your clatter."
"Alas!" cries the daughter, "here's dainty fine work.
The old woman grown harder than a Jew or than Turk."

"She be damned," says the farmer, and to her he goes,
First roars in her ears, then tweaks her old nose.
"Hallo, Goody, what ails you? Wake! woman, I say;
I am come to make peace in this desperate fray.

"Adzooks, ope thine eyes, what a pother is here!
You've no right to compel her, you have not, I swear;
Be ruled by your friends, kneel down and ask pardon,
You'd be sorry, I'm sure, should she walk Covent Garden."

"Alas!" cries the old woman, "and must I comply?
But I'd rather submit than the huzzy should die."
"Pooh, prithee be quiet, be friends and agree,
You must surely be right, *if you're guided by me*."

Unwillingly awkward, the mother knelt down,
While the absolute farmer went on with a frown,
"Come, kiss the poor child, there come, kiss and be friends!
There, kiss your poor daughter, and make her amends."

"No thanks to you, Mother," the daughter replied;
"But thanks to my friend here, I've humbled your pride."
                                    —*Gentleman's Magazine,* XXXVI, 140-141.

CHAPTER THIRTY-THREE

Winning the Peace

THE SUCCESSFUL *negotiation of the treaty of peace with Great Britain still stands as the greatest achievement in the history of American diplomacy. The United States obtained all its principal objectives—independence, adequate continental territory, access to international waterways, and fisheries. That solid achievement is a tribute to the perspicacity and stubbornness of the American peace negotiators—Benjamin Franklin, John Jay and John Adams. The fourth commissioner, Henry Laurens, who had been captured and confined to the Tower of London, was released, but was strangely dilatory in joining his fellow commissioners. He arrived at the very last hour of the negotiations and signed the preliminary articles of peace. At times it seemed as though they were being obstructed by their friends and helped by their enemies. It is an intriguing speculation that had the Americans been less adamant on one point, the insistence on the preliminary acknowledgment of independence, an even more favorable treaty might have been secured. These British-American negotiations were but a fragment of a larger world peace, in which belligerents and neutrals all had a substantial stake. The ability of the American negotiators to hold out against the world for indispensable terms of peace is a dramatic and inspiring story, portions of which are told in the following accounts by the men who made the peace.*

I. FRANCE SEEKS TO DICTATE THE AMERICAN PEACE

Toward the latter part of the American Revolution it was clear that the principal American objective of the war, the recognition of independence, was not an indispensable condition to peace to the Continental powers. Temporary recognition of de facto *independence subject to subsequent readjustments within the British Empire was as much as most of the European powers were ready to demand of England. Spain had sought to mediate the conflict before declaring war on Britain. Then a combined Austro-Russian mediation attempt was made and bogged down. Meantime, Vergennes, who was balancing half a dozen balls on the head of a cane, became concerned about the prolonged and costly character of the war. He was anxious to bring belligerency to an end and willing to compromise to do so. Blocking the road to compromise was American intransigence on the subject of independence, along with her insistence on the navigation of the Mississippi, her territorial ambitions, and her demand to share in the fisheries.*

By February 1781, Vergennes was prepared to end the war between the

United States and Britain on the basis of a long-time truce accepting the actual war map at the beginning of that year. This would have left the British in possession of Maine, New York City, part of the Old Northwest, Charleston and Savannah. In order to carry through a program so objectionable to Americans, Vergennes needed a more pliant peace commission. At that moment it consisted of only one man, the stubborn, independent and irascible John Adams. Vergennes instructed the French minister to America, the Chevalier de la Luzerne, that changes should be made in the peace mission, that Adams should be instructed to take the advice of the King of France, and that the United States should moderate its terms.

As early as December 1775, Bonvouloir, a French agent in America, had boasted of Congress, "I can do what I please with them." Through influence and probably bribery Luzerne was to make substantial headway. For example, Luzerne, according to his own letter to Vergennes, advanced money to General Sullivan, then a member of Congress. Sullivan later insisted that this sum was accepted as a loan, but there is no evidence that he ever paid back a cent of the money.

Luzerne prevailed with Congress. Adams was no longer sole peace commissioner, but was given three colleagues—Franklin, Jay and Laurens (Jefferson did not accept the assignment). Congress on June 15, 1781, instructed the commissioners to be governed in peace-making by the French court. These instructions evoked an eloquent protest from John Jay. Luzerne claimed to have great influence with Robert R. Livingston, Secretary of Foreign Affairs, and to have worked with him on the drafts of instructions which went out from his office. In his instructions of January 7, 1782, Livingston repeated Congress' earlier instruction that the commissioners should in effect be governed by the advice and opinions of their ally, the King of France.

1. "No Step Without the Approbation of His Majesty"

Statement of Chevalier de la Luzerne, minister to the United States.

May 28, 1781

The minister communicated to the committee several observations respecting the conduct of Mr. Adams; and in doing justice to his patriotick character, he gave notice to the committee of several circumstances which proved it necessary that Congress should draw a line of conduct to that minister of which he might not be allowed to lose sight. The minister dwelt especially on a circumstance already known to Congress, namely, the use which Mr. Adams thought he had a right to make of his powers to treat with Great Britain. The minister concluded on this subject that if Congress put any confidence in the king's friendship and benevolence; if they were persuaded of his inviolable attachment to the principle of the alliance, and of his firm resolution constantly to support the cause of the United States, they would be impressed with the necessity of prescribing to their plenipotentiary a perfect and open confidence in the French ministers, and a thorough reliance on the king; and would direct him to take no step without the approbation of his Majesty; and after giving him, in his instructions, the principal and most important outlines for his conduct, they would order him, with respect to the manner of carrying them into execution, to receive his directions from the Count de Vergennes, or from the person who might be charged with the negotiation in the name of the king. The minister observed that this matter is the more important, because, being allied with the United States, it is the business of the king to support their cause with those powers with whom Congress has no connexion, and can have none, until their independence is in a fair train to be acknowledged. That the king would make it a point of prudence and justice to support the minister of Congress; but in case this minister, by aiming at impossible things, forming exorbitant demands which disinterested mediators might think ill-founded, or perhaps by misconstruing his instructions, should put the French negotiators under the necessity of proceeding in the course of the negotiation without a constant connexion with him, this would give rise to an unbecoming contradiction between France and the thirteen United States, which could not but be of very bad effect in the course of the negotiation. . . .

He further observed that whatever might be the resolution of Congress, they would do well to recommend to their plenipotentiary to adopt a line of conduct that would deprive the British of every hope of causing divisions between the allies, and to assume a conciliating character as much as can be consistent with the dignity of his constituents, and to show such a confidence in the plenipotentiary of his Most Christian Majesty as is due to a power so much interested to support the dignity and honour of a nation whose independence they have acknowledged.

—*Journals of the Continental Congress*, XX, 562 ff.

2. CONGRESS AGREES TO BE GOVERNED BY FRENCH ADVICE

Thomas Rodney to Caesar Rodney.

Philadelphia, June 15, 1781

Yesterday I wrote you respecting the Congress of Mediation but when I shall have an opertunity by which I may safely trust the conveyance of such intelligence is uncertain. This important business has chiefly taken up the time of Congress since I last came up and is now completed. It was closed by the decision of an important article in the instructions to our Commissioners which requires them, after having obtained an independence, in all things else to be ultimately governed by the advice of the French Court or Minister. It was moved to reconsider this clause and to strike it out as being too abject and humiliating. It was argued some hours and at last rejected so that the clause stands and the French Court is thereby in possession of full and sufficient power to make a peace, for there is not the least doubt but the mediating powers will readily consent to our independence provided they may make it as simple as possible and it will be ever the interest of France that they should do this lest we should at a future day form an alliance with Great Britain.

I was against this clause because I think it must convince even the French Court that we are reduced to a weak and abject state and that we have lost all that spirit and dignity which once appeared in the proceedings of Congress. . . .

—BURNETT, *Letters of Members of the Continental Congress*, VI, 121-122.

3. Jay Protests "Casting America into the Arms of France"

John Jay to Thomas McKean, President of Congress.

St. Ildefonso, September 20, 1781

. . . As an American I feel an interest in the dignity of my country, which renders it difficult for me to reconcile myself to the idea of the sovereign independent States of America submitting, in the persons of their ministers, to be absolutely governed by the advice and opinions of the servants of another sovereign, especially in a case of such national importance.

That gratitude and confidence are due to our allies is not to be questioned, and that it will probably be in the power of France almost to dictate the terms of peace for us is but too true. That such an extraordinary extent of confidence may stimulate out allies to the highest efforts of generous friendship in our favor is not to be denied, and that this instruction receives some appearance of policy from this consideration may be admitted.

I must, nevertheless, take the liberty of observing that however our situation may in the opinion of Congress render it necessary to relax their demands on every side, and even to direct their commissioners ultimately to concur (if nothing better could be done) in any peace or truce not subversive of our independence which France determined to accede to, yet that this instruction, besides breathing a degree of complacency not quite republican, puts it out of the power of your ministers to improve those chances and opportunities which in the course of human affairs happens more or less frequently to all men. Nor is it clear that America, thus casting herself into the arms of the King of France, will advance either her interest or reputation with that or other nations. . . .

—Wharton, *Revolutionary Diplomatic Correspondence*, IV, 716-717.

II. BRITAIN SUES FOR PEACE

The surrender at Yorktown sealed the doom of the North ministry. During the last few months of his regime Lord North, who had been making futile efforts to relinquish his post ever since Saratoga, repeatedly tendered his resignation to the King. The latter went so far as to prepare a draft of his own abdication. North's action was spurred by a resolution of the Commons of March 4, 1782, to consider as enemies of the King and country all those who should further attempt to carry on the war, and to grant leave to bring in an "Enabling Act" authorizing the King to make a peace or truce with America. Finally, on March 20, the North Ministry resigned. A member of Parliament, Sir Nathaniel Wraxall, has left us a stirring account of the impact on the Commons of North's announcement, which anticipated the passage of a motion of want of confidence in the government.

North was succeeded by Lord Rockingham, a stalwart friend of America. His foreign secretary, Charles James Fox, was a long-time advocate of American independence. Most of the other cabinet posts were given to pro-Americans, but the crucial post of Secretary of Colonial Affairs went to Shelburne, an opponent of independence. William Lee testified to Shelburne's perhaps largely undeserved reputation for duplicity when he declared that "no one will trust for a farthing that knows him, farther than he is bound in black and white." Burke, with the vituperation he customarily reserved for his political adversaries, stigmatized him as "a Catiline or a Borgia in morals."

A fierce rivalry ensued between Fox and Shelburne to control the peace negotiations. Shelburne dispatched Richard Oswald, a retired Scottish merchant and slave trader with family ties in America, to start preliminary talks with Franklin. Fox sent Thomas Grenville to open negotiations with Vergennes. Fox favored the immediate recognition of American independence, as his emissary informed Franklin. Privately he felt that this would split the allies, and, once America was recognized as a foreign power and no longer a colony, it would bring the negotiations entirely into his own hands.

At the start Franklin unlimbered his heaviest artillery and requested the cession of Canada, to which Shelburne was not in the least agreeable. The latter countered with an equally objectionable demand for securing debts due British subjects and the indemnification of the Tories. Then fate determined the issue between the rivals, Fox and Shelburne. On July 1 Rockingham died. Shelburne became Prime Minister. Fox quit the cabinet, leaving his rival in complete control.

Shelburne was taking a calculated risk on negotiating directly with the American commissioners, in whom, he told Oswald, "we have put the greatest confidence," adding, "It is now to be seen how far they or America are to be depended upon." He conceded ruefully, "There never was a greater risk run. I hope the public will be the gainer else our heads must answer for it, and deservedly."

1. LORD NORTH RESIGNS: "GOOD NIGHT, GENTLEMEN"

Memoirs of Sir Nathaniel Wraxall.

... On Tuesday, the 19th of March, [1782,] the First Minister, apprehensive of the event of the debate which was fixed for the ensuing day in the House of Commons, wrote to the King in the most decided terms, resigning his employment; and His Majesty being down at Windsor, Lord North despatched a messenger with the letter. When it arrived, the King was going out to hunt; having perused its contents, for which he was probably not unprepared, he calmly put it into his pocket, made no observation, and mounted his horse. But he had not proceeded more than a few paces when a page came running after him to say that Lord North's messenger had received orders to bring back a reply.

"Tell him," said the King, "that I shall be in town to-morrow morning, and will then give Lord North an answer."

Two noblemen were with him at the time, one of whom was the late Duke of Dorset; the other, Lord Hinchinbrook (afterwards Earl of Sandwich), related to me these particulars. Turning immediately to them, "Lord North," observed His Majesty, "has sent me in his resignation; but I shall not accept it."

If, however, the King was apprised of Lord North's intention or determination to resign, it was by no means known in London, and on the morning of the very day I believe that few individuals of either party entertained a doubt of the continuance of the struggle. Still less did any person conceive that the First Minister would spontaneously lay down his office without giving notice to his friends, and contrary to his own recent professions. He went soon after one o'clock to the Treasury, from whence he was to repair to St. James's, where the King, as usual, had a levee. . . .

It is probable that the conversation which took place between the King and Lord North, on that occasion, was never minutely reported by either to any third person: but we may safely assume that His Majesty endeavoured to prevail on his minister not to abandon him. Robinson profesed himself ig-norant of all the particulars, though he entertained no doubt that Lord North, whether from weariness and disgust, or apprehension of the consequences that might accrue to his sovereign, to himself and to the country, had made up his mind as he drove to St. James's to state at once to the King the determina-tion that he had irrevocably embraced of laying down immediately his power, a resolution which he had notified under his hand on the preceding day. It is certain that the interview between them was long, lasting above an hour and a half, without any witness present; at the end of which time the Minister withdrew, in order to attend the House of Commons.

I have rarely witnessed so full an attendance, at so early an hour, as on that day, not less than four hundred members having taken their seats before five o'clock; both parties appearing impatient to proceed to business. The only delay arose from the absence of the First Minister, and he being every instant expected to arrive from St. James's, all eyes were directed towards the door each time that it opened. The members on both sides, who, it was generally understood, would speak in the course of the ensuing debate, were well known; and as the ground of controversy had been so often gone over, as well as on account of many invalids who attended and who were unable to remain long, it was thought that the question would be brought on before midnight.

At length Lord North entering in a full dressed suit, his riband over his coat, proceeded up the House, amidst an incessant cry of "order, and places!" As soon as he had reached the Treasury Bench, he rose and attempted to ad-dress the chair, but Lord Surrey, who had given notice of a motion for that day, being consequently in possession of the right to speak first, and having likewise risen, a clamour began from all quarters of the most violent descrip-tion. It lasted for some moments in defiance of every effort made by the speaker to enforce silence, till in consequence of the earnestness with which the Minister besought a hearing, and some expressions relative to the impor-tance of the communication that he had to make, which pervaded the tumult, the members opposite allowed him the precedence.

He then stated, after a short preface, that "his object was to save the time and trouble of the House, by informing them that the administration was virtually at an end; that His Majesty had determined to change his confidential servants; and that he should propose an adjournment, in order to allow time for the new ministerial arrangements which must take place."

It is not easy to describe the effect which this declaration produced in a popular assembly, scarcely an individual of which did not hear it with lively

sentiments of exultation, or of concern, both of which emotions were height-
ened by surprise. No painter could have done justice to the expression depic-
tured in many countenances. The opposition, without much difficulty, consented to the proposed adjournment; and the members, actuated by very opposite emotions, soon dispersed in all directions, to carry the intelligence
through the capital. Not, however, till Burke, assuming the part of a moder-
ator, had endeavoured to temper and restrain the vociferous joy of his friends
on so sudden and unexpected an event. But scarcely could he obtain a hearing, amidst the impatience of men who for the first time beheld before their
eyes the promised land. Courteney, on the other side of the House, pronounced a panegyric, or more properly, an encomium, on the personal virtues
and amiable qualities of the First Minister, which he did not suspend on account of the violent indications of dissatisfaction exhibited from the opposition benches.

A more interesting scene had not been acted within the walls of the
House of Commons since February 1743, when Sir Robert Walpole retired
from power. Nor did the First Minister of George the Second by any means
display in the last moments of his political life the equanimity, suavity and dignity manifested by his successor. Lord North ordered his coach to remain at
the House of Commons in waiting on that evening. In consequence of so unexpected an event as his resignation, and the House breaking up at such an
early hour, the housekeeper's room became crowded to the greatest degree,
few persons having directed their carriages to be ready before midnight. In
the midst of this confusion, Lord North's coach drove up to the door, and as
he prepared to get into it, he said, turning to those persons near him with that
unalterable equanimity and good temper which never forsook him, "Good
night, gentlemen, you see what it is to be in the secret."

—WRAXALL, *Historical and Posthumous Memoirs*, pp. 282-284.

2. FRANKLIN PROPOSES THAT BRITAIN CEDE CANADA

Benjamin Franklin to Lord Shelburne.

Passy, April 18, 1782

I have received the letter your Lordship did me the honour of writing to
me on the 16th instant. I congratulate you on your new appointment to the
honourable and important office you formerly filled so worthily, which must
be so far pleasing to you as it affords you more opportunities of doing good,
and of serving your country essentially in its great concerns.

I have conversed a good deal with Mr. Oswald and am much pleased with
him. He appears to me a wise and honest man. I acquainted him that I was
commissioned, with others, to treat of and conclude a Peace. . . .

I leave the rest of the conversation to be related to your Lordship by Mr.
Oswald; and, that he might do it more easily and fully than he could by letter,
I was of opinion with him that it would be best he should return immediately
and do it *viva voce*. Being myself but one of the four persons, now in Europe,
commissioned by the Congress to treat of Peace, I can make no propositions of

BOUNDARIES PROPOSED IN THE NEGOTIATIONS OF 1782,
BETWEEN THE UNITED STATES AND ENGLAND

much importance without them. I can only express my wish that, if Mr. Oswald returns hither, he may bring with him the agreement of your Court to treat for a general Peace, and the proposal of place and time, that I may immediately write to Messrs. Adams, Laurens and Jay. . . . He appeared much struck with my discourse, and as I frequently looked at my paper, he desired to see it. After some little delay, I allowed him to read it; the following is an exact copy:

"NOTES FOR CONVERSATION"

"To make a Peace durable, what may give occasion for future wars should if practicable be removed.

"The territory of the United States and that of Canada, by long extended frontiers, touch each other.

"The settlers on the frontiers of the American Provinces are generally the most disorderly of the people, who, being far removed from the eye and controll of their respective governments, are more bold in committing offences against neighbours, and are for ever occasioning complaints and furnishing matter for fresh differences between their States.

"By the late debates in Parliament, and publick writings, it appears that Britain desires a *reconciliation* with the Americans. It is a sweet word. It means much more than a mere Peace, and what is heartily to be wished for. Nations make a Peace whenever they are both weary of making war. But, if one of them has made war upon the other unjustly, and has wantonly and unnecessarily done it great injuries, and refuses reparation, though there may, for the present, be peace, the resentment of those injuries will remain, and will break out again in vengeance when occasions offer. These occasions will be watched for by one side, feared by the other, and the peace will never be secure; nor can any cordiality subsist between them.

"Many houses and villages have been burnt in America by the English and their allies, the Indians. I do not know that the Americans will insist on reparation; perhaps they may. But would it not be better for England to offer it? Nothing could have a greater tendency to conciliate, and much of the future commerce and returning intercourse between the two countries may depend on the reconciliation. Would not the advantage of reconciliation by such means be greater than the expence?

"If then a way can be proposed which may tend to efface the memory of injuries, at the same time that it takes away the occasions of fresh quarrel and mischief, will it not be worth considering, especially if it can be done, not only without expence, but be a means of saving?

"Britain possesses Canada. Her chief advantage from that possession consists in the trade for peltry. Her expences in governing and defending that settlement must be considerable. It might be humiliating to her to give it up on the demand of America. Perhaps America will not demand it; some of her political rulers may consider the fear of such a neighbour as a means of keeping 13 States more united among themselves, and more attentive to military discipline. But on the minds of the people in general would it not have an excellent effect, if Britain should voluntarily offer to give up this Province; tho'

on these conditions, that she shall in all times coming have and enjoy the right
of free trade thither, unincumbered with any duties whatsoever; that so much
of the vacant lands there shall be sold as will raise a sum sufficient to pay for
the houses burnt by the British troops and their Indians; and also to indemnify
the royalists for the confiscation of their estates?"

This is mere conversation matter between Mr. O. and Mr. F., as the former
is not impowered to make propositions, and the latter cannot make any without the concurrence of his colleagues.

—SMYTH, Writings of Franklin, VIII, 465-472.

3. LORD SHELBURNE DOES NOT FAVOR FRANKLIN'S SUGGESTIONS

Memorandum to Mr. Oswald, April 28, 1782.
Remarks on the Private Paper

1st. Why does he [Franklin] say that he does not know of the Americans
having any intentions of making claims of indemnification, he and others having full powers. That is not open. No reparation to be thought of. The
money spent in America is more than sufficient indemnification for all particular losses. Lord Shelburne has a manuscript of Sir William Petty to send in
return for this paper. The title of it is to show that Ireland would have been
in a state of poverty and uncivilised savageness if it had not been for the
money expended by the English in their wars in that country.

All ideas of a supposed justice in claims of indemnification to be disowned;
and if started, to be waived as much as possible.

It is reasonable to expect a free trade, unencumbered with duties, to every
part of America.

Make early and strict conditions, not only to secure all debts whatever due
to British subjects, but likewise to restore the Loyalists to a full enjoyment of
their rights and privileges. And their indemnification to be considered. Lord
Shelburne will never give up the Loyalists. The Penn family have been sadly
used, and Lord Shelburne is personally interested for them, and thinks it is
duty to be so for all.

The private paper desires Canada for three reasons:—

1st. By way of reparation.—Answer. No reparation can be heard of.

2nd. To prevent future wars.—Answer. It is to be hoped that some more
friendly method will be found.

3rd. Loyalists as a fund of indemnification to them.—Answer. No independence to be acknowledged without their being taken care of.

A compensation expected for New York, Charlestown and Savannah.
Penobscott to be always kept.

—LEWIS, Administrations of Great Britain, pp. 47-48.

4. THE ENGLISH LOOK TO FRANKLIN TO EXTRICATE THEM

Benjamin Franklin's Journal of the Negotiation for Peace.

Saturday, June 1st [1782]. Mr. Grenville came according to appointment.
Our conversation began by my acquainting him that I had seen the Count de
Vergennes, and had perused the copy left him of the power to treat; that
after what he, Mr. Grenville, told me of its being to treat with France *and her*

Allies, I was a little surprized to find in it no mention of the Allies, and that it was only to treat with the King of France and his Ministers. . . .

He answered that . . . the greatest part of those instructions related to treating with me. That to convince me of the sincerity of his court respecting us, he would acquaint me with one of his instructions, tho' perhaps the doing it now was premature, and therefore a little inconsistent with the character of a politician, but he had that confidence in me that he should not hesitate to inform me (tho' he wished that at present it should go no further) *he was instructed to acknowledge the independence of America, previous to the commencement of the treaty.*

Mr. Grenville then spoke much of the high opinion the present Ministry had of me, and their great esteem for me, their desire of a perfect reconciliation between the two countries, and the firm and general belief in England that no man was so capable as myself of proposing the proper means of bringing about such a reconciliation; adding that if the old Ministers had formerly been too little attentive to my counsels, the present were very differently disposed, and he hoped that in treating with them, I would totally forget their predecessors. . . .

Mr. G. then discoursed of our resolution not to treat without our Allies. "This," says he, "can properly only relate to France, with whom you have a Treaty of Alliance, but you have none with Spain, you have none with Holland. If Spain and Holland, and even if France should insist on unreasonable terms of advantage to themselves, after you have obtained all you want and are satisfied, can it be right that America should be dragged on in a war for their interests only?" He stated this matter in various lights and pressed it earnestly.

I resolved from various reasons to evade the discussion and therefore answered that the intended treaty not being yet begun, it appeared unnecessary to enter at present into considerations of that kind. The preliminaries being once settled and the treaty commenced, if any of the other powers should make extravagant demands on England, and insist on our continuing the war till those were complyed with, it would then be time enough for us to consider what our obligations were, and how far they extended. . . .

We then spoke of the reconciliation; but his full power not being yet come, I chose to defer entering upon that subject at present. I told him, I had thoughts of putting down in writing the particulars that I judged would conduce to that end, and of adding my reasons, that this required a little time and I had been hindered by accidents; which was true, for I had begun to write, but had postponed it on account of his defective power to treat. But I promised to finish it as soon as possible. He pressed me earnestly to do it, saying an expression of mine in a former conversation, that there still remained *roots of good will* in America towards England, which if properly taken care of might produce a reconciliation, had made a great impression on his mind and given him infinite pleasure, and he hoped I would not neglect furnishing him with the information of what would be necessary to nourish those *roots,* and could assure me, that my advice would be greatly regarded. . . .

On Monday the 3rd, Mr. Oswald came according to appointment. He told me he had seen and had conversation with Lord Shelburne, Lord Rockingham and Mr. Fox. That their desire of peace continued uniformly the same, tho' he thought some of them were a little too much elated with the late victory in the West Indies;* and when observing his coolness, they asked him if he did not think it a very good thing. "Yes," says he, "if you do not rate it too high." He went on with the utmost frankness to tell me that peace was absolutely necessary for them. That the nation had been foolishly involved in four wars, and could no longer raise money to carry them on, so that if they continued, it would be absolutely necessary for them to stop payment of the interest money on the Funds, which would ruin their future credit. He spoke of stopping on all sums above £1000, and continuing to pay on those below, because the great sums belonged to the rich, who could better bear the delay of their interest, and the smaller sums to poorer persons, who would be more hurt and make more clamour, and that the rich might be quieted by promising them interest upon their interest. All this looked as if the matter had been seriously thought on.

Mr. Oswald has an air of great simplicity and honesty, yet I could hardly take this to be merely a weak confession of their deplorable state, and thought it might be rather intended as a kind of intimidation, by showing us they had still that resource in their power, which he said could furnish five millions a year. But he added, our enemies may now do what they please with us—*they have the ball at their foot*, was his expression—and we hope they will show their moderation and their magnanimity. He then repeatedly mentioned the great esteem the Ministers had for me, that they, with all the considerate people of England, looked to and depended on me for the means of extricating the nation from its present desperate situation; that perhaps no single man had ever in his hands an opportunity of doing so much good as I had at this present, with much more to that purpose. . . .

—SMYTH, ed., *Writings of Franklin*, VIII, 516-525, *passim.*

III. "THE POINT OF INDEPENDENCE"

Franklin had made it clear to Oswald at the start that there must be a preliminary acknowledgment of American independence before any settlement could be negotiated. But Oswald's commission of August 8 only authorized him to conclude a peace or truce with any commissioner of the "colonies or plantations." Vergennes advised Franklin and Jay to begin negotiations without insisting on preliminary recognition, so long as independence was incorporated in the final treaty. Jay suspected that Vergennes was trying to stall the Anglo-U.S. negotiations until certain objectives of the French and Spanish were obtained, such as the capture of Gibraltar then under siege. Vergennes actually revealed his opposition to the preliminary recognition of American independence in a talk with Alleyne Fitzherbert, British peace commissioner treating with the French government at Versailles.

---

* Rodney's victory over the French fleet, April 12, 1782.

At this point John Jay deliberately ignored Congress' instructions to abide by the advice of the French government and refused to negotiate until the point of independence was settled. John Adams, writing from The Hague, pointed out that American ministers had to make their decisions "amidst all these doublings and windings of European politics." "We ought," he insisted, "have opinions, principles and systems of our own," and Congress should back up its own negotiators. He reached Paris in time to strengthen Jay's hands and save the rights to the fisheries. His suspicions of France confirmed him in his deep-rooted isolationism. "America has been long enough involved in the wars of Europe," he wrote to Livingston on November 11. "She has been a football between contending nations from the beginning, and it is easy to foresee that France and England both will endeavor to involve us in their future wars."

To complicate matters further it was apparent that France also opposed the American annexation of Canada, and that behind the scenes Spain strenuously resisted the territorial demands of the United States to the Mississippi. In fact a Franco-Spanish plan would have left the Mississippi south of the Ohio under exclusive Spanish control and denied to the United States the present states of Kentucky, Tennessee, Mississippi and part of Louisiana, along with Alabama.

To fire Jay's smoldering suspicions the British put into his hands a ciphered dispatch from Barbé-Marbois to Vergennes opposing American claims to fishing off Newfoundland's waters. The young French secretary of legation at Philadelphia denounced the letter as spurious, but a copy is in the French Foreign Archives and Marbois later admitted its authenticity.

Fearing that the United States was on the verge of being sold out by France, Jay, with Franklin's agreement, gave up the demand for immediate recognition of independence and on September 9 asked Oswald to get his commission altered so as to recognize independence constructively by being empowered to treat with the Commissioners of the United States of America. In the negotiations which Jay conducted for a time alone during a period when Franklin was indisposed, the claim to Canada was dropped because Jay was now alarmed that the Franco-Spanish allies would block expansionist aims of the United States to the Mississippi. The fact is that Franklin, by listing Canada among the "advisable" rather than the "necessary" articles of independence in his outline of conditions to Oswald on July 10, had in effect dropped it from serious consideration.

It is hardly likely that Jay lost Canada as a result of his stubborn insistence on the point of independence, but he probably had to settle for a more southerly—though in the long run a more natural and practical—boundary line between Canada and the United States than he might have had if negotiations had not been delayed on this matter of immediate recognition. At the same time the Americans might not have been forced to recognize the debts owing to British creditors or to include the troublesome reference to the Loyalists, had negotiations been carried on at a brisker pace. For on September 30 news reached England of the failure of the attack on Gibraltar. This stiffened the tone of British negotiations thenceforward.

1. RECOGNITION OF INDEPENDENCE IS NOT A FAVOR

Richard Oswald to Lord Shelburne.

Paris, July 12, 1782

I will . . . not scruple to give my opinion as things occur to me, viz.:—that the more anxious we appear to be for Peace, the more backward the people here will be, or the harder in their terms, which is much the same thing; and that having fully satisfied this Court of our desire to put an end to the war, as has been done, the more vigorously our exertions are pushed in the interim, we shall come sooner to our purpose, and on better terms.

With respect to the Commissioners for the Colonies, our conduct towards them, I think, ought to be of a style somewhat different; they have shown a desire to treat, and to end with us on a separate footing from the other powers, and I must say, in a more liberal way, or at least with a greater appearance of feeling for the future interests and connections of Great Britain, than I expected. I speak so from the text of the last conversation I had with Mr. Franklin, as mentioned in my letter of yesterday. And therefore we ought to deal with them tenderly, and as supposed conciliated friends, or at least well disposed to conciliation; and not as if we had anything to give them that we can keep from them, or that they are very anxious to have. Even Dr. Franklin himself, as the subject happened to lead that way, as good as told me yesterday, that they were their own masters, and seemed to make no account of the grant of Independence as a favour. I was so much satisfied beforehand of their ideas on that head that I will own to your Lordship I did not read to the Doctor that part of your letter wherein you mention that grant as if it in some shape challenged a return on their part. . . .

I cannot but say I was much pleased, upon the whole, with what passed upon the occasion of this interview. And I really believe the Doctor sincerely wishes for a speedy settlement; and that after the loss of Dependence, we may lose no more; but, on the contrary, that a cordial reconciliation may take place over all that country.

Amongst other things, I was pleased at his showing me a state of the aids they had received from France, as it looked as if he wanted I should see the amount of the obligations to their ally; and as if it was the only foundation of the ties France had over them, excepting gratitude, which the Doctor owned in so many words, but at the same time said the debt would be punctually and easily discharged, France having given to 1788 to pay it. . . .

I should therefore hope it may be possible soon to bring their business near to a final close, and that they will not be any way stiff as to those articles he calls *advisable*, or will drop them altogether. Those he calls necessary will hardly be any obstacle.* I shall be able to make a better guess when I have

---

* This refers to Franklin's outline of conditions of peace. The "necessary" articles were independence, a boundary settlement, a confinement of the boundaries of Canada, and fishing rights off the banks of Newfoundland and elsewhere. The "advisable" articles were an indemnity to those who had suffered by the war, a public acknowledgment of England's error, equality of commercial privileges, and the cession of Canada.

another meeting with him, jointly with Mr. Jay, which I hope to have by the time this courier returns. Allow me, my Lord, to observe that if I continue here any time, I would wish to have a messenger attending. This Potter is a proper man.

—Fox, *Memorials and Correspondence*, IV, 246-252.

2. To Preserve National Dignity John Jay Violates Instructions

Partly decoded letter from John Jay, peace commissioner, to Gouverneur Morris, assistant to the Secretary of Finance. The decoded section is in italics.

Paris, October 13, 1782

Dear Morris

I have received your *festina lente* letter, but wish it had been, at least partly, in cypher; you need not be informed of my reasons for this wish, as by this time you must know that seals are, on this side of the water, rather matters of decoration than of use. It gave me nevertheless great pleasure to receive that letter, it being the first from you that had reached me the Lord knows when. —Except indeed a few lines covering your correspondence with a don. I find you are industrious, and of consequence useful. So much the better for yourself, for the public, and for our friend Morris, whom I consider as the pillar of American credit.

The King of Great Britain, by letters patent under the Great Seal, has authorized Mr. Oswald to treat with the Commissioners of the United States of America. His first Commission litterally pursued the enabling act, and the authority it gave him was expressed in the very terms of that act, viz. to treat with the Colonies, and with any or either of them, and any part of them, and with any description of men in them, and with any person whatsoever, of and concerning Peace, etc.——

Had I not violated the instructions of Congress their dignity would have been in the dust, for the French Minister even took pains not only to persuade us to treat under that commission but to prevent the second by telling Fitzherbert that the first was sufficient. I told the Minister that we neither could nor would treat with any nation in the world on any other than an equal footing.

We may, and we may not, have a peace this winter—act as if the war would certainly continue—keep proper garrisons in your strong posts and preserve your army sufficiently numerous and well appointed until every idea of hostility and surprize shall have compleatly vanished.

I could write you a volume, but my health admits only of short intervals of application.

Present my best wishes to Mr. and Mrs. Morris, Mr. and Mrs. Meredith, and such other of our friends as may ask how we do.

I am, dear Morris, very much

Yours

John Jay

—Gouverneur Morris Papers, Columbia University Lib.

3. ADAMS ARRIVES JUST IN TIME TO STRENGTHEN JAY'S HANDS

John Adams to Robert R. Livingston.

Paris, October 31, 1782

I set off for Paris, where I arrived on Saturday, the 26th of this month, after a tedious journey, the roads being, on account of long-continued rains, in the worst condition I ever knew them.

I waited forthwith on Mr. Jay, and from him learned the state of the conferences. It is not possible at present to enter into details. All I can say is, in general, that I had the utmost satisfaction in finding that he had been all along acting here upon the same principles upon which I had ventured to act in Holland, and that we were perfectly agreed in our sentiments and systems. I can not express it better than in his own words: "to be honest and grateful to our allies, but to think for ourselves." I find a construction put upon one article of our instructions by some persons which, I confess, I never put upon it myself. It is represented by some as subjecting us to the French ministry, as taking away from us all right of judging for ourselves, and obliging us to agree to whatever the French ministers should advise us to do, and to do nothing without their consent. I never supposed this to be the intention of Congress; if I had, I never would have accepted the commission, and if I now thought it their intention I could not continue in it. I can not think it possible to be the design of Congress; if it is I hereby resign my place in the commission, and request that another person may be immediately appointed in my stead.

Yesterday we met Mr. Oswald at his lodgings; Mr. Jay, Dr. Franklin, and myself on one side, and Mr. Oswald, assisted by Mr. Strachey, a gentleman whom I had the honor to meet in company with Lord Howe upon Staten Island in the year 1776, and assisted also by a Mr. Roberts, a clerk in some of the public offices, with books, maps and papers relative to the boundaries.

I arrived in a lucky moment for the boundary of Massachusetts, because I brought with me all the essential documents relative to that object, which are this day to be laid before my colleagues in conference at my house, and afterwards before Mr. Oswald.

It is now apparent, at least to Mr. Jay and myself, that in order to obtain the western lands, the navigation of the Mississippi, and the fisheries, or any of them, we must act with firmness and independence, as well as prudence and delicacy. With these there is little doubt we may obtain them all.

—WHARTON, *Revolutionary Diplomatic Correspondence*, V, 838.

4. "WE HAVE NO DEPENDENCE EXCEPT ON GOD AND OURSELVES"

John Jay to Robert R. Livingston.

Paris, November 17, 1782

... These are critical times, and great necessity there is for prudence and secrecy.

So far, and in such matters as this court [the French government] may think it their interest to support us, they certainly will, but no further, in my opinion.

They are interested in separating us from Great Britain, and on that point we may, I believe, depend upon them; but it is not their interest that we should become a great and formidable people, and therefore they will not help us to become so.

It is not their interest that such a treaty should be formed between us and Britain as would produce cordiality and mutual confidence. They will therefore endeavor to plant such seeds of jealousy, discontent and discord in it as may naturally and perpetually keep our eyes fixed on France for security. This consideration must induce them to wish to render Britain formidable in our neighborhood, and to leave us as few resources of wealth and power as possible.

It is their interest to keep some point or other in contest between us and Britain to the end of the war, to prevent the possibility of our sooner agreeing, and thereby keep us employed in the war, and dependent on them for supplies. Hence they have favored and will continue to favor the British demands as to matters of boundary and the Tories.

The same views will render them desirous to continue the war in our country as long as possible, nor do I believe they will take any measures for our repossession of New York unless the certainty of its evacuation should render such an attempt advisable. The Count de Vergennes lately said that there could be no great use in expeditions to take places which must be given up to us at a peace.

Such being our situation, it appears to me advisable to keep up our army to the end of the war, even if the enemy should evacuate our country; nor does it appear to me prudent to listen to any overtures for carrying a part of it to the West Indies in case of such an event.

I think we have no rational dependence except on God and ourselves, nor can I yet be persuaded that Great Britain has either wisdom, virtue or magnanimity enough to adopt a perfect and liberal system of conciliation. If they again thought they could conquer us, they would again attempt it. . . .

It is not my meaning, and therefore I hope I shall not be understood to mean, that we should deviate in the least from our treaty with France; our honor and our interest are concerned in inviolably adhering to it. I mean only to say that if we lean on her love of liberty, her affection for America, or her disinterested magnanimity, we shall lean on a broken reed, that will sooner or later pierce our hands, and Geneva as well as Corsica justifies this observation. . . .

—WHARTON, *Revolutionary Diplomatic Correspondence*, VI, 45-49.

IV. THE BATTLE FOR THE FISHERIES

As 1782 drew to a close John Adams wrote to Elbridge Gerry, "Thanks be to God that our Tom Cod are safe in spite of the malice of enemies, the finesse of allies, and the mistakes of Congress." Nothing had aroused Adams' lively indignation more than the clear evidence that France opposed granting America the right to fish off the banks of Newfoundland and that a faction in Congress was prepared to sell out the interests of the New England fisher-

men. After much wrangling Adams finally agreed at the last moment, against his better instincts, to have the word "liberty" to fish on the high seas substituted in the treaty for "right." This substitution was to cause a century of controversy.

Diary of John Adams.

[*November*] 25, [*1782*], *Monday*. Dr. Franklin, Mr. Jay and myself, at eleven, met at Mr. Oswald's lodgings. Mr. Strachey told us he had been to London and waited personally on every one of the King's Cabinet Council, and had communicated the last propositions to them. . . .

They could not admit us to dry on the shores of Nova Scotia, nor to fish within three leagues of the coast, nor within fifteen leagues of the coast of Cape Breton. . . .

I could not help observing that the ideas respecting the fishery appeared to me to come piping hot from Versailles. I quoted to them the words of our treaty with France, in which the indefinite and exclusive right to the fishery on the western side of Newfoundland was secured against us, according to the true construction of the treaties of Utrecht and Paris. I showed them the twelfth and thirteenth articles of the treaty of Utrecht, by which the French were admitted to fish from Cape Bona Vista to Cape Riche. I related to them the manner in which the cod and haddock come into the rivers, harbors, creeks and up to the very wharves, on all the northern coast of America, in the spring, in the month of April, so that you have nothing to do but step into a boat and bring in a parcel of fish in a few hours; but that in May they begin to withdraw; we have a saying at Boston that when the "blossoms fall, the haddock begin to crawl"; that is, to move out into deep water, so that in summer you must go out some distance to fish. At Newfoundland it was the same; the fish, in March or April, were in shore in all the creeks, bays and harbors, that is, within three leagues of the coasts or shores of Newfoundland and Nova Scotia; that neither French nor English could go from Europe and arrive early enough for the first fare; that our vessels could, being so much nearer, an advantage which God and nature had put into our hands; but that this advantage of ours had ever been an advantage to England, because our fish had been sold in Spain and Portugal for gold and silver, and the gold and silver sent to London for manufactures; that this would be the course again; that France foresaw it, and wished to deprive England of it, by persuading her to deprive us of it; that it would be a master stroke of policy if she could succeed, but England must be completely the dupe before she could succeed.

There were three lights in which it might be viewed: 1. as a nursery of seamen; 2. as a source of profit; 3. as a source of contention. As a nursery of seamen, did England consider us as worse enemies than France? Had she rather France should have the seamen than America? The French marine was nearer and more menacing than ours. As a source of profit, had England rather France should supply the markets of Lisbon and Cadiz with fish, and take the gold and silver, than we? France would never spend any of that money in London; we should spend it all very nearly. As a source of contention, how could we restrain our fishermen, the boldest men alive, from fishing in prohibited places? How could our men see the French admitted to fish, and themselves excluded by the English? It would then be a cause of disputes, and such seeds France might wish to sow. That I wished for two hours conversation on the subject with one of the King's council; if I did not convince him he was undesignedly betraying the interests of his sovereign, I was mistaken.

Strachey said, perhaps I would put down some observations in writing upon it.

I said, with all my heart, provided I had the approbation of my colleagues; but I could do nothing of the kind without submitting it to their judgments, and that whatever I had said, or should say, upon the subject, however strongly I might express myself, was always to be understood with submission to my colleagues. . . .

[*November*] *29, Friday*. Met Mr. Fitzherbert, Mr. Oswald, Mr. Franklin, Mr. Jay, Mr. Laurens and Mr. Strachey at Mr. Jay's Hotel d'Orléans, and spent the whole day in discussions about the fishery and the Tories. I proposed a new article concerning the fishery; it was discussed and turned in every light, and multitudes of amendments proposed on each side; and at last the article drawn as it was finally agreed to.

The other English gentlemen being withdrawn upon some occasion, I asked Mr. Oswald if he could consent to leave out the limitation of three leagues from all their shores, and the fifteen from those of Louisburg. He said, in his own opinion he was for it; but his instructions were such that he could not do it. I perceived by this, and by several incidents and little circumstances before, which I had remarked to my colleagues who were much of the same opinion, that Mr. Oswald had an instruction not to settle the articles of the fishery and refugees without the concurrence of Mr. Fitzherbert and Mr. Strachey.

Upon the return of the other gentlemen, Mr. Strachey proposed to leave out the word "right" of fishing, and make it "liberty." Mr. Fitzherbert said the word "right" was an obnoxious expression. Upon this I rose up and said, "Gentlemen, is there or can there be a clearer right? In former treaties— that of Utrecht and that of Paris—France and England have claimed the right, and used the word. When God Almighty made the banks of Newfoundland, at three hundred leagues distance from the people of America, and at six hundred leagues distance from those of France and England, did he not give as good a right to the former as to the latter? If Heaven in the creation gave a right, it is ours at least as much as yours. If occupation, use and possession give a right, we have it as clearly as you. If war, and blood, and treasure give a right, ours is as good as yours. We have been constantly fighting in Canada, Cape Breton and Nova Scotia for the defence of this fishery, and have expended beyond all proportion more than you. If, then, the right cannot be denied, why should it not be acknowledged and put out of dispute? Why should we leave room for illiterate fishermen to wrangle and chicane? . . .

After hearing all this, Mr. Fitzherbert, Mr. Oswald and Mr. Strachey retired for some time; and returning, Mr. Fitzherbert said that, upon consulting together and weighing every thing as maturely as possible, Mr. Strachey and himself had determined to advise Mr. Oswald to strike with us according to the terms we had proposed as our ultimatum respecting the fishery and the Loyalists. Accordingly, we all sat down and read over the whole treaty, and corrected it, and agreed to meet tomorrow, at Mr. Oswald's house, to sign and seal the treaties, which the secretaries were to copy fair in the mean time.

I forgot to mention that, when we were upon the fishery, and Mr. Strachey and Mr. Fitzherbert were urging us to leave out the word "right" and substitute "liberty," I told them at last—in answer to their proposal, to agree upon all other articles, and leave that of the fishery to be adjusted at the definitive treaty—I never could put my hand to any articles without satisfaction about the fishery. . . .

—ADAMS, ed., *Works of John Adams*, III, 327-332, 333-335.

V. THE SETTLEMENT OF THE LOYALIST QUESTION

The American commissioners were to a man united against any restitution to or indemnification of the hated Tories. The British government, anxious to make a quick peace and split the allies, was charged by its critics with being shamelessly indifferent to the cause of the Loyalists. As Lord North put it, "What, are not the claims of those who—in conformity to their allegiance, their cheerful obedience to the voice of Parliament, their confidence in the proclamation of our generals, invited under every assurance of military, parliamentary, political and affectionate protection—espoused with the hazard to their lives and the forfeitures of their properties, the cause of Great Britain!" The Americans finally agreed to a compromise suggested by Oswald that Congress would merely recommend to the several states that they correct, if necessary, their acts confiscating the estates of British subjects. This in fact gave the Tories little or nothing, as numerous confiscations continued to be carried out in America after the treaty was signed, but it left a vexing question between the two nations in the years to come.

RESTITUTION TO LOYALISTS IS IMMORAL AND IMPOSSIBLE

Benjamin Franklin to Richard Oswald.

Passy, November 26, 1782

You may well remember that in the beginning of our conferences before the other commissioners arrived, on your mentioning to me a retribution for the Royalists whose estates had been confiscated, I acquainted you that nothing of that kind could be stipulated by us, the confiscation being made by virtue of laws of particular States, which the Congress had no power to contravene or dispense with, and therefore could give us no such authority in our commission. And I gave it as my opinion and advice, honestly and cordially, that, if a reconciliation was intended, no mention should be made in our negotiations of those people; for, they having done infinite mischief to our properties by wantonly burning and destroying farm-houses, villages, towns, if compensation for their losses were insisted on, we should certainly exhibit again such an account of all the ravages they had committed, which would necessarily recall to view scenes of barbarity that must inflame instead of conciliating, and tend to perpetuate an enmity that we all profess a desire of extinguishing. . . . Understanding, however, from you that this was a point your ministry had at heart, I wrote concerning it to Congress, and I have lately received the following resolution, viz:

"By the United States, in Congress assembled

10 September 1782

"Resolved, That the Secretary for Foreign Affairs be . . . directed to obtain, as speedily as possible, authentic returns of the slaves and other property which have been carried off or destroyed in the course of the war by the enemy, and to transmit the same to the ministers plenipotentiary for negotiating peace.

"Resolved, That, in the meantime, the Secretary for Foreign Affairs inform said Ministers that many thousands of slaves, and other property, to a very great amount, have been carried off or destroyed by the enemy; and that, in the opinion of Congress, the great loss of property which the citizens of the United States have sustained by the enemy will be considered by the several States as an insuperable bar to their making restitution or indemnification to the former owners of property, which has been or may be forfeited to, or confiscated by, any of the States."

. . . The mass of evidence, . . . not only of the enormities committed by those people, under the direction of the British generals, but of those committed by the British troops themselves, will form a record that must render the British name odious in America to the latest generations. In that authentic record will be found the burning of the fine towns of Charlestown, near Boston; of Falmouth, just before winter, when the sick, the aged, the women and children were driven to seek shelter where they could hardly find it; of Norfolk, in the midst of winter; of New London, of Fairfield, of Esopus, etc., besides near a hundred and fifty miles of well-settled country laid waste; every house and barn burnt, and many hundreds of farmers, with their wives and children, butchered and scalped.

The present British ministers, when they reflect a little, will certainly be too equitable to suppose that their nation has a right to make an unjust war (which they have always allowed this against us to be) and do all sorts of unnecessary mischief, unjustifiable by the practice of any civilized people, while those they make war with are to suffer without claiming any satisfaction; but that if Britons, or their adherents, are in return deprived of any property it is to be restored to them or they are to be imdemnified. The British troops can never excuse their barbarities. They were unprovoked. The Loyalists may say, in excuse of theirs, that they were exasperated by the loss of their estates, and it was revenge. They have, then, had their revenge. *Is it right they should have both?*

Some of those people may have merit in their regard for Britain, those who espoused her cause from affection; these it may become you to reward. But there are many of them who were waverers and were only determined to engage in it by some occasional circumstance or appearances; these have not much of either merit or demerit. And there are others who have abundance of demerit respecting your country, having by their falsehoods and misrepresentations brought on and encouraged the continuance of the war; these, instead of being recompensed, should be punished.

It is usual among Christian people at war to profess always a desire of peace; but if the ministers of one of the parties choose to insist particularly on a certain article which they have known the others are not and can not be empowered to agree to, what credit can they expect should be given to such professions?

Your ministers require that we should receive again into our bosom those who have been our bitterest enemies, and restore their properties who have destroyed ours; and this while the wounds they have given us are still bleeding! It is many years since your nation expelled the Stuarts and their adherents and confiscated their estates. Much of your resentment against them may by this time be abated, yet, if we should propose it, and insist on it as an article of our treaty with you, that that family should be recalled and the forfeited estates of its friends restored, would you think us serious in our professions of earnestly desiring peace?

I must repeat my opinion that it is best for you to drop all mention of the refugees. We have proposed, indeed, nothing but what we think best for you as well as ourselves. But if you will have them mentioned, let it be in an article in which you may provide that they shall exhibit accounts of their losses to the commissioners, hereafter to be appointed, who should examine the same, together with the accounts now preparing in America of the damages done by them, and state the account, and that if a balance appears in their favor it shall be paid by us to you and by you divided among them as you shall think proper. And if the balance is found due to us, it shall be paid by you.

Give me leave, however, to advise you to prevent the necessity of so dreadful a discussion by dropping the article, that we may write to America and stop the inquiry.

—WHARTON, *Revolutionary Diplomatic Correspondence*, VI, 79-80.

VI. THE RECEPTION OF THE PEACE TREATY

The American Commissioners' grand diplomatic achievement in settling the peace evoked mixed reactions. Official French indignation was anticipated. The Commissioners had broken their instructions and signed a separate peace without telling Vergennes until it was all over. The treaty contained a separate secret article stating that in case West Florida should be British at the end of the war, its boundary should be somewhat further north than if it were to remain in the hands of Spain. When, on the day following the signing, Franklin sent a copy of the preliminary articles to Vergennes he prudently omitted including the secret article. "The English buy peace rather than make it," was Vergennes's biting comment on the success of the separate American negotiations. "Their concessions," he added, "exceed all that I could have thought possible." To his secretary, Rayneval, the treaty was a "dream," which had as its object "the defection of the Americans."

Franklin's superb tact prevented an open breach between the allies. In Congress the French party took an even more critical tone than the government at Versailles, but the treaty was ratified none the less. The peace settled, Adams took it upon himself to instruct the British on how to behave to America in the future, and Franklin made some profound comments on the evils of war. While Hamilton and Jefferson were to disagree on many issues, both were united in enthusiastic praise of the treaty. Jefferson paid homage to Jay and his colleagues. "The terms obtained for us are indeed great," he wrote, "and are so deemed by your country, a few ill designing debtors excepted." Hamilton declared that the peace exceeded "in the goodness of its terms the expectations of the most sanguine," and did "the highest honour to those who made it."

Now the Patriots could turn to the work of peace and reconstruction. "We have now happily concluded the great work of independence," Hamilton added in his letter to Jay, "but much remains to be done to reap the fruits of it." To him the solution was a strong central government to replace the inefficient and weak Confederation. "Let us turn our thoughts to what is future," Adams wrote James Warren. "The Union of the states, an affectionate respect and attachment among all their members, the education of the rising generation, the formation of a national system of oeconomy, policy and manners are the great concerns which still lye before us." He cautioned that "we must guard as much as prudence will permit against the contagion of European manners, and that excessive influx of commerce, luxury and inhabitants from abroad which will soon embarrass us."

1. THE TIFF WITH FRANCE

A. "I AM AT A LOSS TO EXPLAIN YOUR CONDUCT"

Comte de Vergennes to Benjamin Franklin.

Versailles, December 15, 1782

I am at a loss, sir, to explain your conduct and that of your colleagues on this occasion. You have concluded your preliminary articles without any communication between us, although the instructions from Congress prescribe that nothing shall be done without the participation of the King. You are about to hold out a certain hope of peace to America without even informing yourself on the state of the negociation on our part.

You are wise and discreet, sir; you perfectly understand what is due to propriety; you have all your life performed your duties. I pray you to consider how you propose to fulfill those which are due to the King. I am not desirous of enlarging these reflections; I commit them to your own integrity. When you shall be pleased to relieve my uncertainty I will entreat the King to enable me to answer your demands.

B. "I HOPE THIS LITTLE MISUNDERSTANDING WILL BE KEPT SECRET"

Benjamin Franklin to Comte de Vergennes.

Passy, December 17, 1782

Nothing has been agreed in the preliminaries contrary to the interests of France; and no peace is to take place between us and England till you have concluded yours. Your observation is, however, apparently just, that in not consulting you before they were signed, we have been guilty of neglecting a point of *bienséance*. But as this was not from want of respect to the King, whom we all love and honor, we hope it will be excused, and that the great work, which has hitherto been so happily conducted, is so nearly brought to perfection, and is so glorious to his reign, will not be ruined by a single indiscretion of ours. And certainly the whole edifice sinks to the ground immediately if you refuse on that account to give us any futher assistance.

We have not yet despatched the ship, and I beg leave to wait upon you on Friday for an answer.

It is not possible for any one to be more sensible than I am of what I and every American owe to the King for the many and great benefits and favors he has bestowed upon us. All my letters to America are proofs of this; all tending to make the same impressions on the minds of my countrymen that I felt in my own. And I believe that no prince was ever more beloved and respected by his own subjects than the King is by the people of the United States. *The English, I just now learn, flatter themselves they have already divided us.* I hope this little misunderstanding will therefore be kept a secret, and that they will find themselves totally mistaken.

—WHARTON, *Revolutionary Diplomatic Correspondence*, VI, 140, 143-144.

2. THE DEBATE IN THE CONGRESS OF CONFEDERATION

A. "THE CONDUCT OF OUR MINISTERS IS A TRAGEDY TO AMERICA"

March 19, 1783 . . . Mr. [John Francis] Mercer said that not meaning to give offence any where he should speak his sentiments freely. He gave it as his clear and decided opinion that the Ministers had insulted Congress by sending them assertions without proof as reasons for violating their instructions and throwing themselves into the confidence of Great Britain. He observed that France in order to make herself equal to the enemy had been obliged to call for aid and had drawn Spain against her interest into the war; that is was not improbable that she had entered into some specific engagements for that purpose; that hence might be deduced the perplexity of her situation, of which advantage had been taken by Great Britain, an advantage in which our Ministers had concurred for sowing jealousies between France and United States and of which further advantage would be taken to alienate the minds of the people of this country from their ally, by presenting him as the obstacle to peace.

The British Court, he said, having gained this point, may easily frustrate the negotiations and renew the war against divided enemies. He approved of the conduct of the Count de Vergennes in promoting a treaty under the 1st Commission to Oswald as preferring the substance to the shadow and proceeding from a desire of peace. The conduct of our Ministers throughout, particularly in giving in writing every thing called for by the British Minister expressive of distrust of France, was a mixture of follies which had no example, was a tragedy to America and a comedy to all the world besides.

He felt inexpressible indignation at their meanly stooping, as it were, to lick the dust from the feet of a nation whose hands were still dyed with the blood of their fellow citizens. He reprobated the chicane and low cunning which marked the journals transmitted to Congress, and contrasted them with the honesty and good faith which became all nations and particularly an infant republic. They proved that America had at once all the follies of youth and all the vices of old age; thinks it would be necessary to recall our Minister; fears that France may be already acquainted with all the transactions of our Ministers, even with the separate article, and may be only waiting the reception given to it by Congress to see how far the hopes of cutting off the right arm of Great Britain by supporting our revolution may have been well founded; and in case of our basely disappointing her, may league with our enemy for our destruction and for a division of the spoils.

He was aware of the risks to which such a league would expose France of finally losing her share, but supposed that the British Islands might be made hostages for her security. He said America was too prone to depreciate political merit and to suspect where there was no danger; that the honor of the King of France was dear to him, that he never would betray or injure us unless he should be provoked and justified by treachery on our part. . . .

B. "CENSURE NOT MINISTERS WHO HAVE NEGOTIATED WELL"

Mr. [Arthur] Lee took notice that obligations in national affairs as well as others ought to be reciprocal, and he did not know that France had ever bound herself to like engagements as to concert of negotiations with those into which America had at different times been drawn. He thought it highly improper to censure ministers who had negotiated well; said that it was agreeable to practice, and necessary to the end proposed, for ministers in particular emergencies to swerve from strict instructions. France, he said, wanted to sacrifice our interests to her own, or those of Spain; that the French answer to the British memorial contained a passage which deserved attention on this subject. She answered the reproaches of perfidy contained in that memorial by observing that, obligations being reciprocal, a breach on one side absolved the other. The Count de Vergennes, he was sure, was too much a master of negotiation not to approve the management of our ministers instead of condemning it. No man lamented more than he did any diminution of confidence between this country and France; but if the misfortune should ensue, it could not be denied that it had originated with France, who had endeavored to sacrifice our territorial rights—those very rights which by the treaty she had guaranteed to us.

—HUNT, ed., *Writings of Madison*, I, 411-412.

3. THE BRITISH ARE INSTRUCTED ON THEIR FUTURE POLICY

Diary of John Adams.

Monday [December 9, 1782]. Visited Count Sarsfield, who lent me his Notes upon America. Visited Mr. Jay. Mr. Oswald came in. We slided from one thing to another into a very lively conversation upon politics. He asked me what the conduct of his Court and nation ought to be in relation to America.

I answered, "The alpha and omega of British policy toward America was summed up in this one maxim:

"See that American independence is independent; independent of all the world; independent of yourselves, as well as of France; and independent of both, as well as of the rest of Europe. Depend upon it, you have no chance for salvation but by setting up America very high. Take care to remove from the American mind all cause of fear of you. No other motive but fear of you will ever produce in the Americans any unreasonable attachment to the House of Bourbon."

"Is it possible," said he, "that the people of America should be afraid of us or hate us?"

"One would think, Mr. Oswald," said I, "that you had been out of the world for these twenty years past. Yes, there are three millions of people in America who hate and dread you more than any thing in the world."

"What!" said he. "Now we come to our senses?"

"Your change of system is not yet known in America," said I.

"Well," said he, "what shall we do to remove these fears and jealousies?"

"In one word," said I, "favor and promote the interest, reputation, and dignity of the United States in every thing that is consistent with your own. If you pursue the plan of cramping, clipping and weakening America, on the supposition that she will be a rival to you, you will make her really so; you will make her the natural and perpetual ally of your natural and perpetual enemies."

"But in what instance," said he, "have we discovered such a disposition?"

"In the three leagues from your shores, and the fifteen leagues from Cape Breton," said I, "to which your ministry insisted so earnestly to exclude our fishermen. Here was a point that would have done us great harm, and you no good—on the contrary, harm; so that you would have hurt yourselves to hurt us. This disposition must be guarded against."

"I am fully of your mind about that," said he; "but what else can we do?"

"Send a minister to Congress," said I, "at the peace—a clever fellow who understands himself and will neither set us bad examples nor inter-meddle in our parties. This will show that you are consistent with yourselves; that you are sincere in your acknowledgment of American independence; and that you don't entertain hopes and designs of overturning it. Such a minister will dissipate many fears, and will be of more service to the least obnoxious refugees than any other measure could be. Let the King send a minister to Congress and receive one from that body. This will be acting consistently, and with dignity, in the face of the universe."

—ADAMS, ed., *Works of John Adams*, III, 344 ff.

4. "THERE NEVER WAS A GOOD WAR OR A BAD PEACE"

Benjamin Franklin to Joseph Banks.

Passy, July 27, 1783

I join with you most cordially in rejoicing at the return of peace. I hope it will be lasting, and that mankind will at length, as they call themselves reasonable creatures, have reason and sense enough to settle their differences without cutting throats; for, in my opinion, *there never was a good war or a bad peace.* What vast additions to the conveniences and comforts of living might mankind have acquired, if the money spent in wars had been employed in works of public utility! What an extension of agriculture, even to the tops of our mountains; what rivers rendered navigable or joined by canals; what bridges, aqueducts, new roads and other public works, edifices and improvements, rendering England a complete paradise, might have been obtained by spending those millions in doing good which in the last war have been spent in doing mischief; in bringing misery into thousands of families, and destroying the lives of so many thousands of working people, who might have performed the useful labor! . . .

—Bigelow, ed., *Works of Franklin*, X, 147-148.

CHAPTER THIRTY-FOUR

Closing Scenes

I. IN ENGLAND DEFEAT SHAKES
THE FOUNDATIONS OF MONARCHY

Writing to Lord North in early November 1781 before the news of York-town had reached England, George III stated: "The dye is now cast whether this shall be a great empire or the least significant of European states." And, he might well have added, whether the King should henceforth rule or reign.

As the war dragged on to its humiliating conclusion powerful voices arose in England, not only demanding peace with the former colonies, but insisting on changes in the constitutional relations between the monarch and Parliament. That rigid, moralistic and censorious ruler, George III, had identified his own interests with those of the state. His close attention to his duties and his propensity to meddle in the tasks of his subordinates made it likely that he would have to shoulder a large part of the responsibility for the impending loss of a huge slice of the old British Empire. He had refused to remove Lord North in 1778, and his prime minister was given a new lease on life by the intervention of France in the war. Now George III's prestige was at a new low. So long as the King's party retained the support of the country gentlemen, his ministry could stay in power. But by 1780 he could no longer count on their support.

The passage of the Dunning motion in a Committee of the Commons to the effect that "the power of the Crown has increased, is increasing, and ought to be diminished," was the handwriting on the wall. The news of York-town strengthened the ranks of the opposition. Great public meetings indicated that the people wanted an end to the war with America. It was only a question of time before the ministry would be overthrown in Parliament. The debate in the Commons of December 12, 1781, seventeen days after the fateful news of Yorktown reached England, revealed how the wind was blowing. Resolutions censuring the administration of the Navy were defeated by a slender margin. An address moved by Conway, petitioning the King to stop the American war, was rejected by only a single vote. Finally on March 20, 1782, North, anticipating the move for his dismissal, announced his resignation, a dramatic episode which we have already reported in the previous chapter. "At last," wrote George III, "the fatal day has come." He went so far as to draft a message of abdication, which he never submitted.

In a curious poem called "The Prophecy," Philip Freneau predicted that after 1785 "you hardly shall know that the king is alive." In one sense this turned out to be true, for in 1788 the King went mad. He had had his first attack of insanity back in 1765, and the long years of crisis finally took their toll of his obstinate mind. But politically, despite Yorktown, he had managed to fend off a drastic reform of the monarchy. A few sinecures and plums, by which the King had in the past manipulated Parliament, were cut out, but the changes were by no means of a root-and-branch character. George warded off Fox's ideas of a cabinet virtually independent of the King by allying his forces with William Pitt, son of the Earl of Chatham. In his later years the King was an object of sympathy and respect. Although a Regency was set up in 1812, George III, the man who lost the American colonies, reigned over England until his death in 1820.

1. "The Influence of the Crown Has Increased, Is Increasing, and Ought to Be Diminished"

Debate on Mr. Dunning's motion respecting the Influence of the Crown, April 6, 1780.

Mr. Dunning: It may be asked, are my propositions to be taken from the petitions on the table? Are they to be worded in the language of this or that petition? By no means. Some may be more extensive, others may be more full and specific; it will suffice that my propositions will not differ from any, as to the principle, though copied from none. My first resolution will be, "That it is the opinion of this committee, that it is necessary to declare, that the influence of the crown has increased, is increasing, and ought to be diminished." My second, "That it is competent to this House, to examine into, and to correct, abuses in the expenditure of the civil list revenues, as well as in every other branch of the public revenue, whenever it shall appear expedient to the wisdom of this House so to do."

He then proceeded to argue the question on the ground of notoriety, that the influence of the crown was increased, and ought to be diminished, having first regularly moved it. He supported his argument, not upon proof, which he said it was idle to require, and must be decided by the conscience of those who as a jury were called upon to determine what was or was not within their own knowledge. He quoted Mr. Hume to prove that he foresaw the increasing influence so early as the year 1742; and also quoted Judge Blackstone as an authority for its existence. He cited a passage from Hume's Essays, to show that that able writer had prophesied that arbitrary monarchy would one day or other be the euthanasia of the British constitution. He could affirm upon his own knowledge, and pledge his honour to the truth of the assertion, that he knew upwards of fifty members in that House who voted always in the train of the noble lord in the blue ribbon; that confessed out of the House that the influence of the crown was increased, and dangerously increased.

He adduced several arguments of a similar nature, and sat down, he said, with his consolation that neither the minority of that House, nor the people at large, would be any longer mocked and insulted with this or that management or trick, this or that evasion; for the certain alternative would be that the decision on the question now proposed by him would declare whether the petitions were to be really attended to or finally and totally rejected. . . .

Mr. Thomas Pitt instanced the present possession of office by the noble lord in the blue ribbon, as an indubitable proof of the enormous influence of the crown. He asked whether that noble lord had not lost America? Whether he had not spent millions of public money, and wasted rivers of blood of the subjects of Great Britan? And yet, the noble lord, now that the whole country with one voice cried out against and execrated the American war, held his place. To what was this ascribable but to the increased influence of the crown? The noble lord has sunk and degraded the honour of Great Britain; the name of an Englishman was now no longer a matter to be proud of; the time had been when it was the envy of all the world; it had been the key to universal respect, but the noble lord had contrived to sink it almost beneath contempt. He had rendered his countrymen and their country despicable in the eyes of every other power. He declared the noble lord would not have been so long at the head of administration but for the efforts of the opposition; it was their regular contest against the fatal measures that had marked the noble lord's administration, which had kept the noble lord in office. The whole business of the minister, for a series of years, had been to make excuses, and to devise expedients; to find supplies from year to year, without inventing any method in finance, any scheme of supply, comprehensive or permanent. The people would bear taxes, though enormous, when they heard of victories and an extension of commerce and territory; but were apt to judge of ministers, not from ingenious excuses made for their conduct either by themselves or others, but from the success that followed their measures.

He noticed the silence of ministers on the present question, and concluded with asserting that the influence of the crown was most offensively increased. The people of England, he said, saw it, and were alarmed. They had expressed their sense of it in their petitions, and begged that it might be diminished. To comply with that request was the duty of that House, and if something effectual was not done upon the present occasion, the consequences that might follow would probably be such as the bare thought of made him tremble at. . . .

Mr. Burke rallied Mr. Rigby a good deal upon his curiosity. He also thought the minister a curiosity, but he was more fit for the British Museum than the British House of Commons.*

—COBBETT, *Parliamentary History of England*, XXI, 347-348, 361-367.

2. THE HOUSE OF COMMONS PASSES THE DUNNING RESOLUTION

Horace Walpole to Sir Horace Mann.

Strawberry Hill, April 8, 1780

. . . On Wednesday, on the question of the new-raised regiments, in which Mr. Fullarton's was comprised, the ministers carried them in the House of Commons by a majority of nearly forty.

---

* Burke's retort to Rigby's observation that "it was one of the curiosities of the present age to see a minister in the minority."

The next day was appointed for consideration of the petitions from the counties and towns; about forty of which, on vast parchments subscribed by thousands of names, were heaped on the table. The opposition had kept secret their intended motions. The very first, made by Mr. Dunning, was a thundering one: the words were "that the influence of the crown has increased, is increasing, and ought to be diminished." The walls could not believe their own ears; they had not heard such language since they had a wainscot. The ministers, as if this winter were at all like the five last, poorly tried that the chairman should leave the chair; but that would not take now. Thomas Pitt, who never spoke so well before, drew a terrible picture of the difference he had felt between his former journey abroad and his last; from what he knew of the dissimilar situations of his country, then so flourishing, now so fallen! and from what he heard foreigners say of it. This apostrophe, addressed very bitterly to Lord North, threw him into a rage against the opposition that produced mighty tumult. The details of all this, and more, you will see in the papers. I have not room for particulars. In short, late at night, Mr. Dunning's motion was carried by 233 to 215, and, as uncommonly, was instantly reported to the House.

The blow seems to me decisive; for this committee is to continue sitting on the petitions, will exclude any other business, will extract from the petitions whatever propositions it pleased, may ground on those what charges it has a mind, and will carry along all those who have already voted on that foundation; so that, if the ministers attempt to make a further stand, nothing seems so probable as their being personally accused. To combat on the same field of battle after being vanquished will, in my opinion, be frenzy. It is to prevent very great mischief that I heartily wish them to retreat before it is too late. The constitution is vigorous enough, when a sudden turn of the tide can, in three months, sweep away a deep-rooted administration. A torrent opposed may damage the foundations of the constitution itself. . . .

—WALPOLE, *Letters*, XI, 151 ff.

3. "BRITAIN SHOWS THE SIGNS OF THE FALL OF A GREAT EMPIRE"

Debate in the Commons on Sir James Lowther's motion for putting an end to the American War, December 12, 1781.

The House was going into a Committee of Supply when *Sir James Lowther* rose to make a previous motion; before the House went into a committee to vote the army supplies, it became them, he said, to enquire whether they were to persevere in this war and feed it with more British blood. It had been obstinately, fatally pursued. The country was drained, exhausted, dejected. Their hearts were against it. They considered it as a struggle against nature, in which every thing was to be hazarded and nothing to be got. The Speech from the Throne had given them a most serious alarm; it shewed them that ministers were determined to persevere in spite of calamity; that they were bigotted to the prosecution of the contest, . . .

They must, if they designed to do their duty, and to discharge their trust to their constituents, come to a specific declaration on the point and put an end to the war by a peremptory resolution. It was for this reason that he recommended to the House to declare "That it is the opinion of this House that the war carried on in the colonies and plantations of North America has proved ineffectual either to the protection of his Majesty's loyal subjects in the said colonies, or for defeating the dangerous designs of our enemies." ...

Mr. Powys seconded the motion with the most heartfelt satisfaction, for so convinced had he been of the propriety and even necessity of such a resolution that like his hon. friend, from whom on account of his great weight in the county it came with so much more grace, he had determined, unconnected as he was, to have made it himself; for he most sincerely believed that it was the only means left to us, in our present situation, by which we could extricate ourselves from our difficulties and retrieve our rank in Europe.

We had persevered in this war against the voice of reason and wisdom, against experience that ought to teach, against calamity that ought to make us feel. It was the idol of his Majesty's ministers, to which they had sacrificed the interests of the empire and almost half the territories: they bowed before it, they made the nation bow; they said that the resources of the empire were not exhausted; they said so because they themselves found no diminution of income. Their annual incomes arose out of the public purse, and instead of diminishing, they increased with the misfortunes and the impoverishment of the country. The illusion which had filled the minds of some gentlemen with the hope of seeing America reduced to her former obedience to this country was now no more; and though at first it might have betrayed honest men into a determination to support the measures of ministers which had that reduction in view, he could not conceive how it came to pass that now, when the illusion was at an end, when repeated disasters and calamities had proved that the reduction of America by force was impracticable, there could be found a set of honest, independent gentlemen who could persevere in supporting those measures by which the empire had been dismembered and destroyed. That ministers should persevere in the mad plan of pursuing the phantom of conquest in America was not at all surprising to him; on the contrary, it was extremely natural, because to the war they owed their situations and their emoluments, and by a peace they must lose them; but this was not the case of independent gentlemen who supported them; and he was ready to confess that among the friends of administration in that House, he could reckon some gentlemen of independent fortunes; from what motives, or on what principles, such men continued to support the present administration, he was really at a loss to guess. Could it be from experience of their abilities? Alas! the whole history of the American war was one of continued proof that system and abilities were not to be found in the management of our force in the colonies: an army was marched from Canada, and captured at Saratoga: another from Charles-town, and surrendered at York-town.

Was it in the strength and number of our allies that they hoped for success from those measures to which they gave their support? Melancholy reflection! We were left to contend alone with our enemies; abandoned by all the world, we could not find a friend from pole to pole.

There were in this country, at this time, all the signs and tokens of a falling state. The descriptions given of the marks and signs of the decay and fall of a great empire, written by one of the ablest historians of the present age, was so applicable to these times, and to this country, that, if the House would give him leave, he would quote the passage. . . . These were the signs given by the historian of *The Decline and Fall of the Roman Empire*. . . . He called upon gentlemen to recollect that the war in which we were engaged in America was not like a war between two rival or two neighboring states about a barrier or a boundary; a contest which, however it ended, could not detract much from the importance or weight of either. It was a war in which every conclusion was against us; in which we had suffered every thing without gaining any thing. We weakened no enemy by our efforts; we exhausted no rival by distressing ourselves; every point of the war was against us. . . .

He called upon gentlemen to say if there was still any hopes, after the disaster in Virginia; if there was still any disposition in their minds to go on? What ray of hope was not blasted! What prospect had not failed! What object was not abandoned! The country gentlemen, who had been deceived in the beginning, could be deluded no more. There was no idea of drawing a revenue from that country; there was no idea of alleviating the burthens of Britain, by carrying it on; there was no other idea, and there could be no other reason, than to preserve the power, the consequence and the emoluments which flowed from it.

It was time, therefore, for parliament to interfere, and to prevent that total ruin which the measures of administration could not fail to bring on, if they should remain unchecked: the motion that had been just made might prevent that ruin; it did not refuse a supply; it did not clog the wheels of government, nor did it criminate any man or set of men; it had no retrospective tendency; it only asserted a fact which nobody could dispute; of the truth of which the whole world was perfectly well acquainted. It did not encroach upon the prerogatives of the executive power; it did not take away from the crown the right to distribute the forces of the state in whatever manner it should think for the benefit of the people; it went no farther than to say that among the operations of the war, America should not be the theatre. . . .

—Cobbett, *Parliamentary History of England*, XXII, 802-808.

4. George III Drafts His Abdication

Draft Message from the King.

March 1782

His Majesty during the twenty one years He has sate on the Throne of Great Britain, has had no object so much at heart as the maintenance of the British Constitution, of which the difficulties He has at times met with from His scrupulous attachment to the Rights of Parliament are sufficient proofs.

His Majesty is convinced that the sudden change of Sentiments of one Branch of the Legislature has totally incapacitated Him from either conducting the War with effect, or from obtaining any Peace but on conditions which would prove destructive to the Commerce as well as essential Rights of the British Nation.

His Majesty therefore with much sorrow finds He can be of no further

Utility to His Native Country which drives Him to the painful step of quitting it for ever.

In consequence of which Intention His Majesty resignes the Crown of Great Britain and the Dominions appertaining thereto to His Dearly Beloved Son and lawful Successor, George Prince of Wales, whose endeavours for the Prosperity of the British Empire He hopes may prove more Successful.

—FORTESCUE, ed., *Correspondence of King George*, V, 425.

5. AN ANCIENT PROPHECY

Philip Freneau, 1781

When a certain great king, whose initial is G.
Shall force stamps upon paper, and folks to drink tea;
When these folks burn his tea and stampt paper, like stubble,
You may guess that this king is then coming to trouble.
But when a petition he treads under his feet,
And sends over the ocean an army and fleet;
When that army, half starvéd, and frantic with rage,
Shall be cooped up with a leader whose name rhymes to cage;
When that leader goes home dejected and sad,
You may then be assured the king's prospects are bad.
But when B. and C. with their armies are taken,
This king will do well if he saves his own bacon.
In the year seventeen hundred and eighty and two,
A stroke he shall get that will make him look blue;
In the years eighty-three, eighty-four, eighty-five,
You hardly shall know that the king is alive;
In the year eighty-six the affair will be over,
And he shall eat turnips that grow in Hanover.
The face of the lion shall then become pale,
He shall yield fifteen teeth, and be sheared of his tail.
O king, my dear king, you shall be very sore;
The Stars and the Lily shall run you on shore,
And your Lion shall growl—but never bite more.

—FRENEAU, *Poems*, II, 56.

II. THE ALTERNATIVES OF DICTATORSHIP
OR REPUBLICAN GOVERNMENT

In America in the winter of 1783 the chances of a military coup seemed by no means remote. Early in January a delegation of army officers memorialized Congress, pointing out that their pay was seriously in arrears, their food and clothing accounts remained unsettled, and that no provision had been made for the life pension of half pay from the time of their discharge which Congress had promised them in October 1780.

One Congressman, Alexander Hamilton, was thoroughly alarmed. In a letter to Washington of February 7, 1783, he warned the general that the army was prepared to take steps "to procure justice to itself" and urged him

to take the lead in advancing the army's claims in order "to keep a complain-
ing and suffering army within the bounds of moderation." Washington ig-
nored Hamilton's advice, and did not sponsor the movement. After Congress
had rejected a proposal to give the officers a commutation of their pension for
six years' full pay, Major John Armstrong wrote an anonymous address which
was circulated in the main camp near Newburgh, New York. Therein he ad-
vised the officers to assume a bold tone and "suspect the man who would advise
to more moderation and longer forbearance." Armstrong's call for a meeting
of officers had the backing of Horatio Gates.

Recognizing the dangers of military dictatorship, Washington quickly
blunted the movement's force. On March 11 he issued an order forbidding
the unauthorized meeting called for by Armstrong, and proposed instead a
regular meeting of the officers for a discussion of grievances on March 15. A
second anonymous letter, also written by Armstrong, was issued on March 12,
expressing the opinion that Washington's action endorsed (the word "sancti-
fied" was actually used) the claims of the officers. But Washington's unex-
pected and dramatic appearance at the meeting of the fifteenth quickly dis-
abused the dissident elements. We are indebted to a spectator, Major Samuel
Shaw, for an account of Washington's speech, which he read. In his journal
the major records that after reading the first paragraph, Washington paused,
took out his spectacles, "and begged the indulgence of his audience while he
put them on, observing at the same time that he had grown gray in their serv-
ice, and now found himself growing blind." "There was something so natural,
so unaffected, in this appeal," Major Shaw continued, "as rendered it superior
to the most studied oratory. It forces its way to the heart, and you might see
sensibility moisten every eye."

After Washington withdrew, the officers adopted resolutions, affirming
their patriotism, their confidence in Congress, and their disdain of the "in-
famous propositions . . . in a late anonymous address." Thus, Washington's
timely intervention prevented what could have been a military coup. Wash-
ington had demonstrated a full measure of courage and a deep sense of public
responsibility. "On other occasions," Shaw remarked, Washington "had been
supported by the exertions of an Army and the countenance of his friends;
but in this he stood single and alone. . . . He appeared, not at the head of his
troops, but as it were in opposition to them; and for a dreadful moment the
interests of the Army and its General seemed to be in competition! He spoke
—every doubt was dispelled, and the tide of patriotism rolled again in its
wonted course."

"One More Distinguished Proof of Unexampled Patriotism"

Washington addresses the officers of the Army, March 15, 1783.

Gentlemen: By an anonymous summons, an attempt has been made to
convene you together; how inconsistent with the rules of propriety! how unmilitary! and how subversive of all order and discipline, let the good sense of
the Army decide.

In the moment of this Summons, another anonymous production was sent
into circulation, addressed more to the feelings and passions, than to the reason

and judgment of the Army. . . . That the Address is drawn with great Art, and is designed to answer the most insidious purposes. That it is calculated to impress the mind, with an idea of premeditated injustice in the Sovereign power of the United States, and rouse all those resentments which must unavoidably flow from such a belief. That the secret mover of this Scheme (whoever he may be) intended to take advantage of the passions, while they were warmed by the recollection of past distresses, without giving time for cool, deliberative thinking, and that composure of Mind which is so necessary to give dignity and stability to measures is rendered too obvious, by the mode of conducting the business, to need other proof than a reference to the proceeding. . . .

It can *scarcely be supposed*, at this late stage of the War, that I am indifferent to its interests. But, how are they to be promoted? The way is plain, says the anonymous Addresser. If War continues, remove into the unsettled Country; there establish yourselves, and leave an ungrateful Country to defend itself. . . . This dreadful alternative, of either deserting our Country in the extremest hour of her distress, or turning our Arms against it, (which is the apparent object, unless Congress can be compelled into instant compliance) has something so shocking in it, that humanity revolts at the idea. My God! what can this writer have in view, by recommending such measures? Can he be a friend to the Army? Can he be a friend to this Country? Rather, is he not an insidious Foe? Some Emissary, perhaps, from New York, plotting the ruin of both, by sowing the seeds of discord and seperation between the Civil and Military powers of the Continent? . . .

For myself . . . a grateful sence of the confidence you have ever placed in me, a recollection of the chearful assistance, and prompt obedience I have experienced from you, under every vicissitude of fortune, and the sincere affection I feel for an Army, I have so long had the honor to Command, will oblige me to declare, in this public and solemn manner, that, in the attainment of compleat justice for all your toils and dangers, and in the gratification of every wish, so far as may be done consistently with the great duty I owe my Country, and those powers we are bound to respect, you may freely command my Services to the utmost of my abilities.

While I give you these assurances, and pledge myself in the most unequivocal manner, to exert whatever ability I am possessed of, in your favor, let me entreat you, Gentlemen, on your part, not to take any measures, which, viewed in the calm light of reason, will lessen the dignity, and sully the glory you have hitherto maintained; let me request you to rely on the plighted faith of your Country, and place a full confidence in the purity of the intentions of Congress; that, previous to your dissolution as an Army they will cause all your Accts. to be fairly liquidated. . . .

And let me conjure you, in the name of our common Country, as you value your own sacred honor, as you respect the rights of humanity, and as you regard the Military and National character of America, to express your utmost horror and detestation of the Man who wishes, under any specious pretences, to overturn the liberties of our Country, and who wickedly attempts to open the flood Gates of Civil discord, and deluge our rising Empire in Blood. By thus determining, and thus acting, you will pursue the plain and direct road to the attainment of your wishes. You will defeat the insidious designs of our Enemies, who are compelled to resort from open force to secret artifice. You will give one more distinguished proof of unexampled patriotism and patient virtue, rising superior to the pressure of the most complicated sufferings; And you will, by the dignity of your Conduct, afford occasion for Posterity to say, when speaking of the glorious example you have exhibited to Mankind, "had this day been wanting, the World had never seen the last stage of perfection to which human nature is capable of attaining."

—FITZPATRICK, ed., *Writings of Washington*, XXVI, 222-227.

III. WASHINGTON'S PARTING ADVICE TO THE NEW NATION

In several papers and addresses announcing the termination of the war and his own imminent retirement Washington summed up the meaning of the Revolution and the problems facing America in peacetime. The first document included in this section is his "Circular to the States," in which he listed four objectives as "essential to the well being," even to "the very existence" of the United States as "an independent power." They were "an indissoluble union of the states under one Federal Head"; "a sacred regard to public justice"; "the adoption of a proper peace establishment"; and "the prevalence of that pacific and friendly disposition among the people of the United States which will induce them to forget their local prejudices and policies, to make those mutual concessions which are requisite to the general prosperity, and in some instances, to sacrifice their individual advantages to the interest of the community."

The rear guard of the British troops evacuated New York on December 4, 1783. Washington was determined to leave for home as soon as the evacuation was completed, but before departing he had a last meeting with his officers at Fraunces' Tavern. His brief words were reported in Rivington's Tory Gazette. Washington embraced each of his officers in turn, beginning with Knox. "The simple thought," wrote Lieutenant Colonel Benjamin Talmadge, "that we were then about to part from the man who had conducted us through a long and bloody war, and under whose conduct the glory and independence of our country had been achieved, and that we should see his face no more in this world seemed to me utterly insupportable."

Finally, Washington addressed Congress at Annapolis on December 23, and in a few eloquent words submitted his resignation. "The spectators all wept," wrote James McHenry, "and there was hardly a member of Congress who did not drop tears." The preceding evening a ball was given in his honor. "The general," one observer noted, "danced every set, that all the ladies might have the pleasure of dancing with him, or as it has been handsomely expressed, get a touch of him."

1. "WITH OUR FATE WILL THE DESTINY OF MILLIONS BE INVOLVED"

Circular to the States.

Head Quarters, Newburgh, June 8, 1783

Sir: The great object for which I had the honor to hold an appointment in the Service of my Country, being accomplished, I am now preparing to resign it into the hands of Congress, and to return to that domestic retirement, which, it is well known, I left with the greatest reluctance, a Retirement, for which I have never ceased to sigh through a long and painful absence, and in which (remote from the noise and trouble of the World) I meditate to pass the remainder of life in a state of undisturbed repose. But before I carry this resolution into effect, I think it a duty incumbent on me, to make this my last official communication, to congratulate you on the glorious events which Heaven has been pleased to produce in our favor, to offer my sentiments respecting some important subjects, which appear to me, to be intimately connected with the tranquility of the United States, to take my leave of your Excellency as a public Character, and to give my final blessing to that Country, in whose service I have spent the prime of my life, for whose sake I have consumed so many anxious days and watchfull nights, and whose happiness being extremely dear to me, will always constitute no inconsiderable part of my own.

Impressed with the liveliest sensibility on this pleasing occasion, I will claim the indulgence of dilating the more copiously on the subjects of our mutual felicitation. When we consider the magnitude of the prize we contended for, the doubtful nature of the contest, and the favorable manner in which it has terminated, we shall find the greatest possible reason for gratitude and rejoicing; this is a theme that will afford infinite delight to every benevolent and liberal mind, whether the event in contemplation, be considered as the source of present enjoyment or the parent of future happiness; and we shall have equal occasion to felicitate ourselves on the lot which Providence has assigned us, whether we view it in a natural, a political or moral point of light.

The Citizens of America, placed in the most enviable condition, as the sole Lords and Proprietors of a vast Tract of Continent, comprehending all the various soils and climates of the World, and abounding with all the necessaries and conveniences of life, are now by the late satisfactory pacification, acknowledged to be possessed of absolute freedom and Independency; They are, from this period, to be considered as the Actors on a most conspicuous Theatre, which seems to be peculiarly designated by Providence for the display of human greatness and felicity; Here, they are not only surrounded with every thing which can contribute to the completion of private and domestic enjoyment, but Heaven has crowned all its other blessings, by giving a fairer oppertunity for political happiness, than any other Nation has ever been favored with. Nothing can illustrate these observations more forcibly, than a recollection of the happy conjuncture of times and circumstances, under which our Republic assumed its rank among the Nations; The foundation of our Empire was not laid in the gloomy age of Ignorance and Superstition, but at an Epocha when the rights of mankind were better understood and more clearly defined, than at any former period, the researches of the human mind, after social happiness, have been carried to a great extent, the Treasures of knowledge, acquired by the labours of Philosophers, Sages and Legislatures, through a long succession of years, are laid open for our use, and their collected wisdom may be happily applied in the Establishment of our forms of Government; the free cultivation of Letters, the unbounded extension of Commerce, the progressive refinement of Manners, the growing liberality of sentiment, and above all, the pure and benign light of Revelation, have had a me-liorating influence on mankind and increased the blessings of Society. At this auspicious period, the United States came into existence as a Nation, and if their Citizens should not be completely free and happy, the fault will be intirely their own.

Such is our situation, and such are our prospects: but notwithstanding the cup of blessing is thus reached out to us, notwithstanding happiness is ours, if we have a disposition to seize the occasion and make it our own; yet, it appears to me there is an option still left to the United States of America, that it is in their choice, and depends upon their conduct, whether they will be respect-able and prosperous, or contemptable and miserable as a Nation; This is the time of their political probation, this is the moment when the eyes of the whole World are turned upon them, this is the moment to establish or ruin their national Character forever, this is the favorable moment to give such a tone to our Federal Government, as will enable it to answer the ends of its institution, or this may be the ill-fated moment for relaxing the powers of the Union, annihilating the cement of the Confederation, and exposing us to be-come the sport of European politics, which may play one State against an-other to prevent their growing importance, and to serve their own interested purposes. For, according to the system of Policy the States shall adopt at this moment, they will stand or fall, and by their confirmation or lapse, it is yet to be decided, whether the Revolution must ultimately be considered as a blessing or a curse: a blessing or a curse, not to the present age alone, for with out fate will the destiny of unborn Millions be involved.

—FITZPATRICK, ed., *Writings of Washington*, XXVI, 483-486.

2. "I Now Take Leave of You"

Fraunces' Tavern, New York, December 4, 1783. The following report ap-peared in Rivington's New York *Gazette* of December 6, 1783, and the *Penn-sylvania Packet* of December 12, 1783.

His excellency, having filled a glass of wine, thus addressed his brave fellow-soldiers:

"With an heart full of love and gratitude I now take leave of you. I most devoutly wish that your latter days may be as prosperous and happy as your former ones have been glorious and honorable."

These words produced extreme sensibility on both sides; they were an-swered by warm expressions and fervent wishes from the gentlemen of the army, whose truly pathetic feelings it is not in our power to convey to the reader. Soon after this scene was closed, His Excellency the Governor, the Honorable the Council and citizens of the first distinction waited on the gen-eral and in terms most affectionate took their leave.

The corps of light infantry was drawn up in a line. The commander in chief about two o'clock passed through them on his way to Whitehall, where he embarked in his barge for Powles Hook. He is attended by general le baron de Steuben; proposes to make a short stay at Philadelphia; will thence proceed to Annapolis, where he will resign his commission as General of the American Armies into the hands of the Continental Congress, from whom it was derived, immediately after which His Excellency will set out for his seat named Mount Vernon, in Virginia, emulating the example of his model, the virtuous Roman General, who, victorious, left the tented field, covered with honors, and withdrew from public life, *otium cum dignitate.*

—CLINTON, *Public Papers,* VIII, 306-307.

3. "I RETIRE FROM THE GREAT THEATRE OF ACTION"

Washington's address to Congress resigning his commission.

December 23, 1783

Mr. President:

The great events on which my resignation depended having at length taken place; I have now the honor of offering my sincere Congratulations to Congress and of presenting myself before them to surrender into their hands the trust committed to me, and to claim the indulgence of retiring from the Service of my Country.

Happy in the confirmation of our Independence and Sovereignty, and pleased with the oppertunity afforded the United States of becoming a respectable Nation, I resign with satisfaction the Appointment I accepted with diffidence. A diffidence in my abilities to accomplish so arduous a task, which however was superseded by a confidence in the rectitude of our Cause, the support of the Supreme Power of the Union, and the patronage of Heaven.

The Successful termination of the War has verified the most sanguine expectations, and my gratitude for the interposition of Providence, and the assistance I have received from my Countrymen, encreases with every review of the momentous Contest.

While I repeat my obligations to the Army in general, I should do injustice to my own feelings not to acknowledge in this place the peculiar Services and distinguished merits of the Gentlemen who have been attached to my person during the War. It was impossible the choice of confidential Officers to compose my famliy should have been more fortunate. Permit me Sir, to recommend in particular those, who have continued in Service to the present moment, as worthy of the favorable notice and patronage of Congress.

I consider it an indispensable duty to close this last solemn act of my Official life, by commending the Interests of our dearest Country to the protection of Almighty God, and those who have the superintendence of them, to his holy keeping.

Having now finished the work assigned me, I retire from the great theatre of Action; and bidding an Affectionate farewell to this August body under whose orders I have so long acted, I here offer my Commission, and take my leave of all the employments of public life.

—FITZPATRICK, ed., *Writings of Washington,* XXVII, 284-285.

IV. "PEACE MADE, A NEW SCENE OPENS"

Writing his bosom friend John Laurens on August 15, 1782, Hamilton commented: "Peace made, my dear friend, a new scene opens. The object will be to make our independence a blessing. To do this we must secure our Union on solid foundations—a herculean task—and to effect which mountains of prejudice must be levelled! It requires all the virtue and all the abilities of our country." To Hamilton as to Washington a strong foundation meant a Continental government with power to act. Others reflected the same sentiments. "Say, my friend," Samuel Shaw asked the Reverend Mr. Elliot in February 1783, "is America prepared for the reception of the long wished-for blessing?" There had to be a power vested in some supreme head, he argued. "Thirteen wheels require a steady and powerful regulator to keep them in good order, and prevent the machine from becoming useless. The prospect of peace makes a politician of the soldier. We are thirteen states, and a hoop to the barrel *is the prevailing sentiment."*

Leaders like Washington and Hamilton were concerned about developing and preserving the American character. "We are placed among the nations of the earth," Washington wrote Lafayette from Newburgh on April 5, 1783, "and have a character to establish, but how we shall acquit ourselves time must discover." The great end was "to form a Constitution that will give consistency, stability and dignity to the Union." Washington would give whatever help he could as a private citizen, "for henceforward my mind shall be unbent; and I will endeavor to glide down the stream of life, till I come to that abyss, from whence no traveller is permitted to return."

In a sermon delivered in 1783 Ezra Stiles expatiated on one essential ingredient of nationalism—a common language. He predicted that "the rough, sonorous diction of the English language may here take its Athenian polish, and receive its Attic urbanity; as it will probably become the vernacular tongue of more numerous millions than ever yet spake one language on earth." He also expressed the belief that travel and communication in the United States would prevent the rise of provincial dialects. It was his expectation that "the English language will grow up with the present American population into great purity and elegance, unmutilated by the foreign dialects of foreign conquests."

This aspect of cultural nationalism was stressed by the distinguished South Carolinian, David Ramsay, physician and historian, in his perceptive appraisal of the social and cultural consequences of the Revolution, first published in 1789, and by Thomas Paine in his last Crisis paper. It is fitting that Paine, whose first Crisis paper evoked that unflinching courage and selfless dedication, which for posterity are epitomized in the "spirit of 'seventy-six," should in these volumes have the last word, and that on the noble prospects of the American nation. Paine notwithstanding, "the times that tried men's souls" were not really over. The American people were still to face other trials in the buildings of the new nation, in the preserving of union, and in the effort to achieve a durable peace, but that unconquerable spirit forged in the crucible of Bunker's Hill and Valley Forge and King's Mountain would sustain the nation through crises that lay ahead.

1. AN AMERICAN NATIONALISM AND AN AMERICAN CHARACTER

[1793]

From Dr. Ramsay's *History of the American Revolution.*

The American Revolution, on the one hand, brought forth great vices; but on the other hand, it called forth many virtues, and gave occasion for the display of abilities which, but for that event, would have been lost to the world.

When the war began, the Americans were a mass of husbandmen, merchants, mechanics and fishermen; but the necessities of the country gave a spring to the active powers of the inhabitants, and set them on thinking, speaking and acting in a line far beyond that to which they had been accustomed.

The difference between nations is not so much owing to nature as to education and circumstances. While the Americans were guided by the leading strings of the mother country, they had no scope nor encouragement for exertion. All the departments of government were established and executed for them, but not by them. In the years 1775 and 1776 the country, being suddenly thrown into a situation that needed the abilities of all its sons, these generally took their places, each according to the bent of his inclination. As they severally pursued their objects with ardour, a vast expansion of the human mind speedily followed. This displayed itself in a variety of ways. It was found that their talents for great stations did not differ in kind, but only in degree, from those which were necessary for the proper discharge of the ordinary business of civil society.

In the bustle that was occasioned by the war, few instances could be produced of any persons who made a figure, or who rendered essential services, but from among those who had given specimens of similar talents in their respective professions. Those who from indolence or dissipation had been of little service to the community in time of peace, were found equally unserviceable in war. A few young men were exceptions to this general rule. Some of these, who had indulged in youthful follies, broke off from their vicious courses and on the pressing call of their country became useful servants of the public; but the great bulk of those who were the active instruments of carrying on the Revolution were self-made, industrious men. These who by their own exertions had established or laid a foundation for establishing personal independence, were most generally trusted and most successfully employed in establishing that of their country. In these times of action, classical education was found of less service than good natural parts, guided by common sense and sound judgment.

Several names could be mentioned of individuals who, without the knowledge of any other language than their mother tongue, wrote not only accurately, but elegantly, on public business. It seemed as if the war not only required, but created talents. Men whose minds were warmed with the love of liberty, and whose abilities were improved by daily exercise, and sharpened with a laudable ambition to serve their distressed country, spoke, wrote and acted with an energy far surpassing all expectations which could be reasonably founded on their previous acquirements.

The Americans knew but little of one another previous to the Revolution. Trade and business had brought the inhabitants of their seaports acquainted with each other, but the bulk of the people in the interior country were unacquainted with their fellow citizens. A Continental Army and a Congress composed of men from all the States by freely mixing together were assimilated into one mass. Individuals of both, mingling with the citizens, disseminated principles of union among men. Local prejudices abated. By frequent collision asperities were worn off, and a foundation was laid for the establishment of a nation out of discordant materials. Intermarriages between men and women of different States were much more common than before the war and became an additional cement to the union. Unreasonable jealousies had existed between the inhabitants of the eastern and the southern states; but on becoming better acquainted with each other, these in a great measure subsided. A wiser policy prevailed. Men of liberal minds led the way in discouraging local distinctions, and the great body of the people, as soon as reason got the better of prejudice, found that their best interests would be most effectually promoted by such practices and sentiments as were favorable to union.

Religious bigotry had broken in upon the peace of various sects before the American war. This was kept up by partial establishments, and by a dread that the Church of England through the power of the mother country would be made to triumph over all other denominations. These apprehensions were done away by the Revolution. The different sects, having nothing to fear from each other, dismissed all religious controversy. A proposal for introducing bishops into America before the war had kindled a flame among the dissenters; but the Revolution was no sooner accomplished than a scheme for that purpose was perfected, with the consent and approbation of all those sects who had previously opposed it. Pulpits which had formerly been shut to worthy men, because their heads had not been consecrated by the imposition of the hands of a bishop or of a presbytery, have since the establishment of independence been reciprocally opened to each other, whensoever the public convenience required it. The world will soon see the result of an experiment in politics, and be able to determine whether the happiness of society is increased by religious establishments, or diminished by the want of them.

Though schools and colleges were generally shut up during the war, yet many of the arts and sciences were promoted by it. The geography of the United States before the Revolution was but little known; but the marches of armies and the operations of war gave birth to many geographical enquiries and discoveries which otherwise would not have been made. A passionate fondness for studies of this kind and the growing importance of the country excited one of its sons, the Reverend Mr. Morse, to travel through every State of the Union and amass a fund of topographical knowledge far exceeding any thing heretofore communicated to the public.

The necessities of the States led to the study of tactics, fortifications, gunnery and a variety of other arts connected with war, and diffused a knowledge of them among a peaceable people who would ohterwise have had no inducement to study them.

The abilities of ingenious men were directed to make farther improvements in the art of destroying an enemy. Among these, David Bushnell of Connecticut invented a machine for submarine navigation, which was found to answer the purpose of rowing horizontally at any given depth under water, and of rising or sinking at pleasure. To this was attached a magazine of powder, and the whole was contrived in such a manner as to make it practicable to blow up vessels by machinary under them. Mr. Bushnell also contrived sundry other curious machines for the annoyance of British shipping, but from accident they only succeeded in part. He destroyed one vessel in charge of Commodore Symonds, and a second one near the shore of Long-Island.

Surgery was one of the arts which was promoted by the war. From the want of hospitals and other aids, the medical men of America had few opportunities of perfecting themselves in this art, the thorough knowledge of which can only be acquired by practice and observation. The melancholy events of battles gave the American students an opportunity of seeing and learning more in one day than they could have acquired in years of peace. It was in the hospitals of the United States that Dr. Rush first discovered the method of curing the lock jaw by bark and wine, added to other invigorating remedies, which has since been adopted with success in Europe, as well as in the United States.

The science of government has been more generally diffused among the Americans by means of the Revolution. The policy of Great Britain in throwing them out of her protection induced a necessity of establishing independent constitutions. This led to reading and reasoning on the subject. The many errors that were at first committed by unexperienced statesmen have been a practical comment on the folly of unbalanced constitutions and injudicious laws. The discussions concerning the new constitutions gave birth to much reasoning on the subject of government, and particularly to a series of letters signed Publius, but really the work of Alexander Hamilton, in which much political knowledge and wisdom were displayed, and which will long remain a monument of the strength and acuteness of the human understanding in investigating truth. . . .

As literature had in the first instance favoured the Revolution, so in its turn the Revolution promoted literature. The study of eloquence and of the belles lettres was more successfully prosecuted in America after the disputes between Great Britain and her colonies began to be serious than it had ever been before. The various orations, addresses, letters, dissertations and other literary performances which the war made necessary, called forth abilities where they were, and excited the rising generation to study arts which brought with them their own reward. Many incidents afforded materials for the favourites of the muses to display their talents. Even burlesquing royal proclamations by parodies and doggerel poetry had great effects on the minds of the people. A celebrated historian has remarked that the song of "Lillibullero" forwarded the revolution of 1688 in England. It may be truly affirmed that similar productions produced similar effects in America. Francis Hopkinson rendered essential service to his country by turning the artillery of wit and ridicule on the enemy. Philip Freneau laboured successfully in the same way. Royal proclamations and other productions which issued from royal printing presses were, by the help of warm imaginations, arrayed in such dresses as rendered them truly ridiculous. Trumbull with a vein of original Hudibrastic humour diverted his countrymen so much with the follies of their enemies that for a time they forgot the calamities of war. Humphries twined the literary with the military laurel by superadding the fame of an elegant poet to that of an accomplished officer. Barlow increased the fame of his country and of the distinguished actors in the Revolution by the bold design of an epic poem ably executed on the idea that Columbus foresaw in vision the great scenes that were to be transacted on the theater of that new world which he had discovered. Dwight struck out in the same line and at an early period of life finished an elegant work entitled *The Conquest of Canaan*, on a plan which has rarely been attempted. The principles of their mother tongue were first unfolded to the Americans since the Revolution by their countryman Webster. Pursuing an unbeaten track, he has made discoveries in the genius and construction of the English language which had escaped the researches of preceding philologists.

These and a group of other literary characters have been brought into view by the Revolution. It is remarkable that of these Connecticut has produced an unusual proportion. In that truly republican state, every thing conspires to adorn human nature with its highest honours.

From the latter periods of the Revolution till the present time, schools, colleges, societies, and institutions for promoting literature, arts, manufactures, agriculture, and for extending human happiness, have been increased far beyond any thing that ever took place before the Declaration of Independence. Every state in the union has done more or less in this way, but Pennsylvania has done the most. . . .

To overset an established government unhinges many of those principles which bind individuals to each other. A long time, and much prudence, will be necessary to reproduce a spirit of union and that reverence for government without which society is a rope of sand. The right of the people to resist their rulers, when invading their liberties, forms the corner stone of the American republics. This principle, though just in itself, is not favourable to the tranquility of present establishments. The maxims and measures which in the years 1774 and 1775 were successfully inculcated and adopted by American patriots for oversetting the established government, will answer a similar purpose when recurrence is had to them by factious demagogues for disturbing the freest governments that were ever devised.

War never fails to injure the morals of the people engaged in it. The American war, in particular, had an unhappy influence of this kind. Being begun without funds or regular establishments, it could not be carried on without violating private rights; and in its progress it involved a necessity for breaking solemn promises and plighted public faith. The failure of national justice, which was in some degree unavoidable, increased the difficulties of performing private engagements, and weakened that sensibility to the obligations of public and private honor which is a security for the punctual performance of contracts.

In consequence of the war, the institutions of religion have been deranged, the public worship of the Deity suspended, and a great number of inhabitants deprived of the ordinary means of obtaining that religious knowledge which tames the fierceness and softens the rudeness of human passions and manners. Many of the temples dedicated to the service of the Most High were destroyed, and these, from a deficiency of ability and inclination, are not yet rebuilt. The clergy were left to suffer without proper support. The depreciation of the paper currency was particularly injurious to them. It reduced their salaries to a pittance, so insufficient for the maintenance that several of them were obliged to lay down their profession and engage in other pursuits. Public preaching, of which many of the inhabitants were thus deprived, seldom fails of rendering essential service to society by civilising the multitude and forming them to union. No class of citizens have contributed more to the Revolution than the clergy, and none have hitherto suffered more in consequence of it. From the diminution of their number and the penury to which they have been subjected, civil government has lost many of the advantages it formerly derived from the public instructions of that useful order of men.

On the whole, the literary, political and military talents of the citizens of the United States have been improved by the Revolution, but their moral character is inferior to what it formerly was. So great is the change for the worse that the friends of public order are loudly called upon to exert their utmost abilities in extirpating the vicious principles and habits which have taken deep root during the late convulsions.

—RAMSAY, *History of the Revolution*, II, 315 *et seq.*

2. "THE TIMES THAT TRIED MEN'S SOULS ARE OVER!": THOMAS PAINE

The *Crisis*, XIII: "Thoughts on the Peace and the Probable Advantages Thereof."

[1783]

"The times that tried men's souls" are over—and the greatest and completest revolution the world ever knew, gloriously and happily accomplished.

But to pass from the extremes of danger to safety, from the tumult of war to the tranquillity of peace, though sweet in contemplation, requires a gradual composure of the senses to receive it. Even calmness has the power of stunning, when it opens too instantly upon us. The long and raging hurricane that should cease in a moment, would leave us in a state rather of wonder than enjoyment; and some moments of recollection must pass, before we could be capable of tasting the felicity of repose. There are but few instances in which the mind is fitted for sudden transitions: it takes in its pleasures by reflection and comparison and those must have time to act, before the relish for new scenes is complete. . . .

To see it in our power to make a world happy—to teach mankind the art of being so—to exhibit on the theatre of the universe a character hitherto unknown—and to have, as it were, a new creation intrusted to our hands, are honors that command reflection and can neither be too highly estimated nor too gratefully received.

In this pause then of recollection, while the storm is ceasing, and the long agitated mind vibrating to a rest, let us look back on the scenes we have passed and learn from experience what is yet to be done.

Never, I say, had a country so many openings to happiness as this. Her setting out in life, like the rising of a fair morning, was unclouded and promising. Her cause was good. Her principles just and liberal. Her temper serene and firm. Her conduct regulated by the nicest steps, and everything about her wore the mark of honor. It is not every country (perhaps there is not another in the world) that can boast so fair an origin. Even the first settlement of America corresponds with the character of the Revolution. Rome, once the proud mistress of the universe, was originally a band of ruffians. Plunder and rapine made her rich, and her oppression of millions made her great. But America need never be ashamed to tell her birth, nor relate the stages by which she rose to empire. . . .

She is now descending to the scenes of quiet and domestic life. Not beneath the cypress shade of disappointment, but to enjoy in her own land, and under her own vine, the sweet of her labors, and the reward of her toil. In this situation, may she never forget that a fair national reputation is of as much importance as independence! That it possesses a charm that wins upon the world, and makes even enemies civil! That it gives a dignity which is often superior to power, and commands reverence where pomp and splendor fail!

It would be a circumstance ever to be lamented and never to be forgotten, were a single blot, from any cause whatever, suffered to fall on a revolution which to the end of time must be an honor to the age that accomplished it; and which has contributed more to enlighten the world, and diffuse a spirit of freedom and liberality among mankind, than any human event (if this may be called one) that ever preceded it. . . .

—CONWAY, ed., *Writings of Paine*, I, 370-375, *passim.*

Thus, almost eight years after the opening shots at Lexington and Concord, Britain acknowledged the independence of the American States, and the war came to an end. The sage Franklin might say that there never was a good war, but he had never for a moment questioned the necessity of this one, nor did he ever doubt that its ultimate consequences were beneficial to mankind. Who now can doubt that John Adams was justified in seeing, "through all the gloom, the rays of ravishing light and glory," or that posterity did indeed "triumph in the transactions of that day" of independence? The American Revolution was costly in lives and in property, and more costly in the terror and the fear and the violence that, as in all wars, fell so disproportionately on the innocent and the weak. Yet by comparison with other wars of comparable magnitude, before and since, the cost was not high. Notwithstanding the ruthlessness and even the ferocity with which it was waged, it did little lasting damage, and left few lasting scars. Population increased all through the war; the movement into the West was scarcely interrupted; and within a few years of peace, the new nation was bursting with prosperity and buoyant with hope. Independence stimulated both material and intellectual enterprise, and five years after the Treaty of Paris Americans brought the Revolution to a triumphant conclusion by writing the first national constitution and setting up the most enduring of national unions.

Of few other wars can it be said that so much was gained at so little lasting cost, either in lives snuffed out, or in a heritage of hatred. As victory did not make Americans ruthless or militaristic, so defeat did not impair British power or undermine British character. In time British statesmen and historians came to look upon the American Revolution as a proud chapter in their own his-

tory, and to rejoice that Washington triumphed over George the Third. The war dramatized for them the necessity of a new and more wholesome relationship between Crown and Parliament; it vindicated seventeenth-century political theories and principles that were to survive and flourish into the nineteenth and twentieth centuries; it foreshadowed a more enlightened relationship between mother country and colony, one that was eventually to evolve into that notable institution, the Commonwealth of Nations.

The United States, born out of the travail of what John Adams called "this mighty Revolution," was the first colony to break away from a mother country and started a process whose end is not yet. It was the first of the new nations of the modern world, and for a long time a model to other new nations. It was the first to realize the great principle that men make government; the first to provide effective limits on government through written constitutions; the first to create a workable federal system; the first to do away with the age-old subordination of colony to mother country and substitute for this a system of equal and co-ordinate states; the first to abolish the interdependence of church and state and institute full religious freedom; the first to encourage and provide for a society without overt class distinctions (except for the tragic one of Negro slavery), and to inaugurate the great experiment of equality in circumstances auspicious to its success.

The Revolution was, therefore, in a very real sense, the first war whose nonmilitary consequences were of significance to the rest of mankind. In the words of Jefferson, Americans undertook "to make a communication of grandeur and freedom" to all the peoples of the globe; it was for this reason that the Great Declaration had asserted the rights not just of Americans or of Englishmen, but of Man. This concern for something more than private and local interests; this sense of obligation to the welfare of mankind, and of posterity, was common to the generation that fought and won the Revolution. Thus Tom Paine thought it was "the opportunity of beginning the world anew and of bringing forward a new system of government in which the rights of all men should be preserved that gave value to independence." Thus Ethan Allen rejoiced that "to see it in our power to make a world happy, to teach mankind the art of being so, to exhibit on the theatre of the universe, a character hitherto unknown, to have . . . a new creation entrusted to our hands, are honors that can neither be too highly estimated nor too greatly received." And thus Washington admonished us that "with our fate will the destiny of unborn millions be involved." The American Revolution was not an event in American history alone, but in world history, and the new nation which came out of it was destined to play on the great stage of history a part more influential than that played by Athens or Rome in the ancient world, by Spain or England in the modern. That this role has been, on the whole, a benevolent one can be explained in part by the principles of conduct laid down at the very beginning by the great good fortune of leadership by men like Washington, Franklin, Jefferson, Hamilton, Adams and Paine, and by the courage and fortitude of thousands of plain men and women who fought and endured that the nation might live.

THE END

Acknowledgments and Bibliography

An enterprise of this character, stretching over many years, naturally incurs many and deep debts and obligations. Mr. Warren Carroll was notably helpful in the tracking down and transcribing of sources, and we are also appreciative of the assistance rendered by Mr. Robert Christen, Dr. Catherine Crary and Mr. Jesse Lemisch in research and verification. We could not have completed this book without the cheerful help of the staffs of the Columbia University and the Amherst College libraries, who endured with good humor continuous raids upon their collections. We are indebted, too, to libraries and librarians elsewhere: the Massachusetts Historical Society; the Widener Library; the New York Historical Society; the Morristown National Historical Park, and to Mr. Francis Ronalds its director, as well as to his associate, Dr. Walter Hugins; the Library of Congress; the library of the University of North Carolina and many others. The editorial and production departments of The Bobbs-Merrill Company have worked indefatigably with us and for us: Mrs. Nancy L. Bentley, Mrs. Elizabeth McCain, Mr. Walter Hurley, Mr. Harrison Platt, and above all that prince among publishers, Mr. Laurance Chambers, whose help, far beyond the call of duty, is more fittingly acknowledged elsewhere. To the many publishers, historical societies, university presses, government agencies, and private individuals who, by giving us permission to reproduce material in their possession or their control, displayed the operation of the great community of scholarship, we are deeply grateful. An asterisk (*) before a title indicates that special permission was obtained from the publisher, proprietor, or other copyright owner to use the excerpts published in these volumes. Our mapmaker has sometimes found assistance or reassurance through study of the fine maps in *History of the United States and Its People* by Elroy M. Avery. Our wives did not type the manuscript or compile the index or do the other chores so commonly associated with matrimony in academic circles. They did much more: they shared our enjoyment in the undertaking.

HENRY STEELE COMMAGER
RICHARD B. MORRIS

MANUSCRIPTS

American Loyalist Audit Office Transcripts. New York Public Library.
*Baldwin, Loammi. Papers. Houghton Library, Harvard University.
Bancroft Collection. New York Public Library.
Boudinot, Elias. Papers. Library of Congress.

Convention of the New England States with Accompanying Resolutions, 1776-80. Rhode Island State Archives.

*Davie-Weems Collection. University of North Carolina.

Duane, James. Papers. New York Historical Society.

*Eggleston, Joseph, Jr. Letter. The J. Pierpont Morgan Library.

Emmet Collection. New York Public Library.

Gansevoort, Peter, Jr. Military Papers. Lansing-Gansevoort Collection. New York Public Library.

Gates, Horatio. Papers. New York Historical Society.

Greene, Nathanael. Papers. William L. Clements Library.

Hamilton, Alexander. Papers. Library of Congress.

*Hamilton, Lieutenant-Governor Henry. Journal. Houghton Library. Harvard University.

*Howe, Sir William. Orderly Book. Lloyd W. Smith Collection. Morristown National Historical Park.

Jay, John. Papers and Letter Books. Special Collections, Columbia University Library.

Lamb, John. Papers. New York Historical Society.

Lincoln, Benjamin. Papers on the Siege of Savannah. New York Public Library.

McDougall, Alexander. Papers. New York Historical Society.

*McGinnis, Richard. Journal. Privately owned.

McLane, Allen. Papers and Journal. New York Historical Society.

Massachusetts. Town Resolutions, Petitions and Memorials. State Archives, Boston.

Morris, Gouverneur. Papers. Special Collections, Columbia University Library.

Morris, Lewis. Letters. Morristown National Historical Park.

Morris, Robert. Papers. Library of Congress.

Peebles, Captain John, of 42nd or Royal Highland Regiment. Journal, April 13-June 26, 1780, covering siege and capture of Charleston, etc. Cunningham Papers, National Register Office, Edinburgh. Courtesy of Mrs. Inglis Fletcher.

Records of the Court of Appeals in Cases of Capture, 1776-1787. Revolutionary War Prize Cases. National Archives, Washington.

Reed, Joseph. Papers. New York Historical Society.

Rhode Island Records, 1772-1777. State Archives, Providence.

Rush, Benjamin. Diary. Philadelphia Free Library, Ridgeway Branch.

*Schuyler, Philip. Letters. Lloyd W. Smith Collection, Morristown National Historical Park.

———. Papers. New York Public Library.

*Seeley, Sylvanus. Diary. Morristown National Historical Park.

Steuben, Friedrich Wilhelm von. Papers. New York Historical Society.

Stirling, Lord (William Alexander). Papers. New York Historical Society.

*Trumbull, Benjamin. Letters. Lloyd W. Smith Collection, Morristown National Historical Park.

Washington, George. Papers. Library of Congress.
*Weedon, George. Letter of September 5, 1781. "Siege of Yorktown and Surrender of Cornwallis Collection." J. Pierpont Morgan Library.
*Weedon, George. Papers. Chicago Historical Society.

NEWSPAPERS

(Boston) *Continental Journal and Weekly Advertiser,* 1776-1780.
Independent Chronicle and Universal Advertiser, 1776-1783.
(Kingston, N. Y.) *New York Journal, and the General Advertiser,* 1777.
(London)*Morning Post and Daily Advertiser,* 1778.
New York Gazette and Weekly Mercury, 1776-1782.
(New York) *Royal Gazette,* 1777-1783.
(Philadelphia) *Pennsylvania Evening Post,* 1775-1784.
(Philadelphia) *Pennsylvania Gazette,* 1776-1781.
(Philadelphia) *Pennsylvania Packet,* 1775.
(Poughkeepsie, N. Y.) *New York Journal and General Advertiser,* 1778.
(Trenton) *New Jersey Gazette,* 1778.

BOOKS, PERIODICALS AND HISTORICAL COLLECTIONS

*Adams, Charles Francis. "Contemporary Opinion on the Howes." *Massachusetts Historical Society Proceedings,* XLIV, 118-120.
———, ed. *Familiar Letters of John Adams and His Wife, Abigail Adams, During the Revolution, with a Memoir of Mrs. Adams.* New York: Hurd and Houghton, 1876.
———. ed. *Letters of Mrs. Adams, the Wife of John Adams.* 3rd ed. Boston: C. C. Little and J. Brown, 1841.
———, ed. *The Works of John Adams, Second President of the United States: With a Life of the Author, Notes and Illustrations.* 10 vols. Boston: Little, Brown and Company, 1850-1856.
*Adams, John. "Letter." *Massachusetts Historical Society Proceedings,* VIII, 403-405.
*Ainslee, Thomas. "Journal of the Most Remarkable Occurrences in the Province of Quebec from the Appearance of the Rebels in September 1775 Until Their Retreat on the Sixth of May." *Seventh Series of Historical Documents, 1905,* pp. 11-89. Published by the Literary and Historical Society of Quebec.
Allen, Ethan. "Diary." *Pennsylvania Magazine of History and Biography,* IX, 295-296.
———. *A Narrative of Colonel Ethan Allen's Captivity.* 4th ed. Burlington: 1846.
*Allen, Gardner Weld. *Massachusetts Privateers of the Revolution.* Cambridge: Massachusetts Historical Society, 1927.

——. *Naval History of the American Revolution.* 2 vols. Boston: 1913.

Almon, John, ed. *The Parliamentary Register; or, History of the Debates and Proceedings of the Houses of Lords and Commons.* 17 vols. London: J. Almon, 1775-1780.

——. *The Remembrancer; or Impartial Repository of Public Events.* 17 vols. London: J. Almon, 1775-1784.

Anburey, Thomas. *Travels through the Interior Parts of America; in a Series of Letters. By an Officer.* New ed.; 2 vols. London: W. Lane, 1791.

Anderson, Enoch. *Personal Recollections of Captain Enoch Anderson, an Officer of the Delaware Regiments in the Revolutionary War. Papers of the Historical Society of Delaware, No. XVI.* With notes by Henry Hobart Bellas. Wilmington, Del.: Historical Society of Delaware, 1896.

André, Major John. *Major André's Journal; Operations of the British Army under Lieutenant Generals Sir William Howe and Sir Henry Clinton, June, 1777, to November, 1778, to Which Is Added "The Ethics of Major André's Mission," by C. DeW. Willcox.* Tarrytown, N. Y.: William Abbatt, 1930. Copyright 1904 by the Bibliographical Society.

——. *Papers Concerning the Capture and Detention of Major John André.* Collected by Henry B. Dawson. *The Gazette Series,* I, Henry B. Dawson, ed. Yonkers, N. Y.: 1866.

Andrews, Evangeline McLean, ed., in collaboration with Charles McLean Andrews. *Journal of a Lady of Quality; Being the Narrative of a Journey from Scotland to the West Indies, North Carolina, and Portugal in the Years 1774 to 1776.* New Haven: Yale University Press, 1921.

*Andrews, John. "Letters of John Andrews, Esq., of Boston, 1772-1776." Edited by Winthrop Sargent. *Massachusetts Historical Society Proceedings,* VIII (1866), 316-412.

The Annual Register, or a View of the History, Politics, and Literature for the years 1777, 1778, 1781. London: Printed for J. Dodsley, in Pall-Mall, 1778, 1779, 1782.

*Anonymous. *A Brief Narrative of the Ravages of the British and Hessians at Princeton in 1776-1777—A Contemporary Account of the Battles of Trenton and Princeton.* Edited by Varnum Lansing Collins. Princeton Historical Association, Extra Publications, Number One. Princeton, N. J.: The University Library, 1906.

*Anonymous. "A Contemporary British Account of General Sir William Howe's Military Operations in 1777." Contributed by Robert F. Seybolt. *Proceedings of the American Antiquarian Society,* New Series, XL (1931), 69-92.

Arnold, Benedict. "Letters Written while on an Expedition across the State of Maine to Attack Quebec in 1775." *Maine Historical Society Collections,* I (1831), 341-387.

Arnold, Isaac Newton. *Life of Benedict Arnold.* Chicago: Jansen, McClurg & Co., 1880.

Austin, James Trecothick. *Life of Elbridge Gerry.* 2 vols. Boston: Wells, 1828-1829.

Ballagh, James Curtis, ed. *The Letters of Richard Henry Lee.* 2 vols. New York: The Macmillan Company, 1911-1914.

Bancroft, Edward. "Letter." *American Historical Review,* XXIX, 493-494.

Barham, Lord. *Letters and Papers of Charles, Lord Barham, Admiral of the Red Squadron, 1758-1813.* Edited by Sir Henry Knox Laughton. London: Publications of the Navy Records Society, 1907-1911.

Barnes, G. R., & Owen, J. H., eds. *The Private Papers of John, Earl of Sandwich, First Lord of the Admiralty, 1771-1782.* London: Printed for the Navy Records Society, 1932-1938.

Bartlett, John Russell, ed. *Records of the State of Rhode Island and Providence Plantations in New England.* VII and VIII. Providence: Greene, Jackson & Co., 1863.

*Bass, Robert D. *The Green Dragoon.* New York: Henry Holt, 1957. Courtesy of Mr. Robert D. Bass.

Baxter, James Phinney. *The British Invasion from the North; The Campaigns of Generals Carleton and Burgoyne from Canada, 1776-1777, With the Journal of Lieut. William Digby, of the 53d. or Shropshire Regiment of Foot.* Albany: Joel Munsell's Sons, 1887.

Beardsley, Ebenezer. "Effects of Stagnant Air." *Memoirs of American Academy of Arts and Sciences,* I.

Beebe, Lewis. "Journal." *Pennsylvania Magazine of History and Biography,* LIX, 321-361.

*Bemis, Samuel F. "British Secret Service, and the French-American Alliance." *American Historical Review,* XXIX (1923-1924), 474-495.

*Besom, Philip. "Narrative." *Massachusetts Historical Society Proceedings,* V (1862), 357-360.

Bezanson, Anne, assisted by Blanche Daley, Marjorie C. Denison and Miriam Hussey. *Prices and Inflation During the American Revolution, Pennsylvania, 1770-1790.* Philadelphia: University of Pennsylvania Press, 1951.

Bigelow, John, ed. *Benjamin Franklin, Complete Works.* 10 vols. New York: Putnam, 1887-1889.

Boardman, Rev. Samuel W. *Log-Book of Timothy Boardman . . . also, A Biographical Sketch of the Author.* Albany: Joel Munsell's Sons, 1885.

Bolton, Charles Knowles, ed. *Letters of Hugh, Earl Percy, from Boston and New York, 1774-1776.* Boston: C. E. Goodspeed, 1902.

Boswell, James. *The Life of Samuel Johnson, LL.D., with his correspondence and conversations.* New York: 1872.

Boudinot, Elias. *Journal; or Historical Recollections of American Events During the Revolutionary War, from his own original manuscript.* Philadelphia: Bourquin, 1894.

———. *Life, Public Services, Addresses, and Letters.* Edited by J. J. Boudinot. 2 vols. Boston: Houghton Mifflin, 1896.

*———. "Report on American Prisoners of War in New York." *William & Mary Quarterly,* 3rd Series, XIII (1956), 379-393.

Boyd, Julian P., ed. *The Declaration of Independence; The Evolution of the Text as Shown in Facsimiles of Various Drafts by Its Author.* Issued in conjunction with an exhibit of these drafts at the Library of Congress on the two-hundredth anniversary of the birth of Thomas Jefferson. Washington: Library of Congress, 1943.

*————. *The Papers of Thomas Jefferson.* 10 vols. to date. Princeton, N. J.: Princeton University Press, 1950-1954.

Bradford, William. "Letter." *Pennsylvania Archives,* 1st Series, V (1853), 207-209.

*Brooks, John. "Letter." *Massachusetts Historical Society Proceedings,* XIII (1874), 243-245.

Brooks, Noah. *Henry Knox, A Soldier of the Revolution; Major-General in the Continental Army, Washington's Chief of Artillery, First Secretary of War Under the Constitution, Founder of the Society of the Cincinnati, 1750-1806.* New York and London: G. P. Putnam's Sons, 1900.

Brown, Tarleton. *Memoirs, written by himself.* With a preface and notes by Charles I. Bushnell. New York: Privately printed, 1862.

*Buell, Augustus C. *History of Andrew Jackson.* 2 vols. New York: Charles Scribner's Sons, 1904.

Bullock, Charles Jesse. *Finances of the United States, 1775-89, with Especial Reference to the Budget.* University of Wisconsin Bulletin, Vol. 1, No. 2. Madison: 1895.

Burgoyne, Lieut. Gen. John. *A State of the Expedition from Canada, as Laid Before the House of Commons, by Lieutenant-General Burgoyne, and Verified by Evidence; with a Collection of Authentic Documents, and an Addition of Many Circumstances Which Were Prevented from Appearing Before the House by the Prorogation of Parliament.* London: J. Almon, 1780.

*————. "Proclamation." *Massachusetts Historical Society Proceedings,* XII, 89-90.

Burnett, Edmund C., ed. *Letters of Members of the Continental Congress.* 8 vols. Washington, D. C.: Carnegie Institution of Washington, 1921-1936.

Butler, Colonel Richard. "Journal of the Siege of Yorktown." *Historical Magazine,* VIII, 102 et seq.

*Butterfield, L. H., ed. *Letters of Benjamin Rush.* 2 vols. Princeton: Published for the American Philosophical Society by The Princeton University Press, 1951.

Campbell, Mrs. Maria Hull. *Revolutionary Services and Civil Life of General William Hull; Prepared from His Manuscripts, . . . Together with the History of the Campaign of 1812, and Surrender of the Post of Detroit, by James Freeman Clarke.* New York: D. Appleton & Co., 1848.

*Carter, Clarence Edwin, ed. *The Correspondence of General Thomas Gage.* 2 vols. New Haven: Yale University Press, 1931-1933.

Carter, Landon. "Diary." *William & Mary Quarterly*, XVI (1907), 149-152, 258-264.

Chase, Frederick. *A History of Dartmouth College and the Town of Hanover, N. H.* Edited by J. K. Lord. 2 vols. Cambridge: J. Wilson and Son, 1891.

Chastellux, François Jean, Marquis de. *Travels in North America, 1780-82.* Translated by J. Kent. London: 1787; 2 vols, New York: White, 1827.

*Clark, George Rogers. "George Rogers Clark Papers, 1771-1781." *Collections of the Illinois State Historical Library*, VIII (1912); Virginia Series, III, James Alton James, ed.

Clark, Joseph. "Diary." *New Jersey Historical Society Proceedings*, VII (1855), 95-110.

Clinton, George. *Public Papers of George Clinton, First Governor of New York, 1777-1795—1801-1804.* VIII. Edited by Hugh Hastings. Albany: Oliver A. Quayle, State Legislative Printer, 1904.

*Clinton, Sir Henry. *The American Rebellion: Sir Henry Clinton's Narrative of His Campaigns, 1775-1782.* With an Appendix of Original Documents. Edited by William B. Willcox. New Haven: Yale University Press, 1954.

Cobbett, William. *The Parliamentary History of England from the Earliest Period to the Year 1803. . . .* 36 vols. London: Hansard, 1806-1820.

Collier, Sir George. "Extract . . . from the Journal and Papers of Sir George Collier." *Long Island Historical Society, Memoirs*, II (1869), 413-414.

Collins, James. *Autobiography of a Revolutionary Soldier.* Edited by John M. Roberts. Clinton, La.: Feliciana Democrat, 1859.

Columbian Magazine, or Monthly Miscellany. Philadelphia. August, 1789.

Condorcet, Le Marquis de. "Vie de Voltaire." *Oeuvres de Voltaire.* Edited by M. Beuchot. Paris: Chez Lefevre, Libraire, 1834.

Conway, Moncure Daniel, ed. *The Writings of Thomas Paine.* 4 vols. New York: G. P. Putnam's Sons, 1894-1896.

Cook, Frederick, ed. *Journals of the Military Expedition of Major General John Sullivan Against the Six Nations of Indians in 1779 with Records of Centennial Celebrations.* Auburn, N. Y.: Knapp, Peck & Thompson, 1887.

*Corner, George W., ed. *Autobiography of Benjamin Rush; His "Travels Through Life" Together with His Commonplace Book for 1789-1813.* Princeton, N. J.: Published for The American Philosophical Society by Princeton University Press, 1948.

*"Correspondence between a committee of the town of Boston and Contributors of Donations for the Relief of the Sufferers by the Boston Port Bill," *Massachusetts Historical Society Collections*, IV, 4-6, 38-40, 50-52, 71-72, 75-76, 83, 144-145, 251.

*Cresswell, Nicholas. *The Journal of Nicholas Cresswell, 1774-1777.* New York: Dial Press, 1924.

*Crèvecoeur, Hector St. John de. *Sketches of Eighteenth Century America.* New Haven: Yale University Press, 1925.

Curwen, Samuel. *The Journal and Letters of Samuel Curwen, an American in England, from 1775 to 1783.* With an Appendix of Biographical Sketches. By George Atkinson Ward. 4th ed. Boston: Little, Brown and Company, 1864.

Dana, R. H., Jr., ed. "Diary of a British Officer." *Atlantic Monthly*, XXXIX (1877), 394-398.

*Dandridge, Danske. *American Prisoners of the Revolution.* Charlottesville, Va.: The Michie Company, 1911.

Darlington, William. "Letter." *Historical Society of Pennsylvania Bulletin*, I (1845), 58-59.

Davis, Joshua. *A Narrative of Joshua Davis, an American Citizen Who Was Pressed and Served on Board Six Ships of the British Navy.* Boston: 1811.

Dawson, Henry B. *Battles of the United States, by Sea and Land: Embracing Those of the Revolutionary and Indian Wars, the War of 1812, and the Mexican War; with Official Documents, and Biographies of the Most Distinguished Military and Naval Commanders.* 2 vols. New York: Johnson, Fry and Company, 1858.

Deane, Silas. "Correspondence of Silas Deane, Delegate of the First and Second Congress at Philadelphia, 1774-1776." *Connecticut Historical Society Collections*, II. Hartford: 1870.

———. *Silas Deane Papers, 1774-1790.* 5 vols. *New York Historical Society Collections*, "Publication Fund Series," XIX-XXIII. New York: 1887-1891.

De Fonblanque, Edward Barrington. *Political and Military Episodes in the Latter Half of the Eighteenth Century; Derived from the Life and Correspondence of the Right Hon. John Burgoyne, General, Statesman, Dramatist.* London: Macmillan and Co., 1876.

De Lomenie, Louis Leonard. *Beaumarchais and His Times.* Translated by Henry S. Edwards. 4 vols. London: 1856.

Deshon, John. "Letter." *Rhode Island Historical Society Publications*, New Series, VIII (1900), 214-216. Providence: 1900.

Detail and Conduct of the American War, under Generals Gage, Howe, Burgoyne, and Vice-Admiral Lord Howe: With a very Full and Correct State of the Whole of the Evidence, as Given Before a Committee of the House of Commons: And the Celebrated Fugitive Pieces, which are said to have given Rise to that Important Enquiry. The whole Exhibiting a Circumstantial, Connected and Complete History of the Real Causes, Rise, Progress and Present State of the American Rebellion. 3rd. ed. London: Richardson and Urquhart, 1780.

Dexter, Franklin Bowditch, ed. *The Literary Diary of Ezra Stiles, D.D., LL.D., President of Yale College.* New York: Charles Scribner's Sons, 1901.

Dolph, Edward Arthur, ed. *Sound Off, Soldier Songs from Yankee Doodle to Parlez-Vous.* New York: Cosmopolitan Book Corp., 1929.

Donne, W. Bodham, ed. *Correspondence of George III with Lord North, 1768-83.* 2 vols. London: Murray, 1867.

*Douglas, Colonel William. "Revolutionary War Letters of Colonel William Douglas." *The New York Historical Society Quarterly Bulletin*, XIII (1929), 37-40, 79-82, 118-122, 157-163.

Drake, Francis Samuel. *Life and Correspondence of Henry Knox, Major-General in the American Revolutionary Army*. Boston: S. G. Drake, 1873.

Dring, Captain Thomas. *Recollections of the Jersey Prison-Ship; from the Original Manuscripts*. Rewritten by Albert Greene; edited by Henry Dawson. Morrisania, N. Y.: 1865.

Drinker, Mrs. Henry. "Journal." *Pennsylvania Magazine of History and Biography*, XIII (1889), 298-308.

Duncan, James. "Diary of Captain James Duncan, of Colonel Moses Hazen's Regiment, in the Yorktown Campaign, 1781." Edited by William H. Egle. Pennsylvania Archives, 2nd Series, XV. Harrisburg: E. K. Myers, 1890.

Du Ponceau, Pierre. "Autobiography." *Pennsylvania Magazine of History and Biography*, LXIII (1939), 195-227.

Ellery, William. "Letter," *Publications of the Rhode Island Historical Society*, New Series, VIII (1900), 200-201. Providence: 1900.

*Emerson, William. "Diary." In Ralph Waldo Emerson, *Miscellanies*. Boston, New York: Houghton Mifflin & Co., 1863.

Ewing, Thomas. *George Ewing, Gentleman, a Soldier of Valley Forge*. Yonkers, N. Y.: Privately printed by Thomas Ewing, 1928.

Fanning, Nathaniel. *Memoirs of the Life of Captain Nathaniel Fanning, an American Naval Officer. . . .* New York: 1808.

Fanning, Nathaniel. *Narrative of the Adventures of an American Navy Officer*. New York: Printed for author, 1806.

*Farnsworth, Amos. "Diary." Edited by Dr. Samuel A. Greene. *Massachusetts Historical Society Proceedings*, 2nd Series, XII (1899), 74-107.

Field, Edward. *Esek Hopkins, Commander-in-Chief of the Continental Navy. . . .* Providence: 1898.

*Fithian, Philip Vickers. *Journal, 1775-1776, Written on the Virginia-Pennsylvania Frontier in the Army around New York*. Edited by Robert Greenbalgh Albion and Leonidas Dodson. Princeton, N. J.: Princeton University Press, 1934.

Fitzpatrick, John C., ed. *The Writings of George Washington, from the Original Manuscript Sources, 1745-1799*. 39 vols. Washington: United States Government Printing Office, 1931-1944.

*———. *The Diaries of George Washington, 1748-1799*. 4 vols. Boston: Houghton Mifflin Company, 1925. Courtesy of the Mt. Vernon Ladies Association.

Foner, Philip S., ed. *The Complete Writings of Thomas Paine*. 2 vols. Citadel Press, 1945.

Foote, William Henry. *Sketches of Virginia, Historical and Biographical*. Philadelphia: Martier, 1850; 2nd Series, Lippincott, 1855.

Force, Peter, ed. *American Archives: Fourth Series, Containing a Documentary History of the English Colonies in North America from the*

King's Message to Parliament of March 7, 1774, to the Declaration of Independence by the United States. 6 vols. Washington: M. St. Clair Clarke and Peter Force, 1837-1846.

———. *American Archives: Fifth Series, Containing a Documentary History of the United States of America from the Declaration of Independence, July 4, 1776, to the Definitive Treaty of Peace with Great Britain, September 3, 1783.* 3 vols. Washington: M. St. Clair Clarke and Peter Force, 1848-1853.

Ford, Paul Leicester. "Lord Howe's Commission to Pacify the Colonies." *Atlantic Monthly,* LXXVII (1896), 758-766.

———, ed. *Writings of Thomas Jefferson.* 10 vols. New York: Putnam, 1892-1899.

Ford, Worthington Chauncey, ed. *Defences in Philadelphia in 1777.* Brooklyn, N.Y.: Historical Printing Club, 1897.

———. *Letters of Jonathan Boucher to George Washington.* Brooklyn, N.Y.: Historical Printing Club, 1897.

———. *Letters of William Lee, 1766-1783.* 2 vols. Brooklyn, N.Y.: Historical Printing Club, 1892.

*Fortescue, Sir John, ed. *The Correspondence of King George the Third, from 1760 to December 1783.* 6 vols. London: Macmillan and Co., 1927-1928. Courtesy of Librarian, Windsor Castle.

Fox, Charles James. *Memorials and Correspondence of Charles James Fox.* IV. Edited by Lord John Russell. London: R. Bentley, 1857.

*French, Allen. *The First Year of the American Revolution.* Boston: Houghton Mifflin, 1934.

*———. *The Taking of Ticonderoga in 1775: The British Story; A Study of Captors and Captives.* Cambridge, Mass.: Harvard University Press, 1928. Reprinted by permission of the Publishers and the President and Fellows of Harvard College.

Freneau, Philip Morin. *Poems Written and Published During the American Revolutionary War.* . . . 3rd. ed.; 2 vols. Philadelphia: From the Press of Lydia R. Bailey, No. 10, North-Allen, 1809.

Frothingham, Richard. *History of the Siege of Boston and of the Battles of Lexington, Concord, and Bunker Hill. Also, an Account of the Bunker Hill Monument. With illustrative Documents.* 2nd ed. Boston: Charles C. Little and James Brown, 1851.

———. *Rise of the Republic of the United States.* Boston: Little, Brown and Co., 1872.

Gavett, William. "Account of the Affair at North Bridge." *Essex Institute Proceedings,* I (1859), 126-128.

Gentleman's Magazine, XXXVI (March 1776), London.

Gibbes, R. W., ed. *Documentary History of the American Revolution: Consisting of Letters and Papers Relating to the Contest for Liberty, Chiefly in South Carolina, from Originals in the Possession of the Editor, and Other Sources. 1776-1782.* 3 vols. New York: D. Appleton & Company, 1853-1857.

Gibson, James Edgar. *Dr. Bodo Otto and the Medical Background of the American Revolution.* Baltimore: C. C. Thomas, 1937.

Glich, ——. "Account of the Battle of Bennington." *Vermont Historical Society Collections,* I (1870), 211-223.

*Gordon, William. "Letter of Reverend William Gordon, 1776." Edited by Harold Murdock. *Massachusetts Historical Society Proceedings,* LX (1927), 360-366.

Goss, Elbridge Henry. *The Life of Colonel Paul Revere.* I. Boston: Joseph George Cupples, 1891.

*Gottschalk, Louis, ed. *The Letters of Lafayette to Washington, 1777-1779.* New York: Privately printed by Helen F. Hubbard, 1944. Courtesy of Professor Louis Gottschalk.

Graham, James. *The Life of General Daniel Morgan, with Portions of his Correspondence.* New York: 1859.

*Graves, Admiral Lord Thomas. *The Graves Papers and other Documents Relating to the Naval Operations of the Yorktown Campaign, July to October, 1781.* Edited by French Ensor Chadwick. *Publications of the Naval History Society,* VII. New York: The Naval History Society, 1916.

Graydon, Alexander. *Memoirs of His Own Time, with Reminiscences of the Men and Events of the Revolution.* Edited by John Stockton Littrell. Philadelphia: Lindsay & Blakiston, 1846.

Great Britain Historical Manuscripts Commission. *The Manuscript of the Earl of Carlisle, Preserved at Castle Howard, Fifteenth Report, Appendix, Part VI.* London: Eyre and Spottiswoode, 1897.

——. *The Manuscripts of the Earl of Dartmouth.* 3 vols. London: 1887-1896.

——. *Report on the Manuscripts of the Late Reginald Rawdon Hastings.* 4 vols. London: H. M. Stationery Office, 1930-1947.

——. *Report on the Manuscripts of Mrs. Stopford-Sackville.* 2 vols. London: H. M. Stationery Office, 1904-1910.

——. *Manuscripts in Various Collections.*

Greene, George Washington. *The Life of Nathanael Greene, Major-General in the Army of the Revolution.* 3 vols. New York: G. P. Putnam's Sons, 1867-1871.

Greene, Nathanael. "Letter." *Rhode Island Historical Society Collections,* XX (1927), 106-107.

——. "Letters of General Nathanael Greene, to Colonel Jeremiah Wadsworth." *Pennsylvania Magazine of History and Biography,* XXII. Philadelphia: Historical Society of Pennsylvania, 1898.

Griffin, Martin I. J. *Commodore John Barry.* Philadelphia: George W. Gibbens, printer, 1903.

Griswold, Charles. "Letter." *American Journal of Science and Arts,* II, No. 2. (November 1820), 94-101.

Guild, Reuben Aldridge. *Chaplain Smith and the Baptists; or, Life, Journals, Letters, and Addresses of the Rev. Hezekiah Smith, D.D., of Haver-*

hill, Massachusetts. 1737-1805. Philadelphia: American Baptist Publication Society, 1885.

Hadden, James M. *A Journal Kept in Canada and Upon Burgoyne's Campaign in 1776 and 1777. Also Orders kept by Him and Issued by Sir Guy Carleton, Lieut. General John Burgoyne and Major General William Phillips in 1776, 1777, and 1778, with an explanatory chapter and notes by Horatio Rogers.* Albany: Joel Munsell's Sons, 1884.

Hamilton, Lieutenant-Governor Henry. "Extracts from a Private Manuscript Written by Governor Paul Hamilton, Sr., During the Period of the Revolutionary War, from 1776-1800." *Year Book—1898, City of Charleston, S. C.,* pp. 299-327.

Hamilton, J. C., ed. *History of the Republic . . . as Traced in the Writings of Alexander Hamilton.* New York: 1857-1864; Boston, 1879.

*Hammond, Otis G., ed. *Letters and Papers of Major-General John Sullivan, Continental Army.* 3 vols. *Collections of the New Hampshire Historical Society.* XIII, XIV, XV. Concord: New Hampshire Historical Society, 1930-1931, 1939.

"Hand Papers." *Pennsylvania Archives,* 2nd Series, X, 308-309.

Harcourt, Edward William, ed. *The Harcourt Papers.* 13 vols. Oxford: Parker, 1880-1905.

Harrison, Richard. "Testimony." *New York Historical Society Collections,* VI (1783), 71-75.

[Hawkes, James, supposed author]. *A Retrospect of the Boston Tea-Party, with a Memoir of George R. T. Hewes, Survivor of the Little Band of Patriots Who Drowned the Tea in Boston Harbour in 1773. By a citizen of New-York. . . .* New York: S. S. Bliss, printer, 1834.

Hay, Samuel. "Letter." *Pennsylvania Archives,* 2nd Series, I (1879), 598-599.

Heath, William. *Memoirs of Major-General William Heath, by Himself, to which is added the Accounts of the Battle of Bunker Hill by Generals Dearborn, Lee and Wilkinson.* Edited by William Abbatt. New York: William Abbatt, 1901.

Hening, William Waller, ed. *The Statutes at Large; Being a Collection of all the Laws of Virginia from the First Session of the Legislature in the Year 1619.* Richmond: 1819-1823.

Henry, John Joseph. *Account of Arnold's Campaign Against Quebec, and of the Hardships and Sufferings of that Band of Heroes who Traversed the Wilderness of Maine from Cambridge to the St. Lawrence, in the Autumn of 1775.* Albany: Joel Munsell, 1877.

Hill, G. Birkbeck, ed. *Letters of David Hume to William Strahan.* Oxford: Clarendon Press, 1888.

Hopkinson, Francis. *The Miscellaneous Essays and Occasional Writings.* III. Philadelphia: 1792.

Hough, Franklin B. *The Siege of Savannah, by the Combined American and French Forces, under the Command of Gen. Lincoln, and the Count d'Estaing, in the Autumn of 1779.* Albany, N. Y.: Joel Munsell, 1866.

Hovey, Alvah. *A Memoir of the Life and Times of the Rev. Isaac Backus, A. M.* Boston: Gould & Lincoln, 1858.

*Hudson, Charles. *History of the Town of Lexington, Middlesex County, Massachusetts, from Its First Settlement to 1868.* I. Boston: Houghton Mifflin Company, 1913. Courtesy of the Lexington Historical Society.

*Hughes, Thomas. *A Journal by Thos. Hughes for his Amusement, and Designed only for his Perusal by the Time he Attains the Age of 50 if he Lives so Long (1778-1789).* Edited by E. A. Benians. Cambridge, England: The University Press, 1947.

*Hulton, Ann. *Letters of a Loyalist Lady; Being the Letters of Ann Hulton, Sister of Henry Hulton, Commissioner of Customs at Boston, 1767-1776.* Cambridge: Harvard University Press, 1927. Reprinted by permission of the publisher and the President and Fellows of Harvard College.

Hunt, Gaillard, ed. *The Writings of James Madison, comprising his public papers and his private correspondence, for the first time printed.* 9 vols. New York: G. P. Putnam's Sons, 1900-1910.

Hunter, Sir Martin. *The Journal of Gen. Sir Martin Hunter, G.C.M.G., G.C.H., and some Letters of his Wife, Lady Hunter.* Edited by Miss Anne Hunter and Miss Bell. Edinburgh: The Edinburgh Press, 1894.

Huntington, Ebenezer. *Letters Written by Ebenezer Huntington During the American Revolution.* Edited by Charles Frederick Heartman. New York: Privately printed, 1914.

Hutchinson, Thomas, ed. *Diary and Letters of Thomas Hutchinson, with an Account of his Administration.* Compiled from the original documents by P. O. Hutchinson. 2 vols. Boston: Houghton, 1884-1886.

———. *The History of Massachusetts-Bay.* . . . Printed by Thomas and John Fleet at the Heart and Crown in Cornhill, 1764-1767.

Hutton, James. "Some Account of James Hutton's Visit to Franklin, in France, in December of 1777." *Pennsylvania Magazine of History and Biography,* XXXII (1908), 223-232.

James, William Dobein. *A Sketch of the Life of Brig. Gen. Francis Marion and a History of His Brigade.* Charleston, S.C.: Gould and Milet, 1821.

Jay, John. *The Correspondence and Public Papers of John Jay, First Chief-Justice of the United States, Member and President of the Continental Congress, Minister to Spain, Member of Commission to Negotiate Treaty of Independence, Envoy to Great Britain, Governor of New York, etc.* Edited by Henry P. Johnson. 4 vols. New York: G. P. Putnam's Sons, 1896.

Jefferson, Thomas. *Notes on the State of Virginia* in *Writings.* Collected and edited by Paul Leicester Ford. III, 68-295. New York: G. P. Putnam's Sons, 1894.

Johnson, Samuel. *Taxation No Tyranny, an answer to the resolutions and address of the American Congress.* 4th ed. London: Printed for T. Cadell, 1775.

Johnson, William. *Sketches of the Life and Correspondence of Nathanael Greene, Major General of the Armies of the United States, in the War of the Revolution. Compiled Chiefly from Original Materials.* 2 vols. Charleston, S. C.: A. E. Miller, 1822.

Johnston, Henry P. *The Battle of Harlem Heights, September 16, 1776, With a Review of the Events of the Campaign.* New York: The Macmillan Company, 1897.

————. *The Campaign of 1776 Around New York and Brooklyn. Including a New and Circumstantial Account of the Battle of Long Island and the Loss of New York, With a Review of Events to the Close of the Year. Memoirs of the Long Island Historical Society,* III. Brooklyn: Long Island Historical Society, 1878.

————. *The Storming of Stony Point on the Hudson, midnight, July 15, 1779; its Importance in the Light of Unpublished Documents.* New York: J. T. White & Co., 1900.

————. *The Yorktown Campaign and the Surrender of Cornwallis, 1781.* New York: Harper & Bros., 1881.

Jones, Charles C., Jr., ed. *The Siege of Savannah in 1779, as Described in Two Contemporaneous Journals of French Officers in the Fleet of Count d'Estaing.* Albany: Joel Munsell, 1874.

Journals of the Continental Congress, 1774-1789. Edited by Gaillard Hunt. 34 vols. Washington: Government Printing Office, 1904-1937.

Kapp, Friedrich. *The Life of John Kalb, Major-General in the Revolutionary Army.* New York: Henry Holt and Company, 1884.

*Kellogg, Louise Phelps, ed. *Frontier Advance on the Upper Ohio. State Historical Society of Wisconsin Collections,* XXIII, Draper Series, IV. Madison: 1916.

*————. *Frontier Retreat on the Upper Ohio. State Historical Society of Wisconsin Collections,* XXIV, Draper Series, V. Madison: 1917.

Kidder, Frederic and Gould, Augustus A. *The History of New Ipswich from Its First Grant in MDCCXXXVI to the Present Time.* Boston: Gould and Lincoln, 1852.

Knox, Major Henry. "Diary." *New England Historical and Genealogical Register,* XXX, 321-326.

Lacey, John. "Memoirs of Brigadier-General John Lacey, of Pennsylvania." *Pennsylvania Magazine of History and Biography,* XXV (1901), 1-13, 191-207, 341-354, 498-515.

Lafayette, Marquis de. *Memoirs, Correspondence and Manuscripts of General Lafayette.* Published by his family. Vol I. New York: Saunders and Otley, 1837.

Lamb, R. *An Original and Authentic Journal of Occurrences During the Late American War from its Commencement to the Year 1783.* Dublin: Wilkinson & Courtney, 1809.

————. *Memoir of His Own Life.* Dublin: J. Jones, 1811.

Laurens, Henry. "Narrative of his Capture, of his Confinement in the Tower of London, etc., 1780, 1781, 1782." *South Carolina Historical Society Collections,* I (1857), 18-83.

Laurens, John. *The Army Correspondence of Colonel John Laurens in the Year 1777-8, Now First Printed from Original Letters Addressed to his Father, Henry Laurens, President of Congress, with a Memoir by William Gilmore Simms.* New York: The Bradford Club, 1867.

Lauzun, Duc de. "Memoirs." *Magazine of American History*, VI (1881), 51-53.

Leach, John. "Journal." *New England Genealogical Register*, XIX (July 1863), 255-263.

Lee, Charles. "The Lee Papers." *New York Historical Society Collections*, V (1872) and VI (1873). The New York Historical Society.

Lee, Henry. *The Campaign of 1781 in the Carolinas.* Philadelphia: E. Littell, 1824.

———. *Memoirs of the War in the Southern Department of the United States.* 2 vols. Philadelphia: Bradford and Inskeep, 1812; 3rd. ed., New York: University Publishing Company, 1869.

Lee, Richard Henry. *Life of Arthur Lee, L.L.D., Joint Commissioner of the United States to the Court of France, and Sole Commissioner to the Courts of Spain and Prussia, During the Revolutionary War. With his Political and Literary Correspondence and his Papers on Diplomatic and Political Subjects, and the Affairs of the United States During the Same Period.* I. Boston: Wells & Lilly, 1829.

Lewis, Sir George Cornewall. *Essays on the Administrations of Great Britain from 1783 to 1830.* Edited by Sir Edmund Head. London: 1864.

*Literary and Historical Society of Quebec. *Manuscripts Relating to the Early History of Canada. Historical Documents*, 2nd Series, V. Quebec: Middleton & Dawson, 1866; reprinted for the Society by T. J. Moore, 1927.

Livesey, Rev. R. *The Prisoners of 1776; a Relic of the Revolution compiled from the Journal of Charles Herbert.* Boston: G. C. Rand, 1854.

Lodge, Henry Cabot, ed. *Complete Works of Alexander Hamilton.* 9 vols. New York: Putnam, 1885-1886.

———. *The Works of Alexander Hamilton.* Constitutional Edition, 12 vols. New York: G. P. Putnam's Sons, n.d.

Lukens, Jesse. "Letter." *American Historical Record*, I, 547-548.

*Lydenberg, Harry Miller, ed. *Diaries and Sketches of Archibald Robertson, 1762-1780.* New York: New York Public Library, 1930.

Lyman, Simeon. "Journal of Simeon Lyman of Sharon, Aug. 10 to Dec. 28, 1775." *Connecticut Historical Society Collections*, VII (1899), 111-133.

Macaulay, Catherine. "Address." *Magazine of History*, Extra No. 114, XXIX, No. 2, 16-18.

Machias Committee of Correspondence. *Maine Historical Society Collections and Proceedings*, 2nd Series, VI (Portland, 1895), 129-131.

*Mackenzie, Frederick. *Diary of Frederick Mackenzie, Giving a Daily Narrative of his Military Service as an Officer of the Regiment of Royal Welsh Fusiliers During the Years 1775-1781 in Massachusetts, Rhode Island and New York.* 2 vols. Cambridge, Mass.: Harvard University Press, 1930. Reprinted by permission of the publishers, and the President and Fellows of Harvard College.

Mackenzie, Roderick. *Strictures on Lt. Col. Tarleton's History "Of the Campaigns of 1780 and 1781, in the Southern Provinces of North America."* Wherein Military Characters and Corps are Vindicated From injurious Aspersions, and Several important Transactions placed in their Proper Point of View. In a Series of Letters to a Friend. To Which is added, a Detail of the Siege of Ninety Six, and the Re-Capture of the Island of New-Providence. London: Privately printed, 1787.

[Martin, Joseph P.] *A Narrative of Some of the Adventures, Dangers and Sufferings of A Revolutionary Soldier.* Hallowell, Me., 1830.

Mathis, Samuel. "Samuel Mathis to General W. R. Davie, June 26, 1819." *American Historical Record.* II. Edited by Benson J. Lossing. Philadelphia: Samuel P. Town, 1873.

Miles, Col. Samuel. "Journal of Col. Samuel Miles, Concerning the Battle of Long Island—1776." *Pennsylvania Archives*, 2nd Series, I (1879), 519-522.

Montresor, John. "The Montresor Journals." Edited by G. D. Scull. *Collections of the New York Historical Society for the year 1881*, XIV. New York: New York Historical Society, 1882.

Moore, Frank, ed. *Diary of the American Revolution. From Newspapers and Original Documents*, 2 vols. New York: Charles Scribner, 1860.

———. *Materials for History, Printed from Original Manuscripts.* 1st Series. New York: Printed for the Zenger Club, 1861.

———. *Songs and Ballads of the American Revolution. With Notes and Illustrations.* New York: D. Appleton & Company, 1855.

Morris, Lewis, Jr. "Letters to General Lewis Morris." *New York Historical Society Collections*, VIII (1875), 433-512.

*Morris, Richard B., ed. *Alexander Hamilton and the Founding of the Nation.* New York: Dial Press, 1957.

"Morris, Robert, Letters to, 1775-1782." *Collections of the New York Historical Society for the Year 1878*, XI, 397-488. New York: New York Historical Society, 1879.

Morton, Robert. "The Diary of Robert Morton. Kept in Philadelphia While that City was Occupied by the British Army in 1777." *Pennsylvania Magazine of History and Biography*, I (1871), 1-39.

Mott, Edward. Journal. *Connecticut Historical Society Collections*, I, 165-172.

Moultrie, William. *Memoirs of the American Revolution, so far as it Related to the States of North and South Carolina, and Georgia. Compiled from the most authentic Materials, the Author's Personal Knowledge of the various Events, and including an Epistolary Correspondence on Public Affairs, with Civil and Military Officers, at that Period.* 2 vols. New York: David Longworth, 1802.

Muhlenberg, Rev. Henry M. "Journal." *Pennsylvania Historical Society Collections*, I (1853), 147-186.

Munro, Wilfred H. *The History of Bristol, Rhode Island: The Story of the Mt. Hope Lands.* Providence: J. A. and R. A. Reid, 1880.

Murphey, Archibald D. *The Papers of Archibald D. Murphey*. Edited by William Henry Hoyt. 2 vols. *Publications of the North Carolina Historical Commission*. Raleigh, N. C.: E. M. Uzzell & Co., State Printers, 1914.

*Navarro, Martin. "Letter." *Wisconsin State Historical Society Collections*, XVIII, 406-408.

*Neeser, Robert Wilden, ed. *Letters and Papers Relating to the Cruises of Gustavus Conyngham, a Captain of the Continental Navy, 1777-1779*. New York: Printed for the Naval History Society by the DeVinne Press, 1915.

Neilson, Charles. *An Original, Compiled and Corrected Account of Burgoyne's Campaign, and the Memorable Battles of Bemis's Heights, Sept. 19, and Oct. 7, 1777, from the most Authentic Sources of Information; Including many Interesting Incidents connected with the Same: and a Map of the Battle Ground*. Albany: J. Munsell, 1844.

*Newell, Timothy. "A Journal Kept During the Time that Boston was Shut Up in 1775-6." *Massachusetts Historical Society Collections*, 4th Series, I (1852), 261-276.

Nicholson, Capt. James. "Letter." *Naval History Society Publications*, I, 125-126. London: 1911.

Niles, Hezekiah, ed. *Centennial Offering. Republication of the Principles and Acts of the Revolution in America*. New York: A. S. Barnes & Co., 1876.

North Carolina (State). *The State Records of North Carolina. Published under the Supervision of the Trustees of the Public Libraries. By Order of the General Assembly*. Edited by Walter Clark. XI-XXVI (1776-1790). Winston, N. C.: M. I. & J. C. Stewart, 1895-1906.

O'Callaghan, E. B., ed. *Documents Relative to the Colonial History of the State of New-York: Procured in Holland, England and France, by John Romeyn Brodhead, Esq.* 9 vols. Albany: Weed, Parsons and Company, 1853-1858.

Onderdonk, Henry. *Revolutionary Incidents of Suffolk and Kings Counties: With an Account of the Battle of Long Island and the British Prisons and Prison-Ships at New-York*. New York: Leavitt & Company, 1849.

Paine, Thomas. *Additions to Common Sense: Addressed to the Inhabitants of America*. Printed in Philadelphia; reprinted in London for J. Almon, 1776.

Paullin, Charles O. *Out-Letters of the Continental Marine Committee and Board of Admiralty August 1776-September 1780*. Publications of the Naval History Society. 2 vols. New York: 1914.

Pausch, Captain Georg. *Journal of Captain Pausch, Chief of the Hanau Artillery During the Burgoyne Campaign*. Translated and annotated by William L. Stone. Albany: Joel Munsell's Sons, 1886.

Pennsylvania (State). *Pennsylvania Archives. Selected and Arranged from original Documents in the office of the Secretary of the Commonwealth, conformably to Acts of the General Assembly, February 15,*

1851 & March 1, 1852, by Samuel Hazard, Commencing 1776, V. Philadelphia: Joseph Severns, 1853.

Pennsylvania Archives. Second Series. "Pennsylvania in the War of the Revolution, Battalions and Line, 1775-1783." Edited by John Blair Linn and William H. Egle. XI, 629-674. 1880.

Pennsylvania Archives. Eighth Series. VIII. 1931-1935.

————. *Statutes at Large, from 1682-1801.* Compiled by J. T. Mitchell and Henry Flanders. 12 vols. Harrisburg: 1896-1908.

Pickering, Octavius. *The Life of Timothy Pickering.* 4 vols. Boston: Little, Brown and Company, 1867.

Price, Richard. *Observations on the Nature of Civil Liberty, the Principles of Government, and the Justice and Policy of the War with America. To which is added an Appendix, containing a State of the National Debt, and Estimate of the money drawn from the Public by the Taxes: and an account of the national Income and Expenditures since the last War.* London: 1776; New York: Reprinted by S. Loudon, 1776.

Proud, R. "On the Violation, etc." *Pennsylvania Magazine of History and Biography*, XX, 515-519.

Ramsay, David. *History of the American Revolution.* 2 vols. London: John Stockdale, 1793.

Reed, Joseph. *Remarks on Governor Johnstone's Speech in Parliament; With a Collection of all the Letters and Authentic Papers, relative to his Propositions to engage the Interest of one of the Delegates of the State of Pennsylvania, in the Congress of the States of America, to Promote the Views of the British Commissioners.* Philadelphia: Francis Barley, 1779.

Reed, William B. *Life and Correspondence of Joseph Reed, Military Secretary of Washington, at Cambridge: Adjutant-General of the Continental Army: Member of the Congress of the United States: and President of the Executive Council of the State of Pennsylvania.* 2 vols. Philadelphia: Lindsay and Blakiston, 1847.

Reeves, Enos. "Extracts from the Letter-Books of Lieutenant Enos Reeves, of the Pennsylvania Line." *Pennsylvania Magazine of History and Biography*, XXI (1897), 72-85, 235-256, 376-391, 466-476 (concluding installment).

*Reid, W. Max. *The Story of Old Fort Johnson.* New York: G. P. Putnam's Sons, 1906.

*Revere, Paul. "Letter of Paul Revere to Dr. Belknap." Edited by Charles Deane. *Proceedings of the Massachusetts Historical Society*, XVI (1879), 370-376.

Riedesel, Baroness Frederike von. *Letters and Journals relating to the War of the American Revolution, and the Capture of the German Troops at Saratoga.* Translated by William L. Stone. Albany: Joel Munsell, 1867.

Robinson, Thomas P., and Leder, Lawrence H., eds. "Governor Livingston and the 'Sunshine Patriots.'" *William & Mary Quarterly*, 3rd Series, XIII (1956), 394-397.

*Rodney, Caesar, and others. *Letters to and from Caesar Rodney, 1756-1784.* Edited by George Herbert Ryden. Philadelphia: University of Pennsylvania Press, 1933.

*Rodney, Sir George. *Letter-Books and Order-Book.* 2 vols. New York: New York Historical Society, 1932.

Rodney, Thomas. *Diary of Captain Thomas Rodney, 1776-1777.* With an Introduction by Caesar A. Rodney. *Papers of the Historical Society of Delaware, No. VIII.* Wilmington, Del.: The Historical Society of Delaware, 1888.

Ross, Charles, ed. *Correspondence of Cornwallis.* 3 vols. London: Murray, 1859.

Rush, Richard. *Occasional Productions, Political, Diplomatic, and Miscellaneous. Including, among others, A Glance at the Court and Government of Louis Philippe and the French Revolution of 1848. While the Author Resided as Envoy Extraordinary and Minister Plenipotentiary from the United States at Paris.* Edited by Rush's executors. Philadelphia: J. B. Lippincott & Company, 1860.

Sargent, Winthrop, ed. *Loyalist Poetry of the Revolution.* Albany, 1860.

——. *The Loyal Verses of Joseph Stansbury and Doctor Jonathan Odell, relating to the American Revolution.* Albany: J. Munsell, 1860.

Saunders, William L., ed. *Colonial Records of North Carolina.* 10 vols. Raleigh: P. M. Hale, 1886-1890.

Scull, G. D., ed. *Memoir and Letters of Captain W. Glanville Evelyn, of the 4th Regiment ("King's Own") From North America, 1774-1776.* Oxford: James Parker and Co., 1879.

Seabury, Reverend Samuel. *Letters of a Westchester Farmer.* Edited by Clarence H. Vance. Published for Westchester County by the Westchester County Historical Society. White Plains, N. Y., 1930.

Senter, Isaac. "The Journal of Isaac Senter, M. D., on a Secret Expedition against Quebec, 1775." *The Magazine of History with Notes and Queries,* Extra No. 42, 1915.

*Serle, Ambrose. *The American Journal of Ambrose Serle, Secretary to Lord Howe, 1776-1778.* Edited by Edward H. Tatum, Jr. San Marino, California: The Huntington Library, 1940.

Shaw, Major Samuel. *The Journals of Major Samuel Shaw, the First American Consul at Canton, With a Life of the Author,* by Joseph Quincy. Boston: Wm. Crosby and H. P. Nichols, 1847.

Shea, J. G., ed. *The Operations of the French Fleet under the Count de Grasse in 1781-2 as Described in two Contemporaneous Journals.* New York: The Bradford Club, 1864.

Sherburne, Andrew. *Memoirs of Andrew Sherburne: A Pensioner of the Navy of the Revolution.* Providence, 1831.

Sherburne, John Henry. *Life and Character of the Chevalier John Paul Jones.* Washington, 1825.

Simcoe, J. G. *Simcoe's Military Journal, A History of the Operations of a Partisan Corps, Called the Queen's Rangers, Commanded by Lieut. Col. J. G. Simcoe, During the War of the American Revolution: Illustrated* by ten engraved plans of action, etc. *Now first Published, with a Memoir of the Author and other Additions.* New York: Bartlett & Welford, 1844.

*Sinclair, Patrick. "Letter." *Wisconsin State Historical Society Collections,* XI, 147-148.

Smith, William Henry, ed. *The St. Clair Papers. The Life and Public Services of Arthur St. Clair, Soldier of the Revolutionary War; President of the Continental Congress; and Governor of the North-Western Territory, with his Correspondence and other Papers.* 2 vols. Cincinnati: Robert Clarke, 1882.

*Smyth, Albert Henry, ed. *The Writings of Benjamin Franklin.* 10 vols. New York: The Macmillan Company, 1905-1907.

Sparks, Jared, ed. *Correspondence of the American Revolution: Being Letters of Eminent Men to George Washington. From the time of his Taking Command of the Army to the End of his Presidency.* 4 vols. Boston: Little, Brown and Co., 1853.

——. *Diplomatic Correspondence of the American Revolution.* 12 vols. Boston, 1829-1830.

——. *Life of Gouverneur Morris.* 3 vols. Boston: 1832.

Stedman, Edmund C., and Hutchinson, E. M. *Library of American Literature.* 11 vols. New York: Webster, 1891.

Stevens, Benjamin Franklin. *B. F. Stevens's Facsimiles of Manuscripts in European Archives Relating to America, 1773-1783.* London: Malby & Sons, 1889-1895.

——. *The Campaigns in Virginia 1781, An Exact Reprint of Six rare pamphlets on the Clinton-Cornwallis Controversy with very Numerous Important unpublished manuscript notes by Sir Henry Clinton K. B. and the Omitted and hitherto unpublished portions of the letters in their appendixes added from the original manuscripts with a supplement. . . .* 2 vols. London: 1888.

Stillé, Charles J. *Major-General Anthony Wayne and the Pennsylvania Line in the Continental Army.* Philadelphia: J. B. Lippincott Company, 1893.

Stocking, Abner. "An Interesting Journal of the Expedition Against Quebec, 1775." *The Magazine of History with Notes and Queries,* Extra No. 75, 1921.

*Stone, Joel. "The Narrative of Joel Stone." *Loyalist Narratives from Upper Canada.* Edited by James Talmon. Toronto: The Champlain Society, 1946.

Stone, William Leete, ed. *Ballads and Poems relating to the Burgoyne Campaign.* Albany: Joel Munsell, 1893.

——. *The Campaign of Lieut. Gen. John Burgoyne, and the Expedition of Lieut. Col. Barry St. Leger.* Albany: Joel Munsell, 1877.

Story, Joseph. "Account Dictated." *Essex Institute Proceedings,* I, 134-135.

Stryker, William S. *The Battles of Trenton and Princeton.* Boston and New York: Houghton, Mifflin and Company, 1898.

Tallmadge, Benjamin. *Memoir of Col. Benj. Tallmadge, prepared by himself, at the request of his children.* New York: 1858.

Tarleton, Lt.-Col. Banastre. *A History of the Campaigns of 1780 and 1781, in the Southern Provinces of North America.* Dublin: Colles, Exshaw, et al., 1787.

Taylor, Jeannette. *Life and Correspondence of John Paul Jones, including his Narrative.* New York: 1830.

Thacher, James, M. D. *A Military Journal During the American Revolutionary War, from 1775-1783; Describing interesting events and transactions of this period; With Numerous Historical Facts and Anecdotes, from the original manuscript. To Which is added, an Appendix, Containing Biographical sketches of several general officers.* 2nd ed. Boston: Cottons & Barnard, 1827.

Thacher, Rev. Peter. "Narrative." *Historical Magazine,* 2nd Series, III, 382-384.

Thorpe, Francis Newton, ed. *The Federal and State Constitutions, Colonial Charters, and other organic Laws of the states, territories, and colonies now or heretofore forming the United States of America.* 7 vols. Washington: Government Printing Office, 1909.

Tilghman, Tench. *Memoir of Lieut. Col. Tench Tilghman, Secretary and aide to Washington Together with an appendix containing Revolutionary Journals and Letters Hitherto Unpublished.* Albany, N. Y.: J. Munsell, 1876.

Tower, Charlemagne, Jr. *The Marquis de La Fayette in the American Revolution.* 2 vols. Philadelphia: Lippincott, 1895.

Trumbull, Benjamin. "Benjamin Trumbull's Journal of the Expedition against Canada, 1775." *Connecticut Historical Society Collections,* VII (1899), 137-173.

————. "Journal of the Campaign at New York, 1776-7." *Orderly Books and Journals Kept by Connecticut Men While Taking Part in the American Revolution, 1775-1778,* pp. 177-220. *Collections of the Connecticut Historical Society,* VII. Hartford, Conn.: Connecticut Historical Society, 1899.

Trumbull, John. *The Poetical Works of John Trumbull, LL. D. Containing M'Fingal, A Modern Epic Poem, Revised and corrected with copious explanatory notes: The Progress of Dulness; and a collection of Poems on various subjects written before and during the Revolutionary War.* 2 vols. Hartford: 1820.

*Trumbull, Jonathan. "Minutes of Occurrences Respecting the Siege and Capture of York in Virginia, extracted from the Journal of Colonel Jonathan Trumbull, Secretary to the General, 1781." *Proceedings of the Massachusetts Historical Society,* IV (1876), 331-338.

Tucker, St. George. "The Southern Campaign, 1781, From Guilford Court House to the Siege of York, Narrated in the Letters from Judge St. George Tucker to his Wife." Edited by Charles Washington

Coleman, Jr. *The Magazine of American History with Notes and Queries*, VII (1881), 36-46, 201-216.

*Tyler, J. E., ed. "Account of Lexington." *William & Mary Quarterly*, 3rd Series, X (January 1953), 99-107.

*Uhlendorf, Bernard A., ed. and trans. *The Siege of Charleston, with an Account of the Province of South Carolina: the Von Jungkenn Papers in the William L. Clements Library*. Ann Arbor, Mich.: University of Michigan Press, 1938.

—— and Vosper, Edna, eds. *Letters from Major Baurmeister to Colonel Von Jungkenn Written during the Philadelphia Campaign, 1777-1778*. Philadelphia: The Historical Society of Pennsylvania, 1937.

Universal Magazine of Knowledge and Pleasure. London: 1747-1803.

*Van Doren, Carl. *Secret History of the American Revolution; an Account of the Conspiracies of Benedict Arnold and Numerous Others drawn from the Secret Service Papers of the British Headquarters in North America now for the first time examined and made public*. New York: The Viking Press, 1941.

Van Schaak, Henry Cruger. *Life of Peter Van Schaak*. New York: Appleton, 1842.

Vernon, William. "Papers of William Vernon and the Navy Board, 1776-1794." *Rhode Island Historical Publications*, New Series, VIII (1900), 197-277. Providence: 1900.

Waldo, Albigence. "Valley Forge, 1777-1778. Diary of Surgeon Albigence Waldo, of the Connecticut Line." *Pennsylvania Magazine of History and Biography*, XXI (1897), 299-323.

Walpole, Horace. *Journal of the Reign of George III from 1771 to 1783*. John Doran, ed. 2 vols. London: Bentley, 1859.

——. *The Letters of Horace Walpole*. Arranged and edited by Mrs. Paget Toynbee. Oxford: Clarendon Press, 1903-1905.

——. *The Letters of Horace Walpole, Earl of Oxford, including numerous letters now first published from the original manuscripts*. John Wright, ed. London: R. Bentley, 1840.

*Ward, Samuel. *Correspondence of Governor Samuel Ward, May 1775—March 1776, with a biographical introd., based chiefly on the Ward Papers covering the period 1725-1776*. Edited by Bernhard Knollenberg. Providence: Rhode Island Historical Society, 1952.

Warren-Adams Letters; Being Chiefly a Correspondence among John Adams, Samuel Adams, and James Warren. 2 vols. *Collections of the Massachusetts Historical Society*, Vols. LXXII (1917) and LXXIII (1925).

Watkins, George. *Digest of the Laws of Georgia, from its First Establishment as a British Province down to the Year 1800, inclusive. . . .* Philadelphia: Aitken, 1801.

Webb, Samuel Blachley. *Correspondence and Journals of Samuel Blachley Webb*. Collected and edited by Worthington C. Ford. 3 vols. New York: Burnett, 1894.

Wharton, Francis, ed. *The Revolutionary Diplomatic Correspondence of the United States.* Edited under direction of Congress with Preliminary Index, and Notes Historical and Legal. 6 vols. Washington: Government Printing Office, 1889.

Whipple, William. "Letter." "Stray Leaves from an Autograph Collection: Correspondence of Josiah Bartlett, of N. H. during the American Revolution." *Historical Magazine*, VI (March 1862), 73-78.

White, George. *Historical Collections of Georgia: Containing the Most Interesting Facts, Traditions, Biographical Sketches, Anecdotes, etc. relating to its History and Antiquities, from its First Settlement to the Present Time.* Compiled from Original Records and Official Documents. New York: Pudney & Russell, 1855.

White, John. "Extracts." *Essex Institute Historical Collections*, XLIX (Jan. 1913), 92-94.

White, Joseph. *A Narrative of Events.* Charlestown, Mass.: 1833.

Wilkinson, Eliza. *Letters of Eliza Wilkinson during the Invasion and Possession of Charlestown, S. C. by the British in the Revolutionary War.* Edited by Carolina Gripman. New York: 1839.

Wilkinson, James. *Memoirs of My Own Times.* 3 vols. Philadelphia: A. Small, 1816.

*Willard, Margaret Wheeler, ed. *Letters on the American Revolution, 1774-1776.* Boston: Houghton Mifflin Company, 1925.

Willett, Marinus. *A Narrative of the Military Actions of Colonel Marinus Willett, taken chiefly from his own manuscript.* Prepared by his son, William M. Willett. New York: Carvill, 1831.

Wirt, William. *Sketches of the Life and Character of Patrick Henry.* Philadelphia: Claxton, 1818.

*Wortley, Mrs. E. Stuart, ed. *Correspondence of 3rd Earl of Bute and of Lt. Gen. The Hon. Sir Charles Stuart.* London: John Murray Company, 1923.

Wraxall, Sir Nathaniel William. *The Historical and the Posthumous Memoirs of Sir Nathaniel William Wraxall, 1772-1784.* Edited by Henry B. Wheatley. 5 vols. New York: Scribner and Welford, 1884.

Zeisberger, David. *Diary of David Zeisberger, a Moravian Missionary among the Indians of Ohio.* Translated from the German ms. and edited by Eugene F. Bliss. Historical and Philosophical Society of Ohio Publications, New Series, II, III. Cincinnati: Clarke, 1885.

Index

American Farmers forming
at Concord, Massachusetts.
1775

First Georgia Regiment,
Continental Line,
1777. (Private in
Field Dress)

Second
South Carolina
Regiment, 1776.
(Private)

Fourth Connec
Regiment,
Continental L
1777. (Corpora

Third North Carolina
Regiment, Continental Line,
1778. (Private in Field Dress)

Green Mountain Rangers,
1776.
(Privates in Dress Uniform)

Sherburne's
Continental Regiment.
1778-1780. (Private)

Second New Ham
Regiment, Contin
Line, 1777. (Priv